ex·ploring
SERIES

1. Investigating in a systematic way: examining. 2. Searching into or ranging over for the purpose of discovery.

Microsoft®

Office 365® Word™ 2019

COMPREHENSIVE

Series Editor **Mary Anne Poatsy**

Hogan | Lau

Vice President of Courseware Portfolio Management: Andrew Gilfillan
Executive Portfolio Manager: Samantha Lewis
Team Lead, Content Production: Laura Burgess
Content Producer: Alexandrina Wolf
Development Editor: Barbara Stover
Portfolio Management Assistant: Bridget Daly
Director of Product Marketing: Brad Parkins
Director of Field Marketing: Jonathan Cottrell
Product Marketing Manager: Heather Taylor
Field Marketing Manager: Bob Nisbet
Product Marketing Assistant: Liz Bennett
Field Marketing Assistant: Derrica Moser
Senior Operations Specialist: Maura Garcia
Senior Art Director: Mary Seiner
Interior and Cover Design: Pearson CSC
Cover Photo: Courtesy of Shutterstock® Images
Senior Product Model Manager: Eric Hakanson
Manager, Digital Studio: Heather Darby
Digital Content Producer, MyLab IT: Becca Golden
Course Producer, MyLab IT: Amanda Losonsky
Digital Studio Producer: Tanika Henderson
Full-Service Project Management: Pearson CSC (Amy Kopperude)
Composition: Pearson CSC

Credits and acknowledgments borrowed from other sources and reproduced, with permission, in this textbook appear on the appropriate page within text.

Microsoft and/or its respective suppliers make no representations about the suitability of the information contained in the documents and related graphics published as part of the services for any purpose. All such documents and related graphics are provided "as is" without warranty of any kind. Microsoft and/or its respective suppliers hereby disclaim all warranties and conditions with regard to this information, including all warranties and conditions of merchantability, whether express, implied or statutory, fitness for a particular purpose, title and non-infringement. In no event shall Microsoft and/or its respective suppliers be liable for any special, indirect or consequential damages or any damages whatsoever resulting from loss of use, data or profits, whether in an action of contract, negligence or other tortious action, arising out of or in connection with the use or performance of information available from the services.

The documents and related graphics contained herein could include technical inaccuracies or typographical errors. Changes are periodically added to the information herein. Microsoft and/or its respective suppliers may make improvements and/or changes in the product(s) and/or the program(s) described herein at any time. Partial screen shots may be viewed in full within the software version specified.

Microsoft® and Windows® are registered trademarks of the Microsoft Corporation in the U.S.A. and other countries. This book is not sponsored or endorsed by or affiliated with the Microsoft Corporation.

Copyright © 2020 by Pearson. All rights reserved. Manufactured in the United States of America. This publication is protected by copyright and permission should be obtained from the publisher prior to any prohibited reproduction, storage in a retrieval system, or transmission in any form or by any means, electronic, mechanical, photocopying, recording, or likewise. For information regarding permissions, request forms and the appropriate contacts within the Pearson Education Global Rights & Permissions department, please visit www.pearsoned.com/permissions/.

Many of the designations by manufacturers and sellers to distinguish their products are claimed as trademarks. Where those designations appear in this book, and the publisher was aware of a trademark claim, the designations have been printed in initial caps or all caps.

Cataloging-in-Publication Data is available on file at the Library of Congress.

2 2019

ISBN 10: 0-13-543640-0
ISBN 13: 978-0-13-543640-0

Dedications

For my husband, Ted, who unselfishly continues to take on more than his share to support me throughout the process; and for my children, Laura, Carolyn, and Teddy, whose encouragement and love have been inspiring.

Mary Anne Poatsy

For my father, Lawrence Conwill, a lifelong educator and administrator who has inspired so many both in and out of a classroom. His legacy in education and his love of family can never be truly matched, but is something I will always aspire to and admire in him. He is my hero.

Lynn Hogan

I dedicate this book to my only child, Catherine Shen, who taught me that there is another wonderful life outside of my work. My life has been more fulfilling and exciting with her in it. I also dedicate this book to the loving memory of my dog, Harry, who was by my side, through thick and thin, for 16 years. I miss him dearly every day.

Linda K. Lau

About the Authors

Mary Anne Poatsy, Series Editor, Common Features Author

Mary Anne is a senior faculty member at Montgomery County Community College, teaching various computer application and concepts courses in face-to-face and online environments. She holds a B.A. in Psychology and Education from Mount Holyoke College and an M.B.A. in Finance from Northwestern University's Kellogg Graduate School of Management.

Mary Anne has more than 20 years of educational experience. She has taught at Gwynedd Mercy College, Bucks County Community College, and Muhlenberg College. She also engages in corporate training. Before teaching, she was Vice President at Shearson Lehman in the Municipal Bond Investment Banking Department.

Dr. Lynn Hogan, Word Author

Dr. Lynn Hogan currently teaches at the University of North Alabama, providing instruction in the area of computer applications. Prior to her current assignment, she taught for more than 25 years at the community college level, serving in academic administration and teaching applications, programming, and concepts courses in both online and classroom environments. She has served as an author for several Pearson publications over the past 14 years, including Exploring 2010, 2013, and 2016. She also contributed Word chapters for the first edition of Your Office, and developed and wrote Practical Computing. She received an M.B.A. from the University of North Alabama, and a Ph.D. from the University of Alabama.

Lynn has two daughters and resides with her husband, Paul, in Alabama. Her interests include creative writing, photography, traveling, and helping manage a family horse farm.

Dr. Linda K. Lau, Word Author

Since 1994, Dr. Linda K. Lau is a Management Information Systems (MIS) faculty at the College of Business and Economics, Longwood University, located in Farmville, Virginia. She received the Outstanding Academic Advisor Award in 2006. Besides teaching and advising, Linda has authored and co-authored numerous journal and conference articles and textbooks, edited two books, and sat on several editorial boards. Her current research interest focuses on cyber security and forensics, and she is a member of the *Journal of Digital Forensics, Security and Law (JDFSL)* editorial board. Linda earned her Ph.D. from Rensselaer Polytechnic Institute in 1993, and her M.B.A. and B.S. from Illinois State University in 1987 and 1986, respectively. In her younger days, Linda worked as a flight attendant for Singapore International Airlines for six years before coming to America to pursue her academic dream. She also worked as a financial consultant with Salomon Smith Barney from 1999 to 2000 before returning to the academic world. Linda resides in Richmond with her family.

Dr. Robert T. Grauer, Creator of the Exploring Series

Bob Grauer is an Associate Professor in the Department of Computer Information Systems at the University of Miami, where he is a multiple winner of the Outstanding Teaching Award in the School of Business, most recently in 2009. He has written numerous COBOL texts and is the vision behind the Exploring Office series, with more than three million books in print. His work has been translated into three foreign languages and is used in all aspects of higher education at both national and international levels. Bob Grauer has consulted for several major corporations including IBM and American Express. He received his Ph.D. in Operations Research in 1972 from the Polytechnic Institute of Brooklyn.

Brief Contents

Office		Office 365 Common Features	2
Word	CHAPTER 1	Introduction to Word	70
	CHAPTER 2	Document Presentation	128
	CHAPTER 3	Document Productivity	194
	CHAPTER 4	Research and Collaboration	250
	CHAPTER 5	Document Publications	310
	CHAPTER 6	Time-Saving Tools	362
	CHAPTER 7	Document Automation	416
	CHAPTER 8	Word and the Internet	472
Application Capstone Exercise		Word Application Capstone Exercise (Chs. 1–4)	520
		Word Comprehensive Capstone Exercise (Chs. 5–8)	523

Microsoft Office 2019 Specialist Word	527
GLOSSARY	534
INDEX	539

Contents

Microsoft Office 2019

■ CHAPTER ONE Office 365 Common Features: Taking the First Step — 2

CASE STUDY SPOTTED BEGONIA ART GALLERY	2
GET STARTED WITH OFFICE APPLICATIONS	4
Starting an Office Application	5
Working with Files	6
Using Common Interface Components	9
Getting Help	15
Installing Add-ins	17
HANDS-ON EXERCISE 1	19
FORMAT DOCUMENT CONTENT	25
Using Templates and Applying Themes	25
Modifying Text	27
Relocating Text	30
Reviewing a Document	32
Working with Pictures	34
HANDS-ON EXERCISE 2	37
MODIFY DOCUMENT LAYOUT AND PROPERTIES	45
Changing Document Views	45
Changing the Page Layout	46
Creating a Header and a Footer	49
Configuring Document Properties	50
Previewing and Printing a File	51
HANDS-ON EXERCISE 3	53
CHAPTER OBJECTIVES REVIEW	58
KEY TERMS MATCHING	60
MULTIPLE CHOICE	61
PRACTICE EXERCISES	62
MID-LEVEL EXERCISES	65
RUNNING CASE	67
DISASTER RECOVERY	67
CAPSTONE EXERCISE	68

Microsoft Office Word 2019

■ CHAPTER ONE Introduction to Word: Organizing a Document — 70

CASE STUDY SWAN CREEK NATIONAL WILDLIFE REFUGE	70
INTRODUCTION TO WORD PROCESSING	72
Beginning and Editing a Document	73
Customizing Word	79
HANDS-ON EXERCISE 1	82
DOCUMENT ORGANIZATION	86
Using Features That Improve Readability	86
Viewing a Document in Different Ways	91
HANDS-ON EXERCISE 2	96
DOCUMENT SETTINGS AND PROPERTIES	103
Modifying Document Properties	103
Preparing a Document for Distribution	105
HANDS-ON EXERCISE 3	113
CHAPTER OBJECTIVES REVIEW	117
KEY TERMS MATCHING	118
MULTIPLE CHOICE	119
PRACTICE EXERCISES	120
MID-LEVEL EXERCISES	124
RUNNING CASE	125
DISASTER RECOVERY	126
CAPSTONE EXERCISE	127

CHAPTER TWO Document Presentation: Editing and Formatting — 128

CASE STUDY PHILLIPS STUDIO L PHOTOGRAPHY	128
TEXT AND PARAGRAPH FORMATTING	130
Applying Font Attributes	130
Formatting a Paragraph	134
HANDS-ON EXERCISE 1	144
DOCUMENT APPEARANCE	149
Formatting a Document	149
Applying Styles	152
HANDS-ON EXERCISE 2	158
OBJECTS	164
Inserting and Formatting Objects	164
HANDS-ON EXERCISE 3	174
CHAPTER OBJECTIVES REVIEW	180
KEY TERMS MATCHING	181
MULTIPLE CHOICE	182
PRACTICE EXERCISES	183
MID-LEVEL EXERCISES	188
RUNNING CASE	190
DISASTER RECOVERY	191
CAPSTONE EXERCISE	192

CHAPTER THREE Document Productivity: Working with Tables and Mail Merge — 194

CASE STUDY TRAYLOR UNIVERSITY ECONOMIC IMPACT STUDY	194
TABLES	196
Inserting a Table	196
Formatting a Table	200
HANDS-ON EXERCISE 1	204
ADVANCED TABLE FEATURES	210
Managing Table Data	210
Enhancing Table Data	214
HANDS-ON EXERCISE 2	219
MAIL MERGE	226
Creating a Mail Merge Document	226
Completing a Mail Merge	230
HANDS-ON EXERCISE 3	232
CHAPTER OBJECTIVES REVIEW	236
KEY TERMS MATCHING	237
MULTIPLE CHOICE	238
PRACTICE EXERCISES	239
MID-LEVEL EXERCISES	244
RUNNING CASE	247
DISASTER RECOVERY	248
CAPSTONE EXERCISE	249

CHAPTER FOUR Research and Collaboration: Communicating with and Producing Professional Papers — 250

CASE STUDY LITERATURE ANALYSIS	250
RESEARCH PAPER BASICS	252
Using a Writing Style and Acknowledging Sources	252
Creating and Modifying Footnotes and Endnotes	258
Exploring Special Features	260
HANDS-ON EXERCISE 1	264
DOCUMENT TRACKING	271
Tracking Changes	271
Reviewing a Document	273
HANDS-ON EXERCISE 2	280
ONLINE DOCUMENT COLLABORATION	284
Using OneDrive	284
Sharing Documents	286
Collaborating with Word and Word Online	290
HANDS-ON EXERCISE 3	294
CHAPTER OBJECTIVES REVIEW	297
KEY TERMS MATCHING	298
MULTIPLE CHOICE	299
PRACTICE EXERCISES	300
MID-LEVEL EXERCISES	304
RUNNING CASE	306
DISASTER RECOVERY	307
CAPSTONE EXERCISE	308

■ CHAPTER FIVE Document Publications: Designing Newsletters and Working with Graphics — 310

CASE STUDY ALONG THE GREENWAYS	310
DESKTOP PUBLISHING	312
Designing a Newsletter	313
Applying Design Features	316
HANDS-ON EXERCISE 1	**320**
GRAPHIC OBJECTS	326
Inserting Graphic Objects	326
Manipulating Graphic Objects	333
HANDS-ON EXERCISE 2	**336**
DOCUMENT VERSATILITY	342
Using OLE to Insert an Object	342
HANDS-ON EXERCISE 3	**345**
CHAPTER OBJECTIVES REVIEW	348
KEY TERMS MATCHING	349
MULTIPLE CHOICE	350
PRACTICE EXERCISES	351
MID-LEVEL EXERCISES	356
RUNNING CASE	358
DISASTER RECOVERY	359
CAPSTONE EXERCISE	360

■ CHAPTER SIX Time-Saving Tools: Automating Document Creation and Using Multiple Documents and Themes — 362

CASE STUDY COMPUTER TRAINING CONCEPTS, INC.	362
AUTOMATE DOCUMENT CREATION	364
Selecting a Template	364
Creating a Word Template	366
Using Building Blocks	367
HANDS-ON EXERCISE 1	**371**
MULTIPLE DOCUMENTS	376
Viewing Two Documents Side by Side	376
Merging Documents	377
Using Navigational Tools	384
HANDS-ON EXERCISE 2	**389**
DOCUMENT THEMES	396
Applying a Document Theme and Style Set	396
Customizing Theme Colors and Theme Fonts, and Applying Theme Effects	397
HANDS-ON EXERCISE 3	**400**
CHAPTER OBJECTIVES REVIEW	405
KEY TERMS MATCHING	406
MULTIPLE CHOICE	407
PRACTICE EXERCISES	408
MID-LEVEL EXERCISES	411
RUNNING CASE	413
DISASTER RECOVERY	413
CAPSTONE EXERCISE	414

■ CHAPTER SEVEN Document Automation: Using Forms, Macros, and Security Features — 416

CASE STUDY OAK GROVE PRODUCTS	416
FORMS	418
Creating an Electronic Form	419
Enabling Form Protection	424
HANDS-ON EXERCISE 1	**426**
MACROS	432
Creating a Macro	432
Understanding Macro Security	437
HANDS-ON EXERCISE 2	**441**
DOCUMENT PROTECTION AND AUTHENTICATION	445
Applying Document Restrictions	445
Working with Passwords	449
Using a Digital Signature to Authenticate a Document	451
HANDS-ON EXERCISE 3	**453**
CHAPTER OBJECTIVES REVIEW	459
KEY TERMS MATCHING	460
MULTIPLE CHOICE	461
PRACTICE EXERCISES	462
MID-LEVEL EXERCISES	465
RUNNING CASE	467
DISASTER RECOVERY	469
CAPSTONE EXERCISE	470

CHAPTER EIGHT Word and the Internet: Creating and Enhancing Webpages and Blogs 472

CASE STUDY A MATH TUTORING CLUB	472	CHAPTER OBJECTIVES REVIEW	509
WEBPAGE CREATION	474	KEY TERMS MATCHING	510
Customizing the Ribbon	474	MULTIPLE CHOICE	511
Building and Publishing a Webpage	478	PRACTICE EXERCISES	512
HANDS-ON EXERCISE 1	487	MID-LEVEL EXERCISES	515
WEBPAGE ENHANCEMENT	496	RUNNING CASE	516
Enhancing a Webpage	496	DISASTER RECOVERY	517
Creating a Blog Post	499	CAPSTONE EXERCISE	518
HANDS-ON EXERCISE 2	502		

Application Capstone Exercises

Word Application Capstone Exercise (Chs. 1–4) 520

Word Comprehensive Capstone Exercise (Chs. 5–8) 523

Microsoft Office 2019 Specialist Word 527

GLOSSARY 534

INDEX 539

Acknowledgments

The Exploring team would like to acknowledge and thank all the reviewers who helped us throughout the years by providing us with their invaluable comments, suggestions, and constructive criticism.

A. D. Knight
Northwestern State University
Natchitoches–Louisiana

Aaron Montanino
Davenport University

Adriana Lumpkin
Midland College

Alan S. Abrahams
Virginia Tech

Alexandre C. Probst
Colorado Christian University

Ali Berrached
University of Houston–Downtown

Allen Alexander
Delaware Technical & Community College

Amy Rutledge
Oakland University

Andrea Marchese
Maritime College
State University of New York

Andrew Blitz
Broward College; Edison State College

Angel Norman
University of Tennessee–Knoxville

Angela Clark
University of South Alabama

Ann Rovetto
Horry–Georgetown Technical College

Astrid Todd
Guilford Technical Community College

Audrey Gillant
Maritime College, State University of New York

Barbara Stover
Marion Technical College

Barbara Tollinger
Sinclair Community College

Ben Brahim Taha
Auburn University

Beverly Amer
Northern Arizona University

Beverly Fite
Amarillo College

Biswadip Ghosh
Metropolitan State University of Denver

Bonita Volker
Tidewater Community College

Bonnie Homan
San Francisco State University

Brad West
Sinclair Community College

Brian Kovar
Kansas State University

Brian Powell
West Virginia University

Carmen Morrison
North Central State College

Carol Buser
Owens Community College

Carol Roberts
University of Maine

Carol Wiggins
Blinn College

Carole Pfeiffer
Southeast Missouri State University

Carolyn Barren
Macomb Community College

Carolyn Borne
Louisiana State University

Cathy Poyner
Truman State University

Charles Hodgson
Delgado Community College

Chen Zhang
Bryant University

Cheri Higgins
Illinois State University

Cheryl Brown
Delgado Community College

Cheryl Hinds
Norfolk State University

Cheryl Sypniewski
Macomb Community College

Chris Robinson
Northwest State Community College

Cindy Herbert
Metropolitan Community College–Longview

Craig J. Peterson
American InterContinental University

Craig Watson
Bristol Community College

Dana Hooper
University of Alabama

Dana Johnson
North Dakota State University

Daniela Marghitu
Auburn University

David Noel
University of Central Oklahoma

David Pulis
Maritime College, State University of New York

David Thornton
Jacksonville State University

Dawn Medlin
Appalachian State University

Debby Keen
University of Kentucky

Debra Chapman
University of South Alabama

Debra Hoffman
Southeast Missouri State University

Derrick Huang
Florida Atlantic University

Diana Baran
Henry Ford Community College

Diane Cassidy
The University of North Carolina at Charlotte

Diane L. Smith
Henry Ford Community College

Dick Hewer
Ferris State College

Don Danner
San Francisco State University

Don Hoggan
Solano College

Don Riggs
SUNY Schenectady County Community College

Doncho Petkov
Eastern Connecticut State University

Donna Ehrhart
Genesee Community College

Elaine Crable
Xavier University

Elizabeth Duett
Delgado Community College

Erhan Uskup
Houston Community College–Northwest

Eric Martin
University of Tennessee

Erika Nadas
Wilbur Wright College

Evelyn Schenk
Saginaw Valley State University

Floyd Winters
Manatee Community College

Frank Lucente
Westmoreland County Community College

G. Jan Wilms
Union University

Gail Cope
Sinclair Community College

Gary DeLorenzo
California University of Pennsylvania

Gary Garrison
Belmont University

Gary McFall
Purdue University

George Cassidy
Sussex County Community College

Gerald Braun
Xavier University

Gerald Burgess
Western New Mexico University

Gladys Swindler
Fort Hays State University

Gurinder Mehta
Sam Houston State University

Hector Frausto
California State University Los Angeles

Heith Hennel
Valencia Community College

Henry Rudzinski
Central Connecticut State University

Irene Joos
La Roche College

Iwona Rusin
Baker College; Davenport University

J. Roberto Guzman
San Diego Mesa College

Jacqueline D. Lawson
Henry Ford Community College

Jakie Brown, Jr.
Stevenson University

James Brown
Central Washington University

James Powers
University of Southern Indiana

Jane Stam
Onondaga Community College

Janet Bringhurst
Utah State University

Janice Potochney
Gateway Community College

Jean Luoma
Davenport University

Jean Welsh
Lansing Community College

Jeanette Dix
Ivy Tech Community College

Jennifer Day
Sinclair Community College

Jill Canine
Ivy Tech Community College

Jill Young
Southeast Missouri State University

Jim Chaffee
The University of Iowa Tippie College of Business

Joanne Lazirko
University of Wisconsin–Milwaukee

Jodi Milliner
Kansas State University

John Hollenbeck
Blue Ridge Community College

John Meir
Midlands Technical College

John Nelson
Texas Christian University

John Seydel
Arkansas State University

Judith A. Scheeren
Westmoreland County Community College

Judith Brown
The University of Memphis

Juliana Cypert
Tarrant County College

Kamaljeet Sanghera
George Mason University

Karen Priestly
Northern Virginia Community College

Karen Ravan
Spartanburg Community College

Karen Tracey
Central Connecticut State University

Kathleen Brenan
Ashland University

Ken Busbee
Houston Community College

Kent Foster
Winthrop University

Kevin Anderson
Solano Community College

Kim Wright
The University of Alabama

Kirk Atkinson
Western Kentucky University

Kristen Hockman
University of Missouri–Columbia

Kristi Smith
Allegany College of Maryland

Laura Marcoulides
Fullerton College

Laura McManamon
University of Dayton

Laurence Boxer
Niagara University

Leanne Chun
Leeward Community College

Lee McClain
Western Washington University

Lewis Cappelli
Hudson Valley Community College

Linda D. Collins
Mesa Community College

Linda Johnsonius
Murray State University

Linda Lau
Longwood University

Linda Theus
Jackson State Community College

Linda Williams
Marion Technical College

Lisa Miller
University of Central Oklahoma

Lister Horn
Pensacola Junior College

Lixin Tao
Pace University

Loraine Miller
Cayuga Community College

Lori Kielty
Central Florida Community College

Lorna Wells
Salt Lake Community College

Lorraine Sauchin
Duquesne University

Lucy Parakhovnik
California State University–Northridge

Acknowledgments xi

Lynn Baldwin
Madison College

Lynn Keane
University of South Carolina

Lynn Mancini
Delaware Technical Community College

Lynne Seal
Amarillo College

Mackinzee Escamilla
South Plains College

Marcia Welch
Highline Community College

Margaret McManus
Northwest Florida State College

Margaret Warrick
Allan Hancock College

Marilyn Hibbert
Salt Lake Community College

Mark Choman
Luzerne County Community College

Mary Beth Tarver
Northwestern State University

Mary Duncan
University of Missouri–St. Louis

Maryann Clark
University of New Hampshire

Melissa Nemeth
Indiana University–Purdue University Indianapolis

Melody Alexander
Ball State University

Michael Douglas
University of Arkansas at Little Rock

Michael Dunklebarger
Alamance Community College

Michael G. Skaff
College of the Sequoias

Michele Budnovitch
Pennsylvania College of Technology

Mike Jochen
East Stroudsburg University

Mike Michaelson
Palomar College

Mike Scroggins
Missouri State University

Mimi Spain
Southern Maine Community College

Muhammed Badamas
Morgan State University

NaLisa Brown
University of the Ozarks

Nancy Grant
Community College of Allegheny County–South Campus

Nanette Lareau
University of Arkansas Community College–Morrilton

Nikia Robinson
Indian River State University

Pam Brune
Chattanooga State Community College

Pam Uhlenkamp
Iowa Central Community College

Patrick Smith
Marshall Community and Technical College

Paul Addison
Ivy Tech Community College

Paul Hamilton
New Mexico State University

Paula Ruby
Arkansas State University

Peggy Burrus
Red Rocks Community College

Peter Ross
SUNY Albany

Philip H. Nielson
Salt Lake Community College

Philip Valvalides
Guilford Technical Community College

Ralph Hooper
University of Alabama

Ranette Halverson
Midwestern State University

Richard Blamer
John Carroll University

Richard Cacace
Pensacola Junior College

Richard Hewer
Ferris State University

Richard Sellers
Hill College

Rob Murray
Ivy Tech Community College

Robert Banta
Macomb Community College

Robert Dusek
Northern Virginia Community College

Robert G. Phipps, Jr.
West Virginia University

Robert Sindt
Johnson County Community College

Robert Warren
Delgado Community College

Robyn Barrett
St. Louis Community College–Meramec

Rocky Belcher
Sinclair Community College

Roger Pick
University of Missouri at Kansas City

Ronnie Creel
Troy University

Rosalie Westerberg
Clover Park Technical College

Ruth Neal
Navarro College

Sandra Thomas
Troy University

Sheila Gionfriddo
Luzerne County Community College

Sherrie Geitgey
Northwest State Community College

Sherry Lenhart
Terra Community College

Shohreh Hashemi
University of Houston–Downtown

Sophia Wilberscheid
Indian River State College

Sophie Lee
California State University–Long Beach

Stacy Johnson
Iowa Central Community College

Stephanie Kramer
Northwest State Community College

Stephen Z. Jourdan
Auburn University at Montgomery

Steven Schwarz
Raritan Valley Community College

Sue A. McCrory
Missouri State University

Sumathy Chandrashekar
Salisbury University

Susan Fuschetto
Cerritos College

Susan Medlin
UNC Charlotte

Susan N. Dozier
Tidewater Community College

Suzan Spitzberg
Oakton Community College

Suzanne M. Jeska
County College of Morris

Sven Aelterman
Troy University

Sy Hirsch
Sacred Heart University

Sylvia Brown
Midland College

Tanya Patrick
Clackamas Community College

Terri Holly
Indian River State College

Terry Ray Rigsby
Hill College

Thomas Rienzo
Western Michigan University

Tina Johnson
Midwestern State University

Tommy Lu
Delaware Technical Community College

Troy S. Cash
Northwest Arkansas Community College

Vicki Robertson
Southwest Tennessee Community

Vickie Pickett
Midland College

Vivianne Moore
Davenport University

Weifeng Chen
California University of Pennsylvania

Wes Anthony
Houston Community College

William Ayen
University of Colorado at Colorado Springs

Wilma Andrews
Virginia Commonwealth University

Yvonne Galusha
University of Iowa

Special thanks to our content development and technical team:

Barbara Stover

Lisa Bucki

Lori Damanti

Sallie Dodson

Morgan Hetzler

Ken Mayer

Joyce Nielsen

Chris Parent

Sean Portnoy

Steven Rubin

LeeAnn Bates
MyLab IT content author

Becca Golden
Media Producer

Jennifer Hurley
MyLab IT content author

Kevin Marino
MyLab IT content author

Ralph Moore
MyLab IT content author

Jerri Williams
MyLab IT content author

Preface

The Exploring Series and You

Exploring is Pearson's Office Application series that requires students like you to think "beyond the point and click." In this edition, the *Exploring* experience has evolved to be even more in tune with the student of today. With an emphasis on Mac compatibility, critical thinking, and continual updates to stay in sync with the changing Microsoft Office 365, and by providing additional valuable assignments and resources, the *Exploring* series is able to offer you the most usable, current, and beneficial learning experience ever.

The goal of *Exploring* is, as it has always been, to go farther than teaching just the steps to accomplish a task—the series provides the theoretical foundation for you to understand when and why to apply a skill. As a result, you achieve a deeper understanding of each application and can apply this critical thinking beyond Office and the classroom.

New to This Edition

Continual eText Updates: This edition of *Exploring* is written to Microsoft® Office 365®, which is constantly updating. In order to stay current with the software, we are committed to twice annual updates of the eText and Content Updates document available as an instructor resource for text users.

Focus on Mac: Mac usage is growing, and even outstripping PC usage at some four-year institutions. In response, new features such as Mac Tips, On a Mac step boxes, Mac Troubleshooting, and Mac tips on Student Reference Cards help ensure Mac users have a flawless experience using *Exploring*.

Expanded Running Case: In this edition, the Running Case has been expanded to all applications, with one exercise per chapter focusing on the New Castle County Technical Services case, providing a continuous and real-world project for students to work on throughout the semester.

Pre-Built Learning Modules: Pre-built inside MyLab IT, these make course setup a snap. The modules are based on research and instructor best practices, and can be easily customized to meet your course requirements.

Critical Thinking Modules: Pre-built inside MyLab IT, these pair a Grader Project with a critical thinking quiz that requires students to first complete a hands-on project, then reflect on what they did and the data or information they interacted with, to answer a series of objective critical thinking questions. These are offered both at the chapter level for regular practice, as well as at the Application level where students can earn a Critical Thinking badge.

What's New for MyLab IT Graders

Graders with WHY: All Grader project instructions now incorporate the scenario and the WHY to help students critically think and understand why they're performing the steps in the project.

Hands-On Exercise Assessment Graders: A new Grader in each chapter that mirrors the Hands-On Exercise. Using an alternate scenario and data files, this new Grader is built to be more instructional and features Learning Aids such as Read (eText), Watch (video), and Practice (guided simulation) in the Grader report to help students learn, remediate, and resubmit.

Auto-Graded Critical Thinking Quizzes:

- Application Capstones that allow students to earn a Critical Thinking badge
- Chapter-level quizzes for each Mid-Level Exercise Grader project

Improved Mac Compatibility in Graders: All Graders are tested for Mac compatibility and any that can be made 100% Mac compatible are identified in the course. This excludes Access projects as well as any that use functionality not available in Mac Office.

Autograded Integrated Grader Projects: Based on the discipline-specific integrated projects, covering Word, Excel, PowerPoint, and Access in various combinations.

Final Solution Image: Included with Grader student downloads, final output images allows students to visualize what their solution should look like.

What's New for MyLab IT Simulations

Updated Office 365, 2019 Edition Simulations: Written by the *Exploring* author team, ensures one-to-one content to directly match the Hands-On Exercises (Simulation Training) and mirror them with an alternate scenario (Simulation Assessment).

Student Action Visualization: Provides a playback of student actions within the simulation for remediation by students and review by instructors when there is a question about why an action is marked as incorrect.

Series Hallmarks

The **How/Why Approach** helps students move beyond the point and click to a true understanding of how to apply Microsoft Office skills.

- **White Pages/Yellow Pages** clearly distinguish the theory (white pages) from the skills covered in the Hands-On Exercises (yellow pages) so students always know what they are supposed to be doing and why.
- **Case Study** presents a scenario for the chapter, creating a story that ties the Hands-On Exercises together and gives context to the skills being introduced.
- **Hands-On Exercise Videos** are tied to each Hands-On Exercise and walk students through the steps of the exercise while weaving in conceptual information related to the Case Study and the objectives as a whole.

An **Outcomes focus** allows students and instructors to know the higher-level learning goals and how those are achieved through discreet objectives and skills.

- **Outcomes** presented at the beginning of each chapter identify the learning goals for students and instructors.
- **Enhanced Objective Mapping** enables students to follow a directed path through each chapter, from the objectives list at the chapter opener through the exercises at the end of the chapter.
  - **Objectives List:** This provides a simple list of key objectives covered in the chapter. This includes page numbers so students can skip between objectives where they feel they need the most help.
  - **Step Icons:** These icons appear in the white pages and reference the step numbers in the Hands-On Exercises, providing a correlation between the two so students can easily find conceptual help when they are working hands-on and need a refresher.
  - **Quick Concepts Check:** A series of questions that appear briefly at the end of each white page section. These questions cover the most essential concepts in the white pages required for students to be successful in working the Hands-On Exercises. Page numbers are included for easy reference to help students locate the answers.
  - **Chapter Objectives Review:** Located near the end of the chapter and reviews all important concepts covered in the chapter. Designed in an easy-to-read bulleted format.
- **MOS Certification Guide** for instructors and students to direct anyone interested in prepping for the MOS exam to the specific locations to find all content required for the test.

End-of-Chapter Exercises offer instructors several options for assessment. Each chapter has approximately 11–12 exercises ranging from multiple choice questions to open-ended projects.

- **Multiple Choice, Key Terms Matching, Practice Exercises, Mid-Level Exercises, Running Case, Disaster Recovery, and Capstone Exercises** are at the end of all chapters.
  - **Enhanced Mid-Level Exercises** include a **Creative Case** (for PowerPoint and Word), which allows students some flexibility and creativity, not being bound by a definitive solution, and an **Analysis Case** (for Excel and Access), which requires students to interpret the data they are using to answer an analytic question.
- **Application Capstone** exercises are included in the book to allow instructors to test students on the contents of a single application.

The Exploring Series and MyLab IT

The *Exploring Series* has been a market leader for more than 20 years, with a hallmark focus on both the *how* and *why* behind what students do within the Microsoft Office software. In this edition, the pairing of the text with MyLab IT Simulations, Graders, Objective Quizzes, and Resources as a fully complementary program allows students and instructors to get the very most out of their use of the *Exploring Series*.

To maximize student results, we recommend pairing the text content with MyLab IT, which is the teaching and learning platform that empowers you to reach every student. By combining trusted author content with digital tools and a flexible platform, MyLab personalizes the learning experience and helps your students learn and retain key course concepts while developing skills that future employers are seeking in their candidates.

Solving Teaching and Learning Challenges

Pearson addresses these teaching and learning challenges with *Exploring* and MyLab IT 2019.

Reach Every Student

MyLab IT 2019 delivers trusted content and resources through easy-to-use, Prebuilt Learning Modules that promote student success. Through an authentic learning experience, students become sharp critical thinkers and proficient in Microsoft Office, developing essential skills employers seek.

Practice and Feedback: What do I do when I get stuck or need more practice?

MyLab IT features **Integrated Learning Aids** within the Simulations and now also within the Grader Reports, allowing students to choose to Read (via the eText), Watch (via an author-created hands-on video), or Practice (via a guided simulation) whenever they get stuck. These are conveniently accessible directly within the simulation training so that students do not have to leave the graded assignment to access these helpful resources. The **Student Action Visualization** captures all the work students do in the Simulation for both Training and Assessment and allows students and instructors to watch a detailed playback for the purpose of remediation or guidance when students get stuck. MyLab IT offers **Grader project reports** for coaching, remediation, and defensible grading. Score Card Detail allows you to easily see where students were scored correctly or incorrectly, pointing out how many points were deducted on each step. Live Comments Report allows you and the students to see the actual files the student submitted with mark-ups/comments on what they missed and now includes Learning Aids to provide immediate remediation for incorrect steps.

Application, Motivation, and Employability Skills: Why am I taking this course, and will this help me get a job?

Students want to know that what they are doing in this class is setting them up for their ultimate goal—to get a job. With an emphasis on **employability skills** like critical thinking and other soft skills, **digital badges** to prove student proficiency in Microsoft skills and critical thinking, and **MOS Certification practice materials** in MyLab IT, the *Exploring Series* is putting students on the path to differentiate themselves in the job market, so that they can find and land a job that values their schools once they leave school.

Application: How do I get students to apply what they've learned in a meaningful way?

The *Exploring Series* and MyLab IT offer instructors the ability to provide students with authentic formative and summative assessments. The realistic and hi-fidelity **simulations** help students feel like they are working in the real Microsoft applications and allow them to explore, use 96% of Microsoft methods, and do so without penalty. The **Grader projects** allow students to gain real-world context as they work live in the application, applying both an understanding of how and why to perform certain skills to complete a project. New **Critical Thinking quizzes** require students to demonstrate their understanding of why, by answering questions that force them to analyze and interpret the project they worked on to answer a series of objective questions. The new **Running Case** woven through all applications requires students to apply their knowledge in a realistic way to a long-running, semester-long project focused on the same company.

Ease of Use: I need a course solution that is easy to use for both me and my students

MyLab IT 2019 is the easiest and most accessible in its history. With new **Prebuilt Learning** and **Critical Thinking Modules** course set-up is simple! **LMS integration capabilities** allow users seamless access to MyLab IT with single sign-on, grade sync, and asset-level deep linking. Continuing a focus on accessibility, MyLab IT includes an **integrated Accessibility Toolbar** with translation feature for students with disabilities, as well as a **Virtual Keyboard** that allows students to complete keyboard actions entirely on screen. There is also an enhanced focus on Mac compatibility with even more Mac-compatible Grader projects,

Developing Employability Skills

High-Demand Office Skills are taught to help students gain these skills and prepare for the Microsoft Office Certification exams (MOS). The MOS objectives are covered throughout the content, and a MOS Objective Appendix provides clear mapping of where to find each objective. Practice exams in the form of Graders and Simulations are available in MyLab IT.

Badging Digital badges are available for students in Introductory and Advanced Microsoft Word, Excel, Access, and PowerPoint. This digital credential is issued to students upon successful completion (90%+ score) of an Application Capstone Badging Grader project. MyLab IT badges provide verified evidence that learners have demonstrated specific skills and competencies using Microsoft Office tools in a real project and help distinguish students within the job pool. Badges are issued through the Acclaim system and can be placed in a LinkedIn ePortfolio, posted on social media (Facebook, Twitter), and/or included in a résumé. Badges include tags with relevant information that allow students to be discoverable by potential employers, as well as search for jobs for which they are qualified.

> "The badge is a way for employers to actually verify that a potential employee is actually somewhat fluent with Excel."—Bunker Hill Community College Student

The new **Critical Thinking Badge** in MyLab IT for 2019 provides verified evidence that learners have demonstrated the ability to not only complete a real project, but also analyze and problem-solve using Microsoft Office applications. Students prove this by completing an objective quiz that requires them to critically think about the project, interpret data, and explain why they performed the actions they did in the project. Critical Thinking is a hot button issue at many institutions and is highly sought after in job candidates, allowing students with the Critical Thinking Badge to stand out and prove their skills.

Soft Skills Videos are included in MyLab IT for educators who want to emphasize key employability skills such as Accepting Criticism and Being Coachable, Customer Service, and Resume and Cover Letter Best Practices.

Resources

Instructor Teaching Resources	
Supplements Available to Instructors at www.pearsonhighered.com/exploring	**Features of the Supplement**
Instructor's Manual	Available for each chapter and includes: • List of all Chapter Resources, File Names, and Where to Find • Chapter Overview • Class Run-Down • Key Terms • Discussion Questions • Practice Projects & Applications • Teaching Notes • Additional Web Resources • Projects and Exercises with File Names • Solutions to Multiple Choice, Key Terms Matching, and Quick Concepts Checks
Solutions Files, Annotated Solution Files, Scorecards	• Available for all exercises with definitive solutions • Annotated Solution Files in PDF feature callouts to enable easy grading • Scorecards to allow for easy scoring for hand-grading all exercises with definitive solutions, and scoring by step adding to 100 points.
Rubrics	For Mid-Level Exercises without a definitive solution. Available in Microsoft Word format, enabling instructors to customize the assignments for their classes
Test Bank	Approximately 75–100 total questions per chapter, made up of multiple-choice, true/false, and matching. Questions include these annotations: • Correct Answer • Difficulty Level • Learning Objective Alternative versions of the Test Bank are available for the following LMS: Blackboard CE/Vista, Blackboard, Desire2Learn, Moodle, Sakai, and Canvas
Computerized TestGen	TestGen allows instructors to: • Customize, save, and generate classroom tests • Edit, add, or delete questions from the Test Item Files • Analyze test results • Organize a database of tests and student results
PowerPoint Presentations	PowerPoints for each chapter cover key topics, feature key images from the text, and include detailed speaker notes in addition to the slide content. PowerPoints meet accessibility standards for students with disabilities. Features include, but are not limited to: • Keyboard and Screen Reader access • Alternative text for images • High color contrast between background and foreground colors

Scripted Lectures	• A lecture guide that provides the actions and language to help demonstrate skills from the chapter • Follows the activity similar to the Hands-On Exercises but with an alternative scenario and data files
Prepared Exams	• An optional Hands-On Exercise that can be used to assess students' ability to perform the skills from each chapter, or across all chapters in an application. • Each Prepared Exam folder includes the needed data files, instruction file, solution, annotated solution, and scorecard.
Outcome and Objective Maps	• Available for each chapter to help you determine what to assign • Includes every exercise and identifies which outcomes, objectives, and skills are included from the chapter
MOS Mapping, MOS Online Appendix	• Based on the Office 2019 MOS Objectives • Includes a full mapping of where each objective is covered in the materials • For any content not covered in the textbook, additional material is available in the Online Appendix document
Transition Guide	A detailed spreadsheet that provides a clear mapping of content from Exploring Microsoft Office 2016 to Exploring Microsoft Office 365, 2019 Edition
Content Updates Guide	A living document that features any changes in content based on Microsoft Office 365 changes as well as any errata
Assignment Sheets	Document with a grid of suggested student deliverables per chapter that can be passed out to students with columns for Due Date, Possible Points, and Actual Points
Sample Syllabus	Syllabus templates set up for 8-week, 12-week, and 16-week courses
Answer Keys for Multiple Choice, Key Terms Matching, and Quick Concepts Check	Answer keys for each objective, matching, or short-answer question type from each chapter

Student Resources

Supplements Available to Students at www.pearsonhighered.com/exploring	Features of the Supplement
Student Data Files	All data files needed for the following exercises, organized by chapter: • Hands-On Exercises • Practice Exercises • Mid-Level Exercises • Running Case • Disaster Recovery Case • Capstone Exercise
MOS Certification Material	• Based on the Office 2019 MOS Objectives • Includes a full mapping of where each objective is covered in the materials • For any content not covered in the textbook, additional material is available in the Online Appendix document

Office 365 Common Features

Common Features

LEARNING OUTCOME
You will apply skills common across the Microsoft Office suite to create and format documents and edit content in Office 365 applications.

OBJECTIVES & SKILLS: After you read this chapter, you will be able to:

Get Started with Office Applications

OBJECTIVE 1: START AN OFFICE APPLICATION   5
Use Your Microsoft Account, Use OneDrive
OBJECTIVE 2: WORK WITH FILES   6
Create a New File, Save a File, Open a Saved File
OBJECTIVE 3: USE COMMON INTERFACE COMPONENTS   9
Use the Ribbon, Use a Dialog Box and Gallery, Customize the Ribbon, Use the Quick Access Toolbar, Customize the Quick Access Toolbar, Use a Shortcut Menu, Use Keyboard Shortcuts
OBJECTIVE 4: GET HELP   15
Use the Tell Me Box, Use the Help Tab, Use Enhanced ScreenTips
OBJECTIVE 5: INSTALL ADD-INS   17
Use an Add-in from the Store
HANDS-ON EXERCISE 1   19

Format Document Content

OBJECTIVE 6: USE TEMPLATES AND APPLY THEMES   25
Open a Template, Apply a Theme
OBJECTIVE 7: MODIFY TEXT   27
Select Text, Format Text, Use the Mini Toolbar

OBJECTIVE 8: RELOCATE TEXT   30
Cut, Copy, and Paste Text; Use the Office Clipboard
OBJECTIVE 9: REVIEW A DOCUMENT   32
Check Spelling and Grammar
OBJECTIVE 10: WORK WITH PICTURES   34
Insert a Picture, Modify a Picture
HANDS-ON EXERCISE 2   37

Modify Document Layout and Properties

OBJECTIVE 11: CHANGE DOCUMENT VIEWS   45
Change Document Views Using the Ribbon, Change Document Views Using the Status Bar
OBJECTIVE 12: CHANGE THE PAGE LAYOUT   46
Change Margins, Change Page Orientation, Use the Page Setup Dialog Box
OBJECTIVE 13: CREATE A HEADER AND FOOTER   49
Insert a Footer, Insert a Header
OBJECTIVE 14: CONFIGURE DOCUMENT PROPERTIES   50
View and Enter Document Properties
OBJECTIVE 15: PREVIEW AND PRINT A FILE   51
Preview a File, Change Print Settings, Print a File
HANDS-ON EXERCISE 3   53

CASE STUDY | Spotted Begonia Art Gallery

You are an administrative assistant for Spotted Begonia, a local art gallery. The gallery does a lot of community outreach to help local artists develop a network of clients and supporters. Local schools are invited to bring students to the gallery for enrichment programs.

As the administrative assistant for Spotted Begonia, you are responsible for overseeing the production of documents, spreadsheets, newspaper articles, and presentations that will be used to increase public awareness of the gallery. Other clerical assistants who are familiar with Microsoft Office will prepare the promotional materials, and you will proofread, make necessary corrections, adjust page layouts, save and print documents, and identify appropriate templates to simplify tasks. Your experience with Microsoft Office is limited, but you know that certain fundamental tasks that are common to Word, Excel, and PowerPoint will help you accomplish your oversight task. You are excited to get started with your work!

CHAPTER 1

Taking the First Step

FIGURE 1.1 Spotted Begonia Art Gallery Documents

CASE STUDY | Spotted Begonia Art Gallery

Starting Files	Files to be Submitted
cf01h1Letter.docx Seasonal Event Flyer Template	cf01h1Letter_LastFirst.docx cf01h3Flyer_LastFirst.docx

MyLab IT Grader An alternate version of this project is available as a MyLab IT Grader Assessment

Get Started with Office Applications

Organizations around the world rely heavily on Microsoft Office software to produce documents, spreadsheets, presentations, and databases. **Microsoft Office** is a productivity software suite that includes a set of software applications, each one specializing in a specific type of output. There are different versions of Office. Office 365 is purchased as a monthly or annual subscription and is fully installed on your PC, tablet, and phone. With Office 365, you receive periodic updates of new features and security measures. Office 365 also includes access to OneDrive storage. Office 2019 is a one-time purchase and fully installed on your PC. Periodic upgrades are not available. Both Office 365 and Office 2019 have versions that run on a Mac.

All versions of Microsoft Office include Word, Excel, and PowerPoint, as well as some other applications. Some versions of Office also include Access. Office 365 for Mac and Office for Mac include Word, Excel, and PowerPoint, but not Access. **Microsoft Word** (Word) is a word processing application, used to produce all sorts of documents, including memos, newsletters, reports, and brochures. **Microsoft Excel** (Excel) is a financial spreadsheet program, used to organize records, financial transactions, and business information in the form of worksheets. **Microsoft PowerPoint** (PowerPoint) is presentation software, used to create dynamic presentations to inform and persuade audiences. Finally, **Microsoft Access** (Access) is a database program, used to record and link data, query databases, and create forms and reports. The choice of which software application to use really depends on what type of output you are producing. Table 1.1 describes the major tasks of the four primary applications in Microsoft Office.

TABLE 1.1 Microsoft Office Applications

Office Application	Application Characteristics
Word	Word processing software used with text and graphics to create, edit, and format documents.
Excel	Spreadsheet software used to store quantitative data and to perform accurate and rapid calculations, what-if analyses, and charting, with results ranging from simple budgets to sophisticated financial and statistical analyses.
PowerPoint	Presentation graphics software used to create slide shows for presentation by a speaker or delivered online, to be published as part of a website, or to run as a stand-alone application on a computer kiosk.
Access	Relational database software used to store data and convert it into information. Database software is used primarily for decision making by businesses that compile data from multiple records stored in tables to produce informative reports.

These programs are designed to work together, so you can integrate components created in one application into a file created by another application. For example, you could integrate a chart created in Excel into a Word document or a PowerPoint presentation, or you could export a table created in Access into Excel for further analysis. You can use two or more Office applications to produce your intended output.

In addition, Microsoft Office applications share common features. Such commonality gives a similar feel to each software application so that learning and working with each Office software application is easier. This chapter focuses on many common features that the Office applications share. Although Word is primarily used to illustrate many examples, you are encouraged to open and explore Excel and PowerPoint (and to some degree, Access) to examine the same features in those applications. As a note, most of the content in this chapter and book are for the Windows-based Office applications. Some basic information about Office for Mac is included in TIP boxes and in the Step boxes when there are significant differences to point out.

In this section, you will learn how to log in with your Microsoft account, open an application, and open and save a file. You will also learn to identify interface components common to Office software applications, such as the ribbon, Backstage view, and the Quick Access Toolbar. You will experience Live Preview. You will learn how to get help with an application. You will also learn about customizing the ribbon and using Office add-ins.

Starting an Office Application

Microsoft Office applications are launched from the Start menu. Select the Start icon to display the Start menu and select the app tile for the application in which you want to work (see Figure 1.2). Note: The Start menu in Figure 1.2 may show different tiles and arrangement of tiles than what is on your Start menu. If the application tile you want is not on the Start menu, you can open the program from the list of all apps on the left side of the Start menu, or alternatively, you can use search on the taskbar. Just type the name of the program in the search box and press Enter. The program will open automatically.

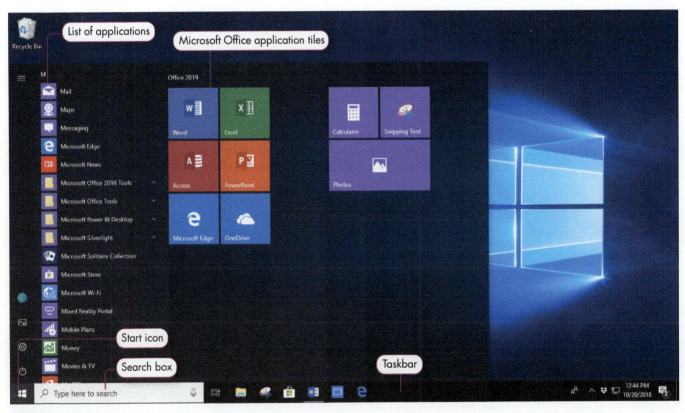

FIGURE 1.2 Windows Start Menu

Use Your Microsoft Account

When you have a Microsoft account, you can sign in to any Windows computer and you will be able to access the saved settings associated with your Microsoft account. That means any computer can have the same familiar look that you are used to seeing on your home or school computers and devices. Your Microsoft account will automatically sign in to all the apps and services that use a Microsoft account, such as OneDrive and Outlook. If you share your computer with another user, each user can have access to his or her own Microsoft account, and can easily switch between accounts by logging out of one Microsoft account and logging in to another Microsoft account. You can switch accounts within an application as well.

To switch between accounts in an application such as Word, complete the following steps:

1. Click the profile name at the top-right of the application.
2. Select Switch account.
3. Select an account from the list, if the account has already been added to the computer, or add a new account.

On a Mac, to switch between accounts in an application, complete the following steps:

1. Click the application menu (Word, Excel, etc.), click Sign Out, and then click Sign Out again.
2. Click File, click New From Template, and then click Sign in at top of the left pane.
3. Click Sign in again, type your user email, click Next, type password, and then click Sign in.

Use OneDrive

Having a Microsoft account also provides additional benefits, such as being connected to all of Microsoft's resources on the Internet. These resources include an Outlook email account and access to OneDrive cloud storage. **Cloud storage** is a technology used to store files and work with programs that are stored in a central location on the Internet. **OneDrive** is a Microsoft app used to store, access, and share files and folders on the Internet. OneDrive is the default storage location when saving Office files. Because OneDrive stores files on the Internet, when a document has been saved in OneDrive the most recent version of the document will be accessible when you log in from any computer connected to the Internet. Files and folders saved to OneDrive can be available offline and accessed through File Explorer—Windows' file management system. Moreover, changes made to any document saved to OneDrive will be automatically updated across all devices, so each device you access with your Windows account will all have the same version of the file.

OneDrive enables you to collaborate with others. You can share your documents with others or edit a document on which you are collaborating. You can even work with others simultaneously on the same document.

STEP 1 Working with Files

When working with an Office application, you can begin by opening an existing file that has already been saved to a storage medium or you can begin work on a new file or template. When you are finished with a file, you should save it, so you can retrieve it at another time.

Create a New File

After opening an Office application, you will be presented with template choices. Use the Blank document (workbook, presentation, database, etc.) template to start a new blank file. You can also create a new Office file from within an application by selecting New from the File tab.

The File tab is located at the far left of the ribbon. When you select the File tab, you see **Backstage view**. Backstage view is where you manage your files and the data about them—creating, saving, printing, sharing, inspecting for accessibility, compatibility, and other document issues, and accessing other setting options. The File tab and Backstage view is where you do things "to" a file, whereas the other tabs on the ribbon enable you to do things "in" a file.

Save a File

Saving a file enables you to open it for additional updates or reference later. Files are saved to a storage medium such as a hard drive, flash drive, or to OneDrive.

The first time you save a file, you indicate where the file will be saved and assign a file name. It is best to save the file in an appropriately named folder so you can find it easily later. Thereafter, you can continue to save the file with the same name and location using the Save command. If the file is saved in OneDrive, any changes to the file will be automatically saved. You do not have to actively save the document. If you want more control over when changes to your document are saved, you have the option to turn this feature off (or back on) with the AutoSave feature in the Quick Access Toolbar.

There are instances where you will want to rename the file or save it to a different location. For example, you might reuse a budget saved as an Excel worksheet, modifying it for another year, and want to keep a copy of both the old and revised budgets. In this instance, you would save the new workbook with a new name, and perhaps save it in a different folder. To do so, use the Save As command, and continue with the same procedure to save a new file: navigating to the new storage location and changing the file name. Figure 1.3 shows a typical Save As pane that enables you to select a location before saving the file. Notice that OneDrive is listed as well as This PC. To navigate to a specific location, use Browse.

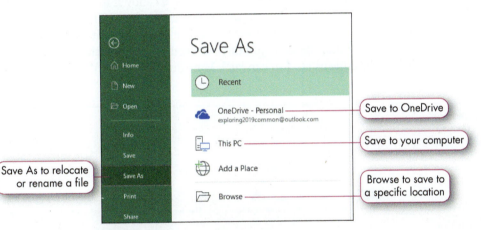

FIGURE 1.3 Save As in Backstage View

> **To save a file with a different name and/or file location, complete the following steps:**
>
> 1. Click the File tab.
> 2. Click Save As.
> 3. Select a location or click Browse to navigate to the file storage location.
> 4. Type the file name.
> 5. Click Save.

STEP 2 Open a Saved File

Often you will need to work on an existing file that has been saved to a storage location. This may be an email attachment that you have downloaded to a storage device, a file that has been shared with you in OneDrive, or a file you have previously created. To open an existing file, navigate in File Explorer to the folder or drive where the document is stored, and then double-click the file name to open the file. The application and the file will open. Alternatively, if the application is already open, from Backstage view, click Open, and then click Browse, This PC, or OneDrive to locate and open the file (see Figure 1.4).

> **MAC TIP:** To open an existing file, navigate in Finder to the folder or drive where the document is stored and double-click the file name to open the file.

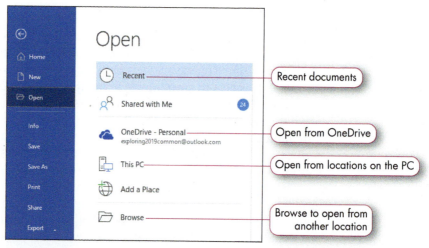

FIGURE 1.4 Open in Backstage View

Office simplifies the task of reopening files by providing a Recent documents list with links to your most recently used files, as shown in Figure 1.5. When opening the application, the Recent list displays in the center pane. The Recent list changes to reflect only the most recently opened files, so if it has been quite some time since you worked with a particular file, or if you have worked on several other files in between and you do not see your file listed, you can click More documents (or Workbooks, Presentations, etc).

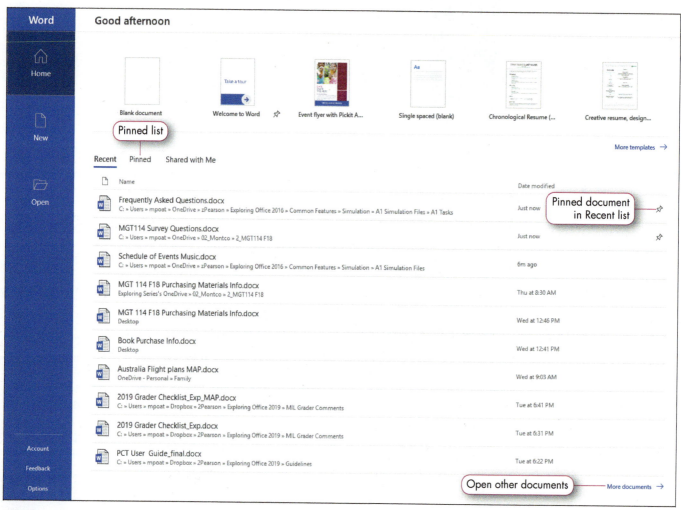

FIGURE 1.5 Recent Documents List

TIP: KEEPING FILES ON THE RECENT DOCUMENTS LIST
The Recent list displays a limited list of only the most recently opened files. However, you might want to keep a particular file in the list regardless of how recently it was opened. In Figure 1.5, note that the *Pin this item to the list* icon displays to the right of each file. Select the icon to pin the file to the list. The pushpin of the "permanent" file will change direction so that it appears to be inserted, indicating that it is a pinned item. Once pinned, you will always have access to the file from the Pinned list. Later, if you want to remove the file from the list, click the pushpin icon. The file will remain on the Recent documents list while it is being used, but will be bumped off the list when other, more recently opened files take its place.

Using Common Interface Components

When you open any Office application, you will first notice the title bar and ribbon (see Figure 1.6) at the top of the document. These features enable you to identify the document, provide easy access to frequently used commands, and controls the window in which the document displays. The **title bar** identifies the current file name and the application in which you are working. It also includes control buttons that enable you to minimize, restore down, or close the application window. The Quick Access Toolbar, on the left side of the title bar, enables you to turn AutoSave on or off, save the file, undo or redo editing, and customize the Quick Access Toolbar. Located just below the title bar is the ribbon. The **ribbon** is the command center of Office applications containing tabs, groups, and commands. If you are working with a large project, you can maximize your workspace by temporarily hiding the ribbon. There are several methods that can be used to hide and then redisplay the ribbon:

- Double-click any tab name to collapse; click any tab name to expand
- Click the Collapse Ribbon arrow at the far-right side of the ribbon
- Use the Ribbon Display Option on the right side of the Title bar. These controls enable you to not only collapse or expand the ribbon, but also to choose whether you want to see the tabs or no tabs at all.

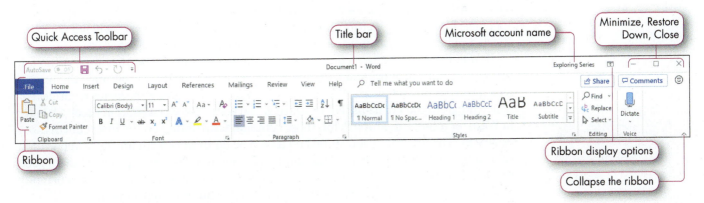

FIGURE 1.6 The Title Bar, Quick Access Toolbar, and Document Controls

Use the Ribbon

The main organizational grouping on the ribbon is tabs. The **tab** name indicates the type of commands located on the tab. On each tab, the ribbon displays several task-oriented groups. A **group** is a subset of a tab that organizes similar commands together. A **command** is a button or task within a group that you select to perform a task (see Figure 1.7). The ribbon with the tabs and groups of commands is designed to provide efficient functionality. For that reason, the Home tab displays when you first open a file in an Office software application and contains groups with the most commonly used commands for that application. For example, because you often want to change the way text is displayed, the Home tab in an Office application includes a Font group, with commands related to modifying text. Similarly, other tabs contain groups of related actions, or commands, many of which are unique to each Office application. The active tab in Figure 1.7 is the Home tab.

> **MAC TIP:** Office for Mac does not display group names in the ribbon by default. On a Mac, to display group names on the ribbon, click the application name menu (Word, Excel, PowerPoint) and select Preferences. Click View and click to select Show group titles in the Ribbon section of the View dialog box.

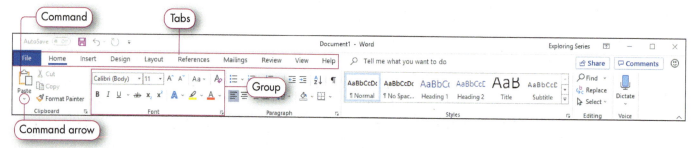

FIGURE 1.7 The Ribbon

As shown in Figure 1.7, some ribbon commands, such as Paste in the Clipboard group, contain two parts: the main command and an arrow. The arrow may be below or to the right of the main command, depending on the command, window size, or screen resolution. When selected, the arrow brings up additional commands or options associated with the main command. For example, selecting the Paste arrow enables you to access the Paste Options commands, and the Font color arrow displays a set of colors from which to choose. Instructions in the *Exploring* series use the command name to instruct you to click the main command to perform the default action, such as click Paste. Instructions include the word *arrow* when you need to select the arrow to access an additional option, such as click the Paste arrow.

Office applications enable you to work with objects such as images, shapes, charts, and tables. When you include such objects in a project, they are considered separate components that you can manage independently. To work with an object, you must first select it. When an object is selected, the ribbon is modified to include one or more **contextual tabs** that contain groups of commands related to the selected object. These tabs are designated as Tool tabs; for example, Picture Tools is the contextual tab that displays when a picture is selected. When the object is no longer selected, the contextual tab disappears.

Word, PowerPoint, Excel, and Access all share a similar ribbon structure. Although the specific tabs, groups, and commands vary among the Office programs, the way in which you use the ribbon and the descriptive nature of tab titles is the same, regardless of which program you are using. For example, if you want to insert a chart in Excel, a header in Word, or a shape in PowerPoint, those commands are found on the Insert tab in those programs. The first thing you should do as you begin to work with an Office application is to study the ribbon. Look at all tabs and their contents. That way, you will have a good idea of where to find specific commands, and how the ribbon with which you are currently working differs from one that you might have used in another application.

STEP 3 Use a Dialog Box and Gallery

Some commands and features do not display on the ribbon because they are not as commonly used. For example, you might want to apply a special effect such as Small caps or apply character spacing to some text. Because these effects are not found on the ribbon, they will most likely be found in a ***dialog box*** (in this case, the Font dialog box). When you open a dialog box, you gain access to more precise or less frequently used commands. Dialog boxes are accessed by clicking a ***Dialog Box Launcher***, found in the lower right corner of some ribbon groups. Figure 1.8 shows the Font group Dialog Box Launcher and the Font dialog box.

> **MAC TIP:** Dialog box launchers are not available in Office for Mac. Instead, click a menu option such as Format, Edit, or Insert for additional options.

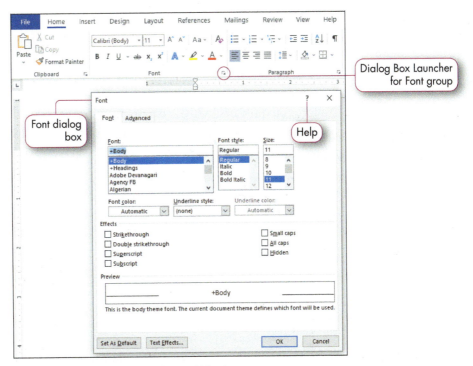

FIGURE 1.8 The Font Dialog Box in Word

> **TIP: GETTING HELP WITH DIALOG BOXES**
> You will find commands or options in a dialog box that you are not familiar with. Click the Help button that displays as a question mark in the top-right corner of the dialog box. The subsequent Help window offers suggestions or assistance in implementing the relevant feature.

Similarly, some formatting and design options are too numerous to include in the ribbon's limited space. For example, the Styles group displays on the Home tab of the Word ribbon. Because there are more styles than can easily display at once, the Styles group can be expanded to display a gallery of additional styles. A ***gallery*** is an Office feature that displays additional formatting and design options. Galleries in Excel and PowerPoint provide additional choices of chart styles and slide themes, respectively. Figure 1.9 shows an example of a PowerPoint Themes gallery. From the ribbon, you can display a gallery of additional choices by clicking More ⏷, which is located at the bottom right of the group's scroll bar found in some ribbon selections (see Figure 1.9).

FIGURE 1.9 The Variants Gallery in PowerPoint

When editing a document, worksheet, or presentation, it is helpful to see the results of formatting changes before you make final selections. The feature that displays a preview of the results of a selection is called **Live Preview**. For example, you might be considering modifying the color of an image in a document or worksheet. As you place the pointer over a color selection in a ribbon gallery or group, the selected image will temporarily display the color to which you are pointing. Similarly, you can get a preview of how theme designs would display on PowerPoint slides by pointing to specific themes in the PowerPoint Themes group and noting the effect on a displayed slide. When you click the item, the selection is applied. Live Preview is available in various ribbon selections among the Office applications.

Get Started with Office Applications • Common Features 2019

Customize the Ribbon

Although the ribbon is designed to put the tasks you need most in an easily accessible location, there may be tasks that are specific to your job or hobby that are on various tabs, or not displayed on the ribbon at all. In this case, you can personalize the ribbon by creating your own tabs and group together the commands you want to use. To add a command to a tab, you must first add a custom group. You can create as many new tabs and custom groups with as many commands as you need. You can also create a custom group on any of the default tabs and add commands to the new group or hide any commands you use less often (see Figure 1.10). Keep in mind that when you customize the ribbon, the customization applies only to the Office program in which you are working at the time. If you want a new tab with the same set of commands in both Word and PowerPoint, for example, the new tab would need to be created in each application.

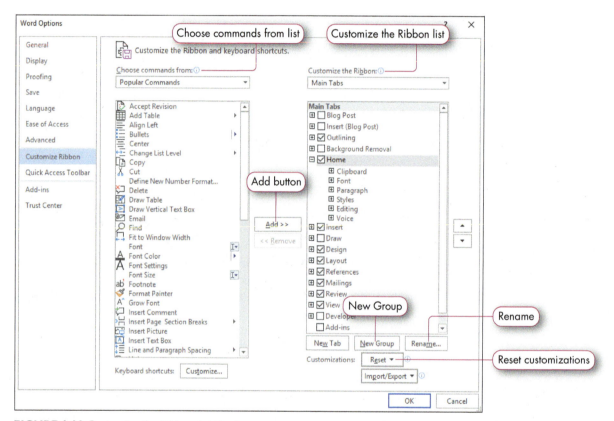

FIGURE 1.10 Customize the Ribbon in Word

There are several ways to access the Customize the Ribbon options:

- Right-click in an empty space in the ribbon and select Customize the Ribbon on the shortcut menu.
- Click the File tab, select Options, and then select Customize Ribbon.
- Click the Customize Quick Access Toolbar button, select More Commands, and then select Customize Ribbon.

The left side of the Customize the Ribbon window displays popular commands associated with the active application, but all available commands can be displayed by selecting All Commands in the *Choose commands from* list. On the right side of the Customize the Ribbon window is a list of the Main Tabs and Groups in the active application. You can also access the contextual Tool tabs by selecting the arrow in the Customize the Ribbon list and selecting Tool Tabs.

To customize the ribbon by adding a command to an existing tab, complete the following steps:

1. Click the File tab, click Options, and then select Customize Ribbon. (Alternatively, follow the other steps above to access the Customize the Ribbon window.)
2. Click the tab name that you want to add a group to under the Customize the Ribbon list. Ensure a blue background displays behind the tab name. Note that checking or unchecking the tab is not selecting the tab for this feature.
3. Click New Group. New Group (Custom) displays as a group on the selected tab.
4. Click Rename and give the new group a meaningful name.
5. Click the command to be added under the Choose commands from list.
6. Click Add.
7. Repeat as necessary, click OK when you have made all your selections.

On a Mac, to customize the ribbon, complete the following steps:

1. Click the Word menu (or whichever application you are working in) and select Preferences.
2. Click Ribbon & Toolbar in the Authoring and Proofing Tools (or in Excel, Authoring).
3. Click the plus sign at the bottom of the Main Tabs box and select New Group.
4. Click the Settings icon and click Rename. Give the new group a meaningful name. Click Save.
5. Continue using steps 5 and 6 in the PC step box above.

To revert all tabs or to reset select tabs to original settings, click Reset, and then click Reset all customizations or Reset only selected Ribbon tab (refer to Figure 1.10).

STEP 4 — Use and Customize the Quick Access Toolbar

The **Quick Access Toolbar (QAT)**, located at the top-left corner of every Office application window (refer to Figure 1.6), provides one-click access to commonly executed tasks. By default, the QAT includes commands for saving a file and for undoing or redoing recent actions. You can recover from a mistake by clicking Undo on the QAT. If you click the Undo command arrow on the QAT, you can select from a list of previous actions in order of occurrence. The Undo list is not maintained when you close a file or exit the application, so you can only erase an action that took place during the current Office session. You can also Redo (or Replace) an action that you have just undone.

You can also customize the QAT to include commands you frequently use (see Figure 1.11). One command you may want to add is Quick Print. Rather than clicking

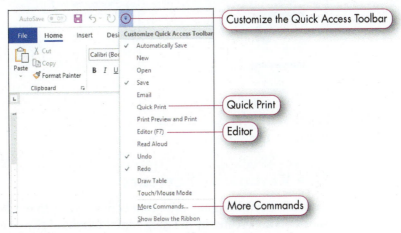

FIGURE 1.11 Customize the Quick Access Toolbar

the File tab, selecting Print, and then selecting various print options, you can add Quick Print to the QAT so that with one click you can print your document with the default Print settings. Other convenient commands can be added, such as Editor to run a spell check of the document.

You customize the QAT by selecting Customize Quick Access Toolbar arrow on the right side of the displayed QAT commands or by right-clicking an empty area on the QAT, and then selecting or deselecting the options from the displayed list of commands. Alternatively, you can right-click any command on the ribbon and select Add to Quick Access Toolbar from the shortcut menu.

To remove a command from the QAT, right-click the command and select Remove from Quick Access Toolbar. If you want to move the QAT to display under the ribbon, select Customize Quick Access Toolbar and click Show below the Ribbon.

STEP 5 Use a Shortcut Menu

In Office, you can usually accomplish the same task in several ways. Although the ribbon and QAT provide efficient access to commands, in some situations you might find it more convenient to access the same commands on a shortcut menu. A ***shortcut menu*** is a context-sensitive menu that displays commands and options relevant to the active object. Shortcut menus are accessed by selecting text or an object or by placing the insertion point in a document and pressing the right mouse button or pressing the right side of a trackpad. (On a Mac, press the Control key when you tap the mouse or use a two-finger tap on a trackpad). The shortcut menu will always include options to cut, copy, and paste. In addition, a shortcut menu features tasks that are specifically related to the document content where the insertion point is placed. For example, if your insertion point is on a selected word or group of words, the shortcut menu would include tasks such as to find a synonym or add a comment. If the active object is a picture, the shortcut menu includes options to group objects, provide a caption, or wrap text. As shown in Figure 1.12, when right-clicking a slide thumbnail in PowerPoint, the shortcut menu displays options to add a new slide, duplicate or delete slides, or to change slide layout.

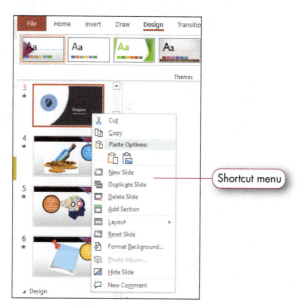

FIGURE 1.12 A Shortcut Menu in PowerPoint

Use Keyboard Shortcuts

Another way to simplify initiating commands is to use ***keyboard shortcuts***. Keyboard shortcuts are created by pressing combinations of two or more keys to initiate a software command. Keyboard shortcuts are viewed as being more efficient because you do not have to take your fingers off the keyboard. Some of the most common keyboard shortcuts in Office include Ctrl+C (Copy), Ctrl+X (Cut), Ctrl+V (Paste), and Ctrl+Z (Undo). Pressing Ctrl+Home moves the insertion point to the beginning of a Word document, to cell A1 in Excel, or to the first PowerPoint slide. To move to the end of those files, press Ctrl+End. There are many other keyboard shortcuts. To discover a keyboard shortcut for a command, point to a command icon on the ribbon to display the ScreenTip. If a keyboard shortcut exists, it will display in the ScreenTip. Many similar keyboard shortcuts exist for Office for Mac applications; however, press the Command key rather than the Ctrl key, such as Command+C for Copy.

> **TIP: USING KEYTIPS**
> Another way to use shortcuts, especially those that do not have a keyboard shortcut, is to press Alt to display KeyTips. You can use KeyTips to do tasks quickly without using the mouse by pressing a few keys—no matter where you are in an Office program. You can get to every command on the ribbon by using an access key—usually by pressing two to four keys sequentially. To stop displaying KeyTips, press Alt again.

Getting Help

No matter whether you are a skilled or a novice user of an Office application, there are times when you need help in either finding a certain ribbon command or need additional assistance or training for a task. Fortunately, there are features included in every Office application to offer you support.

STEP 6 Use the Tell Me Box

To the right of the last ribbon tab is a magnifying glass icon and the phrase "Tell me what you want to do." This is the **Tell me box** (see Figure 1.13). Use Tell me to enter words and phrases to search for help and information about a command or task you want to perform. Alternatively, use Tell me for a shortcut to a command or, in some instances (like Bold), to complete the action for you. Tell me can also help you research or define a term you entered. Perhaps you want to find an instance of a word in your document and replace it with another word but cannot locate the Find command on the ribbon. As shown in Figure 1.13, you can type *find* in the Tell me box and a list of commands related to the skill will display, including Find & Select and Replace. Find & Select gives options for the Find command. If you click Replace, the Find and Replace dialog box opens without you having to locate the command on the ribbon.

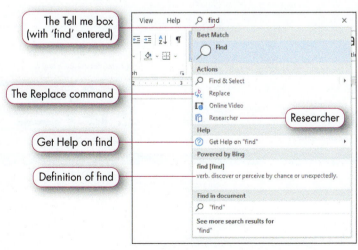

FIGURE 1.13 The Tell Me Box

Should you want to read about the feature instead of applying it, you can click *Get Help on "find,"* which will open Office Help for the feature. Another feature is Smart Lookup on the References tab. This feature opens the Smart Lookup pane that shows results from various online sources based on the search term. **Smart Lookup** provides information about tasks or commands in Office and can also be used to search for general information on a topic, such as *President George Washington*. Smart Lookup is also available on the shortcut menu when you right-click text as well as on the References tab in Word. Depending on your search, Researcher may display instead of, or in addition to, Smart Lookup. Researcher can be used to find quotes, citable sources, and images. Researcher is shown in Figure 1.13.

Use the Help Tab

If you are looking for additional help or training on certain features in any Microsoft Office application, you can access this support on the Help tab (see Figure 1.14). The Help command opens the Help pane with a list of tutorials on a variety of application-specific topics. Show Training displays application-specific training videos in the Help pane. Besides Help and Show Training, the Help tab also includes means to contact Microsoft support and to share your feedback. If you are using Office 365, you receive periodic updates with new features as they are released. To learn more about these features, or simply to discover what a new or previous update includes, use the What's New command. What's New brings you to a webpage that discusses all the newly added features organized by release date. You can also access What's New by clicking Account in Backstage view.

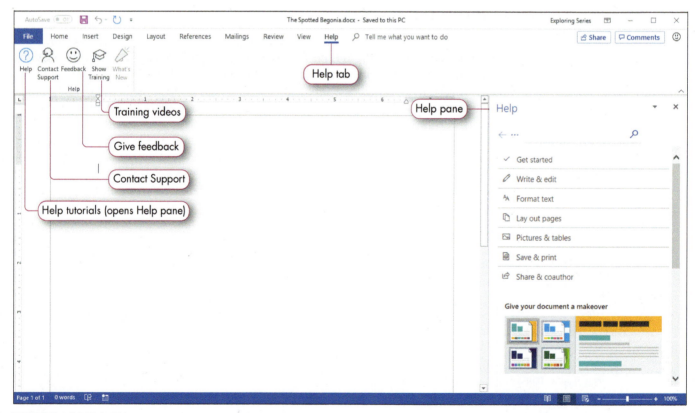

FIGURE 1.14 Help Tab

Use Enhanced ScreenTips

As you use the commands on the ribbon, there may be some that you would like to know more about its purpose, or would like assurance that you are selecting the correct command. For quick summary information on the name and purpose of a command button, point to the command until an **Enhanced ScreenTip** displays, with the name and a brief description of the command. If applicable, a keyboard shortcut is also included. Some ScreenTips include a *Tell me more* option for additional help. The Enhanced ScreenTip, shown for **Format Painter** in Figure 1.15, provides a short description of the command in addition to the steps that discuss how to use Format Painter. Use Format Painter to copy all applied formatting from one set of text to another.

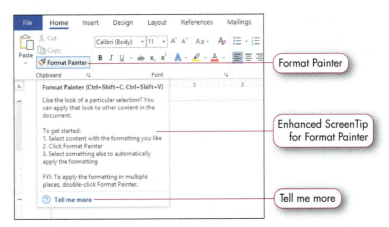

FIGURE 1.15 Enhanced ScreenTip

> **TIP: COPY FORMAT WITH FORMAT PAINTER**
>
> Use Format Painter to quickly apply the same formatting, such as color, font style, and size to other text. Format Painter can also be used to copy border styles to shapes. Format Painter is available in Word, Excel, and PowerPoint, and can be extremely useful when applying multiple formats to other text. Using Format Painter also ensures consistency in appearance between sets of text. To copy formatting to one location, single-click Format Painter, and then click where you want the format applied. To copy formatting to multiple locations, double-click Format Painter. Press Esc or click Format Painter again to turn off the command.

Installing Add-ins

As complete as the Office applications are, you still might want an additional feature that is not a part of the program. Fortunately, there are Microsoft and third-party programs called add-ins that you can add to the program. An **add-in** is a custom program that extends the functionality of a Microsoft Office application (see Figure 1.16). For example, in PowerPoint, you could add capability for creating diagrams, access free images, or obtain assistance with graphic design. In Excel, add-ins could provide additional functionality that can help with statistics and data mining. In Word, add-ins could provide survey or resume-creating capabilities. Some add-ins will be available for several applications. For example, the Pickit image app shown in Figure 1.16 is available for Word and PowerPoint. You can access add-ins through the My Add-ins or Get Add-ins commands on the Insert tab. Some templates may come with an add-in associated with it. Some add-ins are available for free, whereas others may have a cost.

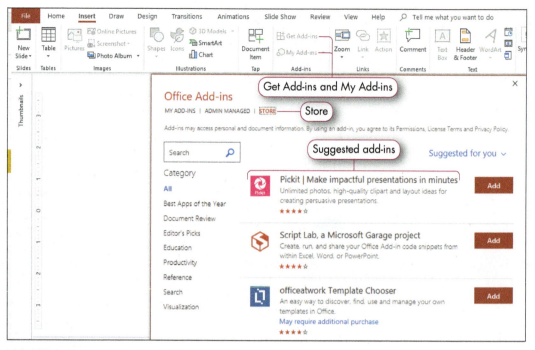

FIGURE 1.16 Add-ins for PowerPoint

1. Explain the benefits of logging in with your Microsoft account. *p. 5*
2. Describe when you would use Save and when you would use Save As when saving a document. *p. 7*
3. Explain how the ribbon is organized. *p. 9*
4. Describe the Office application features that are available to assist you in getting help with a task. *p. 15*

Hands-On Exercises

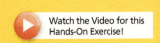
Watch the Video for this Hands-On Exercise!

Skills covered: Open a Saved File • Save a File • Use a Shortcut Menu • Use the Tell me Box

1 Get Started with Office Applications

The Spotted Begonia Art Gallery just hired several new clerical assistants to help you develop materials for the various activities coming up throughout the year. A coworker sent you a letter and asked for your assistance in making a few minor formatting changes. The letter is an invitation to the *Discover the Artist in You!* program Children's Art Festival. To begin, you will open Word and open an existing document. You will use the Shortcut menu to make simple changes to the document. Finally, you will use the Tell me box to apply a style to the first line of text.

STEP 1 OPEN AND SAVE A FILE

You start Microsoft Word and open an event invitation letter that you will later modify. You rename the file to preserve the original and to save the changes you will make later. Refer to Figure 1.17 as you complete Step 1.

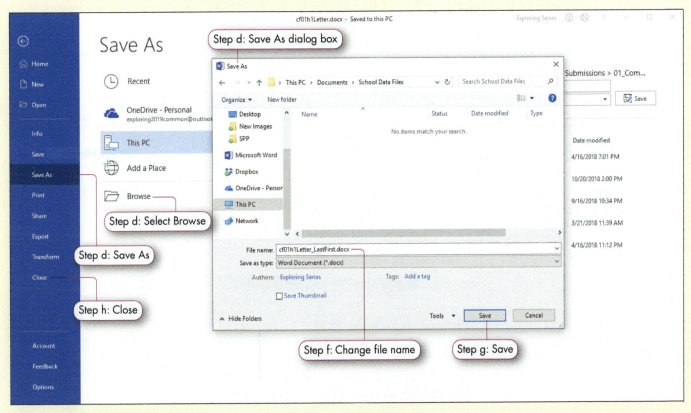

FIGURE 1.17 The Save As Dialog Box

a. Open the Word document *cf01h1Letter*.

   The event invitation letter opens.

   TROUBLESHOOTING: When you open a file from the student files associated with this book, you may see an Enable Content warning in the Message Bar. This is a security measure to alert a user when there is potentially unsafe content in the file you want to open. You may be confident of the trustworthiness of the files for this book, and should click Enable Content to begin working on the file.

b. Click the **File tab**, click **Save As**, and then click **Browse** to display the Save As dialog box.

   Because you will change the name of an existing file, you use the Save As command to give the file a new name. On a Mac, click the File menu and click Save As.

Hands-On Exercise 1   19

c. Navigate to the location where you are saving your files.

If you are saving the file in a different location than that of your data files, then you will also change the location of where the file is saved.

d. Click in the **File name box** (or the Save As box in Office for Mac) and type **cf01h1Letter_LastFirst**.

You save the document with a different name to preserve the original file.

When you save files, use your last and first names. For example, as the Common Features author, I would name my document "cf01h1Letter_PoatsyMaryAnne."

e. Click **Save**.

> **TROUBLESHOOTING:** If you make any major mistakes in this exercise, you can close the file, open *cf01h1Letter* again, and then start this exercise over.

The file is now saved as cf01h1Letter_LastFirst. Check the title bar of the document to confirm that the file has been saved with the correct name.

f. Click **File** and click **Close** to close the file. Keep Word open.

STEP 2 OPEN A SAVED FILE AND USE THE RIBBON

You now have time to modify the letter, so you open the saved file. You use ribbon commands to modify parts of the letter. Refer to Figure 1.18 as you complete Step 2.

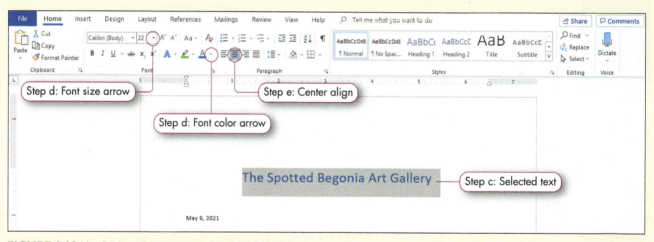

FIGURE 1.18 Use Ribbon Commands to Modify Text

a. Click the **File tab** and click **Open** from the left menu.

The Open window displays.

b. Click **cf01h1Letter_LastFirst** from the list of Recent documents on the right side of the Open window.

The letter you saved earlier opens and is ready to be modified.

c. Place the insertion point in the left margin just before the first line of text *The Spotted Begonia Art Gallery* so an angled right-pointing arrow displays and click.

This is an efficient way of selecting an entire line of text. Alternatively, you can drag the pointer across the text while holding down the left mouse button to select the text.

d. Click the **Font color arrow** in the Font group on the Home tab and select **Blue** in the Standard Colors section. With the text still selected, click the **Font Size arrow** in the Font group and select **22**.

You have changed the color and size of the Art Gallery's name.

e. Click **Center** in the Paragraph group.

f. Click **File** and click **Save**.

Because the file has already been saved, and the name and location are not changing, you use the Save command to save the changes.

STEP 3 USE A DIALOG BOX AND GALLERY

Some of the modifications you want to make to the letter require using tasks that are in dialog boxes and galleries. You will use a Dialog Box Launcher and More to expand the galleries to access the needed commands and features. Refer to Figure 1.19 as you complete Step 3.

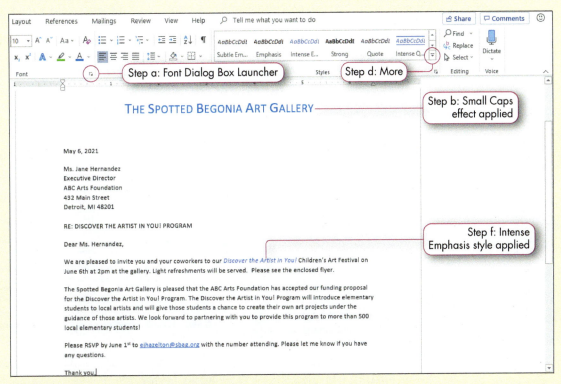

FIGURE 1.19 Use a Dialog Box and Gallery

a. Select the text **The Spotted Begonia Art Gallery**, if it is not already selected. Click the **Font Dialog Box Launcher** in the Font group.

The Font dialog box displays.

> **MAC TROUBLESHOOTING:** Office for Mac does not have Dialog Box Launchers. Instead, open a menu and select an option. For example, to access Font options that display in the Font Dialog Box, click the Format menu, and then click Font.

b. Click the **Small caps check box** in the Effects section to select it and click **OK**.

The Small caps text effect is applied to the selected text.

c. Place the insertion point immediately to the left of the text *Discover the Artist in You!* in the first sentence of the paragraph beginning *We are pleased*. Hold the left mouse button down and drag the pointer to select the text up to and including the exclamation point.

> **TROUBLESHOOTING:** Be sure the file you are working on is displayed as a full window. Otherwise, use the vertical scroll bar to bring the paragraph into view.

d. Click **More** in the Styles group to display the Styles gallery. (On a Mac, click the right gallery arrow or click the down arrow to view more options.)

e. Point to Heading 1 style.

Notice how Live Preview shows how that effect will look on the selected text.

f. Click **Intense Emphasis**.

The Intense Emphasis style is applied to the program name.

g. Click **File** and click **Save**.

STEP 4 USE AND CUSTOMIZE THE QUICK ACCESS TOOLBAR

You make a change to the document and immediately change your mind. You use the Undo button on the QAT to revert to the original word. You also anticipate checking the spelling on the letter before sending it out. Because you use Spell Check often, you decide to add the command to the QAT. Finally, you realize that you could be saving the document more efficiently by using Save on the QAT. Refer to Figure 1.20 as you complete Step 4.

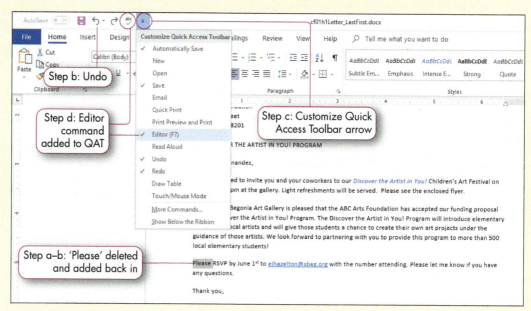

FIGURE 1.20 Customize the Quick Access Toolbar

a. Scroll down so the third paragraph beginning with *Please RSVP* is visible. Double-click **Please** and press **Delete** on the keyboard.

Please is deleted from the letter, but you decide to add it back in.

b. Click **Undo** on the QAT.

Please displays again.

c. Click the **Customize Quick Access Toolbar arrow** on the right side of the QAT.

A list of commands that can be added to the QAT displays.

d. Click **Editor**.

The Editor icon displays on the QAT so you can check for spelling, grammar, and writing issues.

e. Click **Save** on the QAT.

STEP 5: USE A SHORTCUT MENU

The letter inviting Ms. Hernandez also extends the invitation to her coworkers. Ms. Hazelton has asked that you use a different word for coworkers, so you use a shortcut menu to find a synonym. Refer to Figure 1.21 as you complete Step 5.

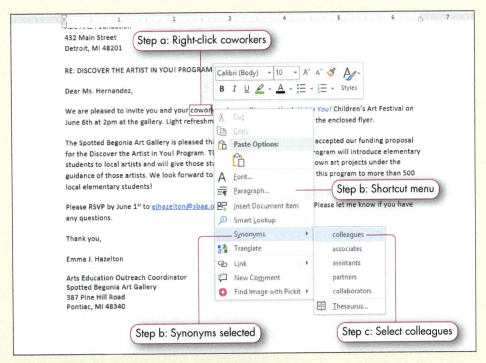

FIGURE 1.21 Use the Shortcut Menu to Find a Synonym

a. Point to and right-click the word **coworkers** in the first sentence of the letter that starts with *We are pleased*.

A shortcut menu displays.

> **MAC TROUBLESHOOTING:** To open a shortcut menu, use Control+click.

b. Select **Synonyms** on the shortcut menu.

A list of alternate words for coworkers displays.

c. Select **colleagues** from the list.

The synonym *colleagues* replaces the word *coworkers*.

d. Click **Save** on the QAT.

Hands-On Exercise 1   23

STEP 6: USE THE TELL ME BOX

You would like to apply the Intense Effect style you used to format *Discover the Artist in You!* to other instances of the program name in the second paragraph. You think there is a more efficient way of applying the same format to other text, but you do not know how to complete the task. Therefore, you use the Tell me box to search for the command and then you apply the change. Refer to Figure 1.22 as you complete Step 6.

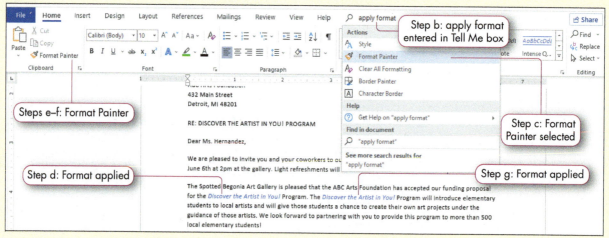

FIGURE 1.22 Use the Tell Me Box

a. Click anywhere in the text **Discover the Artist in You!** in the first sentence of the letter that starts with *We are pleased*.

b. Click the **Tell me box** and type **apply format**.

The Tell me box displays a list of options related to apply format.

c. Select **Format Painter** from the list of options in the Tell Me results.

Notice that the Format Painter command in the Clipboard group is selected and a paintbrush is added to the insertion point.

d. Drag the pointer over the first instance of **Discover the Artist in You!** in the second line of the second paragraph beginning with *The Spotted Begonia*.

The Intense Emphasis style was applied to the selected text.

> **TROUBLESHOOTING:** If the format is not applied to the text, move to the next step, but double-click Format Painter and apply the format to both instances of Discover the Artist in You!

e. Point to **Format Painter** in the Clipboard group and read the Enhanced ScreenTip.

You notice that to apply formatting to more than one selection, you must double-click Format Painter, but because you need to apply the format to only one more set of text, you will single-click the command.

f. Click **Format Painter** in the Clipboard group.

g. Drag the pointer over the second instance of **Discover the Artist in You!** in the second paragraph beginning with *The Spotted Begonia*.

You used the Format Painter to copy the formatting applied to text to other text.

> **TROUBLESHOOTING:** Press Esc on the keyboard to turn off Format Painter if you had to double-click Format Painter in Step d above.

h. Save and close the document. You will submit this file to your instructor at the end of the last Hands-On Exercise.

Format Document Content

In the process of creating a document, worksheet, or presentation, you will most likely make some formatting changes. You might center a title, or format budget worksheet totals as currency. You can change the font so that typed characters are larger or in a different style. You might even want to bold text to add emphasis. Sometimes, it may be more efficient to start with a document that has formatting already applied or apply a group of coordinated fonts, font styles, and colors. You might also want to add, delete, or reposition text. Inserting and formatting images can add interest to a document or illustrate content. Finally, no document is finished until all spelling and grammar has been checked and all errors removed.

In this section, you will explore themes and templates. You will learn to use the Mini Toolbar to quickly make formatting changes. You will learn how to select and edit text, as well as check your grammar and spelling. You will learn how to move, copy, and paste text, and how to insert pictures. And, finally, you will learn how to resize and format pictures and graphics.

Using Templates and Applying Themes

You can enhance your documents by using a template or applying a theme. A ***template*** is a predesigned file that incorporates formatting elements and layouts and may include content that can be modified. A ***theme*** is a collection of design choices that includes colors, fonts, and special effects used to give a consistent look to a document, workbook, or presentation. Microsoft provides high-quality templates and themes, designed to make it faster and easier to create professional-looking documents.

STEP 1 ### Open a Template

When you launch any Office program and click New, the screen displays thumbnail images of a sampling of templates for that application (see Figure 1.23). Alternatively, if you are already working in an application, click the File tab and select New on the Backstage

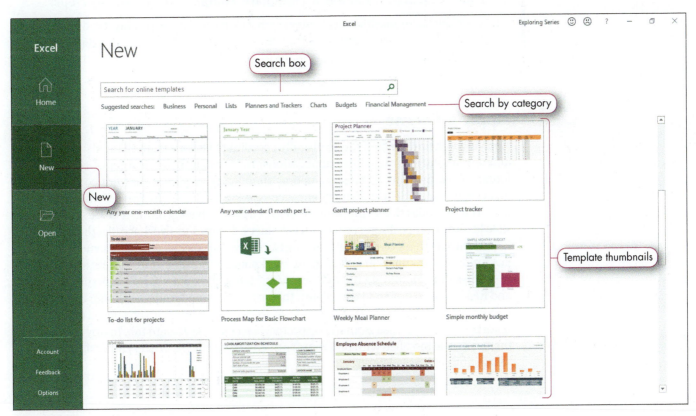

FIGURE 1.23 Templates in Excel

Navigation Pane. One benefit of starting with a template is if you know only a little bit about the software, with only a few simple changes you would have a well-formatted document that represents your specific needs. Even if you know a lot about the program, starting with a template can be much more efficient than if you designed it yourself from a blank file. Templates in Excel often use complex formulas and formatting to achieve a dynamic workbook that would automatically adjust with only a few inputs. Using a resume template in Word greatly simplifies potentially complex formatting, enabling you to concentrate on just inputting your personal experiences. PowerPoint templates can include single element slides (such as organization charts) but also include comprehensive presentations on topics such as Business Plans or a Quiz show game presentation similar to *Jeopardy!*

The Templates list is composed of template groups available within each Office application. The search box enables you to locate other templates that are available online. When you select a template, you can view more information about the template, including author information, a general overview about the template, and additional views (if applicable).

To search for and use a template, complete the following steps:

1. Open the Microsoft Office application with which you will be working. Or, if the application is already open, click File and click New.
2. Type a search term in the *Search for online templates box* or click one of the Suggested searches.
3. Scroll through the template options or after selecting a search term, use the list at the right to narrow your search further.
4. Select a template and review its information in the window that opens.
5. Click Create to open the template in the application.

On a Mac, to search for and use a template, complete the following steps:

1. Open the Microsoft Office application with which you will be working. Or, if the application is already open, click the File menu and click New from Template.
2. Continue with steps 2 through 5 in the PC steps above.

STEP 2 Apply a Theme

Applying a theme enables you to visually coordinate various page elements. Themes are different for each of the Office applications. In Word, a theme is a set of coordinating fonts, colors, and special effects, such as shadowing or glows, that are combined into a package to provide a stylish appearance (see Figure 1.24). In PowerPoint, a theme is a file that includes the formatting elements such as a background, a color scheme, and slide layouts that position content placeholders. Themes in Excel are like those in Word in that they are a set of coordinating fonts, colors, and special effects. Themes also affect any SmartArt or charts in a document, workbook, or presentation. Access also has a set of themes that coordinate the appearance of fonts and colors for objects such as Forms and Reports. In Word and PowerPoint, themes are accessed from the Design tab. In Excel, they are accessed from the Page Layout tab. In Access, themes can be applied to forms and reports and are accessed from the respective object's Tools Design tab. In any application, themes can be modified with different fonts, colors, or effects, or you can design your own theme and set it as a default.

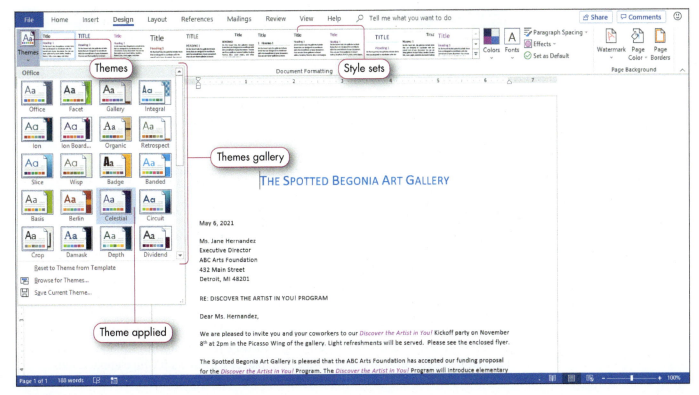

FIGURE 1.24 Themes in Word

Modifying Text

Formatting and modifying text in documents, worksheets, or presentations is an essential function when using Office applications. Centering a title, formatting cells, or changing the font color or size are tasks that occur frequently. In all Office applications, the Home tab provides tools for editing text.

STEP 3 Select Text

Before making any changes to existing text or numbers, you must first select the characters. A common way to select text or numbers is to place the pointer before the first character of the text you want to select, hold down the left mouse button, and then drag to highlight the intended selection. Note that in Word and PowerPoint when the pointer is used to select text in this manner, it takes on the shape of the letter *I*, called the *I-beam*.

Sometimes it can be difficult to precisely select a small amount of text, such as a few letters or a punctuation mark. Other times, the task can be overwhelmingly large, such as when selecting an entire multi-page document. Or, you might need to select a single word, sentence, or paragraph. In these situations, you should use one of the shortcuts to selecting large or small blocks of text. The shortcuts shown in Table 1.2 are primarily applicable to text in Word and PowerPoint. When working with Excel, you will more often need to select multiple cells. To select multiple cells, drag the selection when the pointer displays as a large white plus sign.

Once you have selected the text, besides applying formatting, you can delete or simply type over to replace the text.

TABLE 1.2	Shortcut Selection in Word and PowerPoint
Item Selected	**Action**
One word	Double-click the word.
One line of text	Place the pointer at the left of the line, in the margin area. When the pointer changes to an angled right-pointing arrow, click to select the line.
One sentence	Press and hold Ctrl and click in the sentence to select it.
One paragraph	Triple-click in the paragraph.
One character to the left of the insertion point	Press and hold Shift and press the left arrow on the keyboard.
One character to the right of the insertion point	Press and hold Shift and press the right arrow on the keyboard.
Entire document	Press and hold Ctrl and press A on the keyboard.

Format Text

At times, you will want to make the font size larger or smaller, change the font color, or apply other font attributes, for example, to emphasize key information such as titles, headers, dates, and times. Because formatting text is commonplace, Office places formatting commands in many convenient places within each Office application.

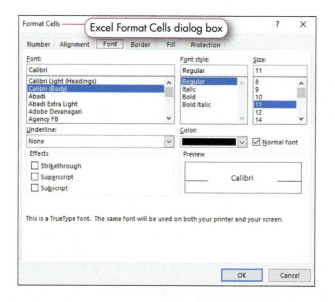
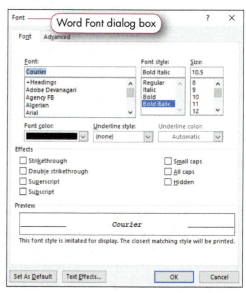
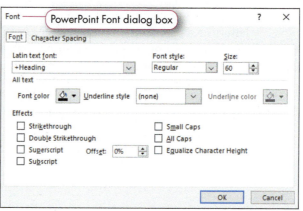

FIGURE 1.25 The Font Dialog Boxes

You can find the most common formatting commands in the Font group on the Home tab. As noted earlier, Word, Excel, and PowerPoint all share very similar Font groups that provide access to tasks related to changing the font, size, and color. Remember that you can place the pointer over any command icon to view a summary of the command's purpose, so although the icons might appear cryptic at first, you can use the pointer to quickly determine the purpose and applicability to your potential text change.

If the font change that you plan to make is not included as a choice on the Home tab, you may find what you are looking for in the Font dialog box. If you are making many formatting choices at once, using the Font dialog box may be more efficient. Depending on the application, the contents of the Font dialog box vary slightly, but the purpose is consistent—providing access to choices related to modifying characters (refer to Figure 1.25).

The way characters display onscreen or print in documents, including qualities such as size, spacing, and shape, is determined by the font. When you open a Blank document, you are opening the Normal template with an Office theme and the Normal style. The Office theme with Normal Style includes the following default settings: Calibri font, 11-point font size, and black font color. These settings remain in effect unless you change them. Some formatting commands, such as Bold and Italic, are called **toggle commands**. They act somewhat like a light switch that you can turn on and off. Once you have applied bold formatting to text, the Bold command is highlighted on the ribbon when that text is selected. To undo bold formatting, select the bold formatted text and click Bold again.

Use the Mini Toolbar

You have learned that you can always use commands on the Home tab of the ribbon to change selected text within a document, worksheet, or presentation. Although using the ribbon to select commands is simple enough, the **Mini Toolbar** provides another convenient way to accomplish some of the same formatting changes. When you select or right-click any amount of text within a worksheet, document, or presentation, the Mini Toolbar displays (see Figure 1.26) along with the shortcut menu. The Mini Toolbar provides access to the most common formatting selections, as well as access to styles and list options. Unlike the QAT, you cannot add or remove options from the Mini Toolbar. To temporarily remove the Mini Toolbar from view, press Esc. You can permanently disable the Mini Toolbar so that it does not display in any open file when text is selected by selecting Options on the File tab. Ensure the General tab is selected and deselect *Show Mini Toolbar on selection* in the User Interface options section.

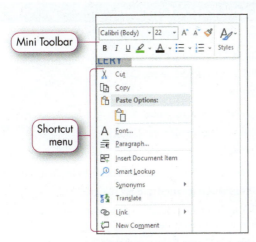

FIGURE 1.26 The Mini Toolbar and Shortcut Menu

Relocating Text

On occasion, you may want to relocate a section of text from one area of a Word document to another. Or suppose that you have included text on a PowerPoint slide that you believe would be more appropriate on a different slide. Or perhaps an Excel formula should be copied from one cell to another because both cells should show totals in a similar manner. In all these instances, you would use the cut, copy, and paste features found in the Clipboard group on the Home tab. The **Office Clipboard** is an area of memory reserved to temporarily hold selections that have been cut or copied and enables you to paste the selections to another location.

STEP 4 · Cut, Copy, and Paste Text

To **cut** means to remove a selection from the original location and place it in the Office Clipboard. To **copy** means to duplicate a selection from the original location and place a copy in the Office Clipboard. To **paste** means to place a cut or copied selection into another location in a document. It is important to understand that cut or copied text remains in the Office Clipboard even after you paste it to another location. The Office Clipboard can hold up to 24 items at one time.

> **To cut or copy text, and paste to a new location, complete the following steps:**
>
> 1. Select the text you want to cut or copy.
> 2. Click the appropriate command in the Clipboard group either to cut or copy the selection.
> 3. Click the location where you want the cut or copied text to be placed. The location can be in the current file or in another open file within most Office applications.
> 4. Click Paste in the Clipboard group on the Home tab.

You can paste the same item multiple times, because it will remain in the Office Clipboard until you power down your computer or until the Office Clipboard exceeds 24 items. It is best practice to complete the paste process as soon after you have cut or copied text.

In addition to using the commands in the Clipboard group, you can also cut, copy, and paste by using the Mini Toolbar, a shortcut menu (right-clicking), or by keyboard shortcuts. These methods are listed in Table 1.3.

TABLE 1.3	Cut, Copy, and Paste Options
Command	**Actions**
Cut	• Click Cut in Clipboard group. • Right-click selection and select Cut. • Press Ctrl+X.
Copy	• Click Copy in Clipboard group. • Right-click selection and select Copy. • Press Ctrl+C.
Paste	• Click in destination location and select Paste in Clipboard group. • Click in destination location and press Ctrl+V. • Right-click in destination location and select one of the choices under Paste Options in the shortcut menu. • Click Clipboard Dialog Box Launcher to open Clipboard pane. Click in destination location. With Clipboard pane open, click the arrow beside the intended selection and select Paste.

> **TIP: USE PASTE OPTIONS**
> When you paste text, you may not want to paste the text with all its formatting. In some instances, you may want to paste only the text, unformatted, so that special effects such as hyperlinks are not copied. In other instances, you might want to paste and match the formatting in the destination location or keep the current formatting in the new location. Paste Options commands are displayed when you click the Paste arrow or use the shortcut menu. Paste Options are different in each application, but in general, they include pasting contents without any formatting applied, pasting contents using the source formats, or pasting contents using the destination formats. In Excel, Paste Options also include pasting values to replace formulas, and transposing columns and rows to rows and columns. There are also options related to pasting pictures.

Use the Office Clipboard

When you cut or copy selections, they are placed in the Office Clipboard. Regardless of which Office application you are using, you can view the Office Clipboard by clicking the Clipboard Dialog Box Launcher, as shown in Figure 1.27.

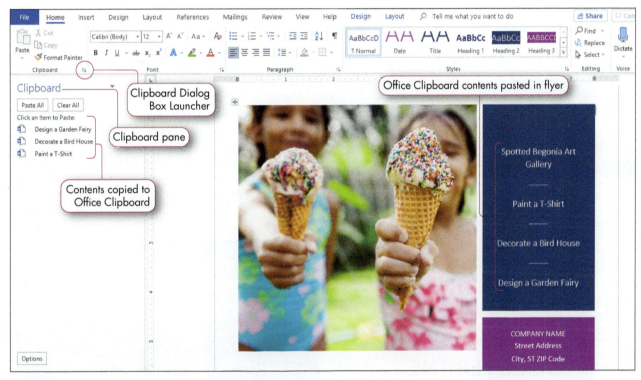

FIGURE 1.27 The Office Clipboard

Unless you specify otherwise when beginning a paste operation, the most recently added item to the Office Clipboard is pasted. If you know you will be cutting or copying and then pasting several items, rather than doing each individually, you can cut or copy all the items to the Office Clipboard, and then paste each or all Office Clipboard items to the new location. This is especially helpful if you are pasting the Office Clipboard items to a different Office file. Just open the new file, display the Clipboard pane, and select the item in the list to paste it into the document. The Office Clipboard also stores graphics that have been cut or copied. You can delete items from the Office Clipboard by clicking the arrow next to the selection in the Clipboard pane and selecting Delete. You can remove all items from the Office Clipboard by clicking Clear All. The Options button at the bottom of the Clipboard pane enables you to control when and where the Office Clipboard is displayed. Close the Clipboard pane by clicking the Close button in the top-right corner of the pane or by clicking the arrow in the title bar of the Clipboard pane and selecting Close.

Reviewing a Document

As you create or edit a file, and certainly as you finalize a file, you should make sure no spelling or grammatical errors exist. It is important that you carefully review your document for any spelling or punctuation errors, as well as any poor word choices before you send it along to someone else to read. Word, Excel, and PowerPoint all provide standard tools for proofreading, including a spelling and grammar checker and a thesaurus.

STEP 5 Check Spelling and Grammar

Word and PowerPoint automatically check your spelling and grammar as you type. If a word is unrecognized, it is flagged as misspelled or grammatically incorrect. Misspellings are identified with a red wavy underline, and grammatical or word-usage errors (such as using *bear* instead of *bare*) have a blue double underline. Excel does not check spelling as you type, so it is important to run the spelling checker in Excel. Excel's spelling checker will review charts, pivot tables, and textual data entered in cells.

Although spelling and grammar is checked along the way, you may find it more efficient to use the spelling and grammar feature when you are finished with the document. The Check Document command is found on the Review tab in the Proofing group in Word. In Excel and PowerPoint the Spelling command is on the Review tab in the Proofing group. When it is selected, the Editor pane will open on the right. For each error, you are offered one or more suggestions as a correction. You can select a suggestion and click Change, or if it is an error that is made more than one time throughout the document, you can select Change All (see Figure 1.28). If an appropriate suggestion is not made, you can always enter a correction manually.

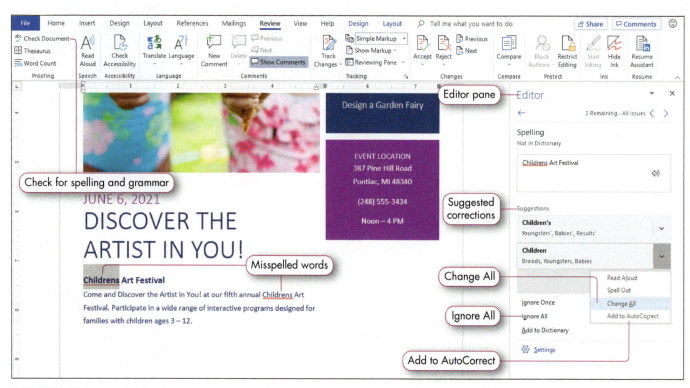

FIGURE 1.28 Using the Editor Pane to Correct Spelling

It is important to understand that the spelling and grammar check is not always correct, so you still need to proof a document thoroughly and review the errors carefully. For example, you might have a word that is truly misspelled in its context, but perhaps is still a valid word in the dictionary. Spell check might not pick it up as a misspelled word, but a careful read through would probably pick it up. There are times when the spelling and grammar check will indicate a word is misspelled and it really is not. This often happens with names or proper nouns or with new technical terms that may not be in the application's dictionary. In these instances, you can choose to Ignore, Ignore All, or Add. Choosing Ignore will skip the word without changing it. If you know there are multiple instances of that word throughout the document, you can choose Ignore All, and it will skip all instances of the word. Finally, if it is a word that is spelled correctly and that you use it often, you can choose to Add it to the dictionary, so it will not be flagged as an error in future spell checks.

If you right-click a word or phrase that is identified as a potential error, you will see a shortcut menu similar to that shown in Figure 1.29. The top of the shortcut menu will identify the type of error, whether it is spelling or grammar. A pane opens next to the shortcut menu with a list of options to correct the misspelling. These would be the same options that would display in the Editor pane if you ran the Spelling & Grammar command from the ribbon. Click on any option to insert it into the document. Similarly, you have the choices to Add to Dictionary or Ignore All. Each alternative also has options to Read Aloud or Add to AutoCorrect.

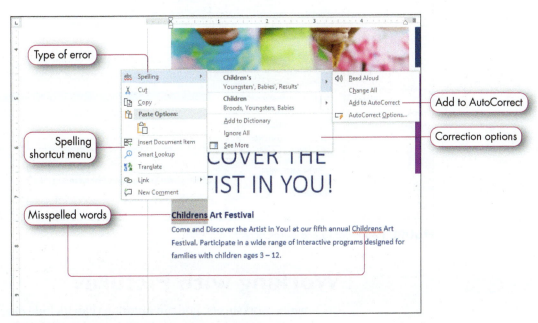

FIGURE 1.29 Spell Check Shortcut Menu options

You can use AutoCorrect to correct common typing errors, misspelled words, and capitalization errors, as well as to insert symbols (see Figure 1.30). There is a standard list of common errors and suggested replacements that is used in Excel, Word, and PowerPoint. So, if you type a word that is found in the Replace column, it will automatically be replaced with the replacement in the With column. For example, if you typed *accross* it would automatically correct to *across*. If you typed (tm) it would automatically change to the trademark symbol ™. You can add or delete terms and manage AutoCorrect by selecting Options from the File tab, and then in the Options dialog box, select Proofing and then click AutoCorrect Options.

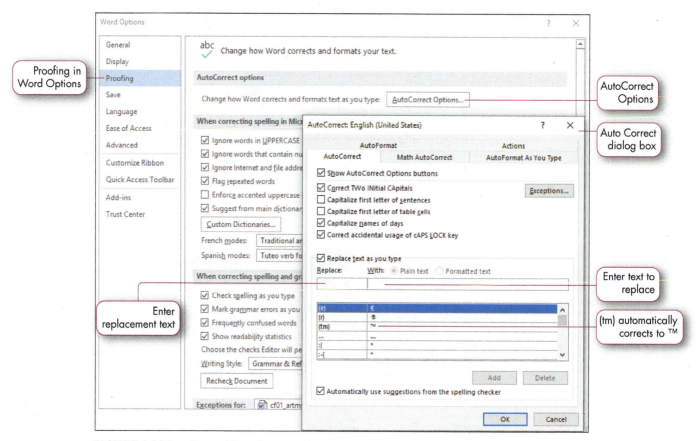

FIGURE 1.30 Proofing and AutoCorrect

Working with Pictures

Documents, worksheets, and presentations can include much more than just words and numbers. You can add energy and additional description to a project by including pictures and other graphic elements. A ***picture*** is just that—a digital photo. A picture can also be considered an illustration. Illustrations can also be shapes, icons, SmartArt, and Charts. While each of these types of illustrative objects have definitive differences, they are all handled basically the same when it comes to inserting and resizing. For the purposes of simplicity, the following discussion focuses on pictures, but the same information can be applied to any illustrative object you include in your document, worksheet, or presentation.

STEP 6 Insert Pictures

In Word, Excel, and PowerPoint, you can insert pictures from your own library of digital photos you have saved on your hard drive, OneDrive, or another storage medium. If you want a wider variety of pictures to choose from, you can search directly inside the Office program you are using for an online picture using Bing. Pictures and Online Pictures are found on the Insert tab.

To insert an online picture, complete the following steps:

1. Click in the file where you want the picture to be placed.
2. Click the Insert tab.
3. Click Online Pictures in the Illustrations group.
4. Type a search term in the Bing search box and press Enter.
5. Select an image and click Insert.

When the picture is inserted into a document, the Picture Tools Format tab displays. You can use these tools to modify the picture as needed.

> **TIP: CREATIVE COMMONS LICENSE**
> The Bing search filters are set to use the Creative Commons license system so the results display images that have been given a Creative Commons license. These are images and drawings that can be used more freely than images found directly on websites. Because there are different levels of Creative Commons licenses, you should read the Creative Commons license for each image you use to avoid copyright infringement.

STEP 7 Modify a Picture

Once you add a picture to your document, you may need to resize or adjust it. Before you make any changes to a picture, you must first select it. When the picture is selected, eight sizing handles display on the corners and in the middle of each edge (see Figure 1.31) and the Picture Tools tab displays on the ribbon. To adjust the size while maintaining the proportions, place your pointer on one of the corner sizing handles, and while holding the left mouse button down, drag the pointer on an angle upward or downward to increase or decrease the size, respectively. If you use one of the center edge sizing handles, you will

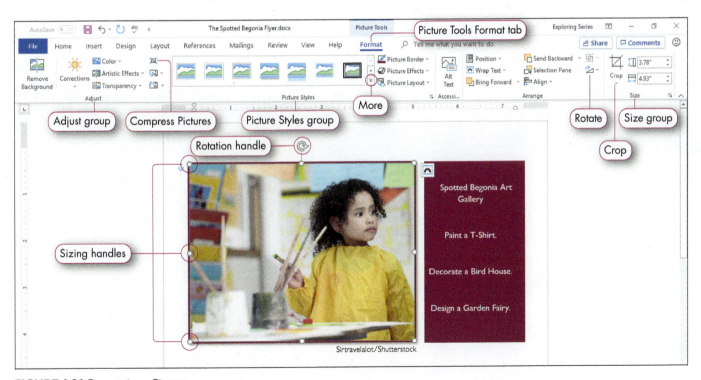

FIGURE 1.31 Formatting a Picture

stretch or shrink the picture out of proportion. In addition to sizing handles, a rotation handle displays at the top of the selected image. Use this to turn the image. For more precise controls, use the Size and Rotate commands on the Picture Tools Format tab. When a picture is selected, the Picture Tools Format tab includes options for modifying a picture. You can apply a picture style or effect, as well as add a picture border, from selections in the Picture Styles group. Click More to view a gallery of picture styles. As you point to a style, the style is shown in Live Preview, but the style is not applied until you select it. Options in the Adjust group simplify changing a color scheme, applying creative artistic effects, and even adjusting the brightness, contrast, and sharpness of an image (refer to Figure 1.31).

If a picture contains areas that are not necessary, you can crop it, which is the process of trimming edges that you do not want to display. The Crop tool is located on the Picture Tools Format tab (refer to Figure 1.31). Even though cropping enables you to adjust the amount of a picture that displays, it does not actually delete the portions that are cropped out. Therefore, you can later recover parts of the picture, if necessary. Cropping a picture does not reduce the file size of the picture or the document in which it displays. If you want to permanently remove the cropped portions of a figure and reduce the file size, you must compress the picture. Compress Pictures is found in the Adjust group on the Picture Tools Format tab (refer to Figure 1.31).

5. Discuss the differences between themes and templates. *p. 25*

6. Discuss several ways text can be modified. *p. 27*

7. Explain how the Office Clipboard is used when relocating text. *p. 31*

8. Explain how to review a document for spelling and grammar. *p. 32*

9. Explain why it is important to use the corner sizing handles of a picture when resizing. *p. 35*

Hands-On Exercises

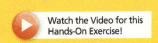
Watch the Video for this Hands-On Exercise!

Skills covered: Open a Template • Apply a Theme • Select Text • Format Text • Cut, Copy, and Paste Text • Check Spelling and Grammar • Insert a Picture • Modify a Picture

2 Format Document Content

As the administrative assistant for the Spotted Begonia Art Gallery, you want to create a flyer to announce the *Discover the Artist in You!* Children's Art Festival. You decide to use a template to help you get started more quickly and to take advantage of having a professionally formatted document without knowing much about Word. You will modify the flyer created with the template by adding and formatting your own content and changing out the photo.

STEP 1 OPEN A TEMPLATE

To facilitate making a nice-looking flyer, you review the templates that are available in Microsoft Word. You search for flyers and finally choose one that is appropriate for the event, knowing that you will be able to replace the photo with your own. Refer to Figure 1.32 as you complete Step 1.

FIGURE 1.32 Search for a Template

a. Ensure Word is open. Click **File** and click **New**.

b. Type the search term **seasonal event flyer** in the *Search for online templates* box to search for event flyer templates. Click **Start searching**.

Your search results in a selection of event flyer templates.

c. Locate the Seasonal event flyer template as shown in Figure 1.32 and click to select it.

The template displays in a preview.

Hands-On Exercise 2   37

> **TROUBLESHOOTING:** If you do not find the template, you may access the template from the student data files – *cf01h2Flyer.dotx* and skip to Step f.

  d. Click **Create** to open the flyer template.

  The flyer template that you selected opens in Word.

  e. Click **Save** on the QAT.

  Because this is the first time you save the flyer file, clicking Save on the QAT opens the Save As window, in which you must indicate the location of the file and the file name.

  f. Click **Browse** to navigate to where you save your files. Save the document as **cf01h2Flyer_LastFirst**.

STEP 2 APPLY A THEME

You want to change the theme of the template for a different font effect and theme color that matches more of the Spotted Begonia Art Gallery's other documents. Refer to Figure 1.33 as you complete Step 2.

FIGURE 1.33 Select and Edit Text

  a. Click the **Design tab** and click **Themes** in the Document Formatting group.

  The Themes gallery displays.

  b. Point to a few themes and notice how the template changes with each different theme.

  c. Click **Gallery**.

  The Gallery theme is applied, changing the color of the banners, and modifying the font and font size.

  d. Save the document.

STEP 3 SELECT AND FORMAT TEXT

You will replace the template text to create the flyer, adding information such as a title, date, and description. After adding the text to the document, you will modify the formatting of the organization name in the flyer. Refer to Figure 1.34 as you complete Step 3.

FIGURE 1.34 Edit Placeholder Text

a. Scroll to see the **Date placeholder** in the main body of the text, click, and then type **June 6, 2021** in the placeholder.

b. Click the **Event Title Here placeholder** and type **Discover the Artist in You!** in the placeholder.

c. Press **Enter** and continue typing **Spotted Begonia Art Gallery**.

d. Click the **Event Description Heading placeholder** and type **Childrens Art Festival**. (Ignore the misspelling for now.)

e. Select each text placeholder in the bottom box of the right table column and replace the content in each text placeholder with the content from the right column below.

Hands-On Exercise 2   39

Placeholder	Text Typed Entry
Company Name	**Event Location**
Street Address City ST Zip Code	**387 Pine Hill Road** **Pontiac, MI 48340**
Telephone	**(248) 555-3434**
Web Address	**Noon – 4 PM**
Dates and Times	**Delete the text**

You modify the placeholders to customize the flyer.

f. Select the title text **Discover the Artist in You!**. Click the **Font arrow** on the Mini Toolbar. Select **Franklin Gothic Medium**.

The font is changed.

> **TROUBLESHOOTING:** If the Mini Toolbar does not display after selecting the text, right-click the selected text and select the font Franklin Gothic Medium.

g. Select the text **June 6, 2021**. Click the **Font Size arrow** on the Mini Toolbar. Select **26** on the Font Size menu.

The font size is changed to 26 pt.

h. Click **Save** on the QAT to save the document.

STEP 4 CUT, COPY, AND PASTE TEXT

You add descriptive text about the event. You then decide to move some of the text to the banner panel on the right. You also copy the sponsor's name to the top of the banner. Finally, you delete some unwanted placeholders. Refer to Figure 1.35 as you complete Step 4.

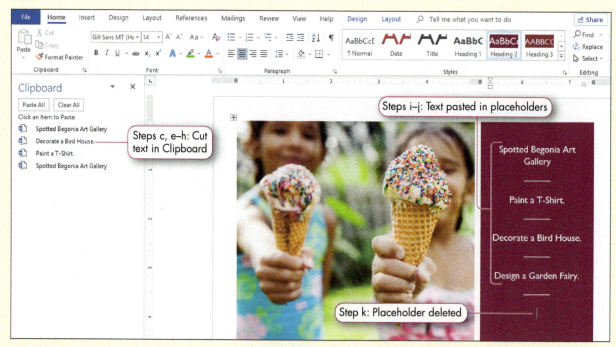

FIGURE 1.35 Use the Clipboard Commands

a. Select the **placeholder text** below Childrens Art Festival that begins with *To get started* and press **Delete**. Enter the following text and ignore any intentional misspellings. They will be corrected later.

   Come and Discover the Artist in You! at our fifth annual Childrens Art Festival. Participate in a wide range of interactive programs designed for families with children ages 3–12. Paint a T-Shirt. Decorate a Bird House. Design a Garden Fairy.

b. Click the **YOUR LOGO HERE placeholder** and press **Delete**.

c. Select the text **Spotted Begonia Art Gallery**. Right-click the selected text and click **Cut** from the shortcut menu.

d. Scroll to the top of the flyer. Click the **Add Key Event Info Here! placeholder** in the right column. Click the **Home tab** and click **Paste** in the Clipboard group to paste the previously cut text.

   The text is now moved to the banner.

e. Click the **Clipboard Dialog Box Launcher**.

   The Office Clipboard displays. The cut text displays in the Clipboard pane.

> **MAC TROUBLESHOOTING:** For Step e, use Command+X. Select the Don't be Shy . . . placeholder text and press Command+V. Repeat for Steps f and g below, using Command+X to cut the indicated text, and Command+V to paste the text in the two placeholders below Paint a T-Shirt.

f. Scroll to the paragraph at the bottom of the flyer beginning with Come and Discover. Select the text **Paint a T-Shirt.** (include the period) and press **Ctrl+X**.

   Notice that the cut text selection is in the Office Clipboard.

g. Select the text **Decorate a Bird House.** from the text you entered in Step a and press **Ctrl+X**.

h. Select the text **Design a Garden Fairy.** from the text you entered in Step a and press **Ctrl+X**.

   The Office Clipboard displays the three cut selections of text.

i. Scroll to the top of the flyer. Select the **Don't Be Shy . . . placeholder text** and click **Paint a T-Shirt** from the Office Clipboard.

   The text in the Office Clipboard is pasted in a new location.

j. Repeat Step i, replacing **One More Point Here! placeholder text** with **Decorate a Bird House** and **Add More Great Info Here placeholder text** with **Design a Garden Fairy**.

k. Select the last **placeholder text** in the banner and press **Delete**.

l. Click **Clear All** in the Clipboard pane and close the Office Clipboard. Save the document.

STEP 5 CHECK SPELLING AND GRAMMAR

Because this flyer will be seen by the public, it is important to check the spelling and grammar in your document. Refer to Figure 1.36 as you complete Step 5.

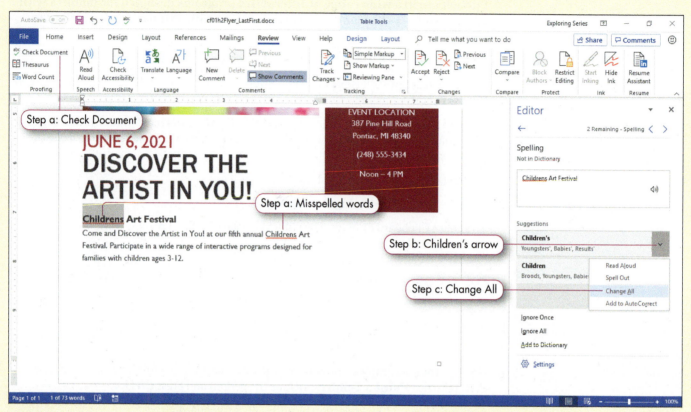

FIGURE 1.36 Check Spelling and Grammar

a. Press **Ctrl+Home**. Click the **Review tab** and click **Check Document** in the Proofing group.

The Editor pane opens and two spelling errors are identified.

b. Click Spelling in the Corrections box and click the **arrow** to the right of Children's in the Editor pane.

c. Select **Change All** to accept the suggested change to *Children's* in the Spelling pane for all instances. Make any other changes as needed. Click **OK** to close the dialog box.

The spelling and grammar check is complete.

d. Save the document.

STEP 6 INSERT A PICTURE

You want to change the template image to an image that better reflects the children's event being held at the gallery. You use an image the Art Gallery director has provided you. Refer to Figure 1.37 as you complete Step 6.

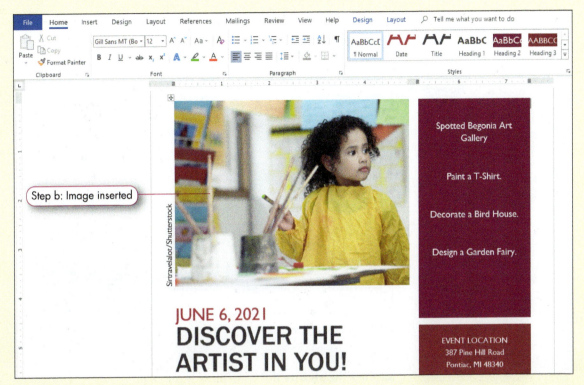

FIGURE 1.37 Insert Picture

a. Scroll to the top of the flyer. Click the **image** to select it and press **Delete**.

You have deleted the image you want to replace.

b. Click **Pictures** in the Illustrations group on the Home tab. Navigate to your Student Data files and select *cf01h2Art.jpg*. Click **Insert**.

The new image is placed in the document.

c. Save the document.

STEP 7 MODIFY A PICTURE

You want to make the picture stand out better, so you decide to add a border frame around the image. Refer to Figure 1.38 as you complete Step 7.

FIGURE 1.38 Modify a Picture

a. Click the **picture** if it is not already selected.

The Picture Tools Format tab displays on the ribbon and sizing handles display around the image. The Table Tools Design and Layout tabs also display. The flyer template uses a table to place the elements. Selecting the picture also selects the table.

b. Click the **Format tab** and click **More** in the Picture Styles group.

A gallery of Picture Styles displays.

c. Point to a few different Picture Styles to see the effects in Live Preview and select **Simple Frame, Black**. Keep the image selected.

A black border is applied around the image.

d. Click the **Picture Border arrow** and select **Pink, Accent 2, Darker 50%** under Theme Colors.

The border color is changed to coordinate with the colors on the flyer.

e. Save the document. Keep the document open if you plan to continue with the next Hands-On Exercise. If not, close the document and exit Word.

Modify Document Layout and Properties

When working with a document, before you send or print it, you will want to view the final product to make sure that your margins and page layout are as they should be. Moreover, you might want to add some details in a header or footer, or in document properties to help identify the author and contents of the document to help in later searches. Although you can always print a document using the default printer settings, you may want to change printer settings or page layout settings before printing.

In this section, you will explore how to view and edit document properties. You will learn about views and how to change a document view to suit your needs. In addition, you will learn how to modify the page layout, including page orientation and margins as well as how to add headers and footers. Finally, you will explore Print Preview and the various printing options available to you.

STEP 1 Changing Document Views

As you prepare or read a document, you may find that you want to change the way you view it. A section of your document may be easier to view when you can see it magnified, or you might want to display more of your document than what is showing onscreen. You can also select a different *view*, the way a file appears onscreen, to make working on your project easier.

Change Document Views Using the Ribbon

Views for Word, Excel, and PowerPoint are available on the View tab. Each application has views that are specific to that application. PowerPoint and Excel each have a Normal view, which is the typical view used to create and view presentation slides and workbooks. Word's Print Layout view is like Normal view in that it is the view used to create documents. Print Layout view is useful when you want to see both the document text and such features margins and page breaks. Table 1.4 outlines the other views in each application. Access does not have a View tab, but rather incorporates unique views that are visible when working with any Access object.

TABLE 1.4 Office Views

Application	View	Description
Word	Print Layout	The default view used when creating documents.
	Read Mode	All editing commands are hidden. Arrows on the left and right sides of the screen are used to move through the pages of the document.
	Web Layout	All page breaks are removed. Use this view to see how a document will display as a webpage.
	Outline View	If Style Headings are used in a document, the document is organized by level. Otherwise, the document will display with each paragraph as a separate bullet.
	Draft View	A pared-down version of Print Layout view.
Excel	Normal	The default view used when creating worksheets.
	Page Break Preview	Displays a worksheet with dashed lines that indicate automatic page breaks. Used to adjust page breaks manually.
	Page Layout	Displays the worksheet headers and margins.
	Custom Views	Create custom views.
PowerPoint	Normal	The default view used when creating presentations.
	Outline View	Displays a presentation as an outline using titles and main text from each slide.
	Slide Sorter	Displays presentation slides in thumbnail form making it easier to sort and organize slide sequence.
	Notes Page	Makes the Notes pane, which is located under the Slide pane, visible. You can type notes that apply to the current slide. Notes do not display during a presentation.
	Reading View	Displays the presentation in full screen like Slide Show.

Change Document Views Using the Status Bar

The ***status bar***, located at the bottom of the program window, displays information relevant to the application and document on which you are working, as well as some commands. On the left side of the status bar is application- and document-specific information. When you work with Word, the status bar informs you of the number of pages and words in an open document. Excel shows the status of the file and a Macro recording command. The PowerPoint status bar shows the slide number and total number of slides in the presentation. Word and PowerPoint also display a proofing icon that looks like an opened book. An x in the icon indicates there are proofing errors that need to be fixed. Clicking the icon will start the spelling and grammar check.

Other pertinent document information for PowerPoint and Excel display on the right side of the status bar. The Excel status bar displays summary information, such as average and sum, of selected cells, and the PowerPoint status bar provides access to slide notes.

The right side of the status bar also includes means for changing the view and for changing the zoom size of onscreen file contents. The view buttons (see Figure 1.39) on the status bar of each application enable you to change the view of the open file. These views correspond to the most commonly used views in each application.

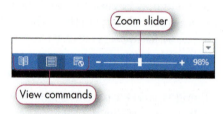

FIGURE 1.39 The Status Bar

The ***Zoom slider*** is a horizontal bar on the right side of the status bar that enables you to increase or decrease the size of the document onscreen. You can drag the tab along the slider in either direction to increase or decrease the magnification of the file (refer to Figure 1.39). Be aware, however, that changing the size of text onscreen does not change the font size when the file is printed or saved.

STEP 2 Changing the Page Layout

When you prepare a document or worksheet, you are concerned with the way the project appears onscreen and possibly in print. The Layout tab in Word and the Page Layout tab in Excel provide access to a full range of options such as margin settings and page orientation. PowerPoint does not have a Page Layout tab, because its primary purpose is displaying contents onscreen rather than in print.

Because a document or workbook is most often designed to be printed, you may need to adjust margins and change the page orientation, or to center a worksheet vertically or horizontally on a page for the best display. In addition, perhaps the document text should be aligned in columns. You will find these and other common page settings in the Page Setup group on the Layout (or Page Layout) tab. For less common settings, such as determining whether headers should print on odd or even pages, you use the Page Setup dialog box.

Change Margins

A ***margin*** is the area of blank space that displays to the left, right, top, and bottom of a document or worksheet. Margins display when you are in Print Layout or Page Layout view (see Figure 1.40), or in Backstage view previewing a document to print. There are Normal, Wide, and Narrow default margin settings for Word and Excel. Word also includes Moderate and Mirrored margins. If you want more customized margin settings, use the Custom Margins option at the bottom of the Margins gallery to display the Page Setup dialog box.

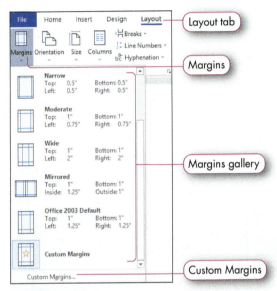

FIGURE 1.40 Page Margins in Word

> **To change margins in Word and Excel, complete the following steps:**
>
> 1. Click the Layout (or Page Layout) tab.
> 2. Click Margins in the Page Setup group.
> 3. Do one of the following:
>   - Select a preset margin option.
>   - Click Custom Margins (refer to Figure 1.40) and set the custom margin settings. Click OK to accept the custom margin settings.

Change Page Orientation

Documents and worksheets can be displayed or printed in different page orientations. A page in ***portrait orientation*** is taller than it is wide. A page in ***landscape orientation*** is wider than it is tall. Word documents are usually displayed in portrait orientation, whereas Excel worksheets are often more suited to landscape orientation. In PowerPoint, you can change the orientation of slides as well as notes and handouts. Orientation is also an option in the Print page of Backstage view.

Use the Page Setup Dialog Box

Page Orientation settings for Word and Excel are found in the Layout (or Page Layout) tab in the Page Setup group. The Page Setup group contains Margins and Orientation settings as well as other commonly used page options for each Office application. Some are unique to Excel, and others are more applicable to Word. Other less common settings are available in the Page Setup dialog box only, displayed when you click the Page Setup Dialog Box Launcher. The Page Setup dialog box includes options for customizing margins, selecting page orientation, centering horizontally or vertically, printing gridlines, and creating headers and footers. Figure 1.41 shows both the Excel and Word Page Setup dialog boxes.

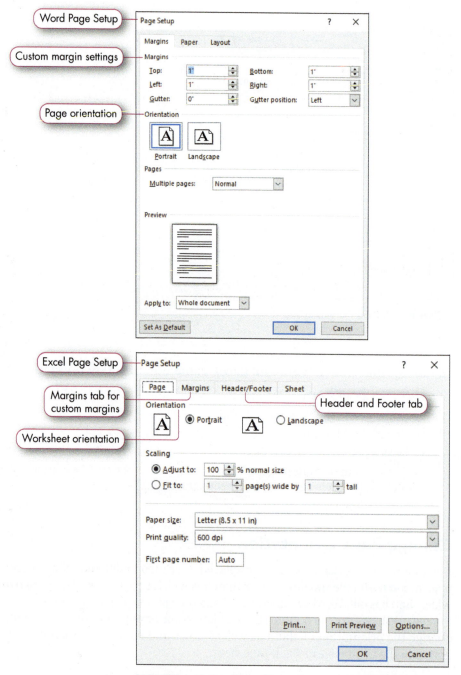

FIGURE 1.41 Page Setup Dialog Boxes in Word and Excel

Although PowerPoint slides are generally set to landscape orientation, you can change to portrait orientation by accessing the Slide Size controls on the Design tab and selecting Custom Slide Size. When choosing to print Notes Pages, Outline, or Handouts, the page orientation can be changed in Print Settings in Backstage view.

STEP 3 Creating a Header and a Footer

The purpose of including a header or footer is to better identify the document and give it a professional appearance. A **header** is a section in the top margin of a document. A **footer** is a section in the bottom margin of a document. Generally, page numbers, dates, author's name, or file name are included in Word documents or PowerPoint presentations. Excel worksheets might include the name of a worksheet tab, as well. Company logos are often displayed in a header or footer. Contents in a header or footer will appear on each page of the document, so you only have to specify the content once, after which it displays automatically on all pages. Although you can type the text yourself at the top or bottom of every page, it is time-consuming, and the possibility of making a mistake is great.

Header and footer commands are found on the Insert tab. In Word, you can choose from a predefined gallery of headers and footers as shown in Figure 1.42. To create your own unformatted header or footer, select Edit Header (or Edit Footer) at the bottom of the gallery. You can only add footers to PowerPoint slides (see Figure 1.42). You can apply footers to an individual slide or to all slides. To add date and time or a slide number, check each option to apply. Check the Footer option to add in your own content. In PowerPoint, the location of a footer will depend on the template or theme applied to the presentation. For some templates and themes, the footer will display on the side of the slide rather than at the bottom. Headers and footers are available for PowerPoint Notes and Handouts. Select the Notes and Handouts tab in the Header and Footer dialog box and enter in the content

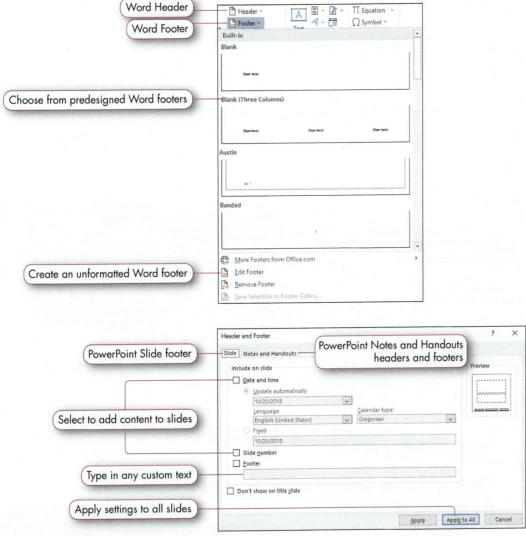

FIGURE 1.42 Insert Footer in Word and PowerPoint

similarly to how you would enter footer information on slides. In Excel, headers and footers are separated into left, center, and right sections. You can type your own contents or use a predefined header or footer element, such as date, file name, or sheet name.

After typing a header or a footer, it can be formatted like any other text. It can be formatted in any font or font size. In Word or Excel, when you want to leave the header and footer area and return to the document, click Close Header and Footer or double-click in the body of the document.

STEP 4 Configuring Document Properties

Recall that Backstage view is a component of Office that provides a collection of commands related to a file. Earlier in this chapter, you used Backstage view to open and save a file and template and to customize ribbon settings. Using Backstage view, you can also view or specify settings related to protection, permissions, versions, and properties of a file. A file's properties include the author, file size, permissions, and date modified. Backstage view also includes options for customizing program settings, signing in to your Office account, and exiting the application. In addition to creating a new document and opening and saving a document, you use Backstage view to print, share, export, and close files.

All the features of Backstage view are accessed by clicking the File tab and then selecting Info in the Backstage Navigation Pane (see Figure 1.43). The Info page will occupy the entire application window, hiding the file with which you are working. You can return to the file in a couple of ways. Either click the Back arrow in the top-left corner or press Esc on the keyboard.

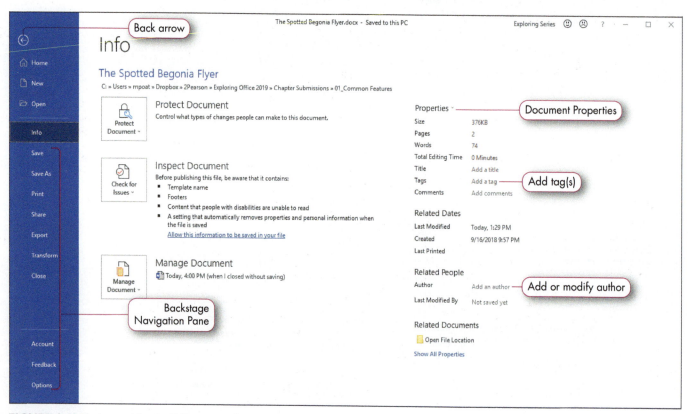

FIGURE 1.43 Backstage View and Document Properties

View and Edit Document Properties

The Info page of Backstage view is where you can protect, inspect, and manage your document as well as manage specific document properties. It is good to include information that identifies a document, such as the author and title. You can also add one or more tags (refer to Figure 1.43). A ***tag*** is a data element or metadata that is added as a document property. Like a keyword, you can search for a file based on tags you assign a document. For example, suppose you apply a tag of *Picasso* to all documents you create that are associated with that artist. Later, you can use that keyword as a search term, locating all associated documents. Statistical information related to the current document such as file size, number of pages, and total words are located on the Info page of Backstage view.

STEP 5 Previewing and Printing a File

When you want to print an Office file, you can select from various print options, including the number of copies and the specific pages to print. It is a good idea to look at how your document or worksheet will appear before you print it. When you select Print from Backstage view, the file previews on the right, with print settings located in the center of the Backstage view. Figure 1.44 shows a typical Backstage Print view. If you know that the page setup is correct and that there are no unique print settings to select, you can simply print without adjusting any print settings.

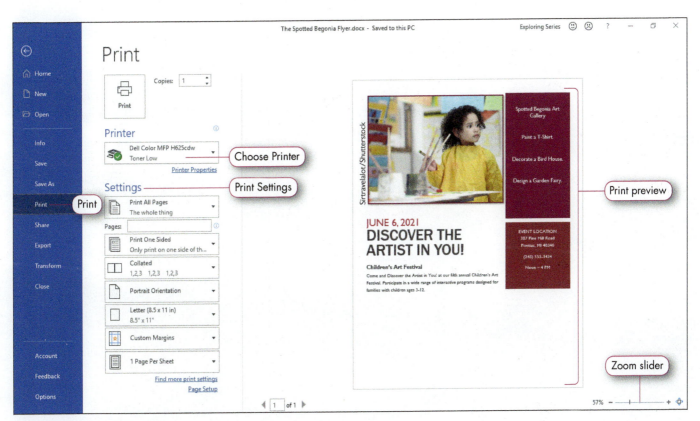

FIGURE 1.44 Backstage Print View in Word

> **TIP: CHANGING THE SIZE OF PRINT PREVIEW**
> Sometimes the preview image of your document shows only a part of the document page or shows a smaller image of the document page. You can change the size of the print preview by using the zoom slider in the bottom-right corner of the preview (refer to Figure 1.44).

Other options in the Backstage Print view vary depending on the application in which you are working. For example, PowerPoint's Backstage Print view includes options for printing slides and handouts in various configurations and colors, whereas Excel's focuses on worksheet selections and Word's includes document options. Regardless of the Office application, you will be able to access Settings options from Backstage view, including page orientation (landscape or portrait), margins, and paper size. To print a file, click the Print button (refer to Figure 1.44).

Quick Concepts

10. Discuss why you would need to change the view of a document. ***p. 45***
11. Discuss the various ways you can change a page layout. ***p. 46***
12. Explain what functions and features are included in Backstage view. ***p. 50***
13. Discuss some document properties and explain why they are helpful. ***p. 50***

Hands-On Exercises

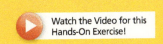
Watch the Video for this Hands-On Exercise!

Skills covered: Change Document Views Using the Ribbon • Change Document Views Using the Status Bar • Change Margins • Change Page Orientation • Insert a Footer • View and Enter Document Properties • Preview a File • Change Print Settings

3 Modify Document Layout and Properties

You continue to work on the flyer. You will review and add document properties, and prepare the document to print and distribute by changing the page setup. You will also add a footer with Spotted Begonia's information. As the administrative assistant for the Spotted Begonia Art Gallery, you must be able to search for and find documents previously created. You know that by adding tags to your flyer you will more easily be able to find it later. Finally, you will explore printing options.

STEP 1 CHANGE THE DOCUMENT VIEW

To get a better perspective on how your flyer would look if posted to the Gallery's website, you explore the Web Layout view available in Word. Refer to Figure 1.45 as you complete Step 1.

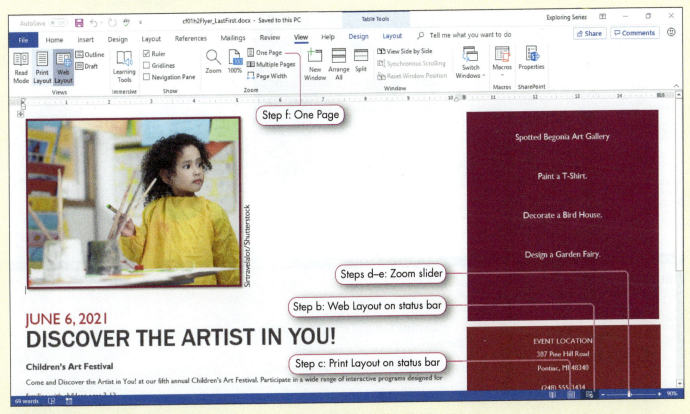

FIGURE 1.45 The Flyer in Web Layout View

a. Open *cf01h2Flyer_LastFirst* if you closed it at the end of Hands-On Exercise 2, and save it as **cf01h3Flyer_LastFirst**, changing h2 to h3.

b. Click **Web Layout** on the status bar. Observe the changes to the view.

The view is changed to Web Layout and simulates how the document would display on the Web.

c. Click **Print Layout** on the status bar. Observe the changes to the view.

The document has returned to Print Layout view.

d. Drag the **Zoom slider** to the left so you can see the full page of the flyer.

e. Drag the **Zoom slider** to the right to zoom in on the image.

f. Click the **View tab** and click **One Page** in the Zoom group.

The entire flyer is displayed.

STEP 2: CHANGE THE PAGE LAYOUT

You show the flyer to the Program Director. You both wonder whether changing the orientation and margin settings will make the flyer look better when it is printed. You change the orientation setting, but ultimately revert to Portrait orientation. You modify the margins in Portrait orientation to improve the spacing around the edges of the page. Refer to Figure 1.46 as you complete Step 2.

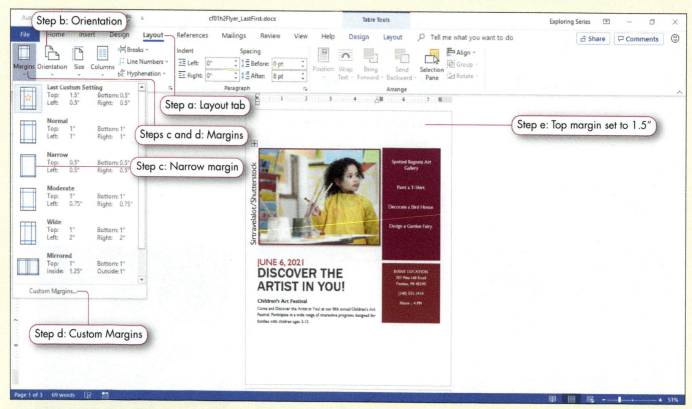

FIGURE 1.46 Change Margins and Orientation

a. Click the **Layout tab** and click **Orientation** in the Page Setup group. Select **Landscape**.

The document is now wider than it is tall.

b. Click **Orientation** and select **Portrait**.

The document returns to Portrait orientation.

c. Click **Margins** in the Page Setup group. Select **Narrow**.

The document margins were changed to Narrow. The Narrow margin allows for better spacing horizontally, but you would like the flyer to be centered better vertically on the page.

d. Click **Margins** and select **Custom Margins**.

The Page Setup dialog box opens.

e. Change the Top margin to **1.5"** Click OK.

f. Click the **View tab** and click **One Page** in the Zoom group.

   The document looks well balanced on the page.

g. Save the document.

STEP 3 INSERT A HEADER AND A FOOTER

You decide to add the Gallery's name and website URL to the flyer as a footer so anyone who is looking for more information on the Spotted Begonia Art Gallery can access the website. Refer to Figure 1.47 as you complete Step 3.

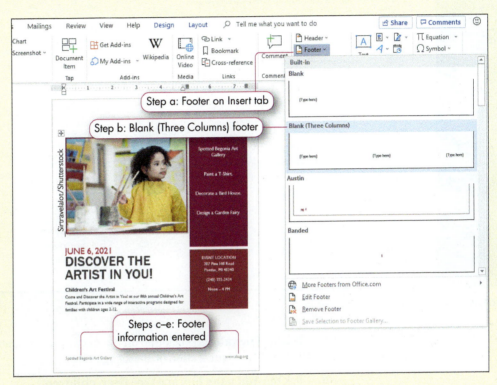

FIGURE 1.47 Insert a Footer

a. Click the **Insert tab** and click **Footer** in the Header & Footer group.

   A footer gallery displays.

b. Click the **Blank (Three Columns) footer**.

   You select a footer with three areas to add your own information.

c. Click **[Type here]** on the left side of the footer. Type **Spotted Begonia Art Gallery**.

d. Click **[Type here]** on the center of the footer. Press **Delete**.

e. Click **[Type here]** on the right side of the footer. Type **www.sbag.org**.

f. Click **Close Header and Footer** in the Close group.

   The footer information is entered.

g. Save the document.

STEP 4: ENTER DOCUMENT PROPERTIES

You add document properties, which will help you locate the file in the future when performing a search of your files. Refer to Figure 1.48 as you complete Step 4.

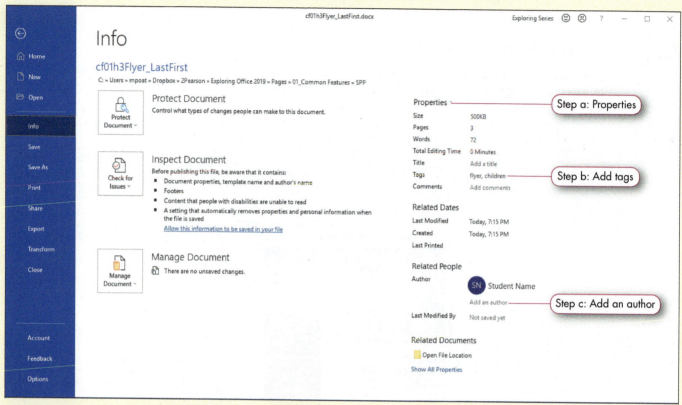

FIGURE 1.48 Enter Document Properties

a. Click the **File tab** and click Info on the Backstage Navigation Pane. Locate Properties at the top of the right section of Backstage view.

b. Click the **Add a tag box** and type **flyer, children**.

> **MAC TROUBLESHOOTING:** On a Mac, to add a tag click the File menu and select Properties. Click the Summary tab and enter text in the Keywords box.

You added tag properties to the flyer.

c. Click the **Add an Author box** and type your first and last name.

You added an Author property to the flyer.

d. Click **Save** in the Backstage Navigation Pane.

STEP 5 PREVIEW A FILE AND CHANGE PRINT SETTINGS

You have reviewed and almost finalized the flyer. You want to look at how it will appear when printed. You also want to look over Print Settings to ensure they are correct. Refer to Figure 1.49 as you complete Step 5.

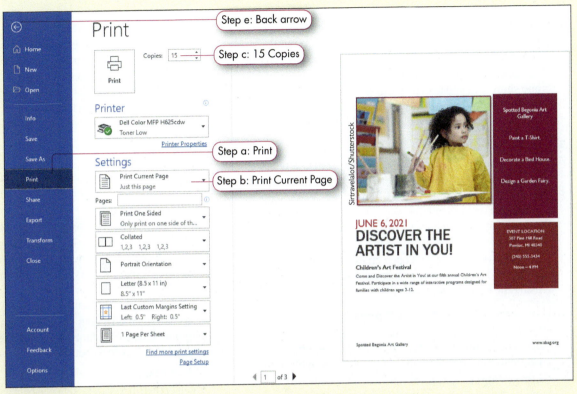

FIGURE 1.49 Backstage Print View

a. Click **Print** in the Backstage Navigation Pane.

It is always a good idea before printing to use Print Preview to check how a file will look when printed.

b. Click **Print All Pages arrow** and select **Print Current Page**.

You notice that the template created extra pages. You only want to print the current page.

c. Select the **1** in the Copies box and type **15**.

The orientation and custom margins settings match what was done previously. Even though you will not print the document now, the print settings will be saved when you save the document.

d. Click the **Back arrow**.

e. Save and close the file. Based on your instructor's directions, submit the following:

cf01h1Letter_LastFirst
cf01h3Flyer_LastFirst

Hands-On Exercise 3   57

Chapter Objectives Review

After reading this chapter, you have accomplished the following objectives:

1. **Start an Office application.**
   - Use your Microsoft account: Your Microsoft account connects you to all of Microsoft's Internet-based resources.
   - Use OneDrive: OneDrive is an app used to store, access, and share files and folders on the Internet. OneDrive is the default storage location for Microsoft Office files. OneDrive is incorporated directly in File Explorer.

2. **Work with files.**
   - Create a new file: You can create a document as a blank document or from a template.
   - Save a file: Saving a file enables you to open it later for additional updates or reference. Files are saved to a storage medium such as a hard drive, CD, flash drive, or to OneDrive.
   - Open a saved file: You can open an existing file using the Open dialog box. Recently saved files can be accessed using the Recent documents list.

3. **Use common interface components.**
   - Use the ribbon: The ribbon, the long bar located just beneath the title bar containing tabs, groups, and commands, is the command center of Office applications.
   - Use a dialog box and gallery: Some commands are not on the ribbon. To access these commands, you need to open a dialog box with a Dialog Box Launcher. A gallery displays additional formatting and design options for a command. Galleries are accessed by clicking More at the bottom of a gallery scroll bar
   - Customize the ribbon: You can personalize the ribbon by creating your own tabs and custom groups with commands you want to use. You can create a custom group and add to any of the default tabs.
   - Use and Customize the Quick Access Toolbar: The Quick Access Toolbar, located at the top-left corner of any Office application window, provides one-click access to commonly executed tasks, such as saving a file or undoing recent actions.
   - You can add additional commands to the QAT.
   - Use a Shortcut menu: When you right-click selected text or objects, a context-sensitive menu displays with commands and options relating to the selected text or object.
   - Use keyboard shortcuts: Keyboard shortcuts are keyboard equivalents for software commands. Universal keyboard shortcuts in Office include Ctrl+C (Copy), Ctrl+X (Cut), Ctrl+V (Paste), and Ctrl+Z (Undo). Not all commands have a keyboard shortcut. If one exists, it will display in the command ScreenTip.

4. **Get help.**
   - Use the Tell me box: The Tell me box not only links to online resources and technical support but also provides quick access to commands.
   - Use the Help tab: The Help tab includes resources for written and video tutorials and training, a means to contact Microsoft Support, and a way to share feedback. What's New displays a webpage that discusses all newly added features organized by release date.
   - Use Enhanced ScreenTips: An Enhanced ScreenTip describes a command and provides a keyboard shortcut, if applicable.

5. **Install add-ins.**
   - Add-ins are custom programs or additional commands that extend the functionality of a Microsoft Office program.

6. **Use templates and apply themes.**
   - Open a template: Templates are a convenient way to save time when designing a document. A gallery of template options displays when you start any application. You can also access a template when you start a new document, worksheet, presentation, or database.
   - Apply a theme: Themes are a collection of design choices that include colors, fonts, and special effects used to give a consistent look to a document, workbook, or presentation.

7. **Modify text.**
   - Select text: Text can be selected by a variety of methods. You can drag to highlight text and select individual words or groups of text with shortcuts.
   - Format text: You can change the font, font color, size, and many other attributes.
   - Use the Mini Toolbar: The Mini Toolbar provides instant access to common formatting commands after text is selected.

8. **Relocate text.**
   - Cut, copy, and paste text: To cut means to remove a selection from the original location and place it in the Office Clipboard. To copy means to duplicate a selection from the original location and place a copy in the Office Clipboard. To paste means to place a cut or copied selection into another location.
   - Use the Office Clipboard: When you cut or copy selections, they are placed in the Office Clipboard. You can paste the same item multiple times; it will remain in the Office Clipboard until you exit all Office applications or until the Office Clipboard exceeds 24 items.

9. **Review a document.**
   - Check spelling and grammar: As you type, Office applications check and mark spelling and grammar errors (Word only) for later correction. The Thesaurus enables you to search for synonyms. Use AutoCorrect to correct common typing errors and misspelled words and to insert symbols.

10. Work with pictures.
- Insert a picture: You can insert pictures from your own library of digital photos saved on your hard drive, OneDrive, or another storage medium, or you can initiate a Bing search for online pictures directly inside the Office program you are using.
- Modify a picture: To resize a picture, drag a corner-sizing handle; never resize a picture by dragging a center sizing handle. You can apply a picture style or effect, as well as add a picture border, from selections in the Picture Styles group.

11. Change document views.
- Change document views using the ribbon: The View tab offers views specific to the individual application. A view is how a file will be seen onscreen.
- Change document views using the status bar: In addition to information relative to the open file, the Status bar provides access to View and Zoom level options.

12. Change the page layout.
- Change margins: A margin is the area of blank space that displays to the left, right, top, and bottom of a document or worksheet.
- Change page orientation: Documents and worksheets can be displayed in different page orientations. Portrait orientation is taller than it is wide; landscape orientation is wider than it is tall.
- Use the Page Setup dialog box: The Page Setup dialog box includes options for customizing margins, selecting page orientation, centering horizontally or vertically, printing gridlines, and creating headers and footers.

13. Create a header and a footer.
- A header displays at the top of each page.
- A footer displays at the bottom of each page.

14. Configure Document Properties.
- View and edit document properties: Information that identifies a document, such as the author, title, or tags can be added to the document's properties. Those data elements are saved with the document as metadata, but do not appear in the document as it displays onscreen or is printed.

15. Preview and print a file.
- It is important to preview your file before printing.
- Print options can be set in Backstage view and include page orientation, the number of copies, and the specific pages to print.

Key Terms Matching

Match the key terms with their definitions. Write the key term letter by the appropriate numbered definition.

- **a.** Add-in
- **b.** Backstage view
- **c.** Cloud storage
- **d.** Footer
- **e.** Format Painter
- **f.** Group
- **g.** Header
- **h.** Margin
- **i.** Microsoft Access
- **j.** Microsoft Office
- **k.** Mini Toolbar
- **l.** Office Clipboard
- **m.** OneDrive
- **n.** Quick Access Toolbar
- **o.** Ribbon
- **p.** Status bar
- **q.** Tag
- **r.** Tell me box
- **s.** Template
- **t.** Theme

1. _____ A productivity software suite including a set of software applications, each one specializing in a type of output. **p. 4**
2. _____ The long bar located just beneath the title bar containing tabs, groups, and commands. **p. 9**
3. _____ A custom program or additional command that extends the functionality of a Microsoft Office program. **p. 17**
4. _____ A collection of design choices that includes colors, fonts, and special effects used to give a consistent look to a document, workbook, or presentation. **p. 25**
5. _____ A data element or metadata that is added as a document property. **p. 51**
6. _____ A component of Office that provides a concise collection of commands related to an open file and includes save and print options. **p. 6**
7. _____ A tool that displays near selected text that contains formatting commands. **p. 29**
8. _____ Relational database software used to store data and convert it into information. **p. 4**
9. _____ A feature in a document that consists of one or more lines at the bottom of each page. **p. 49**
10. _____ A predesigned file that incorporates formatting elements, such as a theme and layouts, and may include content that can be modified. **p. 25**
11. _____ A feature that enables you to search for help and information about a command or task you want to perform and will also present you with a shortcut directly to that command. **p. 15**
12. _____ A tool that copies all formatting from one area to another. **p. 17**
13. _____ Stores up to 24 cut or copied selections for use later in your computing session. **p. 30**
14. _____ A task-oriented section of a ribbon tab that contains related commands. **p. 9**
15. _____ An online app used to store, access, and share files and folders. **p. 6**
16. _____ Provides handy access to commonly executed tasks, such as saving a file and undoing recent actions. **p. 13**
17. _____ The long bar at the bottom of the screen that houses the Zoom slider and various View buttons. **p. 46**
18. _____ The area of blank space that displays to the left, right, top, and bottom of a document or worksheet **p. 47**
19. _____ A technology used to store files and to work with programs that are stored in a central location on the Internet. **p. 6**
20. _____ A feature in a document that consists of one or more lines at the top of each page. **p. 49**

Multiple Choice

1. In Word or PowerPoint, a quick way to select an entire paragraph is to:
   (a) place the pointer at the left of the line, in the margin area, and click.
   (b) triple-click inside the paragraph.
   (c) double-click at the beginning of the paragraph.
   (d) press Ctrl+C inside the paragraph.

2. When you want to copy the format of a selection but not the content, you should:
   (a) double-click Copy in the Clipboard group.
   (b) right-click the selection and click Copy.
   (c) click Copy Format in the Clipboard group.
   (d) click Format Painter in the Clipboard group.

3. Which of the following is *not* a benefit of using One Drive?
   (a) Save your folders and files to the cloud.
   (b) Share your files and folders with others.
   (c) Hold video conferences with others.
   (d) Simultaneously work on the same document with others.

4. What does a red wavy underline in a document or presentation mean?
   (a) A word is misspelled or not recognized by the Office dictionary.
   (b) A grammatical mistake exists.
   (c) An apparent formatting error was made.
   (d) A word has been replaced with a synonym.

5. Which of the following is *true* about headers and footers?
   (a) They can be inserted from the Layout tab.
   (b) Headers and footers only appear on the last page of a document.
   (c) Headers appear at the top of every page in a document.
   (d) Only page numbers can be included in a header or footer.

6. You can get help when working with an Office application in which one of the following areas?
   (a) The Tell me box
   (b) The Status bar
   (c) Backstage view
   (d) The Quick Access Toolbar

7. To access commands that are not on the ribbon, you need to open which of the following?
   (a) Gallery
   (b) Dialog box
   (c) Shortcut menu
   (d) Mini Toolbar

8. To create a document without knowing much about the software, you should use which of the following?
   (a) Theme
   (b) Live Preview
   (c) Template
   (d) Design Style

9. Which is the preferred method for resizing a picture so that it keeps its proportions?
   (a) Use the rotation handle
   (b) Use a corner-sizing handle
   (c) Use a side-sizing handle
   (d) Use the controls in the Adjust group

10. Which is *not* a description of a tag in a Word document?
    (a) A data element
    (b) Document metadata
    (c) Keyword
    (d) Document title

Practice Exercises

1 Designing Webpages

You have been asked to make a presentation at the next Montgomery County, PA Chamber of Commerce meeting. With the Chamber's continued emphasis on growing the local economy, many small businesses are interested in establishing a Web presence. The business owners would like to know more about how webpages are designed. In preparation for the presentation, you will proofread and edit your PowerPoint file. You decide to insert an image to enhance your presentation and use an add-in to include a map and contact information for the Chamber of Commerce. Refer to Figure 1.50 as you complete this exercise.

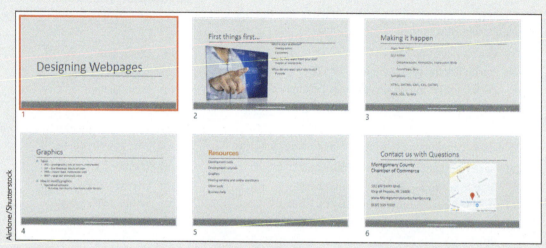

FIGURE 1.50 Designing Webpages Presentation

a. Open the PowerPoint presentation *cf01p1Design*.
b. Click the **File tab**, click **Save As**, and then save the file as **cf01p1Design_LastFirst**.
c. Click the **Design tab** and click **More** in the Themes group. Scroll through the themes to find and select **Retrospect theme**. Select the **third Variant** in the Variants group. Close the Design Ideas pane if it opens.
d. Click **Slide 2** in the Slides pane on the left. Double-click to select **Resources** on the slide title. Use the Mini Toolbar to click the **Font Color arrow**. Select **Orange, Accent 2** in the Theme Colors group. Click **Bold** on the Mini Toolbar.
e. Click **Slide 3** in the Slides pane. Click the **Pictures icon** in the left content placeholder. Browse to the student data files, locate and select *cf01p1Website.jpg*, and then click **Insert**. Close the Design Ideas pane if it opens.
f. Select the picture. Click the **Format tab** and click **More** in the Picture Styles group to open the Pictures Style Gallery. Click the **Reflected Perspective Right**. Click the **Height box** in the Size group and type **4**. Press **Enter**. Place the pointer over the image to display a 4-headed arrow and drag to position the image so it is centered vertically in the open space.
g. Click the **Home tab** and click the **Clipboard Dialog Box Launcher**. Click **Slide 7** and select all the placeholder content. Right-click the selected text and click **Cut** from the shortcut menu.

> **TROUBLESHOOTING:** If there is content in the Office Clipboard, click Clear All to remove all previously cut or copied items from the Office Clipboard.

> **MAC TROUBLESHOOTING:** On a Mac, select the text and press Control+X. Click Slide 4 and press Control+V. Repeat for Step h. Skip to Step j.

h. Click **Slide 5** and select all the placeholder content. Press **Ctrl+X**.
i. Click **Slide 4** and click the **content placeholder**. Click **Paste All** in the Office Clipboard. Close the Office Clipboard.

j. Click **Slide Sorter** on the status bar. Click **Slide 5** and press **Delete**. Click **Slide 6** and press **Delete**. Drag **Slide 2** to the right of **Slide 5**. Click the **View tab** and click **Normal**.

k. Click **Slide 6** in the Slides pane. Click the **Insert tab**, point to **My Add-ins** in the Add-ins group, and read the Enhanced Screen Tip to find out more about Add-ins. Click **My Add-ins**, click the **Store tab**, and then in the search box, type **map**. Press **Enter**.

l. Click **Add** to add OfficeMaps - Insert maps quick and easy!

m. Click Open OfficeMaps on the Insert tab. Click in the Enter a location box and type the address shown on Slide 6. Click Insert Map. Close the OfficeMaps pane.

n. Select the map, click the **Height box** in the Size group, and type **4**. Press **Enter**. Position the map attractively in the slide.

o. Click **Slide 1**. Click **Header & Footer** in the Text group on the Insert tab. Click the **Slide number check box** to select it. Click the **Footer box** to select it and type **Business Owners Association Presentation**. Click **Don't show on title slide check box** to select it. Click **Apply to All**.

p. Click the **Review tab** and click **Spelling** in the Proofing group. In the Spelling pane, click **Change** or **Ignore** to make changes as needed. The words *KompoZer* and *Nvu* are not misspelled, so you should ignore them when they are flagged. Click **OK** when you have finished checking spelling.

q. Click the **File tab**. Click the **Add a Tag box** and type **business, BOA, web design**.

r. Click **Print**. Click the **Full Page Slides arrow** and select **6 Slides Horizontal** to see a preview of all the slides as a handout.

> **MAC TROUBLESHOOTING:** Click the File menu, click Print, and then click Show Details. In the Print dialog box, click the Layout arrow and select Handouts (6 slides per page).

s. Click the **Portrait Orientation arrow** and select **Landscape Orientation**. Click the **Back arrow**.

t. Save and close the file. Based on your instructor's directions, submit cf01p1Design_LastFirst.

2 Upscale Bakery

You have always been interested in baking and have worked in the field for several years. You now have an opportunity to devote yourself full time to your career as the CEO of a company dedicated to baking cupcakes and pastries. One of the first steps in getting the business off the ground is developing a business plan so that you can request financial support. You will use Word to develop your business plan. Refer to Figure 1.51 as you complete this exercise.

FIGURE 1.51 Upscale Bakery Business Plan

a. Open the Word document *cf01p2Business*. Click the **File tab**, click **Save As**, and save the file as **cf01p2Business_LastFirst**.
b. Click the **Design tab**, click **Themes**, and then select **Slice**.
c. Select the paragraphs beginning with *Our Staff* and ending with *(Nutritionist)*. Click the **Home tab** and click **Cut** in the Clipboard group. Click to the left of *Our Products* and click **Paste**.
d. Select the text **Your name** in the first bullet in the *Our Staff* section and replace it with your first and last names. Select the entire bullet list in the *Our Staff* section. On the Mini Toolbar, click the **Font Size arrow** and select **11**.
e. Click **Format Painter** in the Clipboard group. Drag the Format Painter pointer across all four *Our Products* bullets to change the bullets' font size to 11 pt.
f. Click the **Tell me box** and type **footer**. Click **Add a Footer**, scroll to locate the **Integral footer**, and click to add it to the page. Keep the footer open.
g. Right-click the **page number box** in the footer. Click the **Shading arrow** in the Paragraph group on the Home tab and select **White Background 1 Darker 50%**. Click **Close Header and Footer** on the Header & Footer Tools Design tab.
h. Triple-click to select the last line in the document, which says *Insert and position picture here*, and press **Ctrl+X**. Click the **Insert tab** and click **Online Pictures** in the Illustrations group.
i. Click in the **Bing Image search box**, type **Cupcakes**, and then press **Enter**.
j. Select any **cupcake image** and click **Insert**. Do not deselect the image.
k. Ensure the Picture Tools Format tab is active, and in the Picture Styles group, select the **Drop Shadow Rectangle**.

> **TROUBLESHOOTING:** If you are unable to find a cupcake image in Bing, you can use *cf01p2Cupcake* from the student data files.

l. Click the **Size Dialog Box Launcher** and ensure that Lock aspect ratio is selected. Click **OK**. Click the **Shape width box** in the Size group and change the width to **2.5**.
m. Click outside the picture.
n. Press **Ctrl+Home**. Click **Customize Quick Access Toolbar** and select **Spelling & Grammar** (ignore if present). Click **Spelling & Grammar** from the QAT. Correct the spelling error and click **OK**.
o. Click the **View tab** and select **Draft** in the Views group. Click **Print Layout** in the Views group and click **One Page** in the Zoom group.
p. Click the **Layout tab** and click **Margins** in the Page Setup group. Change to **Moderate Margins**.
q. Click the **File tab**. In the Properties section, click in Add a tag box and add the tag **business plan**. Click **Add an author** and add your first and last name to the Author property. Right-click the **current author** (should say Exploring Series) and click **Remove Person**.
r. Click **Print** in Backstage view. Notice the author name has changed in the footer. Change the number of copies to **2**. Click the **Back arrow**.
s. Save and close the file. Based on your instructor's directions, submit cf01p2Business_LastFirst.

Mid-Level Exercises

1 Reference Letter
MyLab IT Grader

You are an instructor at a local community college. A student asked you to provide her with a letter of reference for a job application. You have used Word to prepare the letter, but now you want to make a few changes before it is finalized.

a. Open the Word document *cf01m1RefLetter* and save it as **cf01m1RefLetter_LastFirst**.

b. Change the theme to **Gallery**. Point to Colors in the Document Formatting group and read the Enhanced ScreenTip. Click **Colors** and select **Red**.

c. Insert a **Blank footer**. Type **410 Wellington Parkway, Huntsville, AL 35611**. Center the footer. Close the footer.

d. Place the insertion point at the end of Professor Smith's name in the signature line. Press **Enter** twice. Insert a picture from your files using *cf01m1College.png*. Resize the image to **1"** tall. Click **Color** in the Adjust group and select **Dark Red, Accent color 1 Light**. Click **Center** in the Paragraph group on Home tab.

e. Press **Ctrl+Home**. Select the **date** and point to several font sizes on the Mini Toolbar. Use Live Preview to view them. Click **12**.

f. Right-click the word **talented** in the second paragraph starting with *Stacy is a* and click **Synonyms** from the shortcut menu. Replace *talented* with **gifted**.

g. Move the last paragraph—beginning with *In my opinion*—to position it before the second paragraph—beginning with *Stacy is a gifted*.

h. Press **Ctrl+Home**. Use Spelling & Grammar to correct all errors. Make any spelling and grammar changes that are suggested. Stacy's last name is spelled correctly.

i. Change the margins to **Narrow**.

j. Customize the QAT to add **Print Preview and Print**. Preview the document as it will appear when printed. Stay in Backstage view.

k. Click **Info** in Backstage view. Add the tag **reference** to the Properties for the file in Backstage view.

l. Save and close the file. Based on your instructor's directions, submit cf01m1RefLetter_LastFirst.

2 Medical Monitoring
MyLab IT Grader

You are enrolled in a Health Informatics study program in which you learn to manage databases related to health fields. For a class project, your instructor requires that you monitor your blood pressure, recording your findings in an Excel worksheet. You have recorded the week's data and will now make a few changes before printing the worksheet for submission.

a. Open the Excel workbook *cf01m2Tracker* and save it as **cf01m2Tracker_LastFirst**.

b. Change the theme to **Crop**.

c. Click in the cell to the right of *Name* and type your first and last names. Press **Enter**.

d. Select **cells H1, I1, J1, and K1**. Cut the selected cells and paste to **cell C2**. Click **cell A1**.

e. Press **Ctrl+A**. Use Live Preview to see how different fonts will look. Change the font of the worksheet to **Arial**.

f. Add the Spelling feature to the QAT and check the spelling for the worksheet to ensure that there are no errors.

g. Select **cells E22, F22, and G22**. You want to increase the decimal places for the values in cells so that each value shows one place to the right of the decimal. Use **Increase Decimal** as the search term in the Tell me box. Click **Insert Decimal** in the results to increase the decimal place to **1**.

h. Press **Ctrl+Home** and insert an **Online Picture** of your choice related to blood pressure. Resize and position the picture so that it displays in an attractive manner. Apply the **Drop Shadow Rectangle** picture style to the image.

i. Insert a footer. Use the Page Number header and footer element in the center section. Use the File Name header and footer element in the right section of the footer. Click in a cell on the worksheet. Return to Normal view.

j. Change the orientation to **Landscape**. Change the page margins so Left and Right are **1.5"** and Top and Bottom are **1"**. Center on page both vertically and horizontally. Close the dialog box.

k. Add **blood pressure** as a tag and adjust print settings to print two copies. You will not actually print two copies unless directed by your instructor.

l. Save and close the file. Based on your instructor's directions, submit cf01m2Tracker_LastFirst.

Running Case

New Castle County Technical Services

New Castle County Technical Services (NCCTS) provides technical support for companies in the greater New Castle County, Delaware, area. The company has been in operation since 2011 and has grown to become one of the leading technical service companies in the area. NCCTS has prided itself on providing great service at reasonable costs, but as you begin to review the budget for next year and the rates your competitors are charging, you are realizing that it may be time to increase some rates. You have prepared a worksheet with suggested rates and will include those rates in a memo to the CFO. You will format the worksheet, copy the data to the Office Clipboard, and use the Office Clipboard to paste the information into a memo. You will then modify the formatting of the memo, check the spelling, and ensure the document is ready for distribution before sending it on to the CFO.

a. Open the Excel workbook *cf01r1NCCTSRates* and save as **cf01r1NCCTSRates_LastFirst**.
b. Select **cells A4:C4**. Click **More** in the Styles group on the Home tab and select **Heading 2**.
c. Select **cells A5:C5**. Press **Ctrl** and select cells **A7:C7**. Change the font color to **Red** in Standard Colors.
d. Select **cells A5:C10** and increase the font size to **12**.
e. Select cells **A4:C10**. Open the **Office Clipboard**. Clear the Office clipboard if items display. Click **Copy** in the Clipboard group. Keep Excel open.
f. Open the Word document *cf01r1NCCTSMemo* and save it as **cf01r1NCCTSMemo_LastFirst**.
g. Change Your Name in the From: line to your own name.
h. Press **Ctrl+Home**. Insert image *cf01r1Logo.jpg*. Resize the height to **1"**.
i. Change the document theme to **Retrospect**.
j. Place insertion point in the blank line above the paragraph beginning with *Please*.
k. Open Office Clipboard and click the item in the Office Clipboard that was copied from the NCCTS Rates workbook. Clear then close the **Office Clipboard**.
l. Check the spelling. Correct all grammar and spelling mistakes.
m. Increase left and right margins to **1.5"**.
n. Insert a footer and click **Edit Footer**. Click **Document Info** in the Insert group on the Header and Footer Tools Design tab. Click **File Name**. Click **Close Header and Footer**.
o. Enter **2022**, **rates** as tags.
p. Save and close the files. Based on your instructor's directions, submit the following files:
cf01r1NCCTSMemo_LastFirst
cf01r1NCCTSRates_LastFirst

Disaster Recovery

Resume Enhancement

You are applying for a new position and you have asked a friend to look at your resume. She has a better eye for details than you do, so you want her to let you know about any content or formatting errors. She has left some instructions pointing out where you can improve the resume. Open the Word document *cf01d1Resume* and save it as **cf01d1Resume_LastFirst**. Add your name, address, phone and email in the placeholders at the top of the document. Change the theme of the resume to Office. Bold all the job titles and dates held. Italicize all company names and locations. Use Format Painter to copy the formatting of the bullets in the Software Intern description and apply them to the bullets in the other job description. Bold the name of the university and location. Apply italics to the degree and date. Change the margins to Narrow. Add resume as a tag. Check the spelling and grammar. Save and close the file. Based on your instructor's directions, submit cf01d1Resume_LastFirst.

Capstone Exercise

MyLab IT Grader

Social Media Privacy

You have been asked to create a presentation about protecting privacy on social media sites. You have given the first draft of your presentation to a colleague to review. She has come up with several suggestions that you need to incorporate before you present.

Open and Save Files
You will open, review, and save a PowerPoint presentation.

1. Open the PowerPoint presentation *cf01c1SocialMedia* and save it as **cf01c1SocialMedia_LastFirst**.

Apply a Theme and Change the View
You generally develop a presentation using a blank theme, and then when most of the content is on the slides, you add a different theme to provide some interest.

2. Apply the **Quotable theme** to the presentation and use the **Purple variant**.
3. Change to **Slide Sorter view**. Drag **Slide 2** to become **Slide 3** and drag **Slide 8** to become **Slide 6**.
4. Return to **Normal view**.

Select Text, Move Text, and Format Text
You make some changes to the order of text and change some word choices.

5. Click **Slide 5** and cut the second bullet. Paste it so it is the first bullet.
6. Right-click the second use of **regularly** in the first bullet to find a synonym. Change the word to **often**.
7. Double-click **location** in the fourth bullet. Drag it so it comes after *Disable* and add a space between the two words. Delete the word *of* so the bullet reads *Disable location sharing*.
8. Use the Mini Toolbar to format **Never** in the fifth bullet in italics.

Insert and Modify a Picture
You think Slide 2 has too much empty space and needs a picture. You insert a picture and add a style to give it a professional look.

9. Click **Slide 2** and insert the picture *cf01c1Sharing.jpg* from your data files.
10. Resize the picture height to **4.5"**.
11. Apply the **Rounded Diagonal Corner, White Picture Style**.

Use the Tell me Box
You also want to center the picture on Slide 2 vertically. You use the Tell Me box to help with this. You also need help to change a bulleted list on Slide 5 to SmartArt because many of your slides use SmartArt. You know that there is a way to convert text to SmartArt, but you cannot remember where it is. You use the Tell me box to help you with this function, too.

12. Ensure the picture on Slide 2 is still selected. Type **Align** in the Tell me box. Click **Align Objects** and select **Align Middle**.
13. Select the bulleted text on **Slide 5**. Use the Tell me box to search **SmartArt**.
14. Click the first instance of Convert text to SmartArt from your search and click **More SmartArt Graphics** to convert the text to a **Lined List**.

Insert Header and Footer
You want to give the audience printed handouts of your presentation, so you add a header and footer to the handouts, with page numbers and information to identify you and the topic.

15. Add **page numbers** to all Handouts.
16. Add **Social Media Privacy** as a Header in all Handouts.
17. Add **your name** as a Footer in all Handouts.

Customize the Quick Access Toolbar
You know to review the presentation for spelling errors. Because you run spell check regularly, you add a button on the QAT. You also add a button to preview and print your presentation for added convenience.

18. Add **Spelling** to the QAT.
19. Add **Print Preview and Print** to the QAT.

Check Spelling and Change View
Before you call the presentation complete, you will correct any spelling errors and view the presentation as a slide show.

20. Press **Ctrl+Home** and check the spelling.
21. View the slide show. Click after reviewing the last slide to return to the presentation.

Use Print Preview, Change Print Layout, and Adjust Document Properties

You want to print handouts of the presentation so that 3 slides will appear on one page.

22. Click the **Print Preview and Print command** on the QAT to preview the document as it will appear when printed.
23. Change Full Page Slides to **3 Slides**.

> **MAC TROUBLESHOOTING:** Click the File menu and click Print. Click Show Details. Click Layout and choose Handouts (3 slides per page).

24. Change the Page Orientation to **Landscape**.
25. Adjust the print settings to print **two** copies. You will not actually print two copies unless directed by your instructor.
26. Change document properties to add **social media** as a tag and change the author name to your own.
27. Save and close the file. Based on your instructor's directions, submit cf01c1SocialMedia_LastFirst.

Word | Introduction to Word

LEARNING OUTCOME You will develop a document using features of Microsoft Word.

OBJECTIVES & SKILLS: After you read this chapter, you will be able to:

Introduction to Word Processing

OBJECTIVE 1: BEGIN AND EDIT A DOCUMENT   73
Create a Document, Reuse Text, Use a Template, Add Text and Navigate a Document, Review Spelling and Grammar

OBJECTIVE 2: CUSTOMIZE WORD   79
Explore Word Options

HANDS-ON EXERCISE 1   82

Document Organization

OBJECTIVE 3: USE FEATURES THAT IMPROVE READABILITY   86
Insert Headers and Footers, Adjust Margins, Change Page Orientation, Insert a Watermark, Insert a Symbol

OBJECTIVE 4: VIEW A DOCUMENT IN DIFFERENT WAYS   91
Select a Document View, Change the Zoom Setting, Preview a Document, Manage Page Flow

HANDS-ON EXERCISE 2   96

Document Settings and Properties

OBJECTIVE 5: MODIFY DOCUMENT PROPERTIES   103
Customize Document Properties, Print Document Properties

OBJECTIVE 6: PREPARE A DOCUMENT FOR DISTRIBUTION   105
Ensure Document Accessibility, Ensure Document Compatibility, Understand Document Retrieval, Run the Document Inspector, Select Print Options

HANDS-ON EXERCISE 3   113

CASE STUDY | Swan Creek National Wildlife Refuge

You are fascinated with wildlife in its natural habitat. For that reason, you are excited to work with Swan Creek National Wildlife Refuge, assigned the task of promoting the refuge's educational outreach programs. Emily Traynom, Swan Creek's site director, is concerned that children in the city have little opportunity to interact with nature. She fears that a generation of children will mature into adults with little appreciation of the role of our country's natural resources in the overall balance of nature. Her passion is encouraging students to visit Swan Creek and become actively involved in environmental activities.

Ms. Traynom envisions summer day camps where children explore the wildlife refuge and participate in learning activities. She asked you to use your expertise in Microsoft Word to produce documents such as flyers, brochures, memos, contracts, and letters. You will design and produce an article about a series of summer camps available to children from fifth through eighth grades. From a rough draft, you will create an attractive document for distribution to schools.

CHAPTER 1

Organizing a Document

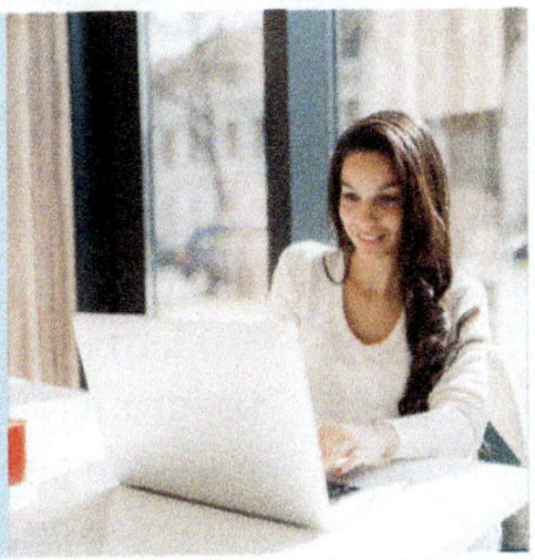

Nd3000/Shutterstock

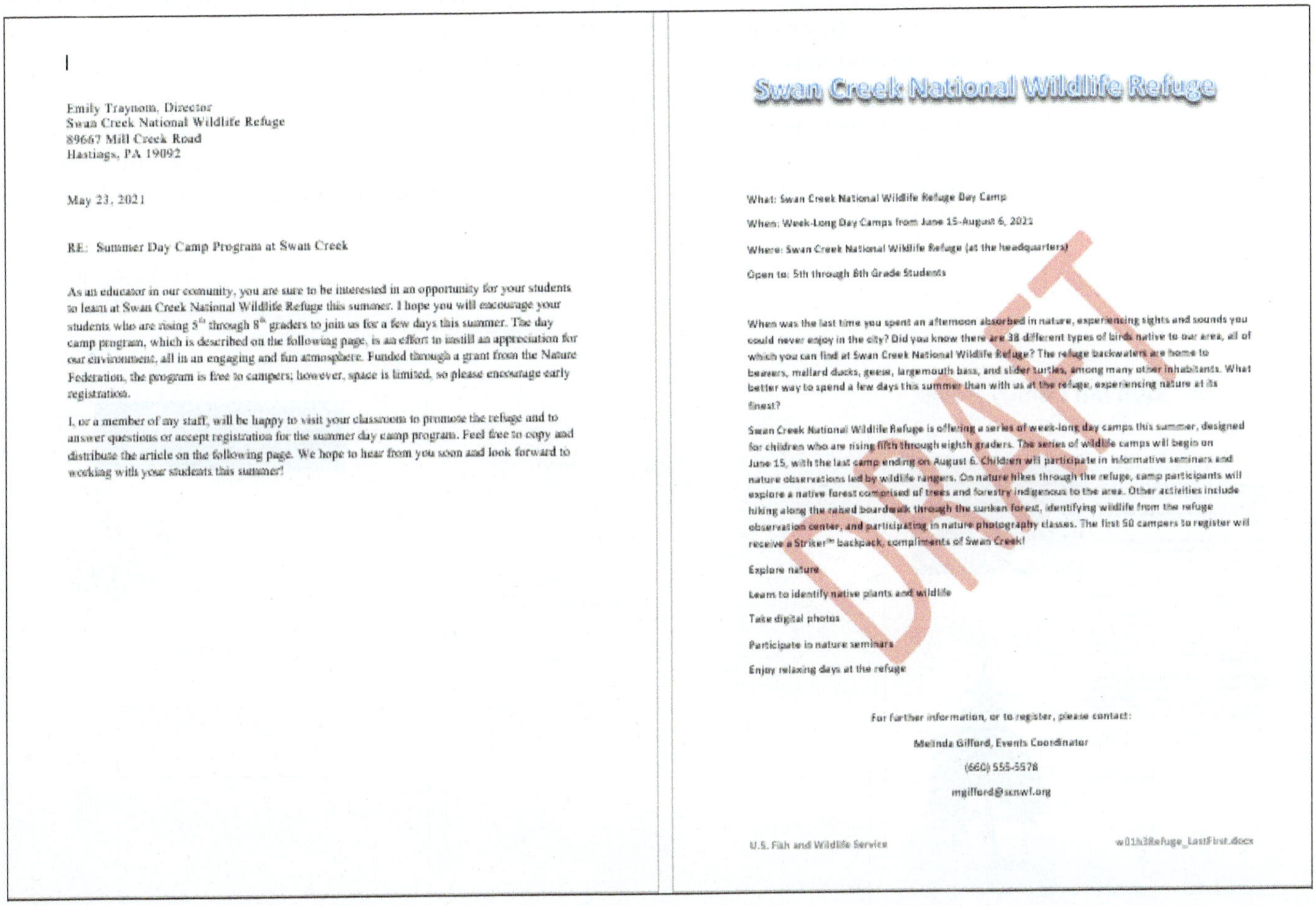

Emily Traynom, Director
Swan Creek National Wildlife Refuge
89667 Mill Creek Road
Hastings, PA 19092

May 23, 2021

RE: Summer Day Camp Program at Swan Creek

As an educator in our community, you are sure to be interested in an opportunity for your students to learn at Swan Creek National Wildlife Refuge this summer. I hope you will encourage your students who are rising 5th through 8th graders to join us for a few days this summer. The day camp program, which is described on the following page, is an effort to instill an appreciation for our environment, all in an engaging and fun atmosphere. Funded through a grant from the Nature Federation, the program is free to campers; however, space is limited, so please encourage early registration.

I, or a member of my staff, will be happy to visit your classroom to promote the refuge and to answer questions or accept registration for the summer day camp program. Feel free to copy and distribute the article on the following page. We hope to hear from you soon and look forward to working with your students this summer!

Swan Creek National Wildlife Refuge

What: Swan Creek National Wildlife Refuge Day Camp

When: Week-Long Day Camps from June 15-August 6, 2021

Where: Swan Creek National Wildlife Refuge (at the headquarters)

Open to: 5th through 8th Grade Students

When was the last time you spent an afternoon absorbed in nature, experiencing sights and sounds you could never enjoy in the city? Did you know there are 38 different types of birds native to our area, all of which you can find at Swan Creek National Wildlife Refuge? The refuge backwaters are home to beavers, mallard ducks, geese, largemouth bass, and slider turtles, among many other inhabitants. What better way to spend a few days this summer than with us at the refuge, experiencing nature at its finest?

Swan Creek National Wildlife Refuge is offering a series of week-long day camps this summer, designed for children who are rising fifth through eighth graders. The series of wildlife camps will begin on June 15, with the last camp ending on August 6. Children will participate in informative seminars and nature observations led by wildlife rangers. On nature hikes through the refuge, camp participants will explore a native forest comprised of trees and forestry indigenous to the area. Other activities include hiking along the raised boardwalk through the sunken forest, identifying wildlife from the refuge observation center, and participating in nature photography classes. The first 50 campers to register will receive a Striker™ backpack, compliments of Swan Creek!

Explore nature

Learn to identify native plants and wildlife

Take digital photos

Participate in nature seminars

Enjoy relaxing days at the refuge

For further information, or to register, please contact:

Melinda Gifford, Events Coordinator

(660) 555-5578

mgifford@scnwl.org

U.S. Fish and Wildlife Service

w01h3Refuge_LastFirst.docx

DRAFT

FIGURE 1.1 Swan Creek Documents

CASE STUDY | Swan Creek National Wildlife Refuge

Starting Files	Files to be Submitted
Blank document w01h1Camps w01h2Letter w01h3NewEmployee	w01h2Flyer_LastFirst w01h3NewEmployee_LastFirst w01h3Refuge_LastFirst

MyLab IT Grader An alternate version of this project is available as a MyLab IT Grader Assessment

Introduction to Word Processing

Word processing software, often called a word processor, is one of the most commonly used types of software in homes, schools, and businesses. People around the world—students, office assistants, managers, and professionals in all fields—use word processing programs such as **Microsoft Word** for a variety of tasks. You can create letters, reports, research papers, newsletters, brochures, and all sorts of documents with Word. You can even create and send email, produce webpages, post to social media sites, and update blogs with Word. Figure 1.2 shows examples of documents created in Word. If a project requires collaboration online or between offices, Word facilitates sharing documents, tracking changes, viewing comments, and efficiently producing a document to which several authors can contribute. By using Word to develop a research paper, you can create citations, a bibliography, a table of contents, a cover page, an index, and other reference pages. To enhance a document, you can change colors, add interesting styles of text, insert graphics, and use tables to present data. With emphasis on saving documents to the cloud, Word enables you to share these documents with others or access them from any device. Word is a comprehensive word processing solution, to say the least.

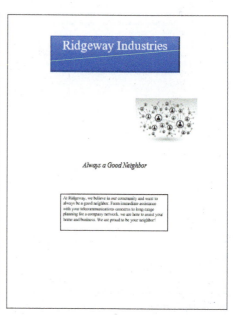

FIGURE 1.2 Sample Word Processing Documents

Communicating through the written word is an important, in fact, vital, task for any business or organization. Word processing software, such as Word, simplifies the technical task of preparing documents, but a word processor does not replace the writer. Be careful when phrasing a document so you are sure it is appropriate for the intended audience. Always remember that once you distribute a document, either on paper or electronically, you cannot retract the words. Therefore, you should never send a document that you have not carefully checked several times to be sure it conveys your message in the best way possible. Also, you cannot depend completely on a word processor to identify all spelling and grammatical errors, so be sure to closely proofread every document you create. Although several word processors, including Word, provide predesigned documents (called templates) that include basic layouts for various tasks, it is ultimately up to you to compose well-worded documents. The role of business communication, including the written word, in the success or failure of a business cannot be overemphasized.

In this section, you will explore Word's interface, learn how to create a document, explore the use of templates, and perform basic editing operations. You will learn to adjust document settings and to modify document properties. Using Word options, you will explore ways to customize Word to suit your preferences.

Beginning and Editing a Document

When you open Word, your screen will be similar to Figure 1.3, although it may vary a bit depending upon whether Office has recently updated. You can create a blank document, or you can select from several types of templates. In addition, you can open a previously created document, perhaps selecting from the list of recent files, and then edit and print a document as desired.

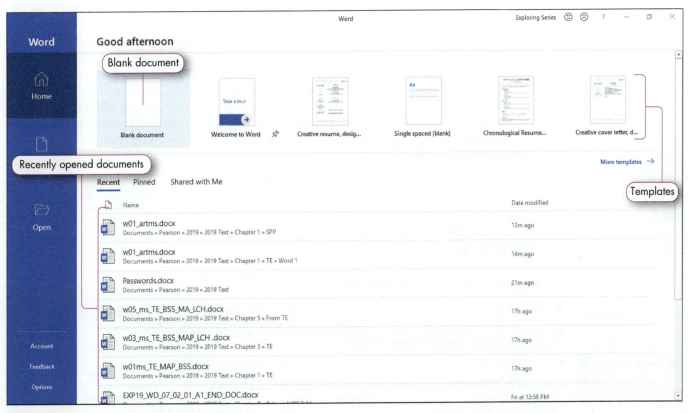

FIGURE 1.3 Word Document Options

STEP 1 Create a Document

To create a blank document, click Blank document when Word opens. As you type text, the **word wrap** feature automatically pushes words to the next line when you reach the right margin, creating what is known as a soft return. The location of automatically generated soft returns changes as text is inserted or deleted, or as page features or settings, such as objects or margins are added or changed. Such soft returns cannot be deleted.

Although word wrap is convenient, you may occasionally want to control when one line ends and another begins, such as at the end of a paragraph or a major section. Or perhaps you are typing several lines of an address or bulleted lines. In those cases, you can indicate that a line should end before text reaches the right margin. To do so, you can either insert a hard return or a soft return. When you press Enter, Word inserts a hard return. As a hard return is entered, a new paragraph begins, with any associated paragraph spacing separating the two paragraphs. In the case of multiple address lines, bulleted text, or text associated with objects such as SmartArt, however, you might want to avoid the paragraph space that results from a hard return. You can insert a manual soft return, or line break, when you press Shift+Enter at the end of any line of text. A new line begins after the soft return, but without any associated paragraph spacing. Manual soft returns, as opposed to the automatic soft returns generated by Word when the right margin is reached, are considered characters and can be deleted. Hard returns are also nonprinting characters that can be removed.

Actions such as a hard return, manual soft return, or even a tab or space are included in a document as nonprinting characters that are only visible when you make a point to display them. To show nonprinting characters, click Show/Hide ¶ on the Home tab (see Figure 1.4). The display of nonprinting characters can assist you with troubleshooting a document and modifying its appearance before printing or distributing. For example, if lines in a document end awkwardly, some not even extending to the right margin, you can check for the presence of poorly placed, or perhaps unnecessary, hard returns (if nonprinting characters are displayed). Deleting the hard returns might realign the document so that lines end in better fashion. Just as you delete any other character by pressing Backspace or Delete (depending on whether the insertion point is positioned to the right or left of the item to remove), you can delete a nonprinting character. To turn off the display of nonprinting characters, click Show/Hide again.

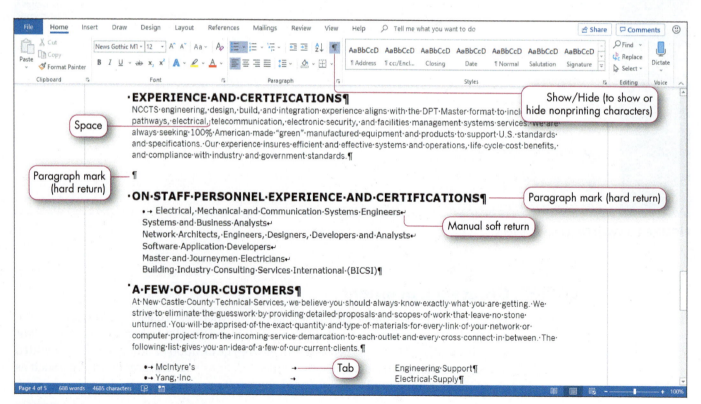

FIGURE 1.4 Displaying Nonprinting Characters

As you work with Word, you must understand that Word's definition of a paragraph and your definition are not likely to be the same. You would probably define a paragraph as a related set of sentences, which is correct in a literary sense. When the subject or direction of thought changes, a new paragraph begins. However, Word defines a paragraph as text that ends in a hard return. Even a blank line, created by pressing Enter, is considered a paragraph. Therefore, as a Word student, you will consider every line that ends in a hard return a paragraph. When you press Enter, a paragraph mark is displayed in the document if you choose to show nonprinting characters (refer to Figure 1.4).

Reuse Text

You might find occasion to reuse text from a previously created document. For example, a memo to employees describing new insurance benefits might borrow all wording from another document describing the same benefits to company retirees. Word facilitates the addition of all text from a saved document to any location within a document that is being developed. Inserting text in that way can save development time, as existing text is inserted without the need to type it again and can also avoid typing errors that are likely to occur if text is typed instead of inserted.

Inserting text from a previously saved document into one that is currently open incorporates all text from the saved document, unlike the copy and paste procedure that is often used to acquire only a portion of text from another document. Text that is copied and pasted must be drawn from a currently open document, whereas text that is reused is retrieved from a saved document without the need to first open it. If the intention is to include all text from a saved file into one that is being created, you will find that inserting text is an efficient way to accomplish that.

To insert text from another document, complete the following steps:

1. Position the insertion point where the inserted text is to be placed.
2. Click the Insert tab. Click the Object arrow (see Figure 1.5).
3. Click Text from File.
4. Navigate to the location of the source document and double-click the file name.

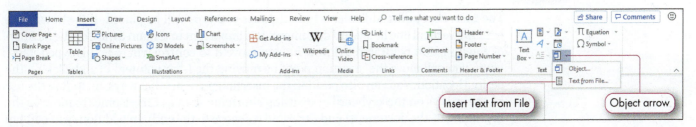

FIGURE 1.5 Inserting Text from Another File

Use a Template

Developing a new document related to a specific scenario or with precise or elaborate formatting can be difficult. With that in mind, the developers of Word have included a library of **templates** from which you can select a predesigned document. You can then modify the document to suit your needs. Various types of templates are displayed when you first open Word, or when you click the File tab and click New. In addition to local templates—those that are available offline with a typical Word installation—Microsoft provides many more online. All online templates are displayed or searchable within Word, as shown in Figure 1.6. Microsoft continually updates content in the template library, so you are assured of having access to all the latest templates each time you open Word.

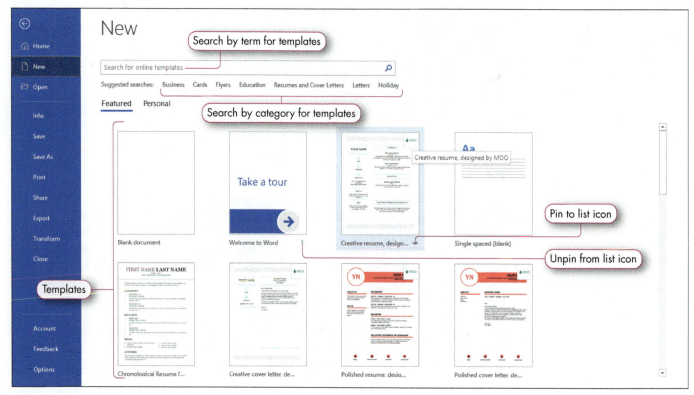

FIGURE 1.6 Working with Templates

Some templates are likely to become your favorites. Because you will want quick access to those templates, you can pin them to the top of the templates menu so they will always be available. Having pinned a template, you can also unpin it when it is no longer necessary. To pin a template, either right-click a favorite template and then pin it to the list or point to a template and click the horizontal Pin to list icon (refer to Figure 1.6). Unpin a template by completing the same steps but choosing to unpin.

STEP 2 Add Text and Navigate a Document

The ***insertion point*** indicates where the text you type will be placed. It is shown as a blinking vertical line in a Word document. It is important to remain aware of the location of the insertion point and to know how to move it to control where text is typed. Most often, you will move the insertion point by moving the I-bar pointer and clicking the desired location. You can also position the insertion point in other ways, including the use of arrow keys on the keyboard or by using shortcuts such as Ctrl+Home (to move to the beginning of the document) and Ctrl+End (to move to the end). In addition, you can tap a touchscreen with a finger or stylus to reposition the insertion point.

If a document contains more text than will display onscreen at one time, click the horizontal or vertical scroll arrows (or drag a scroll bar) to view different parts of the document. An alternative is to press the Page Up or Page Down keys. Then, when the text you want to see displays, position the insertion point and continue editing the document. Be aware that using the scroll bar or scroll arrows to move the display does not reposition the insertion point. It merely enables you to see different parts of the document, leaving the insertion point where it was last positioned. Only when you click or tap in the document, or use a keyboard shortcut, is the insertion point moved.

STEP 3 **Review Spelling and Grammar**

It is important to create a document that is free of spelling and grammatical errors. One of the easiest ways to lose credibility with readers is to allow such errors to occur. Choose words that are appropriate and that best convey your intentions in writing or editing a document. Word provides tools on the Review tab that simplify the tasks of reviewing a document for errors, identifying proper wording, and providing insight into unfamiliar words.

A word considered by Word to be misspelled is underlined with a red wavy line. A possible grammatical mistake or word usage error is underlined in blue. Both types of errors are shown in Figure 1.7. To correct possible grammatical or word usage errors in a document, right-click an underlined error and complete one of the following steps:

- Select the correct spelling from one or more options that may be displayed.
- Ignore the misspelled word.
- Add the word to the Office dictionary so it will be recognized as a valid term.

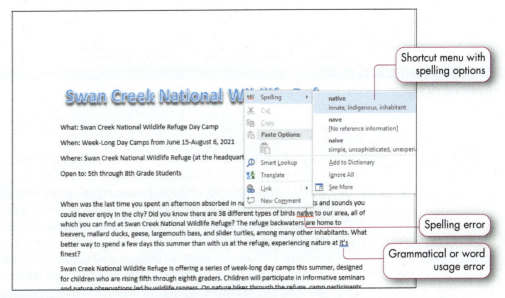

FIGURE 1.7 Correcting Spelling and Grammatical Errors

Correcting each error individually by right-clicking can become time-consuming, especially if the mistakes are many. In that case, Word can check an entire document, pausing at each identified error so that you can determine whether to correct or ignore the problem. To check an entire document for spelling, grammatical, and writing errors, use the Review tab to check the document (see Figure 1.8). Review each error as it is displayed, selecting an identified correction or ignoring the error if it is correct (as might be the case with a name or medical term). If a correct spelling is not displayed, and a word is misspelled, you can manually make the correction.

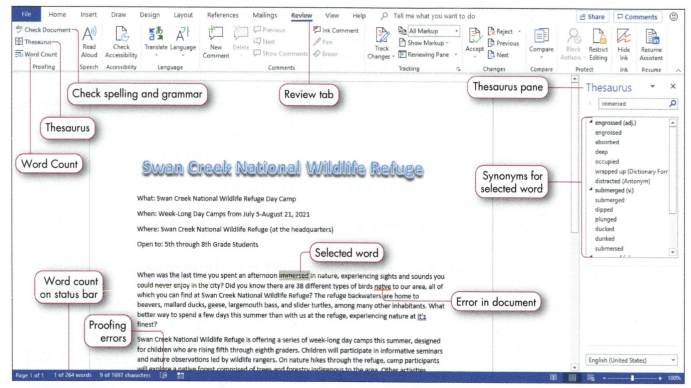

FIGURE 1.8 Options for Proofing a Document

As an alternative to identifying errors, check the Proofing errors icon on the status bar (refer to Figure 1.8). By default, Word automatically checks the entire open document for spelling, grammatical, and word usage errors, displaying on the status bar if errors are found. Click the Proofing errors icon and choose a category of error (Spelling or Grammar) to either change or ignore all errors, one at a time. If, instead, you see a check mark on the Proofing errors icon, the document appears to be error free. The document in Figure 1.8 contains at least one error, as indicated by the Proofing errors icon on the status bar.

Never depend completely on Word to catch all errors; always proofread a document yourself. For example, typing the word *fee* when you meant to type *free* is not an error that Word would typically catch, because *fee* is not actually misspelled and might not be flagged as a word usage error, depending upon the sentence context.

Words do not always come easily. Occasionally, you might want to find a synonym (a word with the same meaning as another) for a particular word. Word provides a handy **thesaurus** for just such an occasion. In addition to providing synonyms, Word's thesaurus also includes antonyms (words with the opposite meaning) for a selected word, if any are available. To identify a synonym, select a word in a document and choose Thesaurus on the Review tab (refer to Figure 1.8). Point to a synonym and click the arrow that displays to insert the word. You can also right-click a selected word and point to Synonyms on the shortcut menu. Select a synonym from a subsequent list of words or click Thesaurus to open the Thesaurus pane for more options.

You can identify a synonym for a word that is not in the current document. In that case, open the thesaurus, type the word for which you want a synonym in the Thesaurus pane, and begin a search. The Thesaurus pane is shown in Figure 1.8. Select from the list presented. If a dictionary is installed, the Thesaurus pane also displays a definition of a selected or typed search term.

> **TIP: COUNTING WORDS**
> Occasionally, you might need to know how many words are included in a document, or in a selected portion of a document. For example, your English instructor might require a minimum word count for an essay. The status bar provides a running total of the number of words typed in a document thus far, or the total number of words for a completed document. You can also find Word Count on the Review tab in the Proofing group (refer to Figure 1.8). To display character count, right-click the status bar and ensure that Character Count (with spaces) is selected.

Especially when editing or collaborating on a document created by someone else, you might come across a word with which you are unfamiliar. Select Smart Lookup on the References tab to peruse additional information in the Smart Lookup pane related to a selected word (see Figure 1.9).

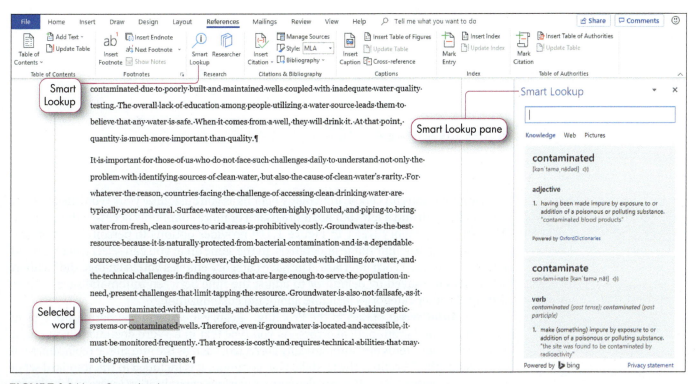

FIGURE 1.9 Using Smart Lookup

Customizing Word

As installed, Word is immediately useful. However, you might find options that you would prefer to customize so that your Word installation is personalized and effective. You might prefer to change the default location to which documents are saved, or maybe you prefer a particular theme or background. These and other options are available for customization within Word.

Explore Word Options

By default, certain Word settings are determined and in place when you begin a Word document. For example, unless you specify otherwise, Word will automatically check spelling as you type. Similarly, the Mini Toolbar will automatically display when text is selected. Although those and other settings are most likely what you will prefer, there may be occasions when you want to change them. When you change Word options, you change them for all documents—not just the currently open file. To modify Word options, click the File tab and click Options. Then select from categories of options, as shown in Figure 1.10.

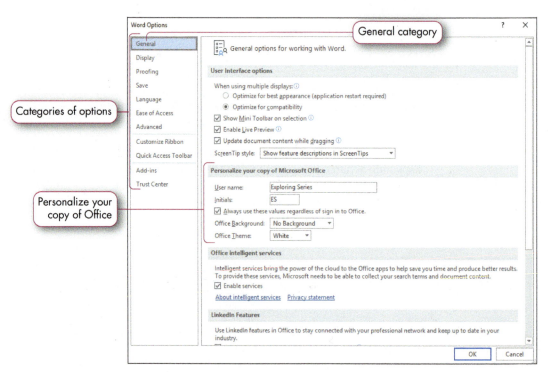

FIGURE 1.10 Accessing Word Options

Although you can choose from many options as you customize your Word installation, you are likely to find a few that are more useful or more commonly accessed than others. The General category (refer to Figure 1.10) provides options to personalize Word by associating a particular name and initials. In the same area, you can select a background and theme for the Word interface. The Save category enables you to change the location where files are saved by default or to adjust the time between automatic saves. Other settings in other categories facilitate additional customization.

The **AutoCorrect** option in the Proofing category includes a standard list of typical misspellings and grammatical errors. As you type text in a Word document, you might notice that some items are automatically corrected, such as the automatic replacement of "teh" with "the." Because the mistake is so common, it is included in the standard set of AutoCorrect entries. AutoCorrect also corrects various capitalization errors and facilitates the inclusion of certain symbols. For example, typing (c) in a document automatically results in the copyright symbol of © because those keystrokes are included in AutoCorrect's standard set of replacements. You can check the list of automatic corrections or changes when you click AutoCorrect Options in the Proofing category in Word Options (see Figure 1.11).

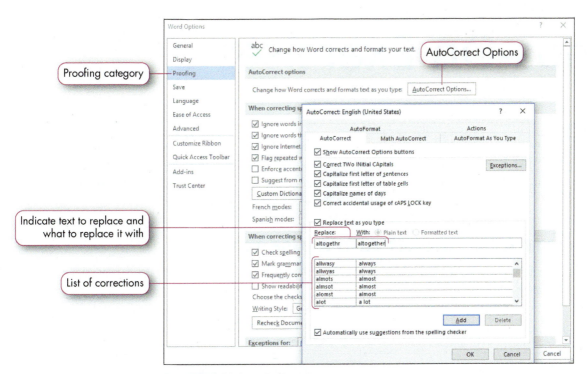

FIGURE 1.11 AutoCorrect Options

In the same dialog box (refer to Figure 1.11), you can customize AutoCorrect entries to include words or names that you often misspell or changes that you choose to make based on text typed. You might even consider using AutoCorrect to simplify the production of documents by replacing abbreviations with whole words. For example, you could include an entry that replaces an abbreviation for your company with the entire company name. That way, whenever you type the initials for a lengthy law firm name, for example, Word could automatically display the entire law firm name. To add AutoCorrect entries, indicate what to replace and what to replace it with in the AutoCorrect dialog box.

> **TIP: SETTING WORD OPTIONS**
> Word options that you change will remain in effect until you change them again, even after Word is closed and reopened. Keep in mind that if you are working in a school computer lab, you might not have permission to change options permanently.

1. Explain how the way you are likely to define a paragraph and the way Word defines a paragraph can differ. *p. 75*

2. Describe the process of reusing text from another document and compare the process to that of copying and pasting text. Provide an example of when reusing text would be preferable to copying and pasting. *p. 75*

3. Describe an advantage of using Word templates to begin document production. *p. 75*

4. Explain why a document might still contain spelling or word usage errors even after Word has checked a document for errors. Provide an example of an error that Word might not identify. *p. 78*

Introduction to Word Processing • **Word 2019**

Hands-On Exercises

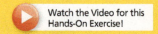

MyLab IT HOE1 Sim Training

Watch the Video for this Hands-On Exercise!

Skills covered: Create a Document • Reuse Text • Add Text and Navigate a Document • Review Spelling and Grammar

1 Introduction to Word Processing

As an office assistant working with the wildlife refuge, you prepare a document publicizing the summer day camps at Swan Creek. Your supervisor provided a few paragraphs that you modify, creating an article for distribution to schools in the area.

STEP 1 CREATE A DOCUMENT AND REUSE TEXT

As you create a new document, you insert text provided by your supervisor and save the document for later editing. Refer to Figure 1.12 as you complete Step 1.

FIGURE 1.12 Beginning a Document

a. Open Word. Click **Blank document**. Click **Save** on the Quick Access Toolbar. In the right pane, click the location where you save your files, or click **Browse** and navigate to the location. Change the file name to **w01h1Refuge_LastFirst**. Click **Save**.

When you save files, use your last and first names. For example, as the Word author, I would name my document "w01h1Refuge_HoganLynn."

> **TROUBLESHOOTING:** If you make any major mistakes in this exercise, you can close the file without saving, open a blank document, and then start this exercise over.

b. Click the **Insert tab** and click the **Object arrow** in the Text group. Click **Text from File**. Navigate to your student data files for this chapter and double-click *w01h1Camps*. Press **Ctrl+Home** to move the insertion point to the beginning of the document.

c. Click **Save** on the Quick Access Toolbar.

This saves the document without changing the name or the location where it is saved.

d. Click the **File tab** and click **Close**.

STEP 2: ADD TEXT AND NAVIGATE A DOCUMENT

Although Ms. Traynom provided you with a good start, you add a bit more detail to the wildlife refuge article. Refer to Figure 1.13 as you complete Step 2.

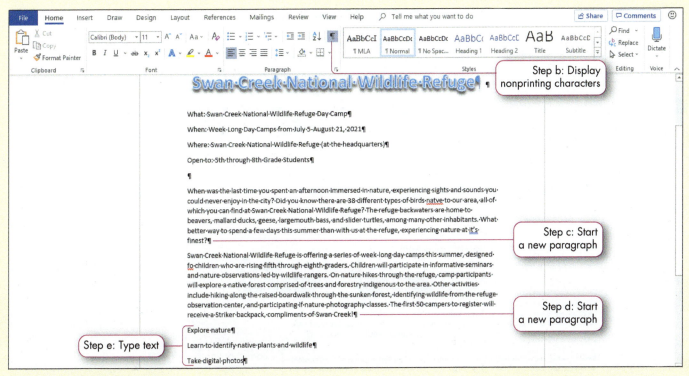

FIGURE 1.13 Editing a Document

a. Click the **File tab**. In the Recent list, click **w01h1Refuge_LastFirst**.

b. Click **Show/Hide** in the Paragraph group on the Home tab to display nonprinting formatting marks (unless they are already displayed).

c. Click after the sentence ending in *finest?*—immediately after the question mark and before the nonprinting space character (that is not shown in Figure 1.13) at the end of the fourth sentence in the body text. Press **Enter**. Press **Delete**.

TROUBLESHOOTING: There will be no space before Swan if you clicked after the space instead of before it when you pressed Enter. In that case, there is no space to delete, so leave the text as is.

d. Scroll down and click after *Creek!*—immediately after the exclamation point after the second body paragraph—and press **Enter**.

e. Type the following text, pressing **Enter** at the end of each line:

explore nature

learn to identify native plants and wildlife

take digital photos

participate in nature seminars

enjoy relaxing days at the refuge

As you type each line, the first letter is automatically capitalized.

Hands-On Exercise 1   83

f. Press **Ctrl+End**. Press **Delete**.

The final paragraph mark is deleted and the second blank page is removed.

g. Save the document.

STEP 3 REVIEW SPELLING AND GRAMMAR

As you continue to develop the article, you check for spelling, grammar, and word usage mistakes. You also identify a synonym and get a definition. Refer to Figure 1.14 as you complete Step 3.

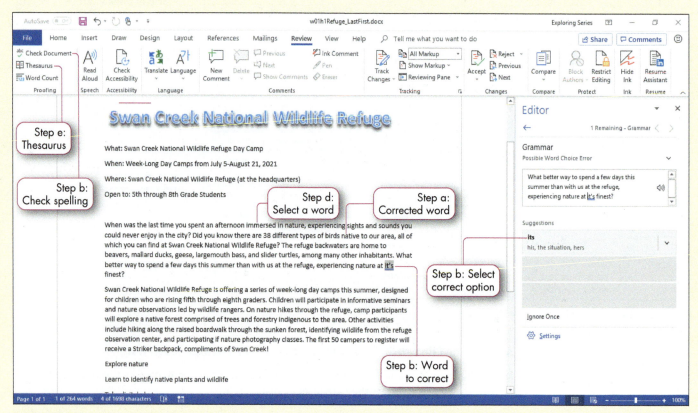

FIGURE 1.14 Proofing a Document

a. Press **Ctrl+Home**. Right-click the red underlined word **natve** in the second line of the first body paragraph in the document. Click **native** on the shortcut menu.

b. Click the **Review tab** and click **Check Document** (or Spelling & Grammar) in the Proofing group. Click **Spelling** in the Editor pane, if shown. As an error is displayed, click to select the correct option. The word *fo* should be *for*. Click **Grammar** in the Editor pane. The word *birds* is not possessive, so ignore the suggested error. The word *it's* should not include an apostrophe, so click the correct option (refer to Figure 1.14). Click **OK** when the check is complete. Close the Editor pane.

c. Read through the document. At least one error in the document is not identified as a spelling or word usage error by Word. Identify and correct the error. The error is a word that is not misspelled but is misused. It is located near the end of the second body paragraph.

d. Select the word *immersed* in the first sentence of the first body paragraph. Click the **References tab**. Click **Smart Lookup** in the Research group.

A definition is shown in the Smart Lookup pane.

TROUBLESHOOTING: If the Smart Lookup pane has not been used before, you may have to respond to a privacy prompt before the Smart Lookup pane will open.

e. Close the Smart Lookup pane. With the word *immersed* still selected, click the **Review tab** and click **Thesaurus** in the Proofing group. Point to the word *absorbed*, click the arrow at the right, and then select **Insert**.

> **TROUBLESHOOTING:** If you click the word *absorbed* instead of the arrow at the right, you will see related word choices, but the word will not be inserted. Click the back arrow at the top of the Thesaurus pane, and repeat Step e.

f. Close the Thesaurus pane.

g. Save the document. Keep the document open if you plan to continue with the next Hands-On Exercise. If not, close the document and exit Word.

Document Organization

Most often, the reason for creating a document is for others to read; therefore, the document should be designed to meet the needs of the reading audience. It should not only be well worded and structured, but also might include features that better identify it, such as headers, footers, and watermarks. In addition, adjusting margins and changing page orientation might better suit a document's purpose and improve its readability. Depending on its purpose, a document might need to fit on one page, or it could be very lengthy.

Before printing or saving a document, review it to ensure that it is attractive and appropriately organized. Word has various views, including Read Mode, Print Layout, Web Layout, Outline, and Draft, that you can use to get a good feel for the way the entire document looks, regardless of its length. The view selected can also give a snapshot of overall document organization, so you can be assured that the document is well structured and makes all points. Using options on the View tab on the ribbon, you can display a document in various ways, showing all pages, only one page, or zooming to a larger view, among other selections.

In this section, you will explore features that improve readability, and you will learn to change the view of a document.

Using Features That Improve Readability

Choosing your words carefully will result in a well-worded document. However, no matter how well worded, a document that is not organized in an attractive manner so that it is easy to read and understand is not likely to impress an audience. Consider not only the content, but also how a document will look when printed or displayed. Special features that can improve readability, such as headers, footers, and symbols, are located on Word's Insert tab. Other settings, such as margins, page orientation, and paper size, are found on the Layout tab. The Design tab provides access to watermarks, which can help convey the purpose or originator of a document.

STEP 1 Insert Headers and Footers

Headers and ***footers*** are sections of text that appear in the top or bottom margin of a document. Although headers and footers typically contain such information as a page number, date, or document title, they can also contain graphics, multiple paragraphs, and fields. Typically, the purpose of including a header or footer is to better identify the document. As a header, you might include an organization name or a class number so that each page identifies the document's origin or purpose. A page number is a typical footer, although it could just as easily be included as a header. You can specify that a header or footer does not appear on the first page, as might be the case if a document includes a title page, or you might create a different header or footer for odd and even pages. If a document is divided into sections, each section could include a different header or footer.

One advantage of using headers and footers is that you specify the content only once, after which it displays automatically on all pages. Although you can type the text yourself at the top or bottom of every page, it is time-consuming, and the possibility of making a mistake is great. Insert a header or footer by making selections on the Insert tab. You can select from a gallery of predefined header or footer styles that include graphics, borders, color, and text areas (see Figure 1.15). However, if you plan to design a simple unformatted header, you can select Edit Header and then type and align text as you like. Alternatively, to begin a simple unformatted header or footer, you can double-click in the top or bottom margin.

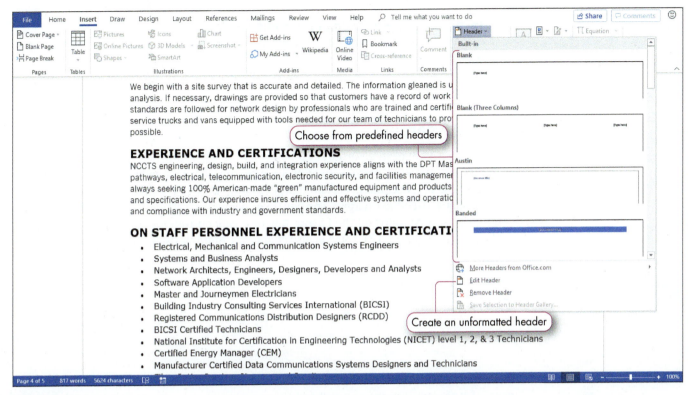

FIGURE 1.15 Inserting a Header

A header or footer can be formatted like any other text. It can be left-, center-, or right-aligned and formatted in any font or font size. When working with a header or footer, the main body text of the document is grayed out temporarily. When you return to the document, the body text is active, with the header or footer text dimmed.

Word provides fields, such as author, date, and file name, that you can include in headers and footers. Some header and footer fields, such as page numbers, will change from one page to the next. Other fields, such as author name and date, will remain constant. Regardless, selecting fields (instead of typing the actual data) simplifies the task of creating headers and footers. Some of the most frequently accessed fields, such as Date & Time and Page Number, are available on the Header & Footer Tools Design contextual tab as separate commands (see Figure 1.16). Others, including Author, File Name, and Document Title, are available when you click Document Info in the Insert group. Depending on the field selected, you might have to indicate a specific format and/or placement. For example, you could display the date as Monday, August 16, 2021, or you might direct that a page number is centered. Document Info also includes a Field option, which provides access to a complete list of fields from which to choose (see Figure 1.16). The same fields are available when you click Quick Parts in the Insert group and click Field.

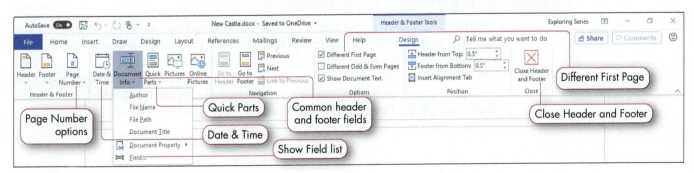

FIGURE 1.16 Header and Footer Fields and Options

Document Organization • **Word 2019**   87

> **TIP: REMOVING A HEADER FROM THE FIRST PAGE**
> Occasionally, you will want a header or footer on all pages except the first, such as when the first page is a report's cover page. In that case, select Different First Page (refer to Figure 1.16) in the Options group on the Header & Footer Tools Design tab (when a header or footer is selected).

STEP 2 Adjust Margins

Although a 1" margin all around the document is the default setting, you might want to change a document's margins to improve appearance and readability. Also, depending on the purpose of a document, certain margin settings may be required for formal papers and publications. To change margins, you have two options. You can select from predefined margin settings using Margins on the Layout tab, or create custom margins by clicking Custom Margins (see Figure 1.17). You can also change the margins using File tab print options.

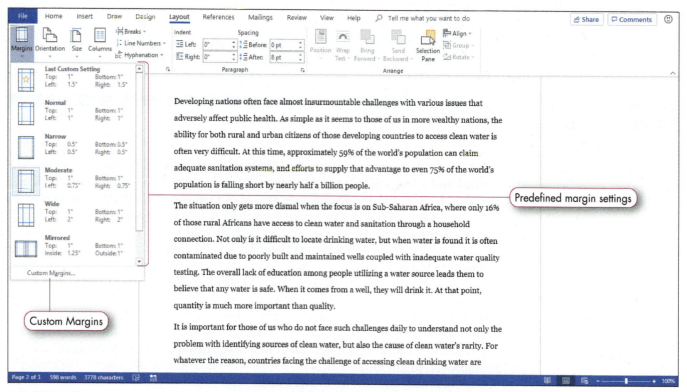

FIGURE 1.17 Setting Margins

STEP 3 Change Page Orientation

Some documents are better suited for portrait orientation, whereas others are more attractive in landscape. For example, certificates are typically designed in landscape orientation, in which a document is shown wider than it is tall; letters and memos are more often in portrait orientation. You can change page orientation on the Layout tab or on the Margins tab in the Page Setup dialog box (see Figure 1.18), which is accessible when you click the Page Setup Dialog Box Launcher on the Layout tab. Print options on the File tab also enable you to adjust page orientation.

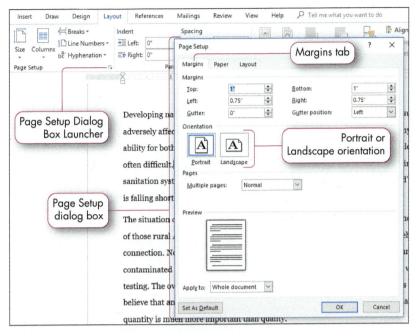

FIGURE 1.18 Changing Page Orientation

STEP 4 Insert a Watermark

A ***watermark***, which is text or a graphic that displays behind text on a page, is often used to include a very light, washed-out logo for a company within a document, or to indicate the status of a document. For example, a watermark displaying *Draft* indicates that a document is not in final form. The document shown in Figure 1.19 contains a watermark. Watermarks do not display on a document that is saved as a webpage, nor will they display in Word's Web Layout view (discussed later in this chapter).

population is falling short by nearly half a billion people.

The situation only gets more dismal when the focus is on Sub-Saharan Africa, where only 16% of those rural Africans have access to clean water and sanitation through a household connection. Not only is it difficult to locate drinking water, but when water is found it is often contaminated due to poorly built and maintained wells coupled with inadequate water quality testing. The overall lack of education among people utilizing a water source leads them to believe that any water is safe. When it comes from a well, they will drink it. At that point, quantity is much more important than quality.

It is important for those of us who do not face such challenges daily to understand not only the problem with identifying sources of clean water, but also the cause of clean water's rarity. For whatever the reason, countries facing the challenge of accessing clean drinking water are typically poor and rural. Surface water sources are often highly polluted, and piping to bring water from fresh, clean sources to arid areas is prohibitively costly. Groundwater is the best resource because it is naturally protected from bacterial contamination and is a dependable source even during droughts. However, the high costs associated with drilling for water, and the technical challenges in finding sources that are large enough to serve the population in

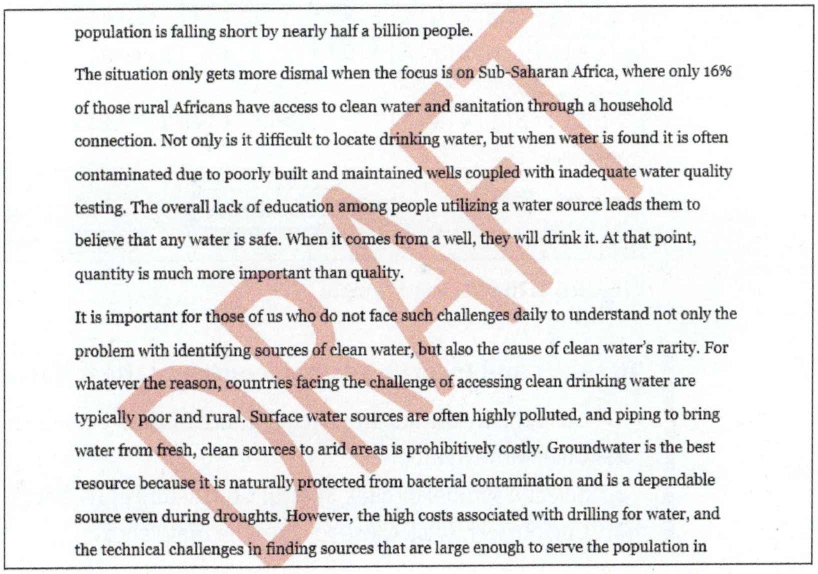

FIGURE 1.19 Using a Watermark

Insert a watermark by selecting Watermark in the Page Background group on the Design tab. Select from predesigned styles or click Custom Watermark to create your own, selecting text, color, and transparency settings. You can even identify a picture as a watermark if you like. To remove a watermark, follow the same steps, choosing to remove a watermark.

STEP 5 **Insert a Symbol**

A ***symbol*** is text, a graphic, or a foreign language character that can be inserted into a document. Some symbols, such as $ and #, are located on the keyboard; however, others are only available from Word's collection of symbols. Symbols such as © and ™ can be an integral part of a document; in fact, those particular symbols are necessary to properly acknowledge a source or product. Because they are typically not located on the keyboard, you can access them in Word's library of symbols or use a shortcut key combination, if available.

Some symbols serve a very practical purpose. For example, it is unlikely you will want a hyphenated word to be divided between lines in a document. In that case, instead of typing a simple hyphen between words, you can insert a nonbreaking hyphen, which is available as a symbol. That special-purpose symbol, along with others, is located in the Special Characters section of the Symbol dialog box. Similarly, you can insert a nonbreaking space when you do not want words divided between lines. For example, a person's first name on one line followed by the last name on the next line is not a very attractive placement. Instead, make the space between the words a nonbreaking space by inserting the symbol, so the names are never divided. Mathematical symbols, foreign currency marks, and popular emoticons are also available in Word's symbol library.

A typical Microsoft Office installation includes a wide variety of fonts. Depending upon the font selected (normal text is shown in Figure 1.20), your symbol choices will vary. Fonts such as Wingdings, Webdings, and Symbol contain a wealth of special symbols, many of which are actually pictures.

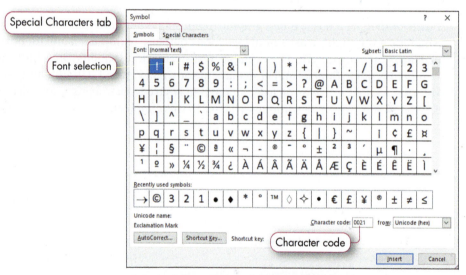

FIGURE 1.20 Selecting a Symbol

To select and insert a symbol, complete the following steps:

1. Click the Insert tab and click Symbol in the Symbols group.
2. Click More Symbols.
3. Select a symbol or click Special Characters and select from the list.
4. Click Insert. Click Close to close the dialog box.

Each symbol is assigned a character code. If you know the character code, you can type the code (refer to Figure 1.20) instead of searching for the symbol itself.

TIP: USING SYMBOL SHORTCUTS
Some symbols, such as © and ™, are included in Word's list of AutoCorrect entries. When you type (c), Word will automatically "correct" it to display ©. Type (tm), and Word shows ™.

Viewing a Document in Different Ways

Developing a document is a creative process. As you create, edit, or review a project, you will want to view the document in various ways. Word provides a view that enables you to see a document as it will print, as well as views that maximize typing space by removing page features. You might review a document in a magazine-type format for ease of reading, or perhaps a hierarchical view of headings and subheadings would help you better understand and proof the structure of a document. The ability to zoom in on text and objects can make a document easier to proofread, while viewing a document page by page helps you manage page flow—perhaps drawing attention to awkward page endings or beginnings. Taking advantage of the various views and view settings in Word, you will find it easy to create attractive, well-worded, and error-free documents.

Select a Document View

When you begin a new document, you see the top, bottom, left, and right margins. This default document view is called **Print Layout view**. You can choose to view a document differently, which is something you might do if you are at a different step in its production. For example, as you type or edit a document, you might prefer **Draft view**, which provides the most typing space possible without regard to margins and special page features. **Outline view** displays a document in hierarchical fashion, clearly delineating levels of heading detail. If a document is destined for the Web, you can view it in **Web Layout view**.

Designed to make a document easy to read and to facilitate access across multiple devices, **Read Mode** presents a document in a left to right flow, automatically splitting text into columns, for a magazine-like appearance. Text often displays in a two-page format. Text adjusts to fit any size screen, flowing easily from page to page with a simple flick of a finger (if using a tablet or touch-sensitive device) or click of the mouse. Users of touch-based devices can rotate the device between landscape and portrait modes, with the screen always divided into equally sized columns. When in Read Mode (see Figure 1.21), the ribbon is removed from view. Instead, you have access to only three menu items: File, Tools, and View. One of the most exciting features of Read Mode is object zooming. Simply double-click an object, such as a table, chart, picture, or video, to zoom in. Press Esc to leave Read Mode.

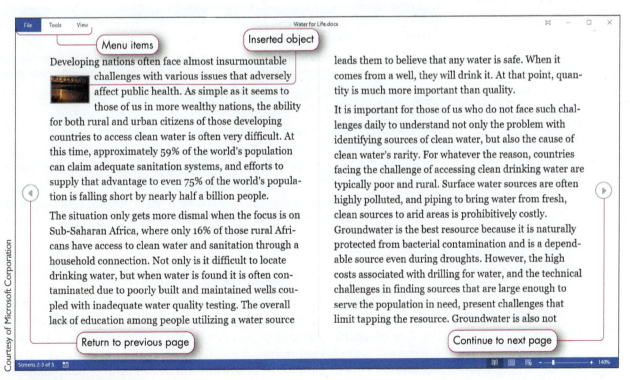

FIGURE 1.21 Read Mode

To change a document's view, click the View tab and select a view from the Views group (see Figure 1.22). Although slightly more limited in choice, the status bar also provides views to choose from (Read Mode, Print Layout, and Web Layout). Word views are summarized in Table 1.1.

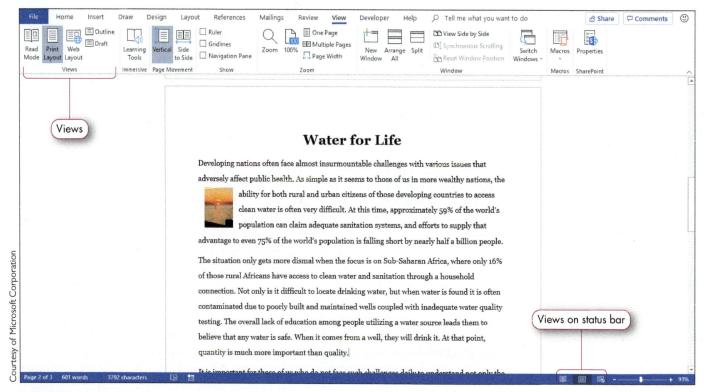

FIGURE 1.22 Word Views

TABLE 1.1	Word Views
View	**Appearance**
Read Mode	Primarily used for reading, with a document shown in pages, much like a magazine. The ribbon is hidden, with only a limited number of menu selections shown.
Print Layout	Shows margins, headers, footers, graphics, and other page features—much like a document will look when printed.
Web Layout	Shows a document as it would appear on a webpage.
Outline	Shows level of organization and detail. You can collapse or expand detail to show only what is necessary. Often used as a springboard for a table of contents or a PowerPoint summary.
Draft	Provides the most space possible for typing. It does not show margins, headers, or other features, but it does include the ribbon.

STEP 6 Change the Zoom Setting

Regardless of the view selected, you can use Word's zoom feature to enlarge or reduce the view of text. Unlike zooming in on an object in Read Mode, the zoom feature available on the View tab enables you to enlarge text, not objects or videos. Enlarging text might make a document easier to read and proofread. However, changing the size of text onscreen does not actually change the font size of a document. Zooming in or out is simply a temporary change to the way a document appears onscreen. The View tab includes options that change the onscreen size of a document (see Figure 1.23). You can also enlarge or reduce the view of text by dragging the Zoom slider on the status bar. Click Zoom In and Zoom Out on the status bar to change the view incrementally by 10% for each click.

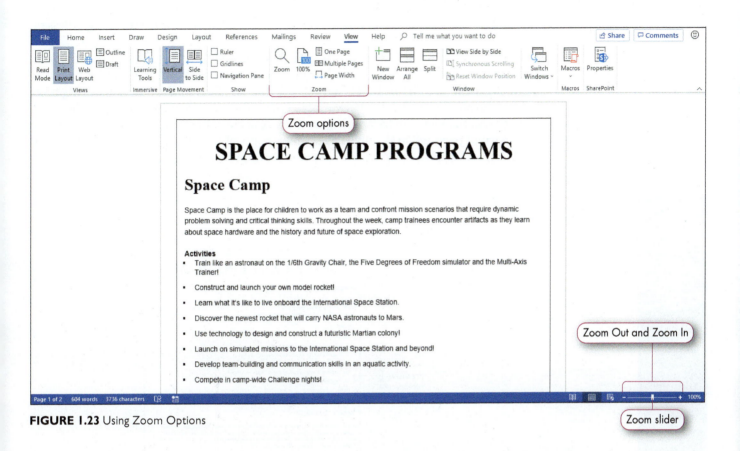

FIGURE 1.23 Using Zoom Options

Use the Zoom command on the View tab to select a percentage of zoom or to indicate a preset width (page width, text width, or whole page). Preset widths are also available as individual options in the Zoom group on the View tab (refer to Figure 1.23).

Preview a Document and Manage Page Flow

Document lengths can vary greatly. A research paper might span 20 pages, whereas a memo is seldom more than a few pages (most often, only one). Obviously, it is easier to view a memo onscreen than an entire research paper. Even so, Word enables you to get a good feel for the way a document will look when printed or distributed, regardless of document length.

Before printing, it is a good idea to view a document in its entirety. One way to do that is to click the File tab and click Print. A document is shown one page at a time in Print Preview (see Figure 1.24). You can use the Next Page or Previous Page navigation arrows to proceed forward or backward in pages. You can also view a document by using options on the View tab (refer to Figure 1.23). Clicking One Page provides a snapshot of the current page, while Multiple Pages shows pages of a multiple-page document side by side (and on separate rows, in the case of more than two pages).

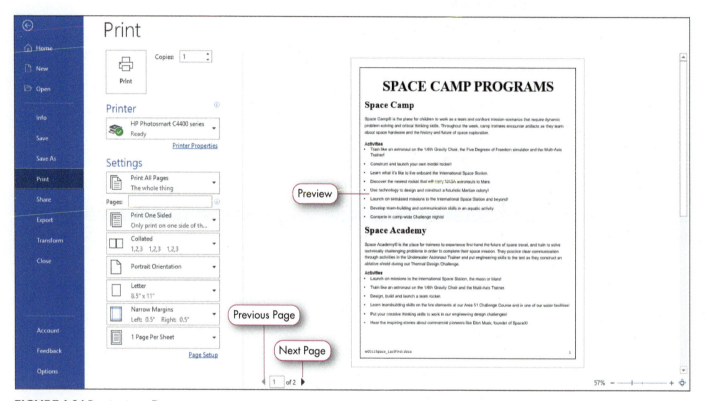

FIGURE 1.24 Previewing a Document

Occasionally, a page will end poorly—perhaps with a heading shown alone at the bottom of a page or with a paragraph split awkwardly between pages. Or perhaps it is necessary to begin a new page after a table of contents, so that other pages follow in the order they should. In those cases, you must manage page flow by forcing a page break where it would not normally occur. To insert a page break, you can use the shortcut Ctrl+Enter or click the Layout tab, click Breaks, and then select Page. Alternatively, click the Insert tab and click Page Break in the Pages group.

With nonprinting characters shown, you will see the Page Break designation (see Figure 1.25). To remove a page break, click the Page Break indicator and press Delete.

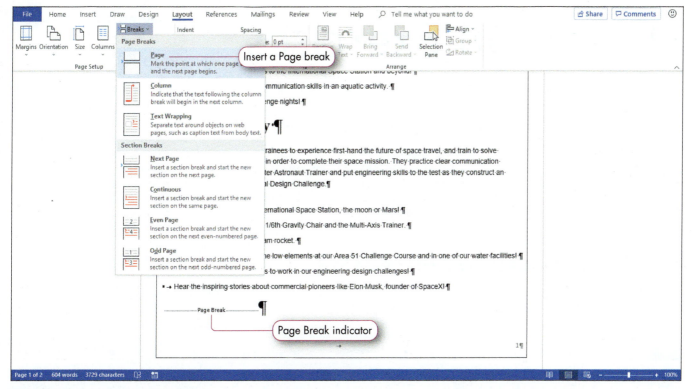

FIGURE 1.25 Inserting a Page Break

5. Provide an example of a header or footer whose value changes from one page to the next. *p. 87*

6. Describe a document that would benefit from the use of a watermark. Explain why that is the case. *p. 89*

7. Explain how, without using a hard or soft return, you might ensure that a person's first name and last name are never separated between lines in a document. *p. 90*

8. Provide an explanation of why Read Mode would be used and how it differs from Print Layout view. *p. 91*

9. Describe a situation in which inserting a page break would be beneficial. *p. 94*

Hands-On Exercises

MyLab IT HOE2 Sim Training

Watch the Video for this Hands-On Exercise!

Skills covered: Insert Headers and Footers • Adjust Margins • Change Page Orientation • Insert a Watermark • Insert a Symbol • Change the Zoom Setting • Preview a Document • Manage Page Flow

2 Document Organization

You are almost ready to submit a draft of the summer day camp article to your supervisor for approval. After inserting a footer to identify the document as originating with the U.S. Fish and Wildlife Service, you adjust the margins and determine the best page orientation for the document. By inserting symbols, you control how words are divided between lines and you give credit through a trademark indication. Next, you insert a watermark to indicate it is a draft document. Finally, you review the document for overall appearance and page flow.

STEP 1 — INSERT HEADERS AND FOOTERS

You insert a footer to identify the article as a publication of the U.S. Fish and Wildlife Service. The footer also includes the file name. Refer to Figure 1.26 as you complete Step 1.

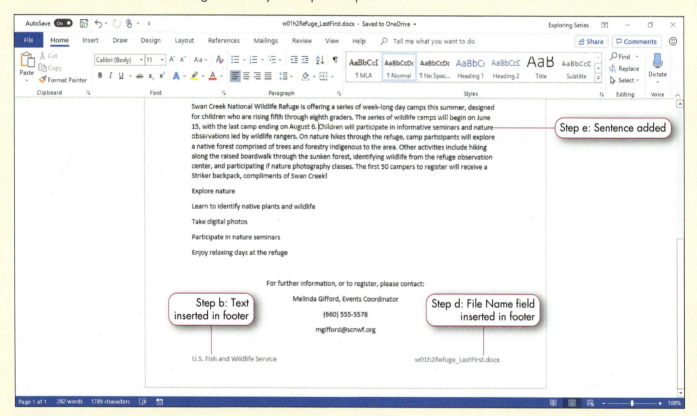

FIGURE 1.26 Designing a Footer

a. Open *w01h1Refuge_LastFirst* if you closed it at the end of Hands-On Exercise 1 and save it as **w01h2Refuge_LastFirst**, changing h1 to h2.

b. Click the **Insert tab**, click **Footer** in the Header & Footer group, and then select **Edit Footer**. Type **U.S. Fish and Wildlife Service**.

> **TROUBLESHOOTING:** If you selected a predefined footer instead of clicking Edit Footer, click Undo on the Quick Access Toolbar and repeat Step b.

c. Click **Insert Alignment Tab** in the Position group on the Header & Footer Tools Design tab. Click **Right** and click **OK**. The Header & Footer Tools Design tab includes several commands in the Position group that facilitate the placement of a header or footer. One of those commands, Insert Alignment Tab, enables you to align text at the right side of an existing header or footer.

> **MAC TROUBLESHOOTING:** The Insert Alignment Tab option is not available on a Mac. You can use tabs to position the footer near the right margin.

d. Click **Document Info** in the Insert group and select **File Name**. Click **Close Header and Footer** in the Close group.

e. Click after the first sentence of the second body paragraph, ending with *through eighth graders*. Be sure to click after the period ending the sentence. Press **Spacebar** and type the following sentence: **The series of wildlife camps will begin on June 15, with the last camp ending on August 6.**

f. Save the document.

STEP 2 ADJUST MARGINS

The article fits on one page, but you anticipate adding text. You suspect that with narrower margins, you might be able to add text while making sure the article requires only one page. You experiment with a few margin settings. Refer to Figure 1.27 as you complete Step 2.

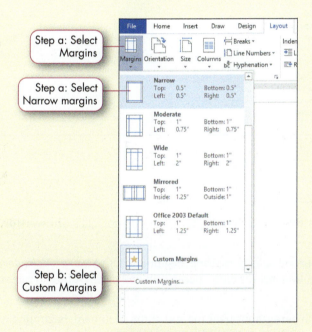

FIGURE 1.27 Working with Margins

a. Click the **Layout tab**, click **Margins** in the Page Setup group, and then select **Narrow**.

At a glance, you determine the right and left margins are too narrow, so you adjust them.

b. Click **Margins** and select **Custom Margins**. Adjust the Left and Right margins to **1"** and click **OK**.

c. Click the **View tab** and click **One Page** in the Zoom group.

The document appears to be well positioned on the page, with room for a small amount of additional text, if necessary.

d. Save the document.

STEP 3 CHANGE PAGE ORIENTATION

Ms. Traynom asked you to prepare an abbreviated version of the article, retaining only the most pertinent information. You prepare and save the shortened version, but you also retain the lengthier version. The shortened article provides a snapshot of the summer activity in an at-a-glance format. Refer to Figure 1.28 as you complete Step 3.

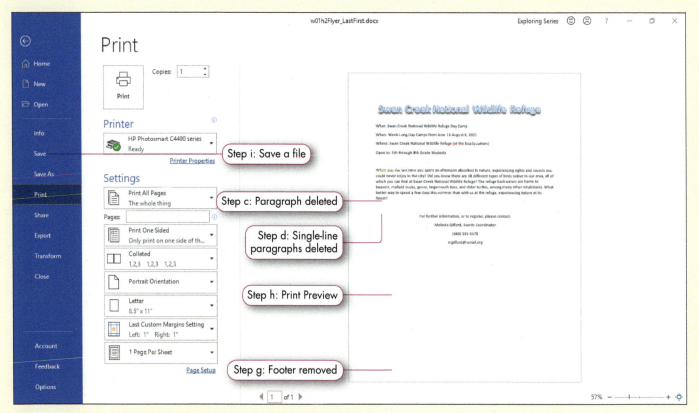

FIGURE 1.28 Previewing a Document

a. Click **100%** in the Zoom group on the View tab.

b. Ensure that nonprinting characters display. If they do not, click **Show/Hide** in the Paragraph group on the Home tab.

c. Triple-click in the second body paragraph, beginning with *Swan Creek National Wildlife Refuge is offering*, to select the entire paragraph and press **Delete** to remove the paragraph.

d. Delete the single-line paragraphs near the end of the document, beginning with *Explore nature* and ending with *Enjoy relaxing days at the refuge*.

e. Click the **File tab** and click **Save As**. Save the file as **w01h2Flyer_LastFirst**.

Because the document is a shortened version of the original, you save it with a different name.

f. Click the **Layout tab** and click **Orientation** in the Page Setup group. Click **Landscape**. Click the **View tab** and click **One Page**. Click **Undo** on the Quick Access Toolbar.

You had suspected the shortened document would be more attractive in landscape orientation. However, since the appearance did not improve, you return to portrait orientation.

g. Select **100%**. Scroll down and double-click in the footer area. Select both footer entries and press **Delete** to remove the footer text. Double-click in the document to close the footer.

The flyer does not require a footer so you remove it.

h. Click the **File tab** and click **Print**. Check the document preview to confirm that the footer is removed.

i. **Save** the document. Click the **File tab** and click **Close**.

You close the flyer without exiting Word. You will submit this file to your instructor at the end of the last Hands-On Exercise.

STEP 4: INSERT A WATERMARK

You open the original article so you can add the finishing touches, making sure to identify it as a draft and not the final copy. To do so, you insert a DRAFT watermark, which can be removed after your supervisor has approved the document for distribution. Refer to Figure 1.29 as you complete Step 4.

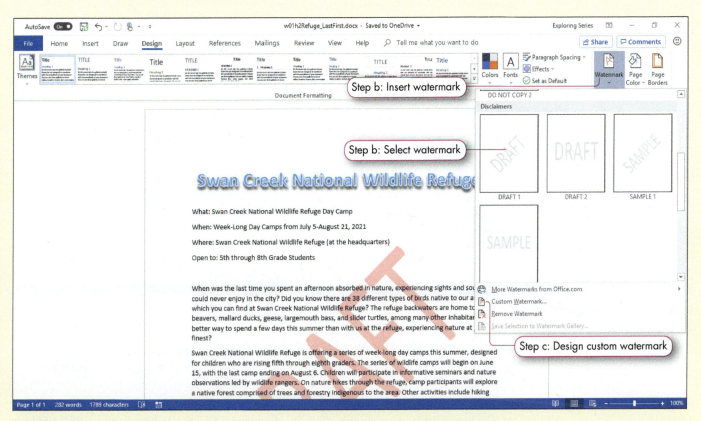

FIGURE 1.29 Inserting a Watermark

a. Click the **File tab**. Select **w01h2Refuge_LastFirst** in the list of Recent Documents.

b. Click the **Design tab** and click **Watermark** in the Page Background group. Scroll through the gallery of watermarks and select **DRAFT 1** (under Disclaimers). The word DRAFT in an angular arrangement displays in the watermark choice.

c. Click **Watermark** again and select **Custom Watermark**. Click the **Color arrow** in the Printed Watermark dialog box and click **Red** (under Standard Colors). Click **OK**.

The watermark is not as visible as you would like, so you change the color.

> **MAC TROUBLESHOOTING:** Select the Text option for a watermark. Ensure DRAFT displays. To slant the watermark, change the orientation to Diagonal.

d. Save the document.

STEP 5 INSERT A SYMBOL

The article you are preparing will be placed in numerous public venues, primarily schools. Given the widespread distribution of the document, you must consider any legality, such as appropriate recognition of name brands or proprietary mentions, by inserting a trademark symbol. You also ensure that words flow as they should, with no awkward or unintended breaks between words that should remain together. Refer to Figure 1.30 as you complete Step 5.

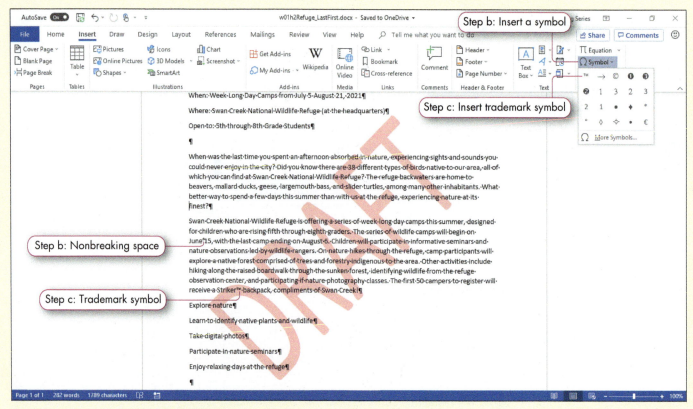

FIGURE 1.30 Working with Symbols

a. Click after the word *June* on the second line in the second body paragraph. Make sure you have placed the insertion point before the space following the word *June*. Press **Delete** to remove the space.

b. Click the **Insert tab** and click **Symbol** in the Symbols group. Click **More Symbols**. Click the **Special Characters tab**. Click **Nonbreaking Space**. Click **Insert** and click **Close**.

Regardless of where the line ends, you want to make sure the phrase June 15 is not separated, with the month on one line and the day on the following line. Therefore, you insert a nonbreaking space.

c. Click after the word *Striker* in the last sentence of the same paragraph. Make sure you have placed the insertion point before the space following the word *Striker*. Click **Symbol** in the Symbols group and click the **Trademark symbol** shown in the list of symbols.

You use the Trademark symbol to indicate that Striker is a brand name.

> **TROUBLESHOOTING:** If you do not find the Trademark symbol in the list of symbols, click More Symbols, click Special Characters, and click the Trademark symbol. Click Insert and click Close.

d. Save the document.

STEP 6 CHANGE THE ZOOM SETTING, PREVIEW A DOCUMENT, AND MANAGE PAGE FLOW

Ms. Traynom provided you with a cover letter to include with the article. You incorporate the letter text into the article as the first page, remove the footer from the first page, proofread the document, and ensure that both pages are attractively designed. Refer to Figure 1.31 as you complete Step 6.

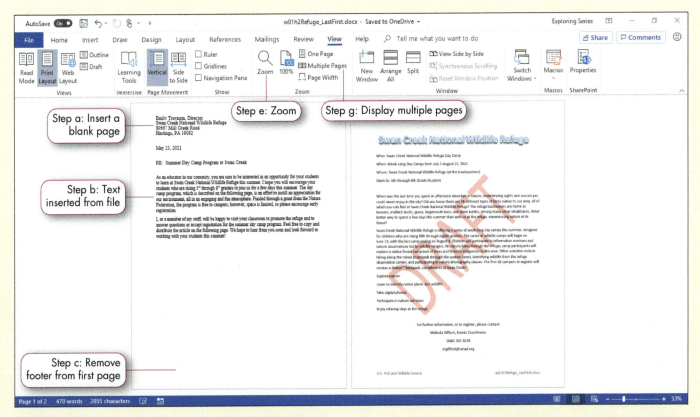

FIGURE 1.31 Modifying and Previewing a Multi-Page Document

a. Press **Ctrl+Home** to position the insertion point at the top of the article. Press **Ctrl+Enter** to insert a blank page at the top. Press **Ctrl+Home** to move to the top of the new page.

Note that both the watermark and the footer display on the new page. That is because those features are designed to appear by default on all pages of a document.

b. Click the **Object arrow** in the Text group on the Insert tab. Click **Text from File**. Navigate to *w01h2Letter* in your student data files and double-click the file name.

You insert text from a previously saved letter as the first page of this document.

c. Double-click in the footer area of the first page. Click **Different First Page** in the Options group of the Header & Footer Tools Design tab.

You indicate that the watermark and footer are not to appear on the first page but will remain on all others.

d. Click **Close Header and Footer** in the Close group.

e. Press **Ctrl+Home**. Click the **View tab** and click **Zoom** in the Zoom group. Click in the **Percent box** and change the Zoom to **125%**. Click **OK**.

f. Scroll through the letter on the first page, proofreading for spelling and grammatical errors. Right-click any underlined error and either correct or ignore it. Manually correct any errors that Word has not flagged. Press **Ctrl+Home**.

Hands-On Exercise 2

g. Click **Multiple Pages** in the Zoom group.

h. Click the **File tab** and click **Print**. Click **Next Page** (the arrow that follows 1 of 2 at the bottom of the screen) to view the article. Click **Previous Page** to return to the letter.

i. Click **Back** ⬅ to return to the document. Click **100%** in the Zoom group. Ensure the insertion point is at the top of the document, and press **Enter** three times to move the text down the page.

The letter appears to be too high on the page, so you move the text down a bit.

j. Click the **File tab** and click **Print**.

The first page is better situated on the page with additional space at the top.

k. Save the document. Keep the document open if you plan to continue with the next Hands-On Exercise. If not, close the document and exit Word.

Document Settings and Properties

After you organize your document and make formatting changes, you save the document in its final form and prepare it for use by others. You can take advantage of features in Word that enable you to manipulate the file in a variety of ways, including ensuring that people with different abilities are able to read and edit the document. You might also choose to include information about the file that does not display in the document, such as a title, author name, subject, and keywords. Such information further identifies the file and can be used as a basis on which to search for or categorize a document later. As you develop a document, you have the option to save the file so that you can access it later, and you should consider methods of document retrieval so that important documents are always available.

In this section, you will explore ways to prepare a document for distribution, including ensuring that a document is as readable as possible, converting a file created in an earlier version to Office 2019, checking for sensitive information included in a file, ensuring adequate document retrieval if a document is lost or corrupted, and working with print options. In addition, you will learn to customize and print document properties.

Modifying Document Properties

Occasionally, you might want to include information to identify a document, such as author, document title, or general comments. Those data elements, or ***document properties***, are saved with the document, but do not appear in the document as it displays onscreen or is printed. Standard document properties that you can assign include author, company, and subject, among others. Such document properties can be useful in categorizing documents and finding them later as the result of a search. For example, suppose you apply a tag of *Computer Applications 225* to all documents you create that are associated with that particular college class. Later, you can use that keyword as a search term, locating all associated documents. Some properties are automatically updated, such as file size and file creation date, while others are optionally created or denoted by the document creator.

If you change the author, or add a title or comments, that information is saved with the file. Comments are notes to yourself or other authors, documenting a process or intention, and they are especially helpful when several authors are collaborating. You can also include tags, or keywords, to help organize and locate document files; however, tags are not saved with the document file. Instead, they are managed by the operating system, making them available across applications. The use of tags facilitates identifying files that are related, albeit from different applications—perhaps identifying related PowerPoint presentations and Word documents.

STEP 1 Customize Document Properties

For statistical information related to the current document, display Backstage view, which is shown when you access the File tab and ensure that Info is selected. Data such as file size, number of pages, and total words are displayed in the right pane on the Info window (see Figure 1.32). You can modify some document information in this view, such as adding a title, tags, or comments. Additional document information can identify a document by author, subject, or title. Tags can assist in organizing files and locating them later. For more possibilities, click Properties and then Advanced Properties (see Figure 1.32). You can then navigate through the file's dialog box, clicking the Summary tab to add or modify properties.

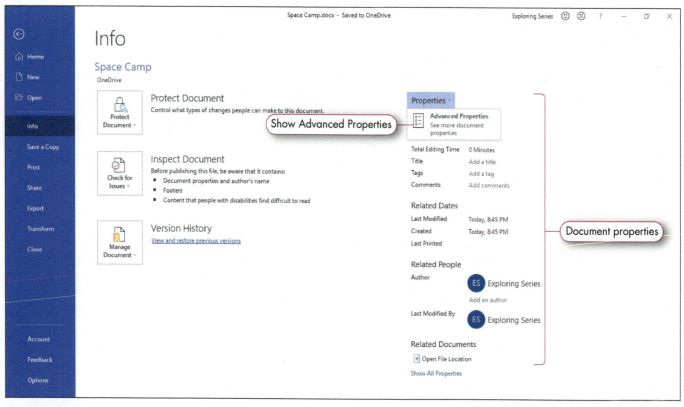

FIGURE 1.32 Working with Document Properties

Although standard document properties, such as title, author, and comments, are helpful in organizing documents by category, you can create your own custom document properties, as well. Suppose you want to identify a document by date assigned, or perhaps as a part of a particular project. Such properties are not considered standard property fields but can be created.

> **To create a custom property, complete the following steps:**
> 1. Click the File tab.
> 2. Ensure that Info is selected. Click Properties.
> 3. Click Advanced Properties.
> 4. Click the Custom tab. Scroll through existing fields or create a custom field, assigning a field type and value.

Print Document Properties

Document properties that were either automatically assigned or that you indicate serve the purpose of identifying and categorizing a document. Because they are not shown onscreen when you open the associated document, you might want to print them for later reference or to include as documentation of the file. From Backstage view (shown when you click File and then click Print), click Print All Pages and then select Document Info (see Figure 1.33). Although the Print Preview pane continues to show the document contents, only document properties will be printed at that point.

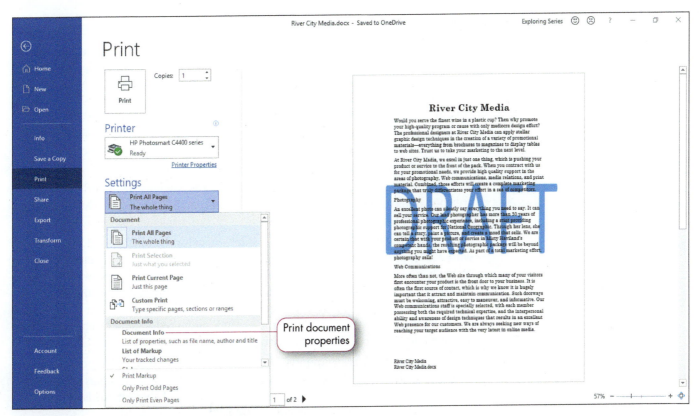

FIGURE 1.33 Printing Document Properties

> **TIP: PRINTING DOCUMENT PROPERTIES WITH ALL DOCUMENTS**
> To print the summary information of document properties with every document that you print, shown as a final page, click the File tab and click Options. Click Display. In the Printing options section, select Print document properties.

Preparing a Document for Distribution

There will be occasions when you want to distribute a document to someone else. Whether it is a report to submit to your instructor or a memo on which you collaborated, most likely the document is something that will be shared with others. Regardless of how you plan to develop, save, and distribute a document, you will not want to chance losing your work because you did not save it properly or failed to make a backup copy. Inevitably, files are lost, systems crash, or a virus compromises a disk. So, the importance of saving work frequently and ensuring that backup copies exist cannot be overemphasized.

A document developed for wide distribution should be readable by people of varying ability levels, even those who are visually challenged or who deal with other disabilities. To assist with that task, Word includes an **Accessibility Checker** that locates elements that might cause difficulty for people with disabilities. As you develop a document for such an audience, keep in mind the possible need to use simple language, ensure that font is sufficiently large, provide enough contrast between font color and background color, and provide other types of appropriate document organization.

As Word versions and updates continue to evolve, there is a chance that someone who needs to read your document is working with an installation that is not compatible with yours, or perhaps the person is not working with Word at all. You can eliminate that source of frustration by saving a document in a compatible format before distributing it.

STEP 2 **Ensure Document Accessibility**

In the United States alone, several million people rely on some sort of assistive technology to access electronic documents and webpages. If documents intended for wide distribution are not created with the need for that technology in mind, it is very likely that those documents will not be readable by many people. It may also be necessary to produce documents in compliance with federal legislation related to accessibility. Word provides assistance with development of accessible documents through the Accessibility Checker, but you should keep the following points in mind as you develop a document so that a check will likely find few suggestions for improvement.

- Use appropriate font style and size. Sans serif fonts, such as Arial and Verdana, are good choices for readability as they are clean and uncluttered. Make sure the font size is at least 12 pt.

- Use contrasting colors and do not rely solely on color to make a point. Readers with a level of color-blindness or those with glaucoma or macular degeneration typically have difficulty reading text that does not contrast strongly with the background. Do not assume that color choice necessarily conveys a message. For example, using a green X to indicate a positive result and a red X as a negative indicator might be less effective than a green Y and a red N, which represent the intended outcome both by color and by letter.

- Add alternative text and captions. Including alternative text and captions for images, pictures, tables, and various objects in a document makes them accessible by screen readers. In that way, the content of those items is understandable to those with certain disabilities.

- Construct simple tables with header rows. When developing a Word table, be sure to use only one row for a header, clearly formatted differently from remaining table text. Do not merge or split table cells and do not leave any rows or columns blank.

- Use meaningful hyperlink text. Do not create hyperlinks with such text as "Click here," as a person using assistive technology might navigate a document by skipping from hyperlink to hyperlink, without access to surrounding text that would provide meaning to such hyperlinks. Instead, make sure a hyperlink provides clear description of the link destination.

- Use built-in formatting styles, especially in the development of headings and lists. Headings that are defined using Word's built-in heading styles enable users to quickly skip through a document by navigating from one heading to another. Use bulleted or numbered lists where appropriate to clearly identify items as included in groups.

Before a document is distributed, run the Accessibility Checker so that questionable areas are first identified and corrected. Select Check Accessibility on the Review tab. As an alternative, you can also choose Check for Issues from the Info group on the File tab and indicate that you want to check accessibility. The Accessibility Checker pane (see Figure 1.34) displays errors (content that is difficult or impossible for those with disabilities), warnings (content that is challenging for those with disabilities), and tips (suggestions for better organization or presentation).

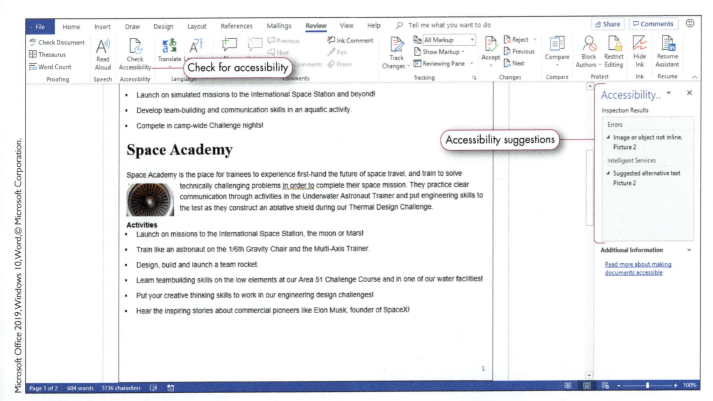

FIGURE 1.34 Using Accessibility Checker

Ensure Document Compatibility

Office 365, a subscription plan that is preferred by many Word users, ensures that Word is continually updated with the most recent additions and software improvements. Whereas historically Microsoft relied solely on major updates—called versions—of its Microsoft Office software for purchase every few years, there is currently less reliance on that form of development and distribution. When that was the norm, however, each new software version was likely to incorporate a different type of file, so that users of early versions might not be able to open files created by newer software installations. While such a challenge is becoming much less likely, you should be aware of the possibility and should understand how to check a document for compatibility before distributing it to those with less up-to-date software installations. From the Info group on the File tab, select Check for Issues and then click Check Compatibility.

You might also consider saving a file in Rich Text Format (RTF) or Portable Document Format (PDF), which adds even more flexibility, as such a file can be opened by other software in addition to Word. Be aware, however, that doing so might compromise the document somewhat because other software types might not be able to accommodate all the current Word features. As you save a Word document, select the file type (see Figure 1.35).

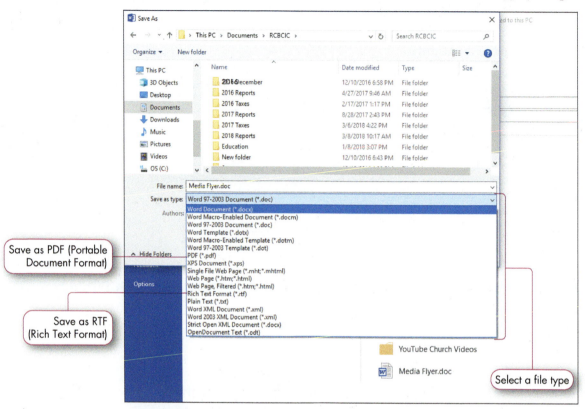

FIGURE 1.35 Selecting a File Type

Occasionally, you might receive a Word document that was created in a much earlier Word version. In that case, the words *Compatibility Mode* are included in the title bar, advising you that some of Word's features may not be available or viewable in the document (see Figure 1.36). While in Compatibility Mode, you might not be able to use new and enhanced Word features; by keeping the file in Compatibility Mode, you ensure that people with earlier Word versions will still have full editing capability when they receive the document. Word simplifies the process of converting a Word document to the newest version. Click the File tab and click Convert (only shown if the file is not in the newest format). Click OK.

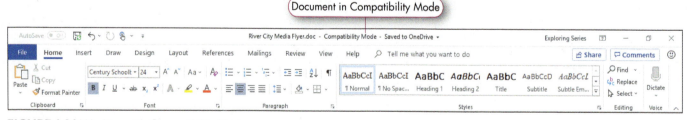

FIGURE 1.36 Working with Compatibility Mode

STEP 3 Understand Document Retrieval

It is inevitable that you will, at some point, lose access to a document before you have saved it, or possibly after you have made a significant amount of progress since the last save. Perhaps the problem is a power disruption or an unexplainable failure that causes Word to become unresponsive. In these instances, the immediate need is to get your document back, without having lost too much content. In a proactive mode, you might have configured

Word to create an automatic backup copy so that you can retrieve most, if not all, of what you have typed. If you are using OneDrive to save the document, you will find that the document was automatically saved and readily available. Even if you have not yet saved a document at all, it is likely that Word can recover much of the document. Obviously, Word is well equipped to address many situations related to recovering documents. Even so, the best practice is to save a document often as you are creating it, perhaps even configuring Word to automatically create a backup copy, so that you are less likely to have to depend on Word's safety nets related to recovering files.

A possible scenario is one in which you close a document without saving it. You may fear that it is gone forever, but that may not be the case. A link to recover unsaved documents is shown at the bottom of the list of recent documents when you click the File tab and click Open, or when you manage documents from the Info selection on the File tab.

> **To locate an unsaved document, complete the following steps:**
>
> 1. Click the File tab and ensure that Info is selected.
> 2. Click Manage Document.
> 3. Select Recover Unsaved Documents.
> 4. Recovered documents are temporarily saved with an ASD extension. If the file you seek is shown, open it and then save it as a Word file, changing the type to Word Document during the save operation.

If you save a document to OneDrive, you do not have to be quite as conscientious about saving often because an open document is automatically saved every few seconds. The **AutoSave** feature is applicable to files saved to OneDrive, OneDrive for Business, and SharePoint Online. If you prefer to save files on local storage, such as a flash drive or a folder on a hard drive, Word provides support through its **AutoRecover** feature, in which you can prescribe an interval of time at which a file should automatically be saved. Word can then recover a document, losing only those changes that might have occurred between saves. Word will be able to recover a previous version of your document when you restart the program, with any files that are recovered shown. By default, file information is saved every 10 minutes (see Figure 1.37), but you can adjust the setting so that the AutoRecover process occurs more or less frequently. You can access controls to adjust the time interval through selections in the Word Options dialog box.

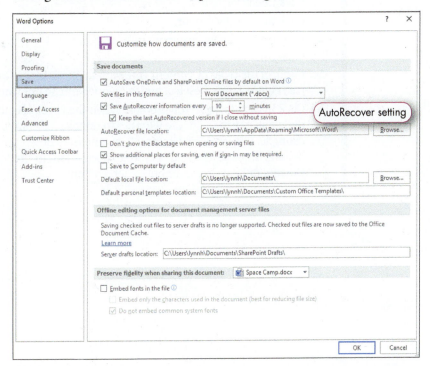

FIGURE 1.37 The AutoRecover Feature

You can also configure Word to create a backup copy each time a document is saved. Although the setting to always create a backup copy is not enabled by default, you can enable it from Word Options in the Advanced category. Even so, creating frequent backup copies can slow your system and may not be altogether necessary, given the excellent File History facility provided by Windows 10. Click the File tab and click Options. Click Advanced. Scroll to the Save group and select Always create backup copy. A backup copy is saved in the same folder as the original, but includes a slightly different file name and the WBK extension, which represents a Word Backup file.

STEP 4 Run the Document Inspector

Before you send or give a document to another person, you should run the **Document Inspector** to reveal any hidden or personal data in the file. For privacy or security reasons, you might want to remove certain items contained in the document such as author name, comments made by one or more people who have access to the document, or document server locations. Word's Document Inspector will check for and enable you to remove various types of identifying information, including:

- Comments, revisions, versions, and annotations
- Document properties and personal information
- Custom XML data
- Headers, footers, and watermarks
- Invisible content
- Hidden text

Because some information removed by the Document Inspector cannot be recovered with the Undo command, you should save a copy of your original document, using a different name, prior to inspecting the document.

> **To inspect a document, complete the following steps:**
>
> 1. Click the File tab and ensure that Info is selected.
> 2. Click Check for Issues.
> 3. Click Inspect Document.
> 4. Respond if a dialog box appears, by clicking Yes if you have not saved the file and want to do so.
> 5. Confirm the types of content you want to check in the Document Inspector dialog box (see Figure 1.38). Deselect any categories you do not want to check.
> 6. Click Inspect to begin the process. When the check is complete, Word lists the results and enables you to choose whether to remove the content from the document. For example, if you are distributing a document to others, you might want to remove all document properties and personal information. In that case, you can instruct the Document Inspector to remove such content.

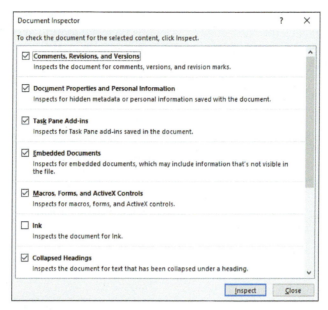

FIGURE 1.38 Inspecting a Document

Select Print Options

Although by default, Word prints one copy of an entire document, you might find it necessary to print multiple copies, or only a few pages. Those settings and others are available when you click the File tab and click Print. The Print settings shown in Figure 1.39 enable you to select the number of copies, the pages or range of pages to print, the printer to use, whether to collate pages, whether to print on only one side of the paper, and how many pages to print per sheet. In addition, you can adjust page orientation, paper size, and even customize a document's margins—all by paying attention to print options. Please note that the wording of some print options will vary, depending on whether you have previously selected the option and indicated a custom setting.

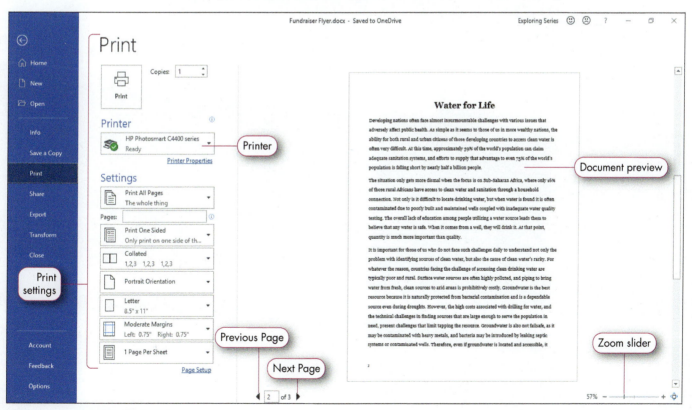

FIGURE 1.39 Word Print Settings

Document Settings and Properties • Word 2019

Print options display to the left of the document preview (refer to Figure 1.39). You can click the Next Page or Previous Page navigation arrows to move among pages in the document preview. You can also drag the Zoom slider to enlarge or reduce the size of the document preview.

10. Explain why document properties are useful in a document, even though they are not actually shown as part of the document onscreen. ***p. 103***

11. Explain the importance of using the Accessibility Checker for a document that you plan to distribute. Provide several examples of suggestions that might occur during the check. ***p. 106***

12. Provide rationale for removing identifying data in a document, such as comments or author name, that might be considered useful in other cases. ***p. 110***

13. Explain why and how you might print document properties. ***p. 104***

Hands-On Exercises

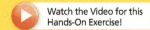

MyLab IT HOE3 Sim Training

Watch the Video for this Hands-On Exercise!

Skills covered: Customize Document Properties • Print Document Properties • Ensure Document Accessibility • Ensure Document Compatibility • Understand Document Retrieval • Run the Document Inspector • Select Print Options

3 Document Settings and Properties

As the office assistant for Swan Creek National Wildlife Refuge, you are responsible for the security, management, and backup of the organization's documents. The article promoting the summer day camps is ready for final approval. Before that happens, however, you will check it one last time, making sure it is saved in a format that others can read. You will also ensure that you have sufficient backup copies. You also want to include appropriate document properties for additional identification, and you will consider print options. Privacy and security are to be considered as well, so you check for identifiers that should be removed before distributing the document. To ensure that the document is readable by as many people as possible, you will check for accessibility.

STEP 1 CUSTOMIZE AND PRINT DOCUMENT PROPERTIES

You assign document properties to the summer camp document to identify its author and purpose. You also create an additional property to record a project identifier. Finally, you prepare to print document properties. Refer to Figure 1.40 as you complete Step 1.

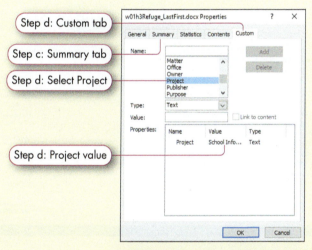

FIGURE 1.40 Customizing Document Properties

a. Open *w01h2Refuge_LastFirst* if you closed it at the end of Hands-On Exercise 2 and save it as **w01h3Refuge_LastFirst**, changing h2 to h3.

b. Click the **File tab**, ensure that Info is selected, click **Properties** in the right pane, and then click **Advanced Properties**.

The Properties dialog box displays.

c. Click the **Summary tab**. Ensure that the Author box contains your name. Click in the **Comments box** and type **Summer Camp Information**.

d. Create a custom property by completing the following steps:
   - Click the **Custom tab** and scroll to select **Project** in the Name list.
   - Type **School Information** in the Value box, and click **Add**.
   - Click **OK** to close the dialog box.

You want to catalog the documents you create for Swan Creek National Wildlife Refuge, and one way to do that is to assign a project identifier using the custom properties that are stored with each document. Because you set up a custom field, you can later perform searches and find all documents in that Project category.

e. Click **Print**, click **Print All Pages**, and then click **Document Info**. Click **Print** if directed to do so by your instructor. Otherwise, continue without printing by clicking **Back**.

STEP 2: ENSURE DOCUMENT ACCESSIBILITY AND COMPATIBILITY

Because the document will be distributed in schools as well as electronically, you check the document for accessibility by those with disabilities. You also convert a document created in an earlier Word version to ensure currency. Refer to Figure 1.41 as you complete Step 2.

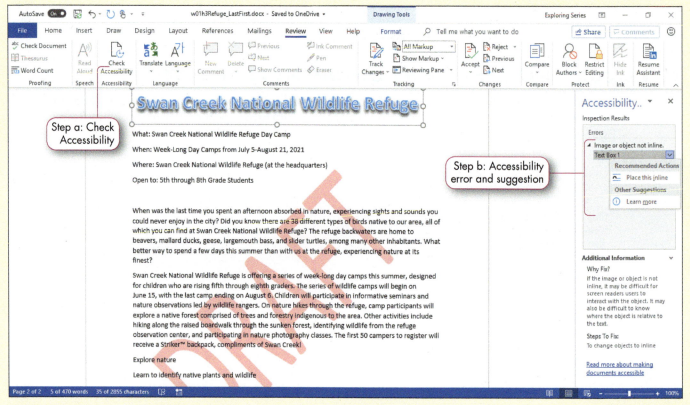

FIGURE 1.41 Check for Accessibility

a. Press **Ctrl+Home** to ensure the insertion point is at the beginning of the document. Click the **Review tab**. Click **Check Accessibility** in the Accessibility group, or alternatively click the File tab, click Check for Issues, and click Check Accessibility.

b. Click **Image or object not inline** in the Accessibility Checker pane, point to Text Box 1, and click the arrow to the right. Click **Place this inline**.

The memo heading is adjusted as it relates to surrounding text. Although other errors may be displayed in the Accessibility Checker pane, you will not address them at this point.

> **TROUBLESHOOTING:** If the adjustment for accessibility results in additional space at the end of the document, perhaps forcing it to another page, delete the extra space to return the display to two pages.

c. Close the Accessibility Checker pane. Save and close w01h3Refuge_LastFirst.

The personnel director has prepared a draft of a memo introducing a new employee. He asked you to proof the document and prepare it for printing. However, he created and saved the memo using an earlier version of Word.

d. Open *w01h3NewEmployee* from the student data files.

The title bar displays *Compatibility Mode* following the file name *w01h3NewEmployee*, indicating that it is not a file saved with a recent installation of Word.

e. Click the **File tab**, ensure that Info is selected, and click **Convert** (beside Compatibility Mode). A message box displays explaining the consequences of upgrading the document. Click **OK**.

The file is converted to the newest Word format. The Compatibility Mode designation is removed from the title bar.

f. Save the document as **w01h3NewEmployee_LastFirst**.

STEP 3 UNDERSTAND DOCUMENT RETRIEVAL

The timeline for preparing for the summer day camps is short. Given the time spent in developing the article, you know that if it were lost, recreating it in a timely fashion would be difficult. In fact, it is critical to ensure appropriate backups and recovery plans for all files for which you are responsible at Swan Creek. You explore document retrieval options on your computer to verify that files are saved periodically and that backups are automatically created. Refer to Figure 1.42 as you complete Step 3.

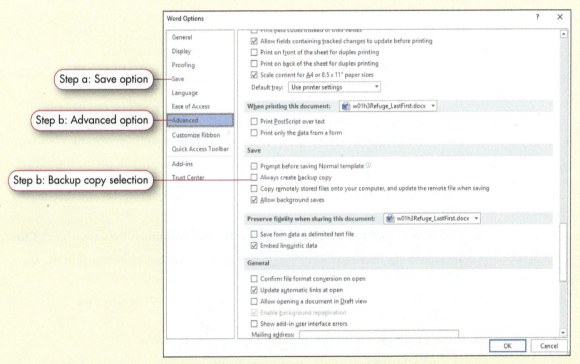

FIGURE 1.42 Exploring Document Retrieval and Recovery Options

a. Click the **File tab** and click **Options**. Click **Save** in the left pane of the Word Options dialog box. If *Save AutoRecover information every* is checked, note the number of minutes between saves.

b. Click **Advanced** in the left pane. Scroll to the Save area and determine whether *Always create backup copy* is selected.

You do not select the setting at this time because you are likely to be in a school computer lab.

c. Click **Cancel**. Close the document.

STEP 4: RUN THE DOCUMENT INSPECTOR AND SELECT PRINT OPTIONS

Before distributing the article, you run the Document Inspector to identify any information that should first be removed. You also prepare to print the document. Refer to Figure 1.43 as you complete Step 4.

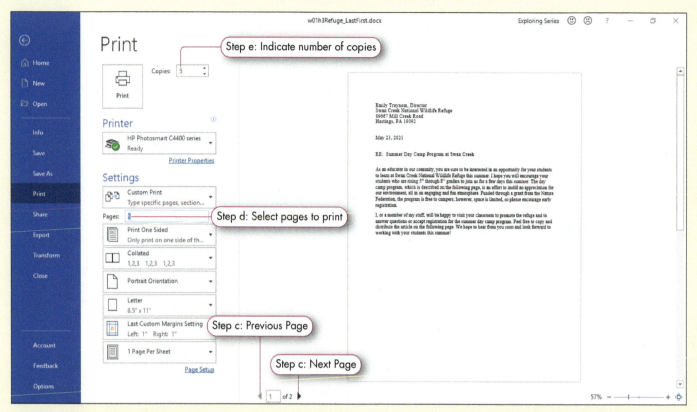

FIGURE 1.43 Working with Print Options

a. Open *w01h3Refuge_LastFirst*. Click the **File tab**, ensure that Info is selected, and click **Check for Issues** (beside Inspect Document). Click **Inspect Document**. Click **Inspect**.

You check for document areas that might display sensitive information. The inspection suggests that the category of Document Properties and Personal Information contains identifying data, as does that of Headers, Footers, and Watermarks, and Custom XML Data.

b. Click **Remove All** beside Document Properties and Personal Information. Click **Close**.

You determine that it would be best to remove all document properties, but you leave headers, footers, and watermarks.

c. Click **Print**. Click **Next Page** to view the next page. Click **Previous Page** to return to the first page.

d. Click in the **Pages box** below Print All Pages. Type **2**.

You indicate that you want to print page 2 only.

e. Click the **Copies up arrow** repeatedly to print five copies.

You indicate that you want to print five copies of page 2.

f. Press **Esc** to return to the document without printing.

g. Save and close the file. Based on your instructor's directions, submit the following:

w01h2Flyer_LastFirst

w01h3Refuge_LastFirst

w01h3NewEmployee_LastFirst

Chapter Objectives Review

After reading this chapter, you have accomplished the following objectives:

1. **Begin and edit a document.**
   - Create a document: Begin a blank document when Word opens and type text.
   - Reuse text: Text from previously created documents can be inserted in another document.
   - Use a template: Predesigned documents save time by providing a starting point.
   - Add text and navigate a document: The insertion point indicates where the text you type will be placed. Use scroll bars or keyboard shortcuts to move around in a document.
   - Review spelling and grammar: Use the Review tab to make sure all documents are free of spelling and grammatical errors.

2. **Customize Word.**
   - Explore Word options: Word options are global settings you can select, such as whether to check spelling automatically, or where to save a file by default.

3. **Use features that improve readability.**
   - Insert headers and footers: Headers and footers provide information, such as page number and organization name, in the top and bottom margins of a document.
   - Adjust margins: You can change margins, selecting predefined settings or creating your own.
   - Change page orientation: Select Landscape to show a document that is wider than it is tall, or Portrait to show a document taller than it is wide.
   - Insert a watermark: A watermark is text or a graphic that displays behind text to identify such items as a document's purpose, owner, or status.
   - Insert a symbol: A symbol is typically a character or graphic that is not found on the keyboard, such as ©.

4. **View a document in different ways.**
   - Select a document view: A view is the way a document displays onscreen; available Word views include Print Layout, Read Mode, Outline, Web Layout, and Draft.
   - Change the zoom setting: By changing the zoom setting, you can enlarge or reduce text size onscreen.
   - Preview a document and manage page flow: Forcing a page break is useful to divide document sections (for example, to separate a cover page from other report pages), or to better manage page flow so that pages do not end awkwardly.

5. **Modify document properties.**
   - Customize document properties: Document properties are items you can add to a document to further describe it, such as author, keywords, and comments.
   - Print document properties: Because document properties are not shown onscreen when you open the associated document, you might consider printing them for later reference or to include as documentation of the file.

6. **Prepare a document for distribution.**
   - Ensure document accessibility: The Accessibility Checker helps ensure that documents are readable by people with disabilities.
   - Ensure document compatibility: Word includes features that assist with converting documents from earlier file formats and saving files so they are easily accessible.
   - Understand document retrieval: Word's AutoSave, AutoRecover, and backup features address file recovery and help ensure that documents are not irretrievably lost.
   - Run the Document Inspector: Word's Document Inspector reveals any hidden or personal data in a file and enables you to remove sensitive information.
   - Select print options: Using Word's print options, you can specify the pages to print, the number of copies, and various other print selections.

Key Terms Matching

Match the key terms with their definitions. Write the key term letter by the appropriate numbered definition.

a. Accessibility Checker
b. AutoCorrect
c. AutoRecover
d. AutoSave
e. Document Inspector
f. Document property
g. Draft view
h. Header or footer
i. Insertion point
j. Microsoft Word
k. Outline view
l. Print Layout view
m. Read Mode
n. Symbol
o. Template
p. Thesaurus
q. Watermark
r. Web Layout view
s. Word processing software
t. Word wrap

1. _____ Text or graphic that displays behind text. **p. 89**
2. _____ A structural view of a document or presentation that can be collapsed or expanded as necessary. **p. 91**
3. _____ The feature that automatically moves words to the next line if they do not fit on the current line. **p. 73**
4. _____ The feature that enables Word to recover a previous version of a document. **p. 109**
5. _____ The tool that checks for document readability by people with disabilities. **p. 105**
6. _____ A computer application, such as Microsoft Word, used primarily with text to create, edit, and format documents. **p. 72**
7. _____ A view in which text reflows to screen-sized pages to make it easier to read. **p. 91**
8. _____ The feature that saves documents automatically so they can be retrieved later. **p. 109**
9. _____ The word processing application included in the Microsoft Office software suite. **p. 72**
10. _____ A predesigned document that may include formats that can be modified. **p. 75**
11. _____ A view that closely resembles the way a document will look when printed. **p. 91**
12. _____ A character or graphic not normally included on a keyboard. **p. 90**
13. _____ A feature that checks for and removes certain hidden and personal information from a document. **p. 110**
14. _____ Information that displays at the top or bottom of each document page. **p. 86**
15. _____ A view that shows a great deal of document space, but no margins, headers, footers, or other special features. **p. 91**
16. _____ A blinking bar that indicates where text that you next type will appear. **p. 76**
17. _____ A tool that enables you to find a synonym for a selected word. **p. 78**
18. _____ A feature that corrects standard misspellings and word errors as they are typed. **p. 80**
19. _____ A view that displays a document as it would appear on a webpage. **p. 91**
20. _____ A data element that is saved with a document but does not appear in the document as it is shown onscreen or is printed. **p. 103**

Multiple Choice

1. Which of the following is a reason to use the Accessibility Checker?
   (a) To ensure compatibility with earlier Word versions.
   (b) To comply with federal legislation related to disabilities.
   (c) To provide access to appropriate document properties.
   (d) To ensure that any headers and footers are visible to everyone.

2. The Document Inspector is useful when you want to:
   (a) troubleshoot a document, identifying and adjusting nonprinting characters.
   (b) check the document for spelling and grammatical errors.
   (c) adjust page layout.
   (d) reveal any hidden or personal data in the file so that it can be removed, if necessary.

3. To keep a first name and last name, such as Susan Barksdale, from being separated between lines of a document, where the word Susan might display on one line, with Barksdale on the next, you could:
   (a) insert a nonbreaking hyphen symbol after the word Susan.
   (b) insert a hard return after Barksdale.
   (c) insert a soft return between Susan and Barksdale.
   (d) insert a nonbreaking space symbol between Susan and Barksdale.

4. To rely on AutoSave to automatically save a document, you must first:
   (a) check the AutoSave setting in Word Options.
   (b) ensure that Word is set to make an automatic backup every few minutes.
   (c) save the document to local storage, such as a flash drive.
   (d) save the document using OneDrive, OneDrive for Business, or SharePoint Online.

5. One reason to use a header or footer is because:
   (a) the header or footer becomes a document property that can be used to search for the document later.
   (b) you only have to specify the content once, after which it displays automatically on all pages.
   (c) most writing style guides require both headers and footers.
   (d) headers and footers are required for all professional documents.

6. Suppose you find that a heading within a report is displayed at the end of a page, with remaining text in that section placed on the next page. To keep the heading with the text, you would position the insertion point before the heading and then:
   (a) press Ctrl+Enter.
   (b) click the Layout tab, click Breaks, and then select Line Numbers.
   (c) insert an automatic soft return.
   (d) press Ctrl+Page Down.

7. In which of the following situations would you consider inserting a soft return instead of a hard return?
   (a) At the end of a single line of an address, with more address lines to follow.
   (b) At the end of a paragraph.
   (c) At the end of a page.
   (d) After words that you prefer not to divide, such as a month name and the date.

8. One reason to display nonprinting characters is to:
   (a) simplify the process of converting a document to an earlier Word version.
   (b) enable document properties to be added to a document.
   (c) assist with troubleshooting a document and modifying its appearance.
   (d) enable spell checking on the document.

9. You want to include all text from another document, which is not currently open, in the document in which you are working. How would you do that?
   (a) Open the document with text to use and append it to the current document.
   (b) Include the file name of the closed file as a header on the last page of the current document.
   (c) Use the Text from File option to reuse text from the closed document at the current location in the open document.
   (d) Create a custom document property listing the file name of the document from which you want to include text and then insert it as an object.

10. To identify a document as a draft, and not in final form, which of the following would you mostly likely add to the document?
    (a) Symbol
    (b) Watermark
    (c) Template
    (d) Document property

Practice Exercises

1 River City Media

Having recently graduated from college with a marketing degree, you are employed by River City Media as a marketing specialist. River City Media provides promotional material in a variety of ways, including print, Web communications, photography, and news releases. It is your job to promote River City Media so that it attracts a large number of new and recurring contacts seeking support with the marketing of products and services. One of your first tasks is updating printed material that describes the specific services that River City Media offers to prospective clients. You modify a brief description of services, first converting the document from an earlier version of Word, in which it was originally saved, to the most current. Refer to Figure 1.44 as you complete this exercise.

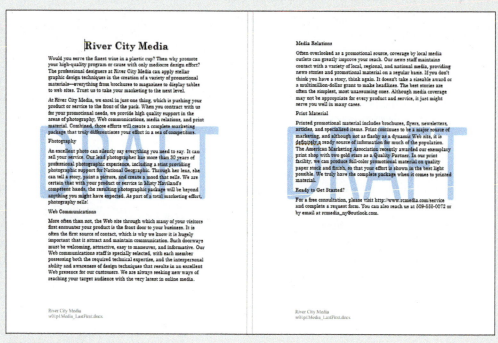

FIGURE 1.44 River City Media Draft

a. Open the *w01p1Media* document. The words *Compatibility Mode* in the title bar inform you the document was created in an earlier version of Word.

b. Click the **File tab**, and click **Save As**. Change the file name to **w01p1Media_LastFirst**. Click in the **Save as type box** and select **Word Document**. Click **Save**. If you are presented with a dialog box letting you know the document will be upgraded to the newest file format, click **OK**.

c. Ensure that nonprinting characters are displayed by clicking **Show/Hide** in the Paragraph group on the Home tab. Press **Ctrl+Home** to ensure that the insertion point is at the beginning of the document. Check the document for errors:

- Click the **Review tab** and check for spelling errors. Correct any identified errors.
- Check for grammatical errors. Correct any identified errors, but ignore any that are flagged for clarity and conciseness.
- Read the document again, checking for errors the spelling check might have missed.

d. Double-click to select the word **maneuver** in the paragraph under the *Web Communications* heading. Click the **References tab** and click **Smart Lookup** in the Research group. Scroll through the Smart Lookup pane to view information related to the selected word. Close the Smart Lookup pane.

e. Double-click **capable** in the paragraph under the *Photography* heading. Click the **Review tab** and click **Thesaurus** in the Proofing group. Locate and insert the word **competent**. Close the Thesaurus pane.

f. Make the following edits in the document:
   - Select the words **When they are** from the second body paragraph on the first page and press **Delete**.
   - Capitalize the word *Combined* in the same sentence.
   - Rearrange the words *We at River City Media* in the same paragraph, so they read **At River City Media, we** (including a comma after the word *Media*).

g. Click after the word **materials** in the first body paragraph on the first page. Delete the following hyphen. Click the **Insert tab** and click **Symbol** in the Symbols group. Click **More Symbols**. Click the **Special Characters tab**. Ensure that Em Dash is selected. Click **Insert** and click **Close**. Click after the word **National** in the paragraph under the *Photography* heading and delete the following space. Press **Ctrl+Shift+Space** to insert a nonbreaking space, ensuring that the magazine title will not be divided between lines. Similarly, insert a nonbreaking space between *Misty* and *Haviland* so the photographer's name will not be divided between lines.

h. Click the **Design tab** and click **Watermark** in the Page Background group. Scroll through the watermarks and click **Draft 2**. Click **Watermark**, click **Custom Watermark**, and then click the **Semitransparent check box** to deselect it. Click **Color**, select **Blue Accent 5** (first row, ninth column under Theme Colors), and then click **OK**.

> **MAC TROUBLESHOOTING:** Select the Text option for a watermark. Ensure Draft displays as the watermark text and transparency is set to 0%.

i. Set up a footer:
   - Click the **Insert tab** and click **Footer** in the Header & Footer group.
   - Click **Edit Footer**. Type **River City Media** and press **Enter**.
   - Click **Document Info** on the Header & Footer Tools Design tab and select **File Name**.
   - Click **Close Header and Footer** (or double-click in the body of the document).

j. Adjust the left and right margins:
   - Click the **Layout tab** and click **Margins** in the Page Setup Group.
   - Click **Custom Margins**.
   - Change the left and right margins to **1.5"**. Click **OK**.
   - Click the **View tab** and click **Multiple Pages** in the Zoom group to see how the text is lining up on the pages.

k. Click before the *Media Relations* heading at the bottom of the first page and press **Ctrl+Enter** to insert a page break.

l. Press **Ctrl+Home**. Click **Read Mode** in the Views group. Click the arrow on the right to move from one page to the next. Press **Esc** to return to the previous document view. Click **100%** in the Zoom group. Save the document.

m. Click the **File tab** and click **Info**. Click **Check for Issues**. Click **Inspect Document** and click **Inspect**. Click **Remove All** beside Document Properties and Personal Information and click **Close**.

n. Save and close the file. Based on your instructor's directions, submit w01p1Media_LastFirst.

2 Freshwater Research

You work with the Office of Media Relations at Tarrant State University. Several faculty researchers have been involved with a study on freshwater analysis, with their findings receiving national recognition. The university plans to post a news release describing the successful research. You will work with a draft of the press release, ensuring that it is properly formatted and readable by all. Refer to Figure 1.45 as you complete this exercise.

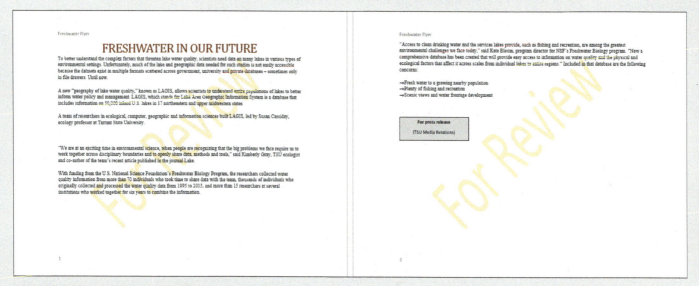

FIGURE 1.45 Freshwater Analysis Document

a. Open *w01p2Lake* and save it as **w01p2Lake_LastFirst**.

b. Press **Ctrl+End** to move the insertion point to the end of the document. Press **Enter**. Click the **Insert tab** and click the **Object arrow** in the Text group. Click **Text from File**. Locate and double-click *w01p2Article*.

c. Click the **Home tab** and click **Show/Hide** to display nonprinting characters. Select the year **1990** in the fifth body paragraph. Change the year to **1995**.

d. Click the **Layout tab**, click **Orientation** in the Page Setup group, and then click **Landscape**. Click the **View tab** and click **Multiple Pages** to view all document pages, noting the poorly situated second page. Return the view to **100%**.

e. Adjust the margins:
   - Click the **Layout tab**. Click **Margins** in the Page Setup group.
   - Click **Custom Margins**.
   - Change the left and right margins to **1.5"**. Click **OK**.

f. Place the insertion point after the word *population* on the second page. Press **Shift+Enter** to insert a soft return. Type **Plenty of fishing and recreation**. (Do not type the period.) Press **Shift+Enter**. Type **Scenic views and water frontage development**. (Do not type the period.)

g. Insert symbols:
   - Place the insertion point before *Fresh water to a growing nearby population*.
   - Click the **Insert tab** and click **Symbol** in the Symbols group.
   - Click **More Symbols**.
   - Change the font in the dialog box to **Symbol**. Locate the **right arrow symbol**, or click in the Character Code box and type **174**.
   - Click **Insert**. Click **Close**.
   - Repeat the process for the remaining two lines of text. Note that you can now select the right arrow symbol from the list of recent symbols shown when you click **Symbol** in the Symbols group.

h. Click before the quotation mark that begins the last body paragraph on the first page (beginning with *Access to clean drinking water*). Click the **Layout tab** and click **Breaks** in the Page Setup group. Click **Page**. Click the **View tab** and click **Multiple Pages** to see how text appears on all pages. Return the view to **100%**.

i. Insert a footer:
- Click the **Insert tab** and click **Footer** in the Header & Footer group.
- Click **Edit Footer**.
- Click **Page Number** in the Header & Footer group, point to **Current Position**, and then click **Plain Number**.
- Double-click in the current page of the document to close the footer.

j. Click the **File tab** and click **Info**. Click **Properties** and click **Advanced Properties**. Click in the **Comments box** and type **Freshwater Flyer**. Click **OK**. Click **Back** to return to the document.

k. Double-click in the **Header area** (top margin). Click **Document Info** in the Insert group, point to **Document Property**, and then click **Comments**. Close the header.

l. Press **Ctrl+Home**. Click the **Review tab** and check spelling. Correct any identified errors, if they are actual errors. There are no misspelled names. Click **OK** when the spelling check is complete. Close the Editor pane.

m. Insert a watermark:
- Click the **Design tab** and click **Watermark** in the Page Background group.
- Click **Custom Watermark**.
- Click to select **Text watermark**. Type **For Review** in the Text box, replacing any existing text.
- Click **Color** and click **Orange** (third selection in Standard Colors).
- Click **OK**.

> **MAC TROUBLESHOOTING:** Select the Text option for a watermark. To slant the watermark, change the orientation to Diagonal.

n. Click the **Review tab**. Click **Check Accessibility** in the Accessibility group. Click **Image or object not inline. (1)** in the Accessibility Checker pane. Point to the Text Box problem shown in the Accessibility Checker pane and click the arrow. Click **Place this inline**. Alternatively, you can follow the directions shown at the bottom of the Accessibility Checker pane. Close the Accessibility Checker pane.

o. Save and close the file. Based on your instructor's directions, submit w01p2Lake_LastFirst.

Mid-Level Exercises

1 Water for Life — MyLab IT Grader

The student organization of which you are a member has selected the supply of clean drinking water to developing nations as a fundraising cause for the current semester. You will design an informational handout that will introduce the current situation and encourage others to become involved with the effort. You begin with a draft and format the document so that it is attractive and informative.

a. Open *w01m1Water* and save it as **w01m1Water_LastFirst**.

b. Change the orientation to **Portrait**. Display nonprinting characters if they are not already shown. Delete the first two lines (*Water for Life* and *Changing Lives Daily*).

c. Change the margin setting to **Moderate**. Preview the document in **Multiple Pages**. Return the view to **100%**.

d. Place the insertion point at the beginning of the document and insert a page break. Place the insertion point at the beginning of the new page. Insert text from *w01m1Cover*. Preview the new page as **One Page**.

e. Return the view to 100%. Insert an unformatted footer containing a page number. The page number should be in the **Current Position** and as a **Plain Number**. Ensure that the footer does not show on the first page. Close the footer.

f. Click after the word *that* in the first line of the second page. Press **Spacebar** and type **adversely**. Ensure that a space precedes and follows the word. Select the words *As long as* in the second paragraph on the second page. Replace the selected words with the word **When**.

g. Select the word **reliable** in the third paragraph on the second page. Use the thesaurus and identify a synonym beginning with the letter *d*. Replace the selected word with the synonym. Close the Thesaurus pane.

h. Modify the watermark so that it displays **DRAFT** in a diagonal fashion. Ensure that the watermark is colored **Red** (second color in Standard Colors).

i. Open Document Properties and add **Flyer for Water for Life** in the Comments section.

j. Insert an unformatted header. Click **Quick Parts** in the Insert group on the Header & Footer Tools Design tab and insert the Comments document property. The header should be left aligned.

k. Check spelling and correct any errors that are found.

l. Run the Accessibility Checker. Correct any problems identified.

m. Save and close the file. Based on your instructor's directions, submit w01m1Water_LastFirst.

2 Backyard Bonanza — MyLab IT Grader

With a degree in horticulture, you have recently been employed to work with Backyard Bonanza, a local outdoor living business specializing in garden gifts, statuary, outdoor fireplaces, landscaping materials, and pavers. The first Friday of each month, Backyard Bonanza participates in a downtown event in which vendors, artists, and musicians set up areas to perform or display products. To encourage those passing by to visit the store, you prepare a document describing a few do-it-yourself backyard projects—all of which can be completed with the help of products sold at Backyard Bonanza. The document is well underway, but you modify it slightly, making sure it is attractive and ready for distribution at the next event.

a. Open *w01m2Backyard*. The document was originally saved in an earlier version of Word, so you should save it as a Word Document with the file name of **w01m2Backyard_LastFirst**. Agree that the upgrade should proceed, if asked.

b. Display nonprinting characters. Preview the document in Multiple Pages to get a feel for the text flow. Change the orientation to **Portrait**.

c. Return to 100% view. Add a page number footer. The page number should be placed at the **Bottom of Page** with the **Plain Number 2** selection. Close the footer.

d. Insert text from *w01m2Fish* at the end of the document.

e. Scroll to the top of page 2. Change the word *Create* to **Build**.
f. Check the document for spelling and grammatical errors. The word *Delite* is not misspelled as it is a brand name. Because there is no correct suggestion for the misuse of the word *layer*, you will need to manually change it. (Hint: You can ignore the error and return to manually correct the mistake, or you can correct the mistake during the spell check and resume the check afterward.) Proofread the document to identify and correct errors that Word might have missed.
g. Preview the document and note the small amount of text on page 3. Change margins to **Narrow**.
h. Insert a page break so that *Build a Backyard Fish Pond* begins on a new page.
i. View the document in Read Mode. Return to Print Layout view.
j. Click after the word *noticed* on page 2 and before the comma in the third sentence of the first body paragraph of directions. Remove the comma and the following space, and insert an **Em Dash**. On page 1, click after the words *Paving Delite*, but before the closing parenthesis (in the first paragraph of directions under *What to do:*). Insert a trademark symbol.
k. Add a watermark with the text **Backyard Bonanza** shown in **Red**. The watermark should be horizontal and semitransparent. Save the document before completing the next step.
l. Run the Document Inspector to identify any information that should be removed before the document is distributed. Remove all document properties and personal information.
m. Save and close the file. Based on your instructor's directions, submit w01m2Backyard_LastFirst.

Running Case

New Castle County Technical Services

New Castle County Technical Services (NCCTS) provides technical services to clients in the greater New Castle County, Delaware area. Founded in 2011, the company is rapidly expanding to include technical security systems, network infrastructure cabling, and basic troubleshooting services. With that growth comes the need to promote the company and to provide clear written communication to employees and clients. Microsoft Word is used exclusively in the development and distribution of documents, including an "About New Castle" summary that will be available both in print and online. You will begin development of the document in this case and continue working with it in subsequent Word chapters.

a. Open *w01r1NewCastle* and save it as **w01r1NewCastle_LastFirst**. Display nonprinting characters. Place the insertion point at the end of the document and insert a page break.
b. Ensure that the insertion point is at the top of the second page. Insert text from *w01r1News*. Preview the document in Multiple Pages. Return to 100% view. Add a left-aligned unformatted footer with the words **New Castle County Technical Services**. On the same line in the footer, but right-aligned, insert a File Name field. Ensure that the footer does not display on the first page. Close the footer.
c. Replace the hyphen after the word *off* in the first sentence of the second body paragraph in the Company Background section with a nonbreaking hyphen. Replace the hyphen after the word *the* in the phrase *off-the-shelf* with a nonbreaking hyphen.
d. Select the words *set up* in the first paragraph on the third page. Change the selected words to **equipped**, ensuring that a space precedes and follows the newly inserted word.
e. Place the insertion point at the end of the first body paragraph on page 1, after the period following the word *offer*. Press **Spacebar** and type **We are proud to include the following new services, added to our inventory this past March.** (Include the period.) Press **Enter**. Type **Desktop troubleshooting**. (Do not type the period.) Insert a soft return. Type **Software training support**. (Do not type the period.)

f. Place the insertion point before the word *We* at the beginning of the first body paragraph on the fourth page (under the *A FEW OF OUR CUSTOMERS* heading). Type **At New Castle County Technical Services,** and press **Spacebar**. Ensure that a comma follows **New Castle County Technical Services**. Change the following word **We** to lowercase, as in *we*.

g. Include a watermark using the *DRAFT 1* selection. Color the watermark **Blue** (eighth color from the left in Standard Colors).

h. Change the page orientation to **Landscape**. Preview the document in Multiple Pages. Note that the first two pages of the document are poorly situated in that orientation, but remaining pages are attractive. You will correct the view of the first pages in a future exercise. Return the view to 100%

i. Check the document for spelling and grammatical errors. Ignore all possible misspellings of company names, but correct any other spelling errors. If grammatical errors are shown, correct them as well. If Clarity and Conciseness concerns are shown, check but ignore any occurrence.

j. Run the Accessibility Checker. Note the comments related to the picture in the first paragraph of the Company Background section. You may also see a warning flagging hard-to-read text contrast, although you will not address that issue at this time. You could correct the issues, but because the picture is not necessary, click the picture of the keyboard and press **Delete** to remove it. Close the Accessibility Checker pane.

k. Open Document Properties, selecting **Advanced Properties** to display the dialog box. Add a Company name of **New Castle County Technical Services**. (Do not type the period.)

l. Save and close the file. Based on your instructor's directions, submit w01r1NewCastle_LastFirst.

Disaster Recovery

Logo Policy

Open *w01d1Policy* and save it as **w01d1Policy_LastFirst**. The document was started by an office assistant, but was not finished. You must complete the document, ensuring that it is error free and attractive. The current header includes a page number at the top right. Remove the page number from the header and create a footer with a centered page number instead. Adjust the font size of any headings throughout the document to ensure consistency and suggest hierarchy. Remove the word *copyright* anywhere it appears in the document and replace it with the copyright symbol. Show nonprinting characters and remove any unnecessary or improperly placed paragraph marks. The AMT Brand section should include only three bulleted items (One name, One voice, and One look). Use solid round black bullets. Insert hard returns where necessary to better space paragraphs. The hyphenated word *non-Association*, in the Improper Use paragraph, should not be divided between lines, so replace the hyphen wherever it occurs in that paragraph with a nonbreaking hyphen. Change the orientation to Landscape. Modify the document properties to include yourself as the author, deleting any other author. Check spelling and grammar, correcting any mistakes. Ensure that all pages begin and end attractively, with no headings standing alone at the end of a page. Insert a page break where necessary. Check spelling and grammar, correcting any mistakes, but ignoring any clarity and conciseness flags. Finally, use a watermark to indicate that the document is not in final form. Save and close the document. Based on your instructor's directions, submit w01d1Policy_LastFirst.

Capstone Exercise

MyLab IT Grader

Space Camp

You are serving as a summer intern at the Space Center. One of the most popular programs offered at the Center is the Space Camp Experience, which is a collection of exploratory programs designed for various age groups. You are using Word to prepare a two-page flyer to promote the camps. In the process, you will apply various formatting and readability features, and will ensure an error-free and informative document.

Inserting Text, Editing a Document, and Changing Margins

Inserting text from another document can save time in creating a document, so you insert text to begin the Space Camp flyer. You also edit the document to ensure attractive arrangement of text. By adjusting margins, you improve readability.

1. Open *w01c1Space* and save it as **w01c1Space_LastFirst**.
2. Display nonprinting characters. In the blank paragraph above *Adult Space Academy* on the second page, insert text from *w01c1Family*.
3. Remove the two blank paragraphs after the Family Space Camp section.
4. Preview the document in **Multiple Pages**. Note the poor placement of the text box on the second page. Remove the five blank paragraphs before the text box so that it moves up the page to better position.
5. Change margins to **Narrow**. Insert a page break before the Family Space Camp heading at the bottom of the first page. Return to 100% view.

Changing Document View, Previewing a Document, Inserting Symbols, and Inserting a Footer

The document contains several sections that are identified by headers. In Outline view, you are able to rearrange sections for better document flow. Because the document contains multiple pages, previewing it in another way facilitates understanding of document layout across pages. A page number footer identifies each page and a symbol is used to ensure that words are not awkwardly divided.

6. Change the view to **Outline**. Click the arrow beside Show Level in the Outline Tools group and click Level 1 to show only major headings. Click + beside *Space Camp* and drag the heading to position it above *Space Academy*. Click **Close Outline View** in the Close group.

7. Preview the document in **Multiple Pages**. Remove the page break on the first page along with the blank paragraph that precedes the Space Academy heading. Insert a page break before the Family Space Camp heading. Return the view to **100%**.
8. Replace the hyphen following the Word *three* in the paragraph below The Adult Space Academy heading with a nonbreaking hyphen.
9. Insert a left-aligned footer with the **File Name** inserted as a field. On the same line, insert a right-aligned footer showing a **Plain Number** page number.

Including a Watermark, Checking Spelling and Grammar, Working with Document Properties, and Checking Accessibility

A watermark is included, identifying the document as a copy. All documents should be checked for spelling and grammatical errors before distribution, so you identify and correct any errors. Document properties are modified so that the document is identified by subject, and text is checked for accessibility by those with disabilities.

10. Insert a horizontal blue watermark with the word **Copy**.
11. Open Document Properties and add **Space Camp Flyer** as the Subject.
12. Check the document for spelling and grammatical errors. Correct any errors, but ignore any clarity and conciseness flags. Use the thesaurus to identify a synonym for the word *exciting* in the first paragraph under the Adult Space Academy heading. The synonym you select should begin with the letter *t*. Change the word *an* that precedes the newly inserted synonym to *a* so that it is grammatically correct.
13. Check for accessibility and correct the error related to alignment of a text box. Disregard other flags at this time.
14. Save and close the document. Based on your instructor's directions, submit w01c1Space_LastFirst.

Word
Document Presentation

LEARNING OUTCOME You will modify a Word document with formatting, styles, and objects.

OBJECTIVES & SKILLS: After you read this chapter, you will be able to:

Text and Paragraph Formatting

OBJECTIVE 1: APPLY FONT ATTRIBUTES 130
Select Font Options, Change Text Appearance

OBJECTIVE 2: FORMAT A PARAGRAPH 134
Select Paragraph Alignment, Select Line and Paragraph Spacing, Select Indents, Set Tab Stops, Apply Borders and Shading, Create Bulleted and Numbered Lists

HANDS-ON EXERCISE 1 144

Document Appearance

OBJECTIVE 3: FORMAT A DOCUMENT 149
Select a Document Theme, Work with Sections, Format Text into Columns

OBJECTIVE 4: APPLY STYLES 152
Select and Modify Styles, Use a Style Set, Create a New Style from Text, Use Outline View

HANDS-ON EXERCISE 2 158

Objects

OBJECTIVE 5: INSERT AND FORMAT OBJECTS 164
Insert a Picture; Move, Align, and Resize a Picture; Modify a Picture; Insert a Text Box; Move, Resize, and Modify a Text Box; Insert WordArt

HANDS-ON EXERCISE 3 174

CASE STUDY | Phillips Studio L Photography

Having recently opened your own photography studio, you are engaged in marketing the business. Not only do you hope to attract customers from the local community who want photos of special events, but you will also offer classes in basic photography for interested amateur photographers. In addition, you have designed a website to promote the business and to provide details on upcoming events and classes. The business is not large enough yet to employ an office staff, so much of the work of developing promotional material falls on you.

Among other projects, you are currently developing material to include in a quarterly mailing to people who have expressed an interest in upcoming studio events. You have prepared a rough draft of a newsletter describing photography basics—a document that must be formatted and properly organized before it is distributed to people on your mailing list. You will modify the document to ensure attractive line and paragraph spacing, and you will format text to draw attention to pertinent points. Formatted in columns, the document will be easy to read. The newsletter is somewhat informal, and you will make appropriate use of colors, borders, and pictures so that it is well received by your audience.

CHAPTER 2

Editing and Formatting

FIGURE 2.1 Phillips Studio L Photography Document

CASE STUDY | Phillips Studio L Photography

Starting Files	File to be Submitted
w02h1Studio w02h3Kayak.jpg w02h3Float.jpg	w02h3Studio_LastFirst

MyLab IT Grader An alternate version of this project is available as a MyLab IT Grader Assessment

Text and Paragraph Formatting

When you format text, you change the way it looks. Your goal in designing a document is to ensure that it is well received and understood by an audience of readers. Seldom will your first attempt at designing a document be the only time you work with it. Inevitably, you will identify text that should be reworded or emphasized differently, paragraphs that might be more attractive in another alignment, or the need to bold, underline, or use italics to call attention to selected text. As you develop a document, or after reopening a previously completed document, you can make all these modifications and more. That process is called ***formatting***.

In this section, you will learn to change font and font size, and format text with character attributes, such as bold, underline, and italics. At the paragraph level, you will adjust paragraph and line spacing, set tab stops, change alignment, and apply bullets and numbering.

Applying Font Attributes

A ***font*** is a combination of typeface and type style. The font you select should reinforce the message of the text without calling attention to itself, and it should be consistent with the information you want to convey. For example, a paper prepared for a professional purpose, such as a resume, should have a standard font, such as Times New Roman, instead of one that looks casual or frilly, such as *Freestyle Script* or *Gigi*. Additionally, more than one font might need to be used to distinguish the purpose of the text, such as paragraph headings, body text, captions, etc., but you will want to minimize the variety of fonts in a document to maintain a professional look. Typically, you should use three or fewer fonts within a document. Word provides default font styles for each of these purposes: Calibri Light is used for headings and Calibri for the body of the text. However, Word enables you to format text in a variety of ways. Not only can you change a font type, but you can also change the font size and apply text attributes, such as bold, italic, or underline, to selected text or to text that you are about to type. Several of the most commonly used text formatting commands are in the Font group on the Home tab.

STEP 1 Select Font Options

A definitive characteristic of any font is the presence or absence of serifs, thin lines that begin and end the main strokes of each letter. A ***serif font*** contains a thin line or extension at the top and bottom of the primary strokes on characters. Times New Roman is an example of a serif font. A ***sans serif font*** (*sans* from the French word meaning *without*) does not contain the thin lines on characters. Calibri is a sans serif font.

Serifs help the eye connect one letter with the next and generally are used with large amounts of text. The paragraphs in this book, for example, are set in a serif font. Body text of newspapers and magazines is usually formatted in a serif font, as well. A sans serif font, such as Calibri, Arial, or Verdana, is more effective with smaller amounts of text such as titles, headlines, corporate logos, and webpages. For example, the heading *Select Font Options*, at the beginning of this section, is set in a sans serif font. Web developers often prefer a sans serif font because the extra strokes that begin and end letters in a serif font can blur or fade into a webpage, making it difficult to read. Examples of serif and sans serif fonts are shown in Figure 2.2.

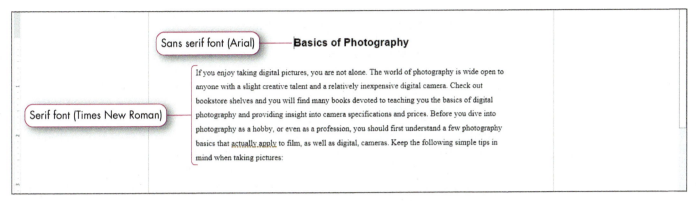

FIGURE 2.2 Serif and Sans Serif Fonts

When you begin a new, blank document, if you do not like the default font for the headings and body text of the document, you can change the fonts for the current document to something that you like. To change the font for selected text, a heading, or for a document you are beginning, click the Font arrow and select a font from those displayed (see Figure 2.3). Each font shown is a sample of the actual font. With text selected, you can point to any font in the list, without clicking, to see a preview of the way the selected text will look in that font. **Live Preview** enables you to select text and see the effects without finalizing the selection.

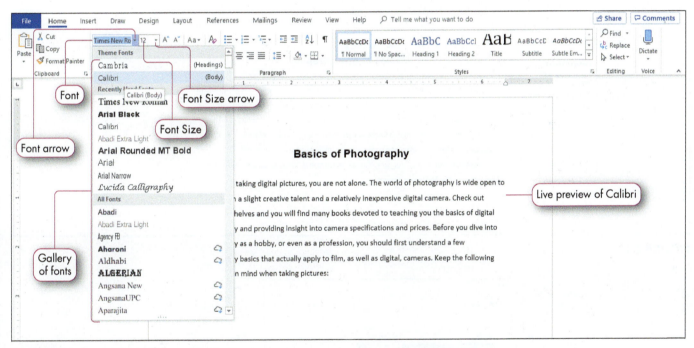

FIGURE 2.3 Select a Font and Font Size

You can also change font size when you click the Font Size arrow (refer to Figure 2.3) and select a point size. Each point size is equivalent to 1/72 of an inch; therefore, the larger the point size, the larger the font. A document often contains various sizes of the same font. For example, a document that includes levels of headings and subheadings might have major headings formatted in a larger point size than lesser headings. The default font size for the body text in a Word document is 11 pt while the default font size for Heading 1 is 16 pt.

> **TIP: FONT FOR BUSINESS DOCUMENTS**
> Most business documents are best formatted in 11- or 12-point serif font. A good font choice is Times New Roman. A document designed for display on the Web is attractive in a blocky sans serif font, such as Arial, regardless of point size.

Change Text Appearance

Commonly accessed commands related to font settings are on the Home tab in the Font group (see Figure 2.4). There are features that enable you to bold, underline, and italicize text; apply text highlighting; change font color; and work with various text effects and other formatting options from commands in the Font group. For even more choices, click the Font Dialog Box Launcher in the Font group and select from additional formatting commands available in the Font dialog box (see Figure 2.5). With text selected, you will see the Mini Toolbar when you move the pointer near the selection, making it more convenient to quickly select a format (instead of locating it on the ribbon or using a keyboard shortcut). Toggle the same command to turn off the formatting effect.

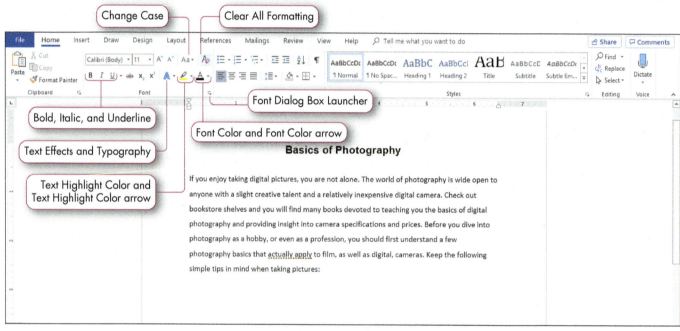

FIGURE 2.4 Font Commands

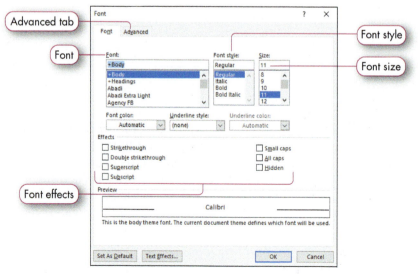

FIGURE 2.5 Font Dialog Box

CHAPTER 2 • Document Presentation

Word includes a variety of text effects that enable you to add a shadow, outline, reflection, or glow to text. The Text Effects and Typography gallery (see Figure 2.6) provides access to those effects as well as to WordArt styles, number styles, ligatures, and stylistic sets that you can apply to text.

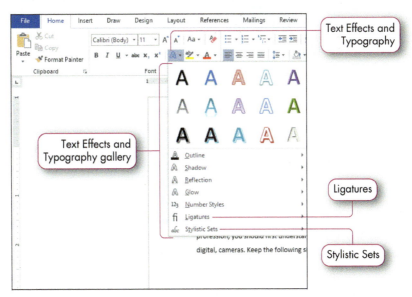

FIGURE 2.6 Text Effects and Typography Gallery

A ligature is two letters that are crafted together into a single character, or glyph. For example, you often see the letters *f* and *i* bound together in a ligature. A stylistic set is a collection of letter styles that you can apply to OpenType fonts. Some fonts include more stylistic sets than others. Stylistic sets and ligatures are often used in the preparation of formal documents such as wedding invitations.

> **TIP: ADVANCED FONT SETTINGS**
> If you intend to use a ligature and/or stylistic set, you may select it via the Advanced tab in the Font dialog box (refer to Figure 2.5). However, the ligatures and stylistic sets are also readily available in the Text Effects and Typography gallery as shown in Figure 2.6.

As a student, you are likely to highlight important parts of textbooks, magazine articles, and other documents. You probably use a highlighting marker to shade the parts of text that you want to remember or to which you want to draw attention. Word provides an equivalent tool with which you can highlight text you want to stand out or to locate easily—the Text Highlight Color command, located in the Font group on the Home tab (refer to Figure 2.4). This highlighting tool can be toggled on to highlight multiple parts of a document, or you can select specific text and apply the highlighter. To highlight text after selecting it, select Text Highlight Color or click the Text Highlight Color arrow and choose another color. You can remove highlights in the same manner, except that you will select No Color.

When creating a document, you must consider when and how to apply capitalization. Titles and headings typically capitalize each key word, but some headings may occasionally be in all capital letters, and sentences begin with a capital letter. Use the Change Case option in the Font group on the Home tab to quickly change the capitalization of selected document text (refer to Figure 2.4).

By default, text color is black. For a bit of interest, or to draw attention to text within a document, you can change the font color of previously typed text or of text that you are about to type. Click the Font Color arrow (refer to Figure 2.4) and select from a gallery of colors. For even more choices, click More Colors and select from a variety of hues or shades. As shown in Figure 2.7, you can click the Custom tab in the Colors dialog box and select a color hue by dragging along a hue continuum.

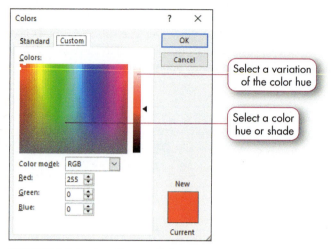

FIGURE 2.7 Apply a Custom Color

> **TIP: MATCHING FONT COLOR**
> If you have created a custom font color, it may be challenging to match that shade later on. It is easy to match a color, however, when you click the Font Color arrow and select the shade from the Recent Colors palette.

Formatting a Paragraph

Formatting selected text is only one way to alter the appearance of a document. You can also change the alignment, indentation, tab stops, or line spacing for any paragraph within the document. Recall that Word defines a paragraph as text followed by a hard return, or even a hard return on a line by itself (indicating a blank paragraph). You can include borders or shading for added emphasis around selected paragraphs, and you can number paragraphs or enhance them with bullets. The Paragraph group on the Home tab contains several paragraph formatting commands (see Figure 2.8). If you are formatting only one paragraph, you do not have to select the entire paragraph. Simply click to place the insertion point within the paragraph and apply a paragraph format. However, if you are formatting several paragraphs, you must select them before formatting.

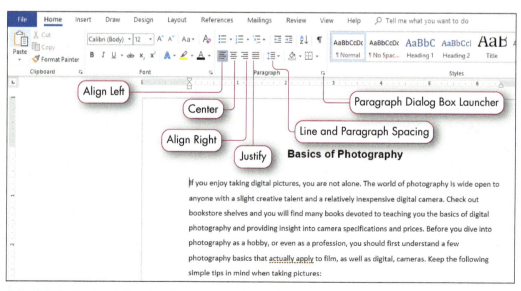

FIGURE 2.8 Paragraph Commands

STEP 2 Select Paragraph Alignment

Alignment refers to how the text is positioned relative to the margins. ***Left alignment*** is the most common alignment, often seen in letters, reports, and memos. When you begin a new blank Word document, paragraphs are left aligned by default. Text begins evenly at the left margin and ends in an uneven ("ragged") right edge. The opposite of left alignment is ***right alignment***, a setting in which text is aligned at the right margin with a ragged left edge. Short lines including dates, figure captions, and headers are often right aligned. A ***center alignment*** positions text horizontally in the center of a line, with an equal distance from both the left and right margins. Report titles and major headings are typically centered. Finally, ***justified alignment*** spreads text evenly between the left and right margins so that text begins at the left margin and ends uniformly at the right margin. Newspaper and magazine articles are often justified. For instance, the text in this book is fully justified. Such text alignment often causes awkward spacing as text is stretched to fit evenly between margins. Figure 2.9 shows examples of paragraph alignments.

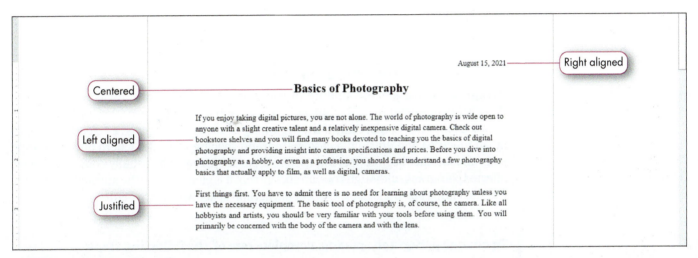

FIGURE 2.9 Paragraph Alignment

To change paragraph alignment, select text (or position the insertion point in a paragraph, if only one paragraph is to be affected) and select an alignment from the Paragraph group on the Home tab (refer to Figure 2.8). You can also change alignment by selecting from the Paragraph dialog box (see Figure 2.10), which opens when you click the Paragraph Dialog Box Launcher (refer to Figure 2.8).

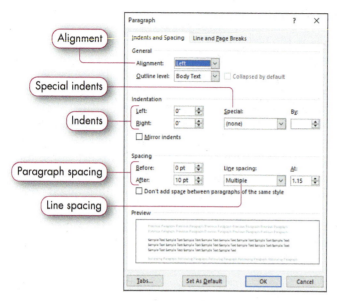

FIGURE 2.10 Paragraph Dialog Box

Select Line and Paragraph Spacing

Paragraph spacing is the amount of space between paragraphs, measured in points. (Recall that one point is 1/72 of an inch.) Paragraph spacing is a good way to differentiate between paragraphs, especially if the beginning of each paragraph is not clearly identified by an indented line. In such a case, paragraph spacing identifies where one paragraph ends and another begins. Spacing used to separate paragraphs usually comes after each affected paragraph, although you can specify that it is placed before the affected paragraph. Use the Paragraph dialog box to select paragraph spacing (refer to Figure 2.10).

> **To change paragraph spacing, complete one of the following steps:**
>
> - Click Line and Paragraph Spacing in the Paragraph group on the Home tab (see Figure 2.11). Click to Add Space Before Paragraph (or to Add Space After Paragraph).
> - Click the Paragraph Dialog Box Launcher in the Paragraph group on the Home tab. Type a number to indicate the amount of Spacing Before or After in the respective areas (refer to Figure 2.10) or click the spin arrows to adjust the spacing. Click OK.
> - Change the Before or After spacing in the Paragraph group on the Layout tab (see Figure 2.12).

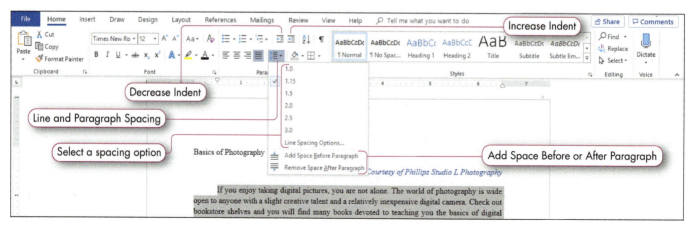

FIGURE 2.11 Spacing Options

CHAPTER 2 • Document Presentation

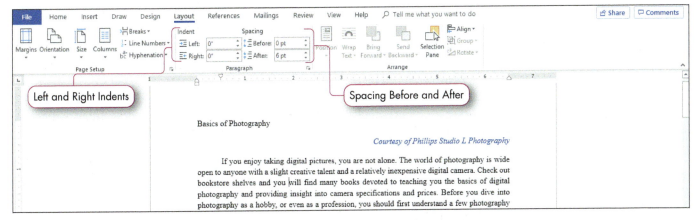

FIGURE 2.12 Paragraph Spacing and Indents

Just as paragraph spacing is the amount of space between paragraphs, *line spacing* is the amount of space between lines. Typically, line spacing is determined before beginning a document, such as when you know that a research paper should be double-spaced, so you identify that setting before typing. Of course, you can change line spacing of a current paragraph or selected text at any point as well.

You can change line spacing using either the Paragraph dialog box or the Line and Paragraph Spacing option in the Paragraph group on the Home tab. The most common line spacing options are single, double, 1.15, or 1.5 lines. Word provides those options and more. From the Paragraph dialog box (refer to Figure 2.10), you can select Exactly, At Least, or Multiple. To specify an exact point size for spacing, select Exactly. If you select At Least, you will indicate a minimum line spacing size while allowing Word to adjust the height, if necessary, to accommodate such features as drop caps (oversized letters that sometimes begin paragraphs). The Multiple setting enables you to select a line spacing interval other than single, double, 1.15, or 1.5 lines.

Select Indents

An *indent* is a setting associated with how part of a paragraph is distanced from the margin. One of the most common indents is a *first line indent*, in which the first line of each paragraph is set off from the left margin. For instance, your English instructor might require that the first line of each paragraph in a writing assignment is indented 0.5" from the left margin, which is a typical first line indent. If you have ever prepared a bibliography for a research paper, you have most likely specified a *hanging indent*, where the first line of a source begins at the left margin, but all other lines in the source are indented. Indenting an entire paragraph from the left margin is a *left indent*, while indenting an entire paragraph from the right margin is a *right indent*. A lengthy quote is often set apart by indenting from both the left and right margins.

Using the Paragraph dialog box (refer to Figure 2.10), you can select an indent setting for one or more paragraphs. First line and hanging indents are considered special indents.

You can select left and right indents from either the Paragraph dialog box or from the Paragraph group on the Layout tab (refer to Figure 2.12).

You can use the Word ruler to set indents. If the ruler does not display above the document space, you can control the ruler display by toggling it on or off on the View tab (see Figure 2.13). The **three-part indent marker** located at the left side of the ruler enables you to set a left indent, a hanging indent, or a first line indent (see Figure 2.14). The marker is comprised of two triangles and a rectangle; the upper triangle is the first line indent marker; the lower triangle is the hanging indent marker. The rectangle below the lower triangle indicates the location of the current left margin. You can exert more complete control of these indents through the Paragraph dialog box. Another way is to drag the indent along the ruler to apply the indent to the current paragraph (or selected paragraphs). Figure 2.13 shows the first line indent moved to the 0.5" mark, resulting in the first line of a paragraph being indented by 0.5".

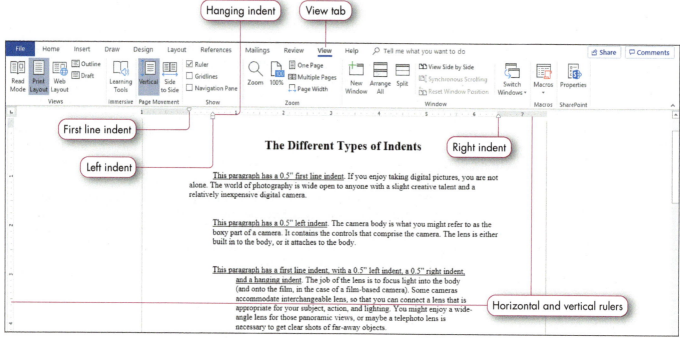

FIGURE 2.13 Set Indents on the Ruler

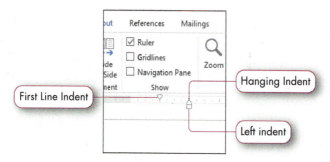

FIGURE 2.14 Three-part Indent Marker on the Ruler

> **TIP: MANAGE A LEFT INDENT AND A HANGING INDENT**
> There might be an occasion where you need to use both a left indent and a hanging indent in your document. When formatting such a paragraph, the text will be indented to the left and then the hanging indent will be applied to the paragraph.

STEP 3 Set Tab Stops

Each time you press Tab, the insertion point moves to the right by 0.5". Typically, you would set a first line indent or press Tab to indent the first line of each new paragraph within a document. When creating a professional document, you can draw attention to certain information by setting the content apart from the body text. There are times when moving the insertion point by different intervals or positions and alignments helps to increase the readability of the document. Tabs enable you to add organization to a document, arranging text in easy-to-read columns. A table of contents and indexes are examples of tabbed text, as is a restaurant menu. In those instances, setting tab stops that overwrite the default tabs is useful. A ***tab stop*** is a marker on the horizontal ruler specifying the location where the insertion point stops after the tab key is pressed to align text in a document. By using tab stops, you can easily arrange text in columns or position text a certain distance from the left or right margins. The most common tab stops are left, right, center, and decimal. By default, a left tab is set every 0.5" when you start a new document.

Table 2.1 describes the types of tabs that are available in the ***tab selector***, which is the small box at the leftmost edge of the horizontal ruler. The tab selector (see Figure 2.15) enables you to repeatedly cycle through tabs, including left, center, right, decimal, bar, first line indent, and hanging indent. Using the tab selector, you can select and apply any of these indents to your document.

TABLE 2.1 Tab Markers

Tab Icon on Ruler	Type of Tab	Function
	Left	Sets the start position on the left, so as you type text moves to the right of the tab setting.
	Center	Sets the middle point of the text you type. Whatever you type will be centered on that tab setting.
	Right	Sets the start position on the right, so as you type text moves to the left of that tab setting and aligns on the right.
	Decimal	Aligns numbers on a decimal point. Regardless of how long the number, each number lines up with the decimal point in the same position.
	Bar	This tab does not position text or decimals but inserts a vertical bar at the tab setting. This bar is useful as a separator for text printed on the same line.
	Hanging	Sets the first line of a paragraph to begin at the left margin, but all other lines in the paragraph are indented.
	First Line	Sets the start position on the left for the first line of each paragraph, so as you type text moves to the right of the tab setting

Tab stops that you set override default tabs. For example, if a 1" left tab is set, when Tab is pressed the insertion point would move directly to a position that is 1" from the left margin without stopping at the 0.5" mark. Tab stops can be inserted and applied in two ways. Tab stops are applied to text you have selected. If you do not select text, the tab stops will apply to the current paragraph and any new paragraphs you type.

To set a tab, click the tab selector on the left of the horizontal ruler until the tab stop option you want displays and click the location of the tab stop on the horizontal ruler. To reposition a tab stop, drag it along the horizontal ruler, or you can drag a tab stop off the ruler to remove it.

A more precise way to set tab stops or to include tab leaders is to use the Tabs dialog box. **Leaders** are the series of dots or hyphens that leads the reader's eye across the page to connect two columns of information, as shown in Figure 2.15. Options for leaders include dots, dashes, and underlines and they are associated with the tab stop to the left. The row of dots that typically connects a food item with its price on a restaurant menu is an example of a leader.

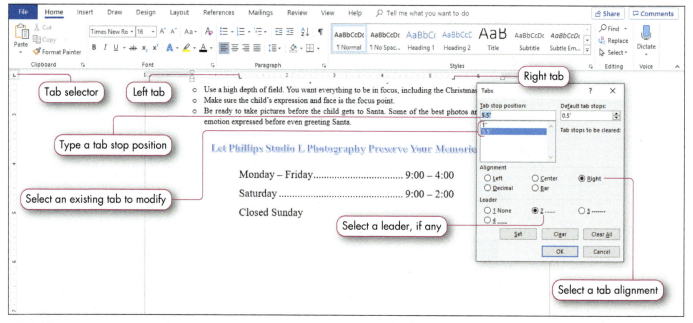

FIGURE 2.15 Set Tab Stops

To set a tab with a leader, complete the following steps:

1. Click the Paragraph Dialog Box Launcher in the Paragraph group on the Home tab and click Tabs in the Paragraph dialog box to open the Tabs dialog box. Alternatively, if a tab has already been set, double-click the tab indicator on the ruler to open the Tabs dialog box.
2. Type in the Tab stop position box the location where you want to set the tab. The number you type is assumed to be in inches, so typing *2* would place a tab at 2".
3. Select a tab alignment (Left, Right, etc.).
4. Specify a leader.
5. Click OK (or click Set and continue specifying tabs).

On a Mac, to set a tab with a leader, complete the following steps:

1. Click the Format menu and click Tabs. Alternatively, if a tab has already been set, double-click the tab indicator on the ruler to open the Tabs dialog box.
2. Follow steps 2-5 above.

> **TIP: DELETING TAB STOPS**
> To manually delete a tab stop you have set, select the text that the tab stop applies to and drag the tab stop off the ruler. An alternative is to click the Paragraph Dialog Box Launcher, click Tabs, select the tab (in the Tab stop position box), and then click Clear. Click OK.

Apply Borders and Shading

You can draw attention to a document or an area of a document by using the Borders and Shading command. A **border** consists of lines that display at the top, bottom, left, or right of a paragraph, a page, a table, or an image, similar to how a picture frame surrounds a photograph or piece of art. **Shading** is a background color behind text in a paragraph, a page, or a table. Shading has more color selections than the Highlight command; it can add a graphical perspective and draw attention to the selected text. Figure 2.16 illustrates the use of borders and shading.

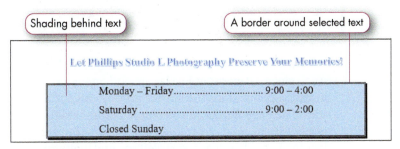

FIGURE 2.16 Borders and Shading

Borders are used throughout this text to surround Tip boxes and Troubleshooting areas. You might surround a particular paragraph with a border, possibly even shading the paragraph, to set it apart from other text on the page, drawing the reader's attention to its contents. You must first select all paragraphs to which you will apply the border or shading formats. If you have not selected text, any border or shading you identify will be applied to the paragraph in which the insertion point is located.

When you click the Borders arrow in the Paragraph group on the Home tab and select Borders and Shading, the Borders and Shading dialog box displays (see Figure 2.17). There are three tabs in the dialog box: Borders, Page Border, and Shading. The paragraph border settings are on the Borders tab. You can format the borders using a Box, Shadow, 3-D, or Custom format. A Box border places a uniform border around a paragraph. A Shadow border places thicker lines at the right and bottom of the bordered area. The 3-D border, on the other hand, adds more dimension to the

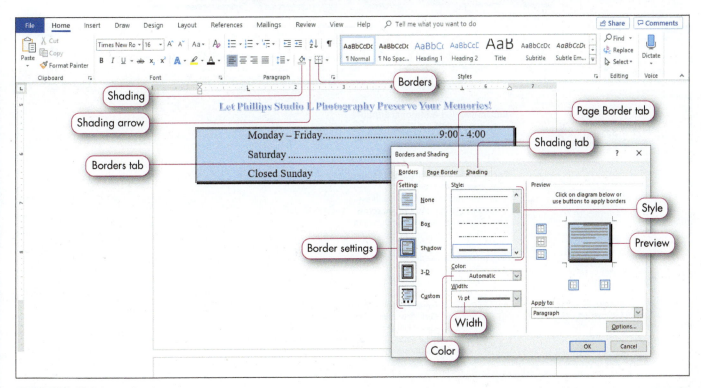

FIGURE 2.17 Select a Border

border. The Custom border enables the user to select a specific style, color, width, and side. The None setting is used to remove borders. The Preview area displays a diagram of the border options that you select.

> **To apply a paragraph border to selected text, complete the following steps:**
> 1. Select text. Click the Borders arrow in the Paragraph group on the Home tab.
> 2. Click Borders and Shading. Ensure that the Borders tab is selected.
> 3. Select a border setting (refer to Figure 2.17).
> 4. Select a style, color, and width of the border.
> 5. Click OK.

The Page Border tab in the Borders and Shading dialog box provides controls that you use to place a decorative border around one or more selected pages. As with a paragraph border, you can place the border around the entire page, or you can select one or more sides. The Page Border tab also provides an additional option to use a preselected image as a border instead of ordinary lines. Note that it is appropriate to use page borders on documents such as flyers, newsletters, and invitations, but not on formal documents such as research papers and professional reports.

You can apply shading to one or more selected paragraphs using the Shading arrow in the Paragraph group on the Home tab. Select a solid color, a lighter or darker variation of the color for the shaded background, or More Colors for even more selections. You can also select shading options from the Shading tab of the Borders and Shading dialog box (refer to Figure 2.17).

STEP 4 Create Bulleted and Numbered Lists

A list organizes information by topic or in a sequence. Use a ***numbered list*** if the list is a sequence of steps. If you add or remove items, the list items are automatically renumbered. If the list is a simple itemization of points, use a ***bulleted list*** (see Figure 2.18). A multilevel

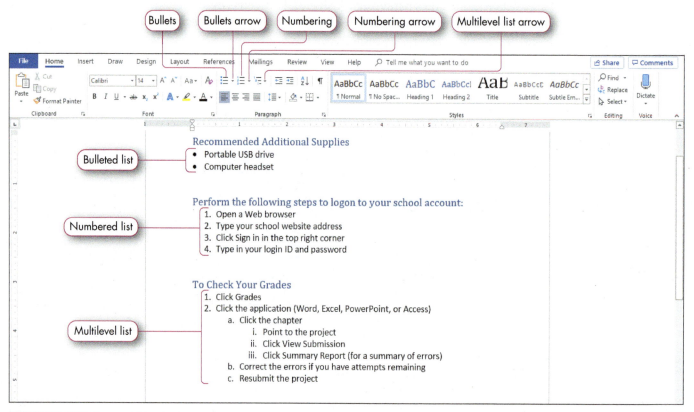

FIGURE 2.18 Bullets and Numbering

list extends a numbered or bulleted list to several levels, and it, too, is updated automatically when topics are added or deleted. A multilevel list is helpful when you have to list major categories as well as subordinate items below each category. You create each of these lists from the Paragraph group on the Home tab.

To apply bullets, numbering, or multiple levels to a list, complete the following steps:

1. Select the items to be bulleted or numbered.
2. Complete one of the following:
   - Click Bullets (or Numbering) to apply the default bullet or numbering style.
   - Click the Bullets (or Numbering) arrow in the Paragraph group on the Home tab and point to one of the predefined symbols or numbering styles in the library. A preview of the style will display in the document. Click the style you want to use.
   - Click Multilevel List and select a style to apply multiple levels to a list.

You can also apply bullets or numbering before you type the items by selecting Bullets (or Numbering) in the Paragraph group, typing the list items, and clicking Bullets (or Numbering) again or press Enter twice to turn off the toggle. In addition, Word can automatically create a list for you in two ways: When you start typing an asterisk followed by a space, Word will create a bulleted list. If you start a new paragraph by typing a number, Word will create a numbered list. There are many different types of bullet styles that you can choose from the Bullet Library. Further, you can also use all kinds of images as bullet styles too. To define a new bullet style or customize the formatting (such as color or special effect) of a selected bullet, click the Bullets arrow in the Paragraph group on the Home tab, click Define New Bullet, and then make selections from the Define New Bullet dialog box.

> **TIP: RENUMBERING A LIST**
> Especially when creating several numbered lists in a document, Word continues the numbering sequence from one list to the next. Instead, if your intention was to begin numbering each list at 1, you can restart the numbering or set the numbering to a specific value. To restart numbering at a new value, right-click the item that is not numbered correctly and click Restart at 1. Alternatively, you can click the Numbering arrow and select Set Numbering Value. Indicate a starting value in the subsequent dialog box and click OK.

1. Describe the difference between a serif and sans serif font. Give examples of when you might use each. *p. 130*
2. Explain what could cause the larger space between lines of bullets and how you would correct it so that the bulleted items are single spaced. *p. 136*
3. If you use Word to create a restaurant menu, describe the type of tabs you would use and approximately how you would space them. *p. 139*
4. You are preparing a document with a list of items to bring for an upcoming camping trip. Describe the Word feature that you could use to draw attention to the list. *p. 142*

Hands-On Exercises

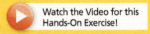

MyLab IT HOE1 Sim Training

Watch the Video for this Hands-On Exercise!

Skills covered: Select Font Options • Change Text Appearance • Select Paragraph Alignment • Select Line and Paragraph Spacing • Select Indents • Set Tab Stops • Apply Borders and Shading • Create Bulleted and Numbered Lists

1 Text and Paragraph Formatting

The newsletter you are developing needs a lot of work. You want to format it so it is much easier to read. After selecting an appropriate font and font size, you will emphasize selected text with bold and italic text formatting. Paragraphs must be spaced so they are easy to read. You know that, to be effective, a document must capture the reader's attention while conveying a message. You will begin the process of formatting and preparing the newsletter in this exercise.

STEP 1 SELECT FONT OPTIONS AND CHANGE TEXT APPEARANCE

The newsletter will be printed and distributed by mail. As a printed document, you know that certain font options are better suited for reading. Specifically, you want to use a serif font in an easy-to-read size. Refer to Figure 2.19 as you complete Step 1.

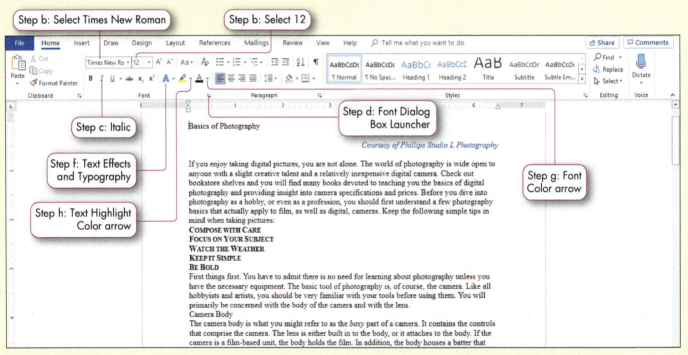

FIGURE 2.19 Format Text

    a. Open *w02h1Studio* and save it as **w02h1Studio_LastFirst**.

> **TROUBLESHOOTING:** If you make any major mistakes in this exercise, you can close the file, open *w02h1Studio* again, and then start this exercise over.

    b. Press **Ctrl+A** to select all the text in the document. Click the **Font arrow** in the Font group on the Home tab and scroll to select **Times New Roman**. Click the **Font Size arrow** in the Font group and select **12**.

        You use a 12-pt serif font on the whole document because it is easier to read in print.

    c. Select the second paragraph in the document, *Courtesy of Phillips Studio L Photography*. Click **Italic** on the Mini Toolbar. Locate and double-click **boxy** in the paragraph below *Camera Body*. Click **Italic** in the Font group.

144 CHAPTER 2 • Hands-On Exercise 1

> **TROUBLESHOOTING:** If the Mini Toolbar does not display or disappears, click Italic in the Font group on the Home tab.

   d. Select the five paragraphs beginning with *Compose with Care* and ending with *Be Bold*. Click the **Font Dialog Box Launcher** in the Font group. (On a Mac, click the Format menu and click Font.)

   The Font dialog box displays with font options.

   e. Ensure that the Font tab is displayed in the Font dialog box and click **Bold** in the Font style box. Click to select the **Small caps check box** under Effects. Click **OK**.

   f. Press **Ctrl+End** to move the insertion point to the end of the document. Select the last paragraph in the document, *Let Phillips Studio L Photography Preserve Your Memories!* Click **Text Effects and Typography** in the Font group. Select **Fill: Blue, Accent color 5; Outline: White, Background color 1; Hard Shadow: Blue, Accent color 5** (third row, third column). Change the font size of the selected text to **16**. Click anywhere to deselect the text.

   g. Press **Ctrl+Home** to position the insertion point at the beginning of the document. Select the second paragraph in the document, *Courtesy of Phillips Studio L Photography*. Click the **Font Color arrow** and select **Blue, Accent 5, Darker 25%** (fifth row, ninth column).

   h. Select the words **you should consider how to become a better photographer** in the paragraph under the *Composition* heading. Click the **Text Highlight Color arrow** and select **Yellow**.

   i. Press **Ctrl+Home**. Click the **Review tab** and click **Check Document** in the Proofing group to check spelling and grammar. Ignore any possible grammatical errors, but correct spelling mistakes.

   j. Save the document.

STEP 2: SELECT PARAGRAPH ALIGNMENT, SPACING, AND INDENTS

The lines of the newsletter are too close together. It is difficult to tell where one paragraph ends and the next begins, and the layout of the text is not very pleasing. Overall, you will adjust line and paragraph spacing, and apply indents where necessary. Refer to Figure 2.20 as you complete Step 2.

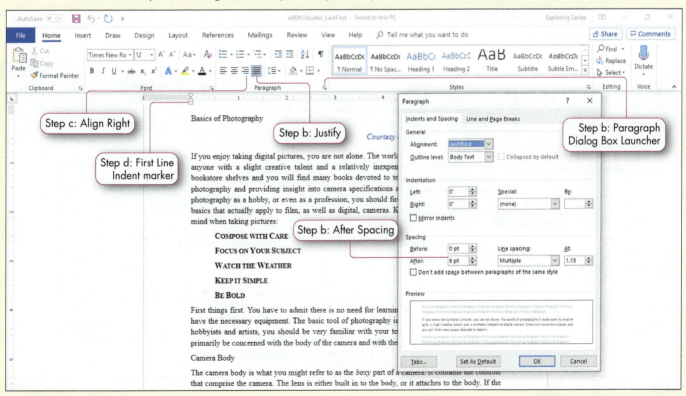

FIGURE 2.20 Adjust Spacing and Indents

a. Select most of the document beginning with the sentence *If you enjoy taking digital pictures* and ending with *emotion expressed before even greeting Santa*. Click the **Home tab**. Click **Line and Paragraph Spacing** in the Paragraph group. Select **1.15**. Do not deselect the text.

All lines within the selected text are spaced by 1.15.

b. Click **Justify** in the Paragraph group. Click the **Paragraph Dialog Box Launcher**. With the Indents and Spacing tab selected, click the **After spin arrow** in the Spacing section to increase spacing after to **6 pt**. Click **OK**. Click anywhere to deselect the text.

You have placed 6 pt spacing after each paragraph in the selected area. Selected paragraphs are also aligned with justify, which means text is evenly distributed between the left and right margins.

c. Press **Ctrl+End**. Click anywhere on the last paragraph in the document, *Let Phillips Studio L Photography Preserve Your Memories!* Click **Center** in the Paragraph group. Press **Ctrl+Home**. Click anywhere on the second paragraph of text in the document, *Courtesy of Phillips Studio L Photography*. Click **Align Right** in the Paragraph group.

d. Click the **View tab** and ensure the ruler check box is selected. Click anywhere in the first body paragraph, beginning with *If you enjoy taking digital pictures*. Click the **Home tab** and click the **Paragraph Dialog Box Launcher**. Click the **Special arrow** in the Indentation group and select **First line**. Click **OK**. Click anywhere in the paragraph beginning with *First things first*. Position the pointer on the First Line Indent marker on the ruler and drag the marker to the **0.5"** mark on the horizontal ruler.

> **MAC TROUBLESHOOTING:** Click the Format menu and click Paragraph.

The first line of both multiline paragraphs that begin the document are indented by 0.5 inches.

e. Save the document.

STEP 3 SET TAB STOPS AND APPLY BORDERS AND SHADING

You realize that you left off the studio hours and want to include them at the end of the document, and you also want to draw attention to the business hours using borders and shading. Refer to Figures 2.21 and 2.22 as you complete Step 3.

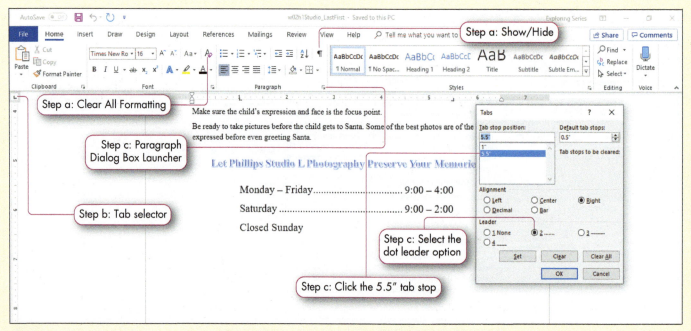

FIGURE 2.21 Set Tab Stops

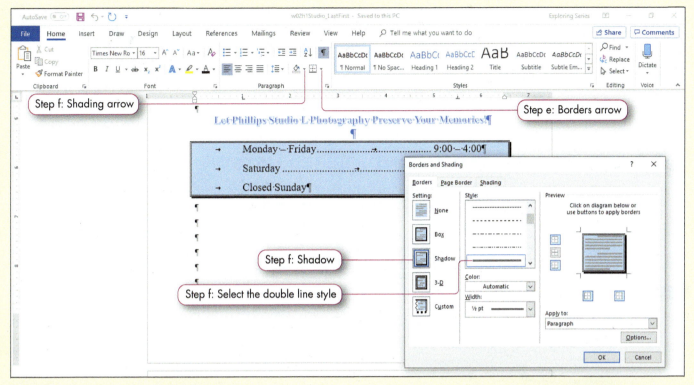

FIGURE 2.22 Apply Borders and Shade Text

a. Press **Ctrl+End**. Click **Show/Hide** in the Paragraph group to display nonprinting characters. Press **Enter** twice. Click **Clear All Formatting** in the Font group on the Home tab. Select **Times New Roman font** and **16 pt size**.

You clicked Clear All Formatting so that the text effect formatting from the paragraph above the insertion point is not carried forward to text that you will type next.

b. Ensure the tab selector (shown at the top of the vertical ruler) specifies a left tab and click at **1"** on the ruler. Click the **tab selector** twice to select a right tab and click at **5.5"** on the ruler.

You set a left tab at 1" and a right tab at 5.5".

TROUBLESHOOTING: If the tabs you set are incorrectly placed on the ruler, click Undo in the Quick Access Toolbar and repeat Step b. You can also drag a tab off the ruler to remove it or drag it along the ruler to reposition it.

c. Click the **Paragraph Dialog Box Launcher** and click **Tabs** at the bottom-left corner. Click **5.5"** in the Tab stop position box. Click **2** in the Leader section and click **OK**.

You modified the right tab to include dot leaders, which means dots will display before text at the right tab.

d. Press **Tab**. Type **Monday – Friday** and press **Tab**. Type **9:00 – 4:00**. Press **Enter**. Press **Tab**. Type **Saturday** and press **Tab**. Type **9:00 – 2:00**. Press **Enter**. Press **Tab**. Type **Closed Sunday**.

e. Select the three paragraphs at the end of the document, beginning with *Monday – Friday* and ending with *Closed Sunday*. Click the **Borders arrow** in the Paragraph group on the Home tab and select **Borders and Shading**.

TROUBLESHOOTING: If you click Borders instead of the Borders arrow, you will not see the Borders and Shading dialog box and the most recent border will be applied to selected text. Click Undo on the Quick Access Toolbar, click the Borders arrow, and then select Borders and Shading.

f. Click **Shadow** in the Setting section. Scroll through the Style box and select the seventh style—**double line**. Click **OK**. Do not deselect the text. Click the **Shading arrow** and select **Blue, Accent 1, Lighter 60%** (third row, fifth column). Click anywhere to deselect the text.

Studio hours are bordered and shaded.

g. Save the document.

STEP 4 CREATE BULLETED AND NUMBERED LISTS

At several points in the newsletter, you include either a list of items or a sequence of steps. You will add bullets to the lists and number the steps. Refer to Figure 2.23 as you complete Step 4.

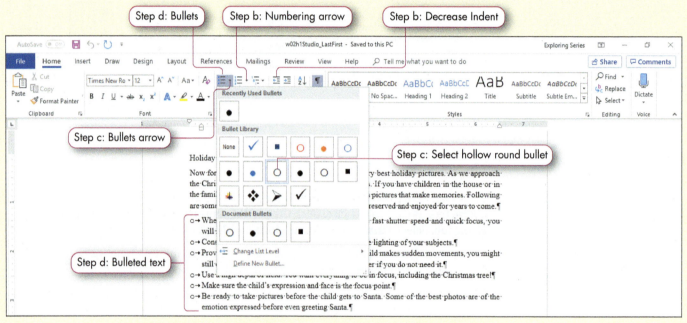

FIGURE 2.23 Add Bullets and Numbers

a. Press **Ctrl+Home**. Select the five boldfaced paragraphs, beginning with *Compose with Care* and ending with *Be Bold*.

b. Click the **Numbering arrow** and select the **Number Alignment** showing each number followed by a right parenthesis. Click **Decrease Indent** in the Paragraph group to move the numbered items to the left margin. Click anywhere to deselect the text.

c. Scroll to the second page and select the four paragraphs following the sentence *Depth of field is determined by several factors*, beginning with *Aperture/F-Stop* and ending with *Point of View*. Click the **Bullets arrow** and select the **hollow round bullet**. Decrease the indent to move the selected text to the left margin. Deselect the text.

d. Press **Ctrl+End** and select the six paragraphs above the last paragraph of text, beginning with *Where kids are involved*, and ending with *even greeting Santa*. Click **Bullets** to apply a hollow round bullet to the selected paragraphs. Decrease the indent so the bullets begin at the left margin.

Clicking Bullets applied the most recently selected bullet style to selected text. You did not have to click the Bullets arrow and select from the Bullet Library.

e. Save the document. Keep the document open if you plan to continue with the next Hands-On Exercise. If not, close the document, and exit Word.

Document Appearance

The overall appearance and organization of a document is the first opportunity to effectively convey your message to readers. You should ensure that a document is formatted attractively with coordinated and consistent style elements. Not only should a document be organized by topic, but also it should be organized by design, so that it is easy to read and that topics of the same level of emphasis are similar in appearance. Major headings are typically formatted identically, with subheadings formatted to indicate a subordinate relationship—in a smaller font, for example. Word includes tools on the Design tab that enable you to create a polished and professional-looking document. You will find options for creating a themed document, with color-coordinated design elements, as well as *style sets*, which are predefined combinations of font, style, color, and font size that can be applied to selected text. Organizing a document into sections enables you to combine diverse units into a whole, formatting sections independently of one another.

In this section, you will explore document formatting options, including themes and style sets. In addition, you will learn to create and apply styles. You will work with sections and columns, learning to organize and format sections independently of one another to create an attractive document that conveys your message.

Formatting a Document

A *document theme* is a set of coordinating fonts, colors, and special effects that are combined into a package to provide a stylish appearance in a Word document. Applying a theme enables you to visually coordinate various page elements. In some cases, adding a page border or page background can also yield a more attractive and effective document. All these design options are available on the Design tab. When formatting a document, you should always keep in mind the document's purpose and its intended audience. Whereas a newsletter might use more color and playful text and design effects, a legal document should be more conservative. With the broad range of document formatting options available in Word, you can be as playful or conservative as necessary.

> **TIP: APPLY DOCUMENT THEME**
> Themes are similar across the Office applications. If a Word document includes a table from Excel, both the Word and Excel files can be formatted with the same document theme, so the effects are consistent across the two applications.

STEP 1 Select a Document Theme

When you open a new blank Word document, it is based on the default Office theme. However, you can select and change the entire theme of the document or just customize the theme fonts, colors, or effects using the Design tab, where you will find a wide selection related to themes, colors, fonts, effects, watermarks, page background, and even page borders (see Figure 2.24). You can choose from a variety of document themes, theme colors, theme fonts, and theme effects, which are in the Document Formatting group. Point to each theme in the Themes gallery to display a preview of the effect on the document and select to change the document theme. Depending on document features and color selections already in place, you might not see an immediate change when previewing a theme.

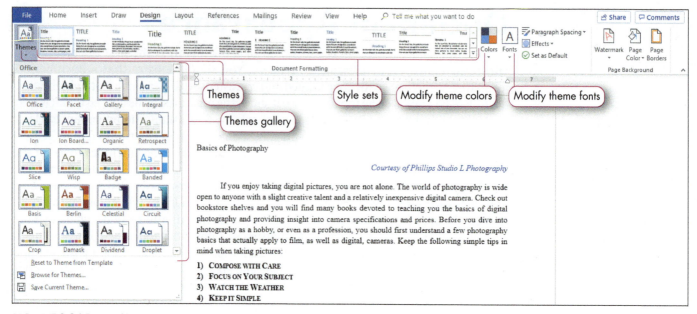

FIGURE 2.24 Design Tab

Modifying a theme color or theme font may be necessary for color coordination and/or to give the document a consistent, professional look. Similarly, you may modify the theme colors or fonts by selecting from a group of coordinated colors or font selections summarized and identified by a unique name. Theme fonts can be applied to headings or body text.

If your document contains objects, you may utilize theme effects to instantly change the general look of the objects in the document. Selections in the theme gallery use lines, borders, fills, and visual effects, such as shading and shadow, to give the objects a unique look, thus drawing attention to the selected item. With the object selected, point to each option in the effects gallery to display a preview of the effect on the object and select to apply the theme effect. You may also add a watermark, page color, or a page border using the tools in the Page Background group.

Work with Sections

As you consider ways to organize a document, you might find it necessary to vary the layout of a document within a page or between pages and incorporate sections into a document with each section arranged or formatted independently of others. For instance, a headline of an article might center horizontally across the width of a page, while remaining article text is divided into columns (see Figure 2.25). In this case, the headline should be situated in one section, while article text resides in another. By arranging text in columns, you can easily create an attractive newsletter or brochure. The Layout tab facilitates the use of sections and formatting in columns. Or, a cover page can be a section by itself that might be centered vertically, while all other pages in the same document are aligned at the top. A *section* is a part of a document that contains its own page format settings, such as those for margins, columns, and orientation. To have text on the same page accommodating both single column and two-column text, break it into sections. So that sections can be managed separately, you must indicate with section breaks where one section ends and another begins. A *section break* is a marker that divides a document into sections. Word stores the formatting characteristics of each section within the section break at the end of a section. Section breaks are often used to change page orientation, add columns to selected text within a document, and add page borders to selected text within a document.

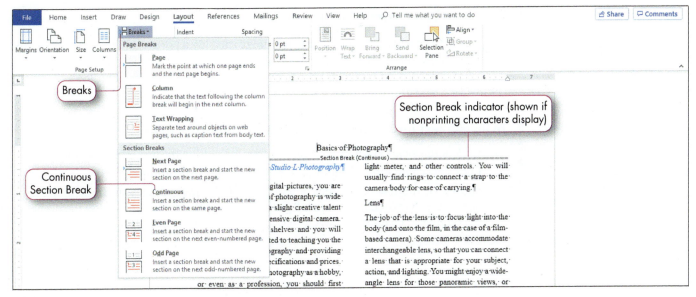

FIGURE 2.25 Select and Display a Section Break

There are four types of section breaks, as shown in Table 2.2. The most common type of section break is the Next Page, which manually forces the text to start at the top of a new page. If you want to format content in a newsletter, then a Continuous section break would be ideal. Even Page and Odd Page section breaks are often used in assembling a book.

TABLE 2.2 Section Breaks

Type	Text that follows...	Use to...
Next Page	must begin at the top of the next page.	force a chapter to start at the top of a page.
Continuous	can continue on the same page.	format text in the middle of the page into columns.
Even Page	must begin at the top of the next even-numbered page.	force a chapter to begin at the top of an even-numbered page.
Odd Page	must begin at the top of the next odd-numbered page.	force a chapter to begin at the top of an odd-numbered page.

To place a section break in a document, complete the following steps:

1. Click at the location where the section break should occur.
2. Click the Layout tab. Click Breaks in the Page Setup group.
3. Select a section break type (refer to Table 2.2). If nonprinting characters are displayed, you will see a section break (refer to Figure 2.25).

If you delete a section break, you also delete the formatting for that section, causing the text above the break to assume the formatting characteristics of the following section. To delete a section break, click the section break indicator (refer to Figure 2.25) and press Delete.

Format Text into Columns

One reason to create a section in a document is to display a portion of the text in columns. Newsletters are often formatted with text in columns. **Columns** format a document or section of a document into side-by-side vertical blocks in which the text flows down the first column and continues at the top of the next column.

To format text into columns, complete the following steps:

1. Click at the location where you want to start formatting the text into columns.
2. Click the Layout tab and click Columns in the Page Setup group.
3. Specify the number of columns or select More Columns to display the Columns dialog box. The Columns dialog box (see Figure 2.26) provides options for setting the number of columns and spacing between columns.
4. Click OK.

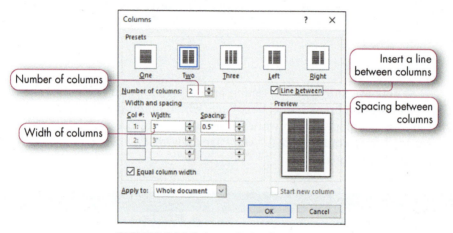

FIGURE 2.26 Columns Dialog Box

Having created a two-column document, you should preview the document to ensure an attractive arrangement of columns. Try to avoid columns that end awkwardly, such as a column heading at the bottom of one column with remaining text continuing at the top of the next column. In addition, columns should be somewhat balanced, if possible, so that one column is not far lengthier than the next. To remedy these kinds of issues, use a column break, which enables you to choose where a column ends. To insert a column break at a specified location in the document, use the Layout tab, select Breaks in the Page Setup group, and then click Column in the Page Breaks section. With nonprinting characters displayed, you will see the Column Break indicator at the location where one column ends and the next begins.

Applying Styles

A characteristic of a professional document is uniform formatting. As you complete reports, assignments, and other projects, you probably apply the same text, paragraph, table, and list formatting for similar elements. Instead of formatting document elements individually, you can apply a style for each element to save time in designing titles, headings, and paragraphs. A *style* is a named collection of formatting characteristics. Styles automate the formatting process and provide a consistent appearance to a document so all major headings look the same, with uniform subheadings. Even paragraphs can be styled to lend consistency to a document. In addition, if styles are appropriately assigned, Word can automatically generate reference pages such as a table of contents and indexes. Although document themes provide a quick way to change the overall color and fonts of a document, styles are more effective when you want to change text formatting quickly and uniformly.

By default, the Normal style is applied to new Word documents. Normal style is a paragraph style with specific font and paragraph formatting, and the features that are set as default are: Calibri (Body) font, 11 pt font size, left alignment, 0 pt Spacing Before, 8 pt Spacing After, and 1.08 Multiple Line spacing. If that style is not appropriate for a document you are developing, you can select another style from Word's Style gallery. The most frequently accessed styles are shown in the Styles group on the Home tab (see Figure 2.27).

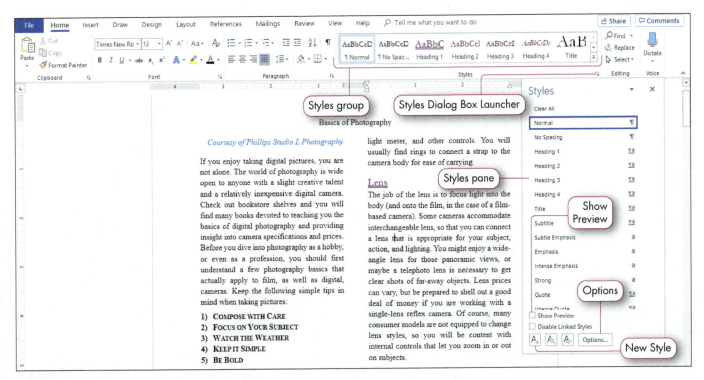

FIGURE 2.27 Styles

STEP 2 Select and Modify Styles

Some styles are considered either character or paragraph styles. Examples of character styles include Emphasis, Quote, Book Title, and List Paragraph, while headings are examples of paragraph styles. A character style formats one or more selected characters within a paragraph, often applying font formats found in the Font group on the Home tab. A paragraph style changes the entire paragraph in which the insertion point is located or changes multiple selected paragraphs. A paragraph style typically includes paragraph formats found in the Paragraph group on the Home tab, such as alignment, line spacing, indents, tabs, and borders. Other styles are neither character nor paragraph but are instead linked styles in which both character and paragraph formatting are included. A linked style applies formatting dependent upon the text selected. For example, when the insertion point is located within a paragraph, but no text is selected, a linked style applies both font characteristics (such as bold or italic) and paragraph formats (such as paragraph and line spacing) to the entire paragraph. However, if text is selected within a paragraph when a linked style is applied, the style will apply font formatting only.

To apply a style to selected text or to an existing paragraph, complete the following steps:

1. Select the text or place the insertion point within the paragraph.
2. Complete one of the following steps:
   - Click a style in the Styles group on the Home tab.
   - Click More for more styles.
   - Click the Styles Dialog Box Launcher (refer to Figure 2.27) to display the Styles pane for more choices.
3. Click to select a style.

Modifying a style, or even creating a new style, affects only the current document, by default. However, you can cause the style to be available to all documents that are based on the current template when you select *New documents based on this template* in the Modify Style dialog box (see Figure 2.28). Unless you make that selection, however, the changes are not carried over to new documents you create or to others that you open. As an example, the specifications for the Title style are shown in Figure 2.28.

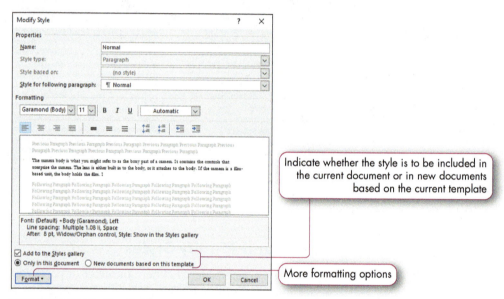

FIGURE 2.28 Modify a Style

To modify a style, complete the following steps:

1. Click the Styles Dialog Box Launcher in the Styles group to open the Styles pane showing all available styles.
2. Point to a style in the Styles pane and click the arrow on the right.
3. Click Modify. The Modify Style dialog box displays (refer to Figure 2.28).
4. Change any font and paragraph formatting or click Format for even more choices.
5. Click Add to the Styles gallery if the style is one you are likely to use often.
6. Indicate whether the style should be available only in the current document, or in new documents based on the current template.
7. Click OK.

> **On a Mac, to modify a style, complete the following steps:**
> 1. Click the Format menu and select Style.
> 2. Click Modify in the Style dialog box.
> 3. Change any font and paragraph settings you want to modify in the Modify Style dialog box. Click Format for more choices.
> 4. Click Add to template to add a new style to the template the current document is based on. For a single use, do not click this option.
> 5. Click Add to Quick Style list to add the new style to the Quick Style list that displays on the Home tab.
> 6. Click OK.

Word provides a gallery of styles from which you can choose. The styles gallery contains a variety of styles that are conveniently located and frequently used. Therefore, you can apply a specific style from the Styles gallery or manage the contents of the gallery by adding or deleting styles that you need or do not need. If a style does not fit with your document design, you can modify almost any component of the style. For example, you might format a Heading 1 style with Black font color instead of the default Blue. When a style is modified, the changes will automatically be applied to all document elements formatted with that style, or you can create your own style. It is possible to store any type of character or paragraph formatting within a style. For example, having formatted a major report heading with various settings, such as font type, color, and size, you can create a style from the heading, calling it Major_Heading. The next time you type a major heading, apply the Major_Heading style so that the two headings are identical in format. Subsequent major headings can be formatted in the same way. If you later decide to modify the Major_Heading style, all text based on that style will automatically adjust as well.

STEP 3 — Use a Style Set

A style set is a combination of title, heading, and paragraph styles that are designed to work together. Using a style set, you can format all elements in a document at one time. Style sets are on the Design tab in the Document Formatting group (refer to Figure 2.24). Click a style set to apply the format combination to the document.

Create a New Style from Text

Having applied several formatting characteristics to text, you can repeat that formatting on other selections that are similar in purpose. For example, suppose you format a page title with a specific font size, font color, and bordering. Subsequent page titles should be formatted identically. To copy formatting from one selection to another, you can certainly use Format Painter. A better alternative is to create a new style from the selection and apply the new style to additional text. For example, you can select the formatted page title and create a new style based on the formatting of the selected text. Then select the next title to which the formatting should be applied and choose the newly created style name from the Styles group or from the Styles pane. You may also check your styles by clicking Style Inspector in the Styles task pane.

Once a style is created, it remains available in both the current document and in other documents based on the same template, if you indicate that preference when you create the style. That way, the same formatting changes can be applied repeatedly in various documents or positions within the same document, even after a document is closed and reopened. Further, styles that indicate a hierarchy (such as Heading 1, Heading 2) can be used to prepare a table of contents or outline.

To create a new style from existing text, complete the following steps:

1. Select text the new style will be based upon.
2. Click More in the Style group.
3. Click Create a Style.
4. Type a name for the new style. Do not use the name of an existing style.
5. Click OK.

On a Mac, to create a new style from existing text, complete the following steps:

1. Select the text the new style will be based upon or click in a paragraph containing paragraph characteristics you want to include in a new style.
2. Click Styles Pane on the Home tab.
3. Click New Style and type a name for the new style. The name must be unique and cannot be the name of an existing style.

STEP 4 Use Outline View

One benefit of applying styles to headings in a long document is the ability to use those headings to view the document in Outline view, making it easier to review and modify the organization of a long document. Outline view in Word displays a document in various levels of detail, according to heading styles applied in a document. Figure 2.29 shows Outline view of a document in which major headings were formatted in Heading 1 style, with subheadings in Headings 2 and 3 styles. You can modify the heading styles to suit your preference. To select a level to view, perhaps only first-level headings, click All Levels (beside Show Level) and select a level. You can display the document in Outline view by clicking the View tab and clicking Outline in the Views group.

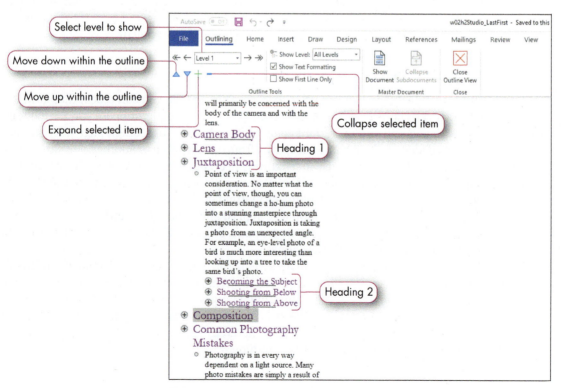

FIGURE 2.29 Outline View

Use Outline view to glimpse or confirm a document's structure. Especially when developing lengthy reports, you will want to make sure headings are shown at the correct level of detail. A document shown in Outline view can also be easily converted to a PowerPoint presentation, with Heading 1 becoming the slide titles, and lower levels becoming bullets on each slide. Also, a table of contents is automatically generated when you select Table of Contents on the References tab.

To collapse or expand a single heading, click the heading in Outline view and click the plus sign (to expand) or the minus sign (to collapse) on the ribbon. For example, having clicked text formatted as Heading 1, click + to show any lower-level headings associated with the particular heading (refer to Figure 2.29). Text other than that associated with the selected heading will remain unaffected. As shown in Figure 2.29, you can move a heading (along with all associated subheadings) up or down in the document. In Outline view, you can also drag the plus or minus sign beside a heading to move the entire group, including all sublevels, to another location.

You can quickly move through and restructure a document in Outline view. Using Outline view to move through a lengthy document can save a great deal of time because it is not necessary to page through a document looking for a particular section heading. To restructure a document in Outline view, drag and drop a heading to reposition it within a document or use Move Up or Move Down. If subheadings are associated, they will move with the heading as well.

Change the view to Print Layout, and when the levels are collapsed so that body text does not display, you can select a heading to move quickly to that section. In Print Layout view, you can collapse everything except the section with which you want to work. Point to a heading and click the small triangle that displays beside the heading (see Figure 2.30) to collapse or expand the following body text and sublevels. Collapsing text in that manner is a handy way to provide your readers with a summary. The document will expand, and the insertion point will be in the section identified by the heading you selected.

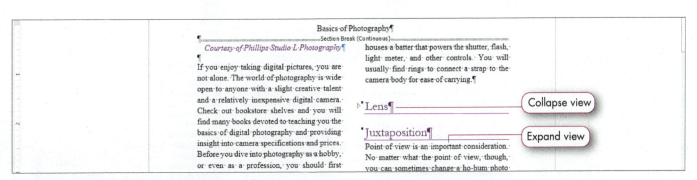

FIGURE 2.30 Expand and Collapse Detail

5. Describe why a document may need to be divided into two or more sections. ***p. 150***

6. Describe a situation where it would be appropriate to insert a column break into a Word document. ***p. 152***

7. Explain the benefit of using styles when formatting several different areas of text. ***p. 152***

8. Discuss how the concept of styles relates to Outline view. ***p. 156***

Hands-On Exercises

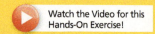

MyLab IT HOE2 Sim Training

Watch the Video for this Hands-On Exercise!

Skills covered: Select a Document Theme • Work with Sections • Format Text into Columns • Select and Modify Styles • Use a Style Set • Create a New Style from Text • Use Outline View

2 Document Appearance

The next step in preparing the photography newsletter for distribution is to apply document formatting to several areas of the document that will make it easier to read. By applying a theme and formatting the document in columns, you will add to the visual appeal. Using styles, you can ensure consistent formatting of document text. Finally, you will check the document's organization by viewing it in Outline view.

STEP 1 SELECT A DOCUMENT THEME, WORK WITH SECTIONS, AND FORMAT TEXT INTO COLUMNS

A document theme provides color and font coordination, simplifying your design task. You will apply a document theme to the newsletter as a simple way to ensure that yours is an attractive document with well-coordinated features. You will format the document as a newsletter. Most often, newsletters display in columns, so you will apply columns to the newsletter. A few items, such as the newsletter heading and the store hours at the end of the document, should be centered horizontally across the page instead of within a column. Using sections, you will format those items differently from column text. Refer to Figures 2.31 and 2.32 as you complete Step 1.

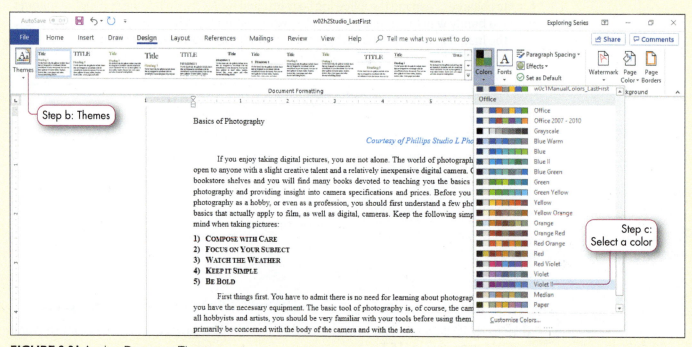

FIGURE 2.31 Apply a Document Theme

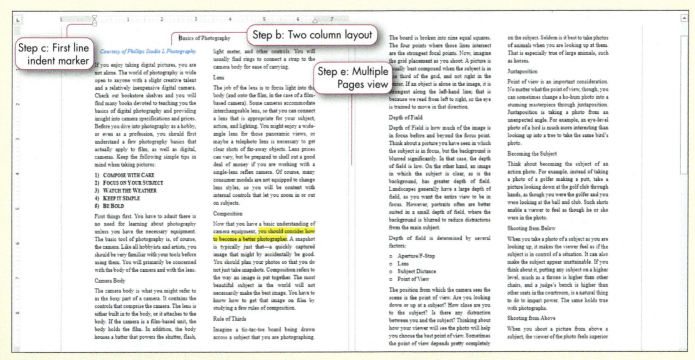

FIGURE 2.32 Format in Columns

a. Open **w02h1Studio_LastFirst** if you closed it at the end of Hands-On Exercise 1, and save it as **w02h2Studio_LastFirst**, changing h1 to h2.

b. Ensure nonprinting characters are displayed. Press **Ctrl+Home**. Click the **Design tab** and click **Themes** in the Document Formatting group. Select **Organic**.

Note the color change applied to the second paragraph of the document, *Courtesy of Phillips Studio L Photography*.

c. Click **Colors** in the Document Formatting group and select **Violet II**.

The second paragraph of the document, *Courtesy of Phillips Studio L Photography*, changed colors because you selected a new color scheme within the theme. The table of studio hours on the last page of the document also changed colors.

d. Select most of the document text, beginning with *Courtesy of Phillips Studio L Photography* and ending with *before even greeting Santa*.

e. Click the **Layout tab** and click **Columns**. Select **Two**.

The selected text is formatted into two columns. A continuous section break is inserted at the beginning of the document, after the document title, and at the end of the document (before the line that precedes the shaded box). The document now has three sections: the title, the middle with the two-column text, and the end.

f. Press **Ctrl+Home**. Click anywhere on the paragraph containing *Basics of Photography*. Click the **Home tab** and click **Center** in the Paragraph group. Click anywhere in the paragraph beginning with *If you enjoy taking digital pictures*. Drag the **First Line Indent marker** on the ruler back to the left margin.

The title of the newsletter is centered horizontally. The first line indent is removed from the first multiline paragraph in the newsletter.

g. Click anywhere in the paragraph beginning with *First things first*. Drag the **First Line Indent marker** to the left margin to remove the indent.

h. Click the **View tab** and click **Multiple Pages** in the Zoom group. Scroll down to view all pages, getting an idea of how text is positioned on all pages. Click **100%** in the Zoom group.

i. Save the document.

STEP 2 SELECT AND MODIFY STYLES

The newsletter is improving in appearance, but you note that the headings (Camera Body, Lens, Composition, etc.) are not as evident as they should be. Also, some headings are subordinate to others, and should be identified accordingly. You will apply heading styles to headings in the newsletter to resolve these issues. Refer to Figure 2.33 as you complete Step 2.

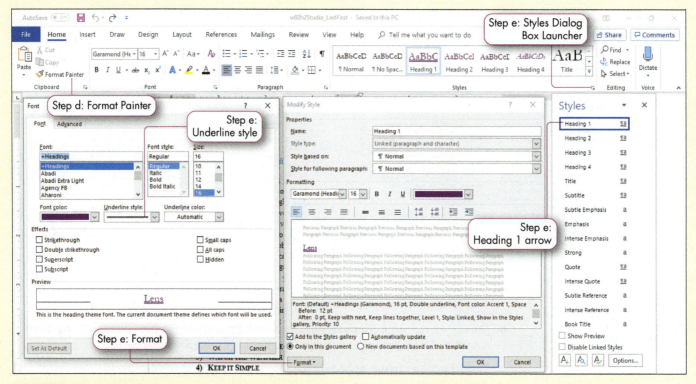

FIGURE 2.33 Work with Styles

a. Select the text **Camera Body** on the first page of the newsletter. Click the **Home tab** and select **Heading 1** in the Styles group. On the same page, in the column on the right, select **Lens** and apply **Heading 1**. Select **Composition** and apply **Heading 1**.

b. Apply **Heading 1** to *Juxtaposition*, *Common Photography Mistakes*, and *Holiday Photography* on the second and third pages of the newsletter.

c. Select **Rule of Thirds** on the first page, and press and hold **Ctrl** as you also select **Depth of Field**, **Becoming the Subject**, **Shooting from Below**, and **Shooting from Above** on the second page. Release Ctrl. Click **Heading 2** in the Styles group on the Home tab. Do not deselect the text.

d. Double-click **Format Painter** in the Clipboard group. Select **Dark Photos** on the third page. Select **Blurry Images**. Press **Esc**. Select **Blurry Images Due to Focus** on the third page. Click **Heading 3** in the Styles group. Select **Blurry Images Due to Camera Shake** on the third page and apply the **Heading 3** style.

TROUBLESHOOTING: If you do not see Heading 3 in the Styles group, click More in the Styles group and select Heading 3.

Using Format Painter, you copied the format of the Heading 2 style to a few headings. Headings throughout the newsletter are formatted according to their hierarchy, with major headings in Heading 1 style and others in correct order beneath the first level.

e. Click the **Styles Dialog Box Launcher** to display the Styles pane. Point to **Heading 1** and click the **Heading 1 arrow**. Click **Modify**. (On a Mac, click the Format menu and select Styles. Select Heading 1 in the Styles list and click Modify.) Click **Format** in the Modify Style dialog box and click **Font**. Click the **Underline style arrow** and click the second underline style (double underline). Click **OK**. Click **OK** again.

You modified Heading 1 style to include a double underline. Every heading formatted in Heading 1 style is automatically updated to include an underline.

f. Close the Styles pane. Save the document.

STEP 3: USE A STYLE SET AND CREATE A NEW STYLE FROM TEXT

Although you are pleased with the heading styles you selected in the previous step, you want to explore Word's built-in style sets to determine if another style might be more attractive. You will also create a style for all bulleted paragraphs in the newsletter. Refer to Figure 2.34 as you complete Step 3.

FIGURE 2.34 Use a Style Set

a. Press **Ctrl+Home**. Click the **Design tab**. Point to any style set in the Document Formatting group, without clicking, to view the effect on the document. Specifically, see how the previewed style affects the Lens heading shown in the right column. Click **More** in the Document Formatting group and select **Lines (Simple)**.

When you apply a style set, headings are formatted according to the style settings, overriding any formatting characteristics you might have set earlier.

b. Click the **View tab** and click **One Page** in the Zoom group to view the first page.

Note that the format of the major headings—Camera Body, Lens, and Composition—has been modified, removing the underline you set earlier, and now displays the format of the Lines (Simple) style set.

c. Click **100%** in the Zoom group. Select the second paragraph in the document, *Courtesy of Phillips Studio L Photography*. Click the **Home tab**. Click the **Font Color arrow** and select **Plum, Accent 1, Darker 25%** (fifth row, fifth column).

You select a coordinating text color for the second paragraph in the document.

d. Scroll to the second page and click anywhere in the bulleted paragraph containing the text *Aperture/F-Stop*. Click the **Bullets arrow** and select a **solid round black bullet**. Click the **Bullets arrow** and click **Define New Bullet**. Click **Font**. Click the **Font color arrow** and select **Plum, Accent 1, Darker 25%**. Click **OK**. Click **OK** again.

Having modified the format of one bulleted item, you will create a style from that format to apply to all other bulleted items in the document.

e. Open the Styles pane. Click **New Style** in the Styles pane. Type **Bullet Paragraph** in the Name box and click **OK**.

You should see a new style in the Styles pane titled Bullet Paragraph.

> **TROUBLESHOOTING:** If you do not see the Styles pane, you may have closed it; click the Styles Dialog Box Launcher to open the Styles pane.

f. Select the three bulleted paragraphs below *Aperture/F-Stop* and click **Bullet Paragraph** in the Styles pane. Scroll to the third page, select the three bulleted paragraphs at the bottom of the right column, and then click **Bullet Paragraph** in the Styles pane. Scroll to the fourth page, select the three bulleted paragraphs at the top of the page (in both columns), and then apply the **Bullet Paragraph style**. Close the Styles pane.

g. Save the document.

STEP 4: USE OUTLINE VIEW

The newsletter spans four pages, with headings identifying various levels of detail. You will check to make sure you have formatted headings according to the correct hierarchy. To do so, you will view the newsletter in Outline view. Refer to Figure 2.35 as you complete Step 4.

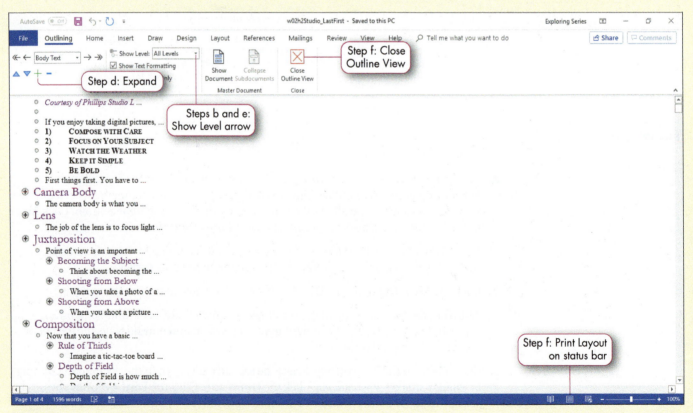

FIGURE 2.35 View an Outline

a. Press **Ctrl+Home**. Click the **View tab** and click **Outline** in the Views group. Scroll down slightly to see the first major heading (with a plus sign on the left)—Camera Body.

b. Click the **Show Level arrow** and click **Level 3**.

You formatted headings in the newsletter as headings, in three levels of detail. Because you did so, you are able to view the document structure according to the hierarchy of headings.

c. Position the pointer on the plus sign that precedes *Blurry Images Due to Camera Shake* (so the pointer becomes a four-headed arrow). Drag the heading above the preceding level (*Blurry Images Due to Focus*). When you see a small black triangle above the preceding level, release the mouse button to reposition the section.

d. Use the same procedure as in Step c to move the *Juxtaposition* section above *Composition*. Click **Expand** in the Outline Tools group to view the content of the *Juxtaposition* section.

e. Click the **Show Level arrow** and select **Level 1** to display Level 1 headings only. Select **Holiday Photography** and click **Expand** in the Outline Tools group.

The *Holiday Photography* section is expanded. Other Level 1 headings remain collapsed.

f. Click **Close Outline View** in the Close group on the Outlining tab. If both columns do not display, click **Print Layout** on the status bar.

g. Save the document. Keep the document open if you plan to continue with the next Hands-On Exercise. If not, save and close the document, and exit Word.

Objects

An ***object*** is an item that can be individually selected and manipulated within a document. Objects, such as pictures, icons, clip art, tables, and other graphic types, are often included in documents to add interest or convey a point (see Figure 2.36). Newsletters typically include pictures and other decorative elements to liven up what might otherwise be a somewhat mundane document. As you work with a document, you can search for appropriate pictures and graphics online—all without ever leaving your document workspace.

FIGURE 2.36 Word Objects

One thing all objects have in common is that they can be selected and worked with independently of surrounding text. You can resize them, add special effects, and move them to other locations within the document. Word includes convenient text wrapping controls so that you can adjust the way text wraps around an object. With Live Layout and alignment guides, you can line up pictures and other diagrams with existing text.

In this section, you will explore the use of objects in a Word document. Specifically, you will learn to include pictures, searching for them online as well as obtaining them from your own storage device. You will create text boxes and learn to create impressive text displays with WordArt.

Inserting and Formatting Objects

Objects such as pictures, icons, and illustrations can be selected from the Web or a storage device. When you select an image using Bing Search on Microsoft Word, the image is set to use the Creative Commons license system, which enables you to use the image more freely than other online images. It is important that you read the Creative Commons license on copyright infringement before using the image. You can also create other objects, such as WordArt, text boxes, screenshots, charts, and tables. A ***text box*** is a bordered area you can use to draw attention to specific text. When you insert an object, it is automatically selected so that you can manipulate it independently of surrounding text. An additional tab displays on the ribbon with options related to the selected object, making it easy to quickly modify and enhance an object.

STEP 1 **Insert a Picture**

A ***picture*** is a graphic image, such as a drawing or photograph. You can insert pictures in a document from your own library of digital pictures you have saved, or you can access abundant picture resources from the Internet. For instance, you can use Bing Search in Word to conduct a Web search to locate picture possibilities. Once incorporated into your document, a picture can be resized and modified with special borders and artistic effects. Other options enable you to easily align a picture with surrounding text, rotate or crop it if necessary, and even recolor it so it coordinates with an existing color scheme.

> **To insert an online picture, complete the following steps:**
>
> 1. Click to place the insertion point in the document in the location where the picture is to be inserted.
> 2. Click the Insert tab and click Online Pictures in the Illustrations group (see Figure 2.37).
> 3. Complete one of the following steps:
>   - **Use Bing Search:**
>   1. Click in the Bing Search box.
>   2. Type a search term (for example, type *school* to identify school-related images), and press Enter.
>   3. Ensure that the *Creative Commons only* check box is selected if you choose to use only Creative Commons approved images.
>   4. Review any relevant licensing information and select an image.
>   5. Click Insert.
>   6. Select and delete any additional text boxes from the online picture.
>   - **Use OneDrive:**
>   1. Click the Bing arrow and select OneDrive.
>   2. Navigate to the folder containing the picture you want to insert.
>   3. Click the picture and click Insert.

There are several hundreds of icons available online to users, and these icons can be searched and inserted similarly to any image by selecting Icons in the Illustrations group (see Figure 2.37). You may enhance the icons by changing the icon's fill or outline, or add a special visual effect such as glow or reflection to match the rest of the document using the formatting options provided on the Graphics tab.

Microsoft has made it so much easier for users to find and insert permission-approved images from the Internet. For instance, Pickit Images is a quick and convenient add-in app that contains images that you are legally allowed to use for any purpose. However, PickIt requires a fee after a brief free trial period. If you believe you will use this resource quite often, it may be a good idea to add it to your ribbon by clicking Store in the Add-ins group of the Insert tab and then selecting Pickit Free Images.

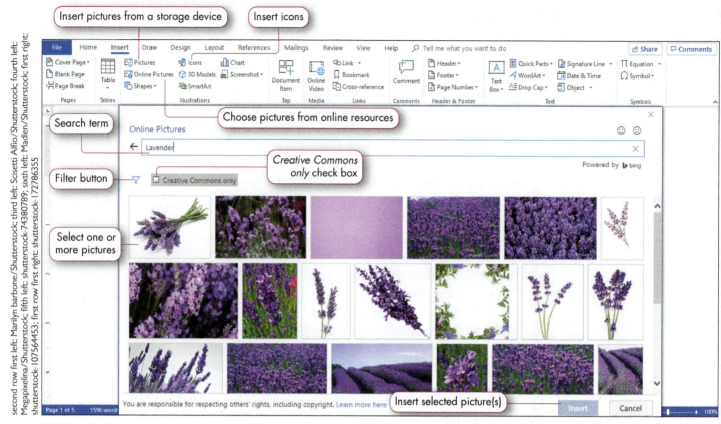

FIGURE 2.37 Insert an Online Picture

To insert pictures from a storage device, complete the following steps:

1. Position the insertion point in the document where the picture is to be inserted.
2. Click the Insert tab and click Pictures in the Illustrations group (refer to Figure 2.37).
3. Navigate to the folder in which your photos are stored.
4. Select a photo to insert and click Insert.

Insert a Screenshot

To capture information that displays on your monitor, whether from a website, another program, or another document that you have open on your computer, you can take a screenshot without leaving Word. You can capture the whole screen and insert it in a document as an object from the Available Windows gallery under Screenshot in the Illustrations group on the Insert tab. The Available Windows gallery will display any open window, but not those that are minimized. You open the document in which you plan to place the screenshot. Position the pointer at the location where you want to insert the whole screen, click Screenshot in the Illustrations group, and pick your selection from the thumbnails in the Available Windows gallery. The selection is automatically inserted into the document as an object.

To capture part of a screen display, you use Screen Clipping. After you open the item to be captured, you open the Word document where you want to add the screen capture (see Figure 2.38). Using Screen Clipping, the document is removed from view, leaving the original screen display. Drag to select any part of the screen display. The document displays again, with the selection now included as an object.

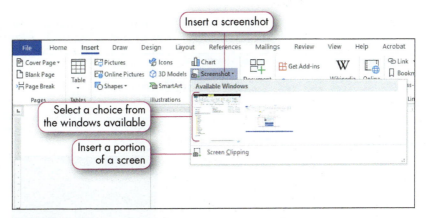

FIGURE 2.38 Insert a Screenshot

> **TIP: SNIP & SKETCH**
> Another useful tool available on your computer to capture a screenshot is the Snip & Sketch. It is an alternative to the Snipping tool with slightly more drawing features. On a Mac, to get a full screenshot, use the Grab tool or press Shift+Command+3.

STEP 2 Move, Align, and Resize a Picture

When a picture is inserted and selected, the Picture Tools Format tab displays, and includes settings and selections related to the inserted picture, as shown in Figure 2.39. You should position the picture so that it flows well with document text and does not appear to be a separate unit. One way to make that happen is to wrap text around the picture, using text wrap options to arrange text evenly around the object. The Format tab includes Wrap Text in the Arrange group (see Figure 2.39). You can select from the text wrapping styles shown in Table 2.3 when you click Wrap Text. You can also choose to allow the object to move with text as text is added or deleted, or you can keep the object in the same place on the page, regardless of text changes.

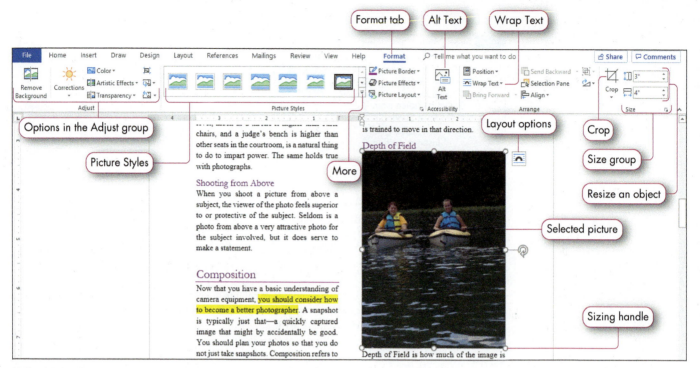

FIGURE 2.39 Picture Tools Format Tab

TABLE 2.3	Text Wrap Options
Type	**Effect**
In Line with Text	The image is part of the line of text in which it is inserted. Typically, text wraps above and below the object.
Square	Text wraps on all sides of an object, following an invisible square.
Tight	Text follows the shape of the object, but it does not overlap the object.
Through	Text follows the shape of the object, filling any open spaces in the shape.
Top and Bottom	Text flows above and below the borders of the object.
Behind Text	The object is positioned behind text. Both the object and text are visible (unless the fill color exactly matches the text color).
In Front of Text	The object is positioned in front of text, often obscuring the text.

Word has a feature that simplifies text wrapping around an object—Layout Options. Located next to a selected object, the Layout Options control (see Figure 2.40) includes the same selections shown in Table 2.3. The close proximity of the control to the selected object streamlines adjusting text wrapping.

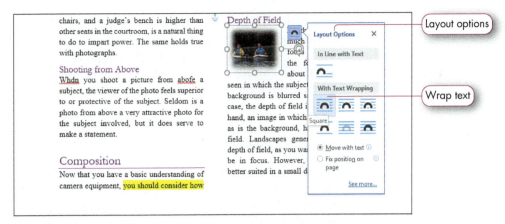

FIGURE 2.40 Text Wrap Options

Word has two interesting features to assist you as you wrap text: Live Layout and alignment guides. **Live Layout** enables you to watch text flow around an object as you move it, so you can position the object exactly as you want it. **Alignment guides** are horizontal or vertical green bars that display as you drag an object, so you can line up an object with text or with another object. The green alignment guide shown in Figure 2.41 helps align the picture object with paragraph text.

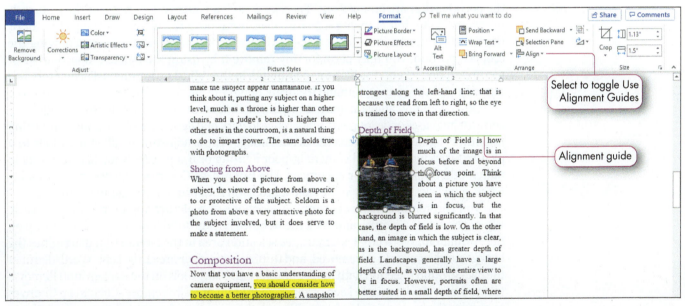

FIGURE 2.41 Alignment Guides

> **TIP: TURNING OFF THE ALIGNMENT GUIDES**
> If you decide that you do not need to use the alignment guides anymore, you can manually turn off this feature by selecting the alignment guides in the Align command and clicking Delete.

Often, a picture is inserted in a size that is too large or too small for your purposes. There are two ways to shrink the picture to fit it in a smaller space or enlarge it to fill some white space. To resize a picture, you can drag a **sizing handle**, which is a dot on each corner and in the center of each side of the selected object. When you drag the corner sizing handles, the image will be resized proportionally. Resizing a picture by dragging a center sizing handle is generally not recommended, as doing so distorts the picture. You can also resize a picture with more precise measurements by adjusting settings in the Size group of the Format tab (refer to Figure 2.39).

By default, the Lock aspect ratio setting is on, which means that when you change a dimension—either width or height—of a picture, the other dimension is automatically adjusted as well. To confirm or deselect the Lock aspect ratio, click the Size Dialog Box Launcher and adjust the setting in the Layout dialog box. Unless you deselect the setting, you cannot change both width and height distinctly from each other, as that would distort the picture.

STEP 3 — Modify a Picture

The Format tab includes options for modifying a picture. You can apply a picture style or effect, as well as add a picture border, from selections in the Picture Styles group. The More arrow (refer to Figure 2.39) provides a gallery of picture styles. As you point to a style, the style is shown in Live Preview, but the style is not applied until you click it. Options in the Adjust group simplify changing a color scheme, applying creative artistic effects, and even adjusting the brightness, contrast, and sharpness of an image.

If a picture contains more detail than is necessary, you can **crop** it, which is the process of trimming edges that you do not want to display. The Crop tool is in the Size group on the Format tab (refer to Figure 2.39). When the Crop tool is used, it will surround the selected object with eight **cropping handles**, evident by dark, thick lines—around the four corners and on the left, right, top, and bottom sides of the selected image. Click on any of these eight handles and drag to remove a portion of the selected object. Even though cropping enables you to adjust the amount of a picture that displays, it does not actually delete the portions that are cropped out. Therefore, you can later restore parts of the picture, if necessary. Note that cropping a picture does not reduce the file size of the picture or of the Word document in which it displays. However, if you are adamant on removing the cropped portion, you may permanently remove it by using the Delete cropped areas of pictures option, Compress Pictures command, in the Adjust group on the Format tab. You may also use the same command to shrink down the file size of high-resolution photos.

Other common adjustments to a picture include contrast and/or brightness. Adjusting contrast increases or decreases the difference in dark and light areas of the image. Adjusting brightness lightens or darkens the overall image. These adjustments often are made to a picture taken with a digital camera in poor lighting or if a picture is too bright or dull to match other objects in your document. The Brightness/Contrast adjustment is available when you click Corrections in the Adjust group on the Format tab (refer to Figure 2.39).

You can remove the background or portions of a picture you do not want to keep. When you select a picture and click the Remove Background tool in the Adjust group on the Format tab, Word creates a marquee selection area in the picture that determines the background, or area to be removed, and the foreground, or area to be kept. Word identifies the background selection with magenta coloring. Using tools on the Background Removal tab, you can mark areas to keep or mark additional areas to remove. Click Keep Changes to remove the background. After making all the necessary formatting to a picture, if you decide to use another image without having to reformat it, you can easily replace the picture using the Change Picture command.

STEP 4 — Insert a Text Box

A **text box** is bordered, sometimes shaded, and the text in the text box is set apart from other text in a document. Depending on the outline selected, a border might not even be visible, so it is not always possible to identify a text box in a document. In most cases, however, you will find a text box as a conspicuously boxed area of text—usually providing additional details or drawing attention to an important point. A text box could contain a pull quote, which is a short text excerpt that is reinforced from a document, or a text box could be used as a banner for a newsletter. Place any text you want to draw attention to or set apart from the body of a document in a text box. Figure 2.42 shows a simple text box that provides business information.

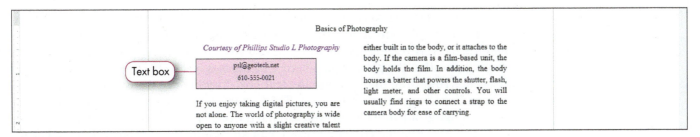

FIGURE 2.42 Text Box

You can select a preformatted text box style or draw your own text box from the gallery in the Text group on the Insert tab (see Figure 2.43). If you select a predefined text box style, the text box will be automatically drawn. If you want to draw your own text box, select Draw Text Box, go to the location where you want the text box to be, and then drag to draw a box. The dimensions of the text box are not that critical, as you can adjust the size using the ribbon. Finally, type your text in text box.

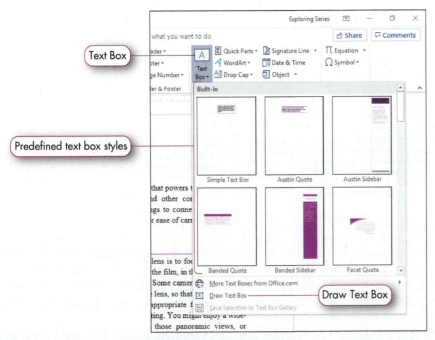

FIGURE 2.43 Insert a Text Box

You can be creative when designing a text box. Options in the Shape Styles group on the Format tab enable you to add fill color, outline, background, and effects to a text box or to select from a gallery of predefined shape styles. The Shape Styles gallery has a selection of styles that uses colors, lines, and special effects to change the shape's appearance. You can preview each style by hovering over a Quick Style in the gallery.

Move, Resize, and Modify a Text Box

Remember that a text box is an object. As such, you can select, move, resize, and modify it, much as you learned you could do with pictures in the preceding sections of this chapter. Layout Options enable you to wrap text around a text box, and alignment guides assist with positioning a text box within existing text.

You can move a text box by dragging it from one area to another. Similar to a picture, you will want to control how the text flows around the text box. When you select or confirm a text wrapping option, text will wrap automatically around the text box as you move it. Position the pointer on a border of the text box so it appears as a small, four-headed arrow. Drag to reposition the text box. As you drag the box, green alignment guides assist in positioning it neatly. The Format tab includes a Position command in the Arrange group that enables you to align the text box in various ways within existing text. You can even indicate the exact height and width of a text box using the Format tab (see Figure 2.44).

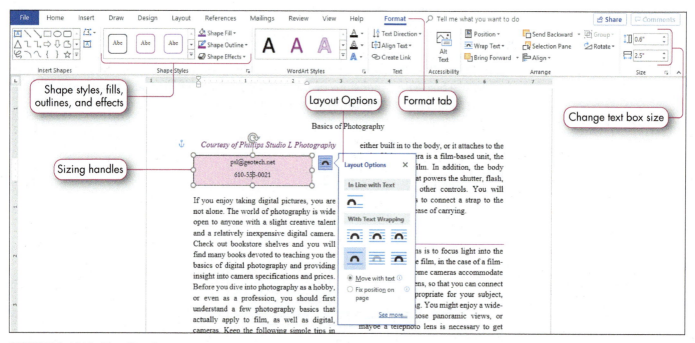

FIGURE 2.44 Modify a Text Box

Like a picture, a text box can be resized using the Size dialog box for precise sizing, or by using the sizing handles. Unlike a picture that can become distorted when using the center sizing handles, the center sizing handles are best used to modify the height or width of a text box. When these are used, the text inside repositions, but does not get distorted.

The text inside the text box can also be formatted. Before formatting text in a text box, select the text to be affected. To do so, drag to select the text to be formatted. Or, if you want to select all text, you can click the dashed border surrounding the text box (when the pointer is a small four-headed arrow). The dashed line should become solid, indicating that all text is selected. Once the text is selected, you may select an alignment option on the Home tab to left-align, right-align, center, or justify text. At that point, any formatting selections you make related to text are applied to all text in the text box.

STEP 5 Insert WordArt

WordArt is a feature that modifies text to include special effects, including colors, shadows, gradients, and 3-D effects (see Figure 2.45). It is a quick way to format text so that it is vibrant and eye-catching. Of course, WordArt is not appropriate for all documents, especially more conservative business correspondence, but it can give life to newsletters, flyers, and other more informal projects, especially when applied to headings and titles. WordArt is well suited for single lines, such as document headings, where the larger print and text design draws attention and adds style to a document title. However, it is not appropriate for body text, because a WordArt object is managed independently of

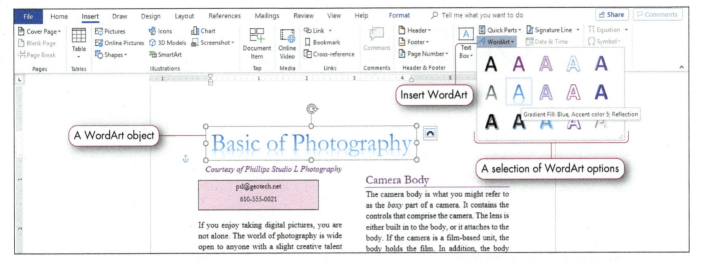

FIGURE 2.45 WordArt

surrounding text and cannot be formatted as a document (with specific margins, headers, footers, etc.). Instead, styles and headings are would be more appropriately used to format body text. In addition, if WordArt were incorporated into body text, the more ornate text design would adversely affect the readability of the document.

You can format existing text as WordArt, or you can insert new WordArt text into a document by selecting WordArt in the Text group on the Insert tab. WordArt is considered an object; as such, the preceding discussion related to positioning pictures and text boxes applies to WordArt as well. Also, Live Layout and alignment guides are available to facilitate ease of positioning, and you can select a text wrapping style with layout options. You may also use the options in the WordArt Styles group to add fills, outline colors, and effects to the WordArt text itself.

To insert new text as WordArt, complete the following steps:

1. Place the insertion point at the point where WordArt will be added.
2. Click the Insert tab.
3. Click WordArt in the Text group.
4. Select a WordArt style.
5. Type text.

Depending on the purpose of a document and its intended audience, objects such as pictures, text boxes, and WordArt can help convey a message and add interest. As you learn to incorporate objects visually within a document so that they appear to flow seamlessly within existing text, you will find it easy to create attractive, informative documents that contain an element of design apart from simple text.

Quick Concepts

9. Describe how you would determine the type of text wrapping to use when positioning a picture in a document. *p. 168*

10. Describe two methods to modify the height and width of a picture. *p. 169*

11. Explain how a text box differs from simple shaded text. *p. 170*

12. Explain why WordArt is most often used to format headings or titles, and not text in the body of a document. *p. 172*

Objects • Word 2019   173

Hands-On Exercises

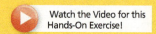

MyLab IT HOE3 Sim Training

Watch the Video for this Hands-On Exercise!

Skills covered: Insert a Picture • Move, Align, and Resize a Picture • Modify a Picture • Insert a Text Box • Move, Resize, and Modify a Text Box • Insert WordArt

3 Objects

After you format the document for easier reading, you want to insert objects into the document to make it more professional looking. You will add interest to the newsletter by including pictures that illustrate points, a text box with business information, and WordArt that livens up the newsletter heading.

STEP 1 INSERT A PICTURE

You will include pictures in the newsletter to represent photographs shot from various angles, as well as holiday graphics. The pictures will be formatted with appropriate picture styles and effects and positioned within existing text. Refer to Figure 2.46 as you complete Step 1.

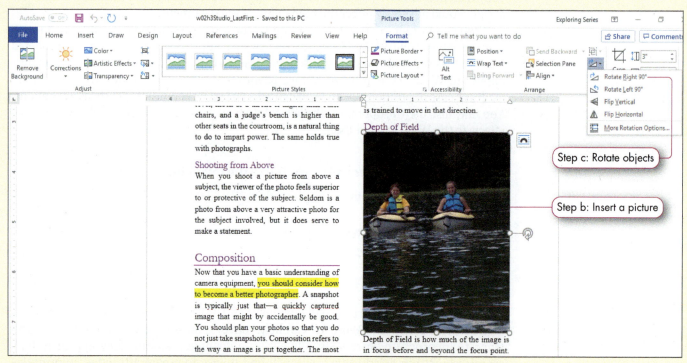

FIGURE 2.46 Insert and Rotate a Picture

a. Open *w02h2Studio_LastFirst* if you closed it at the end of Hands-On Exercise 2, and save it as **w02h3Studio_LastFirst**, changing h2 to h3.

b. Scroll to the second page of the document and click to place the insertion point before the words *Depth of Field is how much of the image*. Click the **Insert tab** and click **Pictures** in the Illustrations group. Navigate to the location of your student data files and double-click *w02h3Kayak.jpg*.

The picture is inserted from your storage.

c. Ensure the picture is selected (surrounded by a border and sizing handles), click **Rotate Objects** in the Arrange group on the Format tab, and then click **Rotate Right 90°**. Click outside the picture to deselect it.

> **TROUBLESHOOTING:** If you do not see Rotate Objects or the Format tab, click the picture to select it, and then click the Format tab.

d. Scroll to the third page and click to place the insertion point before *The most common reason for a blurred image* under the *Blurry Images Due to Focus* heading. Click the **Insert tab**, click **Pictures** in the Illustrations group, and then double-click *w02h3Float.jpg* in your student data files. Rotate the picture to the right. Click outside the picture to deselect it.

> **TROUBLESHOOTING:** The placement of the picture will vary, so it is OK if it is not positioned directly below the *Blurry Images Due to Focus* heading. You will move it later.

e. Scroll to the *Holiday Photography* section and click to place the insertion point before *Now for the fun part*. Click the **Insert tab**. Click **Online Pictures** in the Illustrations group. In the Bing Search box, type **Ski** and press **Enter**. Select the picture shown in Figure 2.48 on the next page (or one that is very similar). Click **Insert**. Click on the border of the text box and delete any additional text boxes that may display when the image is inserted.

The picture is placed within or very near the *Holiday Photography* section. You will reposition it and resize it later.

f. Save the document.

STEP 2 MOVE, ALIGN, AND RESIZE A PICTURE

The pictures you inserted are a bit large, so you will resize them. You will also position them within the column and select an appropriate text wrapping style. Refer to Figure 2.47 and Figure 2.48 as you complete Step 2.

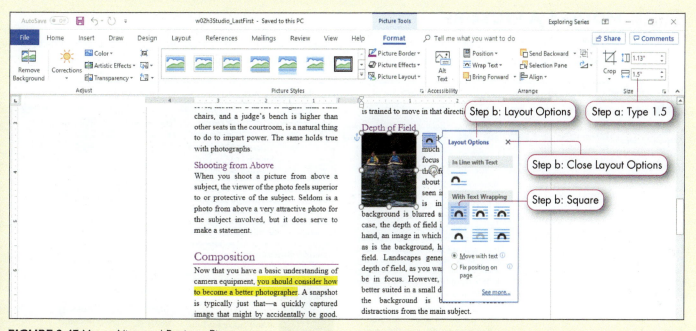

FIGURE 2.47 Move, Align, and Resize a Picture

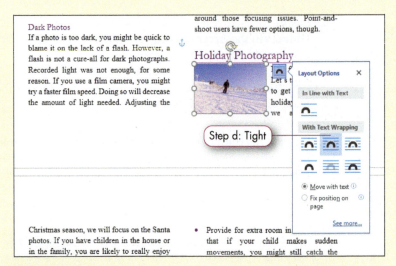

FIGURE 2.48 Align a Picture

a. Scroll up and click to select the picture near the *Depth of Field* section. Click the Format tab. Click in the **Width box** in the Size group on the Format tab and type **1.5**. Press **Enter**.

b. Click **Layout Options** (beside the selected picture) and select **Square** (first selection under *With Text Wrapping*). Close Layout Options. Check the placement of the image with that shown in Figure 2.47 and adjust if necessary.

c. Scroll down and select the second picture, near the *Blurry Images Due to Focus* heading. Change the text wrapping to **Square** and change the width to **1.5**. Close Layout Options.

d. Scroll down and select the ski picture in, or near, the *Holiday Photography* section. Change text wrapping to **Tight**, change the width to **1.5**, close Layout Options, and then drag to position the picture as shown in Figure 2.48. Words may not wrap exactly as shown in Figure 2.48, but they should be approximately as shown.

e. Save the document.

STEP 3 MODIFY A PICTURE

You will apply a picture style and picture effects to the pictures included in the newsletter. You will also crop a picture to remove unnecessary detail. Refer to Figures 2.49 and 2.50 as you complete Step 3.

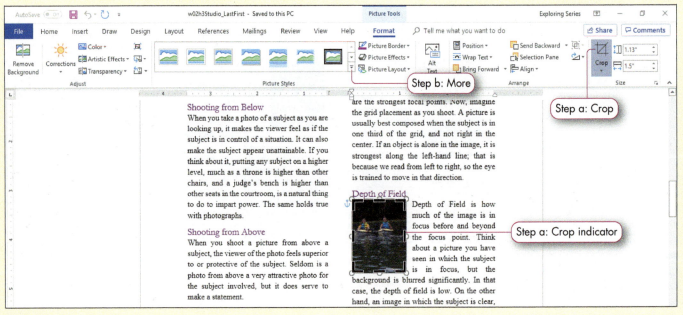

FIGURE 2.49 Crop a Picture

176 CHAPTER 2 • Hands-On Exercise 3

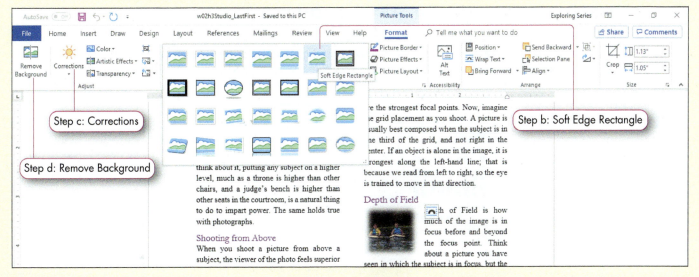

FIGURE 2.50 Select a Picture Style

a. Select the picture in the *Depth of Field* section. Click **Crop** in the Size group on the Format tab. (Be sure to click Crop, not the Crop arrow.)

The crop handles consist of dark thick lines surrounding the selected picture.

TROUBLESHOOTING: If you do not see options related to the picture, make sure the picture is selected and click the Format tab.

b. Drag the crop indicator in the bottom center of the photograph up slightly to remove some of the water, as shown in Figure 2.49. Click **Crop** to toggle the selection off. If necessary, drag to position the picture as shown in Figure 2.50. Do not deselect the picture. Click **More** in the Picture Styles gallery in the Picture Styles group. Select **Soft Edge Rectangle**.

TROUBLESHOOTING: If the picture becomes distorted as you drag, instead of simply shading the water to remove, you are dragging a sizing handle instead of the crop indicator. Only drag when the pointer is a thick black T, not a two-headed arrow. Click Undo and repeat the crop action.

c. Select the picture in the *Blurry Images Due to Focus* section. Click **Corrections** in the Adjust group on the Format tab. Select **Brightness: 0% (Normal), Contrast: +20%** (fourth row, third column under Brightness/Contrast).

You used Word's image editing feature to change brightness and contrast.

d. Select the ski picture. Click **Remove Background** in the Adjust group on the Format tab. Wait a few seconds until the background is shaded in magenta. Click **Keep Changes**. Deselect the picture.

e. Save the document.

STEP 4: INSERT, MOVE, RESIZE, AND MODIFY A TEXT BOX

By placing text in a text box, you can draw attention to information you want your readers to notice. You will insert a text box, including the studio's contact information, near the beginning of the document. You will then resize and modify the text to coordinate with other page elements. Refer to Figure 2.51 as you complete Step 4.

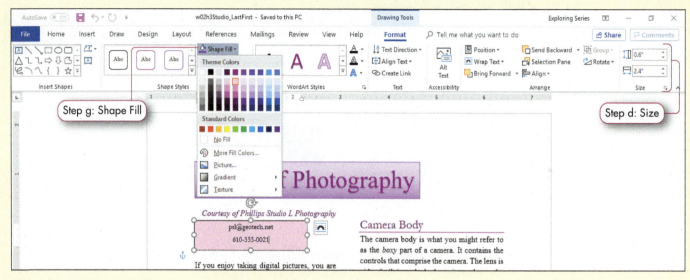

FIGURE 2.51 Insert a Text Box

a. Press **Ctrl+Home**. Ensure nonprinting characters are displayed.

b. Click the **Insert tab** and click **Text Box** in the Text group. Click **Draw Text Box**. Point to the blank paragraph mark below *Courtesy of Phillips Studio L Photography* and drag to draw a small box. The dimensions are not important, as you will resize the text box later.

A small text box is drawn in the document.

c. Click **Layout Options** (beside the text box) and select **Top and Bottom** (second row, first column under Text Wrapping). Close Layout Options.

Text wraps above and below the text box.

d. Click the **Height box** in the Size group on the Format tab and type **0.6** and press **Enter**. Click the **Width box** and type **2.5**. Press **Enter**.

e. Ensure that insertion point is in the text box. Type **psl@geotech.net** and press **Enter**. Type **610-555-0021**. Right-click the underlined email link in the text box and select **Remove Hyperlink**.

f. Click the **dashed line** surrounding the text box to make it solid, so that all text in the text box is selected (although it is not shaded). Click the **Home tab** and click **Center** in the Paragraph group.

All text is centered in the text box.

g. Click the **Format tab**. Click **Shape Fill** in the Shape Styles group. Select **Plum, Accent 1, Lighter 80%** (second row, fifth column).

The text box background is shaded to match the document theme.

h. Click **Use Alignment Guides** in the Arrange Group. Position the pointer near a border of the text box so that the pointer displays as a four-headed arrow. Drag to the left of the column, until the green alignment guide indicates the text box is aligned at that edge. Release the mouse button. The text box should display as shown in Figure 2.51.

i. Save the document.

STEP 5 INSERT WORDART

The newsletter is near completion, but you need to work with the heading—*Basics of Photography*. You will format the heading with WordArt to add some visual appeal. Refer to Figure 2.52 as you complete Step 5.

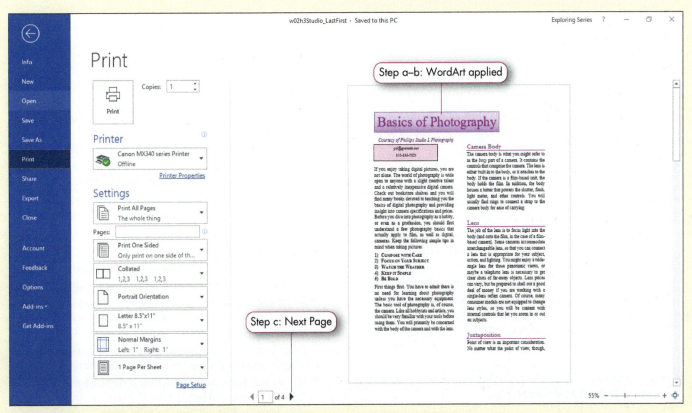

FIGURE 2.52 Insert WordArt

a. Select *Basics of Photography* on the first paragraph of the newsletter, including the following paragraph mark. Be careful not to select the Section Break indicator following the paragraph mark. Click the **Insert tab** and click **WordArt** in the Text group. Select **Fill: Plum, Accent 1 color; Shadow** (first row, second column).

> **TROUBLESHOOTING:** If you do not see a Section Break indicator, click Show/Hide in the Paragraph group on the Home tab to display the nonprinting characters.

The heading is formatted in WordArt in a shade that coordinates with other text formatting in the newsletter.

b. Ensure that the WordArt object is still selected, click **More** in the Shape Styles group on the Format tab, and select **Subtle Effect – Purple Accent 2** (fourth row, third column).

The WordArt object is now formatted with a shading, giving it a special effect. Mac users may use any other similar effect.

c. Click **Layout Options** and click **Top and Bottom**. Close Layout Options.

d. Click outside the WordArt object to deselect it. Click the **File tab** and click **Print**. The first page shows in preview in the right pane (refer to Figure 2.52). Click **Next Page** (at the bottom of the preview page) to move to the next page.

e. Save and close the file. Exit Word. Based on your instructor's directions, submit w02h3Studio_LastFirst.

Chapter Objectives Review

After reading this chapter, you have accomplished the following objectives:

1. **Apply font attributes.**
   - Select font options: Font options include serif or sans serif fonts, and you can change the font type and font size of the body text and headings using the options in the Font group on the Home tab.
   - Change text appearance: Format characters by applying bold, italics, underline, font color, text highlighting, and text effects.

2. **Format a paragraph.**
   - Select paragraph alignment: Paragraph alignment can be applied as left or right aligned, centered, or justified.
   - Select line and paragraph spacing: Line spacing refers to the amount of space between lines within a paragraph, whereas paragraph spacing is the amount of space between paragraphs.
   - Select indents: Options for indenting paragraphs include left indent, right indent, hanging indent, and first line indent.
   - Set tab stops: Use tabs to indent the first line of the paragraph, or to arrange text in columns, including leaders as needed.
   - Apply borders and shading: Borders and shading draw attention to selected paragraphs.
   - Create bulleted and numbered lists: Itemized lists can be set apart from other text with bullets, while sequential lists are formatted with numbers.

3. **Format a document.**
   - Select a document theme: Use a theme to create a color-coordinated document, with page elements based on theme settings.
   - Work with sections: Divide a document into sections, so that each area can be formatted independently of others.
   - Format text into columns: Some documents, such as newsletters, are formatted in two or more columns.

4. **Apply styles.**
   - Select and modify styles: Styles enable you to apply identical formatting to page features, such as headings. When a style is modified, changes apply to all text formatted in that style.
   - Use a style set: Select a style set to quickly format page elements, such as headers and paragraph text.
   - Create a new style from text: Format text and create a style from the text so that formatting characteristics can be easily applied to other text in the document.
   - Use Outline view: Expand and collapse sections, view document structure, and easily rearrange document sections in Outline view.

5. **Insert and format objects.**
   - Insert a picture: Insert pictures from online sources or from a storage device connected to your computer.
   - Insert a screenshot: Capture the whole or a portion of a computer screen and insert it into a document as an object.
   - Move, align, and resize a picture: Reposition objects easily using Live Layout and alignment guides. You can also resize objects and wrap text around objects.
   - Modify a picture: Apply a picture style or effect, adjust the color, contrast, and brightness of a picture, and crop a picture to modify a picture's appearance.
   - Insert a text box: Include text in a bordered area by inserting a text box. You can format a text box with shape styles and effects, and you can align text within a text box.
   - Move, resize, and modify a text box: As an object, a text box can be moved, resized, and modified with options on the Format tab.
   - Insert WordArt: A WordArt object displays text with special effects, such as color, size, gradient, and 3-D appearance.

Key Terms Matching

Match the key terms with their definitions. Write the key term letter by the appropriate numbered definition.

a. Alignment guide
b. Border
c. Bulleted list
d. Column
e. Document theme
f. First line indent
g. Font
h. Hanging indent
i. Line spacing
j. Live Preview
k. Object
l. Paragraph spacing
m. Section break
n. Sizing handle
o. Style
p. Style set
q. Tab stop
r. Text box
s. Three-part indent marker
t. WordArt

1. _____ A feature that modifies text to include special effects, such as color, shadow, gradient, and 3-D appearance. **p. 172**

2. _____ A series of faint dots on the outside border of a selected object; enables the user to adjust the height and width of the object. **p. 169**

3. _____ A list of points that is not sequential. **p. 142**

4. _____ An item, such as a picture or text box, that can be individually selected and manipulated. **p. 164**

5. _____ A unified set of design elements, including font style, color, and special effects, that is applied to an entire document. **p. 149**

6. _____ A typeface or complete set of characters. **p. 130**

7. _____ A named collection of formatting characteristics that can be applied to characters or paragraphs. **p. 152**

8. _____ A mark that indicates the location to indent only the first line in a paragraph. **p. 137**

9. _____ The horizontal or vertical green bar that displays as you move an object, assisting with lining up an object. **p. 169**

10. _____ A combination of title, heading, and paragraph styles that can be used to format selected text. **p. 149**

11. _____ A format that separates document text into side-by-side vertical blocks, often used in newsletters. **p. 152**

12. _____ Lines that display at the top, bottom, left, or right of a paragraph, a page, a table, or an image. **p. 141**

13. _____ The amount of space before or after a paragraph. **p. 136**

14. _____ An Office feature that provides a preview of the results of a selection when you point to it. **p. 131**

15. _____ The vertical space between the lines in a paragraph. **p. 137**

16. _____ An indicator that divides a document into parts, enabling different formatting in each section. **p. 150**

17. _____ A boxed object that can be bordered and shaded, providing space for text. **p. 170**

18. _____ A marker on the horizontal ruler specifying the location where the insertion point stops after Tab is pressed to align text in a document. **p. 139**

19. _____ An icon located at the left side of the ruler that enables you to set a left indent, a hanging indent, or a first line indent. **p. 138**

20. _____ The first line of a paragraph begins at the left margin, but all other lines in the source are indented. **p. 137**

Multiple Choice

1. How does a document theme differ from a style?
   (a) A theme applies an overall design to a document, with no requirement that any text is selected. A style applies formatting characteristics to selected text or to a current paragraph.
   (b) A theme applies color-coordinated design to selected page elements. A style applies formatting to an entire document.
   (c) A theme and a style are actually the same feature.
   (d) A theme applies font characteristics, whereas a style applies paragraph formatting.

2. To identify a series of sequential steps to several levels, you could use:
   (a) tabs.
   (b) a bulleted list.
   (c) a multilevel list.
   (d) a numbered list.

3. The feature that is a collection of formatting characteristics that can be applied to text or paragraphs is:
   (a) WordArt.
   (b) themes.
   (c) style.
   (d) text box.

4. What kind of indent is often used in preparing a bibliography for a research paper?
   (a) First line indent
   (b) Hanging indent
   (c) Right indent
   (d) Left indent

5. To draw attention to such items as contact information or store hours, you could place text in a bordered area called a:
   (a) text box.
   (b) dot leader.
   (c) section.
   (d) tabbed indent.

6. To divide a document into side-by-side vertical blocks so that the text flows down one side and then continues at the top of the other side, you can use a(n):
   (a) column.
   (b) indent.
   (c) section break.
   (d) page break.

7. Which of the following features is best for drawing attention to text with special effects?
   (a) WordArt
   (b) Theme effects
   (c) Text box
   (d) Border

8. Which of the following statement is *true* regarding theme effects?
   (a) It can be applied to headings and body text in a document.
   (b) It enables you to quickly customize the font for the body text and headings in the document.
   (c) It automatically applies a 3-dimensional watermark to a document.
   (d) It gives an object in a document a unique look.

9. Which of the following statement is *true* regarding Outline view?
   (a) The document cannot be edited or formatted.
   (b) It displays only first-level headings.
   (c) It enables you to easily convert the outline to a PowerPoint presentation.
   (d) It does not allow you to move text around.

10. When you crop a picture,
    (a) you can restore the cropped portion later.
    (b) the cropped portion is permanently deleted from the file.
    (c) the file size of the picture is reduced.
    (d) you cannot compress it later.

Practice Exercises

1 Campus Safety

You are the office assistant for the police department at a local university. As a service to students, staff, and the community, the police department publishes a campus safety guide, available both in print and online. With national emphasis on homeland security, and local incidents of theft and robbery, it is obvious that the safety guide should be updated and distributed. You will work with a draft document, formatting it to make it more attractive and ready for print. Refer to Figure 2.53 as you complete this exercise.

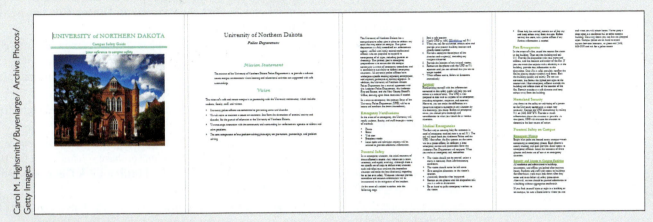

FIGURE 2.53 Format a Document

a. Open *w02p1Campus* and save the document as **w02p1Campus_LastFirst**. Click **Show/Hide** in the Paragraph group to ensure nonprinting characters are displayed.

b. Click the **Design tab**. Click **Themes** in the Document Formatting group and select **Ion Boardroom**. Click **Colors** in the Document Formatting group and select **Green Yellow**. Click **Fonts** in the Document Formatting group and select **Garamond**.

c. Click the **Home tab**. Select the first paragraph in the document and click **Center** in the Paragraph group. Click the **Font Color arrow** in the Font group and select **Green, Accent 3**. Click the **Font Size arrow** and select **26**. Click **Change Case** in the Font group and select **UPPERCASE**. Double-click **OF** in the first paragraph in the document, click **Change Case**, and then select **lowercase**. Select the second paragraph in the document. Center the paragraph, change the font color to **Green, Accent 3**, change the font size to **16**, and then change the case to **Capitalize Each Word**. Do not deselect the text.

d. Click the **Borders arrow** in the Paragraph group and click **Borders and Shading**. Click **Custom** in the Setting section of the Borders and Shading dialog box. Click the **Color arrow** and select **Green, Accent 3**. Scroll through the styles in the Style box and select the seventh style (double line). Click the **Width arrow** and select **1 1/2 pt**. Click **Bottom** in the Preview group and click **OK**.

e. Select the paragraph containing the text *Your reference to campus safety*. Click **Font Color** on the Mini Toolbar to apply the most recent font color selection. Use either the Mini Toolbar or selections on the Home tab to change the font to **Lucida Calligraphy** and center the selection.

f. Click at the end of the currently selected paragraph to position the insertion point immediately after *Your reference to campus safety*. Click the **Insert tab** and click **Pictures** in the Illustrations group. Navigate to the location of your student data files and double-click *w02p1Campus.jpg*.

g. Click **Height** in the Size group on the Format tab and type **5**. Press **Enter**. Click **Corrections** in the Adjust group and select **Brightness: 0% (Normal), Contrast: +20%** under Brightness/Contrast.

h. Click before the words *University of Northern Dakota* immediately below the picture and press **Ctrl+Enter** to insert a manual page break. Scroll up and select the first paragraph on page 1 of the document. Click the **Home tab** and click **Format Painter** in the Clipboard group. Scroll to the second page and select the first paragraph (*University of Northern Dakota*) to copy the formatting. (Note that the Format Painter does not copy the Uppercase format.) Change the font color of the selected line to **Black, Text 1**.

i. Complete the following steps on page 2 to format the text:
   - Select the second paragraph containing the text *Police Department*. Apply **Center**, **Bold**, and **Italic** to the selection. Change the font size to **16 pt**. Click to position the insertion point after the words *Police Department* and press **Enter** twice.
   - Select text in the document beginning with *Mission Statement* and ending with *prevention, partnerships, and problem solving* (on the same page). Click **Line and Paragraph Spacing** in the Paragraph group and select **1.5**. Click the **Paragraph Dialog Box Launcher** and change Spacing After to **6 pt**. Click **OK**.

j. Select the *Mission Statement* heading near the top of page 2 and change the font color to **Green, Accent 3**. Center the selection and change the font size to **16** and the font to **Lucida Calligraphy**. Copy the format of the selection to the *Vision* heading on the same page. Insert a page break after the sentence ending with the words *problem solving* on page 2.

k. Select the paragraph in the *Mission Statement* section, and apply a **0.5" left and right indents** and **full justification**.

l. Select the paragraphs on page 2 in the *Vision* section, beginning with *University police officers are committed to* and ending with *prevention, partnerships, and problem solving*. Click the **Bullets arrow** in the Paragraph group and select the **square filled bullet**. Click **Decrease Indent** in the Paragraph group to move the bullets to the left margin.

m. Scroll to page 3. Click the **Styles Dialog Box Launcher**. Complete the following steps to apply styles to selected text.
   - Click in the paragraph containing *Emergency Notifications*. Click **Heading 1** in the Styles pane. Scroll down and apply the Heading 1 style to the headings *Personal Safety*, *Medical Emergencies*, *Fire Emergencies*, *Homeland Security*, and *Personal Safety on Campus*.
   - Click in the paragraph on page 3 containing the text *Summary*. Click **Heading 2** in the Styles pane. Scroll down and apply Heading 2 style to the headings *Security and Access to Campus Facilities* and *Emergency Phones*.

n. Point to Heading 2 in the Styles pane and click the **Heading 2 arrow**. Click **Modify**. Click **Underline** and click **OK**.

o. Scroll to page 3 and select the five paragraphs in the *Emergency Notifications* section, beginning with *Phone* and ending with *provide additional information*. Apply **square filled bullets** to the selection. Decrease indent to the left margin. Click **New Style** in the Styles pane, type **Bulleted Text** in the Name box, and then click **OK**.

p. Select the seven paragraphs in the *Medical Emergencies* section, beginning with *The victim should not be moved* and ending with *information is needed*. Click **Bulleted Text** in the Styles pane to apply the style to the selection. Close the Styles pane.

q. Select the seven paragraphs in the *Personal Safety* section, beginning with *Seek a safe location* and ending with *follow all directions immediately*. Apply the **numbered list format** (1., 2., 3.) to the selection.

r. Press **Ctrl+Home** to move to the beginning of the document. Spell check the document. The word *of* in the university name is correct in lowercase, so do not correct it.

s. Scroll to page 3 and select all text beginning with *The University of Northern Dakota* and ending at the end of the document. Click the **Layout tab**, click **Columns**, and then select **Two**. Click the **View tab** and click **Multiple Pages** in the Zoom group to view pages of the document. Scroll up or down to check the document for text positioning and any awkward column endings. Click **100%** in the Zoom group.

t. Click **Outline** in the Views group. Click the **Show Level arrow** in the Outline Tools group and click **Level 1**. Click the **plus sign** beside *Personal Safety on Campus* and click **Expand** in the Outline Tools group. Point to the plus sign beside *Emergency Phones* and drag to position the *Emergency Phones* section above *Security and Access to Campus Facilities*. Click **Print Layout** on the status bar.

u. Press **Ctrl+Home** to move to the beginning of the document. Click **Show/Hide** in the Paragraph group to turn off the nonprinting characters feature. Click the **File tab** and click **Print** to preview the document. Click **Next Page** to move through the pages of the document. Click **Back** at the top-left corner of the screen to leave print preview.

v. Compare your work to Figure 2.53. Save and close the file. Based on your instructor's directions, submit w02p1Campus_LastFirst.

2 Drug Abuse

As the director of a local community center, one of your projects is to develop materials on drug addiction, educate teenagers on the dangers of abusing illegal drugs, and warn them about the long-term repercussions of drug dependency. You will also distribute research articles, flyers, and brochures to help convey the message. One such document, a summary of medical facts regarding drug abuse, is near completion. It needs proofreading, formatting, and a few other features that will result in a polished handout for your next presentation. Refer to Figure 2.54 as you complete this exercise.

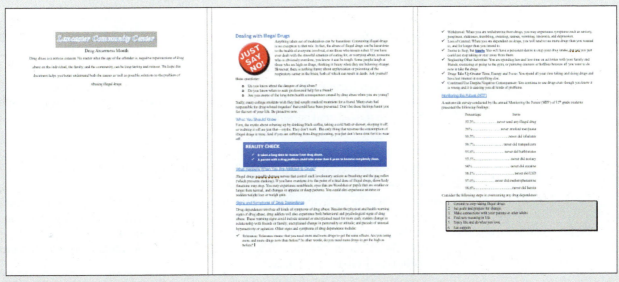

FIGURE 2.54 Finish a Handout

a. Open *w02p2Drug* and save it as **w02p2Drug_LastFirst**.

b. Click the **Home tab** and click **Show/Hide** if nonprinting characters are not displayed. Press **Ctrl+A** to select all document text. Click the **Font arrow** and select **Times New Roman**. Click anywhere to deselect the text. Check the document for spelling and grammatical errors.

c. Press **Ctrl+Home** to move to the beginning of the document. Select the first paragraph in the document, *Lancaster Community Center*. Click the **Insert tab** and select **WordArt** in the Text group. Click **Fill: Blue, Accent color 5; Outline: White, Background color 1; Hard Shadow: Blue, Accent color 5** (third row, third column). Ensure that the WordArt is still selected. Click the **Shape Fill arrow** in the Shape Styles group on the Format tab. Select **White, Background 1, Darker 25%** (fourth row, first column). Click the **Home tab** and change the font size to **24**.

d. Click **Layout Options** and click **Top and Bottom**. Close Layout Options. Point to the WordArt object and drag to visually center it. You should drag when the pointer resembles a four-headed arrow.

e. Select the second paragraph in the document, *Drug Awareness Month*. When you select the text, the WordArt is also selected because it is anchored to the selected paragraph. Center and bold the selected text and change the font size to **14**.

f. Click anywhere in the first paragraph that begins *Drug abuse is a serious concern*. Center the paragraph. Click **Line and Paragraph Spacing** in the Paragraph group and select **2.0**. Click before the paragraph mark ending the paragraph that begins *Drug abuse is a serious concern*. Click the **Layout tab** and click **Breaks**. Click **Next Page** in the Section Breaks group. Press **Delete** to remove the paragraph mark at the top of page 2.

g. Click the **Home tab**. Select the first paragraph on page 2, *Dealing with Illegal Drugs*. Click **Heading 1** in the Styles group. Select *What You Should Know* and click **Heading 2**.

h. Select *What Happens When You Are Addicted to Drugs?* Change the font to **Tahoma**, click **Underline** in the Font group, click the **Font Color arrow**, and then change the font color to **Blue, Accent 1**. Click the **Styles Dialog Box Launcher**. Click **New Style**. Type **Lower Item** in the Name box and click **OK**. Select the heading *Signs and Symptoms of Drug Dependence*. Click **Lower Item** in the Styles pane to apply the newly created style to the selected text. Apply the same format to the heading *Monitoring the Future (MTF)*.

i. Point to Heading 1 in the Styles pane and click the **Heading 1 arrow**. Click **Modify**. Click **Bold** and click **OK**. Scroll up, if necessary, to see that the heading *Dealing with Illegal Drugs* is bold. Close the Styles pane.

j. Select the three paragraphs in the *Dealing with Illegal Drugs* section, beginning with *Do you know about the dangers* and ending with *drug abuse when you are young?* Click the **Bullets arrow** and select the **hollow round bullet**.

k. Select seven paragraphs in the *Signs and Symptoms of Drug Dependence* section, beginning with *Tolerance* and ending with *it is causing you all kinds of problems*. Apply a **check mark bullet** to the selected paragraphs. Click **Decrease Indent** to move the bulleted items to the left margin.

l. Scroll to page 3 and select the last six paragraphs, beginning with *Commit to stop taking illegal drugs* and ending with *Get support*. Click **Numbering** in the Paragraph group to apply default numbers to the selection.

m. Click after the sentence ending with *presented the following findings*: on the same page. Press **Enter**. If the ruler is not displayed above the document area, click the **View tab** and click **Ruler** in the Show group. Ensure that the tab selector, shown just above the vertical ruler, shows a left tab. Click **1″** to set a left tab. Click **3″** to set another left tab. Press **Tab**. Type **Percentage**. Press **Tab**. Type **Items**. Press **Enter**.

n. Drag the 3″ left tab off the ruler to remove it. Click the **tab selector** twice to select a right tab. Click **4″** to set a right tab with the dot leader option.

o. Type the following data, pressing **Tab** at the beginning of each entry and pressing **Enter** at the end of each line except the last line:

53.3%	never used any illegal drug
58%	never smoked marijuana
90.5%	never did inhalants
90.7%	never did tranquilizers
91.8%	never did barbiturates
93.5%	never did ecstasy
94%	never did cocaine
96.1%	never did LSD
97.6%	never did methamphetamine
98.8%	never did heroin

p. Scroll to page 2 and click before the first sentence in the *Dealing with Illegal Drugs* section. Click the **Insert tab** and click **Online Pictures** in the Illustrations group. Type **just say no** in the Bing Search box. Press **Enter**. Double-click the image shown in Figure 2.54 (or select one very similar if it is unavailable). Read the Creative Commons license. Select and delete any additional text boxes that may display when the image is inserted.

q. Change the height of the picture to **1.5** in the Size group on the Format tab. Click **Layout Options** and select **Square**. Close Layout Options.

r. Press **Ctrl+End** to move to the end of the document. Select the six numbered paragraphs. Click the **Home tab** and click the **Borders arrow** in the Paragraph group. Click **Borders and Shading**. Click **Shadow** in the Setting section. Click the **Shading tab**. Click the **Color arrow** in the Fill section and select **White, Background 1, Darker 15%**. Click **OK**.

s. Click after the last sentence in the *What You Should Know* section. Click the **Insert tab** and click **Text Box** in the Text group. Click **Draw Text Box**. Drag to draw a box approximately 1″ high and 6″ wide below the *What You Should Know* section. Adjust the height to **1″** and the width to **6″** exactly in the Size group on the Format tab. Click **Layout Options**. Click **Top and Bottom**. Ensure that the insertion point is in the text box.

t. Click the **Home tab** and click **Bold** in the Font group. Change the font size to **16**. Type **REALITY CHECK** and press **Enter**. Click **Line and Paragraph Spacing** in the Paragraph group and click **1.0**. Click the **Paragraph Dialog Box Launcher**. Change Paragraph Spacing After to **0 pt**. Click **OK**. Change the font size to **10**. Type the following, pressing **Enter** after each line:

It takes a long time to recover from drug abuse.

A person with a drug problem could take more than 5 years to become completely clean.

u. Apply **check mark bullets** to the two sentences you just typed. Click the **Format tab**. Click **More** in the Shape Styles group. Select **Moderate Effect – Blue, Accent 5** (fifth row, sixth column). Point in the text box so that the pointer displays as a four-headed arrow. Drag to position the text box as shown in Figure 2.54. Click **Show/Hide** in the Paragraph group to turn off the nonprinting characters feature.

v. Change the document theme to **Badge** and theme fonts to **Cambria**.

w. Save and close the file. Based on your instructor's directions, submit w02p2Drug_LastFirst.

Mid-Level Exercises

1 Mount Vernon Balloon Festival
MyLab IT Grader

As chair of the Mount Vernon Hot Balloon Festival, you are responsible for promoting the upcoming event. You started a document providing details on the festival. You plan to distribute the document both in print and online. First, you must format the document to make it more attractive and well designed. You will use styles, bullets, and line and paragraph spacing to coordinate various parts of the document. In addition, you will add interest by including objects, such as pictures and WordArt.

a. Open *w02m1Festival* and save it as **w02m1Festival_LastFirst**.

b. Change the document theme to **Organic**. Select the first paragraph in the document, *Mount Vernon Hot Air Balloon Festival*. Insert WordArt, selecting **Fill: Black, Text color 1; Outline: White, Background color 1; Hard Shadow: Orange, Accent color 5** (third row, second column). Change the font size of the WordArt object to **24**.

c. Wrap text around the WordArt object as **Top and Bottom**. Format the WordArt object with Shape Style **Subtle Effect – Teal, Accent 2** (fourth row, third column). Visually center the WordArt object on the first paragraph of the document.

d. Select the second paragraph in the document, *See the Canyon From The Top!* Center and bold the text and apply a font color of **Teal, Accent 2**.

e. Select the remaining text on page 1, beginning with *May 28-29, 2022* and ending with *on the festival grounds*. Format the selected text into two columns with a line in between and equal column width. Change the font of the columned text on page 1 to **Century Schoolbook**. Insert a page break (not a section break) on page 3 after the sentence ending with *inflate balloons on the festival grounds*.

f. Check spelling and grammar—the word *Ballumination* is not misspelled (for the purposes of this document). Also, ignore *From* and *The* in the second paragraph on page 1.

g. Click in the third paragraph on page 1—*May 28-29, 2022*—and right align it. Select all columned text, including the line containing festival dates, and select a line spacing of **1.5** and paragraph spacing after of **6 pt**. Insert a column break before the paragraph beginning with *And don't forget the dogs!*

h. Click to place the insertion point before the paragraph beginning *As for the kids*. Insert an online picture from Bing Search relating to hot air balloons. Note: Alternatively, you can search for an image in a Web browser, and then download and insert a relevant image from the results. Select and delete any additional text boxes from the online picture. Size the picture with a width of **1"**. Select **Square text wrapping** and a picture style of **Reflected Bevel, White**. Position the picture so that it is on the left side of the paragraph beginning with *As for the kids*, but still in the right column.

i. Select the picture and recolor it with **Teal, Accent color 2 Light**. Choose the **Paint Brush Artistic effect**.

j. Scroll to page 3 and select the heading, *When is the best time to see balloons?* Bold the selection and change the font color to **Teal, Accent 2**. Do not deselect the heading. Open the Styles pane and create a new style named **Questions**. Apply the **Questions style** to other questions (headings) on page 3.

k. Scroll to page 4 and apply **solid round bullets** to the first nine paragraphs on the page. Decrease the indent so the bullets begin at the left margin. With the bulleted items selected, click the **Bullets arrow** and click **Define New Bullet**. Click **Font** and change the font color to **Teal, Accent 2**. Click **OK**. Click **OK** again.

l. Insert a page break (not a section break) before the heading *How can I plan for the best experience?* on page 3.

m. Select the schedule of items under the heading *Saturday (5/28/2022)*, beginning with *6:00 AM* and ending with *Balloon Glow*. Set a left tab at **1"** and another left tab with a dot leader at **3"**. Press **Tab** to move selected paragraphs to the left tab, and then move the activities to the 3" tab stop. Select the schedule of items under *Sunday (5/29/2022)*, set a left tab at **1"** and another left tab with a dot leader at **3"**. Press **Tab** to move selected paragraphs to the left tab and move the activities to the 3" tab stop.

n. Save and close the file. Based on your instructor's directions, submit w02m1Festival_LastFirst.

2 Lockwood Pediatric Dentistry

MyLab IT Grader

CREATIVE CASE

You are the office manager for Dr. Lockwood, a general dentist for children, who periodically conducts informational sessions for his young patients. You have written a letter to children in the neighborhood reminding them about the upcoming monthly session, but you want to make the letter more professional looking. You decide to use paragraph formatting such as alignment, paragraph spacing, borders and shading, and bullets that describe some of the fun activities of the day. You also want to add Dr. Lockwood's email address and an appropriate image to the letter.

a. Open the document *w02m2Dentist* and save it as **w02m2Dentist_LastFirst**.

b. Change the capitalization of the recipient *ms. nancy lancaster* and her address so that each word is capitalized and the state abbreviation displays in uppercase. Also capitalize her first name in the salutation. Change Dr. Lockwood's name to your full name in the signature block. Type your email address (or a fictitious email address) on the next line below your name.

c. Show nonprinting characters, if they are not already displayed. Apply **Justify alignment** to body paragraphs beginning with *On behalf* and ending with *September 11*.

d. Select the paragraph mark under the first body paragraph and create a bulleted list, selecting a bullet of your choice. Type the following items in the bulleted list. Do not press Enter after the last item in the list.

   Finding hidden toothbrushes in the dental office
   Participating in the dental crossword puzzle challenge
   Writing a convincing letter to the tooth fairy
   Digging through the dental treasure chest

e. Select text from the salutation *Dear Nancy:* through the last paragraph that ends with *seeing you on September 11*. Set **12 pt Spacing After paragraph**. Remove the paragraph mark just after the *Dear Nancy* paragraph.

f. Select *Dr. Lockwood Pediatric Dentistry Office* in the first paragraph and apply **small caps**.

g. Select the italicized lines of text that give date, time, and location of the meeting. Remove the italics, do not deselect the text, and then complete the following:

   • Increase left and right indents to **1.25** and set **0 pt Spacing After paragraph**.
   • Apply a **double-line box border** with the color **Purple, Accent 4**, and a line width of **3/4 pt**. Shade selected text with the **Purple, Accent 4, Lighter 40% shading color**.
   • Delete the extra tab formatting marks to the left of the lines containing *September 4, 2021*; *4:00 p.m.*; and *Dr. Lockwood Pediatric Dentistry Office* to align them with other text in the bordered area.

h. Remove the paragraph mark before the paragraph that begins with *Please call our office*.

i. Click the paragraph containing the text *Funville, VA 23000* and set **6 pt Spacing After** the paragraph. Click the paragraph containing *Sincerely* and set **6 pt Spacing Before** the paragraph. Add **6 pt Spacing Before** the paragraph beginning with the text *Dr. Lockwood is pleased to let you know*.

j. Select the entire document and change the font to **12 pt Bookman Old Style**.

k. Move to the beginning of the document. Search online for a picture related to **tooth**. Insert the picture, and select and delete any additional text boxes from the online picture.

l. Apply a **Square text wrap** and position the picture in the top-right corner of the document, just below the header area. Resize the graphic to **1.1"** high. Apply the **Beveled Oval, Black Picture Style** (second row, third column) and choose the **Chalk Sketch Artistic Effect**.

m. Move to the end of the document. Insert a **Next Page section break**. Change the orientation to **Landscape**. Change Paragraph Spacing After to **6 pt**. Change the font size to **14**.

n. Move to Section 2 and center the first paragraph. Type **Wellington Water Park & Slide Fun Day!** Press **Enter** and type **September 11, 2021**. Press **Enter** and change the alignment to **Left**. Change the font size to **12**.

o. Set a left tab at **2″** and a right tab at **7″**. Type the following text, with the first column at the 2″ tab and the next column at the 7″ tab. Do not press Enter after typing the last line.

Check-in	9:00
Wave pool	9:30-11:00
Lunch at the pavilion	11:00-12:00
Bungee	12:00-2:00
Water slide	2:00-3:00
Parent pickup at the gate	3:00-3:30

p. Select **Wellington Water Park & Slide Fun Day!** on page 2 and insert WordArt with the style **Gradient Fill: Purple, Accent color 4; Outline: Purple, Accent 4** (second row, third column). Wrap text around the WordArt object at **Top and Bottom**, change the font size of the WordArt object to **24**, and drag to center the object horizontally on the first paragraph.

q. Select the tabbed text, beginning with *Check-in* and ending with *3:00-3:30*. Modify the 7″ right tab to include a dot leader.

r. Check spelling and grammar, correcting any errors and ignoring those that are not errors. Turn off the nonprinting characters feature.

s. Save and close the file. Based on your instructor's directions, submit w02m2Dentist_LastFirst.

Running Case

New Castle County Technical Services

New Castle County Technical Services (NCCTS) provides technical services to clients in the greater New Castle County, Delaware area. Founded in 2011, the company is rapidly expanding to include technical security systems, network infrastructure cabling, and basic troubleshooting services. With that growth comes the need to promote the company and to provide clear written communication to employees and clients. Microsoft Word is used exclusively in the development and distribution of documents, including an "About New Castle" summary that will be available both in print and online. You made a few changes to the document and you are now ready to make this into a professional-looking business document in this exercise.

a. Open *w02r1NewCastle* and save it as **w02r1NewCastle_LastFirst**.

b. Change the document theme to **Facet**, theme colors to **Grayscale**, and theme fonts to **Office**. Show nonprinting characters.

c. Select the first paragraph on page 3 of the document, *About New Castle, Inc.* Insert WordArt, selecting **Fill: Gray, Accent color 3; Sharp Bevel** (second row, fifth column). Ensure that the font size of the WordArt object is **36**.

d. Wrap text around the WordArt object as **Top and Bottom**. Format the WordArt object with Shape Style **Subtle Effect – Light Gray, Accent 2** (fourth row, third column). Visually center the WordArt object on the first paragraph of the document.

e. Place the insertion point in front of the *On Staff Personnel Experience and Certifications* heading on page 4 and insert a page break. Select all the bullets in this section, beginning with *Electrical, Mechanical* and ending with *CompTIA Security+, A+, Server+, Network+*, and format the selected text into two columns with a line in between. Change the font of the columned text to **Century Schoolbook**.

f. Click to place the insertion point before the *Experience and Certifications* heading on page 4. Insert the *w02r1Digital* file from your student data folder. Size the picture with a height of **2"**. Select **Top and Bottom text wrapping** and a picture style of **Reflected Rounded Rectangle**. Position the picture so that it is right below the *Experience and Certifications* heading.

g. Select the picture and recolor it to coordinate with the gray theme of the document. Choose the **Cement Artistic effect**. Delete the blank page if needed.

h. Scroll to page 4, select the 14 bullets right below the *On Staff Personnel Experience and Certifications* heading, and then change the bullets to a **diamond shape**. With the bulleted items selected, click the **Bullets arrow** and click **Define New Bullet**. Change the font color to **Light Gray, Accent 1 Darker 50%**. Open the Styles pane and create a new style named **GrayDiamond**.

i. Select the three sub-items in the last bullet and apply the **square bullet** to them.

j. Scroll to the last page, and select and remove the bullets from the list of 6 companies in the *A Few of Our Customers* section. Delete all the tab stops between company information and time frame information. Set a left tab at **1"** and a right tab with a dot leader at **5"**. Press **Tab** once to move selected paragraphs to the left tab and move the time frame information of each clients to the 5" tab stop.

k. Save and close the file. Based on your instructor's directions, submit w02r1NewCastle_LastFirst.

Disaster Recovery

Fundraising Letter

Each year, you update a letter to several community partners soliciting support for an auction. The auction raises funds for your organization, and your letter should impress your supporters. Open *w02d1Auction* and notice how unprofessional and unorganized the document looks so far. You must make changes immediately to improve the appearance. Consider replacing much of the formatting that is in place now and instead use columns for auction items, apply bullets to draw attention to the list of forms, page borders, and pictures or images—and that is just for starters! Save your work as **w02d1Auction_LastFirst** and close the file. Based on your instructor's directions, submit w02d1Auction_LastFirst.

Capstone Exercise

MyLab IT Grader

Sam's Gym

You are the newly hired membership director of Sam's Gym and one of your responsibilities is to put together a membership package providing essential information to the new members. You quickly collected information from various sources and wrote a draft about the gym and its services. Now you are ready to format the draft to enhance readability and highlight important information. You will use skills from this chapter to format multiple levels of headings, arrange and space text, and insert graphics.

Applying Styles

This document is ready for enhancements, and the Styles feature is a good tool that enables you to add them quickly and easily.

1. Open *w02c1SamGym* and save it as **w02c1SamGym_LastFirst**.
2. Change the document theme to **Integral**, theme colors to **Median**, and theme fonts to **Cambria**.
3. Press **Ctrl+Home**. Create a paragraph style named **Title_Page_1** with these formats: **22 pt** font size and **Ice Blue, Accent 1, Darker 25%** font color (fifth row, fifth column). Ensure that this style is applied to the first paragraph of the document, *Sam's Gym* (including the colon).
4. Select the second paragraph, *Membership Information*, change the font size to **16**, and then apply a font color of **Ice Blue, Accent 1, Darker 25%**.
5. Place the insertion point after the colon in the line *Updated by:* and type your first and last names. Change the capitalization for your name to **Small caps**.
6. Select the remainder of the text in the document, starting with *Introduction* and ending with *MEMBERSHIP FEES*. Justify the alignment of selected text and change line spacing to **1.15**. Place the insertion point on the left side of the *Introduction* paragraph and insert a page break (not a section break).
7. Apply **Heading 1 style** to *Introduction* and *Facility Description* on page 2, *Activities* on page 3, and *Membership Fees* on page 4. Apply **Heading 2 style** to paragraph headings, including *Operational Hours*, *Holiday Hours*, *Childcare Hours*, *Group Exercise Class Description*, and *Individual Training Packages*.
8. Modify the Heading 2 style to use the **Dark Red font color**.

Formatting the Paragraphs

Next, you will apply paragraph formatting to the document. These format options will further increase the readability and attractiveness of your document.

9. Select the second body paragraph in the *Mission Statement* section, which begins with *Mission Statement* and ends with *individual training programs*, and apply these formats: **1"** left and **right indents**, **6 pt** spacing after the paragraph, **boxed double-line**, **3/4 pt** border using the color **Dark Red**, and the shading color **Ice Blue, Accent 1, Lighter 80%**. Delete the blank paragraph above the *Facility Description* heading.
10. Select the nine holidays listed in the *Holiday Hours* section and display them in two columns with a line between the columns.
11. Apply a bulleted list format to the 6 paragraphs in the *Group Exercise Class Description* section on page 3 starting with *Gentle Strength* and ending with *low impact Zumba moves*. Use the symbol of a **diamond**.
12. Apply a **bulleted list format** for the 10-item list in the second paragraph of the *Group Exercise Class Description* section on page 3 starting with *Barre* and ending with *music while burning calories*. Use the symbol of a **solid round circle**.
13. Apply the **numbered list format (1., 2., 3.)** to the four types of packages in the *Individual Training Packages* section.
14. Apply a **1" left tab** and a **4" right tab** with a dot leader to the three schedule items in the *Childcare Hours* section on page 3.

Inserting Graphics

To put the finishing touches on your document, you will add graphics that enhance the explanations given in some paragraphs.

15. Insert the picture file *w02c1Gym.jpg* at the beginning of the paragraph that contains *Welcome to Sam's Gym* in the *Introduction* section. Change the height of the picture to **2"**. Change text wrapping to **Top and Bottom**, and apply the **Center Shadow Rectangle Picture Style** and the **Film Grain Artistic Effect**. Position the picture so that it appears below the *Introduction* heading.
16. Insert the picture file *w02c1Swimming.jpg* at the blank paragraph below the paragraph beginning with *The gym is founded by Sam* in the *Facility Description* section. Change the height of the picture to **2.1"** and text wrapping to **Top and Bottom**. Apply the **Simple Frame, White Picture Style** (first row, first column) to the graphic. Position the picture so that it displays below the *Facility Description* paragraph and ensure that it stays at the bottom of page 2.
17. Insert an online picture from Bing Search using the search word **yoga** at the beginning of the *Group Exercise Class Description* heading. Delete additional text boxes from the online picture. Change the height of the picture to **2.5"** and text wrapping to **Top and Bottom**. Apply the **Reflected Bevel, White Picture Style**. Position the picture so that it is below the *Group Exercise Class Description* heading.

18. Check spelling and grammar, correcting any errors and ignoring those that are not errors, and review the entire document.
19. Display the document in Outline view. Collapse all paragraphs so only lines formatted as Heading 1 or Heading 2 display. Move the *Membership Fees* section to above the *Activities* section and delete the soft return above the *Operational Hours* heading. Close Outline view.
20. Save and close the file. Based on your instructor's directions, submit w02c1SamGym_LastFirst.

Word
Document Productivity

LEARNING OUTCOMES You will demonstrate how tables are used to organize and present information. You will apply mail merge to create personalized letters.

OBJECTIVES & SKILLS: After you read this chapter, you will be able to:

Tables

OBJECTIVE 1: INSERT A TABLE — 196
Create or Draw a Table, Insert and Delete Rows and Columns, Merge and Split Cells, Change Row Height and Column Width

OBJECTIVE 2: FORMAT A TABLE — 200
Apply and Modify Table Styles, Adjust Table Position and Alignment, Format Table Text

HANDS-ON EXERCISE 1 — 204

Advanced Table Features

OBJECTIVE 3: MANAGE TABLE DATA — 210
Calculate Using Table Formulas and Functions, Use a Formula, Use a Function, Sort Data in a Table, Include a Recurring Table Header

OBJECTIVE 4: ENHANCE TABLE DATA — 214
Include Borders and Shading, Convert Text to a Table and Convert a Table to Text, Include a Table Caption

HANDS-ON EXERCISE 2 — 219

Mail Merge

OBJECTIVE 5: CREATE A MAIL MERGE DOCUMENT — 226
Select or Create a Recipient List, Use an Excel Worksheet as a Data Source, Edit a Data Source

OBJECTIVE 6: COMPLETE A MAIL MERGE — 230
Insert Merge Fields, Complete a Merge

HANDS-ON EXERCISE 3 — 232

CASE STUDY | Traylor University Economic Impact Study

As director of marketing and research for Traylor University, a mid-sized university in northwest Nebraska, you have been involved with an economic impact study during the past year. The study is designed to measure as closely as possible the contribution of the university to the local and state economy. An evaluation of data led university researchers to conclude that Traylor University serves as a critical economic driver in the local community and, to a lesser extent, the state of Nebraska. It is your job to summarize those findings and see that they are accurately reflected in the final report.

Your assistant has prepared a draft of an executive summary that you will present to the board of trustees, outlining the major findings and conclusions. The best way to present some of the data analysis will be through tables, which your assistant is not very familiar with, so you will take responsibility for that phase of the summary preparation. You will send an executive summary, along with a cover letter, to community and university leaders. You will use Word's mail merge feature to prepare personalized letters.

Working with Tables and Mail Merge

CHAPTER 3

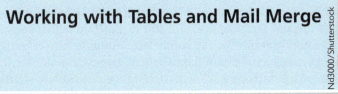

FIGURE 3.1 Traylor University Documents

CASE STUDY | Traylor University Economic Impact Study

Starting Files	Files to be Submitted
w03h1Traylor w03h2KeyFindings w03h2Text w03h3Letter w03h3Trustees.xlsx	w03h2Traylor_LastFirst w03h3Merged_LastFirst

MyLab IT Grader An alternate version of this project is available as a MyLab IT Grader Assessment

Document Productivity • Word 2019   195

Tables

A *table* is a grid of columns and rows that organizes data. As shown in Figure 3.2, a table is typically configured with headings in the first row and related data in the following rows. The intersection of each column and row is a *cell*, in which you can type data. A table is an excellent format in which to summarize numeric data because you can easily align numbers and even include formulas to sum or average numbers in a column or row. Text can be included in a table as well. Although you can use tabs to align text in columns in a Word document, you might find it quicker to create a table than to set tabs, and you have more control over format and design when using a table.

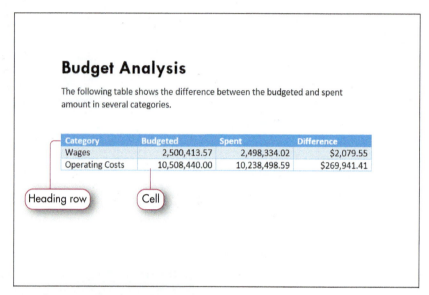

FIGURE 3.2 A Word Table

Word's Table feature is a comprehensive but easy-to-use tool, enabling you to insert a table, add and remove rows and columns, format table elements, include formulas to summarize numbers in a table, and customize borders and shading. You can always change a table, or format it differently, even after it is developed.

In this section, you will learn to insert a table. After positioning the table within a document, you will explore inserting and deleting columns and rows, merging and splitting cells, and adjusting row height and column width. Using table styles, you will modify the appearance of a table, and you will adjust table position and alignment.

Inserting a Table

Inserting a table in a document is an easy task. You can either create a table with uniformly spaced rows and columns, or you can draw a table with the pointer, creating rows and columns of varying heights and widths. Regardless of how a table is created, you can always change table settings so that rows and columns better fit the data included in the table.

When you create a table, you specify the number of columns and rows that should be included. For example, the table shown in Figure 3.2 is a 4×3 table, which means it contains four columns and three rows.

> **TIP: INSERTING AN EXCEL SPREADSHEET**
> If you are familiar with Microsoft Excel, you can insert an Excel spreadsheet into a document and format it as a Word table. The advantage is that when you double-click a cell in the table, it reverts to an Excel spreadsheet, so you can use Excel commands and functionality to modify the table and create formulas. To insert an Excel spreadsheet, click the Insert tab, click Table, and then click Excel Spreadsheet. Enter data in the Excel spreadsheet and click outside the spreadsheet to view it as a Word table. Double-click any cell to return to Excel.

STEP 1 Create or Draw a Table

A table is an object; as such, it can be selected and manipulated independently of surrounding text. You can insert a table in a few ways, beginning by clicking the Insert tab and clicking Table. At that point, you can select from three different methods of creating tables:

- Drag to select the number of columns or rows to include in the table, as shown in Figure 3.3. Click in the bottom-right cell of the selection.
- Click Insert Table to display the Insert Table dialog box, where you can indicate the number of rows and columns you want to include. Click OK.
- Click Quick Tables to insert a predesigned table, including such items as calendars, tabular lists, and matrices.

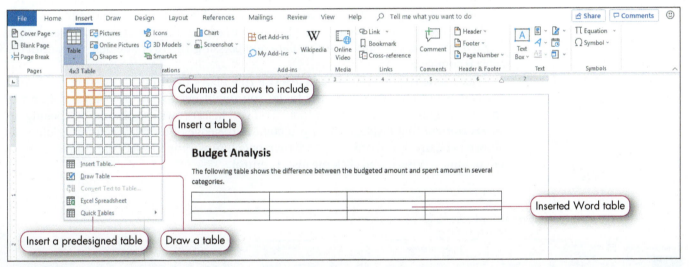

FIGURE 3.3 Inserting a Table

Instead of inserting a table by indicating the number of columns or rows to include, as described in the previous set of steps, you can draw a table. You might choose to draw a table if you know that rows and/or columns should have varying heights or widths. It is sometimes easier to draw rows and columns of varying dimensions when a table is created rather than to modify the dimensions later, as would be necessary if you use the Insert Table feature to create evenly distributed columns and rows.

To draw a table, complete the following steps:

1. Click the Insert tab and click Table in the Tables group.
2. Click Draw Table (refer to Figure 3.3). As you move the pointer over the document, it resembles a pencil.
3. Drag a rectangle and then draw horizontal and vertical lines to create rows and columns within the rectangular table space.
4. Press Esc when the table is complete.

After the table structure is created, you can enter characters, numbers, or graphics in cells, moving from one cell to another when you press Tab or a directional arrow key. You can also click a cell to move to it. As you type text in a cell, it is automatically left-aligned, although you can adjust alignment with options on the Table Tools Layout tab or on the Home tab. If typed text requires more space than is available, the text will wrap and the row height will adjust when it reaches the right edge of the cell. To force text to a new line in a cell (before reaching the right cell border), press Enter. You can instead insert a soft return by pressing Shift+Enter, which forces text to a new line in a cell, but without any additional paragraph spacing.

Insert and Delete Rows and Columns

If a table structure needs to be modified, you can insert or delete columns and rows. For example, suppose you have inserted a table and typed text in cells. As you enter data into a table and complete the last row, you find that an additional row is required. Press Tab to begin a new row. Continue entering data and pressing Tab to create new rows until the table is complete.

Occasionally, you will want to insert a row above or below an existing row, when the row is not the last row in the table. You might even want to insert a column to the left or right of a column in a table. You can insert rows or columns by clicking an *insert control* that displays when you point to the edge of a row or column gridline, as shown in Figure 3.4. To insert several rows or columns, drag to select the number of rows or columns to insert, and click the insert control.

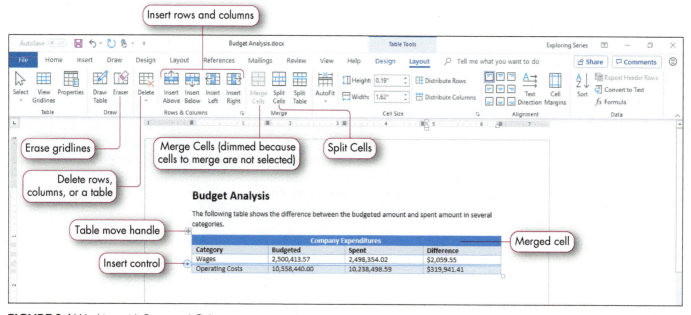

FIGURE 3.4 Working with Rows and Columns

Although it is convenient to use the insert control to insert rows and columns, the Table Tools Layout tab includes more comprehensive options that enable you to insert both columns and rows. Select from options in the Rows & Columns group (refer to Figure 3.4) to insert rows or columns. You can also delete rows or columns.

When you delete a table, you remove the entire table, including all table contents. Although you can select contents and delete them, the table structure remains as an empty set of rows and columns. The key to deleting a table is to first select the table by clicking the table move handle in the top left corner of the table (refer to Figure 3.4). At that point, you can complete any of the following options:

- Right-click the selected table and select Delete Table from the shortcut menu.
- Click Delete in the Rows & Columns group on the Table Tools Layout tab and select Delete Table.
- Press Backspace.

STEP 2 Merge and Split Cells

The first row of the table shown in Figure 3.4 is a merged cell. When several cells are combined into one, the new cell is considered a merged cell. If you want to place a title across the top of a table or center a label over columns or rows of data, you can merge cells. After selecting cells to merge, use Merge Cells on the Table Tools Layout tab to complete the merge. Once cells are merged, you can align data in the merged cells and change the font size to create a table title. You can also erase one or more gridlines within the table. The Eraser tool on the Table Tools Layout tab enables you to remove gridlines (refer to Figure 3.4). Click the Eraser tool and click any table gridline to erase it. Press Esc or click the Eraser tool again to toggle off the eraser.

Conversely, you might want to split a single cell into multiple cells. You can split a selected row or column to provide additional detail in separate cells. Splitting cells is an option on the Table Tools Layout tab (refer to Figure 3.4).

Change Row Height and Column Width

An inserted table is a grid of evenly spaced columns and rows. As mentioned earlier, text automatically wraps within a cell and the row height adjusts to accommodate the entry. Row height is the vertical distance from the top to the bottom of a row, whereas column width is the horizontal space from the left to the right edge of a column. You can manually adjust row height or column width to modify the appearance of a table, perhaps making it more readable or more attractive. Increasing row height can better fit a header that has been enlarged for emphasis. You can increase column width to display a wide area of text, such as a first and last name, to prevent wrapping of text in a cell.

A simple, but not very precise way to change row height or column width is to position the pointer on a border so that it displays as ⊹, which is a line with double pointed arrows, and drag to increase or reduce height or width. For more precision, you can use ribbon commands to adjust row height or column width. After selecting a row or column to be adjusted, change the height or width in the Cell Size group on the Table Tools Layout tab. Alternatively, you can right-click the selected row or column and select Table Properties on the shortcut menu. You can then work with selections from the Column tab or Row tab in the dialog box, as shown in Figure 3.5.

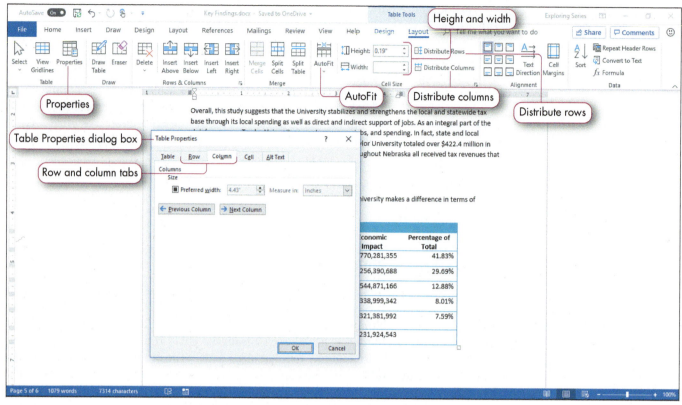

FIGURE 3.5 Changing Row Height and Column Width

You can evenly distribute selected columns and rows to ensure that they are the same height and/or width. Select the columns and rows and click Distribute Rows (or Distribute Columns) in the Cell Size group on the Table Tools Layout tab (refer to Figure 3.5). Distributing rows and columns ensures uniformity within a table.

Instead of adjusting individual columns and rows, you can format a table with column and row dimensions that accommodate all cell entries. The feature, called AutoFit, automatically adjusts rows and columns. After clicking in any cell, select AutoFit on the Table Tools Layout tab (refer to Figure 3.5) and choose to AutoFit Contents.

Formatting a Table

After a table is inserted in a document, you can enhance its appearance by applying coordinated colors, borders, shading, and other design elements. Just as you format other document text by boldfacing, italicizing, or otherwise modifying it, you can format text within a table. You can also align text within cells by selecting an alignment from the Alignment group on the Table Tools Layout tab. Lists or series within cells can be bulleted or numbered, and you can indent table text. A table can be positioned and moved to any location on a page.

STEP 3 Apply and Modify Table Styles

Word provides several predesigned *table styles* that contain borders, shading, font sizes, and other attributes that enhance the readability of a document. Use a table style when you want to create a color-coordinated, professional document or when you do not want to design your own custom borders and shading.

> **TIP: USING TABLE STYLES**
> When you apply a table style or manually modify table shading and color selections, the color choices are associated with the theme in use. Therefore, if you change the document theme, the color selections applied through a table style or manual selections are likely to also change.

As shown in Figure 3.6, the Table Styles gallery provides styles for Plain, List, and Grid tables, although the size of each gallery prohibits all three groups from displaying at once. Select a style from the Table Styles group on the Table Tools Design tab. In Live Preview, the result of a style selection will show as you point to a style in the gallery.

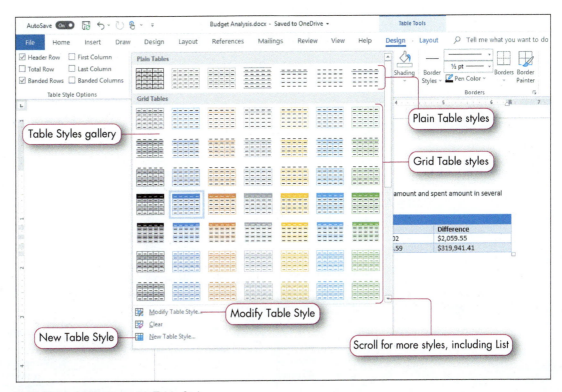

FIGURE 3.6 Working with Table Styles

After choosing a table style, you can modify it, as shown in Figure 3.6. As you modify a table style, you can apply changes to the entire table or to elements such as the header row. In that way, you can adjust a style so that it better suits your purposes. If you have modified a table style and want to make the style available for use in other documents, select New Table Style at the bottom of the Table Styles gallery. Otherwise, choose to save the changes for use only in the current document.

Adjust Table Position and Alignment

Table alignment refers to the horizontal position of a table between the left and right document margins. When you insert a table, it aligns at the left margin, although you can change the alignment, choosing to center the table or align it at the right margin. Right-click any cell and choose Table Properties (or select Properties from the Table Tools Layout tab) to display the Table Properties dialog box shown in Figure 3.7. You can also select alignment options on the ribbon.

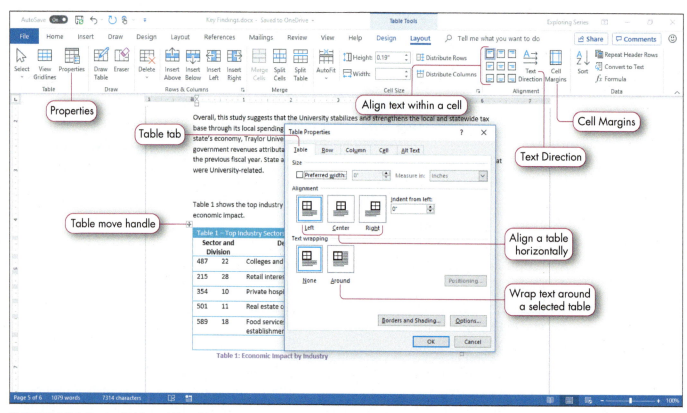

FIGURE 3.7 Adjusting Table and Text Alignment

Move a table to any location within the document when you drag the table move handle. As you move the table, a dashed border displays, indicating the position of the table. Release the mouse button to position the table.

Text within cells can be aligned using alignment options on the Table Tools Layout tab. You can align cell contents both vertically and horizontally within the current cell, as indicated in Figure 3.7. Especially when working with a small table that does not require much document space, you might find it useful to wrap text around the table so that the table is better incorporated visually into the document, much as you would do when wrapping text around a picture or object in a document. Figure 3.7 illustrates the use of text wrapping with a table. Text will wrap on the right side of a left-aligned table, on both sides of a centered table, and on the left side of a right-aligned table. If you select None in the Text Wrapping section, text is prevented from wrapping, ensuring that text displays only above and below a table.

Format Table Text

Text within a cell can be formatted just as any other text in a document. Select text to format and apply one or more font attributes such as font type, font size, underline, boldface, or italics.

> **TIP: SELECTING TEXT IN A TABLE**
> To select a cell's contents, you can drag over the text or click just inside the left edge of a cell.

By default, text within a cell is oriented horizontally so that it reads from left to right. On occasion, you might want to change that direction. Lengthy column headings can be oriented vertically, so that they require less space. Or perhaps a table includes a row of cells repeating a telephone number, with each cell designed to be ripped from the bottom of a printed document. Such cells are often in a vertical format for ease of removal. Cycle through Text Direction options on the Table Tools Layout tab (refer to Figure 3.7) to rotate text in the current cell.

The Cell Margins command in the Alignment group enables you to adjust the amount of white space inside a cell as well as spacing between cells. With additional empty space shown between typed entries, a table can appear more open and readable. Other times, you will want to remove extra space created by cell margins such as when preparing a photo layout in a Word table in which you do not want to display any space at all between photos.

Quick Concepts

1. Explain why it is sometimes beneficial to merge cells in a table, as well as when it might be best to split cells. ***p. 199***

2. Describe a table that would be best designed by drawing instead of inserting. ***p. 197***

3. Describe a situation in which you would want to increase cell margins. Also provide an example of when reducing cell margins would be beneficial. ***p. 203***

Hands-On Exercises

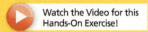

MyLab IT HOE1 Sim Training

Watch the Video for this Hands-On Exercise!

Skills covered: Create or Draw a Table • Insert and Delete Rows and Columns • Merge and Split Cells • Change Row Height and Column Width • Apply and Modify Table Styles • Adjust Table Position and Alignment • Format Table Text

1 Tables

The executive summary is the first section of the economic impact report for Traylor University. Although the summary is already well organized, the data analysis part of the summary needs some attention. Specifically, you develop tables to organize major findings.

STEP 1 CREATE A TABLE AND INSERT AND DELETE ROWS AND COLUMNS

You modify a couple of tables to summarize study findings, including those tables in the executive summary. As you develop or edit the tables, you find it necessary to insert rows to accommodate additional data and to delete columns that are not actually required. Refer to Figure 3.8 as you complete Step 1.

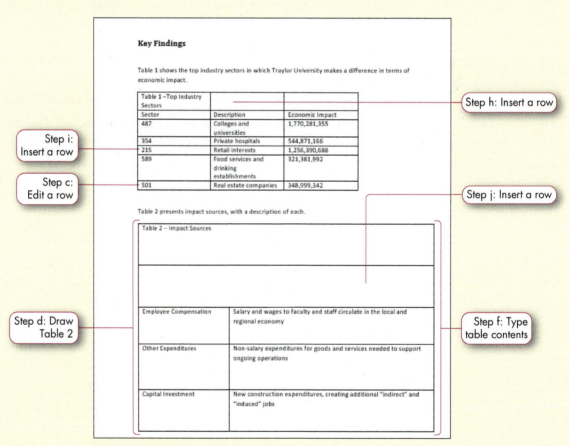

FIGURE 3.8 Report Tables

a. Open *w03h1Traylor* and save it as **w03h1Traylor_LastFirst**.

> **TROUBLESHOOTING:** If you make any major mistakes in this exercise, you can close the file, open *w03h1Traylor* again and then start this exercise over.

b. Click the **View tab** and ensure that Ruler is selected in the Show group. Ensure that non-printing characters are shown. Move to the last page of the document and click in the first cell on the last row of the table.

c. Type the following text on the last row, tabbing between cells. Do not press Tab after the last entry.

| 501 | Real estate companies | Land | 348,999,342 |

You completed the entry of data in a table to indicate community and state interests that are positively impacted by the presence of Traylor University.

> **TROUBLESHOOTING:** If you press Tab after the last entry, a new row is created. Click Undo. If the insertion point moves to a new line within a cell instead of advancing to another cell or row, you pressed Enter instead of Tab between entries. Press Backspace and press Tab. Do not press Tab if you are in the last cell on the last row.

d. Press **Ctrl+End** to position the insertion point at the end of the document. Click the **Insert tab**, click **Table** in the Tables group, and then click **Draw Table**. The pointer displays as 🖉. Drag a box approximately six inches wide and four inches tall, using the vertical and horizontal rulers as guides. Draw one vertical gridline at two inches from the left to create two columns—the first column approximately two inches wide, and the second at four inches wide. Draw three horizontal gridlines to divide the table into four approximately evenly spaced rows of about one inch each. Press **Esc** or click **Draw Table** in the Draw group on the Table Tools Layout tab to toggle the tool off.

> **TROUBLESHOOTING:** It is possible that the lines you draw to form the table are in a color or style other than black. That occurs if someone using the same computer previously selected a different pen color. For this exercise, it will not matter what color the table borders are.

It is OK if the row height is not identical for each row. Simply approximate the required height for each.

e. Click **Eraser** in the Draw group and click to erase the vertical gridline in the first row, so that the row includes only one column. Click **Eraser** to toggle off the eraser.

> **TROUBLESHOOTING:** If you make any mistakes while erasing gridlines, press Esc. Click Undo to undo your actions.

f. Ensure the insertion point is in the first row, type **Table 2 - Impact Sources**. (Do not type the period.) Press **Tab** and complete the table as follows (do not press Tab at the end of the last entry):

Employee Compensation	Salary and wages to faculty and staff circulate in the local and regional economy
Other Expenditures	Non-salary expenditures for goods and services needed to support ongoing operations
Capital Investment	New construction expenditures, creating additional "indirect" and "induced" jobs

Text you type will wrap within some cells. You will resize the columns later, so leave the text as it appears.

g. Position the pointer just above the *Category* column in Table 1, so that the pointer resembles ⬇. Click to select the column. Click **Delete** in the Rows & Columns group on the Table Tools Layout tab and select **Delete Columns**.

h. Click anywhere in **row 1** of Table 1. Click **Insert Above** in the Rows & Columns group. Click in the **first cell** in the new row and type **Table 1 - Top Industry Sectors**. (Do not type the period.)

Text will wrap within the first cell.

Hands-On Exercise 1 205

i. Point to the left edge of the horizontal gridline dividing Sector 354 from 589 to display an insert control. Click the **+ indicator** on the end of the insert control to insert a new row. Click the **first cell** in the new row and type the following. Press **Tab** between cells.

| 215 | Retail interests | 1,256,390,688 |

> **MAC TROUBLESHOOTING:** Use ribbon selections to insert a row instead of the insert control.

j. Click anywhere in **Table 2** to select the table. Point to the left edge of the gridline dividing rows 1 and 2, and click the **insert control** to insert a row above row 2 (*Employee Compensation*). Leave the row blank, for now.

> **TROUBLESHOOTING:** If you do not see an insert control between rows 1 and 2, click in row 1 and click Insert Below in the Rows & Columns group on the Table Tools Layout tab.

> **TROUBLESHOOTING:** Depending on the size of the rows you drew for Table 2, it is possible that Table 2 spans over two pages, with the last row shown on a separate page. You will correct that in the following step.

k. Check spelling and correct any errors. The *Salida* campus is spelled correctly, so ignore the error if presented. Save the document.

STEP 2: MERGE AND SPLIT CELLS AND CHANGE ROW HEIGHT AND COLUMN WIDTH

As you work with the tables in the executive summary, you notice that the first row of Table 1 is not very attractive. The title in that row should not be limited to one small cell. More uniformity of row height and column width would also improve the appearance of Table 2, and you want to add data to the second row. You explore ways to modify both tables by merging and splitting cells and changing row height and column width. Refer to Figure 3.9 as you complete Step 2.

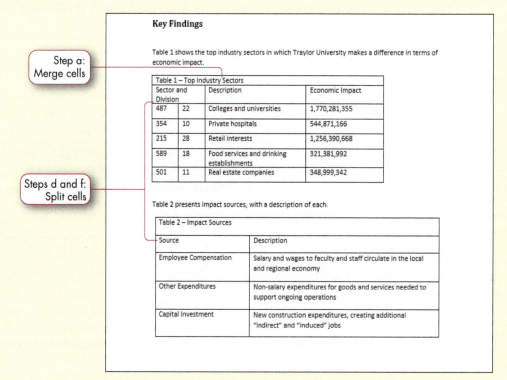

FIGURE 3.9 Merged and Split Cells

a. Position the pointer just outside the left edge of the first row of Table 1, so that it resembles an angled pointing arrow. Click to select **row 1**. Click the Table Tools Layout tab and click Merge Cells in the Merge group.

You merge the cells in row 1 to create one cell in which text can be better positioned across the table.

b. Position the pointer in row 2 on the border between the first and second column of Table 1. The pointer appears as ↔. Drag to the left to reduce the column width to approximately 1 inch to better accommodate the contents of the column.

c. Position the pointer just outside the left edge of row 2 in Table 1 and drag down to select row 2 as well as all remaining rows. With the Table Tools Layout tab selected, use the Height spin arrow in the Cell Size group to change the height to **0.3″**.

Row height of rows 2, 3, 4, 5, and 7 is adjusted to 0.3″. However, because text wraps in row 6, the height of that row is not adjusted to 0.3″. Click anywhere in the table to deselect text.

> **TROUBLESHOOTING:** If items in the first column are selected instead of every cell in every row, you have selected cells instead of rows. Repeat Step c, making sure to position the pointer outside the table and very near the left edge.

The first column of Table 1 lists a sector in which an area of economic impact is identified. Each sector should be further identified by a division, which you now add.

d. Position the pointer just inside the left edge of the third row of Table 1 (containing *487*). The pointer should resemble →. Drag down to select the contents of the first column in row 3 as well as all remaining rows in that column. Click **Split Cells** in the Merge group on the Table Tools Layout tab. Check to ensure that *2* displays as the number of columns and *5* displays as the number of rows. Make necessary adjustments. Uncheck **Merge cells before split**. Click **OK**.

Column 1 is split into two columns so that the first column includes the sector, and the second will contain the associated division.

> **TROUBLESHOOTING:** If all sector numbers appear in the first cell, instead of remaining in separate cells, you did not deselect *Merge cells before split*. Click Undo and repeat Step d.

e. Click in the **first cell** on the second row in Table 1 (containing *Sector*). Type **and Division** after *Sector*. Ensure that a space is included after *Sector*. Type the data underneath the heading as follows, using Figure 3.9 as a guide:

487	22
354	10
215	28
589	18
501	11

f. Click in the **second row** of Table 2. Click **Split Cells** in the Merge group. Ensure that *2* displays as the number of columns and *1* displays as the number of rows. Click **OK**. Place the pointer on the vertical gridline dividing the two columns in row 2. The pointer appears as ↔. Drag to the left to align the gridline with the vertical gridline in row 3.

g. Type **Source**. Press **Tab**. Type **Description**.

h. Click the **table move handle** (at the top-left corner of Table 2) to select the entire table. Use the Height spin arrow in the Cell Size group on the Table Tools Layout tab to reduce the height to **0.01″**.

Row height of all rows in Table 2 is reduced, resulting in a more attractive table.

i. Save the document.

STEP 3 APPLY AND MODIFY TABLE STYLES, ADJUST TABLE POSITION AND ALIGNMENT, AND FORMAT TABLE TEXT

The tables included in the Key Findings section are complete with respect to content, but you realize that they could be far more attractive with a bit of color and appropriate shading. You explore Word's gallery of table styles. You also bold and center column headings and explore aligning the tables horizontally on the page. Refer to Figure 3.10 as you complete Step 3.

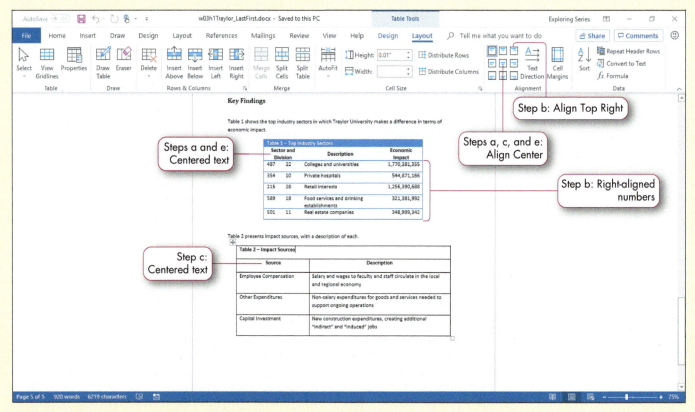

FIGURE 3.10 Formatting and Aligning a Table

a. Select the **second row** in Table 1. Click **Align Center** in the Alignment group on the Table Tools Layout tab.

Text in row 2 is centered both vertically and horizontally within each cell.

b. Select the cells containing numbers in the rightmost column of Table 1 (beginning with 1,770,281,355 and ending with 348,999,342). Click **Align Top Right** in the Alignment group. Click anywhere to deselect the cells. Position the pointer on the right border of the rightmost column of Table 1 so that it resembles ⊹. Drag to the left to reduce the column so that the width is approximately **1"**, better accommodating the contents of the column.

c. Select the **second row** in Table 2, containing column headings. Click **Align Center** in the Alignment group. With the column headings selected, click the **Home tab** and click **Bold** in the Font group. Bold the contents of row 1 in Table 2.

d. Bold the contents of the first two rows in Table 1. Click anywhere in Table 1, click the **Table Tools Design tab**, and click **More** in the Table Styles group. Scroll through the gallery and select **List Table 3 - Accent 1** (row 3, column 2 under List Tables). You must scroll through the list of styles to locate the List Tables area.

The table style removed some of the formatting from Table 1, applying color-coordinated font color, shading, and a colored border. The style also removed the inside vertical borders.

e. Click the **First Column check box** in the Table Style Options group to deselect it. Click the **Table Tools Layout tab**. Select the **second row** in Table 1 (containing column headings) and click **Align Center** in the Alignment group.

f. Click the **View tab** and click **One Page** in the Zoom group to view the current page. Note that the tables are not centered on the page horizontally. Click **100%** in the Zoom group.

g. Right-click anywhere in **Table 1** and select **Table Properties**. Click **Center** in the Alignment group of the Table tab in the Table Properties dialog box to center the table horizontally. Click **OK**. Repeat this technique to center Table 2 horizontally. Click **One Page** in the Zoom group to view the effects of the realignment. Click **100%**.

h. Save the document. Keep the document open if you plan to continue with the next Hands-On Exercise. If not, close the document, and exit Word.

Advanced Table Features

Developing a basic Word table to organize data in columns is a fairly simple task. With a bit more effort, you can enhance a table using features that improve its readability. Many of the tasks typically associated with an Excel spreadsheet can be accomplished in a Word table, such as summing or averaging a numeric column or row. By using advanced table features in Word, you can create tables that not only organize data, but also present table contents in an attractive, easy-to-read format.

In this section, you will enhance tables with borders and shading. In addition, you will sort table data and learn to include formulas and functions in a table. You will learn to include captions with tables, so that tables are correctly identified. By indicating that a header row should recur on each printed page in which a table displays, you will ensure that table contents are easily identified, even if table rows are carried over to another page. Finally, you will simplify the task of creating a table by converting plain text into a table, and you will learn to convert a table to plain text.

Managing Table Data

A table is often used to summarize numeric data. For example, the table shown in Figure 3.11 organizes a list of students receiving college scholarships. The last row of the table shows column totals, calculated using functions, which are discussed in a later section. The table is sorted by student last name. Because the college awards many individual scholarships, there is a likelihood that the table could extend beyond one page. In that case, the first row (containing table headings) should be set to recur across all pages so that table data are identified by column headings, regardless of the page on which the table is continued. You can manage table data to include calculations, sort table contents, and cause header rows to recur across pages. Planning a table ahead of time is always preferable to recognizing the need for a table after text has already been typed. However, in some cases, you can convert plain text into a table. Conversely, after a table has been created, you can convert table text back to plain text.

Recipient Name	Major	Date Awarded	Amount Awarded	Amount Spent
Alim, Nisheeth	Accounting	5/15/2022	1,850	1,200
Diminsha, Ahmed	Finance	4/23/2022	1,200	1,200
Don, Clarke	Management	2/1/2022	1,350	728
Edge, Latisha	Finance	6/4/2022	2,550	1,014
Gonzalez, Patricia	Accounting	3/16/2022	1,500	0
Green, Amber	Entrepreneurship	5/10/2022	1,225	1,225
James, Greg	CIS	4/23/2022	2,850	350
McDonald, June	Accounting	5/15/2022	2,335	2,001
Marish, Tia	CIS	2/10/2022	1,895	1,400
Pintlala, Sarah	Management	8/1/2022	3,950	2,100
Tellez, Anthony	Finance	6/2/2022	2,350	2,300
Wallace, April	Marketing	2/28/2022	1,100	250
		TOTAL	24,155	13,768

FIGURE 3.11 Managing Table Data

STEP 1 Calculate Using Table Formulas and Functions

Organizing numbers in columns and rows within a Word table not only creates an attractive and easy-to-read display, but also simplifies the task of totaling, averaging, or otherwise summarizing those numbers. Although Word is not designed to perform heavy-duty statistical calculations, it is possible to determine basic solutions, such as a sum, an average, or a count of items in cells using built-in functions.

Use a Formula

A *formula* is a calculation that can add, subtract, divide, or multiply cell contents. To use formulas, you must understand the concept of cell addresses. A Word table is very similar to an Excel worksheet, so if you are familiar with Excel, you will understand how Word addresses cells and develops formulas. Each cell in a Word table has a unique address. Columns are designated with letters (although such labeling is understood—letters do not actually display above each column) and rows with numbers. For example, Nisheeth Alim's award amount, shown in Figure 3.12, is in cell D2 (fourth column, second row). The amount he has spent is in cell E2, and the amount remaining is to be calculated in cell F2. The formula to calculate the amount remaining is =D2-E2, which subtracts the amount spent from the award amount. When indicating a cell reference, you do not have to capitalize the address. For example, =A10+A11 is evaluated identically to =a10+a11.

Unlike the way you would manage formulas in an Excel worksheet, you do not actually type a formula or function in a cell. Instead, you use the Formula dialog box to build a formula or use a function (see Figure 3.12).

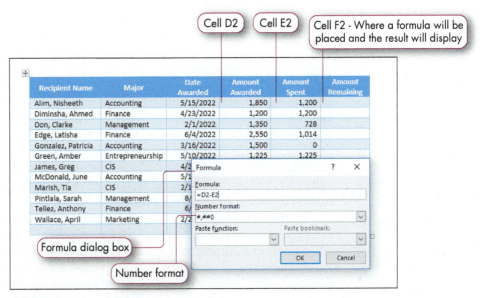

FIGURE 3.12 Using the Formula Dialog Box

> **TIP: NUMBER FORMAT**
> When identifying a number format, you have several options to select from when you click Number Format in the Formula dialog box. A # in a format indicates that leading zeroes will be suppressed. A 0 in a format indicates that leading zeroes will be displayed. Other format options enable you to display dollar signs or percent signs in the formula result.

A formula can contain more than one mathematical operator. The minus sign in the formula described in the preceding steps is considered an operator. Mathematical operators that you can use in creating formulas include exponentiation (^), multiplication (*), division (/), addition (+), and subtraction (-).

When more than one operator is included in a formula, evaluation of the formula follows a set procedure, called the *order of operations*. The order of operations requires that the following operations be evaluated in the following order:

1. Parenthetical information (any calculation in parentheses)
2. Exponentiation
3. Multiplication and Division—evaluated from left to right if both operators are present in a formula
4. Addition and Subtraction—evaluated from left to right if both operators are present in a formula

As an example, the expression =C12+C15*1.8 is evaluated as follows: Multiply cell C15 by 1.8 and add the result to cell C12. If, however, you wanted the addition to be performed first, you would enclose that calculation in parentheses. Because the use of parentheses has a higher order of operation than multiplication, that addition would be done first, and the result would be multiplied by 1.8.

> **TIP: UPDATING A FORMULA**
> Unlike Microsoft Excel, a formula in a table is not automatically updated when the contents of cells referenced by the formula change. However, you can manually update a formula. Right-click the cell containing the formula and select Update Field. On a Mac, you must first select the value and then update the field.

Common equations, such as the area of a circle, and more complex equations, such as the quadratic formula, are available to be incorporated into a document or table. The Equation command on the Insert tab provides a list of equations and enables you to create your own. The formula is created in a placeholder, so you can manage it independently of surrounding text. Most math symbols and operators are not located on the keyboard; however, you can create a formula so that it seamlessly integrates with surrounding text by making selections from the Symbols group on the Insert tab or the Equation Tools Design tab, shown when you click the Insert tab and select Equation from the Symbols group.

Use a Function

Word provides ***functions***, which are built-in formulas, to simplify the task of performing basic calculations. A function uses values in a table to produce a result. For example, the SUM function totals values in a series of cells, whereas the COUNT function identifies the number of entries in a series of cells. The total scholarship amount, that is included in the Total row shown in Figure 3.11, is calculated with a SUM function, which adds the values in the column above. In most cases, a function provides an alternative to what would otherwise be a much lengthier calculation.

To determine a final scholarship amount in the Total row of the table shown in Figure 3.11, you could click in the cell underneath the last scholarship award amount and add all cells individually in the fourth column, as in =D2+D3+D4+D5+D6, continuing to list cells in the range through D13. A ***range*** is a series of adjacent cells. Although the formula would produce a final total, the formula would be extremely lengthy. Imagine the formula length in a more realistic situation in which hundreds of students received a scholarship! A much more efficient approach would be to use a SUM function, in which you indicate, by position, the series of cells to total. For example, the function to produce a total scholarship amount is =SUM(ABOVE). Similarly, a function to produce an average scholarship amount is =AVERAGE(ABOVE). In fact, you can select from various table functions, as shown in Table 3.1. The positional information within parentheses is referred to as an ***argument***. Positional information indicates the position of the data being calculated. You can use positional notation of ABOVE, BELOW, LEFT, or RIGHT as arguments. An argument of ABOVE indicates that data to be summarized is located above the cell containing the function. Although not a comprehensive list, the functions shown in Table 3.1 are commonly used. Note that an argument will be included within parentheses in each function.

TABLE 3.1 Table Functions

Function	Action
=SUM(argument)	Totals a series of cells
=AVERAGE(argument)	Averages a series of cells
=COUNT(argument)	Counts the number of entries in a series of cells
=MAX(argument)	Displays the largest number in a series of cells
=MIN(argument)	Displays the smallest number in a series of cells

To place a formula or function in a table cell, complete the following steps:

1. Click in the cell that is to contain the result of the calculation. For example, click in cell D14 of the table shown in Figure 3.11 to include a function totaling all scholarship amounts.
2. Click Formula in the Data group on the Table Tools Layout tab.
3. Type a formula or edit the suggested function. Alternatively, you can click the Paste function, select a function, and then type an argument. Click OK.

> **TIP: COMBINING ARGUMENTS**
> Combine arguments in a function to indicate cells to include. For example, =SUM(ABOVE,BELOW) totals numeric cells above and below the current cell. =SUM(LEFT,ABOVE) totals numeric cells to the left and above the current cell, whereas =SUM(RIGHT,BELOW) totals numeric cells to the right and below the current cell. Combine any two arguments, separated by a comma, to indicate cells to include.

STEP 2 Sort Data in a Table

Columns of text, dates, or numbers in a Word table can be sorted alphabetically, chronologically, or numerically. The table shown in Figure 3.11 is sorted alphabetically in ascending order by student name. It might be beneficial to sort the data in Figure 3.11 by date, so that scholarship awards are shown in chronological order. Or you could sort table rows numerically by award amount, with highest awards shown first, followed in descending order by lesser award amounts. You might even want to sort awards alphabetically by major, with scholarship award amounts within programs of study shown in order from low to high. Such a sort uses a primary category (major, in this case) and a secondary category (award amount). You can sort a Word table by up to three categories.

A table is often designed so that the first row contains column headings. Those column headings, also called a header row, serve as categories that you can sort by. As you conduct a sort, described in the following steps, you should first indicate whether the table has a header row. In doing so, you can then select one or more sort categories. Even if a table has no header row, you can select rows to sort and indicate which column to sort by.

To sort table rows, complete the following steps:

1. Click anywhere in the table (or click in the column to sort by).
2. Click Sort in the Data group on the Table Tools Layout tab.
3. Specify whether the table includes a header row.
4. Indicate or confirm the primary category, or column, to sort by (along with the sort order, either ascending or descending), as shown in Figure 3.13.
5. Select any other sort columns and indicate or confirm the sort order. Click OK.

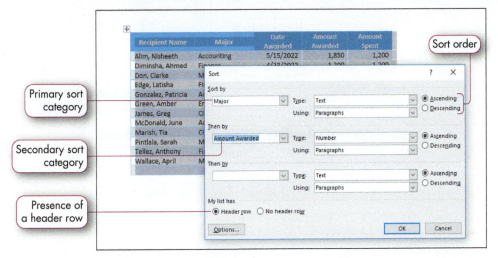

FIGURE 3.13 Sorting a Table

Include a Recurring Table Header

A table is typically comprised of a header row followed by several rows of data. The header row in Figure 3.11 includes text identifying the first column as Recipient Name, the second as Major, and so forth. With a large number of students receiving scholarships, the table could easily extend beyond one page. If the document is to be printed, table rows on the additional pages would have no identifying header row. To remedy that situation, you can cause one or more rows of headings to repeat at the top of every page on which a table extends. Select the header row(s) and choose to repeat header rows on the Table Tools Layout tab. Repeated table header rows are visible only in Print Layout view.

Enhancing Table Data

You include data in a table to organize it in a way that makes it easy for a reader to comprehend. Using table styles and table formulas, you have learned to configure a table so it is attractive and so that it provides any necessary summary information. To further enhance table data, you can select custom shading and borders. Certain writing styles require the use of captions to identify tables included in reports; you will also learn to work with captions in this section.

STEP 3 Include Borders and Shading

Enhancing a table with custom borders and shading is a simple task when you use Word's Border tools. A *border* is a line style you can apply to individual cells, to an entire table, or to individual areas within a table. You can design your own border, selecting a pen color, line style, and line weight, or you can select from a gallery of predesigned borders that coordinate with existing table styles. When a table is inserted, it is automatically formatted in Table Grid style, with all cells bordered with a ½ pt single line border.

Word makes use of **Border Painter**, a tool that enables you to apply border settings you have identified (or a border style selected from the Borders gallery) to one or more table borders. Using Border Painter, you can apply preselected borders by "brushing" them on a table border with the pointer. Figure 3.14 shows various border selections that are available on the Table Tools Design tab when a table is selected.

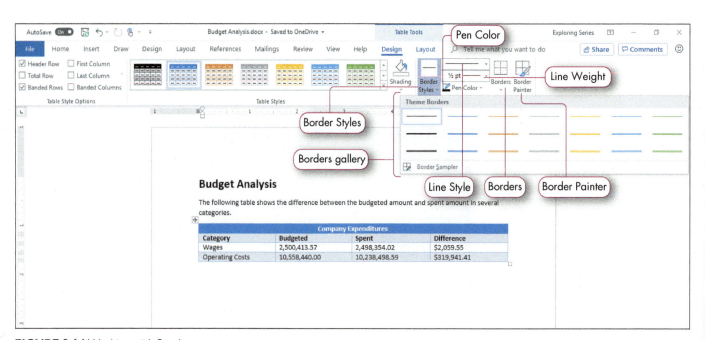

FIGURE 3.14 Working with Borders

In most cases, using the Borders and Shading dialog box is the simplest approach to changing borders and shading within a table. Options include border style, color, line weight, and shading (background) color.

> **To use the Borders and Shading dialog box to change borders in a table, complete the following steps:**
>
> 1. Select the cells to modify (or click the table move handle to select the entire table).
> 2. Click the Borders arrow in the Borders group on the Table Tools Design tab. Click Borders and Shading to display the Borders and Shading dialog box (see Figure 3.15).
> 3. Select from options in the dialog box to add, remove, or modify table and cell borders. In addition, you can select shading when you click the Shading tab in the dialog box.

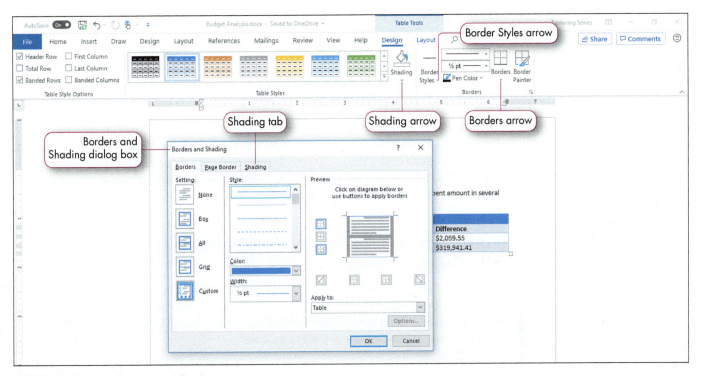

FIGURE 3.15 Using Borders and Shading

For more specificity than what might be found in the Borders and Shading dialog box, you can design a custom border. You can create a custom border by selecting a pen color, line style, and line weight, and then apply it to table borders, or you can select from a gallery of predesigned border styles. You should be aware that if you change the document theme later, the border style and color choice will change to match the theme. Regardless of whether you are applying a custom border or a predesigned style, you can select the borders to apply the selection to when you click the Borders arrow (refer to Figure 3.15) and select a type (Outside Borders, Right Border, Left Border, etc.).

> **To design and apply custom borders, select a table and complete the following steps:**
>
> 1. Choose a pen color, line style, and line weight (refer to Figure 3.14). The pointer displays as a pen. Alternatively, click Border Styles and select a border style. Each border style combines border width, color, and size.
> 2. Click the Borders arrow (refer to Figure 3.15) and select a border to apply the border selections to. Alternatively, drag the insertion pointer across a border to apply the selected border design.
> 3. Click Border Painter to toggle off the border application or press Esc.

As shown in Figure 3.15, the Design tab also includes options for selecting shading. ***Shading*** applies color or a pattern to the background of a cell or group of cells. You might want to apply shading to a header row to emphasize it, setting it apart from the rows beneath. Apply shading to selected areas by choosing from options on the Table Tools Design tab. The Shading option provides various color selections, whereas the Borders option enables you to open the Borders and Shading dialog box, from which you click the Shading tab for shading choices.

> **TIP: USING BORDER SAMPLER**
> After applying a custom border or border style to one or more borders in a table, you can copy the selection to other table borders. You can easily accomplish this task using Border Sampler. Click the Border Styles arrow (refer to Figure 3.15) and click Border Sampler. The pointer becomes an eyedropper tool; click a table border that you want to copy. The pointer automatically switches to the Border Painter tool, as indicated by the ink pen designation or a paintbrush, if using a Mac, so you can brush another border to apply the border selection.

STEP 4 Convert Text to a Table and Convert a Table to Text

Suppose you are working with a list of items organized into two areas, with each item separated from the next by a comma, tab, or a paragraph marker. For example, you develop a list of items in a sale along with each respective price, with the items and prices separated by a tab. You know that if the areas, or columns, were organized as a table, you could easily apply a table style, sort rows, and even use formulas to summarize numeric information. In that case, you can convert text to a table.

> **To convert text to a table, complete the following steps:**
> 1. Select text to be converted.
> 2. Click the Insert tab and click Table in the Tables group.
> 3. Click Convert Text to Table.
> 4. Select options from the Convert Text to Table dialog box (see Figure 3.16), including the number of columns and rows to include.
> 5. Click OK.

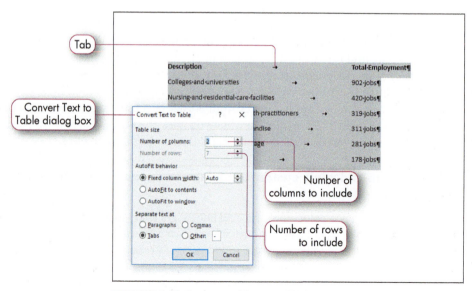

FIGURE 3.16 Converting Text to a Table

Conversely, you might identify a need to convert table text to plain text, removing special table features, and then organizing columns into simple tabbed columns.

To convert a table to text, complete the following steps:

1. Click anywhere in the table.
2. Click Convert to Text in the Data group on the Table Tools Layout tab.
3. Indicate how table text is to be divided in the Convert Table to Text dialog box (see Figure 3.17).
4. Click OK.

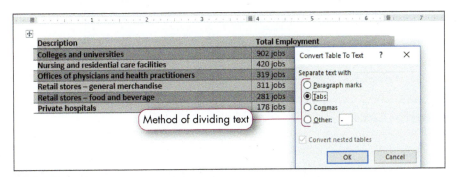

FIGURE 3.17 Converting a Table to Text

Include a Table Caption

A *caption*, such as *Table 1*, is a numbered item of text that identifies a table, figure, or other object in a Word document. A particular writing style may be required for class papers or published works. This style will prescribe a standard set of guidelines, including the usage of captions. A caption is often used to cite a table that came from a research source. A caption typically includes a label, such as the word *Figure* or *Table*, followed by a sequential number that can be automatically updated with the addition of new tables or captioned objects.

To include a table caption, complete the following steps:

1. Click a cell in the table.
2. Click the References tab and click Insert Caption in the Captions group. The Caption dialog box displays, as shown in Figure 3.18. Because you are providing a caption to a table, the word *Table* displays in the Label box, although that can be changed to *Figure* or *Equation*. Depending on the wording of the caption, you might find that a label is unnecessary or even redundant. In that case, select the check box to exclude the label from the caption.
3. Click the Position arrow and indicate a caption position—above or below the table.
4. Click Numbering to select a numbering style (1, 2, 3, or A, B, C, for example).
5. Click OK to close the dialog box.

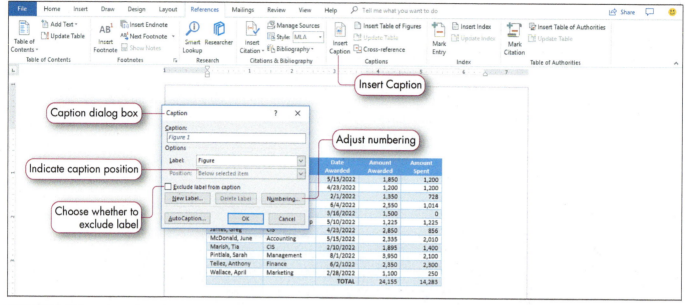

FIGURE 3.18 Inserting a Caption

When a caption is created, it is formatted in Caption style. You can use the Styles pane to modify the Caption style applied to all captions in the document. You can identify and modify the caption style in the Styles gallery on the Home tab.

As you continue to add captions to tables in a document, each caption is shown in sequence. For example, if the first caption is Table 1, then the second caption you add will automatically be labeled Table 2. If you should insert a table between existing tables, the caption you add to the table will automatically be shown in sequence, with captions on following tables updated accordingly. However, if you delete a table from a document, remaining captions are not automatically renumbered. In that case, you must manually update the captions. To update all captions in a document, select all document text, right-click anywhere in the selection, and then select Update Field. Or to update only one caption, right-click the caption number, and then click Update Field.

Quick Concepts

4. Differentiate between the use of a function and a formula in a table. When would one be preferable to another? Provide several examples. *p. 212*

5. Provide an explanation of why a table formula that sums row data does not include data from a newly added row. Explain what can be done to cause the sum to be correct. *p. 212*

6. Describe a situation in which it would be beneficial to convert an existing list of tabbed text into a table. *p. 216*

Hands-On Exercises

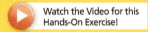

MyLab IT HOE2 Sim Training

Watch the Video for this Hands-On Exercise!

Skills covered: Use a Formula • Use a Function • Sort Data in a Table • Include a Recurring Table Header • Include Borders and Shading • Convert Text to a Table • Include a Table Caption

2 Advanced Table Features

As you continue to work with the Key Findings section of the executive summary, you modify the two tables you previously created. The first table, showing major areas in which the university contributed to the economy, is modified to include a total row and to indicate the percentage represented by each sector. You also explore Word's Borders gallery and design options as you customize the tables to reflect the color scheme of the university. Adding a caption to each table serves to identify the table and will be useful for your assistant when she prepares a Table of Figures later. You also apply a sort order to each table to organize each in a more understandable manner.

STEP 1 USE A FORMULA AND USE A FUNCTION

Table 1 includes a numeric column showing Traylor University's economic impact in several sectors. You add a row showing the total for all of the sectors. You also insert a column showing the percentage of the total represented by each sector's value. Refer to Figure 3.19 as you complete Step 1.

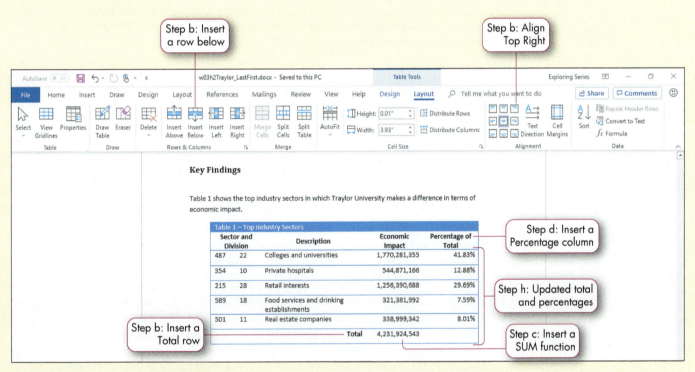

FIGURE 3.19 Working with Table Formulas

a. Open *w03h1Traylor_LastFirst* if you closed it after Hands-On Exercise 1 and save it as **w03h2Traylor_LastFirst**, changing h1 to h2.

b. Ensure that page 5 is shown, displaying Table 1 and Table 2. Click in the **last row** of Table 1. Click **Insert Below** in the Rows & Columns group on the Table Tools Layout tab. Click in the **third column** of the new row (the Description column), type **Total**, and then apply bold formatting to the word Total. With the word still selected, click **Align Top Right** in the Alignment group on the Table Tools Layout tab.

You add a row in which to place a total economic impact figure.

c. Click in the **cell** immediately below the last economic impact number. Click **Formula** in the Data group. The suggested function, =SUM(ABOVE) is correct. Click the **Number format arrow** and select **#,##0**. Click **OK**.

The total economic impact is 4,241,924,543.

> **TROUBLESHOOTING:** If the total is incorrect, you most likely typed a number incorrectly in the column above. Refer to Figure 3.9 in the previous Hands-On Exercise for the correct numbers. Make any necessary corrections in Table 1. The total will not show the correct number until you complete Step h to update the field.

d. Click **Insert Right** in the Rows & Columns group. Click the **last cell** in the second row of the new column and type **Percentage of Total**.

Text will wrap in the cell. You added a new column that will show the percentage each sector's value represents of the total economic impact.

e. Click in the **last column** of the third row (in the *Colleges and universities* row). Click **Formula** in the Data group. Drag to select the suggested function in the Formula box. Type **=D3/D8*100**. Click the **Number format arrow**, scroll through the options, and then select **0.00%**. Click **OK**.

You create a formula to obtain the result. The formula divides the value in the cell to the left (cell D3) by the total value of economic impact in the last row of the table (cell D8). The result is multiplied by 100 to convert it to a percentage. The format you chose displays the result with a percent sign and two places to the right of the decimal. The percentage represented by Colleges and universities is 41.73%.

> **TROUBLESHOOTING:** If an error message displays in the cell instead of a percentage, or if the percentage is incorrect, click Undo and repeat Step e.

f. Click in the **last column** of the *Private hospitals* row. Click **Formula** in the Data group. Press **Backspace** repeatedly to remove the suggested function from the Formula box. Type **=D4/D8*100**. Click **OK**.

The number format remains at 0.00%, so there is no need to change it.

g. Click in the **last column** of the *Retail interests* row and repeat Step f, changing *D4* in the formula to **D5** (because you are working with a value on the fifth row). Create a formula for *Food services and drinking establishments* and *Real estate companies*, adjusting the row reference in each formula.

h. Change the number in *Economic Impact* for *Real estate companies* in the second to last row in the table from *348,999,342* to **338,999,342**. Right-click the total in the next row, *4,241,924,543*, and click **Update Field** to update the total. Right-click the percentage of total for Real estate companies in the last column of the second to last row. Click **Update Field**. Right-click each remaining percentage figure in the last column, updating each field.

i. Save the document.

STEP 2 SORT DATA IN A TABLE AND INCLUDE A RECURRING TABLE HEADER

You will sort Table 1 so that the dollar amounts are arranged in descending order. That way, it is very clear in which sectors the university had the most impact. You will also sort Table 2 in alphabetical order by Source. The resulting table appears well organized. After inserting text from another file, Table 2 is split between two pages. You will repeat Table 2 header rows to better identify table rows that are carried over to another page. Refer to Figure 3.20 as you complete Step 2.

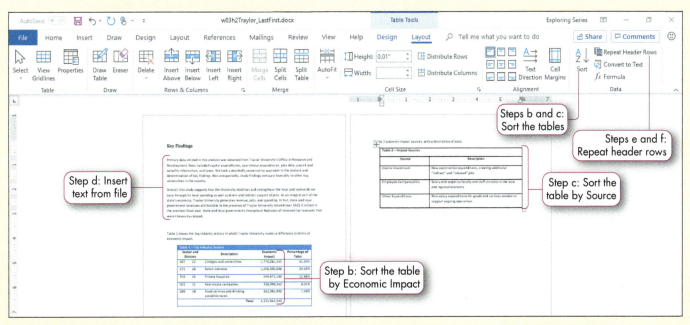

FIGURE 3.20 Sorted Tables

a. Show nonprinting characters if they are not already displayed. Position the pointer just outside the left edge of the third row of Table 1 (beginning with 487). The pointer should be a right-directed white arrow. Select the third through the seventh row. Do not include the final total row.

The table rows that are to be sorted are selected. You do not want to include the first two rows or the final total row in the sort because they do not contain individual values to sort.

b. Click **Sort** in the Data group on the Table Tools Layout tab. Click the **Sort by arrow** and select **Column 4**. Click **Descending**. Click **OK**.

The five rows containing a sector name (Colleges and universities, Retail interests, etc.) are sorted in descending order by the value in the fourth column (Economic Impact). It is clear that the sector most affected is Colleges and universities.

c. Position the pointer just outside the left edge of the third row of Table 2. Drag to select the remaining rows. Click **Sort** in the Data group. Click the **Sort by arrow** and select **Column 1**. Click **Ascending** and click **OK**.

The three rows containing a source (Capital Investment, etc.) are sorted in ascending order alphabetically.

d. Click before the words *Table 1* in the first paragraph on page 5. Press **Enter**. Place the insertion point before the second blank paragraph under *Key Findings*. Click the **Insert tab**, click the **Object arrow** in the Text group, and then select **Text from File**. Navigate to your student data files and double-click *w03h2KeyFindings*.

> **TROUBLESHOOTING:** If you see an Object dialog box instead of text from the inserted file, you clicked Object instead of the Object arrow. Close the dialog box and repeat Step d.

e. Scroll to the bottom of page 5 and note that Table 2 is now split between pages, with several rows on page 6. Those rows are not identified by column headings (Source and Description). Select the first two rows of Table 2 (on page 5). Click the **Table Tools Layout tab**. Click **Repeat Header Rows** in the Data group.

The first two rows of Table 2 repeat above the remaining rows of Table 2 shown on page 6.

f. Click **Repeat Header Rows** again to return to the previous table arrangement in which header rows are not repeated on page 6. Click before the words *Table 2 presents impact sources* on page 5. Press **Ctrl+Enter** to insert a manual page break.

You determine that the way Table 2 is divided between pages 5 and 6 is very unattractive, even with repeating header rows, so you remove the repeating rows and insert a manual page break to force the entire table onto another page.

g. Save the document.

STEP 3 INCLUDE BORDERS AND SHADING AND A TABLE CAPTION

You expect to add more tables later but decide to format Tables 1 and 2 so they are more attractive and color-coordinated. You explore border and shading options, learning to "paint" borders and considering border selections from the Borders gallery. Because you expect to include numerous figures throughout the report, you insert captions to identify those tables. Refer to Figure 3.21 as you complete Step 3.

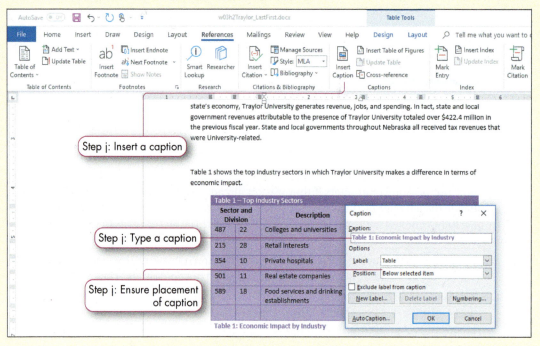

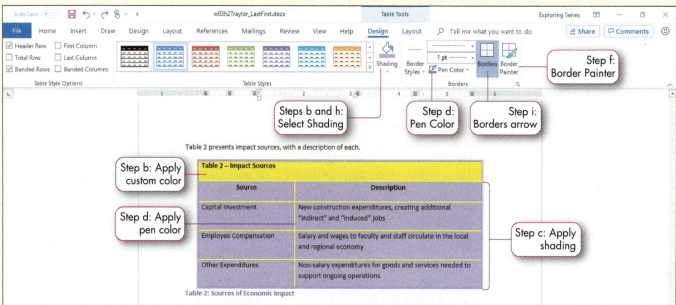

FIGURE 3.21 Including Borders, Shading, and Captions

a. Click the **table move handle** to select Table 2. Click the **Table Tools Design tab** and click **Border Styles** in the Borders group. Select **Double solid lines, ½ pt, Accent 4** (row 3, column 5 of under Theme Borders). Click the **Borders arrow** in the Borders group and select **All Borders**.

> **TROUBLESHOOTING:** If you do not see the table move handle, point to or click any cell in the table and move to the top-left corner of the table to click the table move handle (or click the Table Tools Layout tab, click Select in the Table group, and then click Select Table).

b. Select **row 1** in Table 2. Click the **Shading arrow** in the Table Styles group on the Table Tools Design tab and select **More Colors**. Click the **Custom tab** and adjust Red to **240**, Green to **239**, and Blue to **29**. Click **OK**.

> **MAC TROUBLESHOOTING:** Click Color Sliders and select RGB Sliders from the list to identify a custom color.

c. Select **rows 2, 3, 4,** and **5** in Table 2. Click the **Shading arrow** and select **Purple, Accent 4, Lighter 40%** (fourth row, eighth column).

> **MAC TROUBLESHOOTING:** The particular purple shade may not be available, so select another that is similar.

Traylor University's school colors are purple and gold, so you design tables with that color combination.

d. Click **Pen Color** in the Borders group. Select the **Yellow color** shown under Recent Colors. The pointer displays as an ink pen, or as a paintbrush if using a Mac, indicating that Border Painter is active. The line style and line weight retain the earlier settings (double line at ½ pt), although if not, select a double line style and ½ pt weight. Drag the pen along the horizontal border dividing row 1 from row 2 in Table 2. Next, drag the pen along the horizontal border dividing row 2 from row 3. Do the same for the next two horizontal borders dividing row 3 from row 4, and row 4 from row 5. Drag the pen along the vertical border dividing the first column from the second (in the purple shaded area). Press **Esc** to turn off Border Painter or click Border Painter to toggle off the tool.

> **TROUBLESHOOTING:** If you make a mistake as you color borders, press Esc or click Border Painter to turn off the pen and click Undo to undo your action(s). Repeat Step d.

e. Select the **first two rows** in Table 2. Click the **Table Tools Layout tab** and increase the row height in the Cell Size group to **0.4"**.

The first two rows in Table 2 are resized slightly.

f. Click the **Table Tools Design tab**. Click **Border Painter** in the Borders group. Scroll to page 5 and drag the pen along the horizontal border dividing row 2 from row 3 in Table 1. Do the same for the horizontal borders dividing all other rows, but do not drag the bottom border of the table or the horizontal border dividing row 1 from row 2. Drag the pen along the vertical gridlines dividing all columns, but do not drag the outside borders of the table, and do not drag any vertical line in row 1. Press **Esc** or click Border Painter to toggle off the tool.

> **TROUBLESHOOTING:** If you make a mistake as you color borders, press Esc to turn off the pen and click Undo to undo your action(s). Repeat Step f.

Border Painter was used to "paint" the currently selected yellow border on the gridlines dividing rows and columns in Table 1.

g. Click anywhere in **Table 1** and click the **table move handle** to select Table 1. Click the **Border Styles arrow**. Select **Double solid lines, ½ pt, Accent 4** (row 3, column 5). Click the **Borders arrow** and select **Outside Borders**.

A border style was applied to the outside borders of the selected table.

h. Select **row 1** in Table 1. Click the **Shading arrow** in the Table Styles group and click **Purple, Accent 4** (row 1, column 8 under Theme Colors). Select **rows 2 through 8** in Table 1. Click the **Shading arrow** and select **Purple, Accent 4, Lighter 40%** (row 4, column 8 under Theme Colors).

> **MAC TROUBLESHOOTING:** The particular purple shade may not be available, so select another that is similar.

i. Click the **table move handle** to select Table 1. Click the **Borders arrow** and select **Borders and Shading**. In the Borders and Shading dialog box, ensure that the Borders tab is selected, click **All** in the Setting area, and then scroll up and click the **first selection** in the Style box (single purple line). Click **Width** and select **1 pt**. Click **OK**.

You decide a more conservative format would be attractive, so you use the Borders and Shading dialog box to apply a purple border between all cells.

j. Click anywhere in **Table 1**. Click the **References tab**. Click **Insert Caption** in the Captions group. With the insertion point immediately after the phrase *Table 1* in the Caption box, type **:** and press **Spacebar**. Type **Economic Impact by Industry**. (Do not type the period.) Ensure that *Below selected item* is shown as the caption position. Click **OK**. Click the **Home tab** and click **Increase Indent** in the Paragraph group. Click anywhere in **Table 2** and insert a caption below the selected item that reads **Table 2: Sources of Economic Impact**. (Do not type the period.)

k. Click the **Home tab**. Click the **Styles Dialog Box Launcher**. Scroll down and point to Caption in the Styles pane. Click the **Caption arrow** and select **Modify**. Change the font size to **11** and the font color to **Purple, Accent 4**. Click **OK**. Close the Styles pane.

The Caption style was modified to include purple font so the caption text coordinates with the table color scheme.

l. Save the document.

STEP 4: CONVERT TEXT TO A TABLE

One additional table is necessary to complete the executive summary, but the necessary data are arranged in a tabbed format instead of a table. You convert the columns of data into a table. Refer to Figure 3.22 as you complete Step 4.

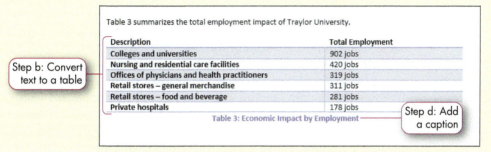

FIGURE 3.22 Working with Tables and Captions

a. Press **Ctrl+End** to move to the end of the document. Press **Enter** twice. Click the **Insert tab**, click the **Object arrow**, and then select **Text from File**. Navigate to the location of your student data files and double-click *w03h2Text*.

   Columned text is inserted in the document, with each column separated by a tab.

b. Select the newly inserted text, beginning with *Description* and ending with *178 jobs*. It does not matter whether you also select the paragraph mark following the words *178 jobs* but do not select the paragraph mark on the following line. Click **Table** in the Tables group and click **Convert Text to Table**. Click **OK** to accept the default settings of two columns and seven rows.

> **TROUBLESHOOTING:** If the Convert Text to Table dialog box suggests another setting, such as one column and nine rows, you selected the blank paragraphs below the tabbed text in addition to the text. Click Cancel and repeat Step b, selecting only the tabbed text.

c. Click **More** in the Table Styles group. Click **Grid Table 2 - Accent 4** (row 2, column 5 under Grid Tables).

d. Click in the newly created table, click the **References tab**, and then click **Insert Caption** in the Captions group. Add the caption **Table 3: Economic Impact by Employment**. (Do not type the period.) Ensure that the position is *Below selected item*. Click **OK**. Modify the Caption style to center captions.

   Note that the caption is formatted with the purple font that you indicated earlier and that all captions are centered.

e. Click before the blank paragraph preceding Table 3 (above the table), press **Enter**, and then type **Table 3 summarizes the total employment impact of Traylor University.** (Include the period.)

f. Check the document for spelling errors, addressing any that might be identified.

g. Save and close the document. You will submit this file to your instructor at the end of the last Hands-On Exercise.

Mail Merge

At some point in your personal or professional life, you may want to send the same document to a number of different people. The document might be an invitation, a letter, or a memo. For the most part, document text will be the same, regardless of how many people receive it. However, certain parts of the document may contain personalized information, such as the inside address included in a letter. Consider the task of conducting a job search. You have created a cover letter and want to personalize the letter with the recipient's name and address, include the recipient's name in the salutation, and perhaps reference the company name in the body of the cover letter for all companies you are sending your resume and cover letter to. In addition, you want to generate envelopes with each recipient's address. Word's **Mail Merge** feature enables you to easily generate those types of personalization within one common document. Mail merge is a process that combines content from a main document and a data source, with the option of creating a new document. A data source is a list of variable data to include in the document, effectively personalizing it, such as recipient name and address.

You can use mail merge to create a set of form letters, personalizing or modifying each one for the recipient. A ***form letter*** is a document that is often mass produced and sent to multiple recipients. The small amount of personal information included in the form letter—perhaps the salutation or the recipient's address—can be inserted during the mail merge procedure.

Mail merge may also be used to send personalized email messages to multiple recipients. Unlike sending email to a group of recipients or listing recipients as blind carbon copies, creating a mail-merged email makes it appear as if each recipient is the sole addressee. You can also use mail merge to send an email in which the message is personalized for each recipient, referring to the recipient by name within the body of the message.

In this section, you will learn to use Mail Merge to create a main document and select a recipient list. You will then combine, or merge, the main document and data source to produce a document that is personalized for each recipient.

Creating a Mail Merge Document

The mail merge process begins with a ***main document*** that contains wording that remains the same for all recipients. In the case of the cover letter used in your job search, the main document would include paragraphs that are intended for all recipients to read—perhaps those that describe your qualifications and professional goals. Placeholders are also included in the main document. They are intended to contain variable data, which might include a recipient's address or a salutation directed to a particular person. During the mail merge process, a data source that contains variable data is combined with the main document to produce personalized documents. You can merge a data source of employer names and mailing addresses with a main document to produce a personalized letter for each potential employer. Mail merge also enables you to print labels or envelopes, obtaining addresses from a data source.

If creating a form letter in which certain variable data will be inserted, you can begin with the main document, or letter, open. If you have not yet created the form letter, you will begin with a blank document. Similarly, you would begin with a blank document when creating envelopes or labels.

The main document used in a mail merge process can be a new or existing document. In creating a document to be merged with a data source, you can select from ribbon options or you can work with the Mail Merge Wizard, which is a step-by-step approach. In either case, begin with a main document (or a blank document) and select from options on the Mailings tab.

Select or Create a Recipient List

The ***data source*** that is merged with the main document is often referred to as a recipient list. It provides variable data to include in the document, such as recipient name, address, phone number, and company information. Each item of information is referred to as a ***field***. For example, the data source might include a last name field, a first name field, a street address field, etc. A group of fields for a person or thing, presented as a row in the data source, is called a ***record***. Figure 3.23 illustrates a sample data source. Note that each record in the data source represents a person, with each record subdivided into fields. The data source shown in Figure 3.23 is an Access database table.

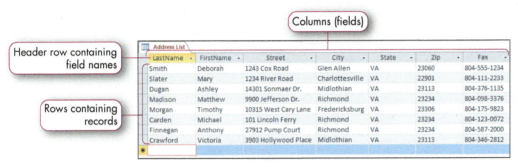

FIGURE 3.23 Mail Merge Data Source

A data source can be obtained from:
- A Word document that contains records stored in a table, where each row after the first is a record and the top row contains headings (field names)
- An Access database table or query
- An Excel worksheet, where each row after the first contains records and the top row shows headings (field names)
- A group of Outlook contacts

The first row in the data source is called the ***header row*** and identifies the fields in the remaining rows. Each row beneath the header row contains a record, and every record contains the same fields in the same order—for example, Title, FirstName, LastName, etc.

If you do not have a preexisting list to use as a data source, you can create one during the Word mail merge process.

To create a new data source, complete the following steps:
1. Click Select Recipients in the Start Mail Merge group on the Mailings tab.
2. Click Type a New List. The New Address List dialog box displays with the most commonly used fields for a mail merge.
3. Type data or click Customize Columns to add, delete, or rename the fields to meet your needs.

On a Mac, to create a new data source, complete the following steps:
1. Click Select Recipients on the Mailings tab and select Create a New List.
2. Add a new field name and click the plus sign.
3. Delete any unwanted field names from the field names list by clicking the minus sign.
4. Organize the order of field names by clicking the up and down arrows.
5. Click Create.
6. Give the data source a name and click Save.
7. Populate the fields with data for each recipient using the right arrow to move to the next record.
8. Click OK when complete.

STEP 1 Use an Excel Worksheet as a Data Source

An Excel worksheet organizes data in columns and rows, and it can be used to develop a data source that can be merged with a main document during a mail merge. With only a bit of introduction, you can learn to enter data in an Excel worksheet, designing columns and rows of data so that a lengthy address list can be easily maintained. With many columns and rows available in a single worksheet, Excel can store a huge number of records, making them available as you create a mail merge document. Figure 3.24 shows an Excel worksheet that can be used as a data source. Note the header row, with records beneath.

FIGURE 3.24 Excel Worksheet

Use an Access Database as a Data Source

As a database program, Microsoft Access is designed to manage large amounts of data. An Access database typically contains one or more tables; each table is a collection of related records that contains fields of information. Access enables you to query a table, which is the process of filtering records to show only those that meet certain search criteria. For example, you might want to view only the records of employees who work in the Accounting department. If you want to send a personalized communication, such as a letter or email, to all employees in the Accounting department, you could use the query as a basis for a mail merge. An Access table is well suited for use as a mail merge data source, due to its datasheet design (approximating an Excel worksheet) and its propensity for filtering records. Figure 3.23 shows a sample Access table that could be used as a data source.

Use a Word Table or an Outlook List as a Data Source

Because a Word table is organized in rows and columns, it is ideal for use as a data source in a mail merge. The first row in the Word table should include descriptive headers, with each subsequent row including a record from which data can be extracted during a mail merge process. The document used in a mail merge must contain a single table.

To merge a main document with an existing data source, click Select Recipients in the Start Mail Merge group on the Mailings tab. Click Use Existing List (see Figure 3.25). Navigate to the Excel, Access, or Word data source and double-click the file.

You can also use a list of Outlook contacts as a data source, which is especially helpful when you have bulk mail to send to your contacts. If you have an Outlook account, you can access basic information included with your contacts, including name, email address, mailing address, and phone number. Select Outlook Contacts as a data source when you begin the process of selecting recipients on the Mailings tab.

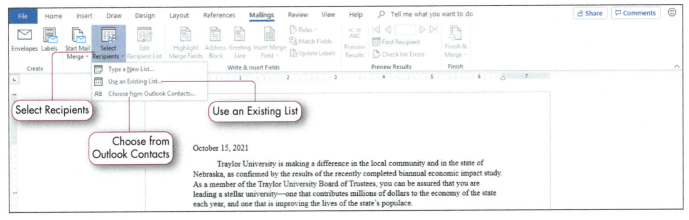

FIGURE 3.25 Selecting an Existing List

STEP 2 Edit a Data Source

Before merging a data source with the main document, you can rearrange records in the data source so that output from a mail merge is arranged accordingly. For example, you can sort the data source in alphabetical order by last name so that letters are arranged alphabetically or so that mailing labels print in order by last name. Or perhaps data in the data source should be updated, as might be the case if a recipient's address has changed. In addition, you could consider filtering a data source to limit the mail merge output based on criteria. You might, for example, want to print letters to send to clients in a specific region or state. Select Edit Recipient List on the Mailings tab and work with the dialog box shown in Figure 3.26 to edit, sort, filter, or otherwise modify the data source before including its contents in the main document during the mail merge process.

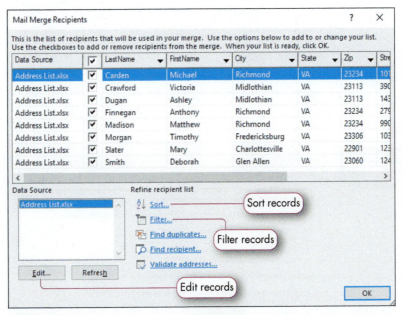

FIGURE 3.26 Editing and Sorting a Data Source

The same data source can be used to create multiple sets of form documents. You could, for example, create a marketing campaign in which you send an initial letter to the entire list, and then send follow-up letters at periodic intervals to the same mailing list. Alternatively, you could filter the original mailing list to include only a subset of names, such as the individuals who responded to the initial letter.

Completing a Mail Merge

After a data source has been identified and prepared for merging with a main document, the mail merge process is near completion. Items of text in the main document that are considered variable, such as an address block or a greeting, must be copied from the data source and inserted so that the resulting document is personalized to the recipient or purpose. Upon completion of the mail merge process, a merged document contains several documents, each uniquely prepared with areas of variable data.

STEP 3 Insert Merge Fields

The goal of a mail merge is often to produce a document or email that is personalized and sent to multiple recipients. As the document is prepared, you will indicate locations of variable data, such as a mailing address or a personalized greeting. Such areas of information are called **merge fields**. When you write a letter or create an email in preparation for a mail merge, you will insert one or more merge fields in the main document in the location(s) of variable data. As shown in Figure 3.27, the Write & Insert Fields group on the Mailings tab enables you to select Address Block, Greeting Line, or other items that can be included as a placeholder in the main document. The data source must contain fields that are recognizably named. For example, a field containing last names is given a field name that is likely to be recognized as containing a person's last name, such as LastName. Because a merge field corresponds with a field in the data source, matching the two fields guarantees that the right data will be inserted into the main document when you complete the merge.

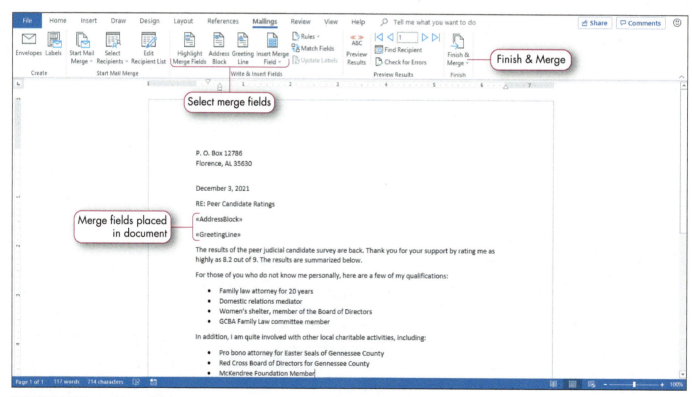

FIGURE 3.27 Insert Merge Fields

Merge fields display in the main document within angle brackets, for example <<AddressBlock>>, <<FirstName>>, or <<Donation>>. Those entries are not typed explicitly but are entered automatically when you select Insert Merge Field on the Mailings tab and then identify a field to include (refer to Figure 3.27) or when you choose from selected merge fields shown in the Write & Insert Fields group. As the document is merged with a data source, data from the data source will be placed in the position of the merge fields. Therefore, <<AddressBlock>> will not display in the merged document; instead a recipient's multi-line mailing address will be shown, followed by the same letter addressed to another recipient in the data source. Having inserted merge fields, you will preview the document to ensure correct placement and content.

STEP 4 Complete a Merge

After you create the main document and identify the source data, you are ready to begin the merge process. The merge process examines each record in the data source, and when a match is found, it replaces the merge field in the main document with the information from the data source. A copy of the main document is created for each record in the data source, creating individualized documents.

Finish the merge by selecting that action from the Mailings tab (refer to Figure 3.27). You can then choose to edit individual documents, providing a preview of each page of the merged document, or you can choose to immediately print the merged items.

Quick Concepts

7. Explain the importance of giving fields in a data source recognizable headings, such as LastName or Title. *p. 230*

8. Provide rationale for using Mail Merge, explaining why it is useful and in what situations. *p. 226*

9. Describe types of data sources that can be used in a mail merge process, explaining strengths of each data source and why you might choose one over the other. *p. 228*

Hands-On Exercises

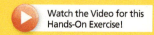

Skills covered: Select or Create a Recipient List • Use an Excel Worksheet as a Data Source • Edit a Data Source • Insert Merge Fields • Complete a Merge

3 Mail Merge

The executive summary is ready for you to send to members of the board of trustees. You merge a form letter with a data source of addresses, merging fields in the process to personalize each letter.

STEP 1 SELECT A RECIPIENT LIST

You select a recipient list, including the names and addresses of members of the board of trustees. Refer to Figure 3.28 as you complete Step 1.

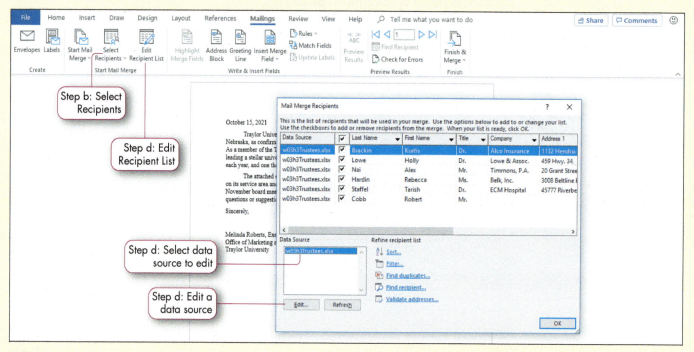

FIGURE 3.28 Selecting a Recipient List

a. Open *w03h3Letter* and save it as **w03h3Letter_LastFirst**.

b. Click the **Mailings tab** and click **Select Recipients** in the Start Mail Merge group.

c. Click **Use an Existing List**. Navigate to the location of your data files and double-click *w03h3Trustees.xlsx*. With **Sheet1$** selected, click **OK**.

d. Click **Edit Recipient List** in the Start Mail Merge group. Click **w03h3Trustees.xlsx** in the Data Source box and click **Edit**. Click **New Entry** and add the following record, leaving the Address 2 area blank.

| Mr. | Robert | Cobb | Tremont Insurance | Rt. 19 | Navarre | NE | 68811 |

e. Click **OK**. Click **Yes**. Click **OK**.

> **MAC TROUBLESHOOTING:** It is possible that you may have to add the record directly to the data source file instead of working through Word's Mailings tab settings.

You inadvertently left off one of the trustees, so you add him to the data source.

STEP 2 › EDIT A DATA SOURCE

You sort the records alphabetically by city and then by recipient last name. Refer to Figure 3.29 as you complete Step 2.

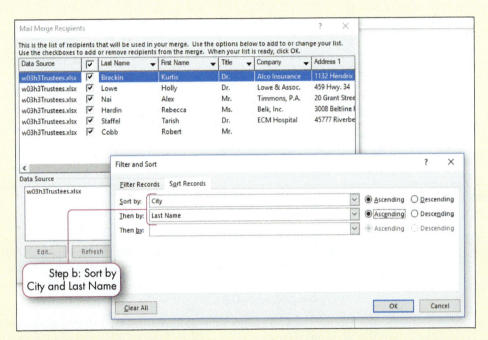

FIGURE 3.29 Sorting a Recipient List

a. Click **Edit Recipient List** in the Start Mail Merge group. Click **Sort** in the *Refine recipient list* area of the Mail Merge Recipients dialog box.

You open the data source in order to sort it.

b. Click the **Sort by arrow**, scroll down, and then click **City**. Ensure that sort order is Ascending. Click the **Then by arrow** and click **Last Name**. Ensure that sort order is **Ascending**. Click **OK**.

c. Scroll to the right to confirm that records are sorted by City. Scroll back to the left and confirm that the two records with a city of Navarre (records 3 and 4) are also sorted by Last Name. Click **OK**.

STEP 3 INSERT MERGE FIELDS

Although the body of the letter will be the same for all recipients, you create merge fields to accommodate variable data, including each recipient's name and address. Refer to Figure 3.30 as you complete Step 3.

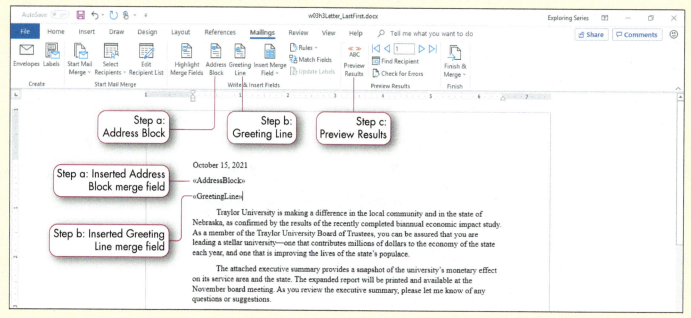

FIGURE 3.30 Inserting Merge Fields

a. Click after *2021* in the first line of the document. Press **Enter** twice. Click **Address Block** in the Write & Insert Fields group. Note the address in the Preview area. Ensure that *Insert recipient's name in this format*, *Insert company name*, and *Insert postal address* are selected. Click **OK**.

The AddressBlock merge field is inserted, with double chevrons on each side, indicating its status.

> **MAC TROUBLESHOOTING:** Because the Address Block and Greeting Line selections may not be available, click Insert Merge Field and choose fields that comprise the address block and greeting line—Title, First Name, Last Name, etc., ensuring that a space is shown between fields where necessary.

b. Press **Enter**. Click **Greeting Line**. Click **OK**.

A salutation is added, using the Greeting Line placeholder.

> **TROUBLESHOOTING:** If you make a mistake when entering merge fields, you can backspace or otherwise delete a field.

c. Click **Preview Results** in the Preview Results group.

d. Select the first four lines of the address block, from Ms. Rebecca Hardin through Suite 10. Click the **Layout tab** and remove any paragraph spacing shown in the Paragraph group.

STEP 4 COMPLETE A MERGE

Now that you have inserted merge fields into the form letter, the letter is complete. You will merge the main document with the data source so that each letter is personally addressed and ready to be printed. Refer to Figure 3.31 as you complete Step 4.

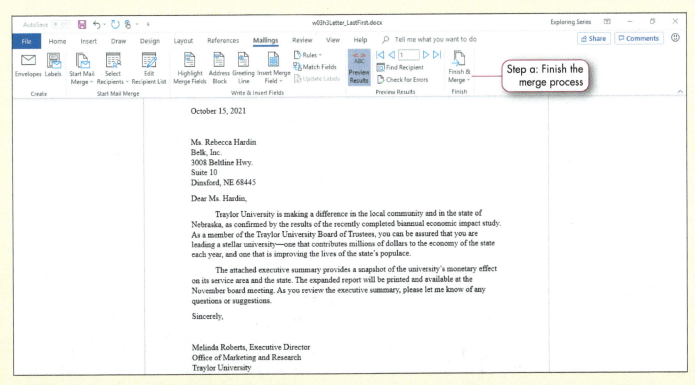

FIGURE 3.31 Completing a Mail Merge

a. Click the **Mailings tab**. Click **Finish & Merge** in the Finish group. Click **Edit Individual Documents**. Ensure that *All* is selected in the *Merge to New Document* dialog box and click **OK**.

Scroll through the letters, noting that each address and salutation is unique to the recipient. The main document and data source were merged to create a new document titled *Letters1*. You will save the document.

b. Save the document as **w03h3Merged_LastFirst** and close the document. Save and close w03h3Letter_LastFirst. Based on your instructor's directions, submit the following:

w03h2Traylor_LastFirst

w03h3Merged_LastFirst

Chapter Objectives Review

1. **Insert a table.**
   - Create or draw a table: You can include a table in a document by indicating the number of rows and columns, enabling Word to create the table, or you can draw the table, designing rows and columns of varying height and width.
   - Insert and delete rows and columns: You can insert or delete rows and columns in a table to accommodate additional data or to otherwise update a table.
   - Merge and split cells: As you update a table, you can merge cells in a row or column, accommodating text that is to be aligned within the row or column, and you can split cells within an existing row or column as well.
   - Change row height and column width: You can increase or decrease row height and column width in several ways—using selections on the Table Tools Layout tab, as well as manually dragging column or row borders.

2. **Format a table.**
   - Apply and modify table styles: Apply predesigned color, borders, and shading to a table by selecting a table style. Modify an existing style to adjust settings that better suit your purposes.
   - Adjust table position and alignment: A table can be aligned horizontally on a page; in addition, you can align cell contents within each cell horizontally and vertically.
   - Format table text: Format text included in a cell just as you would format text outside a table, with bold, italics, underlining, etc. You can also apply paragraph formatting, such as alignment, bullets, and numbering.

3. **Manage table data.**
   - Calculate using table formulas or functions: Numeric data in a table can be summarized through the use of formulas or functions. Formulas refer to table cells as a column and row, such as cell A1.
   - Use a formula: A formula includes table cells and mathematical operators to calculate data in a table.
   - Use a function: A function is a simplified formula, such as SUM or AVERAGE, that can be included in a table cell.
   - Sort data in a table: You can sort table columns in ascending or descending order, including up to three sort categories. For example, you can sort a table by department name, and then by employee name within department.
   - Include a recurring table header: When table rows are divided between pages, you can repeat header rows so that they display at the top of table rows on a new page.

4. **Enhance table data.**
   - Include borders and shading: Use borders and shading to customize a table's design. You can use Word's Borders gallery, Border Painter, or the Borders and Shading dialog box to enhance a table with borders and shading.
   - Convert text to a table and convert a table to text: You can convert text that is arranged in columns, with tabs separating columns, to a table. Conversely, you can convert text arranged in a table into text that is tabbed or otherwise divided into columns.
   - Include a table caption: A table caption identifies a table, numbering each table in a document sequentially. You can modify the caption style and update caption numbering when tables are deleted.

5. **Create a mail merge document.**
   - Select or create a recipient list: To prepare a form letter or other document type so that it is personalized with variable data, such as recipient name and address, you select or create a recipient list that will be merged with the main document.
   - Use an Excel worksheet as a data source: A worksheet, comprised of columns and rows, can be used as a data source containing records used in a mail merge.
   - Use an Access database as a data source: An Access table or query, containing records with data that can be merged with a main document, is often used as a data source for a mail merge.
   - Use a Word table or an Outlook list as a data source: A Word table is often used as a data source, with data merged into a main document. Similarly, Outlook contacts can be incorporated into a main document during a mail merge.
   - Edit a data source: Records in a data source can be sorted or filtered before they are merged with the main document. In addition, you can update records, and add or delete them.

6. **Complete a Mail Merge.**
   - Insert merge fields: Merge fields are placeholders in a main document to accommodate variable data obtained from a data source.
   - Complete a merge: As you complete a mail merge procedure, you update a main document with variable data from a data source, resulting in a new document that is a combination of the two.

Key Terms Matching

Match the key terms with their definitions. Write the key term letter by the appropriate numbered definition.

- a. Argument
- b. Border
- c. Border Painter
- d. Caption
- e. Cell
- f. Data source
- g. Form letter
- h. Formula
- i. Function
- j. Insert control
- k. Mail Merge
- l. Main document
- m. Merge field
- n. Order of operations
- o. Range
- p. Record
- q. Shading
- r. Table
- s. Table alignment
- t. Table style

1. _____ The position of a table between the left and right document margins. **p. 202**
2. _____ A descriptive title for a table. **p. 217**
3. _____ A document used in a mail merge process with standard information that you personalize with recipient information. **p. 226**
4. _____ A line that surrounds a Word table, cell, row, or column. **p. 214**
5. _____ A named collection of color, font, and border design that can be applied to a table. **p. 200**
6. _____ A background color that displays behind text in a table, cell, row, or column. **p. 216**
7. _____ A combination of cell references, operators, and values used to perform a calculation. **p. 211**
8. _____ The intersection of a column and row in a table. **p. 196**
9. _____ A process that combines content from a main document and a data source. **p. 226**
10. _____ Contains the information that stays the same for all recipients in a mail merge. **p. 226**
11. _____ An indicator that displays between rows or columns in a table, enabling you to insert one or more rows or columns. **p. 198**
12. _____ Organizes information in a series of rows and columns. **p. 196**
13. _____ A list of information that is merged with a main document during a mail merge procedure. **p. 227**
14. _____ Determines the sequence by which operations are calculated in an expression. **p. 211**
15. _____ Serves as a placeholder for the variable data that will be inserted into the main document during a mail merge procedure. **p. 230**
16. _____ A pre-built formula that simplifies creating a complex calculation. **p. 212**
17. _____ Feature that enables you to choose border formatting and click on any table border to apply the formatting. **p. 214**
18. _____ A positional reference contained in parentheses within a function. **p. 212**
19. _____ A group of related fields representing one entity, such as a person, place, or event. **p. 227**
20. _____ A series of adjacent cells. **p. 212**

Multiple Choice

1. In which of the following scenarios would you filter a data source in preparation for a mail merge?
   (a) When an Outlook contact list is not readily available
   (b) When mailing a promotional document to recipients in a particular zip code, excluding others
   (c) When records in a data source have not yet been sorted
   (d) When a data source is in a format other than a Word table and must be filtered prior to importing the data source

2. When you use the Table command on the Insert tab, Word inserts a table in a document, automatically aligning it:
   (a) in the center of the page.
   (b) at the right margin.
   (c) at the left margin.
   (d) evenly divided between the right and left margins.

3. Which of the following is true regarding the use of AutoFit to adjust the size of rows and columns in a table?
   (a) Even after AutoFit is enacted, you can still manually adjust rows and columns.
   (b) AutoFit should only be applied after all design is complete, as its settings are final.
   (c) AutoFit is not available on the ribbon, but is located in the Table Properties dialog box.
   (d) AutoFit must be applied before selecting a table style, as it might negate certain style settings.

4. Why might you choose to draw a table instead of using the Table command on the Insert tab?
   (a) The ribbon is temporarily hidden so the Insert tab is not available.
   (b) You know that rows and/or columns will have varying heights or widths.
   (c) The table will contain a minimal number of columns and/or rows so it is much quicker to draw it.
   (d) You know that it is easier to modify a table that is drawn (erasing gridlines or applying table styles).

5. You plan to place a function or formula in cell B4 of a Word table to total the cells in the column above. How would that function or formula appear?
   (a) =SUM(ABOVE)
   (b) =B1+B2+B3+B4
   (c) =TOTAL(ABOVE)
   (d) =SUM(B1-B3)

6. Which of the following is a purpose of a caption?
   (a) To add a comment to a particular table element
   (b) To provide documentation of the style used to design the table
   (c) To provide appropriate citation of a source from which the table was drawn
   (d) To provide a title in the first row of the table

7. Enhancing the appearance of a table by applying colors, borders, shading, and other design elements (as a set) is made possible by which of the following features?
   (a) Table styles
   (b) Border styles
   (c) Caption style
   (d) Border Painter

8. Which of the following best describes the purpose of a mail merge process?
   (a) To produce a document or email message in which variable data is drawn from a data source and combined with a main document
   (b) To produce a document or email message with fields containing data that should not vary from one document to the next
   (c) To produce only printed material, primarily mailing labels and envelopes
   (d) To produce only electronic material that is mass distributed, such as newsletters, for delivery through email

9. Why might you choose to convert text in a document to a table?
   (a) Because you want to manage the data by sorting rows or by applying other table features such as formulas or attractive table design.
   (b) Because text arranged as a table is simpler to include as a main document in a mail merge procedure than other text arrangements.
   (c) Because you can apply such features as borders and shading to text in a table but not to text in a document.
   (d) Because writing styles typically require that tabbed data be included in a table instead of as text in a document.

10. Having applied custom borders to a table, what feature do you use to copy the border style to another table?
    (a) Borders gallery
    (b) Format Painter
    (c) Border Painter
    (d) Border style

Practice Exercises

1 Academics

As an executive assistant working in the Admissions Office at Carnes State University, you are involved with a research project that is exploring the relationship between student GPA and involvement in academic clubs and scholarly activities. Academic and extracurricular data from a random sample of students in the College of Business has been summarized in a Word table that will be included in a brief memo to others on campus. You edit and format the report, preparing it for final submission. Refer to Figure 3.32 as you complete this exercise.

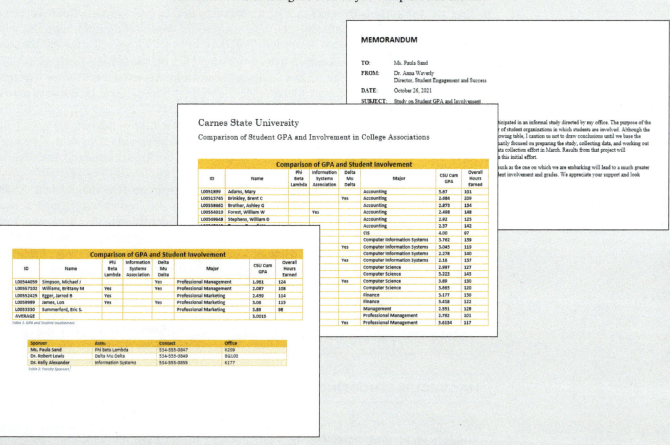

FIGURE 3.32 Academics Documents

a. Open *w03p1Academics* and save the document as **w03p1Academics_LastFirst**. Ensure that nonprinting characters are displayed.

b. Click before the blank paragraph mark at the top of page 2. Using Century Schoolbook font at 20-point size, type **Carnes State University** and press **Enter**. Change the font size to **16**. Type **Comparison of Student GPA and Involvement in College Associations**. Press **Enter**. Check the document for spelling and grammatical errors. All names in the table are correct.

c. Point to the outside left edge of the first row in the table and click to select the entire row. Click the **Table Tools Layout tab** and click **Align Center** in the Alignment group.

d. Click after the last entry in the last row, ending in *115*. Press **Tab**. Type the following data, tabbing between all entries except the last. Do not press Tab after the last item. Do not type the word (blank) but leave the cell empty.

| L0051899 | Adams, Mary | (blank) | (blank) | (blank) | Accounting | 3.67 | 101 |
| L0055558 | Shockney, Maria | Yes | Yes | (blank) | CIS | 4.00 | 97 |

e. Right-click any name identified as misspelled and click **Ignore All**. Click **Sort** in the Data group. In the Sort dialog box, click the **Sort by arrow** and select **Major**. The sort should occur in ascending order. Click the **Then by arrow** and sort by **Name** in ascending order. Click **OK**.

f. Indicate that Michael Simpson and Andrew Sams are both active in Delta Mu Delta by typing **Yes** in the Delta Mu Delta column for each of those students.

g. Click anywhere in the first row. Click **Insert Above** in the Rows & Columns group. Click **Merge Cells** in the Merge group. Change the font size to **16**. Type **Comparison of GPA and Student Involvement**. (Do not type the period.)

h. Click the **Table Tools Design tab**, click the **Shading arrow**, and then click **Gold, Accent 4** (row 1, column 8). Select all text in the third row through the end of the table, beginning with *L0051899* and ending with *98* (on page 3). Bold the selection. Click any cell to deselect the area.

i. Click the **table move handle** to select the entire table. Click the **Table Tools Design tab**. Click the **Pen Color arrow** in the Borders group and select **Gold, Accent 4**. Click the **Line weight arrow** and click **1½ pt**. Ensure that a single line border is shown. Click the **Borders arrow** and click **All Borders**. Click any cell to deselect the area.

j. Click after **98** at the end of the last row. Press **Tab**. Type **AVERAGE**. Press **Tab** six times to reach the *CSU Cum GPA* column. Click the **Table Tools Layout tab**. Click **Formula** in the Data group. Click between **SUM** and **(ABOVE)** in the Formula dialog box. Press **Backspace** repeatedly to remove the word *SUM*, and type **AVERAGE**. The formula should be =*AVERAGE(ABOVE)*. Click **OK**.

k. Click the **View tab** and click **Multiple Pages** in the Zoom group. Note that the table is split between two pages. Click **100%** in the Zoom group. Select the first two rows of the table on page 2. Click the **Table Tools Layout tab** and click **Repeat Header Rows** in the Data group. View the document in multiple pages once more to see the change. Change the view back to **100%**.

l. Click anywhere in the table. Point to the outside left edge of the table between *Frederick Davidson* and *David Stumpe*. Click the **Insert indicator**. Click in the first cell of the new row and type the following record, tabbing between cells. Do not type (blank) in the cell containing that text, but leave the cell empty.

| L00500932 | Johns, Lacey | (blank) | Yes | Yes | Computer Science | 3.89 | 130 |

> **MAC TROUBLESHOOTING:** Insert a new row using ribbon selections.

m. Move to page 3 and right-click the **average** (in the second to last column) in the last row. Click **Update Field**. Click the **References tab** and click **Insert Caption** in the Captions group. Ensure that the caption begins with *Table 1*. Type a colon (:) and press **Spacebar**. Type **GPA and Student Involvement**. (Do not type the period.) Ensure that the caption will display below the table and click **OK**.

> **MAC TROUBLESHOOTING:** Before updating the field, you must first select the value in the cell.

n. Press **Enter** twice. Click the **Insert tab** and click the **Object arrow** in the Text group. Click **Text from File**. Navigate to the location of the student data files and double-click *w03p1Sponsors*.

o. Select the newly inserted text, from *Sponsor* through *K177*. It does not matter whether you select the paragraph mark following *K177*, but do not select the blank paragraph on the next line. Click **Table** in the Tables group and click **Convert Text to Table**. Confirm that the new table will include four columns and four rows. Click **OK**.

p. Ensure that the entire table is selected. Right-click anywhere in the selected table and click **Table Properties**. Click the **Column tab**. Ensure that the Preferred width check box is selected, as indicated by a checkmark in the box. Change the width to **2** and ensure that the measurement is in Inches. Click **OK**. Do not deselect the table. Click **More** in the Table Styles group and select **Grid Table 4 - Accent 4** (row 4, column 5 under Grid Tables). Select the first row of the table and change the font color to **Black, Text 1**.

q. Right-click anywhere in the selected table and click **Table Properties**. Click the **Table tab**. Click **Center**. Click **OK**. Insert a caption below the table that reads **Table 2: Faculty Sponsors**. (Do not type the period.) Click **OK**. Click the **Home tab** and click **Increase Indent** in the Paragraph group to indent the caption.

r. Save the document. Press **Ctrl+Home**.

s. Click the **Mailings tab** and click **Select Recipients** in the Start Mail Merge group. Click **Use an Existing List**. Navigate to your data files and double-click *w03p1Faculty.xlsx*. Click **OK** to select the *Sheet1$* worksheet.

t. Click before the paragraph mark following *TO:*. Click **Insert Merge Field** in the Write & Insert Fields group. Click **Title**. Press **Spacebar**. Click **Insert Merge Field** and click **First_Name**. Press **Spacebar**. Click **Insert Merge Field** and click **Last_Name**. Click before the paragraph mark following *DATE:* and type today's date.

u. Click **Preview Results**. Click **Finish & Merge**. Click **Edit Individual Documents**. Ensure that All is selected and click **OK**. Scroll through the merged document to see that three recipients will receive the memo and tables. The document should include nine pages.

v. Save the document as **w03p1AcademicsMerged_LastFirst** and close the document. Save and close the file w03p1Academics_LastFirst. Based on your instructor's directions, submit w03p1AcademicsMerged_LastFirst.

2 Fitness Matters

As a health sciences graduate, you are coordinating a weight-loss and fitness program for a local health club, Fitness Matters. Participants in the weight-loss program have each set a weight-loss goal that you have recorded in a spreadsheet, along with the actual amount lost at the end of the first six weeks. You want to recognize those who have lost at least 10 pounds by sending a congratulatory letter. Because you already have the participants' information stored in a database table, you decide to create a mail merge document that you can use to quickly create letters to send to each person who has lost at least 10 pounds. Refer to Figure 3.33 as you complete this exercise.

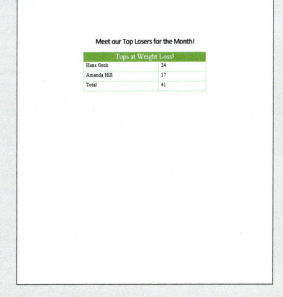

FIGURE 3.33 Fitness Matters Letter

a. Open *w03p2Letter* and save the document as **w03p2Letter_LastFirst**. Show nonprinting characters if they are not already displayed. Click before the blank paragraph mark after the second body paragraph. Click the **Insert tab**. Click **Table**. Drag to select 3 columns and 3 rows and click to insert the table.

b. Type **Pounds Lost** in the first cell on the first row. Press **Tab**. Type **Level**. Press **Tab**. Type **Step Prize**. Press **Tab**. Complete the table as shown below. Do not press Tab after the last entry.

10-15	Bronze	One free gym week
16-20	Silver	$100 gift card

c. Point to the top of the middle column so that the pointer is a downward arrow. Click to select the column. Right-click the selected column and click **Delete Columns**. Click in the first row. Click the **Table Tools Layout tab**. Click **Insert Above** in the Rows & Columns group. Click **Merge Cells**. Change the font size to **16**. Type **Fitness Matters!** Click the **Table Tools Layout tab** and click **Align Center** in the Alignment group.

d. Click anywhere in the fourth row. Click **Insert Below** in the Rows & Columns group. Complete the new row as shown below (contents of the last cell on the right will wrap).

>20	Trail bike from Spinning Spoke

e. Click **AutoFit** in the Cell Size group. Click **AutoFit Contents**. Click the **Table Tools Design tab**. Click **Plain Table 3** in the Table Styles group (fifth style from the left).

f. Right-click any cell in the table. Click **Table Properties**. Click **Center**. Click **OK**.

g. Click the **Pen Color arrow** and select **Green, Accent 6, Darker 25%** (row 5, column 10). Click **Line weight** and select **1 ½ pt**. Ensure that the line style option is a single line. Drag each horizontal gridline in the table, including the top and bottom of the table to paint each border. Press **Esc**.

h. Click the **table move handle**. Click the **Table Tools Layout tab** and click **Align Center** in the Alignment group.

i. Click any cell to deselect the area. Point to the outside left edge of the table between the second and third rows. Click the **Insert indicator**. Click in the first cell on row 3. Type **5-9** and press **Tab**. Type **One free fitness class**. Select row 1. Click the **Table Tools Design tab**. Click the **Shading arrow** and select **Green, Accent 6, Darker 25%**. Change the font color of the text in row 1 to **White, Background 1**.

> **MAC TROUBLESHOOTING:** Insert a new row using ribbon selections.

j. Press **Ctrl+End**. Click the **View tab** and ensure that Ruler is selected. Press **Ctrl+Enter** to insert a page break. Press **Enter** twice. Click the **Home tab** and click **Heading 1** in the Styles group. Type **Meet Our Top Losers for the Month!** Click **Center** in the Paragraph group. Select the heading line, bold the text, and ensure that the font color is **Black, Text 1**. Click after the heading line and press **Enter** twice.

k. Click the **Insert tab**. Click **Table** and select **Draw Table**. The pointer displays as a pencil. Positioning the insertion point below the heading line, drag a box approximately 4 inches wide and 1 ½ inches tall, using the vertical and horizontal rulers as guides. Draw one vertical gridline about 2 ½ inches from the left side of the box. Draw two horizontal gridlines to divide the table into three approximately evenly spaced rows of about ½ inch each. Press **Esc**.

l. Select row 1 and click **Merge Cells** in the Merge group. Type **Tops at Weight Loss!** Complete the remaining table cells as following:

Amanda Hill	17
Hans Groh	24

m. Click the **Table Tools Design tab** and apply the **Grid Table 1 Light - Accent 6 table style** (row 1, column 7 under Grid Tables). With the insertion point positioned after *24* in the last cell on the last row press **Tab**. Type **Total**. Press **Tab**. Click the **Table Tools Layout tab** and click **Formula** in the Data group. Click **OK** to accept the suggested SUM function.

n. Select rows 2 and 3. Click **Sort** in the Data group. Click the **Sort by arrow** and select **Column 2**. Select descending order. Click **OK**. Right-click any cell in the table and select **Table Properties**. Click **Center** and click **OK**.

o. Select row 1. Click **Align Center** in the Alignment group. Change the font size to **16**. Click the **Table Tools Design tab**, click the **Shading arrow**, and then click **Green, Accent 6**. Change the font color of the text in row 1 to **White, Background 1**. Click anywhere to deselect the row.

p. Click the **table move handle**. Right-click any selected cell and click **Table Properties**. Click the **Row tab**. Click the check box to select height and change the row height to **0.3"**. Click **OK**. Check spelling and save the document.

q. Click the **Mailings tab** and click **Select Recipients**. Click **Use an Existing List**.

r. Navigate to the location of your data files and double-click *w03p2Members.xlsx*. Ensure that *Sheet1$* is selected and click **OK**.

s. Click **Edit Recipient List**. Click **Sort** in the Mail Merge Recipients dialog box. Click the **Sort by arrow** and click **City**. Click the **Then by arrow** and select **LastName**. Both selections should be sorted in ascending order. Click **OK**.

t. Click **Filter**. Click in the first **Field box**, scroll down, and then select **Pounds Lost**. Click in the **Comparison box** and click **Greater than or equal**. Click in the **Compare to box** and type **10**. Click **OK**. Click **OK** again.

u. Click before the blank paragraph mark below the date on page 1. Click **Address Block** in the Write & Insert Fields group and click **OK** to insert the default format.

v. Place the insertion point at the left of the colon in the salutation line beginning with *Dear*. Press **Spacebar**. Click **Insert Merge Field** and select **FirstName**. Press **Spacebar**. Click **Insert Merge Field** and select **LastName**.

w. Place the insertion point at the left of the word *pounds* in the second-to-last sentence in the first body paragraph (beginning with *In fact, you have lost*). Click **Insert Merge Field** and select **Pounds_Lost**. Press **Spacebar**.

x. Click **Preview Results**. Click **Finish & Merge**. Click **Edit Individual Documents**. Ensure that *All* is selected and click **OK**. The letters are shown in a new document, titled *Letters1*.

y. Scroll through the pages to ensure that five two-page letters are included. Save the document as **w03p2LetterMerged_LastFirst** and close the document. Save and close w03p2Letter_LastFirst. Based on your instructor's directions, submit w03p2LetterMerged_LastFirst.

Mid-Level Exercises

1 Football Statistics   MyLab IT Grader

As a communication specialist for the Midwest Athletic Conference, you are preparing a summary of football statistics for inclusion in material published by the conference. Specifically, you highlight stats from the offensive units of leading teams in the conference. A Word table is an ideal way to summarize those statistics, so you prepare and populate several tables. Where appropriate, you include formulas to summarize table data. The tables must be attractively formatted, so you use Word's design and bordering tools as well.

a. Open *w03m1Football* and save it as **w03m1Football_LastFirst**.

b. Select text in the document from # (in the top-left corner) to *13.4* (in the bottom-right corner) and convert the text to a table. Whether you include the paragraph mark following 13.4 is irrelevant, but do not include the paragraph mark on the following line. Change page orientation to **Landscape**. Change the font of the second and third lines (Midwest Athletic Conference and Season Statistics) to **Cambria 16 pt**.

c. Delete column 1. Change the font of all table data to **Cambria 10 pt**. AutoFit the contents of the table.

d. Ensure that no team names in column 1 are bold or underlined. However, entries in row 1 should remain bold and underlined.

e. Insert a row above row 1 in the table. Complete the following steps to populate and format the new row:
   - Type **Offensive Statistics** in the first cell on the new row.
   - Type **Rushing Statistics** in the next cell on the first row.
   - Select the second, third, fourth, fifth, and sixth cells on the first row. Merge the selected cells.
   - Align *Rushing Statistics* in the center of the merged cell.
   - Type **Passing Statistics** in the next cell on the first row.
   - Select the cell containing *Passing Statistics* and the next three cells on the first row. Merge the cells.
   - Align *Passing Statistics* in the center of the merged cell.
   - Merge the remaining cells on row 1, type **Total** in the merged cell, and then center the word *Total*.

f. Insert a row between *HARKINSVILLE* and *DAKOTA STATE* and type the following data in the new row:

| JAMES COLLEGE | 38.2 | 41.0 | 220.5 | 4.2 | 19.7 | 32.7 | 0.601 | 199.2 | 7.6 | 57.9 | 449.3 | 5.9 | 12.7 |

g. Select a table style of **Grid Table 5 Dark - Accent 2** (row 5, column 3 under Grid Tables). Select all table text. Apply a Pen Color of **Orange, Accent 2, Darker 50%** (row 6, column 6 under Theme Colors) with a line weight of ½ pt and a line style of a **single line** to outside borders.

h. Ensure that the pen color is Orange, Accent 2, Darker 50% and the line weight is ½ pt. Select a **double-line style** and apply the selection to the border along the horizontal line separating row 1 from row 2, and also along the vertical line separating the first column from the second. The vertical line border should begin in row 2 and continue down the table.

i. Move to the end of the document, press **Enter** twice, and then insert a 3×5 table. Enter the following data in the table.

Calvin Spraggins	SPR	1428
Demaryius Schuster	DEN	1197
Brandon Marchant	CHI	1182
Wayne McAnalley	IND	1156
Sparky Hall	HOU	1114

j. Change the column width of all columns in the table to **1.5"**. Center all entries in the last two columns.

k. Insert a new blank row at the top of the table and complete the following steps:
   - Type **Receiving Yards** in the first cell on row 1.
   - Change the font size of the entry on row 1 to **14 pt**.
   - Merge all cells on row 1.
   - Ensure that *Receiving Yards* is centered.
l. Shade the first row with **Orange, Accent 2, Lighter 60%** (row 3, column 6 under Theme Colors).
m. Add a new blank row at the end of the table and type **Average** in the first cell of the new row. Enter a formula in the last cell of the new row to average all entries in the column above. You do not need to select a number format.
n. Align both tables horizontally in the center of the page. Check for spelling and grammatical errors. All names in both tables are correct.
o. Change the receiving yards for *Calvin Spraggins* to **1451**. Update the average to reflect the change.
p. Click any cell in the first table. Click the **Table Tools Design tab** and click **Border Painter** in the Borders group. With the pointer resembling a pen, click the double-line border that divides the first and second rows of the first table to "sample" it. Drag to apply the sampled border to the border dividing the first and second rows in the second table. Press **Esc** or click Border Painter to toggle off the tool.

> **MAC TROUBLESHOOTING:** When working with Border Painter, the pointer resembles a paintbrush instead of a pen.

q. Add a caption below the first table with the following text: **Figure 1: Midwest Athletic Conference Offensive Statistics**. (Do not include the period.) Add a caption below the bottom of the second table that reads **Figure 2: Total Receiving Yards**. (Do not include the period.) Modify the Caption style to include a font color of **Orange, Accent 2, Darker 50%**. Caption style font should be bold (not italicized) and centered. Save the document.
r. Begin a mail merge procedure, selecting as a recipient list *Sheet1$* of *w03m1Universities.xlsx*.
s. Sort the data source by **University** in ascending order. Merge the University field with the source document so that the university name displays after the text *Draft Prepared for:* on page 1. Ensure that a space is shown before the University placeholder. Preview the results and finish the merge, merging all records.
t. Save the merged document as **w03m1FootballMerged_LastFirst** and close the file. Save and close w03m1Football_LastFirst. Based on your instructor's directions, submit w03m1FootballMerged_LastFirst.

2 Fresh

MyLab IT Grader

Your company has developed a meal planning app that is being marketed in various grocery and food service establishments. You are preparing a one-page flyer promoting the meal planning service and app. The flyer includes information, some of which is shown in a table, describing the new service. You will merge the flyer with a data source so that each grocery store will have personalized copies of the flyer for distribution at those locations.

a. Open *w03m2Fresh* and save the document as **w03m2Fresh_LastFirst**. Ensure that nonprinting characters are displayed. At the second blank paragraph that follows the document logo, insert a 2×1 table.

b. Type **Meal Planning Series** in the first cell of the table. Right-align text in the next cell and type **Volume 24**. Format all text in the table as italics, with a font size of **10 pt**.

c. Adjust the width of both columns in the table to **2″**. Center the table horizontally on the page. Shade the table with **Green, Accent 6, Lighter 60%**.

d. Select text at the end of the page, beginning with *Citrus Salmon Whole Grain Rice Bowl* and ending in *490* (whether you select the paragraph mark that follows 490 is irrelevant). Convert the selected text to a table, accepting all default settings in the dialog box.

e. Adjust the width of the second column to **1″**.

f. Insert a row above the first row and type **Meal Selection** in the first cell. Type **Calories** in the second. Apply **Align Center** alignment to both entries.

g. Insert a column to the right of the second column. Include a heading for the new column in row 1 of **Remaining Calorie Count**. Text will wrap in the cell.

h. Insert a column to the left of the first column and adjust column width of the new column to **1″**. Merge all cells in the new column.

i. Type **FRESH!** in the merged cell. Click **Text Direction** in the Alignment group on the Table Tools Layout tab twice to rotate the text attractively. Click **Align Center**. Change the font size of text in the first column to **26**.

j. Click in the fourth column on the second row (below *Remaining Calorie Count*). Include a formula to subtract Calories from 1200. You do not need to select a Number format. Repeat the formula down the column, adjusting the cell reference for each row.

k. Change the calorie count for Barbecue Chicken Pizza to **550**. Update the field in the next cell to reflect the new amount.

l. Change the table style to **Grid Table 5 Dark – Accent 6** (row 5, column 7 under Grid Tables). Select text in row 1 (but not the merged cell) and choose **Align Center** alignment. Apply Align Center alignment to all numbers in the last two columns.

m. Center the table on the page horizontally. Select the first column. Select the first double line style and a line weight of ½ pt. Select a pen color of **Green, Accent 6**. Apply the border selection to the outside borders of the selected column. Save the document.

n. Place the insertion point at the end of the document (after *Download the Fresh! app from your friends at*). Press **Spacebar**. Click the **Mailings tab** and choose to select recipients from an existing list. You will use the Excel workbook, *w03m2Grocers.xlsx*. Use the *Grocers$* worksheet. Edit the recipient list and sort by Grocery Name in ascending order.

o. Insert a merge field of Grocery_Name. Preview the results and finish the merge of all records, resulting in a document with five pages.

p. Save the merged document as **w03m2FreshMerged_LastFirst** and close the file. Save and close w03m2Fresh_LastFirst. Based on your instructor's directions, submit w03m2FreshMerged_LastFirst.

Running Case

New Castle County Technical Services

You continue to work with promotional material for New Castle County Technical Services (NCCTS). In so doing, you create and modify a couple of tables, further outlining company services for potential clients. In addition, you prepare a cover letter to merge with a data source as you prepare to mail the promotional document.

a. Open *w03r1NewCastle.docx* and save it as **w03r1NewCastle_LastFirst**.

b. Show nonprinting characters. Scroll to page 5. Select the six clients listed in the tabbed area at the bottom of page 5 and near the top of page 6, making sure to include everything from the first nonprinting tab character through the paragraph mark after the words *Since 1999*. Convert the selected text to a table, accepting all dialog box settings.

c. Delete the first column in the table, which is empty. Change the column width of the new second column to **1.5"**.

d. Insert a row above the first row of the table. Type **Our Valued Connections** in the first cell of the newly inserted row. Merge both cells on the first row and apply center alignment to the text in the first row. Change the font size of text in the first row to **16 pt**.

e. Apply **Grid Table 4 – Accent 5 table style** to the table (row 4, column 6 under Grid Tables). Deselect **First Column** in the Table Style Options group. Place the insertion point after the last body paragraph on page 5 (ending in *a few of our current clients*). Press **Enter**. The table should display completely on page 6.

f. Select the table. Select a border style of **Single solid line, 1 ½ pt**. Apply the border style to all borders in the table. Center the table horizontally on the page.

g. Insert a row after the last row in the table and type **Call Us Today at 256-555-7100.** (Include the period.) Merge all cells on the last row and center the text. Apply shading to the last row, selecting a shading color of **Dark Gray, Accent 6, Darker 25%**. Change the font size of text in the last row to **16 pt** and bold the text.

h. Place the insertion point on the blank paragraph that precedes the last paragraph on page 1. Insert a 4×6 table. The table will span two pages. Beginning in the first cell on the first row of the table, type the following data:

Active accounts			
	2019	2020	Increase
Network Security	48	81	
IT Consulting	124	145	
Cloud Integration	38	40	
Disaster Recovery	109	132	

i. Adjust the column widths of columns 2, 3, and 4 to **1"**. Merge all cells in the first row and center the text. Adjust the font size of text in the first row to **16 pt** and bold the text.

j. Apply a table style of **Grid Table 4** (row 4, column 1 under Grid Tables). Bold all table entries in row 2. Center the table horizontally on the page.

k. Click in the last cell on the third row of the table. Insert a formula to determine the percentage increase from 2019 to 2020. The formula is **=(C3-B3)/B3*100**. Change the Number format to **0.00%**. Continue down the column, placing an appropriate formula in each cell to indicate the percentage increase. The Number format for all formulas in the last column is **0.00%**.

l. Change the number in the 2020 column for Cloud Integration to **59**. Update the field on the same row to adjust for the new entry.

m. Add a row at the end of the table. Type **Total** in the first cell on the last row. Include a formula in each of the next two cells to total the active accounts in 2019 and 2020. The formula should be **=SUM(ABOVE)-B2**, which sums the column above but removes the year from the calculation. Include a similar formula in the next cell, adjusting for the year reference. The Number format should be **#,##0**. Do not include a formula in the last cell on the last row.

n. Place the insertion point before the page break designation at the end of page 2. Click the **Layout tab**, click **Breaks**, and then insert a **Continuous** section break. Click anywhere in the body of the letter on page 1 or 2 and change the orientation of the letter to Portrait. All pages following the letter remain in Landscape orientation.

o. Delete the page break on page 3. Delete the first three lines of text (address lines) on page 1 and delete a space that may display before the Date placeholder. Select and replace [Date] on the first line of the letter with the current date by clicking the Insert tab and selecting **Insert Date and Time** in the Text group. Select the **month, day, year** format and do not choose to have the date update automatically. Ensure that the date displays on a line by itself. Save the document. Press **Enter** after the date.

p. Begin a mail merge procedure to combine the data source, *w03r1Clients.xlsx*, with the open document. Use the *Company Addresses$* worksheet. Edit the recipient list to filter records for an Account Manager of **Andrea Macon** and a State of **MS**. Sort the filtered records by **Name** in ascending order.

q. Replace [Recipient Name] on the first line of the address block on page 1 with the merge field of **Name**. Ensure that the square brackets are also removed and that <<Name>> displays on a line by itself. Replace text on the next three lines with merge fields of the same name, ensuring that square brackets are removed. Replace [City, ST Zip] with the merge field of **City**. Type a comma and press **Spacebar**. Insert the merge field of **State**. Press **Spacebar** and insert the merge field of **Zip**.

r. Replace [Business Type] in the first body paragraph (including the square brackets) with the merge field **Business_Type**. Ensure that a space precedes and follows the new insertion. Similarly, replace [Account Manager] and [Account No], with merge fields of the same name.

s. Replace [Your Name] at the end of the letter with your first and last names. Check spelling, correcting any misspellings and ignoring any names or company names that may be identified as errors.

t. Click the **Mailings tab** and click **Preview Results** to view a merged document. Merge all of the records into individual documents. The newly merged document should contain 12 pages.

u. Save the newly merged document as **w03r1NewCastleMerged_LastFirst**. Close the document. Save and close w03r1NewCastle_LastFirst. Based on your instructor's directions, submit w03r1NewCastleMerged_LastFirst.

Disaster Recovery

Assignment Planner

Your computer applications instructor assigned the task of using your Word skills to design an assignment planner. She challenged you to use what you have learned about Word tables to design an attractive document, with a table grid set up so you can enter class assignments for each week. The assignment is a group project, so you and your classmates decide to pattern the assignment planner table after a notebook you already use to record assignments. The first attempt at table design did not go so well, and the classmate who began the project needs help. Open the file *w03d1Planner* and redesign the document to produce an attractive planner that you could actually use. Do not settle for a mundane table. Use what you have learned about table styles, creating borders, and adjusting row height, column width, and alignment to create a stunning table. Make sure your table has enough space for a five-day week and six subjects. Complete the table with a sample week of assignments in classes in which you are enrolled. Save the completed document as **w03d1Planner_LastFirst** and close the document. Based on your instructor's directions, submit w03d1Planner_LastFirst.

Capstone Exercise

MyLab IT Grader

Boston Travels

You are employed with Boston Travels, a company that coordinates travel to various attractions in and around Boston. A recent effort involved consolidating various travel opportunities into travel packages at a steep discount. To promote that new development, you are working with a flyer that will be available at various locations throughout the city. In designing the flyer, you work with table design and formatting features. In addition, you include sponsor names on the flyer through a mail merge process.

Create and Enhance Tables

As a basic letterhead, you design a table consisting of company information and photos of Boston. You also create a table promoting the various travel packages that are now available through Boston Travels.

1. Open *w03c1Boston* and save it as **w03c1Boston_LastFirst**. Display nonprinting characters.

2. Ensure that the insertion point is at the beginning of the document. Press **Enter**. Return to the beginning of the document and insert a 3×2 table. Type **Boston Travels** in the first cell on the first row.

3. Insert the *w03c1Image1.jpg* picture file in the first cell of the second row. Change the picture height to **1"**. (Ensure that you use selections on the Picture Tools Format tab to change the picture height.) In the second cell of the second row, insert the *w03c1Image2.jpg* picture file. Change the picture height to **1"**. In the third cell of the second row, insert the *w03c1Image3.jpg* picture file and resize it to **1"** in height.

4. Select the table and AutoFit table contents. Merge all cells on the first row, and center row contents. Change the font size of text in row 1 to **22 pt**.

5. Apply a table style of **Grid Table 4 – Accent 1** (row 4, column 2 under Grid Tables). Center the table horizontally on the page. Reduce left and right cell margins to **0"**.

6. Select the table. Select a border style of **Double solid lines, ½ pt, Accent 1** (row 3, column 2). Apply the selection to outside borders. Change the font color of text in the first row to White, Background 1 and ensure that it is bold.

7. Press **Enter** after the third paragraph (ending in *fantastic pricing*). Select text at the end of the document, from *Back Bay/Fenway* to *16.00*. Whether you select the ending paragraph mark on the last line is irrelevant. Convert the text to a table, accepting all dialog box settings.

8. Insert a column before the first column in the table. Type **Family Fun Tours** in the first cell of the new column. Select the first three cells in the new column and merge them.

9. Type **Patriot Tours** in the second cell of the first column (below the *Family Fun Tours* merged cell). Select the second, third, and fourth cells in the first column and merge them.

10. Type **JFK/Harvard Tours** in the third cell of the first column (below the *Patriot Tours* merged cell). Select the final three cells in the first column and merge them.

11. Select the third column. Click **Split Cells** and uncheck *Merge cells before split*. Accept all other dialog box settings. Change the width of the second column, containing attractions, to **2"**. Change the width of the last two columns to **0.85"**.

12. Insert a row above the first row. Type **Tour Package** in the first cell of the new row. Type **Attraction** in the second cell on the same row. Type **Discounted Admission** in the third cell on the same row.

13. Merge the last two cells on row 1. Apply **Align Center** alignment to row 1. Create a formula in the last cell on row 2 that subtracts (0.4*admission price) from the admission price. The admission price is shown in cell C2, so the formula should be **=C2-(0.4*C2)**. The Number format should be **#,##0.00**. Adjusting for each row, enter a discounted admission formula for each attraction in the table.

14. Apply a table style of **List Table 4 – Accent 1** (row 4, column 2 under List Tables). Select all tour names in column 1 and apply **Align Center** alignment. Center the table horizontally on the page.

15. Select all numbers in the last column and change the font color to **Red** (second column in Standard colors). Check spelling and correct any errors. Ignore any grammatical error related to the use of the word *So*. Save the document.

Use Mail Merge to Create Personalized Document

You include the name of each sponsor of the tour program at the end of the document so that personalized flyers can be generated and distributed.

16. Begin a mail merge, selecting *w03c1Sponsors.xlsx* as the data source. Data is located on *Sheet1$* of the data source. Edit the recipient list to sort by **Sponsor** in ascending order.

17. Replace [Sponsor] on the last line of the document with the merge field of **Sponsor**. Preview results and finish the merge, editing individual documents and merging all. The merged document should contain seven pages.

18. Save the merged document as **w03c1BostonMerged_LastFirst**. Save and close w03c1Boston_LastFirst. Based on your instructor's directions, submit w03c1BostonMerged_LastFirst.

Word | Research and Collaboration

LEARNING OUTCOME: You will model professional use of research and collaboration tools.

OBJECTIVES & SKILLS: After you read this chapter, you will be able to:

Research Paper Basics

OBJECTIVE 1: USE A WRITING STYLE AND ACKNOWLEDGE SOURCES 252
Select a Writing Style, Format a Research Paper, Create a Source and Include a Citation, Share and Search for a Source, Create a Bibliography

OBJECTIVE 2: CREATE AND MODIFY FOOTNOTES AND ENDNOTES 258
Create Footnotes and Endnotes, Modify Footnotes and Endnotes

OBJECTIVE 3: EXPLORE SPECIAL FEATURES 260
Create a Table of Contents, Create an Index, Create a Cover Page

HANDS-ON EXERCISE 1 264

Document Tracking

OBJECTIVE 4: TRACK CHANGES 271
Use Track Changes, Accept and Reject Changes

OBJECTIVE 5: REVIEW A DOCUMENT 273
Use Markup, Add a Comment, View Comments, Reply to Comments, Work with a PDF Document

HANDS-ON EXERCISE 2 280

Online Document Collaboration

OBJECTIVE 6: USE ONEDRIVE 284
Use OneDrive with File Explorer

OBJECTIVE 7: SHARE DOCUMENTS 286
Invite Others to Share, Share a Document Link, Send as an Attachment

OBJECTIVE 8: COLLABORATE WITH WORD AND WORD ONLINE 290
Use Word Online

HANDS-ON EXERCISE 3 294

CASE STUDY | Literature Analysis

You are a college student enrolled in several classes in which you are required to write papers. One is a literature class, and another is a business management class. Each class requires that you adhere to a specific writing style; each style differs with respect to writing guidelines and the use of citations. As a requirement for the literature class in which you are enrolled, you will prepare an analysis of "A White Heron," a short story by Sarah Orne Jewett. The analysis is a group effort, completed by four students, including you. You are required to develop the paper based on a particular writing style, and you will include citations and a bibliography. Your instructor, Mr. Carpenter, will provide feedback in the form of comments that the group will then incorporate into the paper. Because you are a commuting student with a part-time job, you are not always on campus and your time is very limited. As is typical of many college students, even those in your literature group, time and availability are in short supply. The group is quick to realize that much of the coordination on the project must be done from a distance. You will share the project in such a way that each student can contribute, although not in a group setting. Instead, the document will be available online, with each student reviewing, contributing, and reposting the project. Another project involves a short paper for your business management class in which you will include a cover page as well as footnotes.

CHAPTER 4

Communicating with and Producing Professional Papers

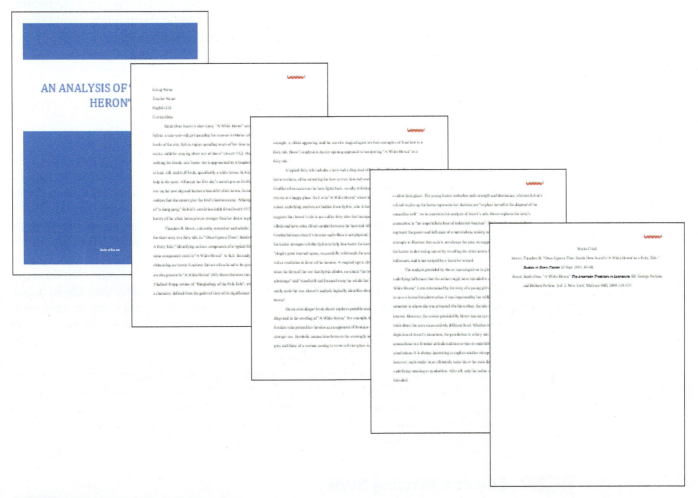

FIGURE 4.1 Literature Analysis Document

CASE STUDY | Literature Analysis

Starting Files	Files to be Submitted
w04h1Analysis w04h1Airlines w04h2WhiteHeron w04h2Entry.pdf	w04h1Airlines_LastFirst w04h2WhiteHeron_LastFirst w04h2Entry_LastFirst.pdf w04h3Analysis_GroupName

MyLab IT Grader An alternate version of this project is available as a MyLab IT Grader Assessment

Research Paper Basics

Researching a topic and preparing a research paper are common components of most college degrees. Although Word cannot replace the researcher, it can provide a great deal of support for properly citing sources and adhering to specific style manuals. A *style manual*, or style guide, is a set of rules and standards for writing documents. In addition, Word assists with preparing footnotes and endnotes and preparing a bibliography. Although the research and wording of a research paper are up to you, Word is an excellent tool in the production of an attractive, well-supported document.

In this section, you will explore the use of Word features that support the preparation of a research paper. Specifically, you will learn how to use style manuals, create source references and insert citations, develop a bibliography, and work with footnotes and endnotes.

Using a Writing Style and Acknowledging Sources

As you write a research paper, you will develop content that supports your topic. The wording you use and the way you present your argument are up to you; however, you will be expected to adhere to a prescribed set of rules regarding page design and the citing of sources. Those rules are spelled out in a style guide that you can refer to as you develop a research paper. A style guide prescribes such settings as margins, line and paragraph spacing, the use of footnotes and endnotes, the way sources are cited, and the preparation of a bibliography.

It is common practice to use a variety of **sources** to supplement your own thoughts when writing a paper, report, legal brief, or other type of research-based document. In fact, the word *research* implies that you are seeking information from other sources to support or explore your topic when writing a research paper. Properly citing or giving credit to your sources of information ensures that you avoid plagiarizing. Merriam-Webster's Collegiate Dictionary's[1] definition of **plagiarizing** is "to steal and pass off (the ideas or words of another) as one's own." Not limited to failure to cite sources, plagiarism includes buying a paper that is already written or asking (or paying) someone else to write a paper for you. In addition to written words, plagiarism applies to spoken words, multimedia works, or graphics. Plagiarism has serious moral and ethical implications and is typically considered as academic dishonesty in a college or university.

STEP 1 Select a Writing Style

When assigning a research paper, your instructor will identify the preferred **writing style**. The choice of writing style is often a matter of the academic discipline in which the research is conducted. A writing style provides a set of rules that results in standardized documents that present citations in the same manner and that include the same general page characteristics. In that way, research documents contain similar page features and settings, so a reader can focus on the content of a paper without the distraction of varying page setups. However, a style manual does not require specific wording within a research paper and it will not assist with developing your topic or conducting research.

The humanities disciplines, including English, foreign languages, philosophy, religion, art, architecture, and literature, favor the **MLA (Modern Language Association)** style, which has been in existence for more than 50 years. Brief parenthetical (synonymous with

---

[1] By permission. From Merriam-Webster's Collegiate Dictionary, 11th edition © 2019 by Merriam-Webster, Inc. (www.Merriam-Webster.com).

in-text) citations throughout a paper identify sources of information, with those sources arranged alphabetically in a Works Cited page. MLA style is used in many countries around the world, including the United States, Brazil, China, India, and Japan. Current MLA guidelines are published in the *MLA Handbook for Writers of Research Papers* and the *MLA Style Manual and Guide to Scholarly Publishing*.

Such disciplines as business, economics, communication, and social sciences promote the use of **APA (American Psychological Association)** writing style. Developed in 1929, APA attempts to simplify the expression of scientific ideas and experiment reports in a consistent manner. Its focus is on the communication of experiments, literature reviews, and statistics. The *Publication Manual of the American Psychological Association* provides current rules and guidelines associated with the writing style.

The **Chicago writing style** is an excellent choice for those who are preparing papers and books for publication. In fact, it is one of the most trusted resources within the book publishing industry. True to its name, the Chicago writing style was developed at the University of Chicago in 1906. It is currently in its 17th edition. The style is often referred to as CMS or CMOS. Often associated with the Chicago writing style, the Turabian writing style originated as a subset of Chicago. The dissertation secretary at the University of Chicago, Kate Turabian, narrowed the Chicago writing style to focus on writing papers. To do so, she omitted much of the information that is relevant for publishing. Currently, Turabian style is used mainly for the development of papers in the field of history. As you start working on your research paper, you may ensure the correct writing style is designated to your Word document from the Citations & Bibliography group on the References tab (see Figure 4.2).

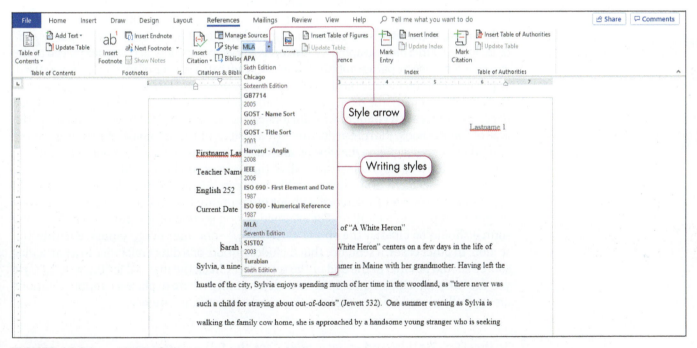

FIGURE 4.2 Select a Writing Style

Format a Research Paper

Regardless of the writing style used, most research papers in academic writing share several common formatting features to maintain some uniformity and consistencies across disciplines and to help produce a professional-looking document. With the exception of the title or cover page, some of these commonly established guidelines for a research paper are described as:

- Align text at the left
- Double-space between lines
- Include no paragraph spacing before or after
- Set all margins (top, bottom, left, and right) at 1" to leave room for comments
- Indent the first line of all body paragraphs by 1/2"
- Indent quotations 1" from the left margin
- Separate sentences by only one space
- Use a serif font, such as Times New Roman, at 12 pt size
- Create a right-aligned header, including the page number in Arabic numerals, positioned 1/2" from the top of the page

Create a Source and Include a Citation

By its very nature, a research paper is a collection of ideas and statements related to a topic. Many of those ideas are your own, summarizing your knowledge and conclusions. However, you will often include facts and results obtained from other sources. When you quote another person, glean ideas from others, or include information from another publication, you must give credit to the source by citing it in the body of your paper and/or including it in a bibliography. A **citation** is a brief, parenthetical reference placed at the end of a sentence or paragraph that directs a reader to a source of information you used. Typically, a citation includes an author or publication name, with an optional page number. For more information, the reader can check the source on your bibliography or Works Cited page. As you create a citation, you add a reference source. A cited reference includes the type of source (book, journal article, report, website, etc.), title, publisher, page number(s), and other items specific to the type of source. At the conclusion of a report, you can use Word to create a bibliography, listing all of the sources you have cited.

Proper placement of a citation within a research paper is critical. A citation should appear near a source of reference without interrupting the flow of a sentence. Use your judgment in placing a citation. For example, a long section of text that comes from one source should be cited at the end of the section—not after every sentence within the section. In other cases, a sentence that includes a quote or a direct reference to a particular source should be cited at the end of the sentence. Check the manual for the writing style you are working with for assistance with determining where to place a citation. Citations are typically placed before a punctuation mark that ends a sentence.

To insert a citation and source, complete the following steps:

1. Place the insertion point at the end of the sentence that you want to cite, typically before the ending punctuation mark.
2. Click the References tab.
3. Click Insert Citation in the Citations & Bibliography group.
4. Click the source if inserting a previously defined source. Click Add New Source and type the new source information if creating a new source (see Figure 4.3).

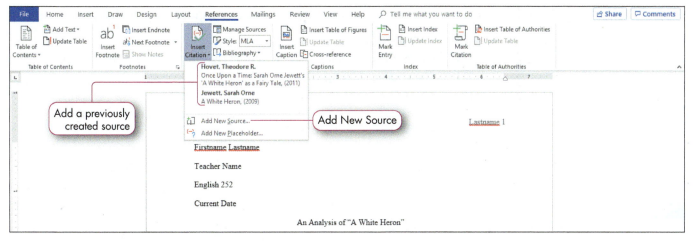

FIGURE 4.3 Add a Source

Depending on the writing style in use, the way a citation is worded may vary. Although Word automatically formats parenthetical citations (citations in parentheses in the body of the text) with the author's last name and some other information, you might need to modify the wording or placement of items to accommodate the writing style. For example, if a sentence you are citing includes the author's name, most writing styles require only the page number in the citation, not the author's name. However, Word will place the author's name in the citation, so you must edit the citation to remove the name. A citation can be edited after selecting it, and options include adding a page reference and/or suppressing the author, year, or title. When you click a parenthetical citation and click the Citation Options arrow, you can do more than simply edit the citation. You can also choose Edit Source (updating the source citation wherever it appears in the document) or Convert citation to static text (removing the field designation from the citation so that you can treat it like normal text). After you convert the citation to text, it will still be included in a bibliography generated by Word.

Share and Search for a Source

When you create a source, it is available for use in the current document, saved in the document's **Current List**. It is also placed in a **Master List**, which is a database of all sources created in Word on a computer. Sources saved in the Master List can be shared in any Word document. This feature is helpful to those who use the same sources on multiple occasions. Suppose you are working on a research paper that addresses a topic similar to that of another paper you created on the same computer, you can access the same source by using Manage Sources.

> **To access a source from the Master List of previously defined sources, complete the following steps:**
>
> 1. Click the References tab.
> 2. Click Manage Sources in the Citations & Bibliography group.
> 3. Select a source in the Master List that you intend to use in the current document (see Figure 4.4).
> 4. Click Copy to move it to the Current List.
> 5. Click Close.
> 6. Click in the location of the citation in the current document and click Insert Citation.
> 7. Select the source reference.

On a Mac, to access previously defined sources, complete the following steps:

1. Click the References tab.
2. Click Citations and click Settings in the bottom right corner of the Citations pane.
3. Click Citation Source Manager.
4. Follow steps 3-5 in the PC step box on the previous page.
5. Click in the location of the citation in the current document and double-click the source to insert in the Citations pane.
6. Close the Citation pane.

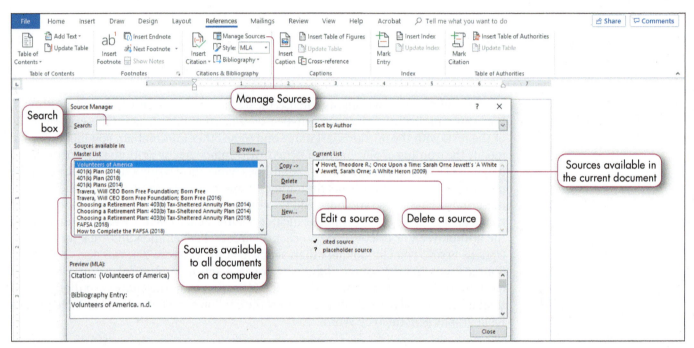

FIGURE 4.4 Manage a Source

The Source Manager not only enables you to share sources among several documents, it also makes it easy to delete and edit sources. In the Source Manager dialog box, select a source from either the Master or Current List, and then click Delete or Edit (refer to Figure 4.4). If sources are numerous, you might appreciate a quick way to search for a particular source. Search by author, title, or year by typing a search term in the Search box of the Source Manager dialog box (refer to Figure 4.4). As you type, Word narrows the results, so you can more easily determine if a source exists that meets your search criteria.

STEP 2 Create a Bibliography

A ***bibliography*** is a list of documents or sources that are consulted by an author during research for a paper. It guides a reader to sources of your research for additional study, and it also provides a reader with an opportunity to validate your references for accuracy. In theory, a bibliography lists not only those references that were cited in parenthetical terms throughout the paper, but also those that were not cited but were helpful as you prepared the paper. A ***Works Cited*** page, on the other hand, is designed to contain only those sources that were cited in the paper, which is the way most research documents are expected to be prepared. However, a bibliography and a Works Cited page are considered synonymous terms when working with Word, and they both include consulted and cited sources. After a bibliography is prepared, you can always edit it to add additional references if required. Figure 4.5 shows a bibliography developed in Word and is formatted according to the MLA writing style, which requires the use of *Works Cited* as a title. Note that all sources include a hanging indent, which is typical of all writing style requirements. Further, entries are listed in alphabetical order by the last names of authors or editors, or by the first words of the titles.

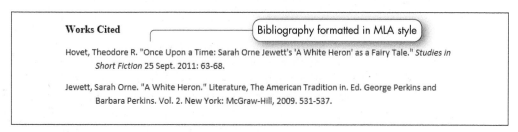

FIGURE 4.5 Bibliography

Depending on the writing style you are following, the term used for the list of references varies. MLA uses the term *Works Cited*, whereas APA requires *References*. Still others prefer *Bibliography*. You should be familiar with the preferred term and organization before using Word to develop the list of references.

The works cited/bibliography should be placed on a separate page by selecting Bibliography, References, or Works Cited (depending on the particular writing style requirement) in the Citations & Bibliography group on the References tab. If you want no heading but simply the formatted references, select Insert Bibliography.

Regardless of which approach you take, you should always confirm that the resulting page meets all requirements of the style to which you are writing. Just as you would proofread a document instead of relying solely on Word's spelling checker, you should also consult a writing style manual to make sure your bibliography is correct.

When Word creates a bibliography page, it formats all citations as a single field. As shown in Figure 4.6, when you insert a bibliography list that Word has prepared, the entire list is shown as a unit, called a Bibliography field. The bibliography page does not update automatically should your sources change. However, the field can be updated at a later time when you include additional sources within the paper by clicking Update Citations and Bibliography (see Figure 4.6) to include the new sources in the bibliography. You can also choose to format the existing bibliography with a different title (perhaps changing from *Works Cited* to *References*), and you can convert the bibliography to static text.

FIGURE 4.6 Update a Bibliography

Creating and Modifying Footnotes and Endnotes

A ***footnote*** is a citation or note that appears at the bottom of a page, while an ***endnote*** serves the same purpose but appears at the end of a document. Like parenthetical citations, the purpose of a footnote and endnote is to draw a reader's attention to a specific source of information. In addition, footnotes and endnotes are often used to further describe a statistic or statement used in the report without including additional detail in the text. For example, a statistic on the number of victims in a natural disaster or the amount of money given through a government program could be further detailed in a footnote. You might also define or illustrate a concept included in the report, providing a personal comment. Much of business writing is persuasive text, in which you explain a situation or encourage others to take some action. Using a footnote is a great way to further describe a statistic used in your text without having to incorporate it into the written paragraph. That way, you do not risk cluttering the document with overly explanatory text, perhaps losing or diverting the attention of the reader. A footnote, providing clarification of a statistic, is shown in Figure 4.7. Note that the footnote is linked by a superscript (elevated number) to the corresponding reference in the paper.

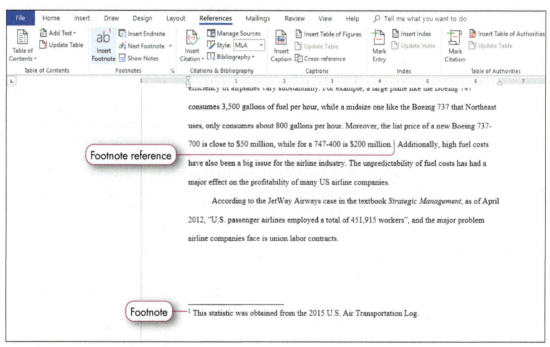

FIGURE 4.7 Include a Footnote

You should never use both footnotes and endnotes in the same paper. Choosing whether to use footnotes or endnotes, if at all, depends in part on the number of citations included and the way you want your reader to process the report's information. Because endnotes are included as a list at the end of the document, they do not add clutter to the bottom of pages. In addition, they might make the report easier to read because a reader's gaze is not constantly shifting back and forth from the bottom of a page to the text. Conversely, a footnote provides immediate clarification of a source and enables the writer to make additional comments related to a statement on the same page as the footnote.

Although you might choose to include footnotes to provide additional information related to a statement on the same page, you will most likely use a bibliography or Works Cited page to provide a complete list of referenced sources in a paper. An advantage to using a bibliography for that task is that each source is listed only once. In contrast, a footnote or endnote appears each time a source is referenced, regardless of how many times the same source is cited in a paper. Although subsequent footnotes and endnotes referencing the same source are abbreviated, they are still listed, often resulting in a cluttered, possibly distracting, arrangement of repetitive information.

> **TIP: FOOTNOTES VERSUS PARENTHETICAL CITATIONS**
> The choice of whether to use a footnote or a parenthetical citation to reference a source depends somewhat on the writing style you are following. Always refer to the writing style guide when considering which to use, as each style tends to prefer one to the other. The choice is also related to the type of document. For example, legal documents almost always rely heavily on footnotes instead of parenthetical citations.

Including a bibliography does not mean that you cannot use footnotes to provide more detailed descriptions of statements or facts in the paper. You should be aware, however, that most writing styles limit a footnote to only one sentence. Therefore, any planned explanation of a report statement must be condensed to just one sentence.

STEP 3 Create Footnotes and Endnotes

Source information in a document that you reference with a footnote or endnote includes a number or symbol in superscript. The reference is then keyed to the same number or symbol at the end of the page (footnote) or at the end of the document (endnote). The References tab includes the Insert Footnote and Insert Endnote commands. By default, Word sequentially numbers footnotes with Arabic numerals (1, 2, and 3) and endnotes with lowercase Roman numerals (i, ii, and iii). If you add or delete footnotes or endnotes, Word renumbers the remaining notes automatically.

> **To insert a footnote or endnote, complete the following steps:**
> 1. Click beside the text to reference (or after ending punctuation, if referencing a sentence).
> 2. Click the References tab.
> 3. Click Insert Footnote (or Insert Endnote) in the Footnotes group.
> 4. Type the footnote or endnote text.
> 5. Double-click the footnote or endnote mark to return to the text reference.

Modify Footnotes and Endnotes

Occasionally, you will determine that different wording better suits a particular footnote or endnote. Or perhaps you want to remove a footnote or endnote completely. You can even change the format of a footnote or endnote, changing the font, font size, or character formatting. To modify a footnote or endnote, double-click the numeric reference in the body of the document. The insertion point will be placed to the left of the footnote or endnote number.

To insert a footnote or endnote while specifying settings other than those selected by default, use the Footnotes launcher on the Reference tab to open the Footnote and Endnote dialog box. As shown in Figure 4.8, you can modify the placement, number format, symbol, and initial number before you insert a new footnote or endnote. On the other hand, you may delete any unwanted footnote or endnote by selecting the numeric footnote or endnote indicator in the document and pressing Delete.

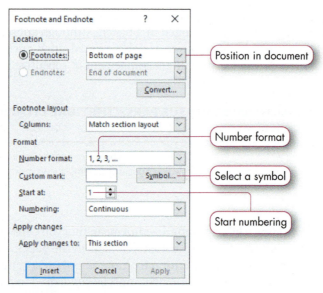

FIGURE 4.8 Footnote and Endnote Dialog Box

You can remove note text and replace it with alternate wording, just as you would adjust wording in a document. If you plan to change the format of a single note, instead of affecting all footnotes or endnotes in a document, you can select the note text and apply different formatting—perhaps italicizing or bolding words. More often, you might want to adjust the format of every footnote or endnote in a document. Footnotes are formatted in Footnote Text style and endnotes are formatted in Endnote Text style. Those styles include a specific font type, font size, and paragraph spacing, and can also be accessed from the Styles pane.

To modify the style of either a footnote or endnote, complete the following steps:

1. Right-click a footnote or endnote and select Style.
2. Click Modify in the Style dialog box.
3. Adjust the font and alignment settings or click Format for more selections.
4. Click OK repeatedly to accept the settings and return to the document.

Exploring Special Features

Although writing a research paper is a typical requirement of a college class, it is not the only type of paper you are likely to write. In the workplace, you might be asked to contribute to technical reports, grant proposals, and other types of business documents. Those reports are not likely to be as strictly bound to writing style rules as are reports written for academic purposes. In fact, you might find it necessary to include special features such as a table of contents, an index, and even a cover page to properly document a paper and make it easier to navigate. Such features are not usually included in a college research report or required by academic writing style guides, but they are common components of papers, chapters, and articles to be published or distributed.

STEP 4 ▸ Create a Table of Contents

For a long, written report or research paper, a ***table of contents*** lists headings and subheadings in the order they appear in the document, along with the page numbers on which the entries begin. The key to enabling Word to create a table of contents is to apply heading styles to headings in the document at appropriate levels. You can apply built-in styles, Heading 1 through Heading 9, or identify your own custom styles to use when generating the table of contents. For example, if you apply Heading 1 style to major headings, Heading 2 style to subordinate headings, and lower-level heading styles to remaining headings as appropriate, Word can create an accurate table of contents. The table of contents is displayed on a separate section of the document.

> **To insert a predefined table of contents, complete the following steps:**
> 1. Ensure that headings in the document are formatted with heading styles according to level.
> 2. Click the References tab.
> 3. Click Table of Contents in the Table of Contents group.
> 4. Select an Automatic table style to create a formatted table of contents that can be updated when heading text or positioning changes (or select Manual Table to create a table of contents that is not updated when changes occur).

For more flexibility as you design a table of contents, you can choose Table of Contents (on the References tab) and select Custom Table of Contents. From the Table of Contents dialog box, select options related to page numbering and alignment, general format, level of headings to show, and leader style (the characters that lead the reader's eye from a heading to its page number).

A table of contents is inserted as a field. When you click a table of contents, the entire table is shown as an entity that you can update or remove. As shown in Figure 4.9, controls at the top of the selection enable you to update, modify, or remove a table of contents. As you make changes to a document, especially if those changes affect the number, positioning, or sequencing of headings, you will want to update any associated table of contents. You will indicate whether you want to update page numbers only or the entire table.

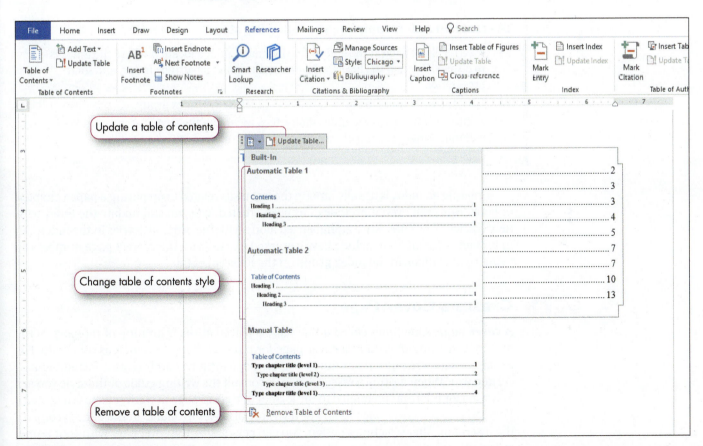

FIGURE 4.9 Update a Table of Contents

Create an Index

No doubt you have used an ***index*** to locate a topic of interest in a book. In doing so, you were able to move quickly to the topic. Most books and many lengthy papers include an index. Typically located at the end of a book or document, an index provides an alphabetical listing of topics included in a document, along with related page numbers. In a document, you can mark items to include and have them automatically formatted as an index. In situations where there are more than one name or term to describe the same content, you can mark the item for cross reference.

To mark items to include in an index, complete the following steps:

1. Select a word or phrase to include in an index.
2. Click the References tab and click Mark Entry in the Index group.
3. Select or confirm settings in the Mark Index Entry dialog box as follows:
   - Ensure that text in the Main entry box is stated exactly as it should appear in the index.
   - Click Mark, if only one occurrence of the selected text is to be noted in the index. Otherwise, click Mark All to include all occurrences of the selected text.
   - Include a cross-reference, if needed. For example, an index entry for appetizers could be cross-referenced with hors d'oeuvres. Click Mark.
4. Close the dialog box.
5. Repeat Steps 1 to 4 for any additional terms to mark as index entries. Close the dialog box when all items have been marked.

As you mark entries for inclusion in the index, they will be coded in the document with a tag. After marking entries to include in an index, you are ready to create the index. There are several layouts available for the Index page, and Word arranges the index entries in alphabetical order and supplies appropriate page references.

To create an index, complete the following steps:

1. Insert a blank page at the end of the document or at a location where the index is to display. Position the insertion point on the blank page, type Index, and then press Enter.
2. Click the References tab and click Insert Index in the Index group.
3. Adjust the settings in the Index dialog box, including the format style, number of columns, language, and alignment.
4. Click OK.

Creating an index is usually among the last tasks related to preparing a paper, chapter, or book. However, even if an index has been created, you can still update the index with new entries. New entries are alphabetized along with the original entries in the index. An index can be updated to include newly marked entries with the correct page numbers by using Update Index in the Index group on the References tab.

STEP 5 Create a Cover Page

A ***cover page***, sometimes called a *title page*, is placed at the beginning of a report. Some writing styles do not require a cover page for a research report, whereas others do. For example, APA writing style requires a cover page for a research report, formatted in a certain way. When writing a research paper, consult the writing guide of the style you are following for information related to the format of a cover page (if a cover page is required). You can create a cover page in any of a variety of styles available in the Pages group on the Insert tab. After selecting a design, you can personalize the cover page with your name, report title, and any other variable data.

While templates are available, some situations merit a plain cover page that you create yourself. For instance, if you want a cover page to be formatted in the same way as the remainder of the report, you might consider creating and customizing a cover page in its own section.

To create a customized cover page from scratch, complete the following steps:

1. Position the insertion point at the beginning of the document. Click the Layout tab.
2. Click Breaks and click Next Page in the Section Breaks group.
3. Position the insertion point at the beginning of the document. Type the content of your cover page to include information such as your name, date, and title of the document.
4. Double-click the header or footer area. Select Different First Page on the Header & Footer Tools Design tab if you create a page number header or footer. You do not want the cover page to include a page number.

Quick Concepts

1. Describe the type of writing style you would be expected to use for a writing assignment in a business class. *p. 253*
2. Explain why you need to cite sources in your work. *p. 252*
3. Describe the purpose of creating a table of contents. *p. 260*
4. Explain a situation where it would be appropriate to use a footnote. *p. 258*

Hands-On Exercises

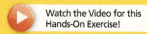

MyLab IT HOE1 Sim Training

Watch the Video for this Hands-On Exercise!

Skills covered: Select a Writing Style • Format a Research Paper • Create a Source and Include a Citation • Share and Search for a Source • Create a Bibliography • Create Footnotes • Modify Footnotes • Create a Table of Contents • Create an Index • Create a Cover Page

1 Research Paper Basics

You have completed a draft of an analysis of the short story "A White Heron." As a requirement for the literature class in which you are enrolled, you must format the paper according to MLA style, including citations and a bibliography. In addition to the literature analysis, you have also completed a marketing plan for a fictional company, required for a business management class. The instructor of that class, Mr. Carpenter, asked you to consider submitting the paper for inclusion in a collection of sample papers produced by the School of Business at your university. For that project, you will include a table of contents, an index, and a cover page.

STEP 1 SELECT A WRITING STYLE, FORMAT A RESEARCH PAPER, CREATE A SOURCE, AND INCLUDE A CITATION

You will format the analysis of "A White Heron" in MLA style and include citations where appropriate. Refer to Figure 4.10 as you complete Step 1.

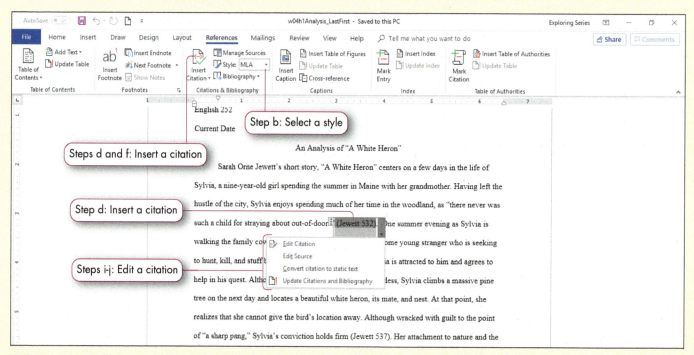

FIGURE 4.10 Add Sources and Insert Citations

a. Open *w04h1Analysis* and save it as **w04h1Analysis_LastFirst**.

> **TROUBLESHOOTING:** If you make any major mistakes in this exercise, you can close the file, open *w04h1Analysis* again, and then start this exercise over.

b. Click the **References tab** and click the **Style arrow** in the Citations & Bibliography group. Select **MLA Seventh Edition**. Apply the following MLA style settings to the whole document:

- Text is **left** aligned.
- Line spacing is **2.0** (or double).
- Paragraph spacing Before and After is **0**.

- Font is **Times New Roman** at **12 pt** size.
- Margins are 1" at the top, bottom, left, and right.
- First line of all body paragraphs are indented 0.5".
- Report title is centered.

c. Insert a right-aligned header that includes your last name, followed by a space and a plain page number. Make sure the page number is inserted as a field, not simply typed. Format the header as **Times New Roman 12 pt**.

d. Place the insertion point after the ending quotation mark and before the ending period in Jewett's notation in the first body paragraph (ending in *straying about out-of-doors*). Click the **References tab** and click **Insert Citation** in the Citations & Bibliography group. Click **Add New Source**. Click the **Type of Source arrow** and click **Book Section**. Complete the citation as follows, but do not click OK after completing the source.

Author: **Jewett, Sarah Orne**

Title: **A White Heron**

Book Title: **The American Tradition in Literature**

Year: **2009**

Pages: **531–537**

City: **New York**

Publisher: **McGraw-Hill**

e. Click to select **Show All Bibliography Fields**. Scroll down and click in the **Editor box** and type **Perkins, George**. Click **Edit** beside Editor. Type **Perkins** in the Last box. Click in the **First box** and type **Barbara**. Click **Add** and click **OK**. Click in the **Volume box** and type **2**. Click **OK**.

You have added a source related to a section of a book in which the short story is printed.

f. Click after the word *firm* and before the ending period in Jewett's notation (that ends in *Sylvia's conviction holds firm*) in the first paragraph. Click **Insert Citation** in the Citations & Bibliography group and click **Jewett, Sarah Orne** to insert a citation to the same source as that created earlier.

> **MAC TROUBLESHOOTING:** Click Citations on the References tab, double-click the citation in the Citations pane, and then close the pane.

g. Place the insertion point after the ending quotation mark and before the ending period in Hovet's notation in the second body paragraph (ending in *functions that are also present in "A White Heron"*). Add a new source, selecting **Article in a Periodical** as the source and type:

Author: **Hovet, Theodore R.**

Title: **Once Upon a Time: Sarah Orne Jewett's 'A White Heron' as a Fairy Tale**

Periodical Title: **Studies in Short Fiction**

Year: **2011**

Month: **Sept.**

Day: **25**

Pages: **63–68**

You have to use single quotes for the title of the source because double quotes will be added around the full title in the Bibliography.

h. Click to select **Show All Bibliography Fields**, set the Volume to **15** and the Issue to **1**, and then click **OK**.

i. Click Jewett's parenthetical citation in the first body paragraph beside the words *straying about out-of-doors*. Click the **Citation Options arrow** and click **Edit Citation**. Type **532** in the Pages box. Click **OK**.

You have added a page number to identify the source as required by MLA writing style.

j. Edit the next citation in the first body paragraph (following the sentence that ends in *Sylvia's conviction holds firm*) to include page number **537**. Click the only Hovet citation in the second body paragraph. Click the **Citation Options arrow** and click **Edit Citation**. Suppress the display of Author, Year, and Title, but include a Page Number of **63**. Click **OK**.

k. Save the document.

STEP 2: SHARE AND SEARCH FOR A SOURCE AND CREATE A BIBLIOGRAPHY

Now that sources are cited and stored in the document, you can quickly insert the bibliography at the end. You will also explore the sharing of sources. Refer to Figure 4.11 as you complete Step 2.

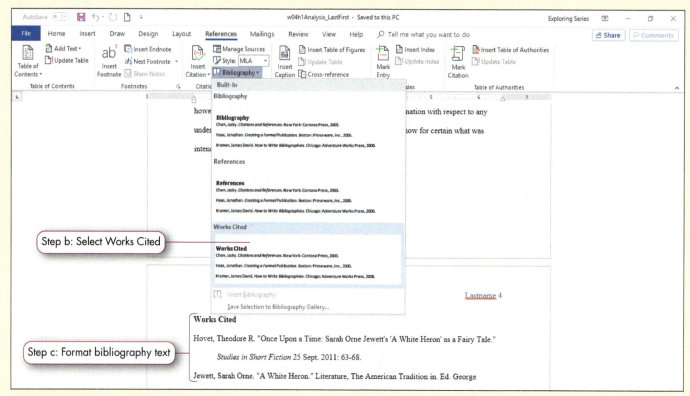

FIGURE 4.11 Create a Bibliography

a. Click **Manage Sources** in the Citations & Bibliography group on the References tab.

Note that the sources you created in the previous step are shown in the Master List and the Current List. They are available for use in other documents, as well as in the current document.

> **MAC TROUBLESHOOTING:** Click Citations on the References tab, click Settings in the Citations pane, and then click Citation Source Manager.

> **TROUBLESHOOTING:** It is possible that sources other than those you just added are also shown in the Master List. The list includes all sources you have included in other documents as well as those in the current document.

b. Click **Close**. Press **Ctrl+End** to move to the end of the document. Press **Ctrl+Enter** to insert a page break. Click **Bibliography** in the Citations & Bibliography group and click **Works Cited**.

A bibliography is always included as a separate page at the end of the document. Therefore, you inserted a page break before adding the bibliography. The bibliography includes the heading Works Cited. The two sources you used in your analysis are listed, although you may have to scroll up to see them.

c. Drag to select all text on the Works Cited page, including the heading *Works Cited* and all sources. Change the line spacing to **2.0** (or double), the paragraph spacing Before and After to **0**, and the font to **Times New Roman 12 pt**. Select the *Works Cited* heading, remove the bold format, and then center the line.

The Works Cited page adheres to MLA writing style guidelines.

d. Save and close the document. Leave Word open for the next step.

STEP 3: CREATE AND MODIFY FOOTNOTES

You are a business major enrolled in a business management class. As a final project, you have prepared a case analysis of a fictional airline. Due to the large amount of statistical data included, you expect to use footnotes to provide additional clarification. Because footnotes and endnotes are mutually exclusive—you only use one or the other in a single paper—you will not use endnotes. However, you know that the way in which endnotes and footnotes are added is very similar. Refer to Figure 4.12 as you complete Step 3.

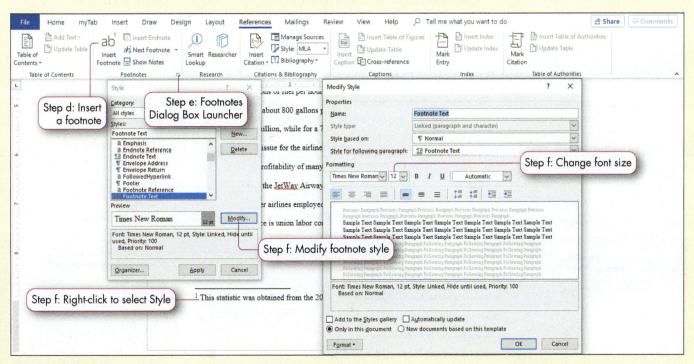

FIGURE 4.12 Modify Footnotes

a. Open *w04h1Airlines* and save it as **w04h1Airlines_LastFirst**.

b. Select the whole document and apply the following formatting:
- Alignment is **left** aligned.
- Line spacing is **2.0** (or double).
- Paragraph spacing Before and After is **0**.
- Sentences separate by only **one space**.
- Font is **Times New Roman** at **12 pt** size.

c. Deselect the text.

d. Click **Find** in the Editing group on the Home tab. The Navigation Pane opens on the left. Type **200 million** in the Search box and press **Enter**. Click after the period ending the sentence in *$200 million*. Close the Navigation Pane. Click the **References tab** and click **Insert Footnote** in the Footnotes group. Type **This statistic was obtained from the 2015 U.S. Air Transportation Log.** (include the period).

You inserted a footnote, numbered it with a superscript, further clarifying the information stated.

e. Scroll to page 4 and place the insertion point after the period ending the first paragraph (ending in *for over 34 years*). Click the **Footnotes Dialog Box Launcher** and click **Insert**. Type **Competitors to Northeast have proven slightly less profitable.** (include the period).

> **MAC TROUBLESHOOTING:** Click the Insert tab, select Footnote, and then click Insert.

You inserted another footnote, numbered sequentially after the first footnote. Using the Footnote and Endnote dialog box, you have options to specify various choices, including numbering and formatting.

f. Right-click the footnote at the bottom of page 4 and click **Style**. Click **Modify**. Change the font type to **Times New Roman** and the font size to **12**. Click **OK** and click **Apply**.

You changed the footnote style for this document to include a font type and size that is similar to the body text. The new format applies to all footnotes in the document.

g. Save the document.

STEP 4 CREATE A TABLE OF CONTENTS AND AN INDEX

The case study is almost complete, but your instructor, Mr. Carpenter, requires a table of contents and an index. You will prepare a table of contents and will begin an index. Refer to Figure 4.13 as you complete Step 4.

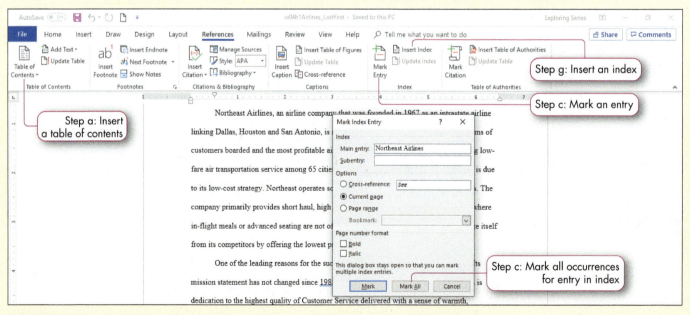

FIGURE 4.13 Create a Table of Contents and an Index

a. Press **Ctrl+Home** to move to the beginning of the document. Press **Ctrl+Enter** to insert a page break. Move the insertion point to the beginning of the new page and press **Enter** twice. Click the **References tab** and click **Table of Contents** in the Table of Contents group. Select **Automatic Table 2**.

You inserted a table of contents comprising of the headings and page numbers from the report.

b. Point to the **Situational Analysis link** in the Table of Contents and **Ctrl+Click** to move to that section of the document. Change the Situational Analysis heading to **Data Analysis**. Press **Ctrl+Home** to move to the beginning of the document and ensure that the table of contents is selected. Click **Update Table** at the top-left corner of the table. Click **Update entire table**. Click **OK**.

You changed the wording of a heading in the report. After updating the table of contents, the new wording is also included there.

c. Point to the **Problem Statement link** in the Table of Contents and **Ctrl+Click** to move to that section of the document. Select **Northeast Airlines** in the first sentence of the first body paragraph. Click **Mark Entry** in the Index group on the References tab, click **Mark All** in the Mark Index Entry dialog box, and then click **Close**.

You marked the phrase Northeast Airlines for inclusion in the index. By selecting Mark All, you have instructed Word to include a page reference to the phrase wherever it occurs in the document. Also, the nonprinting characters are automatically turned on so you can see the code for the marked entry.

d. Select the word **Northeast** in the sentence that begins *Northeast operates solely Boeing 737s* in the same paragraph. Click **Mark Entry** in the Index group on the References tab. Select **Cross-reference** and type **Northeast Airlines** beside the word *See*. Click **Mark**. Click **Close**.

Because you refer to Northeast Airlines throughout the document as either Northeast Airlines or Northeast, you will cross-reference the term so that it appears appropriately in the index.

e. Scroll to page 4 and mark the first word on the page, *Code-sharing*, as an index entry, making sure to mark all occurrences.

f. Press **Ctrl+End** to go to the end of the document and insert a page break. Ensure the insertion point is at the top of the new blank page.

g. Click **Insert Index** in the Index group on the References tab. Click **OK** to accept all default settings and insert the index. Select the index and change the font to **Times New Roman**.

You inserted an index comprising the three terms you marked earlier. A complete index would most likely consist of many more terms, with all terms referenced to pages in the document.

h. Save the document.

STEP 5 CREATE A COVER PAGE

As a final touch, you create a cover page with information related to the report title, your name, the course number, and the current date. Refer to Figure 4.14 as you complete Step 5.

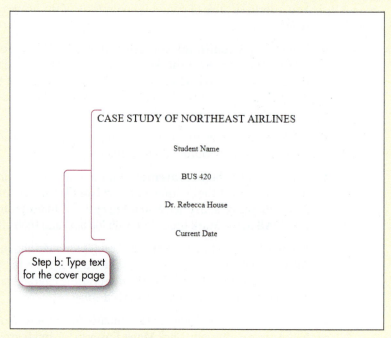

FIGURE 4.14 Create a Cover Page

a. Insert a page break at the beginning of the document and place the insertion point at the top of the new blank page. Click the **Home tab** and click **Center alignment** in the Paragraph group. Change the font size to **16 pt** and font color to **Black, Text 1**. Remove italics.

b. Type **Case Study of Northeast Airlines**. Press **Enter** three times and type your first and last names. Press **Enter** three times again and type **BUS 420**. Press **Enter** three times and type **Dr. Rebecca House**. Press **Enter** three times and type the current date. Ensure that text on the cover page is neither bold nor italicized. Select the text *Case Study of Northeast Airlines*, open the Font dialog box, and then select **All caps**.

Although Word provides many more colorful choices of cover pages, you will design a more conservative cover page to accompany this business report.

c. Click the **Layout tab** and click the **Page Setup Dialog Box Launcher**. Click the **Layout tab**. Click the **Vertical alignment arrow** and click **Center**. Click **OK**.

You centered the cover page vertically.

d. Click the **View tab** and click **One Page** in the Zoom group. Turn off the nonprinting characters feature.

The cover page is centered vertically on the page.

e. Save and close the document. You will submit this file to your instructor at the end of the last Hands-On Exercise.

Document Tracking

Whether in a college class or in the workplace, it is likely that you will seek feedback from others or collaborate with them on the completion of a project. Knowing how to use the **Track Changes** feature to keep track of all additions, deletions, and formatting changes made to the document can help to enhance collaborative efforts. Further, you can use **Markup** to help customize how tracked changes are displayed in a document. With group editing, it is easy to track changes and review any comments that have been made by individuals who have access to the document. Documents are often saved in PDF format to share with others. **PDF (Portable Document Format)** is a file format that captures all elements of a page and stores them electronically. Especially useful for documents like magazine articles, brochures, and flyers, PDF format accurately represents all page elements, including graphics and text effects. You can now convert a PDF document into a Word document and edit the content.

In this section, as you track changes in a document, you will learn to control the level of detail that shows, and how to accept or reject changes made by others. You will also explore reviewing documents, adding and replying to comments in the process. Finally, you will explore ways that you can work with PDF documents.

Tracking Changes

Whether you work individually or with a group, you can monitor any revisions you make to a document. The Track Changes feature in the Tracking group on the Review tab enables you to track all changes (for example, content and formatting) made to a document. Track Changes is particularly useful in situations in which a document must be reviewed by several people—each of whom can offer suggestions or change parts of the document—and these changes and comments are identified by the person making them. When you no longer want your changes to be tracked, you can toggle off the Track Changes feature. You can also lock tracking with or without a password to prevent other authors from turning off Track Changes (see Figure 4.15).

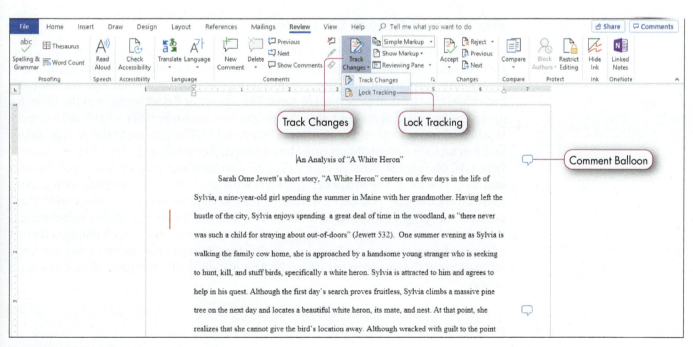

FIGURE 4.15 Lock Tracking

STEP 1 **Use Track Changes**

When Track Changes is not active, any change you make to a document is untraceable, and no one will know what you have changed unless he or she compares your revised document with the previous version. When Track Changes is active, it applies ***revision marks***, which indicate where a person added, deleted, or formatted text. You can use the predefined settings in Track Changes, or you may change the track changes format using the Advanced Track Changes Options dialog box (see Figure 4.16).

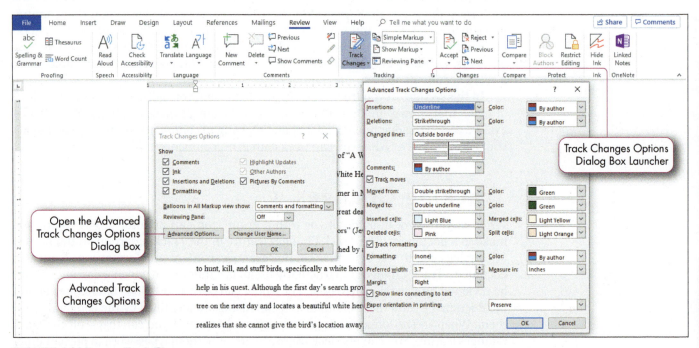

FIGURE 4.16 Format Track Changes

Accept and Reject Changes

As you complete the revisions in a document, you will review all comments and act on them or otherwise reply to the reviewer. You also can view all edits, including changes in wording and formatting. You can move through the document and review each individual change using Previous or Next. The Accept or Reject features in the Changes group enable you to accept or reject all changes, or you can be more specific with respect to which changes to accept or reject (see Figure 4.17). The options in the Accept/Reject features include Accept/Reject and Move to Next; Accept/Reject This Change; Accept/Reject All Changes Shown; Accept/Reject All Changes; and Accept/Reject All Changes and Stop Tracking. For instance, to review with the option of accepting or rejecting individual changes, you can use Accept and Reject. To accept or reject individual changes, the pointer must be in an edited area in the document. Before submitting a final document, ensure that all changes have been accepted and track changes turned off to produce a clean copy. You can use the Accept/Reject All option or you can turn off tracking at the same time by using the Accept/Reject All Changes and Stop Tracking option.

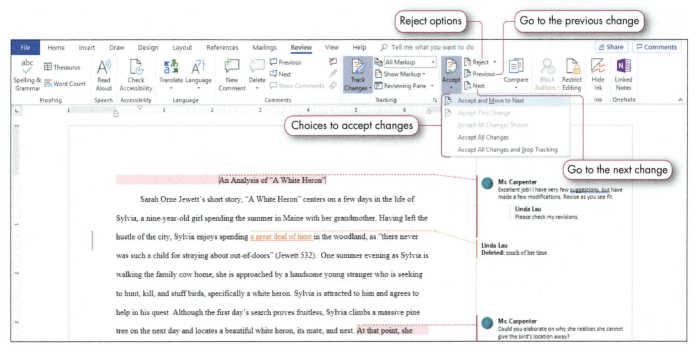

FIGURE 4.17 Accept or Reject Changes

Reviewing a Document

In today's organizational environment, teams of people with diverse backgrounds, skills, and knowledge prepare documents. Team members work together while planning, developing, writing, and editing important documents. A large part of that process is reviewing work begun or submitted by others. No doubt you have focused on a document of your own so completely that you easily overlooked obvious mistakes or alternative wording. A reviewer, bringing a fresh perspective, can often catch mistakes, perhaps even suggest ways to improve readability. In reviewing a document, you will most often find ways to change wording or otherwise edit the format, and you might find an opportunity to provide **comments** related to the content. Although comments are most often directed to the attention of another author or editor, you can even include comments to remind yourself of a necessary action.

STEP 2 Use Markup

Markup is a way of viewing tracked changes. If a lot of changes have been made, they may become distracting as you read through an entire document. Therefore, you can use markup to customize how track changes are displayed. The Show Markup feature (see Figure 4.18) enables readers to view document revisions organized by the type of revisions (such as comments, insertions, deletions, and formatting), how the revisions are shown, as well as by reviewer. There are four markup views that modify how one sees changes made to a document: Simple Markup, All Markup, No Markup, and Original. You can toggle each selection on or off to view the types of markups that you want to see. **Simple Markup** is a clutter-free way to display tracked changes (see Figure 4.19). In Simple Markup, a vertical red bar displays on the left side of any paragraph in which edits have occurred, but the revisions are hidden (see Figure 4.19). Toggle the red bar to display the full changes or to remove them from view.

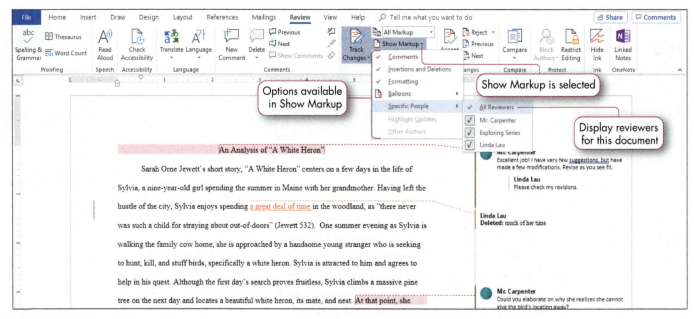

FIGURE 4.18 Show Markup

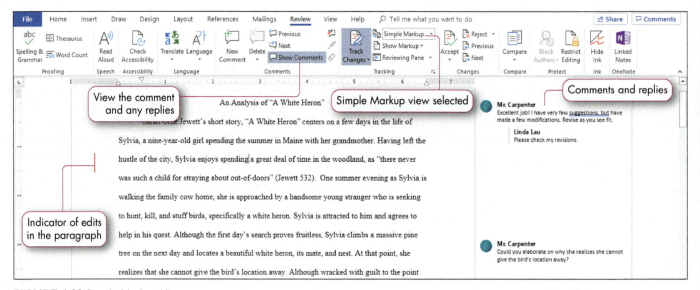

FIGURE 4.19 Simple Markup View

The document in Figure 4.20 is shown with **All Markup** in the Tracking group selected. This view shows the document with all the revisions, markups, and comments using the formats predefined in Track Changes Options. **No Markup** provides a completely clean view of a document, temporarily hiding all comments and revisions, and displays the document as it would if all changes were applied and does not show any of the markups or comments. It enables you to preview the document before accepting the changes. Although no revisions or comments show, keep in mind that they are only hidden. To remove them permanently, you have to accept or reject the changes. Lastly, **Original Markup** displays the document in its original form, as it was before any changes were applied.

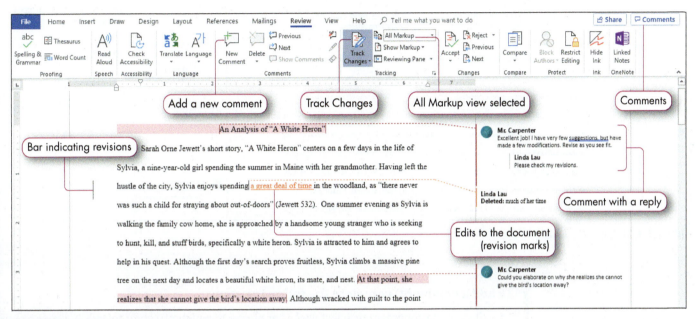

FIGURE 4.20 All Markup View

One of the benefits of Track Changes is that you can filter the changes by reviewer, thereby enabling you to review, accept, or reject individual or all changes recommended by a specific person. You can also use Track Changes Options to select types of revision and to change the settings for track changes and balloons.

Add a Comment

Besides tracking changes and changing the markup view, the Review tab has a Comments group that provides commands to add new comments, delete existing comments, or navigate through the document and review each individual comment using Previous or Next (see Figure 4.21). Comments can also be added using the comment icon on the right side of the window above the ribbon, which displays onscreen no matter what ribbon tab is currently selected. A comment works like a sticky note on a hard copy, enabling you to attach notes or information to various parts of your document. It is also a good way to ask the writer a question, to express concern about a particular sentence, or to remind yourself of a necessary action.

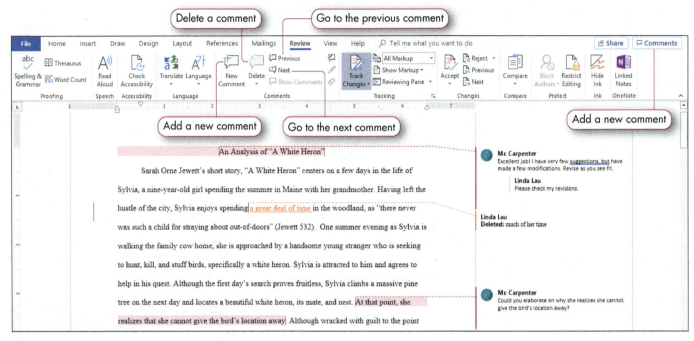

FIGURE 4.21 Add a Comment

> **To add a comment, complete the following steps:**
> 1. Click in the document or select a word or phrase to which you want to add a comment.
> 2. Complete one of the following substeps:
>   - Click New Comment in the Comments group on the Review tab.
>   - Click Comments at the top-right corner of the window and select New Comment.
> 3. Type a comment in the comment balloon that displays in the right margin. You will be identified as the author in the comment balloon, with the date and time of the comment.

If you do not select anything prior to clicking New Comment, the comment is assigned to the word or object closest to the insertion point.

> **TIP: CONFIRMING THE USER NAME**
> Before you use the Comments feature, make sure your name appears as you want it to display in any comments. To do so, click the File tab and click Options. In the General section, confirm that your name and initials display as the user. Word uses that information to identify the person who uses collaboration tools, such as Comments. If you are in a lab environment, you might not have permission to modify settings or change the user name; however, you should be able to change those settings on a home computer.

View Comments

Any comment is displayed on the right side of the document in a **comment balloon**. A comment balloon displays as a boxed note in the margin and when selected highlights the text to which the comment is applied. You can also choose to display revisions in balloons. Font and paragraph options of the comment balloon can be changed using Styles or the shortcut menu.

Comments can be viewed in both Simple Markup and All Markup views, but not in No Markup and Original views. Print Layout is the most common means of viewing a document, but even in other views (e.g., Read Mode and Web Layout), comments display similarly, except in Draft view, where they appear as tags embedded in the document. However, when you point to the embedded tags, the comments show.

Reply to Comments

Replying to a comment is a feature that helps provide a "conversation" around a comment. Move the pointer over the comment and click Reply to type a response (see Figure 4.22). The response will be placed within the original comment balloon. All replies to original comments are indented beneath the original, with the commenter identified by name, making it easy to follow the progression of a comment through its replies. After you have addressed a comment and clicked Resolve, the comment is grayed out. However, you can still reopen the comment again by clicking Reopen on the right of Reply.

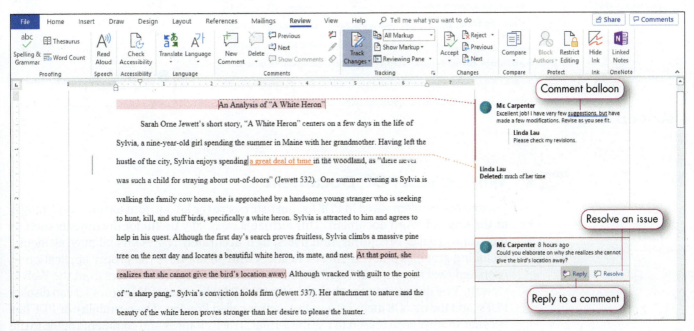

FIGURE 4.22 Reply to a Comment

In any view, you can display the Reviewing Pane, which displays all comments and editorial changes made to the document, as well as statistics regarding the number of changes made. You will find the Reviewing Pane useful when the contents of comments are too lengthy to display completely in a comment balloon. Figure 4.23 shows the Reviewing Pane on the left, although you can also choose to place the Reviewing Pane on the bottom of the window. The Reviewing Pane can be displayed or hidden by toggling the command found in the Tracking group. To display the pane vertically or horizontally, click the Reviewing Pane arrow (see Figure 4.23).

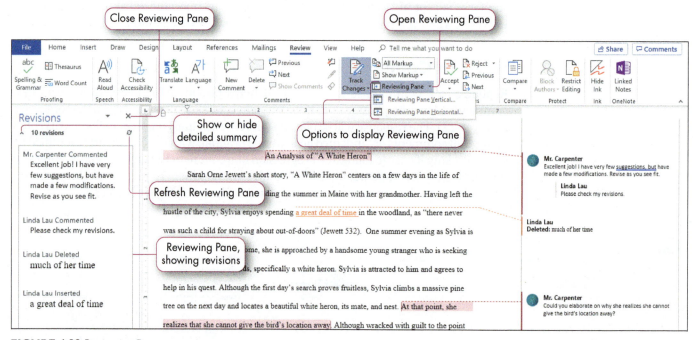

FIGURE 4.23 Reviewing Pane

STEP 3 Work with a PDF Document

Documents are often saved in PDF format to preserve the layout, font formats, and images of the original Word document. This format is especially useful for documents such as magazine articles, brochures, and flyers, as it accurately represents all page elements, including graphics and text effects. Readers who do not have the proper application to open and read the original Word document can download free viewers from the Web to view the PDF documents. Further, the Microsoft Edge browser in Windows 10 can display PDFs, and the macOS includes a native viewer called Preview. The portability of PDF has become another good reason to use the format. Track changes and comments made to the Word document will also be displayed in the PDF document. However, documents that are finalized should not include comments before converting them to PDF.

> **To export a Word document as a PDF file, complete the following steps:**
>
> 1. Open a document in Word.
> 2. Click the File tab and click Export.
> 3. Click Create PDF/XPS under Create a PDF/XPS Document.
> 4. Navigate to the location where you save your files, rename the file, and then ensure that *Open file after publishing* is selected.
> 5. Click Publish. The PDF file automatically opens in the default PDF viewer.
> 6. Close both the PDF and Word documents.

On a Mac, to export a Word document as a PDF file, complete the following steps:

1. Open a document in Word.
2. Click the File menu and click Save As.
3. Click the File Format box to open the list and select PDF.
4. Click Export.

You can now convert a PDF document into a Word document and edit the content. **PDF Reflow** is a built-in capability that produces editable Word documents from PDF files—documents that retain the intended formatting and page flow of the original PDF document. PDF Reflow seeks to convert recognizable features of a PDF document into items that are native to Word. For example, a table in a PDF document is converted into a table in a Word document so you can use Word's table feature to modify and update the item. Similarly, bulleted lines in a PDF file become bulleted paragraphs in a Word document. Although using PDF Reflow does not always convert every feature flawlessly, the result is usually a close imitation of the original. PDF Reflow is more attuned to converting text than graphics.

To convert a PDF document to Word, complete the following steps:

1. Click Open on the File tab.
2. Browse to the folder of the PDF document you want to open and double-click the selected file. (On a Mac, choose encoding settings and click OK.)
3. Click OK if warned that the conversion might take a while and that the PDF document contains interactive features that are not supported by PDF Reflow. Within a few seconds, the PDF file opens as a Word document which you can edit as you would any Word document.

5. Describe why you want to use track changes in your document. *p. 271*
6. When using Track Changes, explain why you want to filter the changes by reviewers. *p. 271*
7. Explain under what situation would you want to use Simple Markup. *p. 273*
8. Explain why you would want to save a Word document in the PDF format. *p. 278*

Hands-On Exercises

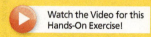

MyLab IT HOE2 Sim Training

Watch the Video for this Hands-On Exercise!

Skills covered: Use Track Changes • Accept Changes • Use Markup • Add a Comment • View Comments, Reply to Comments • Work with a PDF Document

2 Document Tracking

Your literature group submitted a draft copy of the analysis of "A White Heron." Your literature instructor, Mr. Carpenter, made comments and suggested some additional editing before the paper is considered complete. Even at this early stage, however, Mr. Carpenter is very pleased with your group's initial analysis. In fact, he suggested that you prepare to submit the paper to the campus Phi Kappa Phi Honor Society for judging in a writing contest. He will provide a copy of the entry form in PDF format so you can have it on hand when you submit the paper. Now, you will review his comments and changes and act on his suggestions.

STEP 1   USE TRACK CHANGES, USE MARKUP, AND ACCEPT CHANGES

Your instructor, Mr. Carpenter, returned to you an electronic copy of the analysis with a few edits and comments. You are ready to review the paper using track changes and markup, and to accept or reject changes. Refer to Figure 4.24 as you complete Step 1.

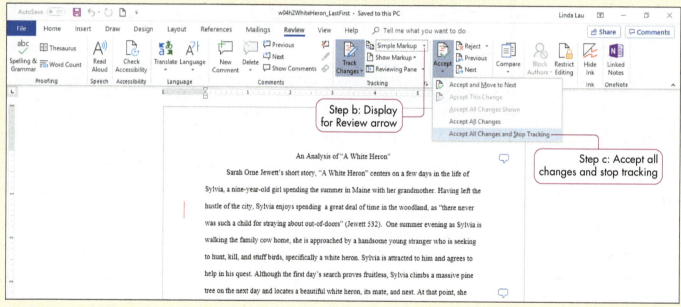

FIGURE 4.24 Track Changes

a. Open *w04h2WhiteHeron* and save it as **w04h2WhiteHeron_LastFirst**.

b. Click the **Review tab**, click the **Display for Review arrow** in the Tracking group, and then click **Simple Markup**. Click the **Home tab**, click **Text Highlight Color**, and then highlight the following terms in the document with the yellow highlighting:

- The word *One* in the third sentence of the first paragraph on page 1.
- The word *facets* in the second sentence of the second paragraph on page 1.
- The word *killing* in the partial first paragraph of page 3.
- The word *interesting* in the last paragraph of the document.

c. Click the **Review tab**, click the **Accept arrow** in the Changes group, and then select **Accept All Changes and Stop Tracking**.

You have accepted all remaining changes.

d. Click the **Display for Review arrow** and click **No Markup**.

The document looks completely clean, without any markups or comments.

e. Save the document.

STEP 2: ADD, VIEW, AND REPLY TO COMMENTS

You will review and reply your instructor's comments, make a few changes, and save the document for final review and group collaboration later. Refer to Figure 4.25 as you complete Step 2.

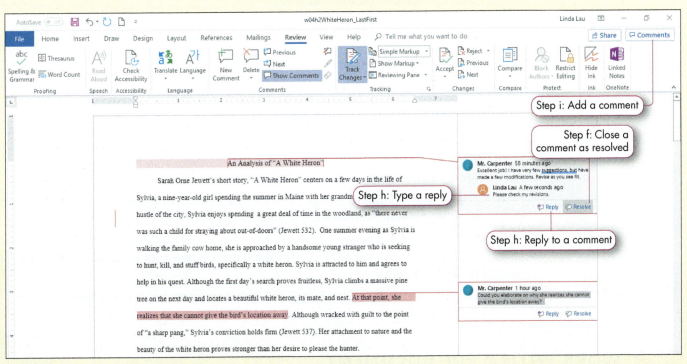

FIGURE 4.25 Work with Comments

a. Click the **Review tab**, click the **Display for Review arrow** in the Tracking group, and then select **All Markup**. Scroll to the top of the document and review the comments made by your instructor. Click the **Display for Review arrow** in the Tracking group and click **Simple Markup** to return to an uncluttered view.

In the Simple Markup view, you may also display the comments by clicking Show Comments.

b. Click the **Reviewing Pane arrow** in the Tracking group and click **Reviewing Pane Vertical**. Review the comments shown in the Reviewing Pane. Close the Reviewing Pane (titled *Revisions*).

> **MAC TROUBLESHOOTING:** There is no arrow for the Reviewing Pane and it can only display vertically. Click Reviewing to toggle the pane on and off.

c. Point to the **first comment balloon** on the right of the report title and note the highlighted text *See Comments*. Click the **comment balloon** to view the comment. Click the **comment balloon** again to close the comment.

d. Click the **third comment balloon** on the first page and note that you need to add a citation. Click **Close** in the markup balloon to close it. Click after the quotation mark and before the period in the sentence in the last paragraph on the first page (ending with *for the course of action*). Add a new source for the following book:

Hands-On Exercise 2   281

Type of Source: **Book Section**

Author: **Propp, Vladimir**

Title: **Morphology of a Folk Tale**

Year: **1994**

City: **New York**

Publisher: **Anniston**

e. Scroll to the end of the document and click anywhere in the bibliography text. Click **Update Citations and Bibliography**.

You added a new source and updated the Works Cited page to include the newly added source.

f. Click on the third comment balloon and click **Resolve**.

You have addressed the comment, so you closed it.

g. Scroll up and click the **second comment balloon** to view the comment. Close the markup balloon. Click before the word *Although* in the sentence in the first body paragraph (that begins with *Although wracked with guilt*). Type **She is too tenderhearted to give up the heron family to the hunter.** (include the period). Press **Spacebar**. Click on the second comment balloon again and click **Resolve**.

h. Click the **first comment** on page 1 and click **Reply** (refer to Figure 4.25). Type **Please check my revisions.** (include the period). Close the comment.

i. Go to the end of the document. Press **Enter**. Click **New Comment** in the Comments group on the Review tab and type **This document is ready for my group to review.** (include the period).

j. Save and close the document. Keep Word open for the next step. You will submit this file to your instructor at the end of the last Hands-On Exercise.

STEP 3 WORK WITH A PDF DOCUMENT

You are ready to finalize the paper, and Mr. Carpenter has let you know that you must include an entry form with the submission. You are not on campus, so Mr. Carpenter has emailed the entry form as a PDF document. You will convert the form to Word and complete it with your name and report information. You will then save it as a PDF document for later submission. Refer to Figure 4.26 as you complete Step 3.

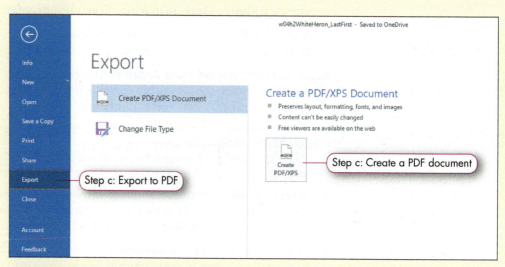

FIGURE 4.26 Work with a PDF Document

a. Click the **File tab**, click **Open**, click **Browse**, and then navigate to the student data files folder. Change the type of files in the Open dialog box to **PDF Files (*.PDF)**. Double-click *w04h2Entry.pdf* to open the file. Click **OK** if warned that the conversion might take a while.

Word has converted the original PDF version of the entry form and opened it in Word so you can modify it.

b. Click after *Date* and type today's date. Complete the remaining information, including your name, instructor's name, college class, email, and the **An Analysis of "A White Heron"** report title.

> **TROUBLESHOOTING:** If the document opened as an Adobe PDF file instead of as a Word document, you opened the file from File Explorer. Instead, you should open the document from within Word. Click the File tab and click Open.

c. Click the **File tab** and click **Export**. (On a Mac, use Save As.) Click **Create PDF/XPS Document** and click **Create PDF/XPS**. Navigate to the location where you save your assignments, rename the file as **w04h2Entry_LastFirst**, and ensure that *Open file after publishing* is checked. Click **Publish**.

You saved the entry form you completed in Word as a PDF file for later submission with the entry.

d. Close the document after the PDF version of the completed entry form is displayed. Close the Word version of the entry form without saving it. You will submit the PDF file to your instructor at the end of the last Hands-On Exercise.

Online Document Collaboration

With its continuing commitment to incorporate collaboration features, Microsoft is simplifying how people in any location can work together in groups to complete projects. The global marketplace and Web 2.0 technologies create a dynamic in which collaboration on projects is the norm, rather than the exception. Marketing proposals, company reports, and all sorts of other documents are often prepared by a group of people working with a shared documents folder, in which all can contribute to the shared documents at any time. Similarly, group projects that are assigned as part of a class requirement may more easily be completed by sharing documents online for review and completion. Recognizing the proliferation of devices that students and professionals use to collaborate on projects, including personal computers and mobile devices, the Office suite has become a complete, cross-platform, cross-device solution for working collaboration. Individuals can work from anywhere and on almost any device. The key to such sharing is online accessibility.

In this section, you will learn how to use OneDrive with File Explorer. You will also learn how to use Word Online. Further, you will explore the various options of sharing your documents and collaborating with your peers in real time using Word and Word Online.

Using OneDrive

Word facilitates document saving and sharing through **OneDrive**, which is a Web-based storage site and sharing utility. Saving a document to OneDrive is sometimes referred to as "saving to the cloud," because the document is saved and stored online (in the cloud) but it is also made available to work offline through File Explorer.

When you use OneDrive as a storage location, you can retrieve documents from any Internet-connected device and share documents with others. You may also want to use OneDrive as a location for backing up documents. Documents saved to OneDrive will not be lost if your hard drive crashes or your flash drive is lost or damaged. OneDrive has ample free storage available to users, making it a viable alternative to a local drive. Another advantage of using OneDrive is the AutoSave feature, which is enabled when you save your files to OneDrive. With AutoSave on, any document saved to OneDrive is automatically saved every few seconds. You can see the auto-saving status in the file name at the top of the window. The AutoSave default is On, but if you do not want to save your work continually you can turn AutoSave off manually by toggling the AutoSave icon on the Quick Access Toolbar. If you accidentally saved changes through AutoSave, you can revert to and restore any older versions of the file and make the older version the current one. Click the file name at the top of the window to see all versions in the Version History pane, open the version that you want, and click Restore to keep the chosen version.

> **TIP: ONEDRIVE FOR MOBILE DEVICES**
> You can download a OneDrive app on your mobile device that enables you to easily access your OneDrive files from the mobile device and upload videos and pictures to OneDrive.

STEP 1 Use OneDrive with File Explorer

Windows 10 incorporates OneDrive into File Explorer, so you can see and easily access files stored on OneDrive. Moreover, files in the OneDrive folder are available offline, so you can access and work with files stored on OneDrive even when you do not have access to the Internet. When access to the Internet becomes available, any changes made to the files will sync to OneDrive. Because there is a OneDrive folder in File Explorer, you can save directly to OneDrive in a similar fashion as you would save to any other storage device. Files and folders can be moved and copied between OneDrive and other storage locations on your computer as shown in Figure 4.27. You can also delete files from OneDrive as easily as you can from any other folder in File Explorer.

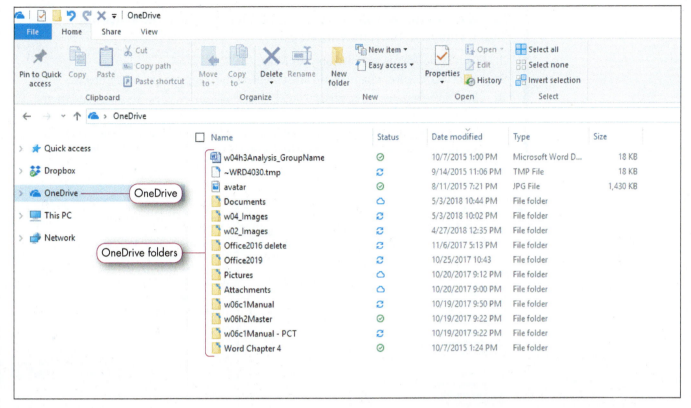

FIGURE 4.27 OneDrive in File Explorer

You can select which folders to sync between the online storage and your computer, and which folders are available only online. Using this feature can help manage storage space on your computing device and save time by only syncing those files that you modify and use most often. You can manage the syncing options through OneDrive settings, found by clicking the OneDrive icon in the Notification area on the taskbar, as shown in Figure 4.28.

FIGURE 4.28 OneDrive Icon

> **To choose and sync files and folders between OneDrive and File Explorer, complete the following steps:**
>
> 1. Sign in to Windows with a Microsoft account and enable OneDrive to display the OneDrive icon in the notification area at the far right of the taskbar (refer to Figure 4.28).
> 2. Click the OneDrive icon, click More Options (three vertical dots), and then click Settings.
> 3. Click the Account tab in the Microsoft OneDrive dialog box and select Choose folders.
> 4. Complete one of the following substeps in the Choose folders dialog box:
>   - Check the *Make all files available* box to make all your OneDrive files available on your computer.
>   - Check the boxes for the folders you want to sync under *Or make these folders visible* (see Figure 4.29). Only checked folders will sync.
> 5. Click OK to sync the files and folders.
> 6. Close the OneDrive dialog box.

On a Mac, to choose and sync files and folders between OneDrive and Finder, complete the following steps:

1. Ensure OneDrive is installed on your Mac.
2. Start OneDrive from Launchpad and complete the setup process by signing in.
3. Click More Options (three vertical dots), click Preferences, click Account, and then click Choose Folders.
4. Choose to sync everything, individual folders, or individual files, and then click OK. New items you add to the OneDrive folder on your Mac will sync to OneDrive.

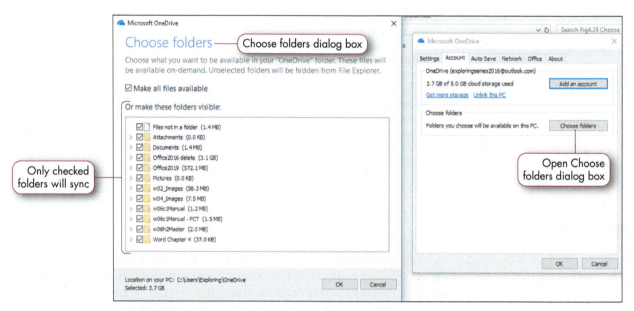

FIGURE 4.29 Choose and Sync Folders between OneDrive and File Explorer

> **TIP: USING A MICROSOFT ACCOUNT**
> To use Microsoft services such as OneDrive, you must have a Microsoft account. If you use Outlook, Hotmail, OneDrive, Office Online, Skype, or Xbox Live, Windows Live, or if you had a Windows Phone, you already have a Microsoft account. If you do not have an account, you can create one at signup.live.com.

Sharing Documents

OneDrive also is a means of online collaboration. Because a document saved in OneDrive is stored online, you can share the document with others who have access to the Internet. Also, sharing via OneDrive removes the hassles of version control, which is a problem created by passing around versions of the same document via email. To use the share feature, the document must be saved to OneDrive and you must also be connected to the Internet.

When viewing a list of files in OneDrive, you can right-click a file and click Share to open a Share dialog box from which you can select a method of sharing (Get a link, Email, or share through a social media site such as Facebook or LinkedIn) and stipulate editing privileges. You can also set an expiration date or a password to manage the accessibility of a document (see Figure 4.30). Alternatively, you can also share files directly from Word or Word Online. After saving a document to OneDrive or if you are working with Word or Word Online, you can share your document with others in several ways. You can share a document through a link or as an attachment via email. As you share a document, you can indicate whether those you share with can edit the document or simply view it.

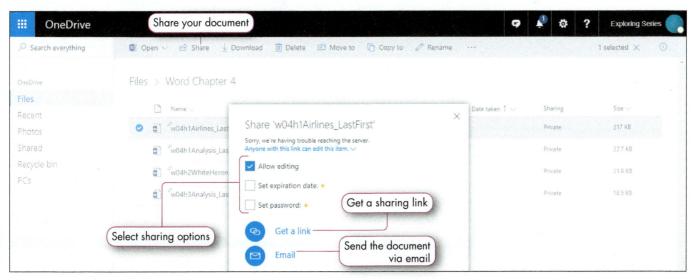

FIGURE 4.30 Share a document on OneDrive

Invite Others to Share

You can invite others to share a document with you by sending them a link to your file using Word or Word Online. You choose whether your invitee can edit or only view the document. Those invited to share receive an email with a link to work on the document. When the link is selected, the document opens in Word Online. If multiple people have been invited to share, everyone can be in the document and make changes at the same time. Because you are working in real time, all changes are synced so all users will be able to see changes in a matter of seconds.

> **To share a Word document already saved to OneDrive, complete the following steps:**
>
> 1. Open the document that you have saved to your OneDrive folder on File Explorer in Word.
> 2. Complete one of the following substeps:
>   - Click the File tab and click Share.
>   - Click Share at the top-right corner of the Word window.
> 3. Complete one of the following substeps (see Figure 4.31):
>   - Type the email addresses of invitees in the Invite people box in the Share pane. Separate each name or email address with a semicolon.
>   - Click *Search the Address Book for contacts* on the right of the Invite people box and find your recipient(s).
> 4. Indicate whether the recipient(s) can edit or only view the shared document.
> 5. Type a message (optional).
> 6. Click Send.

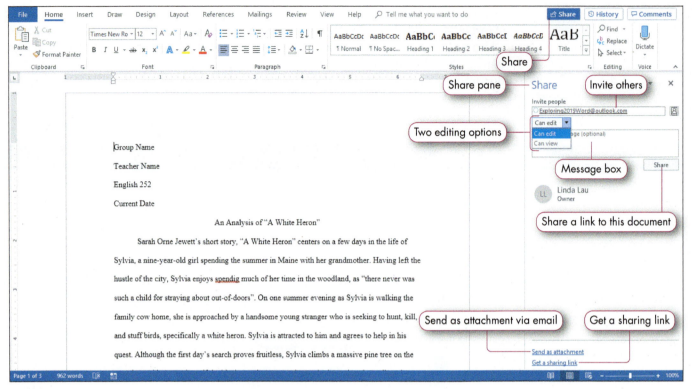

FIGURE 4.31 Invite Others

Share a Document Link

Another way to share your document with your recipients is to generate a sharing link. A sharing link can either grant editing privileges or limit access to view only. Once a link is generated, it is copied and can be pasted to an email message, into another document, or made available in a website or blog. The document opens in Word Online when the link is clicked and all changes made to the document are made in real time and synced simultaneously.

> **To get a sharing link to a OneDrive document, complete the following steps:**
> 1. Open the document that you have saved to your OneDrive folder on File Explorer in Word.
> 2. Complete one of the following substeps:
>   - Click the File tab and click Share.
>   - Click Share at the top-right corner of the window.
> 3. Click Get a sharing link at the bottom of the Share pane (refer to Figure 4.31).
> 4. Complete one of the following substeps (see Figure 4.32):
>   - Click *Create an edit link* under Edit link if you want anyone with the link to edit the shared document.
>   - Click *Create a view-only link* under View-only link if you want anyone with the link to view but not edit the shared document.
> 5. Click Copy and distribute the generated link to intended recipients using your preferred email service provider.

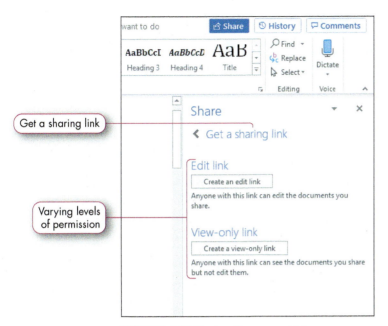

FIGURE 4.32 Share a Document Link

> **TIP: QUICK ACCESS TO SHARED FILES**
> After you click on the link in an email to view a shared file on OneDrive, that document will automatically display in Shared (on macOS and iOS) or Shared with me (on Android, or Windows Desktop). On the File tab, click Open, select Shared with Me, and then you will see a list of files that others have shared with you.

Send as an Attachment

If working in Word, an additional option is to share a document as an email attachment. Using this method, recipients receive a copy of the full document. However, recipients cannot make edits or to view the document online. When you share a document as an email attachment, choose one of the following two formats (see Figure 4.33) and a new email message will open in your default email account:

- Send a copy: In this option, the recipient gets a copy of the original Word document to review. This could be a problem for large files with photos and images, or database files, because there might be some file size limitations with some email accounts. Further, the recipients must have the appropriate application to open and view the attached document.

- Send a PDF: The recipient gets a PDF attachment of the original Word document. The PDF file preserves all layout, formatting, fonts, and images. This is a recommended option if revisions are not expected.

Because email recipients receive a copy of the document, if they want to make changes, the changes must be saved and the revised version emailed back to the primary author. If revisions are received from multiple people, the primary author needs to consolidate all the changes onto one document, which can be a daunting task. Therefore, distributing documents as email attachments is acceptable, but is the least collaborative, most noninteractive method of working together.

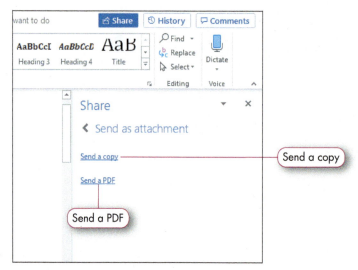

FIGURE 4.33 Send as an Attachment

Collaborating with Word and Word Online

Imagine gathering around a conference table to work on a document with others. The group shares ideas and comments on content, working to produce a collaborative document that is representative of the group's best effort. Now expand that view to include co-authors who are widespread geographically instead of gathered in a conference room. Because the far-flung group members are all online at the same time, they can view a document and collaborate on content, although not simultaneously, ultimately producing a document to which all attendees have had the opportunity to contribute. Whether your goal is to present a document for discussion (but no editing) or to seek input from a group, you will appreciate the ease with which documents saved to OneDrive and opened in Word or Word Online facilitate that task.

After you have saved a document to OneDrive and shared it with others, you are ready to collaborate in real time. As mentioned above, if a recipient was granted editing privileges to a shared document via a link or an email invitation, when the link is selected, the document opens in Word Online. At any point, you can switch to Word to continue working with a shared document. Because Word Online is somewhat limited, you might find that you need to edit a document in Word to access a feature not found in Word Online. For example, you might want to add a bibliography or check a document in Outline view. The option to edit in Word is available with the same collaborative features as with Word Online. Any document saved to OneDrive and shared with editing privileges has real-time, collaborative functionality.

STEP 2 Use Word Online

Word Online is a Web-based version of Word that enables you to edit and format a document online. As a component of Office Online, which also includes Excel Online, PowerPoint Online, and OneNote Online, Word Online is free and is available when you sign in to OneDrive.com. Using Word Online you can begin a new document, open a document previously saved in OneDrive, or open a document shared with you. The document opens in a browser window with a selection of commands. Because it is Web-based, you are not required to purchase or install software on your computer to use Word Online. Using Word Online, you can create and edit Word documents from any Internet-connected computer, and across any platform. Word Online is similar to Word, but with fewer features.

To create a new document in Word Online, complete the following steps:

1. Log in to your Microsoft account at OneDrive.com.
2. Click New (see Figure 4.34). A menu displays enabling you to create a Folder, or a new Word, Excel, PowerPoint, OneNote file, an Excel survey, or a Plain text document.
3. Click and select Word document.
4. Click the default file name, *Document1*, on the title bar and type a file name.
5. Type content in the document, and it is automatically saved to OneDrive.
6. For additional functionality, click Open in Word.

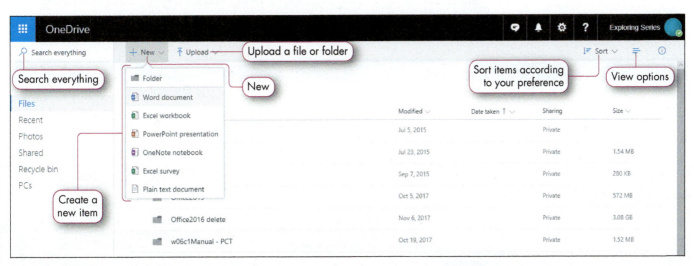

FIGURE 4.34 Create a New Document in Word Online

There are three views in the Document Views group on the View tab: Editing, Reading, and Immersive Reader. By default, all new documents open in Editing View. Editing View enables you to make changes to a document. Click Open in Word to switch to the fully featured version of Word. Reading View shows the document as it will print and enables the addition of comments. You cannot edit in Reading View. To make changes to the document, click Edit Document, and choose Edit in Word or Edit in Browser using Word Online (see Figure 4.35). **Immersive Reader** is another document view that is an add-in learning tool designed to help readers pronounce words correctly, read quickly and accurately, and understand what is read.

FIGURE 4.35 Use Word Online

Word Online has the familiar look and feel of Microsoft Word; however, you will note that the ribbon in Word Online has fewer tabs than the ribbon in Word installed on your computer (see Figure 4.36). In addition, there are also limited, but sufficient, functionality using the Insert, Page Layout, Review, and View tabs that are similar to Word. As you work with Word Online, you will find some other differences and limitations. For example, Dialog Box Launchers are not present for some groups, and certain features such as nonprinting characters, hidden text, Citations and Bibliography, Table of Contents, Cover Page, and Index are not supported. An important advantage of Word and Word Online is it enables authors to collaborate online and author and edit in real-time. Word Online has a new feature called *Simplified Ribbon*, which displays a two-line instead of the classic three-line view to provide more space for users to focus on their work and to collaborate with others. Unlike the installed version of Word, Track Changes is not a feature on the Review tab in Word Online.

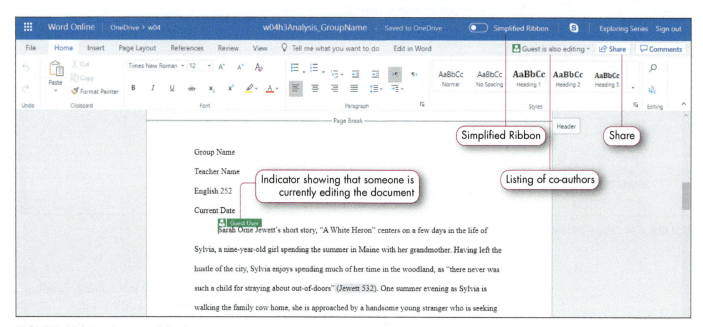

FIGURE 4.36 Notification of Co-Authors

Co-authoring a document is simple, with no specific commands required to begin editing. Simply open a shared document from OneDrive and use either Word or Word Online to modify the document. Of course, the document must be shared in such a way that editing by other authors is permitted. When you save or upload a Word document to OneDrive, anyone with whom you share the document (with editing privileges) can access and edit the document, even if you are also editing the document at the same time. This simultaneous editing is also called **real-time co-authoring**. You will see pictures and initials of co-authors displayed in the top right corner of the window. As you edit a shared document, you will be made aware of others who are editing the same document, identified by color flags associated with each individual. Word Online has a feature called **Real Time Typing**, which enables you to see where in the document your co-authors are working and any contributions they make as they type them (refer to Figure 4.36). For a quick demonstration of this new feature, save a document to OneDrive, and invite your peers to join you in a simultaneous authoring session.

Quick Concepts

9. As you save a document to OneDrive, you will most likely also want to have a copy on your computer for backup purposes. Explain how you can make sure that as you modify one copy, the other is also updated. ***p. 284***

10. Both Word and Word Online enable you to create and edit a document. Explain when one might be preferred over the other. ***p. 290***

11. Describe the advantages of online collaboration. ***p. 290***

12. Editing View and Reading View of Word Online serve different purposes. Describe some extra features of Editing View. ***p. 291***

Hands-On Exercises

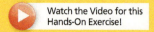

MyLab IT HOE3 Sim Training

Watch the Video for this Hands-On Exercise!

Skills covered: Use OneDrive with File Explorer • Invite Others to Share • Use Word Online

3 Online Document Collaboration

Your literature group will finalize the analysis of "A White Heron" by collaborating on a few last-minute edits online. Your instructor will assign you to work in a group of four students to complete this Hands-On Exercise and you have been selected as the group leader who will assume the task of posting and sharing the document. You will work with a draft of the analysis of the short story, co-authoring the document online, and then addressing final comments with classmates in your group.

STEP 1 USE ONEDRIVE WITH FILE EXPLORER AND INVITE OTHERS TO SHARE

You know that OneDrive provides storage space that can be accessed by others and can be used as a backup. Therefore, you plan to use OneDrive to share the analysis of "A White Heron" so that classmates can collaborate on the project. As the group leader, you will save a copy of the analysis paper to your OneDrive folder on File Explorer because changes made to the document will be synchronized with the online version stored in OneDrive. Because coordinating schedules is difficult for group members, your group decides to edit the document online. That way, each group member can edit the document at any time from any location, while all other group members can see the edits that have been made. As the group leader, you will share the document through Word Online with all group members. Your instructor will assign your group a name. Refer to Figure 4.37 as you complete Step 1.

FIGURE 4.37 Share a Document in Word Online

a. Ensure that you have a Microsoft account and that the OneDrive folder displays in File Explorer.

> **TROUBLESHOOTING:** Before beginning this exercise, you must have a Microsoft account. If you do not have a Microsoft account, create one at signup.live.com.

b. Open *w04h1Analysis_LastFirst* and save it as **w04h3Analysis_GroupName** to your OneDrive folder on File Explorer.

If you do not navigate to a specific folder, Microsoft will automatically save your document to the Documents folder on OneDrive.

c. Click **Share** at the top right corner. Ensure that Invite people is selected in the Share pane.

   An alternative way is to click File and click Share.

d. Type the email addresses of those with whom you want to share the document. Ensure the *Can edit* option is selected.

e. Type an optional message and click **Share**.

f. Click Close.

> **TROUBLESHOOTING:** If no group members have been assigned, consider sharing documents with a friend, family member, or with yourself, using an email address that is different from the email address associated with the current Windows account.

STEP 2 USE WORD ONLINE

Each team member has received an email with a link to the shared document—w04h3Analysis_GroupName. Each person will access w04h3Analysis_GroupName, reviewing and editing the report individually on his or her computer. You do not have to access the report simultaneously, although that is an option. Refer to Figure 4.38 as you complete Step 2.

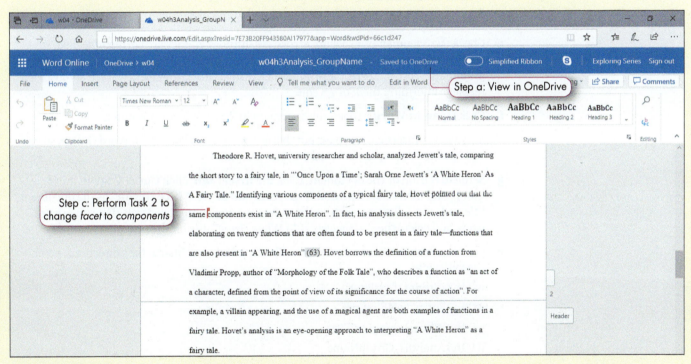

FIGURE 4.38 Collaborate on a Shared Document

> **TROUBLESHOOTING:** To complete all steps of this exercise, every group member must have a Microsoft account. If you do not have a Microsoft account, create one at signup.live.com.

a. Open a browser window and open your email account. Open the email with the shared link and click **View in OneDrive**.

   The document opens in Word Online on your computer.

> **TROUBLESHOOTING:** If the link you use does not display the shared document, repeat Step 1 to produce another link.

b. Click **Edit Document** and select **Edit in Browser** to start editing the shared document. Type the Group Name assigned by the instructor to replace Student Name on the first line of the document.

c. Divide the following tasks among group members, with each task completed by only one team member (unless there are fewer team members than tasks; in that case, assign the tasks as appropriate). As each group member completes a task, it is automatically saved. These tasks can be done simultaneously and you will see indicators showing that someone is currently editing the document as well.

- Task 1: Remove the word *On* from the fourth sentence of the first paragraph and the sentence should begin with the word **One**.
- Task 2: Change the highlighted word *facets* in the second sentence of the second paragraph to **components**.
- Task 3: Change the highlighted word *killing* in the first paragraph of page 3 to **revealing**.
- Task 4: Change the word *helpful* to **interesting** in the last paragraph of the document.

d. Click the **Home tab**, click **Text Highlight Color**, and then toggle the following areas in the document to remove the yellow highlights:

- The word *components* in the second sentence of the second paragraph on page 1.
- The word *revealing* in the first paragraph of page 3.
- The word *interesting* in the last paragraph of the document.

e. Check the document for spelling errors. All authors' names are correctly spelled, so ignore flagged errors of names. The essay begins with a capital *A*, so ignore the apparent grammatical error. Correct any misspelled words. Group members will see an onscreen message informing them of an edit.

f. Click **Open in Word** to open the document in Word on your computer.

You want to insert a cover page but this feature is not available on Word Online, so you will open the document in Word on your computer.

g. Scroll to the top of the document. Click the **Insert tab**, click **Cover Page** in the Pages group, and then select **Banded**. Type **Analysis of "A White Heron"** as the document title and your full name as the author. Remove any content controls that you are not using and delete the *An Analysis of "A White Heron"* title on the next page.

h. Close the browser. Save and close the file. Based on your instructor's directions, submit the following:

w04h1Airlines_LastFirst

w04h2Entry_LastFirst.pdf

w04h2WhiteHeron_LastFirst

w04h3Analysis_GroupName

Chapter Objectives Review

After reading this chapter, you have accomplished the following objectives:

1. **Use a writing style and acknowledge sources.**
   - Select a writing style: A research paper is typically written to adhere to a particular writing style, often dictated by the academic discipline.
   - Format a research paper: Research papers share a set of common formatting features to maintain consistency and help to make the document look more professional.
   - Create a source and include a citation: Each source consulted for a paper must be cited, according to the rules of a writing style.
   - Share and search for a source: Sources are included in a Master List, available to all documents created on the same computer, and a Current List, available to the current document.
   - Create a bibliography: A bibliography, also known as works cited or references, lists all sources used in the preparation of a paper.

2. **Create and modify footnotes and endnotes.**
   - Create footnotes and endnotes: Footnotes (located at the bottom of a page) and endnotes (located at the end of a paper) enable you to expand on a statement or provide a citation.
   - Modify footnotes and endnotes: You can change the format or style of footnotes and endnotes, or delete them.

3. **Explore special features.**
   - Create a table of contents: If headings are formatted in a heading style, Word can prepare a table of contents, listing headings and associated page numbers.
   - Create an index: Mark entries for inclusion in an index, which is an alphabetical listing of marked topics and associated page numbers.
   - Create a cover page: Some writing styles require a cover page, which you can create as the first page, listing a report title and other identifying information.

4. **Track changes.**
   - Use Track Changes: With Track Changes active, all edits in a document are traceable so you can see what has been changed.
   - Accept and reject changes: With Track Changes active, you can evaluate each edit made, accepting or rejecting it.

5. **Review a document.**
   - Use markup: Markup views enable you to customize how tracked changes are displayed in a document. There are four markup views: Simple Markup, All Markup, No Markup, and Original.
   - Add a comment: A comment is located in a comment balloon in the margin of a report, providing a note to the author.
   - View comments: Comments are viewed in comment balloons in the document.
   - Reply to comments: Replying to comments creates a conversation around the comment with the reply placed within the original comment balloon.
   - Work with a PDF document: Documents are saved in PDF format to preserve the layout, format fonts, and images of the original Word document.
   - Reflow is a Word feature that converts a PDF document into an editable Word document.

6. **Use OneDrive.**
   - Use OneDrive with File Explorer: Windows 10 incorporates OneDrive into File Explorer to simplify the process of organizing and managing OneDrive folders (and contents), as well as ensuring that files are synchronized.

7. **Share documents.**
   - Invite others to share: Use Word and Word Online to share documents through links, with varying levels of permission.
   - Share a document link: Word will generate a sharing link with varying levels of permission and send the link to recipients in a separate email.
   - Send as an attachment: Send an email to recipients with an attached document, either in PDF or the original format.

8. **Collaborate with Word and Word Online.**
   - Use Word Online: Word Online is a Web-based version of Word that enables you to create, edit, and format a document online without having to install Word on your computer.

Key Terms Matching

Match the key terms with their definitions. Write the key term letter by the appropriate numbered definition.

- **a.** Bibliography
- **b.** Citation
- **c.** Comment
- **d.** Comment balloon
- **e.** Cover page
- **f.** Endnote
- **g.** Footnote
- **h.** Index
- **i.** Master List
- **j.** MLA
- **k.** OneDrive
- **l.** Plagiarizing
- **m.** Real-time co-authoring
- **n.** Revision mark
- **o.** Simple Markup
- **p.** Source
- **q.** Style manual
- **r.** Table of contents
- **s.** Track Changes
- **t.** Works Cited

1. _____ A database of all sources created in Word on a computer. **p. 255**
2. _____ A list of sources cited by an author in his or her work. **p. 256**
3. _____ A note recognizing a source of information or a quoted passage. **p. 254**
4. _____ A Web-based storage site and sharing utility. **p. 284**
5. _____ An alphabetical listing of topics covered in a document along with the page numbers where the topic is discussed. **p. 262**
6. _____ A Word feature that monitors all additions, deletions, and formatting changes you make in a document. **p. 271**
7. _____ A citation that appears at the end of a document. **p. 258**
8. _____ A Word feature that simplifies the display of comments and revision marks, resulting in a clean, uncluttered look. **p. 273**
9. _____ A page that lists headings in the order they appear in a document and the page numbers where the entries begin. **p. 260**
10. _____ A note, annotation, or additional information to the author or another reader about the content of a document. **p. 273**
11. _____ A list of sources consulted by an author in his or her work. **p. 256**
12. _____ A shape that displays on the right side of a paragraph in which a comment has been made and provides access to the comment. **p. 277**
13. _____ A guide to a particular writing style outlining required rules and conventions related to the preparation of papers. **p. 252**
14. _____ The act of using and documenting the works of another as one's own. **p. 252**
15. _____ A citation that appears at the bottom of a page. **p. 258**
16. _____ A writing style established by the Modern Language Association with rules and conventions for preparing research papers (used primarily in the area of humanities). **p. 252**
17. _____ A Word feature that shows several authors simultaneously editing the document in Word or Word Online. **p. 292**
18. _____ Indicates where text is added, deleted, or formatted. **p. 272**
19. _____ The first page of a report, including the report title, author or student, and other identifying information. **p. 262**
20. _____ A publication, person, or media item that is consulted in the preparation of a paper and given credit. **p. 252**

Multiple Choice

1. When you are working on a group paper with your classmates, members can take turns to write and edit the content of the paper. Which feature must the group use so that members can see the changes made to the same document?
   (a) Mark Index Entries
   (b) Track Changes
   (c) Accept Changes
   (d) Create Cross-References

2. What Word Online view is required when you want to access commands on the tab?
   (a) Editing
   (b) Web Layout
   (c) Print Layout
   (d) Reading

3. Which of the following statements about sharing a document through Word Online is *true*?
   (a) It cannot be simultaneously edited by more than one person.
   (b) It must be a Word document.
   (c) It is available for viewing only, not editing.
   (d) It is available for simultaneous editing and collaboration.

4. The choice of whether to title a list of sources such as Bibliography, Works Cited, or References is dependent upon:
   (a) the writing style in use.
   (b) the version of Word you are using.
   (c) whether the sources are from academic publications or professional journals.
   (d) your own preference.

5. When working with Word Online, how can you tell that someone is editing a shared document at the same time that you are?
   (a) The Reviewing Pane displays, providing the names of others who are editing the document.
   (b) A comment balloon displays in the left margin.
   (c) A note displays at the top right corner of the window.
   (d) There is no way to tell who is editing at the same time.

6. Which of the following is *not* an option on Word's References tab?
   (a) Insert a New Comment
   (b) Update a Table of Contents
   (c) Insert a Footnote
   (d) Manage Sources

7. The writing style you are most likely to use in a business class is:
   (a) APA.
   (b) Chicago.
   (c) Turabian.
   (d) MLA.

8. To ensure that documents you save in OneDrive are synchronized with copies of the same documents saved on your hard drive, you could use:
   (a) the Backup setting in Word Options.
   (b) the Windows 10 Startup screen.
   (c) File Explorer.
   (d) the AutoRecover option.

9. Which feature provides a simple, uncluttered, view of comments and tracked changes made to a document?
   (a) Track All
   (b) Show Markup
   (c) Simple Markup
   (d) All Markup

10. After you create and insert a table of contents into a document:
    (a) any subsequent page changes arising from the insertion or deletion of text to existing paragraphs must be entered manually.
    (b) any additions to the entries in the table arising due to the insertion of new paragraphs defined by a heading style must be entered manually.
    (c) you cannot make any changes to the table of contents.
    (d) you can select a table of contents and click Update Table to bring the table of contents up to date.

Practice Exercises

1 Live. Work. Dine. Shop.

You are the assistant publicity manager of a construction company building a community where residents can live, work, dine, and shop within the community without having to get into a car. You and a team of colleagues are designing promotional materials for this project. You conducted your research online for such communities in other states and wrote a promotional article. You will share your research with your team members online so that they can contribute, comment, and collaborate with you before submitting it to your manager for final approval. Refer to Figure 4.39 as you complete this exercise.

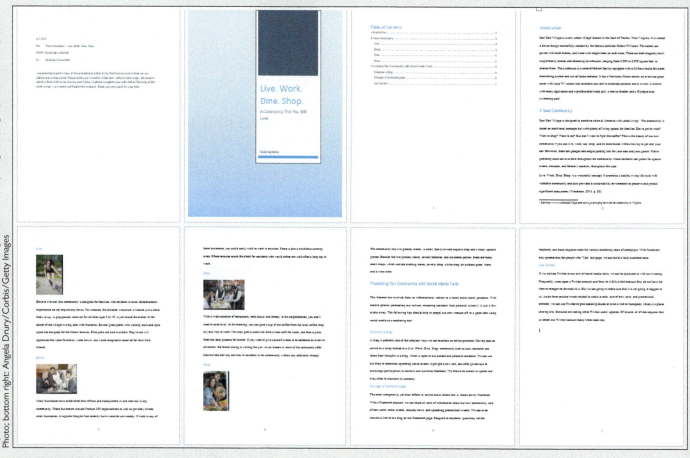

FIGURE 4.39 Design a Promotional Article

a. Open *w04p1Live* and save it as **w04p1Live_LastFirst**.

b. Apply the following formatting to the whole document:
   - Document is double spaced.
   - Font is Times New Roman 12 pt size.
   - No paragraph spacing before or after any paragraph.
   - Margins are 1" at the top, bottom, left, and right.
   - Alignment is left.

c. Press **Ctrl+Home**. Click the **Insert tab**, click **Cover Page**, and then select **Facet**. Complete the cover page by completing the following:
   - Click **Document title** and type **Live. Work. Dine. Shop.** (include the periods).
   - Click **Document subtitle** and type **A Community That You Will Love**.
   - Remove the current author (unless the current author shows your first and last names) and type your first and last names.
   - Right-click the **Abstract paragraph** at the top of the page and click **Remove Content Control**.

d. Click the **Review tab**. Click the **Track Changes arrow** and click **Track Changes**. All of your edits will be marked as you work. Change the view to **All Markup**. Make the following changes to the document:
   - Change the *Promotion* heading on page 5 to **Promoting Our Community Using Social Media Tools**.
   - Scroll to page 5 and select the heading **Maintain a blog**. Click the **Review tab** and click **New Comment**. Type **Susie, do you like what I wrote in this section?**
e. Insert a page break at the beginning of the cover page and move to the beginning of the new page. Open the PDF file *w04p1Invite.pdf* in Word, then copy and paste all the text to the first page of the *w04p1Live_LastFirst* document. Replace Firstname Lastname with your first and last names. Because Track Changes is on, the text you inserted is colored to indicate it is a new edit.
f. Scroll through the document, noting the edits that were tracked. On page 6, you will see the comment you made earlier. Press **Ctrl+Home** to move to the beginning of the document. Click the **Review tab** and change the Display for Review in the Tracking group to **No Markup**. Scroll through the document to note that revision marks (indicating edits) do not display. Move to the beginning of the document and select **Simple Markup**. Scroll through the document once more. Click a bar beside an edited paragraph to display the edits. Click the bar again to remove them from view.
g. Check the document for spelling errors. All names of people and websites are correctly spelled. Scroll to page 6 and click the **comment balloon** beside the *Maintain a blog* section. Click **Reply** in the expanded markup balloon. Type **I will review the document and give you my suggestions on Monday afternoon.** (include the period). Close the comment balloon.
h. Click after the period at the end of the first sentence on page 4, under the *A New Community* heading. The sentence ends with *urban living*. Click the **References tab** and click **Insert Footnote** in the Footnotes group. Type **See http://www.westbroadvillage.com/news_events.php for a similar community in Virginia.** (include the period). Right-click the **hyperlink** in the footnote and click **Remove Hyperlink**.
i. Click the **Review tab** and change the view to **No Markup**. Right-click the footnote at the bottom of page 3 and click **Style**. Click **Modify**. Change the font to **Times New Roman** and the font size to **10**. Click **OK** and click **Close**.
j. Move to the top of page 3 (beginning with the *Introduction* heading) and insert a page break at the top of the page. Move to the top of the new page (page 3). Click the **References tab**, click **Table of Contents** in the Table of Contents group, and then click **Automatic Table 2**.
k. Double-click the *Conclusion* link and press **Ctrl+Click**. Delete the Conclusion section (removing the heading and the paragraph below the heading). Scroll to page 3 and click **Table of Contents**. Click **Update Table** in the content control and select **Update entire table**. Click **OK**. Note that the Conclusion section is no longer included in the table of contents.
l. Click the **Review tab** and change the view to **Simple Markup**. Click the **Accept arrow** and click **Accept All Changes and Stop Tracking**. Scroll through the document and note that edits are no longer marked.
m. Click before the period in the last sentence in the second paragraph in the *A New Community* section that ends *protect significant ecosystems*. Click the **References tab** and click the **Style arrow** in the Citations & Bibliography group. Select **APA Sixth Edition**. Click **Insert Citation** in the Citations & Bibliography group and click **Add New Source**. Add the following source from a Journal Article and click **OK**:

Author: **Woodman, Jennifer Lynn**
Title: **Protecting Ecosystems**
Journal Name: **Journal of Ecosystems Studies**
Year: **2015**
Pages: **23–30**
Volume: **6**
Issue: **4**
(Hint: Click *Show All Bibliography Fields* to enter the volume and issue.)

n. Click the **citation** you just created, click the **Citation Options arrow**, and then click **Edit Citation**. Type **23** in the Pages box. Click **OK**.

o. Sign in to your Microsoft account and save the document to your OneDrive folder on File Explorer. Click **Share** at the top right corner, enter your own email address, and ensure the **Can edit option** is selected in the Share pane. Type an optional message and click **Share**.

p. Open your email with the shared link and click **View in OneDrive**. Scroll through the document on Word Online. Click **Edit Document** and select **Edit in Browser**. Select *MEMO* at the top of the letter. Click **Comments** and click **New Comment**. Type **I have completed my research for this project. Please review this document and make any edits you feel necessary.** (include the period). Click **Post**. Close the Comments pane. Click **Open in Word**.

q. Click the **File tab**, click **Export**, and then select **Create PDF/XPS**. Leave the file name as w04p1Live_LastFirst and ensure that the type is PDF. Click **Publish** to save the document as a PDF file. Scroll through the PDF file and note that the edits and the comment were saved as part of the PDF document.

r. Close all open files, saving a file if prompted to do so. Based on your instructor's directions, submit the following:

w04p1Live_LastFirst
w04p1Live_LastFirst.pdf

2 DREAM Act Letter

You are a partner in a law firm that deals with a large number of potential DREAM Act beneficiaries. The DREAM Act (Development, Relief, and Education for Alien Minors) provides conditional permanent residency to undocumented residents under certain conditions (good moral character, completion of U.S. high school degree, arrival in the United States as minors, etc.). Supporters of the Act contend that it provides social and economic benefits, whereas opponents label it as an amnesty program that rewards illegal immigration. Your law firm has partnered with leading law professors across the country to encourage the U.S. Executive Branch (Office of the President) to explore various options related to wise administration of the DREAM Act. In a letter to the president, you outline your position. Because it is of a legal nature, the letter makes broad use of footnotes and in-text references. Because the letter is to be signed and supported by law professors across the country, you will share the letter online, making it possible for others to edit and approve of the wording. Refer to Figure 4.40 as you complete this exercise.

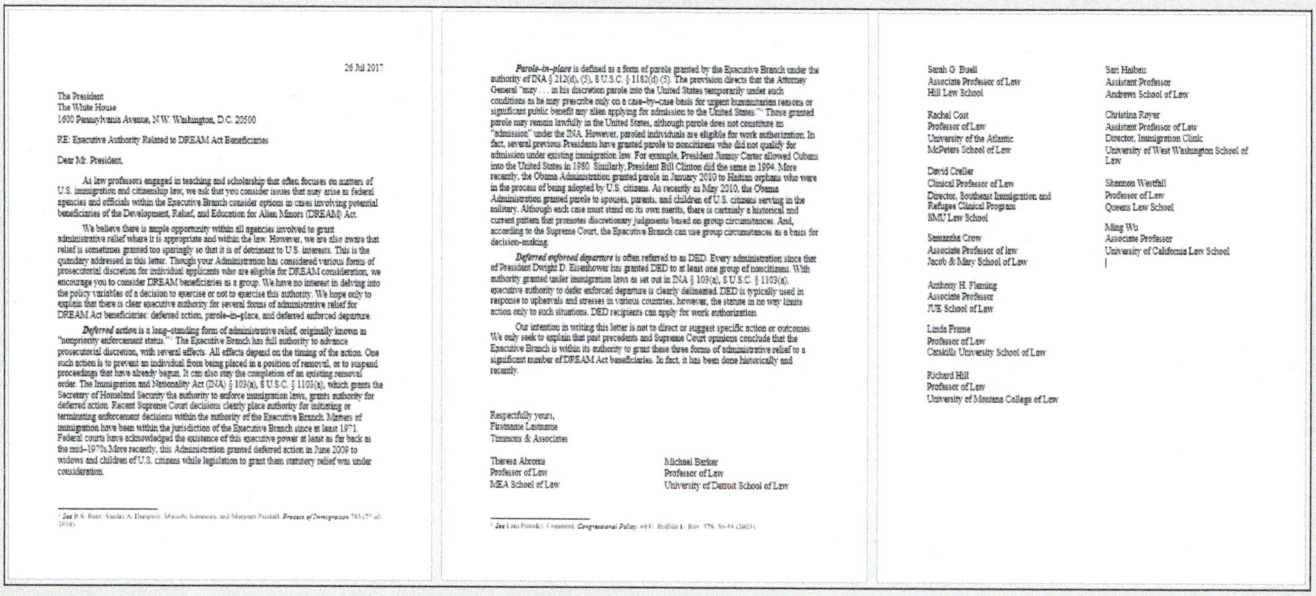

FIGURE 4.40 Format the DREAM Act Letter

a. Open *w04p2Law* and save as **w04p2Law_LastFirst**.
b. Scroll through the document and change *Firstname Lastname* in the closing to your first and last names. Add two blank paragraphs above *Respectfully yours*. Check the document for spelling errors. All names are spelled correctly. The word *parol* should be spelled parole. The word *nonpriority* is not misspelled. Select the text in the document from *As law professors engaged in teaching and scholarship* through *historically and recently*. Ensure the paragraph spacing After is **6 pt**. Deselect the text. Change the margin setting to **Normal**.
c. Scroll down and select the text from *Theresa Abroms* through the end of the document. Format the selected text in two columns. Deselect the text. Ensure that *Rachel Cost* and her information are in the same column by adding a **hard return** in front of her name. Scroll to the last page and place the insertion point to the left of *Sari Haibau*. Click **Breaks** in the Page Setup group on the Layout tab. Click **Column**.
d. Place the insertion point after the ending quotation mark that ends the first sentence in the third body paragraph on page 1. Click the **References tab** and click **Insert Footnote** in the Footnotes group. Type *See* **R.S. Bane, Sandra A. Dempsey, Minoshi Satomura, and Margaret Falstaff,** *Process of Immigration* **785 (7th ed. 2014).** (include the period). Note: the word *See* is italicized in the footnote.
e. Scroll to page 2 and place the insertion point after the quotation mark that ends the second sentence in the paragraph that begins *Parole-in-place is defined*. Click the **Footnotes Dialog Box Launcher** in the Footnotes group and click **Insert**. Type *See* **Lani Parosky, Comment,** *Congressional Policy*, **64 U. Buffalo L. Rev. 578, 56–58 (2003).** (include the period). Note: the word *See* is italicized in the footnote.
f. Sign in to your Microsoft account and save the document to your OneDrive folder on File Explorer. Click **Share** at the top right corner, enter your own email address, and ensure the **Can edit option** is selected in the Share pane. Type an optional message and click **Share**.
g. Open your email with the shared link and click **View in OneDrive**. Scroll through the document and note that Word Online shows a placeholder for the footnotes you created. However, you cannot edit or work with footnotes in Word Online because it is limited in features. Point to a footnote placeholder to read a comment to the effect that you must open Word to work with footnotes.
h. Click **Edit Document** and select **Edit in Browser**. Click the **Review tab**, ensure that **Show Comments** in the Comments group is enabled, and review the comment on the Comments pane.
i. Select *The President* at the top of the letter. Click **New Comment** in the Comment pane. Type **Please review this document very carefully and pay attention to all the names and their associations. Also, please make any edits you feel necessary.** (include the period). Click **Post**. Close the Comments pane.
j. Click **Open in Word**. Click the **Track Changes arrow** in the Tracking group and click **Track Changes**. Click **Reviewing Pane** (not the Reviewing Pane arrow). Reverse the words *to* and *not* in the second body paragraph on page 1. Note the changes in the Reviewing Pane as well as the vertical bar on the right side of the affected paragraph indicating that edits have been made. Click the **vertical bar** to view the changes. Click it again to return to Simple Markup. Close the Reviewing (Revisions) Pane.
k. Ensure that w04p2Law_LastFirst.docx is displayed, click the **Review tab**, click the **Accept arrow** in the Changes group, and then click **Accept All Changes and Stop Tracking**.
l. Save the document. Click **Share** at the top right corner and click **Send as attachment** at the bottom of the Share pane. Click **Send a PDF**. Type your own email address when your default email account opens. Type an optional subject and send the email. Open your own email and download the PDF file to your computer. Open the PDF file and review the whole document for any last-minute revisions.
m. Save and close both files. Based on your instructor's directions, submit the following:
w04p2Law_LastFirst
w04p2Law_LastFirst.pdf

Mid-Level Exercises

1 WWW Web Services Agency

MyLab IT Grader

You work as a Web designer at WWW Web Services Agency and have been asked to provide some basic information to be used in a senior citizens' workshop. You want to provide the basic elements of good Web design and format the document professionally. Use the basic information you have already prepared in a Word document and revise it to include elements appropriate for a research-oriented paper.

a. Open *w04m1Web* and save as **w04m1Web_LastFirst**. Delete the square brackets and change the author name to your own name.

b. Apply the following formatting to the whole document:
   - Alignment is left.
   - Document is double-spaced.
   - The font is Times New Roman 12 pt.
   - Paragraph spacing before or after any paragraph is 0.
   - Margins are 1" at the top, bottom, left, and right.

c. Change citation style to **APA Sixth Edition**. Place the insertion point at the end of the Proximity paragraph (after the period) on the second page of the document. The paragraph ends with *indicates less proximity*. Insert the following footnote: **Max Rebaza, Effective Websites, Chicago: Windy City Publishing, Inc. (2018)**. Do not include the period.

d. Insert a table of contents on a new page after the cover page. Use a style of your choice.

e. Add a bibliography to the document by inserting citation sources from the footnotes already in place. Because you will not use in-text citations, you will use the Source Manager to create the sources. To add new sources, complete the following steps:
   - Click the **References tab** and click **Manage Sources** in the Citations & Bibliography group.
   - Add a source for the footnote you created in Step c (a Book). Click **New** in the Source Manager dialog box and add the source to both the Current List and the Master List.
   - Create citation sources for the two additional sources identified in the document footnotes. The footnote on the fourth page is from an article in a periodical (issue 7) and the footnote on the fifth page cites a journal article.

f. Change the citation style to **Chicago.** Insert a bibliography at the end of the document on a separate page. Select **Bibliography**. Apply **Heading 2 style** to the Bibliography heading and center the heading. Double space the bibliography and ensure that there is no paragraph spacing before or after. Update the table of contents to include this new addition and change the font for Bibliography to **Times New Roman**.

g. Mark all occurrences of *Web*, *content*, and *site* as index entries. Cross-reference *Web pages* with *Web sites*. Create an index on a separate page after the bibliography using the **Formal format**.

h. Check the document for spelling errors. All names are spelled correctly.

i. Begin to track changes. Select the heading **Proximity and Balance** on the third page. Add a new comment, typing **This section seems incomplete. Please check and add content.** (include the period)

j. Add the following sentence as the second sentence in the Contrast and Focus section: **You are most likely familiar with the concept of contrast when working with pictures in an image editor.**

k. Sign in to your Microsoft account and save the document to your OneDrive folder on File Explorer. Click **Share** at the top right corner and click **Get a sharing link** at the bottom of the Share pane. Click **Copy** to create an edit link.

l. Scroll to the end of the document, press **Enter**, and then paste the link.

m. Click the **File tab**, click **Export**, and then select **Create PDF/XPS**. Leave the file name as w04m1Web_LastFirst and ensure that the type is PDF. Click **Publish** to save the document as a PDF file. Scroll through the PDF file and note that the edits and the comment were saved as part of the PDF document.

n. Close all files and based on your instructor's directions, submit the following:
   w04m1Web_LastFirst
   w04m1Web_LastFirst.pdf

2 Study Abroad

MyLab IT Grader

You want to study for a semester in a foreign country. For the application process, you need to write a proposal describing the program that you are interested in. You conducted online research, found a foreign university that appealed to you, and developed a list of activities that you will participate in while away. Now you want to format the Word document to enhance the readability and to include a cover page, table of contents, and index, before submitting it to your academic advisor for discussion.

a. Open *w04m2StudyAbroad* and save it as **w04m2StudyAbroad_LastFirst**.

b. Turn on **Track Changes** so any further changes will be flagged.

c. Apply **Heading 1 style** to section headings that display in all capital letters. Apply **Heading 2 style** (scroll to locate the style) to section headings that display alone on a line in title case (the first letter of each word is capitalized). Format the program fees' items in the *Included in the Tuition* section as a bulleted list.

d. Sign in to your Microsoft account and save the document to your OneDrive folder on File Explorer. Click **Share** at the top right corner, enter your own email address, and then ensure the **Can edit option** is selected in the Share pane. Type an optional message and click **Share**. Open your email with the shared link and click **View in OneDrive**. Scroll through the document on Word Online. Click **Edit Document** and select **Edit in Browser**. Click the **Review tab** and ensure that **Show Comments** in the Comments group is enabled.

e. Type the following reply to the first comment in the document (you will insert the cover page and TOC in a later step): **I have changed this heading to Heading 1, and inserted a cover page and a TOC before this heading.** (include the period). Type the following reply to the third comment: **I have formatted these items as a bulleted list.** (include the period). Close the Comments pane.

f. Click **Open in Word**. Change the citation style to **APA Sixth Edition**. Insert a footnote on page 1 at the end of the first sentence in the first paragraph (after the period), which ends with *Strasbourg, France*. Type the following for the footnote: **EU Studies Program in Strasbourg, France. http://www.eustudiesprogram.eu/resources/eustudies-web.pdf**. Change the number format for footnotes to **a, b, c** in the Footnotes dialog box. (Click **Apply**, not Insert.) Locate the endnote at the end of the document and convert it to a footnote.

g. Create a footer for the document consisting of the title **Study Abroad**, followed by a space and a page number. If the page number already displays as a footer, adjust it so that it follows Study Abroad. Left align the footer in the footer area. Do not display the footer on the first page.

h. Create a cover page of your choosing. Delete any placeholders that you are not using.

i. Create a page specifically for the table of contents right after the cover page and generate a table of contents.

j. Mark all occurrences of the following text for inclusion in the index: Alsace, Black Forest, Classes, European Union, France, Grand Île, and Rhine valley. Cross-reference *Strasbourg* with *France* and *European Union* with *EU*. On a separate page at the end of the document, create the index in **Classic format** and accept all default settings. Accept all changes to the document and turn off Track Changes.

k. Click **Share** at the top right corner and click **Send as attachment** at the bottom of the Share pane. Click **Send a PDF**. Type your own email address when your default email account opens. Type an optional subject and send the email. Open your own email and download the PDF file to your computer. Open the PDF file and review the whole document for any last-minute revisions.

l. Save and close both files. Based on your instructor's directions, submit the following:
w04m2StudyAbroad_LastFirst
w04m2StudyAbroad_LastFirst.pdf

Running Case

New Castle County Technical Services

New Castle County Technical Services (NCCTS) provides technical services to clients in the greater New Castle County, Delaware, area. Founded in 2011, the company is rapidly expanding to include technical security systems, network infrastructure cabling, and basic troubleshooting services. With that growth comes the need to promote the company and to provide clear written communication to employees and clients. Microsoft Word is used exclusively in the development and distribution of documents, including an "About New Castle" summary that will be available both in print and online. You made a few changes to the document and you are now ready to make this into a professional-looking business document in this exercise.

a. Sign in to your Microsoft account. Open *w04r1NewCastle* and save it as **w04r1NewCastle_LastFirst** to your OneDrive folder on File Explorer.

b. Accept the following formatting changes in the document and turn off Track Changes.
   - Font is Times New Roman.
   - Margins are 1" at the top, bottom, left, and right.
   - Alignment is left.

c. Click **Share** at the top right corner, enter your own email address, and then ensure the **Can edit option** is selected in the Share pane. Type an optional message and click **Share**.

d. Open your email with the shared link and click **View in OneDrive**. Scroll through the document on Word Online. Click **Edit Document** and select **Edit in Browser**. Click the **Review tab** and ensure that **Show Comments** in the Comments group is enabled. Select the date at the top of the letter. Click **New Comment** in the Comment pane and type **I have accepted all the formatting changes.** (include the period). Click **Post**.

e. Address the comment in the *Active Accounts* section of the document by typing the following sentence as the third sentence in the paragraph: **It is not surprising to see that network security and cloud integration have a larger increase than IT consulting and disaster recovery.** (include the period) Click **Reply** and click **Resolve** to close the comment since you have taken action on the item. Close the Comments pane.

f. Click **Open in Word**. Insert a footnote on page 6 at the end of the second sentence in the first paragraph (after the period), which ends with *of the past two years*. Type the following for the footnote: **Information for the past five years can be made available upon direct request from the company.** (include the period). Change the number format for footnotes to **1, 2, 3** in the Footnotes dialog box. (Click **Apply**, not Insert.) Use a style to change the font to **Times New Roman, 11 pt size**.

g. Create the **Integral cover page**. Change the document title to **About New Castle** and change the author name to your own name. Delete any placeholders that you are not using.

h. Create a page specifically for the table of contents right after the cover page and generate a table of contents using the **Automatic Table 2 style**.

i. Mark all occurrences of the following text for inclusion in the index: *computer, certification, network, NCCTS, training support,* and *troubleshooting*. Cross-reference *New Castle* with *Technical Services*. On a separate page at the end of the document, create the index in **Classic format**.

j. Click **Share** at the top right corner and click **Send as attachment** at the bottom of the Share pane. Click **Send a PDF**. Type your own email address when your default email account opens. Type an optional subject and send the email. Open your own email and download the PDF file to your computer. Open the PDF file and review the whole document for any last-minute revisions.

k. Save and close both files. Based on your instructor's directions, submit the following:
   w04r1NewCastle_LastFirst
   w04r1NewCastle_LastFirst.pdf

Disaster Recovery

Computer History

You are preparing a brief history of computers for inclusion in a group project. Another student began the project but ran out of time and needs your help. You need to turn the draft into a professional-looking document by applying formatting based on the APA writing style and including proper citations of the sources used in your research. Adding a cover page, a table of contents, and an index to the research paper will also help to enhance the document. Open *w04d1Computers* and save it as **w04d1Computers_LastFirst**. Turn on Track Changes and respond to all comments left for you by the previous student, and then mark the comments as resolved when you are done. Save and close the file. Based on your instructor's directions, submit w04d1Computers_LastFirst.

Capstone Exercise

MyLab IT Grader

Funding a College Education

Funding a college education can be an expensive and daunting task for parents. Being a recent college graduate provides you with first-hand experience on how to finance a four-year education. Upon graduation, you and a fellow student created a consulting business to educate parents on college funding and help them maneuver the maze of scholarships and federal funding. To get things started, your business partner has written a draft of the comprehensive guide to college funding and is ready for you to review it.

Use Word Online, and Apply Formatting

Your business partner sent you the guide in PDF format, so you will open and save it in Word. To apply consistency throughout the draft document, you will format the document in the APA style.

1. Sign in to your Microsoft account. Open *w04c1College* and save it as **w04c1College_LastFirst** to your OneDrive folder on File Explorer.

2. Use Word Online to apply the following formatting to the whole document:
   - Document is double-spaced.
   - Font is Times New Roman 12 pt size.
   - No paragraph spacing before or after any paragraph.
   - Margins are 1" at the top, bottom, left, and right.
   - Alignment is left.

Track Revisions

The document you received has several changes and comments made by your partner. You will review the tracked changes and make a few of your own.

3. Ensure that the markup view is All Markup. In the first paragraph on the first page, reject the addition of the words *2- or*. Reject the *Click here for more* change in the FAFSA section. Accept all other tracked changes in the document and stop tracking.

4. Review and act on the three comments about formatting all headings to the correct heading styles as per the comments left by your business partner. Reply to these comments by typing **I have made the style replacement** and mark them as Resolved.

Credit Sources

You are now ready to add the citations for resources that your partner used when assembling this guide. However, because these features are not available on Word Online, you need to use Word on your computer to perform the rest of the tasks.

5. Select **APA Sixth Edition style**. Click before the period ending in the sentence *More information on how to complete the FASFA is available online* in the FAFSA section. Insert the following website citation:

   Name of Webpage: **How to Complete the FAFSA**
   Name of Website: **Collegeboard**
   Year: **2018**
   Month: **May**
   Day: **03**
   URL: **https://bigfuture.collegeboard. gov/pay-for-college/financial-aid-101/ how-to-complete-the-fafsa**

6. Click before the period ending in the sentence *grants and scholarships, federal loans, and work-study* on page 1 in the FAFSA section. Insert the following website citation:

   Name of Webpage: **FAFSA**
   Name of Website: **fafsa**
   Year: **2018**
   Month: **May**
   Day: **03**
   URL: **https://fafsa.edu.gov**

7. Insert a footnote on page 2 before the period in the sentence ending *for the academic year of 2017-2018*: **The amount of Pell Grant award changes every year. For more information, please consult the Department of Education.** (include the period). Change the number format for footnotes to **a, b, c** in the Footnotes dialog box. (Click **Apply**, not Insert.) Use style to change the font to **Times New Roman, 11 pt size**.

8. Delete the reminder comment at the bottom of the last page. Insert a blank page at the end of the report and insert a bibliography in APA style on the blank page with the title **Works Cited**. Double space the bibliography, with no paragraph spacing and a font of **Times New Roman 12 pt**. Center the *Works Cited* title, apply **12 pt**, but **not bold** formatting. Ensure that all text in the bibliography is formatted to **Black, Text 1 font color**.

Insert a Cover Page, a Table of Contents, Page Number, and Index

To put the finishing touches on your document, you add a cover page, a table of contents, page number, and an index to the document.

9. Insert the **Retrospect cover page**. Change the author name to your own name and delete any placeholders that you are not using. Address the first comment and delete the comment, the title, and the blank paragraphs.

10. Create a page specifically for the table of contents right after the cover page using the **Automatic Table 1** style.
11. Display a centered page number, using **Plain Number 2 format,** in the footer of the document. Do not display the page number footer on the first page. Numbering begins with page 1 on the Table of Contents page.
12. Mark all occurrences of *scholarship*, *grant*, and *FAFSA* as index entries. Cross-reference *college* with *university*. Create an index on a separate page after the bibliography using the **Formal format**. Use all other default settings.

Share the Document and Create a PDF Document

13. Sign in to your Microsoft account, save the document to your OneDrive folder on File Explorer, and then get a sharing link. Scroll to the end of the document, insert a blank paragraph, and then paste the link.
14. Create a PDF document with the same name.
15. Close all files and based on your instructor's directions, submit the following:

    w04c1College_LastFirst

    w04c1College_LastFirst.pdf

Word
Document Publications

LEARNING OUTCOMES You will design and create a newsletter and incorporate graphical elements.

OBJECTIVES & SKILLS: After you read this chapter, you will be able to:

Desktop Publishing

OBJECTIVE 1: DESIGN A NEWSLETTER 313
Develop Overall Document Layout, Apply and Modify Columns Layout, Insert a Section Break, Insert a Column Break

OBJECTIVE 2: APPLY DESIGN FEATURES 316
Create a Masthead, Create a Drop Cap, Apply Borders and Shading, Include Images

HANDS-ON EXERCISE 1 320

Graphic Objects

OBJECTIVE 3: INSERT GRAPHIC OBJECTS 326
Insert SmartArt, Insert WordArt, Insert a Text Box, Create a Pull Quote or Sidebar, Insert Drawing Shapes

OBJECTIVE 4: MANIPULATE GRAPHIC OBJECTS 333
Change Shape Fills and Borders; Resize an Object; Group, Layer, and Rotate Objects

HANDS-ON EXERCISE 2 336

Document Versatility

OBJECTIVE 5: USE OLE TO INSERT AN OBJECT 342
Use the Copy and Paste Method to Embed or Link an Object, Use the Insert an Object Method to Embed or Link an Object, Update a Link

HANDS-ON EXERCISE 3 345

CASE STUDY | Along the Greenways

Kody Allen is director of The Greenways, a nonprofit organization. The organization was formed to generate interest in outdoor activities as well as to provide support and funding for additional walking and biking trails in the city and surrounding counties. Maintaining positive public relations is key to generating support for the organization, and providing a quarterly newsletter is one way to do this.

Mr. Allen has asked you to create a newsletter in a format that is easy to read but also informative. In addition, you will consider including professional design elements and graphics to add visual interest. Mr. Allen wants to limit the newsletter to one page.

CHAPTER 5

Designing Newsletters and Working with Graphics

FIGURE 5.1 Greenways Newsletter

CASE STUDY | Along the Greenways

Starting Files	File to be Submitted
w05h1Bike.jpg	w05h3Greenways_LastFirst
w05h1Greenways	
w05h3Budget.xlsx	
w05h3Funding	

MyLab IT Grader An alternate version of this project is available as a MyLab IT Grader Assessment

Document Publications • Word 2019 311

Desktop Publishing

Desktop publishing is a process that uses software, such as Microsoft Word, to design commercial-quality printed material. Through a combination of technologies and page composition software, desktop publishing enables users to manipulate text and graphics to produce attractive documents. Some desktop publishing tasks, such as a college catalog, require a high level of precision and typesetting capability; in those cases, you might opt for dedicated desktop publishing software that includes sophisticated typesetting and graphic tools. However, Word's comprehensive set of desktop publishing tools is often sufficient for such applications as newsletters, brochures, and other documents requiring unique type and artwork. In fact, Word's enhanced graphic design features have narrowed the gap between typical word processing tasks and desktop publishing flair, such that many companies find that Word is the only tool necessary for the production of high-quality, graphic-rich printed material.

Designing an attractive document that includes eye-catching features and graphics is often time consuming, requiring software proficiency and attention to detail. Although the development of high-quality marketing and informational material often requires the attention of skilled professionals and graphic designers, you can use Word to produce attractive newsletters, brochures, and flyers, without requiring a great deal of desktop publishing skill on your part. With a bit of practice using Word, and basic proficiency in graphic design, you can easily develop professional-looking documents such as the newsletter shown in Figure 5.2.

In this section, you will learn to develop a simple newsletter that includes multiple columns situated in an attractive arrangement. The inclusion of images and other objects, positioned within the flow of newsletter text, adds interest to and enlivens a newsletter, as well.

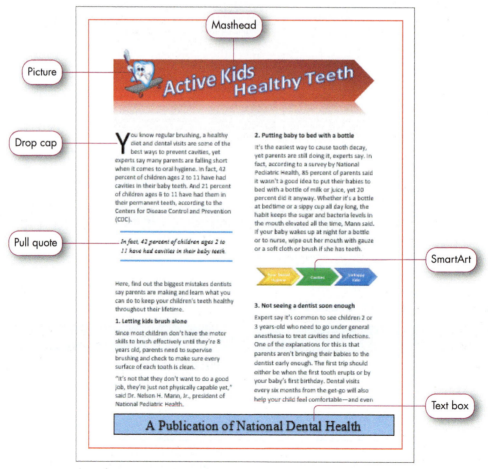

FIGURE 5.2 Sample Newsletter

Designing a Newsletter

Perhaps the most difficult aspect of creating a document is to develop an overall design; the mere availability of desktop publishing software, such as Word, does not guarantee an attractive and effective document. Designing a document is a creative process in which you consider your audience and purpose, combining overall appearance, wording, and specific formatting features to create a document that accomplishes the goal of effectively conveying your message. Let your eye be the judge and follow your instincts. It also helps to seek inspiration from others by collecting samples of documents that succeed in capturing attention and using those document principles as the starting point for an effective design.

> **TIP: LIMIT USE OF TYPOGRAPHY**
> Less is more—a rule that especially applies to typefaces and styles. Too many of either will produce cluttered documents. Try to limit the design to a maximum of two fonts per document but choose multiple sizes or a variety of formatting treatments. Use boldface or italics for emphasis—not underlining—but do so in moderation. Too much emphasis on too many elements is distracting. A simple design is often the best design.

Develop Overall Document Layout

The design of a newsletter is developed on a grid, an underlying set of horizontal and vertical lines that determine the placement of major elements. A grid may be simple or complex, but it is always distinguished by the number of columns it contains. The three-column grid of Figure 5.3 is one of the most common and utilitarian designs. Other grid designs include multiple columns of various widths and heights. You would typically use a one-column grid for term papers and letters. A two-column, wide-and-narrow format is appropriate for some newsletters, textbooks, and manuals.

FIGURE 5.3 Designing on a Grid

The grid concept simplifies a document design task, as it affords a strong foundation upon which you can manage various formatting options. It enables you to develop a plan for positioning newsletter elements appropriately with relation to one another. Moreover, the conscious use of a grid encourages consistency from page to page within a document (or from issue to issue of a newsletter), resulting in a polished publication.

> **TIP: SIDE TO SIDE VIEW**
> As you develop a multi-page publication, a global view of the document in a side-to-side arrangement provides an overview of the page layout that enhances your understanding of the document flow. You can page through a document much like reading a book instead of scrolling through pages vertically. Select the Print Layout view and the Side to Side option in the Page Movement group on the View tab to flip through pages by swiping a touchscreen or using a mouse. For quick navigation or general overview, use the Thumbnails command in the Zoom group (having selected Side to Side movement) and click any page or pinch on a touchscreen to zoom in or out. Click Vertical in the Page Movement group or select another view to return to a single-page view.

Now that you have determined an overall document layout, you will next focus on specific formatting features, such as font style, boldface, and italics. Such formatting not only yields an attractive document but also assists in emphasizing essential points. Consider the following suggestions when formatting text:

- Vary font size and/or font style to delineate various sections, such as major headings and subheadings. Format headings in a font size at least two points larger than that of the body text.
- Use bold and italic formatting sparingly. Both are effective at drawing attention, but excessive variation in font results in a document that looks choppy and disjointed.
- Limit the use of all uppercase letters and underlining. Uppercase letters are often associated with screaming, while underlining typically indicates a hyperlink.
- Avoid overusing such techniques as drop caps, color, and objects. While appropriate use of such items can generate interest and entertainment, overuse can result in a document that is cluttered and difficult to follow.

> **TIP: CUSTOMIZING THE STATUS BAR**
> Designing a document that is intended for publication often requires that you work within certain constraints related to overall document design and placement of page elements. You might even be required to remain within a range of words or characters. Customizing the status bar to provide document information can help. Right-click the status bar and select from various options, including a character and word count that updates immediately as you type.

STEP 1 — Apply and Modify Column Layout

Newsletters often include multiple columns, as illustrated by the document shown in Figure 5.2. A newsletter title is typically located at the top of the first page of a newsletter, followed by text that is formatted in multiple columns. Columns can be equally sized, or you can arrange them in varying widths, even including a line between them for additional interest or definition. You can format text into columns by using Columns in the Page Setup group on the Layout tab and selecting the number of columns you want. If you do not first select text to format, column selections are applied to all text in the document or current section.

For more specificity, click More Columns from the Columns option on the Layout tab to open a dialog box, shown in Figure 5.4, from which you can choose additional settings, such as the inclusion of a line between columns or the selection of a preset column design (One, Two, Three, Left, or Right). Word calculates the width of each column based on the number of columns, the left and right margins, and the space between columns. The One, Two, and Three column selections result in columns of equal width, while the Left and Right options apply two columns of unequal width, with the narrower column on the left or right, respectively. Varying column width can add interest to a newsletter, modifying the predictability of more uniform text design. Regardless of column design, text that has been formatted in columns flows continuously from the bottom of one column to the top of the next.

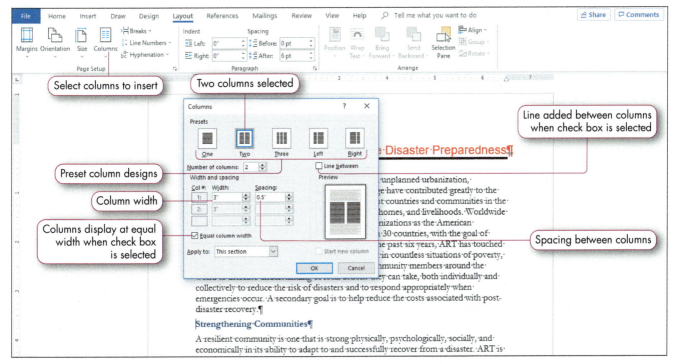

FIGURE 5.4 The Columns dialog box

As you design a newsletter, you can also use the Columns dialog box to specify custom column widths. In the dialog box shown in Figure 5.4, ensure that *Equal column width* is deselected and indicate a measurement for the width of each column and column spacing.

STEP 2 Insert a Section Break

A column setting is applied to selected text, or to all text in the section where the insertion point is located. To change the text layout to a different column arrangement, perhaps from two columns to one column, select the text or click where you want to change the layout and then select the desired column setting. For example, to format a newsletter title as one column, while the remaining newsletter text appears in two columns, the title must be in a separate section. A section break is also required at the end of the last column in the newsletter to ensure that text is balanced within columns. Such a break enables Word to identify column text that should be formatted differently from other text on a single page. As shown in Figure 5.5, you can select from various types of section breaks. With the insertion point at the location where the continuous section break should occur, click Breaks on the Layout tab, and then select Continuous.

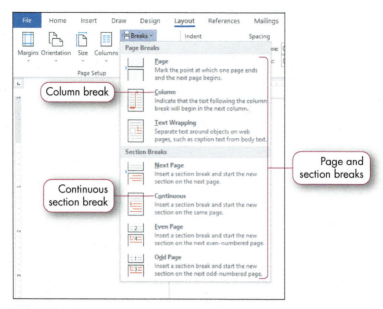

FIGURE 5.5 Page and Section Breaks

Insert a Column Break

As you develop a newsletter in columns, you can control where one column ends and another begins by inserting a column break. Unless you specify otherwise, Word automatically breaks columns, although not always in the most attractive manner. For example, you may find that one column in a newsletter ends with a subheading at the bottom of the column, with remaining text in that section continuing in the next column. In that case, you would insert a column break before the subheading so that the subheading and text begins at the top of the next column. The column break option is included as a break in the Page Setup group on the Layout tab, as shown in Figure 5.5.

Applying Design Features

Companies, civic clubs, churches, and even families use Word to design newsletters. You can create a newsletter using a newsletter document template or design a newsletter from a blank document. Using Word, you can design and format newsletters, arranging text in columns and incorporating such objects as pictures, SmartArt, and text boxes, as shown in Figure 5.2. Objects and formatting features that are often found in newsletters include the following:

- **Images.** Pictures and graphics visually break a long line of text, adding interest and drawing attention to a topic. Images direct the eye to relevant textual information, providing a bit of color and making the document more entertaining to read.
- **WordArt.** WordArt enables you to apply predefined styles to major headings, banners, or other text elements. A WordArt object is often large and colorful, drawing attention to a specific area of a newsletter.
- **SmartArt.** A SmartArt graphic, showing relationships or processes, can enhance understanding. Diagrams tend to convey ideas much more effectively than do words alone.
- **Shapes.** Word's drawing tools simplify the addition of shapes and objects to a document. Such shapes as arrows and callouts enable you to create descriptive drawings or to clarify elements within a document.
- **Tables.** A table provides a grid of columns and rows in which you can summarize data in an understandable way. With Word's comprehensive table design and layout tools, you can add style, color, and structure to a simple table.

- **Charts.** Presentation of data in a chart, such as a pie or column design, often enhances understanding and adds interest to a document. Charts created and formatted using Microsoft Excel can be easily inserted into a Word document.
- **Screenshots.** A screenshot is a graphic image of a screen display. You can use Word to capture a screenshot and include it in a document.
- **Borders.** Documents such as newsletters often include bordered text or even a page border surrounding one or more pages. Not limited to simple lines, borders can be designed with various line thicknesses and colors as well as small graphics.
- **Shading.** When used as the background color of an item, such as a text box or paragraph, shading is an effective way to set an element apart.
- **Lists.** Whether bulleted or numbered, lists help to organize and emphasize information.
- **Typography.** You can use stylized text and enhanced text effects to design document contents that best achieve the desired visual effect and to effectively convey the intended message. Good typography design often goes unnoticed, whereas poor typography detracts from the message. The selection of fonts, font styles, and font sizes that enhance text within a document is a critical, often subtle, element in the success of a document.
- **Styles.** You can use predefined styles in desktop publishing to add personality to your newsletter. Remember that a style is a set of formatting options you apply to characters or paragraphs. A style includes such settings as alignment, line spacing, indents, tabs, borders, and shading. You can use the same styles from one edition of a newsletter to the next to ensure consistency. Additionally, the use of styles in any document promotes uniformity and increases flexibility.

No hard and fast rules exist to dictate how many or which features you should include when designing a newsletter. Your objective should be to create a document that is easy to read and visually appealing. You may find that a design that works well in one document is not at all appropriate for a different document. For example, a technical newsletter on best practices for critical care nurses would not be formatted in the same way as a more informal newsletter developed by a local swim team. Therefore, you should experiment with various design techniques as you develop documents for different purposes.

STEP 3 Create a Masthead

Most often located at the top of a newsletter, a *masthead* typically includes a title, perhaps incorporating graphics or a logo, as well as other identifying information such as company address and contact information, a volume and issue number, and the date of publication. The purpose of the masthead is to communicate the identity of the publication in an easily recognizable fashion, as shown in Figure 5.6. You can employ various Word techniques and formatting features to create a masthead, including designing a WordArt object, text box, or shaded text.

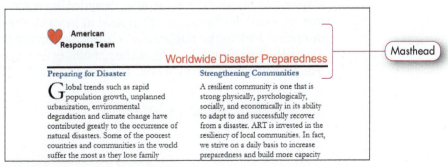

FIGURE 5.6 Newsletter Masthead

STEP 4 Create a Drop Cap

Paragraphs in a newsletter can begin with a ***drop cap***, which is a capital letter formatted in a font size larger than the body text. A drop cap adds interest and a bit of style to text within a document. Drop caps can align with text or display in the margin, and they can be designed in various sizes. The choice depends on the style and design of the newsletter. To insert a drop cap, place the insertion point before the letter that is to be converted to a drop cap and click Drop Cap in the Text group on the Insert tab. You can point to either the Dropped option or In margin to see a preview of the effect before selecting one, or you can select Drop Cap Options to display the dialog box shown in Figure 5.7.

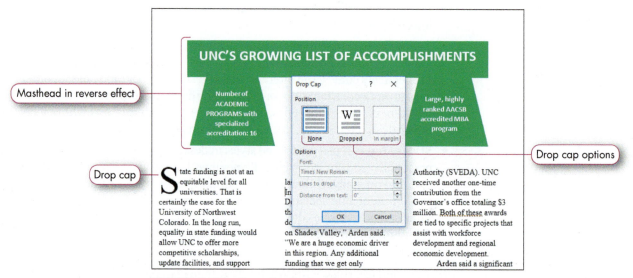

FIGURE 5.7 The Drop Cap Dialog Box and Reverse Masthead

STEP 5 Apply Borders and Shading

Bordered text and/or shading is used to emphasize points and create a welcome variation in a continuous column of text. Horizontal lines, or borders, effectively create a visual separation, such as when dividing one section or topic from another. Bordering and/or shading a single paragraph, text box, or object is an effective visual technique to add color variation or modify the document flow. Both the Borders option and the Shading option in the Paragraph group on the Home tab enable you to apply various shading and bordering to selected text. Using the Borders option, you can select a predesigned border or click Borders and Shading to more precisely define a border or shading setting from a dialog box. The Shading option on the Home tab provides various color selections related to the current theme, or you can design a custom color instead.

Borders and shading are often applied to a masthead. A border around the masthead can be used to distinguish the content from the rest of the document. To add additional emphasis, a masthead is sometimes designed in reverse effect, which uses light-colored text on a dark background. Often used in newsletter mastheads, a reverse provides a distinctive look to the publication, clearly identifying the document and enabling the newsletter title to stand out from the remaining text. Simply format the object or text in a dark background and light text. The masthead shown in Figure 5.7 is an example of a reverse effect.

Include Images

Images are commonly found in newsletters, infusing an informal or relaxed feel to the information presented in the document. An image, such as a photograph or graphic, can stand alone or can be formatted so that text wraps around the image in an attractive manner. Newsletters are seldom developed without such eye-catching features as pictures or graphics.

You can insert pictures from your own library of digital photos that are saved on your hard drive, OneDrive, or another storage medium, or you can insert an online picture using Bing. To insert a picture from a file, click Pictures on the Insert tab, navigate to the location of the image, select the image file, and then click Insert.

Online images are available when you click Online Pictures from the Insert tab and provide a search term for the Bing Search process. You can scroll through Images that meet the search terms, click a picture, and then click Insert to add it to a document. When you access photos from an online search, most of the photos are subject to Creative Commons licensing. It is important that you review the specific license for any image to ensure that you comply with any copyright guidelines. Creative Commons is a nonprofit organization that enables users to share the use of creativity and knowledge through free legal tools. By signing a simple, standardized, copyright license, content owners give the public the permission to use their creative work under certain conditions. They can also easily change copyright terms at any time. Usually, you can use the images for free if it is for personal use.

> **TIP: USING PICKIT IMAGES**
> As you develop documents that require pictures, you may need to locate a source of images. Although you can find images from various online sources, you must consider licensing requirements and copyright limitation. To simplify the process of obtaining pictures that are clear of legal restrictions and readily available in Office applications, Microsoft provides an add-in app called Pickit through which you can access a large library of images and photographs—all through a ribbon selection. To install the Pickit app, make sure you are signed in to your Office account. Then click the Insert tab and My Add-ins. Click Store and search for or locate Pickit. Add the app, which becomes a ribbon selection on the Home tab. When you need an image, click the app on the Home tab to open a pane from which you can search for and add pictures to a document. A fee may be required for continued use of the Pickit app.

Using Layout Options, you can identify the way you want text to wrap around a selected object. You might want text to wrap in a square or tight fashion around the object, or perhaps the object should display with text only above or below. With an object selected, a Layout Options icon displays near the top right corner of the object. Click the icon to choose from various text wrapping options. In addition, the Wrap Text command is in the Arrange group on the Picture Tools Format tab. For more precise text wrapping options, click Wrap Text and select More Layout Options.

1. Describe the difference between a continuous section break and a column break. *p.315*
2. Provide rationale for using a reverse effect when designing a masthead instead of a simple text heading as related to the overall appeal and effectiveness of the masthead. *p.318*
3. Explain how envisioning a grid structure as you design a newsletter could be beneficial. *p.313*

Hands-On Exercises

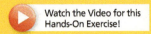

MyLab IT HOE1 Sim Training

Watch the Video for this Hands-On Exercise!

Skills covered: Apply and Modify Column Layout • Insert a Section Break • Insert a Column Break • Create a Masthead • Create a Drop Cap • Apply Borders and Shading • Include Images

1 Desktop Publishing

Kody Allen, the director of The Greenways, forwarded a document with short articles that he would like to include in the newsletter you are preparing. You design a layout that will display the information in an easy-to-read and visually appealing manner. You also consider how to display the masthead and other visual elements.

STEP 1 APPLY AND MODIFY COLUMN LAYOUT

Upon reviewing the file that Mr. Allen provides, you consider the structure necessary to design an attractive newsletter. You decide to modify the margins and to arrange the newsletter in two columns. In considering the best way to arrange the newsletter, you decide it would be more attractive with columns of unequal width in which one column is narrower than the other. You select another column layout and adjust column width. You also add a line to separate columns. Refer to Figure 5.8 as you complete Step 1.

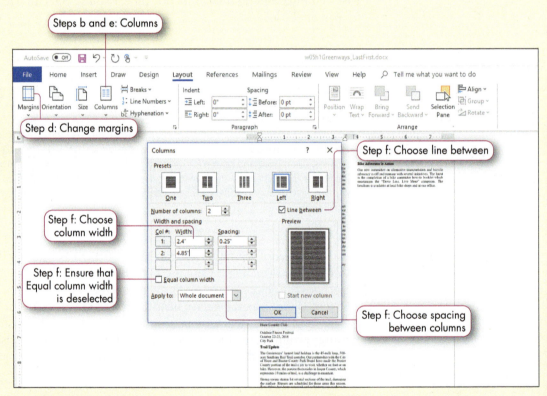

FIGURE 5.8 Modifying Column Layout

    a. Open *w05h1Greenways* and save it as **w05h1Greenways_LastFirst**. Ensure that nonprinting characters are displayed.

> **TROUBLESHOOTING:** If you make any major mistakes in this exercise, you can close the file, open *w05h1Greenways* again and then start this exercise over.

b. Ensure that the insertion point is at the top of the document and click the **Layout tab**. Click **Columns** in the Page Setup group and select **Two**.

The text of the newsletter displays in two columns. The column width for each column and the spacing between columns is determined automatically.

c. Click the **View tab** and view the document as **One Page**.

The one-page view of the document shows two columns, although the left column is significantly longer than the right. You will adjust the column lengths later.

d. Click the **Layout tab** and change the margins to **Narrow**.

Because the newsletter is a bit lengthy, smaller margins provide more working space within the document.

e. Click **Columns** in the Page Setup group and select **More Columns** to display the Columns dialog box.

f. Click **Left** in the Presets section and click to select the **Line between check box** to display a line between the columns. Click in the **Width box** beside Col # 1 and type **2.4**. Change the spacing in the next box to **0.25**. Ensure that Equal column width is deselected. Click **OK**.

The left column is narrower than the right, and a vertical line appears as a column separator.

g. Click the **View tab** and click **100%** in the Zoom group.

STEP 2 INSERT A SECTION BREAK AND A COLUMN BREAK

So that columns on the last page are evenly distributed, you insert a continuous section break at the end of the document. You plan to include a newsletter title that should be configured in one column, so you insert a section break above the two-column layout. By inserting a column break, you ensure that text is not awkwardly divided between columns. Refer to Figure 5.9 as you complete Step 2.

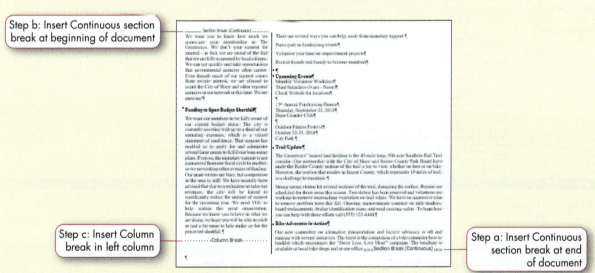

FIGURE 5.9 Inserting Breaks

a. Place the insertion point at the end of the document (after the words *at our office* in the right column). Click the **Layout tab**. Click **Breaks** in the Page Setup group. Select **Continuous** under Section Breaks.

Inserting a Continuous section break at the end of the document ensures more even distribution of columns.

b. Place the insertion point at the beginning of the document. Click **Breaks** in the Page Setup group and click **Continuous** under Section Breaks.

If nonprinting characters are shown, a double dotted line displays, indicating that a section break occurs at the top of the left column in the document. Adding this Continuous section break enables you to format the area of the document that precedes the section break differently from the section that follows it.

c. Place the insertion point before the last paragraph in the left column, beginning with *There are several ways you can help*. Click **Breaks** in the Page Setup group and click **Column**.

You insert a Column break so that the list of ways you can help is not divided between columns.

STEP 3: CREATE A MASTHEAD

The title of your newsletter is a critical element, as it is most likely the first thing a reader will view. You decide to insert a masthead to identify the newsletter. To ensure that the title displays properly as one column, you type the title before the previously inserted section break at the top of the page. Refer to Figure 5.10 as you complete Step 3.

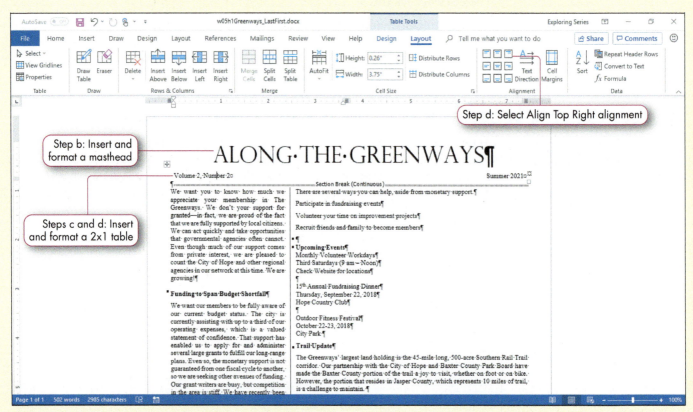

FIGURE 5.10 Creating a Masthead

a. Press **Ctrl+Home** to move the insertion point to the top of the page, click **Columns** in the Page Setup group on the Layout tab, and then select **One**.

The section break extends across the top of the document, creating one column at the top of the page. Information you type there will not be split into two columns like the text in the section below the break.

> **MAC TROUBLESHOOTING:** Press Command + Up Arrow four times to move the insertion point to the top of the document.

b. Type **Along the Greenways** and press **Enter** twice. Select the text you just typed and center it across the width of the page. Change the font of the selected text to **Perpetua Titling** and adjust the font size to **33**.

The large heading is the masthead for the newsletter.

c. Click to the left of the section break just below the masthead. Using the Table command on the Insert tab, insert a **2×1 table**.

A table displays below the masthead and above the section break.

d. Make the following changes in the table:

- Type **Volume 2, Number 2** in the left cell.
- Type **Summer 2021** in the right cell.
- Click the **Table Tools Layout tab**. Click **Align Top Right** in the Alignment group to right align content in the last cell.
- Select the entire row. Click the **Layout tab** (not the Table Tools Layout tab) and change Spacing Before to **6 pt**.
- Click the **Table Tools Design tab**, click the **Borders arrow** in the Borders group, and then click **No Border**.

The border is removed, although with nonprinting characters being displayed, you will see some indication that the text is in a table arrangement. When nonprinting characters are toggled off, the text will look well aligned but will not have borders.

STEP 4 CREATE A DROP CAP

A drop cap is often applied to the first paragraph of a document or article. In this case, you format a paragraph with a drop cap to enhance the newsletter. You also format the document with bullets to further identify topics of interest. Refer to Figure 5.11 as you complete Step 4.

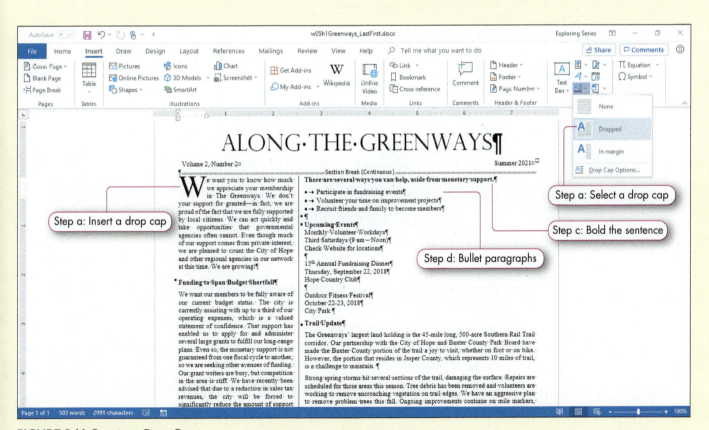

FIGURE 5.11 Creating a Drop Cap

a. Place the insertion point at the left of the first letter in the first paragraph (beginning with *We want you to know*). Click the **Insert tab**, click **Drop Cap** in the Text group, and then select **Dropped**.

> **MAC TROUBLESHOOTING:** Click the Format menu, select Drop Cap, and then click Dropped.

b. Click anywhere outside the drop cap frame.

c. Select the first sentence at the top of the right column, beginning with *There are several ways you can help*. Bold the selection.

d. Select the next three paragraphs, beginning with *Participate in fundraising events* and ending with *Recruit friends and family to become members*. Click **Bullets** in the Paragraph group on the Home tab. Click **Decrease Indent** in the Paragraph group to align the bullets with the left edge of the column. Click the **Layout tab** and view settings in the Paragraph group, removing any paragraph spacing from the bulleted paragraphs.

STEP 5: APPLY BORDERS AND SHADING AND INSERT AN IMAGE

One way to better define and draw attention to the newsletter title is to create a reverse effect in which the background is dark and the font is white. To highlight specific points, you place a border around a paragraph. You also add an image. Refer to Figure 5.12 as you complete Step 5.

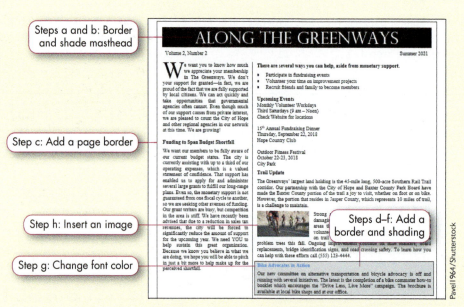

FIGURE 5.12 Working with Shading and a Picture

a. Press **Ctrl+Home**. Click the **Home tab**. Click the **Borders arrow** in the Paragraph group and select **Borders and Shading**.

The Borders and Shading dialog box displays.

b. Click the **Shading tab**, click the **Style arrow**, and then click **Solid (100%)**. Ensure that Paragraph displays in the Apply to box and click **OK**.

The masthead displays white text on a black background.

c. Click the **Design tab** and click **Page Borders** in the Page Background group. Click **Box** in the Setting section. Change the width to **1½ pt**. Ensure that Whole document displays in the Apply to box. Click **OK**.

Because you selected Page Borders from the Design tab, you ensured that the selected border was applied to the whole document. The same selection is available when you click the Borders arrow on the Home tab and select Borders and Shading to open the dialog box. At that point, however, you would have to be sure to click the Page Border tab to indicate that the border should surround the page instead of a paragraph.

d. Select the *Bike Advocates in Action* heading in the right column and the paragraph that follows it.

e. Click the **Home tab**, click the **Borders arrow** in the Paragraph group, and then select **Borders and Shading**. Click **Box** in the Setting group of the Borders tab. Change the width to **1 pt**.

f. Click the **Shading tab**, click the **Style arrow**, click **15%**, ensure that Paragraph displays in the Apply to box, and then click **OK**. Deselect the paragraph.

A black border and gray shading display around and behind the paragraph.

g. Select the heading *Bike Advocates in Action*, click the **Font Color arrow** in the Font group, and then click **Dark Blue, Text 2, Lighter 40%** (row 4, column 4). Deselect the heading.

h. Insert and format an image by completing the following steps:
- Place the insertion point before the paragraph near the end of the right column, beginning with *Strong spring storms*. Insert *w05h1Bike.jpg* from your student data files.
- Click **Wrap Text** in the Arrange group on the Picture Tools Format tab and select **Square**.
- Ensure that the image is selected. Change the height to **0.7**. When you adjust the height, the width automatically adjusts so that the picture is not distorted.
- Use Figure 5.12 as a visual guide and drag the bicycle image so that the bottom of the picture is aligned with the bottom of the paragraph.

i. Save the document. Keep the document open if you plan to continue with the next Hands-On Exercise. If not, close the document and exit Word.

Graphic Objects

Newsletters and other published documents are often more appealing if they include images and other graphic objects. Word simplifies the inclusion of such items with drawing tools and readily available objects such as SmartArt, WordArt, and text boxes. You will find a number of options to choose from in each category, and you can modify selections in terms of color, size, background, and placement. One thing you should keep in mind when adding graphic objects to a document—some objects may display better on the computer screen than in print, so view images with a critical eye before you finalize a document.

In this section, you will insert a variety of graphic objects. You will work with tools that enable you to make adjustments to graphic objects, such as changing colors, layering, and rotation.

Inserting Graphic Objects

Graphic objects—such as stylized text, shapes, diagrams, and text boxes—add visual interest to documents and often illustrate processes in a more understandable way than text alone. Word provides a variety of objects that you can use individually or in combination to illustrate a point or emphasize text. For example, you can insert a process diagram to describe a set of steps. Or perhaps your intent is to provide a callout to better describe an area of text. You can even combine objects for an intended effect, positioning and overlapping shapes.

STEP 1 Insert SmartArt

Although Word provides ample shapes and drawing tools to enable you to create diagrams, it can be extremely time consuming and difficult to create complex, designer-quality illustrations using those tools alone. To simplify that task, Word includes **SmartArt**, which is a visual representation of information that can be created to effectively communicate a message or idea in one of many visually appealing layouts. For example, you might insert a SmartArt diagram of an organization chart, a list, or a process to illustrate an important concept that is difficult to explain with simple text but easier to understand when viewed as an illustration. SmartArt is an option in the Illustrations group on the Insert tab. From the Choose a SmartArt Graphic dialog box, you can select a category in the left pane and any of a number of diagrams to the right. Click a selection in the middle pane to see a short description, as shown in Figure 5.13.

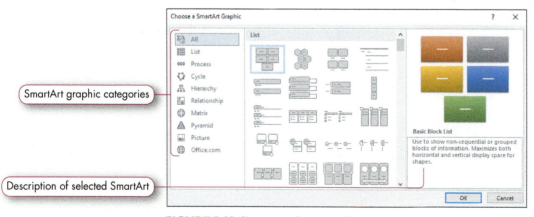

FIGURE 5.13 Choosing a SmartArt Graphic

When a SmartArt diagram is inserted into a document, text placeholders display, as shown in Figure 5.14. You can click a placeholder and type text directly into the diagram. Alternatively, you can click the text pane arrow in the middle left side of the diagram frame to view the text pane if it is not already visible. The SmartArt *text pane*, shown in Figure 5.14, displays an outline view for typing text items that are then placed in the SmartArt diagram. With a SmartArt object selected, SmartArt Tools Design and Format tabs display on the ribbon. The Design tab provides a toggle button for the SmartArt text pane, along with other tools to change the appearance of the diagram, such as changing shapes and style. The Format tab provides tools to modify the appearance of the diagram text.

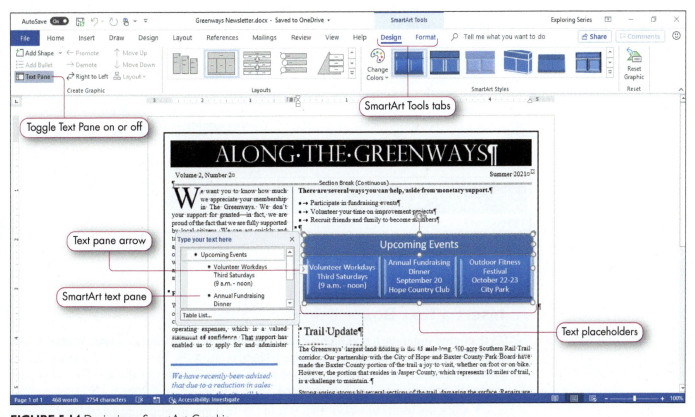

FIGURE 5.14 Designing a SmartArt Graphic

STEP 2 ### Insert WordArt

WordArt is a feature that creates decorative text that is especially useful for designing banners or headings. An advantage of using WordArt is that you can rotate text in any direction, add three-dimensional effects, or modify text orientation (slanted, arched, or even upside down).

WordArt is an option in the Text group on the Insert tab. You can apply WordArt formatting to existing text or type text in a text box with WordArt formatting applied. Choose a style from the WordArt gallery (see Figure 5.15) and type text in the WordArt text box. The resulting text, which is considered a WordArt object, can be moved and resized in the same manner as other graphic objects. The Drawing Tools Format tab provides formatting features that enable you to change alignment, add special effects, and change styles quickly. With WordArt text selected, you can also modify the format from selections on the Home tab, such as font size.

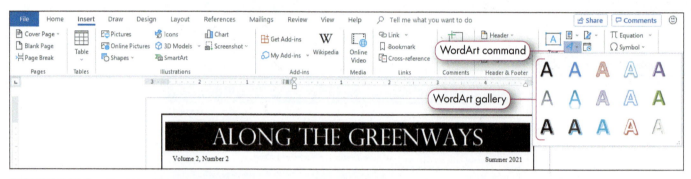

FIGURE 5.15 Creating WordArt

Insert a Text Box

As the name suggests, a ***text box*** is a rectangular object that contains text. Magazine and newspaper articles often use text boxes to help control the placement of text as well as provide a visual tool to entice readers to focus on the contents of the text box. There are several ways to insert a text box, as listed below and shown in Figure 5.16:

- Click the Insert tab, click Text Box in the Text group, and then select Draw Text Box.
- Click the Insert tab, click Shapes in the Illustrations group, and then select Text Box in the Basic Shapes group.
- Click the Insert tab, click Text Box in the Text group, and then select Simple Text Box.

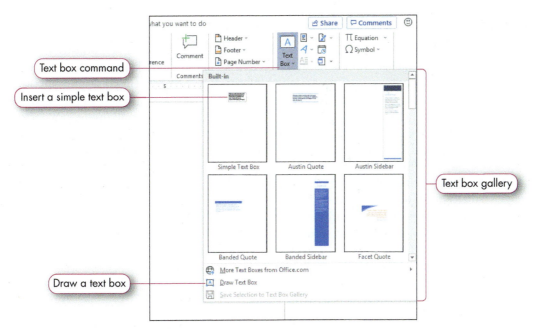

FIGURE 5.16 Inserting a Text Box

> **TIP: TEXT BOXES AND RECTANGLE SHAPES**
> Unlike a rectangle shape that can be selected from the Illustrations group on the Insert tab, a text box modifies its size to accommodate the amount of text included. In contrast, a rectangle shape can also include text, but its size does not automatically adjust for text included.

Like SmartArt and WordArt, a text box is an object that you can select and manage independently of surrounding text. With a text box selected, the Drawing Tools Format tab displays (see Figure 5.17). Commands on the tab enable you to customize the border and background color of a text box, select text effects, and position a text box horizontally and vertically. In addition, you can identify the way text should wrap around the text box object. As with other objects, you can drag the text box to reposition it. With text selected, you can apply font properties from the Home tab, such as font size, type, and alignment, within the text box.

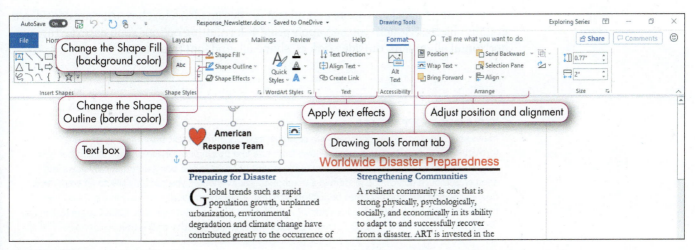

FIGURE 5.17 Formatting a Text Box

Graphic Objects • Word 2019   329

STEP 3 | Create a Pull Quote or Sidebar

A ***pull quote*** is a phrase or sentence taken from an article to emphasize a key point. A ***sidebar*** enables you to call attention to information in a document by displaying it in a space along the side of the featured information. Sidebars might display supplementary information, or they can simply display information of interest to the reader. Several designs in the text box gallery are suitable for a sidebar or pull quote in a document, as shown in Figure 5.16, but you can also create your own.

A pull quote is typically set in larger type, often in a different font or in italics, and may be offset with borders at the top, bottom, or on the sides. Pull quotes are frequently displayed in professional publications, such as newsletters and annual reports, to draw attention to important topics, as shown in Figure 5.18. Sidebar text might display supplementary information such as company data or summary text. To begin the process of creating a pull quote or sidebar, select from preformatted text boxes in the Text Box gallery (shown when you click the Insert tab and click Text Box in the Text group). Then add text in the pull quote or sidebar.

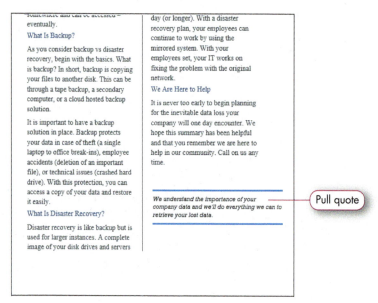

FIGURE 5.18 A Pull Quote

Because a typical pull quote and sidebar are designed in a text box, they are considered graphic objects. As such, you can apply graphic formatting options such as text wrapping, horizontal alignment, outside borders, shape fill, and font treatments.

TIP: LINK TEXT BOXES
Newsletters are sometimes designed with columnar text organized in text boxes instead of being formatted in columns. In that case, text flows from one text box in one column or page to another text box. You can link text boxes so that when text runs out of space in one box it automatically flows into another. Although text can be present in a text box to link to another, you can only link to an empty text box. As the first text box becomes populated with text, it will automatically continue in the linked text box. To link text boxes, place the insertion point in the first text box and type text. Click Create Link in the Text group on the Drawing Tools Format tab. Click in the empty text box to link to it.

STEP 4 **Insert Drawing Shapes**

Occasionally, a predefined object, such as a text box or SmartArt, is not sufficient for your purpose. Perhaps you are designing an award document in which you will include a banner shape with text. Or maybe a thought bubble would be helpful to illustrate a point. In both cases, you use the Shapes gallery to access and modify the shape. A ***shape*** is an object, such as a circle or an arrow, that you can use as visual enhancement in a document. Use one shape or combine multiple shapes to create a more complex image. When you click the Insert tab and click Shapes in the Illustrations group, the Shapes gallery displays, as shown in Figure 5.19. Select a shape from the gallery. The pointer becomes a crosshair. At that point, click in the document to insert the shape or drag to draw the shape in any size.

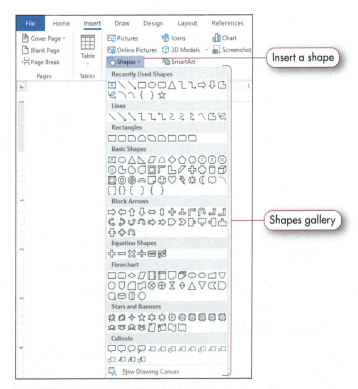

FIGURE 5.19 Using the Shapes Gallery

An object, such as a shape, is treated as a separate entity that can be moved, resized, formatted, or even duplicated. A duplicated object is the same size and appearance as the original. To duplicate an object, including a WordArt selection, text box, shape, image, or SmartArt, select the object, and press Ctrl+D. Once the object is duplicated, you can drag to reposition it or use tools on the ribbon to adjust the appearance.

Although predesigned shapes are readily available when you access the Shapes gallery from the Insert tab, you can also create your own drawings and shapes using the Draw tab. If it is not shown on the ribbon, you can right-click the ribbon and choose to customize the ribbon to include the Draw tab. Using a set of pens, available when you click the Draw tab, you can write, draw, or highlight text. Click a pen once to select it and then click it again to further define color and thickness settings. When you click Add Pen from the Pens group on the Draw tab, you can select a pen, pencil, or highlighter. An eraser is also available to toggle on and use to remove drawn elements. When you click Draw in the Tools group and Ink to Shape in the Convert group, you can draw a shape freehand, and Word will convert the shape into a well-designed and recognizable replica. Having used a drawing tool to illustrate, you can take advantage of Word's Ink Replay command to repeat ink strokes, letting you reinforce a point.

After you have drawn one shape, you might want to continue drawing the same shape. For example, if you are creating a flowchart or organization chart, you might need to use a shape several times, although not necessarily in the exact same size as the first shape that was drawn. Use the Lock Drawing Mode command to quickly draw additional shapes, while retaining the latitude to adjust size or dimensions as the shape is redrawn. Unlike the process of copying and pasting, or duplicating, in which an exact duplicate of an original is created, the process of drawing additional shapes does not necessarily result in shapes that are identical.

To create multiple instances of the same shape, using Lock Drawing Mode, complete the following steps:

1. Click the Insert tab.
2. Click Shapes in the Illustrations group.
3. Right-click a shape in the gallery.
4. Select Lock Drawing Mode. The pointer becomes a crosshair. (Lock Drawing Mode is not available in Word for Mac.)
5. Place the pointer at the location where the shape is to be drawn.
6. Click to duplicate exactly the original shape's size or drag to create a new shape of varying size.
7. Repeat Steps 5 and 6 to create more instances of the same shape. Press Esc when finished.

If you are creating a drawing comprised of several shapes, consider using the Drawing Canvas. This tool assists with arranging multiple shapes, keeping all parts of the drawing together. Click the Insert tab, click Shapes in the Illustrations group, and then select New Drawing Canvas to create a work area. The framed canvas area is considered an object, although it contains no border or background color when it is first created. You can format the canvas with borders and fills just as you would any other object. Then, insert one or more shapes on the canvas and format and position them.

Insert 3D Models

A 3D object can be manipulated in three dimensions, rotated in any direction at any angle. You might find 3D objects useful in online or electronic sales brochures where potential customers can explore facets of an item, such as a house they are considering purchasing. 3D objects can accurately represent items that must be assembled or they can provide detail in technical manuals. Although 3D objects can also be inserted in documents designed for printing, they are especially beneficial in online documents where they can be rotated, resized, panned, and zoomed.

You can create your own 3D images or obtain them from an external source such as Microsoft's Remix3D (www.Remix3D.com). Paint 3D, a desktop app included with Windows 10 or available at the Microsoft Store, enables you to create your own 3D images, saving them for inclusion in a Word document if you like. Insert a 3D image by selecting 3D Models from the Insert tab. If you click the 3D Models arrow, you can choose to obtain an image online or from files on your computer. If you simply click the 3D Models command, you will be directed to Microsoft's collection of online images. Select an image from various categories or navigate to the file you seek and insert the graphic.

After you have inserted a 3D object, you can choose from various formatting options on the 3D Model Tools Format tab, shown in Figure 5.20. The 3D Model Views group includes various three-dimensional views of the selected object. You can change the object's orientation, tilting or rotating it, when you drag the 3D rotation handle that displays in the center of the object. A rotation handle at the top of the object enables you to rotate it clockwise or counter-clockwise, and sizing handles are available if you want to drag to resize. Click Pan & Zoom and then drag the magnifying glass that displays beside

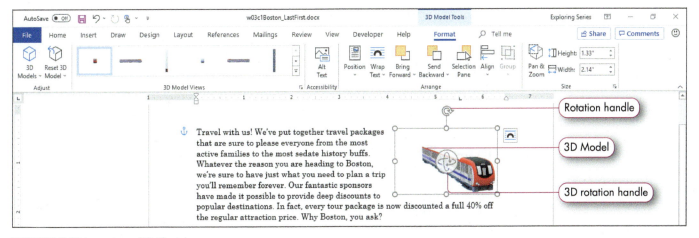

FIGURE 5.20 Inserting a 3D Model

the object up or down to increase or reduce the view. When you pan and zoom, however, the object's dimensions do not change; you merely use more or less of the allocated space for the object's display. As with more traditional images, you can wrap text around a 3D model, position and align it on the page, and adjust the height and width. All of those options are available on the 3D Model Tools Format tab when the object is selected.

Manipulating Graphic Objects

The default format for a shape is a simple blue border and blue fill. Unformatted text boxes contain a dark border and white fill. You will likely want to modify an object's appearance by resizing it or adding text or color. The Format tab includes multiple formatting tools that assist you in that task.

Change Shape Fills and Borders

Shapes and text boxes contain two main components to which color can be applied—the line or border of the object, and the fill or interior space of the object. So that you can customize shapes, Word provides a Shape Styles gallery, which contains predefined styles with a combination of colors, lines, and other effects. As shown in Figure 5.21, the Drawing Tools Format tab includes not only a Styles gallery but also options for individually modifying the shape outline or fill color of a selected object. Some shapes, such as a straight line, obviously do not contain an interior area for applying a fill color, but you can change the color, width, and style of the line itself. You can also enhance the shape by adding visual effects such as shadow, reflection, glow, soft edges, bevel, and 3D rotation.

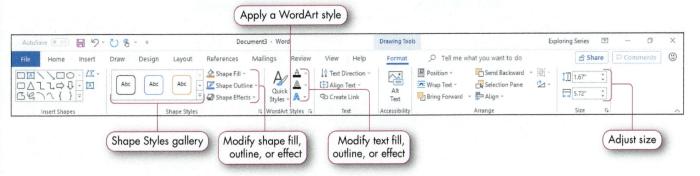

FIGURE 5.21 Drawing Tools Format Tab

Resize an Object

Any object can be resized, including a text box, WordArt, SmartArt, image, or shape. Resizing options are available in the Size group on the Drawing Tools Format tab (refer to Figure 5.21). You can also resize an object by dragging a sizing handle, although such resizing is not as precise as modifying settings on the ribbon. If the object you are resizing is a picture, you should only drag a corner sizing handle so that the image is not distorted.

> **TIP: CROP AN IMAGE**
> When working with images, you may want to crop, or remove unwanted horizontal or vertical edges. Click Crop on the Picture Tools Format tab and drag a cropping handle inward to border the area to keep—press Enter. To crop a picture in a shape click the Crop arrow on the Format tab. Point to Crop to Shape and select a shape. You can resize the picture after cropping it.

STEP 5 Group, Layer, and Rotate Objects

Occasionally, you may need to insert several shapes and combine them into one object. ***Grouping*** shapes or objects combines them into one entity. A single border surrounds all grouped objects when you select the grouped object, so you can move, copy, delete, resize, or adjust the group as one object. Even though several objects are grouped, you can still modify a single item within the group when you double-click the individual item. To group objects, hold Shift as you click each object to be grouped. The objects shown in Figure 5.22 have not yet been grouped into one object, although they have all been selected. Choose to group the objects using the Group command in the Arrange group on the Drawing Tools Format tab.

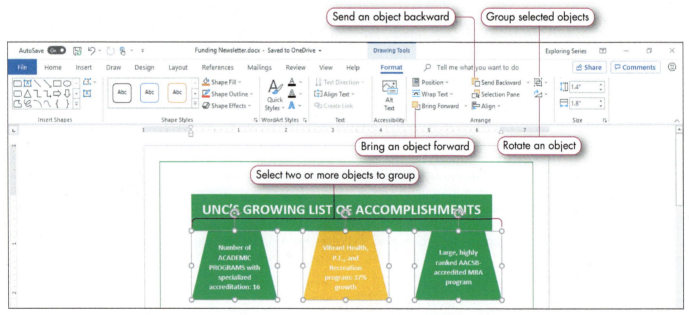

FIGURE 5.22 Grouping Objects

You can separate grouped objects by ungrouping them. **Ungrouping** breaks a grouped object into separate individual objects. You might ungroup objects because you want to make modifications to one individual part of the group rather than to the entire group, such as sizing or repositioning an individual object in the group. Ungrouping also makes it possible to delete an object or add another object to the group. To ungroup objects, select the grouped object and follow the steps to group several objects, selecting Ungroup instead of Group.

When you want to place all or part of an object on top of another, as when an arrow shape is intended to overlap a text box, the objects become layered. **Layering** combines objects into a hierarchy with the most recently added object placed on a higher layer than a previously created object.

When working with layered shapes in Word, you can bring a shape to the front by one layer, push a shape back by one layer, move a shape to the front of all layers, or push a shape to the back of all layers. You can even locate an object behind or in front of text. With multiple objects selected, you can change layering order with commands on the Drawing Tools Format tab. To layer objects, select an object to be rearranged and select from the options described in Table 5.1. After objects are arranged in the order of layers, it might be useful to group them so they can be moved, resized, and adjusted together as one object.

TABLE 5.1 Layering Options on the Drawing Tools Format Tab

Command	Outcome
Bring Forward	Moves an object on top of another object directly in front of it
Bring to Front	Moves an object to the top of all other objects
Bring in Front of Text	Moves an object to display in front of text
Send Backward	Moves an object below the object directly behind it
Send to Back	Moves an object to the back of all other objects
Send Behind Text	Moves an object to display behind text

An object's angle can be adjusted in several different directions by flipping or rotating it. The Rotate Objects command is in the Arrange group on the Drawing Tools Format tab, as shown in Figure 5.22. Select from several commands to rotate the object in a particular direction or to flip horizontally or vertically.

Quick Concepts

4. Describe the purpose of a pull quote and why it might be useful in a document. **p. 330**

5. Describe similarities and differences between grouping and layering. **p. 334**

6. Provide an example of when you might choose to insert a SmartArt diagram in a document instead of creating the illustration using shapes or other graphic elements. **p. 326**

Hands-On Exercises

MyLab IT HOE2 Sim Training

Watch the Video for this Hands-On Exercise!

Skills covered: Insert SmartArt • Insert WordArt • Create a Pull Quote or Sidebar • Insert Drawing Shapes • Group, Layer, and Rotate Objects

2 Graphic Objects

The Greenways newsletter is coming together nicely. You decide to illustrate upcoming events with appropriate graphics. You also plan to display article titles using a combination of graphics and text rather than formatting the font.

STEP 1 INSERT SMARTART

Members of The Greenways should be made aware of several upcoming events. You want to be sure these events stand out in the newsletter, so you use SmartArt to display them. This will give the news item a unique look and will fit in the wider right column. Refer to Figure 5.23 as you complete Step 1.

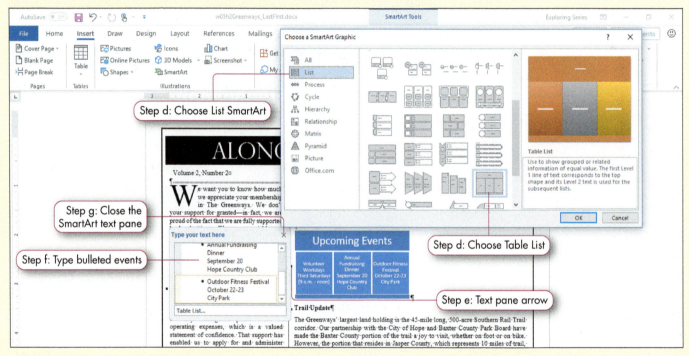

FIGURE 5.23 Using the SmartArt Text Pane

a. Open *w05h1Greenways_LastFirst* if you closed it at the end of Hands-On Exercise 1, and save it as **w05h2Greenways_LastFirst**, changing h1 to h2.

b. Ensure that nonprinting characters are displayed. Delete the heading *Upcoming Events* and the event information that follows, up to but not including the *Trail Update* heading. The insertion point should be at the left of the *Trail Update* heading.

c. Press **Enter**. Place the insertion point beside the newly inserted blank paragraph. Click the **Insert tab** and click **SmartArt** in the Illustrations group.

The Choose a SmartArt Graphic dialog box displays with a list of categories in the left pane.

d. Click **List** in the left pane, scroll down to view the additional designs in the middle pane, and then click **Table List** (row 8, column 4 under List category). Click **OK**.

e. Click the **text pane arrow** at the center left side of the SmartArt object unless the text pane already displays.

The text pane, with bulleted placeholders, displays at the left side of the SmartArt object.

336   CHAPTER 5 • Hands-On Exercise 2

f. Complete the following steps to enter text:

- Type **Upcoming Events** beside the first bullet.
- Click beside the first indented bullet. Type **Volunteer Workdays**, press **Shift+Enter** to move the insertion point to the next line without a bullet, type **Third Saturdays**, press **Shift+Enter**, and then type **(9 a.m. - noon)**. Leave a space before and after the hyphen.

> **TROUBLESHOOTING:** If you press Enter instead of Shift+Enter when entering data, press Backspace twice to remove the new bullet and return to the end of the preceding bullet. Press Shift+Enter and continue to enter data.

- Type the following text in the two remaining panels, pressing **Shift+Enter** as needed to move to a new line as shown for each panel. Refer to Figure 5.23 as needed. Event titles may wrap in the text pane. After typing the first event, you may have to scroll to locate the next indented bullet.

Annual Fundraising Dinner	Outdoor Fitness Festival
September 20	October 22–23
Hope Country Club	City Park

g. Click **Close** in the top right corner of the Text pane.

h. Click an outside border of the SmartArt object so that the entire object is selected. Sizing handles surround the outer edges of the object. Ensure that the SmartArt Tools Design tab is selected and click **More** in the SmartArt Styles group. Click **Inset** (row 1, column 2 under 3-D).

i. Click the **SmartArt Tools Format tab** and change the width in the Size group to **4.8"**. The height should be **1.4"**.

STEP 2 INSERT WORDART

You format a title as WordArt so that it is a bit more eye-catching. As you do so, you make sure the WordArt object coordinates well with the SmartArt object in the newsletter's right column. Refer to Figure 5.24 as you complete Step 2.

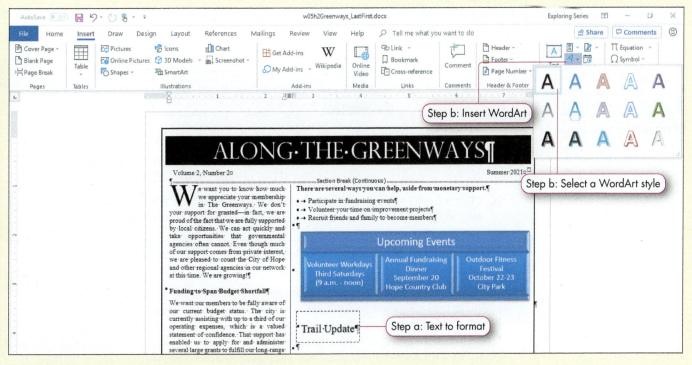

FIGURE 5.24 Inserting WordArt

a. Select the heading *Trail Update* in the right column. Whether you select the following paragraph mark is irrelevant.

b. Click the **Insert tab** and click **WordArt** in the Text group. Click **Fill: Black, Text color 1; Shadow** (row 1, column 1).

c. Click the **Home tab** and change the font size of the WordArt text to **16**.

d. Click the Drawing Tools Format tab. Click **Wrap Text** in the Arrange group and click **Top and Bottom**.

e. Click **Shape Outline** in the Shape Styles group, point to **Dashes**, and then click **Dash** (fourth item in the list). Click anywhere to deselect the WordArt object.

STEP 3: CREATE A PULL QUOTE

You create a pull quote to draw attention to a statement of interest to newsletter readers. Refer to Figure 5.25 as you complete Step 3.

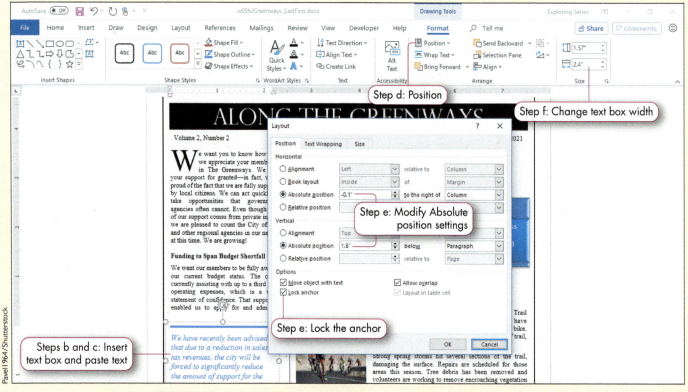

FIGURE 5.25 Positioning an Object

a. Select the sixth sentence in the *Funding to Span Budget Shortfall* section that begins with *We have recently been advised*. Press **Ctrl+C** to copy the selected text.

b. Click before the *Funding to Span Budget Shortfall* heading. Click the **Insert tab**, click **Text Box** in the Text group, and then click **Austin Quote** in the gallery.

> **MAC TROUBLESHOOTING:** To create a pull quote with formatting similar to the Austin Quote, do the following:
> - Click the Insert tab, click Text Box, and then click Draw Text Box.
> - Drag to draw a text box similar to that shown in Figure 5.25. The absolute size does not matter at this point. It will be adjusted later.
> - Adjust Wrap Text to Top and Bottom.
> - Click the Borders arrow on the Home tab, and click Borders and Shading. Apply a 3 pt, Blue Accent 1 border to the top and bottom of the text box.

c. Click the **Home tab**, click the **Paste arrow** in the Clipboard group, and then select **Keep Text Only (T)** (fourth option in the top row).

The text you cut earlier displays in the text box, although the text box is poorly positioned on the page.

d. Click the **Drawing Tools Format tab**, click **Position** in the Arrange group, and then select **More Layout Options**.

> **MAC TROUBLESHOOTING:** Click Shape Format, click Arrange, click Position, and then click More Layout Options.

e. Click **Absolute position** in the Horizontal section and change the value in the adjacent box to **-0.1**. The value should be to the right of Column. Ensure that Absolute position in the Vertical section is selected and change the value in the adjacent box to **1.6**. The value should be below Paragraph. Click to select **Lock anchor** and click **OK**.

f. Change the width in the Size group of the Format tab to **2.4**.

The pull quote fits within the left column.

STEP 4: INSERT AND FORMAT DRAWING SHAPES

You notice there is a significant amount of white space at the bottom of the newsletter, so you add a shape object that spans the width of the newsletter and displays text to remind readers of an upcoming event. Refer to Figure 5.26 as you complete Step 4.

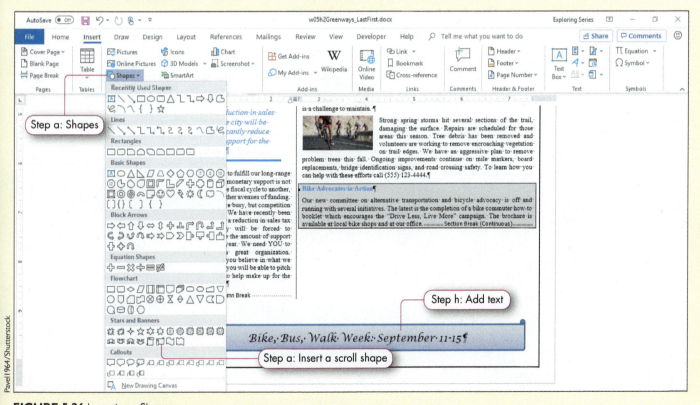

FIGURE 5.26 Inserting a Shape

a. Place the insertion point at the bottom of the page. Click the **Insert tab**, click **Shapes** in the Illustrations group, and then click **Scroll: Horizontal** (row 2, column 6 under Stars and Banners).

The insertion point is displayed as a crosshair.

b. Drag the pointer across the bottom of the newsletter to create a scroll that extends across the width of the page.

The scroll remains selected after releasing the mouse button, as indicated by the sizing handles.

c. Change the height in the Size group on the Format tab to **0.7"**. Change the width to **7.2"**.

d. Click **Wrap Text** in the Arrange group and select **More Layout Options**. Click the **Position tab** and click **Alignment** in the Horizontal section. Click the **Alignment arrow**, click **Centered**, click the **relative to arrow**, and then click **Margin**. Click **OK**.

e. Click the **Shape Fill arrow** in the Shape Styles group. Click **Blue, Accent 1, Darker 25%** (row 5, column 5).

f. Click the **Shape Fill arrow** again, point to **Gradient**, and then click **Linear Up** (row 3, column 2) under the Light Variations section.

The scroll color changes to display a lighter blue color that gradually lightens as it nears the top of the object.

g. Click the **Shape Outline arrow** in the Shape Styles group, point to **Weight**, and then click **2 1/4 pt**.

h. Ensure that the shape is selected. Type **Bike, Bus, Walk Week**. (Do not type the period.) Select the text and change the font size to **16**. Change the font color to **Black, Text 1**. Change the font to **Lucida Calligraphy**.

i. Ensure that the shape is selected and click **Layout Options** at the top right corner of the scroll. Click **Fix position on page**. Close Layout Options.

When you fix the position on a page, you ensure that the object remains at the specified location.

> **MAC TROUBLESHOOTING:** Click Arrange on the Shape Format tab, click Position, and then click More Layout Options. Click the Lock anchor check box to select it.

STEP 5 GROUP OBJECTS

Shapes can be displayed together as layered objects, but moving multiple objects for precise placement can become a tedious process. You group shapes so that you can move them as a unit. Refer to Figure 5.27 as you complete Step 5.

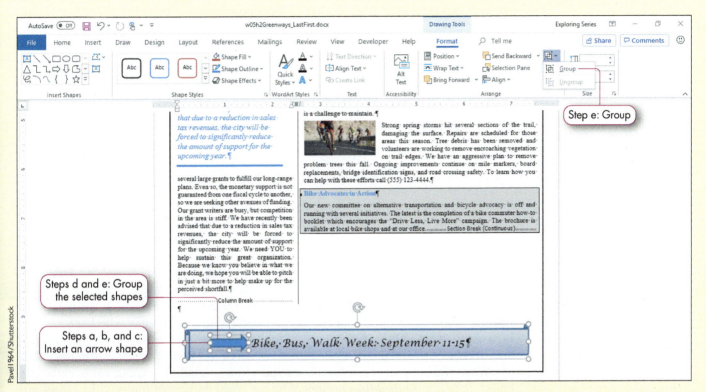

FIGURE 5.27 Grouping Objects

a. Click the **Insert tab**, click **Shapes** in the Illustrations group, and then click **Arrow: Right** from the Block Arrows section. Drag the pointer to create the arrow on the left side of the scroll before the text that displays in the scroll object at the bottom of the page (refer to Figure 5.27).

b. Change the height of the selected arrow to **0.3"** in the Size group on the Format tab. Change the width to **0.8"**.

c. Press a directional key (left, right, up, or down) to nudge the arrow shape so that it rests near the scroll text, as shown in Figure 5.27.

d. Press and hold **Shift** and click the scroll shape, outside the arrow.

The scroll and arrow are both selected, and sizing handles for both objects display.

TROUBLESHOOTING: If either object becomes deselected when you press Shift and select another, click outside both objects, click the scroll shape, and then press Shift and click the arrow shape.

e. Click **Group**, or Group Objects, in the Arrange group on the Drawing Tools Format tab and select **Group**.

Because both objects are now considered one, the grouped object can be treated as one entity.

f. Save the document. Keep the document open if you plan to continue with the next Hands-On Exercise. If not, close the document, and exit Word.

Document Versatility

Word is an extremely versatile application, but not everything in a Word document needs to originate in Word, nor does it need to remain a Word document for others to view its content. Objects and data from other applications can be included in a Word document.

The process of developing a Word document is not necessarily confined to the Microsoft Word application. You might find that a document requires content from another application, such as Excel or PowerPoint, to achieve its purpose. However, you must determine how to incorporate the content within the Word document.

In this section, you will explore methods of accessing data from other applications for inclusion in a Word document. In so doing, you will learn to embed and link data as well as to update linked data when original data changes.

Using OLE to Insert an Object

With Microsoft Office, you can share objects across applications. For example, suppose you are composing a report in Word that explains survey results. You used Excel to summarize the survey results in the form of a worksheet and accompanying chart. The worksheet arrangement of columns and rows enables you to organize data and prepare a chart to graphically illustrate the data. You plan to use the data and chart in a Word document. The process of placing the data and chart in the Word document is not complicated; however, you must first determine whether you want the objects to be automatically updated when the original data changes the data, in this example or whether you prefer to modify them in Word independently of the source. The feature that enables you to insert and link objects into different applications is called ***Object Linking and Embedding (OLE)***.

When you copy an object from one application to another, you can either embed the object or link it. ***Embedding*** an object into a Word document imports the object into the document. After embedded content is inserted into a Word document, it is no longer connected to the source file. Thus, the embedded content can be edited or modified in the Word document without changing the source data. An embedded object is a snapshot of information at the time the data was embedded into the file. For example, suppose a PowerPoint slide contains a table that is relevant to a Word document. Embedding the table in the Word document means that any change to the PowerPoint table would not be reflected in the Word document.

Linking is the process of importing an object from another application so that the object retains a connection to the original data. If you change the data in the original source file, data in the destination file reflects the changes. A data file used as a linked object may be linked to multiple documents. The same Excel chart, for example, can be linked to a Word document and a PowerPoint presentation. Any changes to the Excel chart are reflected and updated in the document and the presentation to which the chart is linked when you update the link in the document or presentation.

The choice of whether to embed or link an inserted object depends upon your purpose. A linked object will reflect the most current information. This might be important, for example, when you insert stock prices for a company into a newsletter. If the current prices that you insert into the document originate from an Excel worksheet, you would want the prices in the Word document to change when the Excel worksheet prices change. If the prices are linked to the original Excel worksheet data, changes to the original price data would reflect in the Word document. On the other hand, if you want to retain the original data, without the possibility of change occurring when the source data is modified, then embedding would be the best choice. You can choose from two methods when linking or embedding—copy and paste an object or insert an object.

STEP 1 ## Use the Copy and Paste Method to Embed or Link an Object

To copy an object or data from a source (such as a chart on a PowerPoint slide) and place it in a Word document, you can copy the data from the source and choose a paste option when placing it in the destination file. When copying and pasting, both the source and destination files must be open; if copying a slide from PowerPoint, for example, the presentation must be open as well as the document to which you are pasting the slide content.

- To embed an object or data, click the Paste arrow in the Clipboard group and select a Paste option (related to formatting).
- To link data, click the Paste arrow in the Clipboard group and select Paste Special. Select Paste link (see Figure 5.28). Select the appropriate object from the right pane of the Paste Special dialog box and click OK.

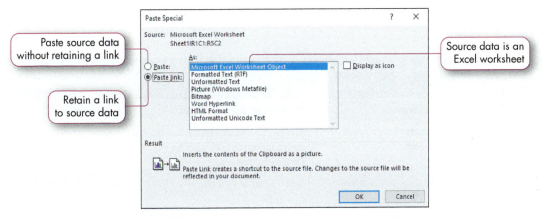

FIGURE 5.28 Using the Copy and Paste Method of Linking

STEP 2 ## Use the Insert an Object Method to Embed or Link an Object

In addition to using copy and paste, Word provides another option for inserting objects or data from other applications. You can insert an entire source file as an object, choosing to display all contents of the source file in the Word document, or simply an icon that can be double-clicked to display the file contents. You might choose this method when you want all contents of a source file included, instead of only a portion, or when you do not want to open the source file before including it in a Word document. Regardless of whether you choose to display all contents or only an icon, you can indicate whether the source file should be embedded or linked.

The choice of whether to include the entire source file or an icon depends in part on the size of the source data. For example, you might want to link or embed an Excel worksheet in a Word document. However, if the worksheet contains a large amount of data that would clutter the Word document or significantly increase the file size of the document, you can insert the Excel workbook as an icon, so the data is available, but without occupying a great deal of document space. On the other hand, if the object you are copying is relatively small and would not clutter the document or be distracting, you can include the contents of the object within the document. Be aware that an icon is relevant only in an electronic document, as to view the source file's contents, you must double-click the icon.

From the Insert tab, click Object in the Text group to display a dialog box with two tabs, as shown in Figure 5.29. The Create from File tab enables you to embed or link a source file, showing either the file contents or a file icon, as described in Table 5.2.

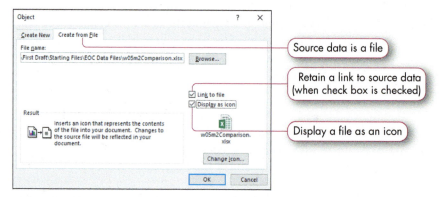

FIGURE 5.29 Using the Insert an Object Method of Embedding or Linking

TABLE 5.2 Using the Insert an Object Method of Embedding or Linking

Outcome	To Embed Source Data	To Link to Source Data
To Display Source File Contents	Browse to the source file but do not select either option (Link to file or Display as icon).	Select Link to file.
To Display as a File Icon	Select Display as icon.	Select Display as icon and also Link to file.

STEP 3 Update a Link

Having linked an object in a document, you can modify the source data, ensuring that any edits are also reflected in the Word document. To begin, open the source file in its native application—Excel, for example—to make modifications. You can also open the application from within the Word document containing the linked object. To do so, double-click the linked object or double-click the application icon if you chose to display one. After making changes in the source file, you must update the linked data in the Word document to reflect the changes there. To update the linked data, right-click the inserted object text or the icon representing inserted text in the document and select Update Link.

Quick Concepts

7. Contrast the processes of embedding and linking, describing when one method might be preferable over another. *p. 342*

8. Explain why linked content in a Word document might not show updates that are made to the source file. Describe steps that must be followed to ensure that linked content is updated. *p. 344*

Hands-On Exercises

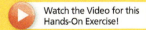

MyLab IT HOE3 Sim Training

Watch the Video for this Hands-On Exercise!

Skills covered: Use the Copy and Paste Method to Embed or Link an Object • Use the Insert an Object Method to Embed or Link an Object • Update a Link

3 Document Versatility

The newsletter for The Greenways is nearly complete. Mr. Allen requests space to display first-quarter financial information and provides the information in an Excel worksheet. You add this information by inserting a worksheet into the newsletter.

STEP 1 USE THE COPY AND PASTE METHOD TO EMBED OR LINK AN OBJECT

The Excel worksheet that contains the first-quarter income sources is to be added to the newsletter; however, changes to the worksheet might be necessary in the future. You decide the proper course of action is to insert the information with a link to the original file so that when data is updated in the worksheet, it is reflected in the document. You also include an icon that is related to funding data for the project. Refer to Figure 5.30 as you complete Step 1.

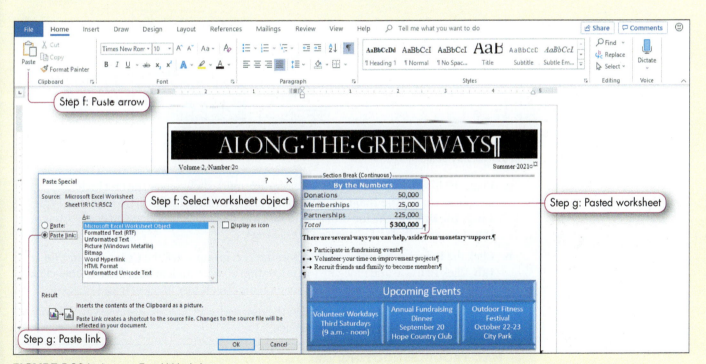

FIGURE 5.30 Linking an Excel Worksheet

a. Open *w05h2Greenways_LastFirst* if you closed it at the end of the Hands-On Exercise 2 and save it as **w05h3Greenways_LastFirst**, changing h2 to h3. Show nonprinting characters if they are not already displayed. Minimize the Word document.

b. Start Excel. Open *w05h3Budget.xlsx*.

c. Drag to select **cells A1:B5** in the Excel worksheet.

d. Click **Copy** in the Clipboard group on the Home tab (or press Ctrl+C).

A moving border displays around the selection, indicating it has been copied to the Clipboard.

e. Click the **Word icon** on the Windows taskbar to return to the Word document. Place the insertion point before the heading *There are several ways you can help, aside from monetary support* in the right column. Press **Enter**. Click before the newly inserted blank paragraph.

f. Click the **Paste arrow** in the Clipboard group. Select **Paste Special** to display the Paste Special dialog box. In the *As* list, click **Microsoft Excel Worksheet Object**.

g. Click **Paste link** and click **OK**. Ensure that Excel is minimized but not closed.

STEP 2: USE THE INSERT AN OBJECT METHOD TO EMBED OR LINK AN OBJECT

Funding data related to the Jasper County portion of the trail is included in a separate Word document that you will embed, but not link, in the newsletter. That way, a reader of the electronic version of the newsletter can double-click an icon in the newsletter for more information. Refer to Figure 5.31 as you complete Step 2.

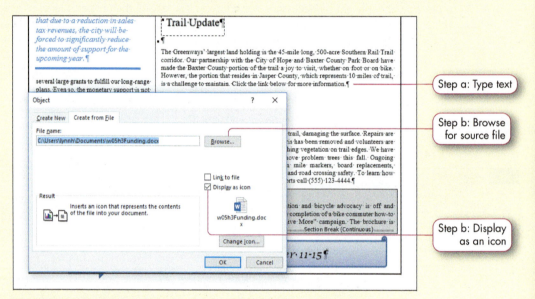

FIGURE 5.31 Embedding Content

a. Place the insertion point before the paragraph mark shown after the first body paragraph under the *Trail Update* heading, ending with *is a challenge to maintain*. Type **Click the link below for more information**. (Include the period and ensure that a space precedes the new sentence.) Press **Enter**.

b. Click the **Insert tab** and click **Object** in the Text group. Click the **Create from File tab**. Click **Browse** and navigate to the location of your student data files. Double-click *w05h3Funding.docx*. Click the **Display as icon check box** to select it and click **OK**.

The funding document is embedded in the newsletter as an icon. Because you did not choose to link the file, it is only embedded.

> **MAC TROUBLESHOOTING:** Click Object on the Insert tab and click Object to display the Object dialog box. Click to select the Display as icon check box and in the Object type box click Microsoft Word Document. Click From File and navigate to your student files. Double-click w05h3Funding.docx. Click OK.

c. Click a border of the scroll shape at the bottom of the page to select the object. Click the Drawing Tools Format tab, click **Position** in the Arrange group and click **More Layout Options**. Adjust the Absolute position in the Vertical section to **9.9"** below Page. Click OK.

When the file icon was inserted, the shape was moved slightly to a different position, which makes the page look unattractive. Therefore, you reposition it.

STEP 3 UPDATE A LINK

You receive changes to be made in the budget worksheet that is linked in the newsletter. Those changes should be reflected in the newsletter as well. Refer to Figure 5.32 as you complete Step 2.

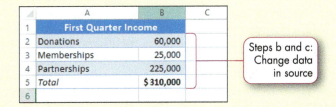

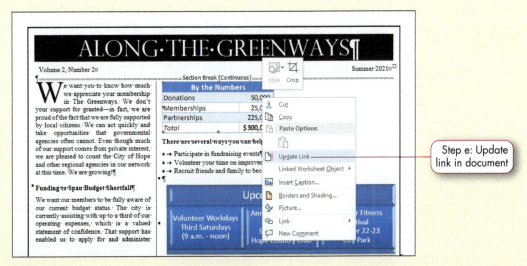

FIGURE 5.32 Updating a Link

a. Click the **Excel icon** on the Windows taskbar to return to the worksheet. Press **Esc** to cancel the moving border.

b. Click **cell A1**, type **First Quarter Income**, replacing *By the Numbers*, and then press **Enter**.

c. Click **cell B2** (beside *Donations*), type **60000**, and then press **Enter**.

d. Minimize Excel.

e. Return to the Word document. Right-click the **Excel worksheet object** at the top of the right column and select **Update Link**.

The linked object reflects the changes you made in the Excel workbook.

f. Save and close w05h3Greenways_LastFirst. Close Excel without saving. Based on your instructor's directions, submit w05h3Greenways_LastFirst.

Chapter Objectives Review

1. **Design a newsletter.**
   - Develop overall document layout: Good design helps convey a message effectively. It is also concerned with the overall appearance and placement of objects and text. Envisioning a grid, in which a document page is divided into columns, can help achieve design excellence.
   - Apply and modify column layout: As is often the case with newsletters, text can be arranged in multiple columns. When you select one of the column preset designs, Word calculates the width of each column based on the number of columns, the left and right margins on the page, and the space between columns. Several preset column designs result in columns of unequal width, in which either the right or left column (of a two-column design) is wider than the other.
   - Insert a section break: A section break separates document areas so they can be arranged independently. For example, a section break after a newsletter heading enables the heading to be situated in a single column, while the remainder of the newsletter is formatted in two columns. A section break at the end of the last column of a multicolumn document balances text within columns.
   - Insert a column break: Use a column break to force text to begin at the top of the next column. You would use a column break if one column ended awkwardly, possibly displaying a subheading alone at the end of a column.

2. **Apply design features.**
   - Create a masthead: A masthead displays at the top of a document, serving as a title. A masthead is often formatted in a one-column format and in a larger or more colorful font to draw attention to the purpose of the newsletter.
   - Create a drop cap: A drop cap is a capital letter formatted in a font size larger than the body text. Drop caps are used to draw attention and add style to a newsletter or article.
   - Apply borders and shading: Borders and shading can be applied to text selections, drawing the eye to areas of critical importance.
   - Include images: Most newsletters include images, such as photographs or graphics, as a means of adding color and interest, and capturing a reader's attention. Images can stand alone, or you can set the text in a document to wrap around them.

3. **Insert graphic objects.**
   - Insert SmartArt: SmartArt is a visual representation of a process, list, or relationship. SmartArt is often more effective than simple text when communicating interconnected ideas or processes.
   - Insert WordArt: WordArt is a feature that creates decorative text that can be used to add interest to document text. It is often used in large elements, such as major titles.
   - Insert a text box: To emphasize text or provide additional information, consider using a text box, which is a rectangular shape containing text. A text box can control the placement of text and allow for layering with other objects and shapes.
   - Create a pull quote or sidebar: A pull quote is a phrase or sentence taken from an article to emphasize a key point. It is typically set in larger type, often in a different font or in italics, and may be offset with borders at the top, bottom, or on the sides. A sidebar displays in a space along the side of a document, containing supplementary information.
   - Insert drawing shapes: A shape is an object, such as a circle or an arrow, which you can use as a visual enhancement. You can use one shape or combine multiple shapes to create a more complex image.

4. **Manipulate graphic objects.**
   - Change shape fills and borders: A shape's fill and outline can be changed with ribbon selections, and shape effects can be applied.
   - Resize an object: Any object can be resized—such as a text box, WordArt, image, or shape—manually (by dragging a sizing handle) or precisely (using size selections).
   - Group, layer, and rotate objects: Grouping is the process of combining selected objects so that they display as a single object. When grouped, objects can be moved simultaneously or otherwise managed as a single unit. Layering is the process of placing one shape on top of another or rearranging the order of stacked objects. Rotating an object means changing the angle of the object.

5. **Use OLE to insert an object.**
   - Use the copy and paste method to embed or link an object: Source data can be copied from one application or file to another. In so doing, you can specify whether the copied content should be pasted as an embedded or linked item. An embedded item is not modified when the source data is changed, whereas a linked object retains a connection to the original file and reflects changes made to the source data.
   - Use the insert an object method to embed or link an object: You can insert all content from another file, with or without creating a link. You can also specify whether the inserted content displays in a document or whether it shows an icon that you can double-click to view the data.
   - Update a link: If you edit the source of a linked object—for example, you might edit the Excel worksheet that was copied and linked in a Word document—those edits can update both the original (Excel) and the linked object (Word). To accomplish that, you must update the link in the Word document.

Key Terms Matching

Match the key terms with their definitions. Write the key term letter by the appropriate numbered definition.

a. Desktop publishing
b. Drop cap
c. Embed
d. Group
e. Layer
f. Link
g. Masthead
h. Object Linking and Embedding (OLE)
i. Pull quote
j. Shape
k. Sidebar
l. SmartArt
m. Text box
n. Text pane
o. Ungroup
p. WordArt

1. _____ A phrase or sentence taken from an article to emphasize a key point. **p. 330**
2. _____ A process that brings an object or data from another application or file into a document, enabling the object to be edited without changing the source. **p. 342**
3. _____ The process of placing one shape on top of another. **p. 335**
4. _____ The identifying information at the top of a newsletter. **p. 317**
5. _____ A feature that creates a decorative text object that is especially useful for designing banners or headings. **p. 328**
6. _____ Supplementary text that appears in a box on the side of a document. **p. 330**
7. _____ The process of combining objects so they appear as a single object. **p. 334**
8. _____ A process that brings an object or data from another application or file into a document, retaining a connection to the source data. **p. 342**
9. _____ A rectangular object that contains text and that can display in any location within a document; if text changes, the box dimensions automatically adjust to accommodate. **p. 328**
10. _____ A very large capital letter at the beginning of a paragraph. **p. 318**
11. _____ A process that divides a combined single object into individual objects that constitute it. **p. 335**
12. _____ The feature that enables you to insert and link objects or information into different applications. **p. 342**
13. _____ A pane that displays beside a SmartArt diagram, enabling you to enter text. **p. 327**
14. _____ A process that uses software, such as Word, to design commercial-quality printed material. **p. 312**
15. _____ An object, such as a circle or an arrow, that you can use as visual enhancement in a document. **p. 331**
16. _____ A visual representation of information that can be created to effectively communicate a list, process, or relationship. **p. 326**

Multiple Choice

1. Wrapping text is relevant when:
   (a) selecting a Transform text effect.
   (b) indicating how text can be positioned around an object.
   (c) positioning a sidebar within a newsletter.
   (d) positioning text within a text box.

2. What color combination comprises a reverse on a masthead?
   (a) Light text on a clear background
   (b) Dark text on a clear background
   (c) Dark text on a light background
   (d) Light text on a dark background

3. You just inserted two shape objects, a triangle and circle, into a document; the circle is larger and was inserted on top of the triangle, so the triangle cannot be seen. What can you do to display the triangle on top of the circle?
   (a) Click the circle and use Bring to Front.
   (b) Click the triangle and use Send to Back.
   (c) Click the circle and use Send to Back.
   (d) Click the circle and use Bring in Front of Text.

4. One method of balancing columns so that each column contains approximately the same amount of text is to:
   (a) insert a continuous section break at the end of the last column.
   (b) insert a page break at the end of the last column.
   (c) manually set column lengths in the Columns dialog box.
   (d) press Enter until the text lines up at the bottom of each column.

5. When you update a link in Word, you:
   (a) create a hyperlink to a Web page.
   (b) check a link for validity.
   (c) create a link to another Word document.
   (d) apply changes to an item in Word when the source data changes.

6. An advantage to grouping several objects together is that the objects can then be:
   (a) managed as a single object.
   (b) formatted using selections in the Paragraph dialog box.
   (c) individually anchored to the next paragraph.
   (d) saved as a backup file with a unique object name.

7. A pull quote is:
   (a) a type of SmartArt.
   (b) a phrase or sentence taken from an article to emphasize a key point.
   (c) a section of text that is linked from one text box to the next.
   (d) a phrase that is usually formatted as a WordArt object.

8. Which feature enables you to quickly insert an organization chart that can be modified or enhanced as needed?
   (a) WordArt
   (b) SmartArt
   (c) Shapes
   (d) Image

9. Which of the following processes inserts content from a PowerPoint presentation in a way that enables you to edit the inserted content in the document without changing the source data?
   (a) Embedding
   (b) Copying and inserting
   (c) Linking
   (d) Find and replace

10. For which of the following would WordArt be a good choice?
    (a) SmartArt shape
    (b) Banner or heading
    (c) Shape text
    (d) Image caption

Practice Exercises

1 You Build It

You are assisting a local chamber of commerce with the development of a promotional page to be included in an upcoming newsletter. The page promotes You Build It—a program that encourages creativity in DIY home building projects. You design the two-column informational page with a variety of eye-catching graphics and visual appeal. Refer to Figure 5.33 as you complete this exercise.

FIGURE 5.33 You Build It Flyer

a. Open *w05p1Build* and save it as **w05p1Build_LastFirst**. Show nonprinting characters if they are not already displayed.

b. Ensure that the insertion point is at the beginning of the document. Change the font to **Book Antiqua** and the font size to **36**. Type **Just Imagine**. (Do not type the period.) Center the text. Select the first line, containing the text *Just Imagine*. Click the **Shading arrow** in the Paragraph group and select **Gold, Accent 4, Darker 50%** (row 6, column 8). Click the **Font Color arrow** in the Font group and select **White, Background 1**. Deselect the text.

c. Press **Ctrl+Home** to move the insertion point to the beginning of the document. Click the **Layout tab**, click **Columns** in the Page Setup group, and then select **Two**. Click the **Insert tab** and click **Pictures** in the Illustrations group. Browse for and select w05p1kitchen.jpg from the student data files. Click **Insert**. Ensure that the image is selected, click the **Picture Tools Format tab**, and then ensure that the picture width is **3"**. Click **Wrap Text** in the Arrange group on the Picture Tools Format tab and click **Square**.

d. Press **Ctrl+End** to move the insertion point to the end of the document and press **Enter**. Minimize the Word document. Start Excel. Open *w05p1Plans.xlsx*. Drag to select cells **A1:B5**. Click **Copy** in the Clipboard group on the Home tab (or press Ctrl+C).

e. Click the **Word icon** on the Windows taskbar to return to the Word document. Click the **Paste arrow** in the Clipboard group and select **Paste Special**. Select **Paste link** and click **Microsoft Excel Worksheet Object** in the *As* list. Click **OK**. Click the Excel worksheet object in the Word document to select it. Click **Center** in the Paragraph group on the Home tab.

f. Select all body paragraph text in the left column, beginning with *Challenge yourself* and ending at the end of the inserted worksheet. Click the **Shading arrow** in the Paragraph group and click **Orange, Accent 2, Darker 25%** (row 5, column 6). Deselect the text.

g. Select all text in the two body paragraphs in the left column (beginning with *Challenge yourself* and ending with *for the building novice*). Do not select the linked worksheet. Change the font to **Arial**. Click anywhere to deselect the text. Click the **Design tab** and click **Page Borders** in the Page Background group. Click **Box** in the Setting section, change the color to **Gold, Accent 4, Darker 50%**, (row 6, column 8), and then change the width to **3 pt**. Click **OK**.

h. Click the **Insert tab**, click **Text Box** in the Text group, and then click **Banded Sidebar**. Click the **SIDEBAR TITLE placeholder** and type **build with us**. (Do not type the period.) Text will automatically display in all caps. Click the paragraph text placeholder in the long blue sidebar to select it. Type the following, pressing **Enter** after each line:

Potting Table
Saturday, September 21
10:00 a.m. - noon (Leave a space before and after the hyphen.)

i. Select the text just typed, including the final paragraph mark after the word *noon*, click the **Layout tab** and reduce the Spacing After to **0**. Click after *noon* and press **Enter** twice. Type the following events, pressing **Enter** twice between each event description. Do not press Enter after the final event. Note that when you type the word *Décor*, the accent mark is automatically added. Use Figure 5.33 as a guide.

Fall Door Décor
Saturday, September 28
10:00 a.m. – noon

Children Build
Saturday, September 28
2:00 p.m. – 3:00 p.m.

Laying Patio Stone
Saturday, October 5
10:00 a.m. – noon

Model Sailboat (Children)
Saturday, October 5
2:00 p.m. – 3:00 p.m.

j. Click the **Insert tab** and click **3D Models**. Click the **Vehicles** category and click the sailboat picture. If that picture is not available, select a similar one. With the picture selected, click **Wrap Text** in the Arrange group on the 3D Model Tools Format tab and click **Square**. Change the height of the picture (in the Size group) to **1.5"**. Click **Left** in the 3D Model Views group (second selection from left). Drag to visually center the sailboat in the text box following the last event typed. Refer to Figure 5.33 for approximate placement. Drag the 3D rotation handle in the center of the sailboat to position it approximately at the 3D placement shown in Figure 5.33. Deselect the sailboat picture by clicking anywhere in the blue sidebar text box.

k. With the blue sidebar selected, click the **Drawing Tools Format tab** and change the height in the Size group to **7"**. Scroll to display the top of the sidebar and click the outermost dashed line surrounding the sidebar. Click the **Shape Fill arrow** in the Shape Styles group and select **Gold, Accent 4, Darker 50%** (row 6, column 8). Select the text **BUILD WITH US**. Change the font color to **White, Background 1** and apply bold formatting.

l. Click the **Excel icon** on the taskbar to display the *w05p1Plans.xlsx* workbook. Click **cell B5**, containing the number *15*. Type **9** and press **Enter**. Minimize the workbook, but do not close it. Ensure that the Word document w05p1Build_LastFirst displays. Right-click the worksheet in the left column and select **Update Link**.

m. Click the **Insert tab**. Click **Shapes** in the Illustrations group. Click **Arrow: Right** in the Block Arrows section. Drag to create an arrow (pointing to the right) approximating the size of that shown in Figure 5.33. Ensure that the Drawing Tools Format tab is selected and change the height and width of the shape to **1"**, using the options in the Size group. Click the **Shape Fill arrow** and select **Orange, Accent 2**.

n. Press **Ctrl+D** to duplicate the arrow. Click **Rotate**, or Rotate Objects, in the Arrange group and select **Flip Horizontal**. Drag the arrow to position it approximately as shown in Figure 5.33.

o. Ensure that an arrow shape is selected. Click **Align** in the Arrange group on the Drawing Tools Format tab and select **View Gridlines**. Using the grid as a guide, drag to more precisely align the arrow shapes. You can also use the arrow keys to nudge a shape in any direction. Click **Align** and select **View Gridlines** to turn off the display of gridlines. Click outside the arrow to deselect it.

p. Click the arrow on the left. Type **Dream It**. Following the same steps, type the words **Do It** in the right arrow. Change the font size of text in both arrows to **10 pt** and bold the text. Click outside the arrow to deselect it.

q. Click the **Insert tab** and click **Insert WordArt** in the Text group. Select **Fill: Orange, Accent color 2; Outline: Orange, Accent color 2** (row 1, column 3). Change the font size to **20 pt** and type **You Build It**. With the WordArt object selected, ensure that the Drawing Tools Format tab is selected. Click **Shape Fill**, and then select **Orange, Accent 2, Darker 25%** (row 5, column 6). Drag the WordArt object to center it below the arrows, as shown in Figure 5.33.

r. Hold **Shift** and click each **arrow shape** above the WordArt. All three objects (the arrows and WordArt) should be selected. Click **Group**, or Group Objects, in the Arrange group on the Drawing Tools Format tab and select **Group**.

s. Click **Position** in the Arrange group and select **More Layout Options**. With the Position tab selected, ensure that Absolute position is selected in the Horizontal section. Adjust the inches to **4.4"** to the right of Column. Select **Absolute position** in the Vertical section and adjust the inches to **0.2"** below Paragraph. Click **OK**. Deselect the grouped object.

t. Click the **Insert tab**, click **Text Box** in the Text group, and then click **Draw Text Box**. Click immediately below the lower left corner of the Excel spreadsheet in the left column. Adjust the height of the text box to **0.5"** and the width to **3"**. Change the font to **Garamond** and the font size to **8 pt**. Click the **Layout tab** and remove any paragraph spacing.

u. Type **Building Matters** and press **Tab** three times. Type **(790) 555-1800**. (Leave a space before *555* and do not type the period.) Press **Enter**. Type **110 Broad Street** and press **Tab** three times. Type **bmatters@tel.net**. (Do not type the period.) Press **Enter**. Type **Austin, TX 78703**. (Do not type the period.) Right-click **bmatters@tel.net** and select **Remove Hyperlink**.

v. Ensure that the text box is selected. Click the **Drawing Tools Format tab**. Click **Shape Outline** and select **No Outline**. Deselect the text box. Turn off the display of nonprinting characters.

w. Select the event information text in the sidebar, beginning with *Potting Table* and ending with the times for the Model Sailboat class (the last line in the sidebar). The model sailboat picture will most likely also be selected. Click the **Home tab** and click **Center** in the Paragraph group.

x. Select the text box at the bottom of the left column. Click the **Format tab**. Click **Position** in the Arrange group and select **More Layout Options**. Change the Absolute position in the Horizontal section to **0"** to the right of Margin. The Absolute position in the Vertical section should be **1.25"** below Paragraph. Click **OK**.

y. Click the **Excel icon** on the Windows taskbar and close the workbook without saving it.

z. Save and close the document. Based on your instructor's directions, submit w05p1Build_LastFirst.

2 Lake Days

Your family owns a small realty firm, TA Realty, in the lake district of North Carolina. Many of your clients seek rental homes or condos on the lakes, so you specialize in promotion of that type of property. A local publication is accepting one-page flyers from businesses in the area, so you plan to prepare a page to promote the rental of lake property. You use Word to design a flyer containing columns and objects that are formatted attractively. Refer to Figure 5.34 as you complete this exercise.

FIGURE 5.34 Lake Property Flyer

a. Open *w05p2Lake* and save the document as **w05p2Lake_LastFirst**. Ensure that nonprinting characters are displayed. With the insertion point at the beginning of the document, insert *w05p2Pier.jpg*. Change the width to **4.5"** and apply the **Soft Edge Rectangle picture style**. Change text wrapping to **Square**. Drag the picture to position it approximately as shown in Figure 5.34.

b. Click the **Insert tab** and click **Text Box** in the Text group. Click **Draw Text Box** and click at the first paragraph mark at the top of the page. Change the text box height to **3.5"** and the width to **4.5"**. Click the **Layout tab** and remove any paragraph spacing

c. Type **lake** in the text box, press **Enter**, and then type **days**. Correct the word *lake* so that the first letter is in lowercase. Change the font size of text in the text box to **90** and change the font to **Times New Roman**.

d. Click before the word *lake* and press **Tab**. Select the word *lake* and change the font color to **Orange, Accent 2, Darker 25%**. Click the **Drawing Tools Format tab**, click **Shape Fill** in the Shape Styles group, and then select **No Fill**. Click **Shape Outline** and select **No Outline**. Drag the text box to position it approximately as shown in Figure 5.34.

e. Place the insertion point at the end of the document. Click the **Layout tab**, click **Breaks**, and then click **Continuous**. Insert text from *w05p2Text.docx*.

f. Select all of the newly inserted text, from *Where to go* through the end of the document. Click the **Layout tab**, click **Columns**, and then click **Three**.

g. Click before the words *Where to stay* in the second column. Click **Breaks** in the Page Setup group and click **Column**. Click before the words *When to go* near the end of the first column. Insert a column break.

h. Select the word **Where** in the heading line of the first column. Click the **Home tab**. Double-click **Format Painter** in the Clipboard group. Double-click the word **When** in the heading at the top of the second column and double-click the word **Where** in the heading at the top of the third column. Press **Esc**.

i. Select the words **to go** in the heading line of the first column. Double-click **Format Painter** in the Clipboard group. Drag to paint the format on the words *to go* in the heading at the top of the second column. Drag to paint the format on the words *to stay* in the heading at the top of the third column. Press **Esc**.

j. Bold the subheadings *FOCUS ON THE OFF-SEASON*, *WIDEN YOUR SEARCH*, *CHECK THE SCHOOL CALENDAR*, and *WEIGH PRICE VS. AMENITIES*.

k. Click after the period after the word *destination* ending the first body paragraph in column 3. Click the **Insert tab** and click **SmartArt** in the Illustrations group. Click **Process** in the left pane. Click **Basic Process** (row 1, column 1). Click **OK**.

l. Click the outermost border of the SmartArt object to ensure that the entire SmartArt diagram is selected. Click the **SmartArt Tools Format tab**. Change the height of the SmartArt diagram to **0.5"** and change the width to **1.8"**. Click in the first shape in the SmartArt diagram and type **Price**. (Do not type the period.) Type **Amenities** in the second shape. Type **Service** in the third shape.

m. Click the **SmartArt Tools Design tab**. Click **Change Colors** in the SmartArt Styles group and select **Colored Fill – Accent 2** (column 2 under Accent 2). Select a SmartArt style of **Subtle Effect**.

n. Click the **Insert tab**, click **Shapes**, and then click **Star: 7 Points** in the Stars and Banners section. Click the first paragraph mark at the top of the document. Ensure that the height is **1"** and the width is **1"**. Type **TA** and press **Enter**. Type **Star**.

o. Select all text in the shape, click the **Layout tab**, and then remove any paragraph spacing. Bold the text in the shape. With the shape selected, click the **Drawing Tools Format tab**, click **Shape Fill**, and then select **Orange, Accent 2, Lighter 40%** (row 4, column 6).

p. Click the outer border of the star shape to select the entire shape. Press **Ctrl+D** to duplicate the shape. Remove text from the new star. With the **Drawing Tools Format tab** selected, click **Send Backward** in the Arrange group.

q. Hold **Shift** and click the **top star** so that both stars are selected. Click **Group**, or Group Objects, in the Arrange group on the Format tab and click **Group**.

r. Drag the grouped object to position it approximately as shown in Figure 5.34. Check the spelling, correcting any errors, but disregarding any clarity errors. View the document as One Page.

s. Click the **Design tab** and click **Page Borders** in the Page Background group. Click **Shadow**, change the color to **Orange, Accent 2, Darker 50%** (row 6, column 6), and then change the weight to **3 pt**. Click **OK**.

t. Save and close the document. Based on your instructor's directions, submit w05p2Lake_LastFirst.

Mid-Level Exercises

1 Book Trends

You work with the National Literary Guild as an analyst and reporter for news publications sponsored by the organization. You are designing a short newsletter that is periodically produced and made available both on the Web and in print.

a. Open *w05m1Books* and save it as **w05m1Books_LastFirst**.
b. Change the font of the first two paragraphs to **Arial Rounded MT Bold**. Center both lines. Change the font size of the first line, *The Trend*, to **48**. Change the font size of the second line to **14**. Shade the first two lines with **Blue, Accent 1, Darker 25%** and change the font color to **White, Background 1**. Deselect the text.
c. Insert the picture file *w05m1Books.jpg*. Wrap text **In Front of Text**. Ensure that the height of the image is **1.2"**. Duplicate the image.
d. Flip the image horizontally so that the stack of books presents a mirror image of the original. Position one book image at the far-right side of the shaded masthead, overlapping the blue shading. Position the other at the far left.
e. Insert a **2x1 Table** under the masthead. In the first cell, type **Volume 1, Number 8**. In the second cell, type **Summer 2022**. Right-align text in the second cell. Change all table text to **Arial** font. Set all borders of the table to **No Border**.
f. Insert a page break after the table. Place the insertion point after the table on the first page. Draw a text box at the position of the insertion point. Size the text box to be **6"** in height and **6.5"** in width. Insert text from the file *w05m1Newsletter*.
g. Move to the top of the second page. Draw a text box. Size the text box to **7.5"** in height and **6.5"** in width. Click in the text box on the first page and ensure that the **Drawing Tools Format tab** is selected. Click **Create Link** in the Text group. Click in the text box on the second page. Press **Ctrl+A** to select all text in both text boxes, and change the font to **Comic Sans MS**.
h. Change the font size of all subheadings shown below to **14**.
   - What's New
   - Are You a James Patterson Fan?
   - Check Out The Long Song.
   - Best Selling Books of All Time
   - This Month's Book Club Question
i. Click before one of the blank paragraph marks at the end of the text box on the first page and press Enter. Place the insertion point at the blank paragraph below *Best Selling Books of All Time*. Click **Object** in the Text group on the Insert tab and click the **Create from File tab**. Browse to and select *w05m1BestSellers.xlsx*. Do not select any check box to link or display an icon. Center the inserted worksheet object.
j. Change the shape fill of both text boxes to **Blue, Accent 1, Lighter 80%**. Select the text box on the first page, click **Align** on the Drawing Tools Format tab, and then select **Align Center** to align the text box in the center of the page horizontally. Align the text box on the second page in the middle of the page vertically by selecting **Align** and **Align Middle**. Set the shape outline of both text boxes to **No Outline**. Apply a shape effect of **Shadow, Offset: Bottom Right** to both text boxes.
k. Check the spelling, correcting any mistakes. Ignore the grammatical error suggesting a change to *The Long Song*, if presented. Save the document and exit Word. Based on your instructor's directions, submit w05m1Books_LastFirst.

2 Disaster Response

You are a volunteer with the American Response Team, a global disaster response organization. Your primary responsibility is the development of various publications for print and online access. This project involves the development of a two-page document summarizing the organization's efforts at worldwide disaster relief.

a. Open *w05m2Response* and save it as **w05m2Response_LastFirst**. Ensure that nonprinting characters are displayed.
b. Change the font size of the first paragraph, *Worldwide Disaster Preparedness*, to **18 pt**. Change the font color to **Red** (second column under Standard Colors). Right-align the text.

c. Insert a text box, choosing to draw the text box, above the text *Preparing for Disaster* at the top of the document. Draw the text box approximately 2" wide and 1" high. It is OK if it obscures existing document text, as you will resize and move the text box later in this exercise. Type **American** on one line in the text box and **Response Team** on the next. Remove all paragraph spacing from text in the text box.

d. Change the text box height to **0.77"** and change the width to **2"**. Change the text box font size to **14 pt** and bold and center the text.

e. Click **Position** on the Drawing Tools Format tab and select **More Layout Options**. Change the Absolute position in the Horizontal section to **-0.07"** to the right of Column. Adjust the Absolute position in the Vertical section to **-0.62"** below Paragraph.

f. Insert a heart shape, located in the Basic Shapes section, placing it anywhere on the text box. Adjust the height and width of the heart shape to **0.35"** and change the shape fill to **Red** (second column under Standard Colors). Position the heart in the top-left corner of the text box.

g. Remove the outline from the text box. Add a **1 ½ pt** bottom border to the *Worldwide Disaster Preparedness* line. Ensure that the border is black. The border will extend the width of the document.

h. Change all document text following the *Worldwide Disaster Preparedness* heading to **Garamond 14 pt**. Apply **6 pt** After paragraph spacing to the selected text. Check spelling, correcting any errors, but ignore any grammatical and clarity concerns.

i. Format all subheadings—Preparing for Disaster, Strengthening Communities, Response Readiness, and Developing a Worldwide Disaster Preparedness Center—as **Bold**, with a font color of **Blue, Accent 5, Darker 50%**.

j. Apply a black checkmark bullet to each of the seven paragraphs beginning at the bottom of the first page and ending on the second (beginning with *Increase the resilience of communities* and ending with *Build technical expertise*). Decrease the indent of the bulleted text so that it begins at the left margin.

k. Select all text from *Preparing for Disaster* on page 1 through *www.artdisastercenter.org* on page 2 and format the text in two columns.

l. Add a drop cap to the first letter in the first body paragraph on page 1, beginning with *Global trends*. To do so, open the Drop Cap Options dialog box, select **Dropped**, and then indicate the number of lines to drop as **2**.

> **MAC TROUBLESHOOTING:** Click the Format menu, select Drop Cap, and then click Dropped.

m. Insert *w05m2Crisis.jpg* at any location in column 1. Select **Square** text wrapping and apply **Reflected Perspective Right** picture style. Change the picture width to **2.4"**. Click **Position** on the Drawing Tools Format tab and select **More Layout Options**. Position the picture at an Absolute position of **1.75"** to the right of Column and **2.08"** below Paragraph.

n. View the document in multiple pages. Insert a column break before the heading shown alone at the bottom of the left column on page 1. Insert a column break before the heading shown alone at the bottom of the right column. Return the view to 100%.

o. Insert a SmartArt diagram after the URL, *www.artdisastercenter.org*, at the end of the right column on page 2. Select the **Process category** and select **Step Up Process**. Type **ART** in the lowest step in the diagram, type **STAR Partners** in the middle, and then type **Disaster Center** in the top step.

p. Change the SmartArt colors to **Colorful Range – Accent Colors 4 to 5**. Ensure that the entire SmartArt diagram is selected. Adjust the height of the SmartArt object to **2"** and ensure that the width is **3"**.

q. Select text at the end of the document, from *How You Can Help* through the end. Insert a text box, choosing to draw the text box so that the selected text is in the new text box. Change the text box height to **2.3"** and the width to **6.5"**.

r. Change the text box shape fill to **Gray, Accent 3, Lighter 80%** (row 2, column 7). Change the weight of the shape outline to **1 ½ pt**. Choose a shape effect of **Bevel, Round Convex**.

s. Bold the text box title, *How You Can Help*, and center the title.

t. Save and close the file. Based on your instructor's directions, submit w05m2Response_LastFirst.

Running Case

New Castle County Technical Services

New Castle County Technical Services (NCCTS) provides technical support for companies in the greater New Castle County, Delaware, area. NCCTS has been asked to participate in a technology fair at a local university. The fair is open to students and community members, many of whom are potential clients for New Castle's data and network solutions. You have been asked to take a rough draft of information related to data recovery solutions and use Word to create an attractive multi-page informational handout. You will format the document with various text and paragraph settings, including the use of columns and graphic objects to add interest.

a. Open *w05r1NewCastle* and save it as **w05r1NewCastle_LastFirst**.

b. Show nonprinting characters. Select the first heading on page 1 (*New Castle County Technical Services*) and insert WordArt, selecting **Fill: Black, Text color 1; Outline: White, Background color 1; Hard Shadow: White, Background color 1** (row 3, column 1).

c. Select all text on page 1 and part of page 2, beginning with the first body paragraph (*At New Castle, we recover data . . .*) and ending before the heading *Preserving Data for the Life of Your Company*. Change the font to **Rockwell 12 pt**. For all the selected text, adjust paragraph spacing to **6 pt Before** and ensure that spacing **After** is **0 pt**. Double-space the selected text.

d. Insert a shape, selecting **Arrow: Right**. Drag the arrow so that it points to the approximate left of the second heading line (*Fast, Local, and Experienced Data Recovery*). Change the arrow height to **0.5"** and change the width to **0.5"**. Change the shape fill to **Red** (second column under Standard Colors).

e. Duplicate the arrow and rotate it, choosing to flip it horizontally. Move the duplicated arrow to the opposite end of the same heading and position it in approximate alignment with the arrow on the left. View gridlines to assist in that process. Remove the view of gridlines when the task is complete.

f. Use the Position command on the Drawing Tools Format tab, selecting **More Layout Options**, to finalize placement of the arrow shapes as follows:
   - The left arrow is positioned **-0.3"** to the right of Margin and **1.4"** below Paragraph.
   - The right arrow is positioned **6.3"** to the right of Margin and **1.4"** below Paragraph.

g. Remove bold formatting from the last bulleted item on page 1 and remove the bullet so that the text is a paragraph. With the insertion point before the words *Our goal is to provide*, press **Backspace** to position the text at the left margin.

h. Remove the hard return at the end of the sentence to combine two sentences into one paragraph. Italicize the last sentence in the paragraph, beginning with *We understand the importance*, and ensure that a space precedes the sentence.

i. Insert a page break before the heading near the bottom of page 2, *Preserving Data for the Life of Your Company*. Select all text on pages 3–5 and change the font to **Times New Roman 14 pt**. Ensure that paragraph spacing in the selected text is **6 pt After** and **0 pt Before**.

j. Select text, beginning with the heading *Consider Moving Backup and Disaster Recovery to the Cloud* on page 3, and continuing through the end of the document. Open the Columns dialog box and select **Two columns**, also choosing the **Line between** option.

k. Change the font size of the first heading on page 3, *Preserving Data for the Life of Your Company*, to **24 pt**. Change paragraph spacing After to **18 pt** for the first body paragraph on page 3, beginning with *Where your company is concerned*.

l. Click before the first letter in the first body paragraph on page 3, *W*, and insert a drop cap, selecting **Dropped**.

> **MAC TROUBLESHOOTING:** Click the Format menu, select Drop Cap, and then click Dropped.

m. Select the sentence at the top of page 2, *We understand the importance of your company data and we'll do everything we can to retrieve your lost data*. Copy the selection. Place the insertion point at the end of the document, after the words *Call on us any time*, and press **Enter**. Insert a text box, selecting **Austin Quote**. Paste the copied text in the text box.

- **n.** Drag the text box to position it under the last paragraph in the right column. With the text box selected, click **Position** on the Drawing Tools Format tab and select **More Layout Options**. Adjust the Horizontal absolute position to **4.4"** to the right of Page and adjust the Vertical absolute position to **1.8"** below Paragraph.
- **o.** Place the insertion point after the first paragraph in the right column on page 3, ending in *from one-half to one-third of their costs*. Insert SmartArt, selecting the **Process category** and choosing **Continuous Block Process**.
- **p.** Type **Backup** in the first shape on the left, type **Disaster Recovery** in the middle shape, and then type **Complete Coverage** in the last shape. Select a SmartArt style of **Cartoon** (in the 3-D section) and change the colors to **Transparent Gradient Range – Accent 1** (column 5 under Accent 1). Change the SmartArt height to **1"** and the width to **3"**.
- **q.** Check spelling, correcting any spelling mistakes but ignoring any flagged clarity and conciseness issues.
- **r.** Save the document and exit Word. Based on your instructor's directions, submit w05r1NewCastle_LastFirst.

Disaster Recovery

Auto Sales

You work for a local automotive dealer, who attempted to create a document that describes a vehicle, including a spreadsheet calculation for pricing that can be updated automatically. He thinks this will be a great resource for all sales associates, but his first attempt to create the document was unsuccessful. He did not properly link the document with the source file, and the document lacks graphics that would add interest. You have been assigned the task of repairing the document so that the pricing information from the *w05d1Cooper.xlsx* spreadsheet can be updated easily and automatically. You must also modify the document to include a picture of the Mini Cooper, obtained from Microsoft's collection of online pictures, and any other improvements that would yield a more professional-looking document. Open *w05d1Car* and save it as **w05d1Car_LastFirst**. Correct the document, as previously described. Use your judgment and creativity, producing an attractive, error-free document. The Mini Cooper is sometimes listed as a MINI Cooper, so choose either iteration but be consistent. Based on your instructor's directions, submit w05d1Car_LastFirst.

Capstone Exercise

MyLab IT Grader

Alumni Office Article

As an assistant in the Alumni Office of the University of Northwest Colorado, you are preparing an article for inclusion in an upcoming issue of the Alumni Affairs publication. The article is related to the current university funding situation and is prepared in rough draft form. You will use Word to format the article so that it is attractive and informative, including columns, graphic objects, text formatting, and linking to an external funding worksheet.

Insert and Format Graphic Shapes

As a newsletter heading, you insert and format a series of duplicated shapes, with each shape filled with color and text. The color-coordinated shapes serve as an attractive introduction to newsletter content.

1. Open *w05c1Funding* and save it as **w05c1Funding_LastFirst**. Ensure that nonprinting characters are displayed.
2. Select all text, including any blank paragraphs, and apply a first line indent of **0.5"**. Ensure that there is no paragraph spacing within the selected text.
3. Place the insertion point before the blank paragraph at the top of the document and remove the first line indent from the line. Insert a text box at the top of the document, choosing to draw the text box. Change the height of the text box to **0.75"** and the width to **6.3"**. Choose **Top and Bottom text wrapping**.
4. Type **UNC'S GROWING LIST OF ACCOMPLISHMENTS** in the text box. Center the text horizontally. Click **Align Text** on the Drawing Tools Format tab and select **Middle**. Change the shape fill to **Green** (column 6 in Standard colors). Change the font of text in the text box to **White, Background 1** and change the font size to **22**. Bold the text. Remove the shape outline from the text box.
5. Click **Position** in the Arrange group on the Drawing Tools Format tab and select **More Layout Options**. Adjust the Absolute position in the Horizontal section to **0"** to the right of Column. Adjust the Absolute position in the Vertical section to **0"** below Paragraph.
6. Insert a shape under the text box, selecting **Trapezoid** in the Basic Shapes group. Change text wrapping of the shape to **Top and Bottom**. Change the height of the shape to **1.4"** and the width to **1.8"**. Change the shape fill to **Green** (column 6 in Standard colors) and remove the shape outline.
7. Position the shape, adjusting the Absolute position in the Horizontal section to **0"** to the right of Column. Adjust the Absolute position in the Vertical section to **0.75"** below Paragraph.
8. Type **Number of ACADEMIC PROGRAMS with specialized accreditation: 16**. (Do not type the period.) Bold text in the shape.
9. Duplicate the shape and drag it to just below the approximate center of the text box, positioning it at **2.35"** to the right of Column (Absolute position in the Horizontal section) and **0.75"** below Paragraph (Absolute position in the Vertical section). Change the shape fill to **Gold, Accent 4**. Replace the existing text in the shape with **Vibrant Health, P.E., and Recreation program: 37% growth**. (Do not type the period.)
10. Duplicate the shape and drag it to the right side of the text box, positioning it at **4.7"** to the right of Column (Absolute position in the Horizontal section) and **0.75"** below Paragraph (Absolute position in the Vertical section). Change the shape fill to **Green** and replace the existing text in the shape with **Large, highly ranked AACSB-accredited MBA program**. (Do not type the period.)

Format Text in Columns, Insert a Section Break, and Group Objects

The shapes comprising the newsletter heading are grouped so they can be treated as one object. Newsletter text is arranged in columns, with the grouped object centered above them. A section break, positioned at the end of the document, ensures an even arrangement of columns.

11. Select all text below the shapes, beginning with *State funding is not at an equitable level*, and format in three columns. Change the font of the selected text to **Times New Roman 12 pt**. Change margins to **Narrow**.
12. Check spelling, correcting any mistakes. Ignore all grammatical and clarity concerns.
13. Click the first trapezoid shape at the top of the document, hold Shift, and then click the remaining two shapes as well as the green text box above. With all four objects selected, group the objects. Click **Position** on the Drawing Tools Format tab and select **Position in Top Center with Square Text Wrapping** (row 1, column 2 under Text Wrapping).
14. Insert a Continuous section break at the end of the document so that columns on the last page are in proportion to one another.

Add a Pull Quote and a Drop Cap

To draw attention to an interesting fact, you create a pull quote and position it within the column text. A drop cap adds interest to document text.

15. Click anywhere on page 1 and insert a text box, selecting **Banded Quote**. Change the shape style to **Subtle Effect - Green, Accent 6** (row 4, column 7 under Theme Styles).
16. Replace text in the text box with **UNC HAS A $316 MILLION PER YEAR ECONOMIC IMPACT ON SHADES VALLEY**. (Include the period.) Select the text and change the text fill to **Gold, Accent 4**. Select *$316 Million* in the text box and change the font size to **22**. Ensure that text in the text box is centered horizontally.
17. Click the outer edge of the text box to select the entire object. Change the text box height to **1.11"** and the width to **3.6"**. Position the text box at **0.2"** to the right of Margin (Absolute position in the Horizontal section) and **4.75"** below Margin (Absolute position in the Vertical section).
18. Remove the first line indent from the first body paragraph on page 1, beginning with *State funding is not at an equitable level*. Place the insertion point before the first letter in the paragraph and insert a drop cap, choosing **Dropped**.

Link to a Worksheet and Add a Page Border

A worksheet, with pertinent data, is included in the article and linked so that changes to the worksheet are reflected in the document. Finishing the newsletter with a page border adds polish and professionalism to the document that is intended for publication.

19. Place the insertion point after the first paragraph on page 2, ending in *fall of 2022*. Press **Enter**. Remove the first line indent from the new blank paragraph.
20. Open *w05c1Comparison.xlsx* and select cells **A1 through B4**. Copy the selection. Minimize the Excel workbook but do not close it. Using Paste Special, paste the selection in the document, making sure to paste the link and selecting **Microsoft Excel Worksheet Object**.
21. Display the Excel workbook and change the State Average in cell B3 to **35%**. Press Enter after making the change. Return to the Word document and update the link in the worksheet shown on page 2.
22. Insert a page border, selecting **Box**, and then choosing a color of **Green**. The line weight should be ½ **pt**.
23. Save and close the document. Close the Excel workbook without saving. Based on your instructor's directions, submit w05c1Funding_LastFirst.

Word

Time-Saving Tools

LEARNING OUTCOME You will demonstrate how to use templates, work with multiple documents, and apply and modify themes.

OBJECTIVES & SKILLS: After you read this chapter, you will be able to:

Automate Document Creation

OBJECTIVE 1: SELECT A TEMPLATE 364
Select and Download a Template
OBJECTIVE 2: CREATE A WORD TEMPLATE 366
Save a Document as a Template
OBJECTIVE 3: USE BUILDING BLOCKS 367
Create and Insert a Custom Building Block
HANDS-ON EXERCISE 1 371

Multiple Documents

OBJECTIVE 4: VIEW TWO DOCUMENTS SIDE BY SIDE 376
View Two Documents Side by Side
OBJECTIVE 5: MERGE DOCUMENTS 377
Compare Two Documents, Combine Two Documents, Insert a File as an Object, Create a Master Document and Subdocuments, Modify the Master Document and Subdocuments, Use the Master Document and Subdocuments with Extreme Care

OBJECTIVE 6: USE NAVIGATIONAL TOOLS 384
Use the Navigation Pane, Create Bookmarks
HANDS-ON EXERCISE 2 389

Document Themes

OBJECTIVE 7: APPLY A DOCUMENT THEME AND STYLE SET 396
Apply a Theme to a Document, Apply a Style Set
OBJECTIVE 8: CUSTOMIZE THEME COLORS AND THEME FONTS, AND APPLY THEME EFFECTS 397
Customize Theme Colors, Customize Theme Fonts, Apply Theme Effects, Save a Custom Theme
HANDS-ON EXERCISE 3 400

CASE STUDY | Computer Training Concepts, Inc.

Alexandra Caselman is the director of marketing at Computer Training Concepts, Inc., a business that provides technical training on a variety of computer systems to other companies. Alexandra is responsible for collecting information about a potential training event, such as how much time the training will take, how many instructors will be needed, and how much the training event will cost. She collects this information from her staff and then spends a great deal of time copying and pasting the information into a few documents that she can package together and send to a potential client.

During a recent meeting, she mentions this cumbersome task to you, her assistant director, and you suggest that Microsoft Word has features that make the process of assembling the information more efficient. Alexandra decides to split the job with you because her method of compiling the information is outdated and slow. She will assemble and give you the collected information so that you can set up some of the documents as templates. You will then update the templates with more information and convert the content into one nicely designed, professional-looking document.

CHAPTER 6

Automating Document Creation and Using Multiple Documents and Themes

FIGURE 6.1 Computer Training Proposal

CASE STUDY | Computer Training Concepts, Inc.

Starting Files	Files to be Submitted
Blank document Functional resume template Functional resume reference sheet template w06h2Proposal1 w06h2Proposal2 w06h2Faculty	In the w06h3Master_LastFirst zipped file: w06h1ResumeRW_LastFirst w06h1References_LastFirst w06h1ReferencesTemplate_LastFirst.dotx w06h2FinalProposal_LastFirst w06h3Master_LastFirst w06h3MasterTheme_LastFirst.thmx

MyLab IT Grader An alternate version of this project is available as a MyLab IT Grader Assessment

Time-Saving Tools • Word 2019

Automate Document Creation

Word is useful for creating interesting and complex documents because it provides a variety of formatting features that you can apply to the documents. You can jump-start the formatting process by using professional designs provided in the form of templates. A ***template*** is a predesigned file that contains preformatted text and/or graphics such as a theme or layout, and may include content that can be modified. Word provides a variety of templates for common documents, and additional templates can be downloaded from Office.com. Each template contains an existing framework of formats and text to decrease the time to create a document.

You can also develop your own templates to use when you create certain types of documents that are used frequently. Another way to save time is to use predefined document elements to automate and streamline repetitive tasks such as creating headers, cover pages, tables, and watermarks.

Document templates use the file extensions .dotx or .dotm (if the template contains a macro, which is a program written to execute a repetitive task) in Word. Previous versions of Word (prior to 2007) use .dot as the extension for templates.

> **TIP: SEARCH FOR TEMPLATES**
> When you search for a template on your computer, click the All Word Documents or All Files arrow in the Open dialog box and select All Word Templates. Navigate to the folder containing your template or the custom default directory and select the template.

In this section, you will use a template to start a document so that you do not have to set fonts or bullets, or create a style for the document. You will also create and save a Word document that you use frequently as your own template. Finally, you will work with building blocks that can be reused to automate and streamline repetitive tasks.

Selecting a Template

Word provides several different templates for different types of documents. You can use Word templates to create letters, memos, reports, resumes, agendas, calendars, brochures, and checklists, as well as other documents such as the APA style report and itineraries. Using a template can be an easy way to create a professional-looking document.

> **TIP: NORMAL TEMPLATE**
> A blank document uses the Normal template, which is the framework that defines the default margin (with 1″ left, right, top, and bottom margins), left horizontal alignment, 11 pt Calibri font, 8 pt After spacing, 1.08 Multiple Line spacing, and other settings.

Some templates have features, styles, and placeholders for information that you provide to complete the document. A ***placeholder*** is a field or block of text used to determine the position of objects in a document (see Figure 6.2). A placeholder can also contain filler text, generated to display the visual appeal of a print layout, that you can delete and replace with your own content. The filler text is also frequently used to visually display formatting such as font, typography, and layout. Common examples of placeholders are name and street address. In general, placeholders can also be content controls that you can add and customize to use in templates, forms, and documents. Content controls are covered in a later chapter.

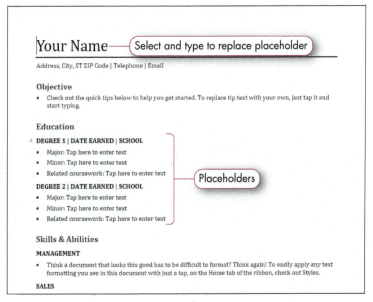

FIGURE 6.2 Replace Placeholders with Text in a Resume Template

> **TIP: USING A RESUME TEMPLATE AND THE RESUME ASSISTANT**
> A variety of resume templates are available in Word and using a template can be an easy way to create a professionally formatted resume. Resume Assistant can help you to create a professional-looking resume. This feature, located in the Resume group on the Review tab, provides information on job description, skills, and work experience based on the profiles of similar jobs listed on LinkedIn.

STEP 1 Select and Download a Template

When you launch Word and go to the New tab, a variety of installed templates are displayed on the start screen. If Word is already open, you can access the installed templates from the File tab. If you do not see a template that you want to use from the installed templates, you can perform a search by clicking one of the suggested search terms or by typing a key term (e.g., resume, letter, or memo) in the Search for online templates search box as shown in Figure 6.3.

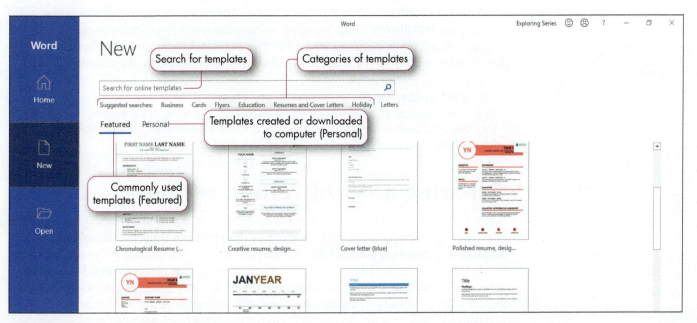

FIGURE 6.3 Select a Document Template

Automate Document Creation • **Word 2019**   365

Template thumbnails are small pictures displayed below the search box that match the search term in the *Search for online templates* search box, and with a list of categories displayed on the right. When the template thumbnails are displayed, click each to preview it as shown in Figure 6.4. You can use the arrows in the template preview mode to view the next or previous templates. Once you find a template you want to use, click Create to download it to your computer.

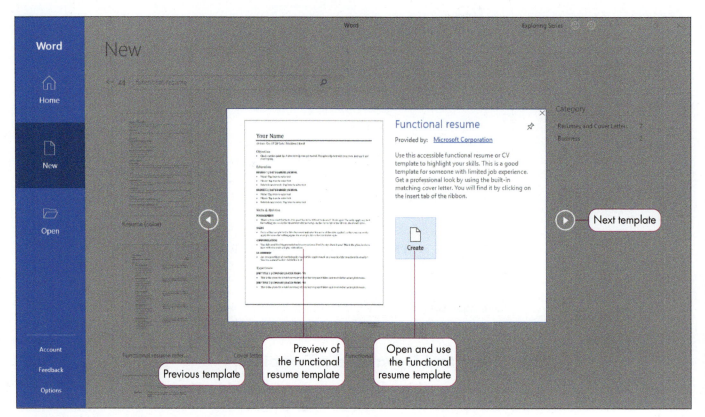

FIGURE 6.4 Preview and Select a Template

After the template downloads, you can open it in a new document window. Then you can modify the template with your own information. When you save the revised template, it will automatically save as a Word document. After you download and save a template, the template will display in the Featured or Personal templates categories on the File tab, so you can access it again more easily. The personal templates are those you have downloaded and saved, while the featured templates are those most commonly used.

> **TIP: INFORMATION ON THE TEMPLATE USED**
> To see which template a document is using, click the File tab, ensure that Info is selected, open the Advanced Properties dialog box, and the template name is displayed on the bottom of the Summary tab.

Creating a Word Template

If you create or use the same document frequently or if you are creating a document for others to use and modify with only minor updates each time, you should modify the document by inserting placeholders for the information you change frequently and save the document as a template. For instance, these placeholders can contain a date, greeting, body, and salutation, thereby requiring you to replace only the changing information. If you have a report that you update on a regular basis that is contained in a very structured and detailed table, you might consider making the report into a template.

STEP 2 **Save a Document as a Template**

When you save a document as a template, Word automatically saves the template to a default location for templates, which is the Custom Office Templates subfolder in the Documents folder. However, you can specify a location on your own hard drive, portable storage device, or OneDrive account by navigating to the folder to your choice. Be aware that templates saved in other locations do not display in the Custom Office Templates subfolder. When you save a document as a template, the file extension changes from *.docx* to *.dotx*.

> **To save a document as a template, complete the following steps:**
> 1. Open the document.
> 2. Click the File tab.
> 3. Click Save As and click Browse.
> 4. Change the *Save as type* to Word Template (see to Figure 6.5).
> 5. Click Browse and navigate to the location where you save your files.
> 6. Click Save.

> **On a Mac, to save a document as a template, complete the following steps:**
> 1. Open the document.
> 2. Click the File menu and select Save As Template.
> 3. Click Save.

FIGURE 6.5 Save as a Word Template

Using Building Blocks

When you create Word documents that frequently contain the same content or objects, you can save the content or objects so that you can use them again without re-creating or retyping them. A variety of building blocks are available for insertion in a Word document. ***Building blocks*** are predefined blocks of text for standardized content that can be placed in any document. Examples of building blocks include disclaimers that display at the bottom of a document, such as a policy about using a company computer for personal matters or business information, such as company address or logo, for a header or footer. Other objects that you can save as a building block include watermarks, tables, or larger objects such as a cover page to a report or a whole page with specific tables and formatting.

You have already worked with many building blocks. The built-in cover pages, headers, footers, bibliographies, table of contents, and watermarks are all considered building blocks and can be accessed through those corresponding galleries. Alternatively, you can preview and insert building blocks through the **Building Blocks Organizer** in the Text group on the Insert tab, which displays a list of all available building blocks (see Figure 6.6). You can sort these building blocks by name, gallery, category, or template storage location. The gallery divides the building blocks into groups. The default galleries include Bibliographies, Cover Pages, Equations, Footers, Headers, Page Numbers, Table of Contents, Tables, Text Boxes, and Watermarks. When you click any of the building blocks in the Building Blocks Organizer, you will see its description. You can also edit entry properties, delete an entry, or insert individual building block into the document using the Building Blocks Organizer.

To access the Building Blocks Organizer, complete the following steps:

1. Click the Insert tab.
2. Click Explore Quick Parts in the Text group.
3. Click Building Blocks Organizer.
4. Select any of the building blocks to preview it and to display its description.

(On a Mac, the Building Block Organizer is not available. However, you can access building blocks from individual galleries such as Cover Page, Table of Contents, Watermarks, etc. You can also use AutoText to create a building block.)

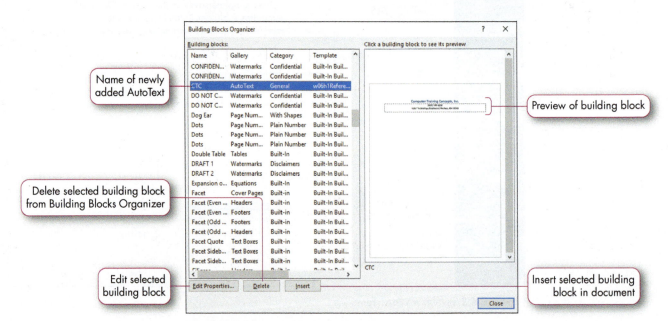

FIGURE 6.6 Building Blocks Organizer

Some of the building blocks from the AutoText, Bibliographies, and Equations galleries must be inserted at a specific location indicated by the insertion point, but other items, such as Cover Page, Header, Footer, or Table of Contents, are inserted without having to place the insertion point at a specific location.

STEP 3 Create and Insert a Custom Building Block

In addition to a predefined set of building blocks created by Microsoft, you may find that you frequently use document content such as logos, specially formatted headers or footers, and standardized tables that are not found in the Building Blocks gallery. In these instances, you can create and customize your own building blocks. By default, when you create a new building block, it is automatically assigned to the Quick Parts gallery, but you can save the building block in other galleries or create your own galleries. You can also save a building block as *AutoText* to store text or graphics that you want to use again, such as a standard contract clause, a long distribution list, or a logo. Figure 6.7 illustrates creating a new building block item.

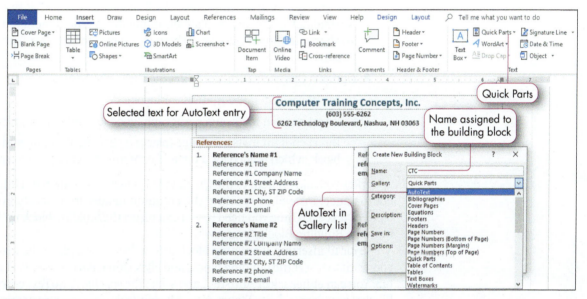

FIGURE 6.7 Add an Entry to the Quick Parts Gallery

To create a new building block, click Quick Parts in the Text group and select Save Selection to Quick Part Gallery. The Create New Building Block dialog box displays. It is where you name, classify, describe, and control the placement of the new building block.

> **MAC TIP: USE AUTOTEXT TO CREATE A BUILDING BLOCK** To create an AutoText entry, select the text or graphic you want to store as AutoText. Click the Insert menu, point to AutoText, and then click New. Enter a name for the AutoText entry and click OK. To use the AutoText, click in the document where you want to insert the AutoText, click the Insert menu, point to AutoText, and then click the name of the entry you want to use.

Automate Document Creation • Word 2019

The Create New Building Block dialog box has the following options:

- **Name:** Assign a name that reflects the object. This name must be unique, although it does not have to match the entry. Building blocks for the same type of document, such as an Annual Report, can be grouped together by naming the building block with the same starting text (for instance, Annual Report table, Annual Report cover page, etc.).
- **Gallery:** Click the arrow and select the gallery in which to store the building block. The building block can be added to an existing gallery (such as Cover Page, Header, or Table). Or, if it is not related to an existing gallery (such as a logo), then it can be added to the Quick Parts gallery.
- **Category:** Select the General category or create your own category to identify your company, department, or project so the building blocks stay grouped together.
- **Description:** Type a short description of the building block. This displays as an Enhanced ScreenTip if that option is selected.
- **Save in:** Select the name of the template as the storage location. Building Blocks can only be saved in templates. A building block is saved in Building Blocks.dotx, Normal.dotm, any other available template, or a document template you create. To share building blocks, save them in a separate template that can be distributed to others.
- **Options:** Choose one of the following three options:
  - Insert content (for equations or logos).
  - Insert content in its own paragraph (good for tables, paragraphs, and headings).
  - Insert content in its own page (places a page break before and after the building block, which is good for a table of contents, cover page, or large tables).

After you add an item to the Quick Parts gallery, you can insert it into any document. For instance, instead of creating the common header from scratch or typing the same block of text each time you need it, you can insert the building block with the same content from the Building Blocks Organizer.

Prior to inserting a building block into a document, place the insertion point where you want to insert the building block, and click Quick Parts in the Text group on the Insert tab. You can either select AutoText and select the specific AutoText entry or select Building Blocks Organizer (refer to Figure 6.6). Alternatively, you can also access any building block in its own gallery, such as Cover Page, on the Insert tab and Table of Contents on the References tab. To review the list of building blocks quickly, you can sort the Quick Parts alphabetically by name, scroll down the list to select the specific Quick Parts item that you want, and then click Insert to use the selected object.

> **TIP: INSERTING A BUILDING BLOCK**
> If you remember the unique name that you assigned to the Quick Parts item, you can quickly insert the building block by typing the unique name and pressing F3 to insert the building block into the document.

1. Explain the advantages of using a predefined template. ***p. 364***
2. Describe the benefits of using a building block. ***p. 367***
3. Explain why you would use the Building Blocks Organizer. ***p. 368***

Hands-On Exercises

MyLab IT HOE1 Sim Training

Watch the Video for this Hands-On Exercise!

Skills covered: Select and Download a Template • Save a Document as a Template • Create and Insert a Custom Building Block

1 Automate Document Creation

After Alexandra Caselman assembles a quote for the cost of training, she then wants you to include the instructor's resume. She also wants you to create a sheet of references—people who have used the services of Computer Training Concepts, Inc. Alexandra wants each resume and reference sheet to have a similar look, so you decide to use templates and building blocks instead of starting with blank documents each time.

STEP 1 SELECT AND DOWNLOAD A TEMPLATE

You recently found the selection of resume templates that comes with Word and learned that you can search for more templates online at Office.com. You decide to select one style and fill in the information for the trainer whom Alexandra will send to the next job. Refer to Figure 6.8 as you complete Step 1.

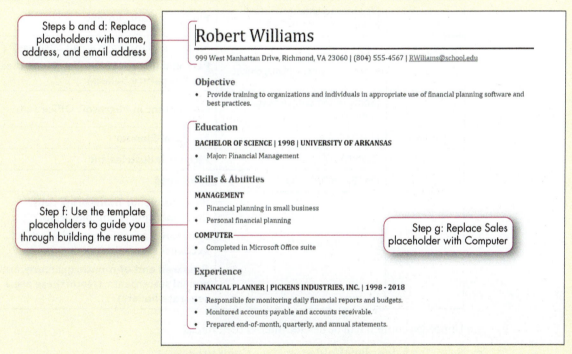

FIGURE 6.8 Select and Use a Resume Template

a. Start Word. Click **New**.

   The New tab displays a list of available templates.

b. Type **resume** in the *Search for online templates* box and press **Enter**. In the New pane, scroll down to locate and click the **Functional resume** template. Click **Create**.

   A download window displays briefly and the Functional resume template opens as a new document. The Resume Assistant pane may display. This feature is used to help gather information as you write your resume. For now, close the Resume Assistant pane. To access the Resume Assistant again, click Resume Assistant in the Resume group on the Review tab.

c. Select **Your Name** at the top of the document and type **Robert Williams**.

   The resume is for the trainer taking on the next job, Robert Williams.

d. Save the document as **w06h1ResumeRW_LastFirst**. Confirm the *Save as type* box displays Word Document. Click **Save**.

You save the file with your last name and first name; the RW initials indicate that the resume is for Robert Williams.

e. Replace the Address, City, ST ZIP Code placeholders with **999 West Manhattan Drive, Richmond, VA 23060**. Replace the phone number placeholder with **(804) 555-4567** and the email address placeholder with **RWilliams@school.edu**, and press **Space** after the email address.

f. Select the appropriate placeholder and type the following information in the resume for each category:

Category	Placeholder	Type the following information
Objective	[Check out the quick . . . .]	Provide training to organizations and individuals in appropriate use of financial planning software and best practices.
Education	DEGREE	Bachelor of Science
	DATE EARNED	1998
	SCHOOL	University of Arkansas
	[Tap here to enter text] after Major:	Financial Management
Skills & Abilities	[Think a document that looks . . . .] under Management	Financial planning in small business / Personal financial planning (Note: these are 2 separate bullets)
	[Some of the sample text . . .] under Sales	Competent in Microsoft Office suite
Experience	JOB TITLE	Financial Planner
	COMPANY	Pickens Industries, Inc.
	DATES FROM - TO	1998-2018
	[This is the place for a brief . . . .]	Responsible for monitoring daily financial reports and budgets. / Monitored accounts payable and accounts receivable. / Prepared end-of-month, quarterly, and annual statements. (Note: these are 3 separate bullets)

Unneeded content will be deleted later in the exercise.

g. Select the **Sales placeholder** and type **Computer**.

You are replacing the heading to more closely align with Robert's skills.

h. Select the **[Minor: Tap here to enter text] placeholders** below *Major: Financial Management*, right-click, and then select **Remove Content Control**. Also delete the colon and the bullet point.

i. Select and delete all the placeholders, colons, and bullet points that you did not use (refer to Figure 6.8).

j. Save and close the document. Keep Word open for the next step.

STEP 2 SAVE A DOCUMENT AS A TEMPLATE

The next step in compiling the proposal for a potential client is to generate a list of references. This information changes often, so you want to use a template that you can update quickly. Refer to Figure 6.9 as you complete Step 2.

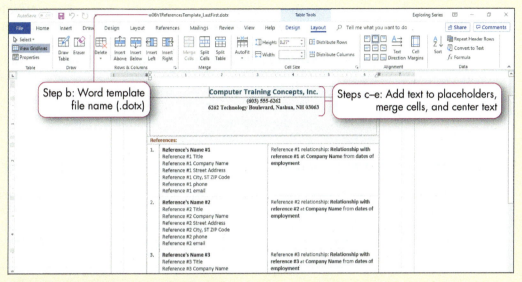

FIGURE 6.9 Save a Document as a Template

a. Click the **File tab** and click **New**. Type **references** in the *Search for online templates* box and press **Enter**. Scroll down and click the **Functional resume reference sheet template**. Click **Create**. Close Resume Assistant if it opens automatically for you.

The Functional resume reference sheet template displays with placeholders and sample text.

> **MAC TROUBLESHOOTING:** Click the File menu and select New from Template.

b. Click the **File tab**, click **Save as**, and then click **Browse**. Click the **Save as type arrow** and select **Word Template** or **Word Template (*.dotx)**. Navigate to the folder where you save your student files, name the document as **w06h1ReferencesTemplate_LastFirst**, and then click **Save**.

Word automatically saves the template to the default Custom Office Templates subfolder in the Documents folder. You want to save it to your own folder so that you can have access to it from any computer. When you save this document as a template, you can open it later and make modifications without changing the original template.

> **MAC TROUBLESHOOTING:** Click the File menu. Select Save as Template. Save the document as w06h1ReferencesTemplate_LastFirst. Click Save.

> **TROUBLESHOOTING:** If you did not change the location, the file will be saved to the Custom Office Templates. Repeat this step to resave the template to the correct location.

> **TROUBLESHOOTING:** If your table gridlines are not visible, you can turn them on by clicking View Gridlines in the Table group on the Table Tools Layout tab.

c. Replace the placeholders at the top of the page:

[Your Name]	**Computer Training Concepts, Inc.** (Include the period.)
[Phone]	**(603) 555-6262**
[Street Address]	**6262 Technology Boulevard**
[City, ST ZIP Code]	**Nashua, NH 03063**

Hands-On Exercise 1   373

d. Select and remove the **[E-Mail]** and **[Website] placeholders** by removing the content controls.

e. Place the insertion point to the left of the phone number until a right-pointing arrow displays. Click to select the row. Click the **Table Tools Layout tab** and click **Merge Cells** in the Merge group. Change the font to **Times New Roman** and change the alignment to **Center**. Select and center the text **Computer Training Concepts, Inc.**

> **TROUBLESHOOTING:** If the Merge Cells command is not available, you may have selected the text and not the cells. Ensure that you select the entire row of the table containing the phone number and address.

f. Save the template.

STEP 3: CREATE AND INSERT A CUSTOM BUILDING BLOCK

Because you also insert the company letterhead frequently, you decide to save that information as a custom building block, which can be inserted with only a few keystrokes instead of retyping the information each time. After the template is set up, you can add the information about companies that will be used as references in this proposal. After adding the references, you save the file as a document instead of a template. Refer to Figure 6.10 as you complete Step 3.

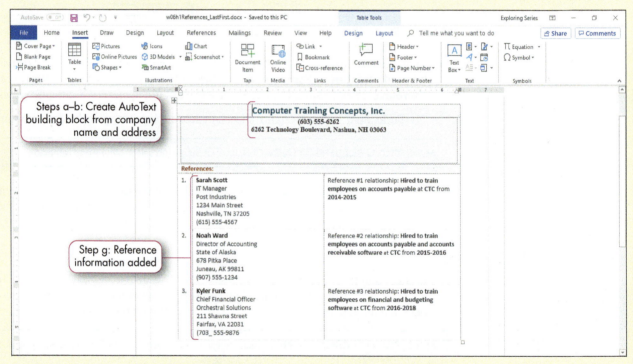

FIGURE 6.10 Create a Custom Building Block

a. Select the content on both rows at the top of the page. Click the **Insert tab**, click **Quick Parts** in the Text group, and then select **Save Selection to Quick Part Gallery**.

> **MAC TROUBLESHOOTING:** Select the content on both rows. Click the Insert menu, point to AutoText, and then click New. Type CTC in the Name box and click OK.

b. Complete the following steps within the Create New Building Block dialog box:
- Type **CTC** in the Name box.
- Click the **Gallery arrow** and select **AutoText**.
- Click the **Save in arrow** and select **Building Blocks.dotx**. Click **OK**.

The building block is added to the Building Blocks template and will be available for use in all documents.

c. Select the two rows containing the company name, phone, and address and press **Delete**. Select the two rows again. Click **Quick Parts** in the Text group, point at AutoText, and then select **CTC** at the top of the gallery list.

You test the building block by deleting the content and inserting the newly created building block from Quick Parts. The CTC building block displays the text exactly the way you formatted it. Now you can use this building block in other documents you design for the company.

> **MAC TROUBLESHOOTING:** After deleting the company name, phone, and address, click the Insert menu, point to AutoText, and then click CTC.

d. Save the template.

e. Click and select the two rows for Reference's Name #4 and #5, right-click, and select **Delete Rows**.

The references are listed in a table. Because you will include only three references, you will delete both rows containing the content for Reference #4 and Reference #5.

f. Remove the email placeholders for the remaining three references because they are not used. Press **backspace** to remove the blank row.

g. Type the following information into the corresponding reference placeholders:

[Reference's Name #1]	**Sarah Scott**
[Reference #1 Title]	**IT Manager**
[Reference #1 Company Name]	**Post Industries**
[Reference #1 Street Address]	**1234 Main Street**
[Reference #1 City, ST Zip Code]	**Nashville, TN 37205**
[Reference #1 Phone]	**(615) 555-4567**
[Reference #1 Relationship:]	**Hired to train employees on accounts payable software at CTC from 2014-2015**
[Reference's Name #2]	**Noah Ward**
[Reference #2 Title]	**Director of Accounting**
[Reference #2 Company Name]	**State of Alaska**
[Reference #2 Street Address]	**678 Pitka Place**
[Reference #2 City, ST Zip Code]	**Juneau, AK 99811**
[Reference #2 Phone]	**(907) 555-1234**
[Reference #2 Relationship:]	**Hired to train employees on accounts payable and accounts receivable software at CTC from 2015-2016**
[Reference's Name #3]	**Kyler Funk**
[Reference #3 Title]	**Chief Financial Officer**
[Reference #3 Company Name]	**Orchestral Solutions**
[Reference #3 Street Address]	**211 Shawna Street**
[Reference #3 City, ST Zip Code]	**Fairfax, VA 22031**
[Reference #3 Phone]	**(703) 555-9876**
[Reference #3 Relationship:]	**Hired to train employees on financial and budgeting software at CTC from 2016-2018**

h. Click the **File tab** and click **Save As**. Click the **Save as type arrow** and select **Word Document**. Type **w06h1References_LastFirst** (remove the word Template from the file name) in the File name box and click **Save** to save the document.

Because you have added specific references, you save the template as a Word document (.docx).

i. Close the document. Leave Word open if you plan to continue with the next Hands-On Exercise.

Multiple Documents

One feature in Word enables you to work with multiple versions of the same document simultaneously—you can view multiple documents at one time as well as combine them into one. By using this feature, you can combine information from several versions of the same document into one document more efficiently.

In this section, you will view multiple documents side by side, as well as compare and combine them. You will create a master document that contains subdocuments and use tools to navigate within lengthy documents. Finally, you will create a bookmark for a location in a document and use the Go To feature to find that marker.

STEP 1 Viewing Two Documents Side by Side

The ***View Side by Side*** feature enables you to display two versions of the same document on the same screen. This feature is useful when you want to compare an original to a revised document or when you want to cut or copy content from one document and paste it to another. When the documents display side by side, synchronous scrolling is active by default. ***Synchronous scrolling*** enables you to scroll through both documents at the same time using either of the two scroll bars. If you want to scroll through each document independently, click Synchronous Scrolling on the View tab to toggle it off, and use the respective scroll bars to navigate through each document.

To view two documents side by side, you must have both documents open. The View Side by Side command is grayed out if only one document is open. When the documents are open, click View Side by Side in the Window group on the View tab; the Word window splits to display each document, as shown in Figure 6.11. If you have more than two documents open, when you click View Side by Side, the Compare Side by Side dialog box displays so you can select which document you want to display beside the active document.

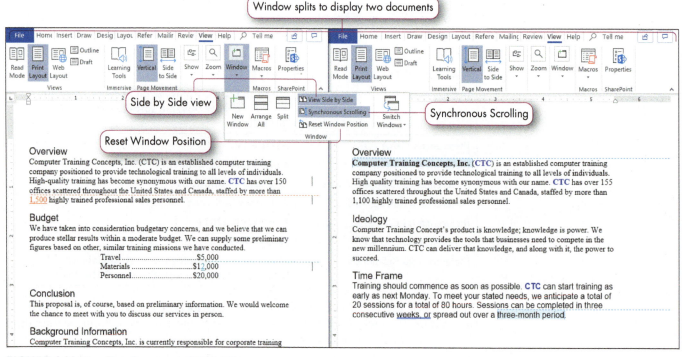

FIGURE 6.11 View Two Documents Side by Side

While in Side by Side view, you can resize and reposition the two document windows so that they share the screen equally. To reset the two document windows to the original side-by-side viewing size, click Reset Window Position on the View tab. To close Side by Side view, click View Side by Side to toggle it off. The document that contains the insertion point when you close Side by Side view will display as the active document.

> **MAC TIP:** View Side by Side and Synchronous Scrolling are not available in Word for Mac. Currently, there are no alternatives or work-arounds for this feature.

Merging Documents

Besides enabling you to view two documents simultaneously, Word also provides different ways to combine multiple documents into one. The method you use depends on the reason you are combining the documents. You might simply want to combine two documents, deciding which portions of each to keep or omit. You might need to add the entire contents of one document into another, or you might want to include the entire contents of several documents in one.

Sometimes, it is necessary to have several people edit their own copy of the document simultaneously before they return it to you. When this occurs, you have several similar documents but with individual changes. Instead of compiling results from printed copies or viewing each one in Side by Side view to determine the differences, you can use the Compare and/or Combine features.

Compare Two Documents

Legal blacklining is a way to compare two documents and to display the changes between the two documents. Legal blacklining enables attorneys to compare versions of documents or contracts, authors and editors to track progress of a manuscript, and financial managers to review changes in large tables. The **Compare** feature automatically evaluates the contents of two versions of a document side by side for a line-by-line comparison and displays a merged version with markup and tracked changes showing the differences between them. The Compare Documents dialog box contains a variety of options you can invoke; however, options display only after clicking the More button—Figure 6.12 is showing the options for the More setting. The options you are most likely to change are in the *Show changes in* section, in which you determine where the combined documents display—in the original document, the revised document, or a new document. You can also display the original and revised documents side by side with the changes in a new document as shown in Figure 6.13.

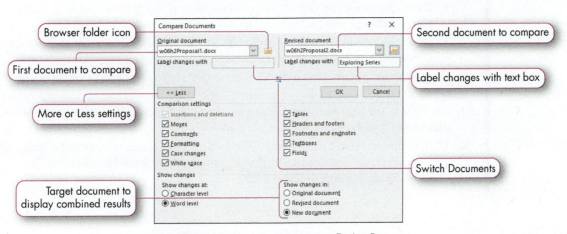

FIGURE 6.12 Compare Documents Dialog Box

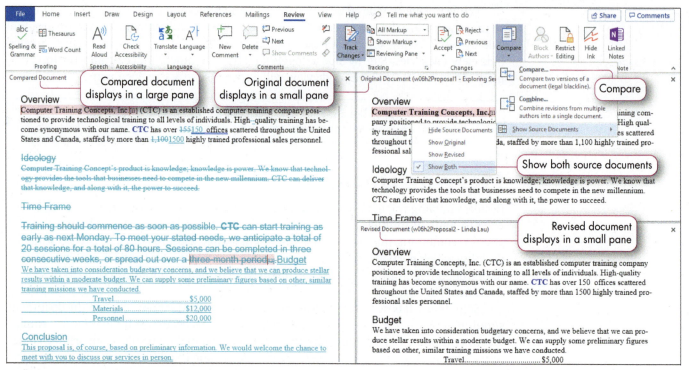

FIGURE 6.13 Result of Comparing Two Documents

> **To compare two documents, complete the following steps:**
>
> 1. Click the Review tab.
> 2. Click Compare in the Compare group and select Compare to display the Compare Documents dialog box (refer to Figure 6.12).
> 3. Click the Original document arrow or the Browse folder icon to navigate to the first document that you want to compare.
> 4. Click the Revised document arrow or Browse folder icon to navigate to the second document that you want to compare.
> 5. Click More to display more options for the following:
>   - Comparison settings: These settings include moves, comments, formatting, case changes, white space, tables, headers and footers, footnotes and endnotes, textboxes, and fields. Deselect the check boxes for any settings that you want to omit.
>   - Show changes at: By default, all revisions are marked at the Word level. However, you can change this to Character level if you prefer.
>   - Show changes in: You can choose to display the combined changes in the Original document, the Revised document, or a New document.
> 6. Click New document below *Show Changes in* to place the result of the comparison into a new document. Click OK.
> 7. Click Yes in the Microsoft Word dialog box about the documents containing tracked changes to continue with the comparison.
> 8. Click Compare in the Compare group and select Show Source Documents. You have four options regarding the two source documents: Hide Source Documents, Show Original, Show Revised, or Show Both.

STEP 2 **Combine Two Documents**

After you compare the content of the two documents and display the result of the comparison in a separate document, you can see the differences between the two documents. However, if you want to go a step farther than just viewing the differences, you can use the ***Combine*** feature to integrate all changes from multiple authors or documents into one single document. Similar to comparing documents, the Combine Documents dialog box contains the same set of options. If you do not want to modify the original documents, you should combine the changes into a new document.

To combine two documents, complete the following steps:

1. Start Word and open a blank document.
2. Click the Review tab.
3. Click Compare in the Compare group.
4. Select Combine to display the Combine Documents dialog box.
5. Click the Original document arrow or the Browse folder icon to navigate to the first document that you want to combine.
6. Click the Revised document arrow or Browse folder icon to navigate to the second document that you want to combine.
7. Click More to display more options for the following:
   - Comparison settings: These settings include moves, comments, formatting, case changes, white space, tables, headers and footers, footnotes and endnotes, textboxes, and fields. Uncheck the check boxes for any settings that you want to omit.
   - Show changes at: By default, all revisions are marked at the Word level. However, you can change this to Character level if you prefer.
   - Show changes in: You can choose to display the combined changes in the Original document, the Revised document, or a New document.
8. Click New document below *Show Changes in* to place the result of the comparison into a new document. Click OK.
9. Click anywhere in the left panel box to activate the Revisions pane.
10. Close the Revisions pane.
11. Click Compare in the Compare group and select Show Source Documents. You have four options regarding the two source documents: Hide Source Documents, Show Original, Show Revised, or Show Both.

TIP: SWITCH DOCUMENTS AND LABEL CHANGES WITH SETTING
When comparing or combining two documents, it does not matter which document you choose to be the original or revised because you can always change the order later by using Switch Documents on the Compare Documents or Combine Documents dialog box. Notice that the *Label changes with* setting listed the author's name. If you want to change the username, you can type a new name in the *Label changes with* text box.

Insert a File as an Object

There are many ways to insert content into a file. In Chapter 1, you learned how to reuse text from another document using Text from File in the Object command on the Insert tab. You can also add the content of one file as an object to another document by using the Object command. This feature does not work on PDFs containing text that was created as an image. However, the majority of forms and other PDFs that you would want to type on will be supported. The Create from File tab in the Object dialog box lists the following two options (see Figure 6.14): (1) the Link to file option inserts the content of the file into your document and also creates a shortcut to the source file; and (2) the Display as icon option inserts an icon that represents the content of the file. If both options are selected, Word inserts an icon that represents the content of the file and also updates your document if changes were made to the source file. If neither of the two options are selected, you can still edit the contents of the object later using the application that created the source file.

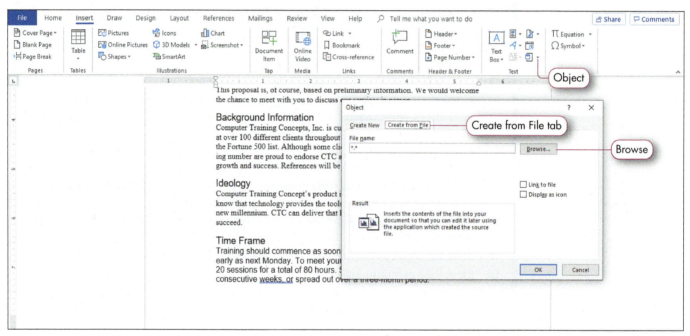

FIGURE 6.14 Insert Content from Another Document into the Current Document

STEP 3   Create a Master Document and Subdocuments

Working with long documents can be cumbersome. You may notice your computer slows down when you are working in a lengthy document—scrolling, finding and replacing, editing, and formatting may take longer to process, especially if the document contains many large images. To improve this situation, you can create a ***master document***, a document that acts like a binder for managing smaller documents. A smaller document that is a part of a master document is called a ***subdocument***. You can create a master document to hold the chapters of a book, where each chapter is stored as a subdocument. You also can use a master document to organize and store multiple documents created by others, such as a group project where each member of the group is responsible for a specific section of the document. You can edit and work with several subdocuments individually and more efficiently without having to even open the master document. Multiple authors can also work on various subdocuments simultaneously.

After you create the master document and insert all the subdocuments into the appropriate locations in the master document, you can insert page numbers into the master document so that the numbers run consecutively from one subdocument to the next. You can navigate quickly to any location within multiple subdocuments, reorganize multiple subdocuments simply by moving headings, display recent changes to multiple subdocuments in one document, and sort or arrange the subdocuments by author or by section. In the master document, you can also create a table of contents, indexes, or cross-references that reflect the entries in all of the subdocuments. Also, within the master document, you can insert any building block you like, such as a page title, company contact information, a masthead, or a page heading. Finally, you can print all the subdocuments directly from the master document.

To create the master document, click Outline in the Views group on the View tab to display the Outlining tab. The Outlining tab contains Show Document and Collapse or Expand Subdocuments in the Master Document group, as well as other tools that enable you to create, add, and arrange subdocuments. After you create the subdocuments, the link or path to the location where the subdocument is stored displays in the master document. You can use the tools in the Outline Tools group to create, promote, and demote headings; expand and collapse body text; and work with subdocuments. Figure 6.15 displays a master document with three subdocuments that are collapsed. In comparison, Figure 6.16 displays the same master document with the three subdocuments expanded. The collapsed structure enables you to see at a glance the subdocuments that contained in the master document as well as the location of where these subdocuments are stored. You can insert additional subdocuments or remove existing subdocuments from the master document. Deleting a subdocument from within a master document does not delete the actual subdocument file. However, if you move or rename the subdocument from the original location, the content no longer displays in the master document.

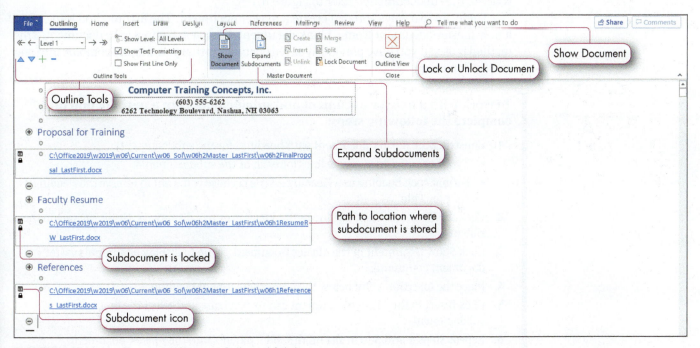

FIGURE 6.15 Master Document Showing Collapsed Subdocuments

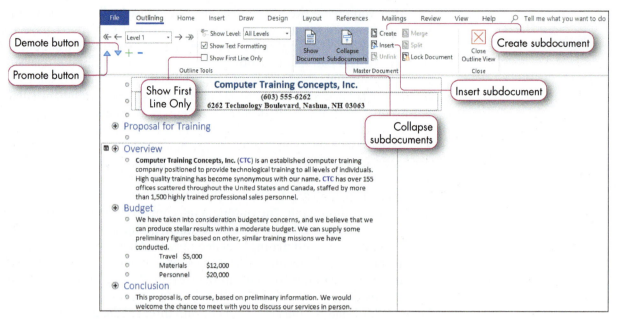

FIGURE 6.16 Master Document Showing Expanded Subdocuments

Word uses the built-in heading styles to create the subdocuments in the master document. For instance, you can choose to reserve Heading 1 in the Styles group for the title of the entire document and keep that text as part of the master document, and then use Heading 2 to start a new subdocument. The Promote and Demote buttons in the Outline Tools group on the Outlining tab can also automatically apply the built-in heading styles to the subdocuments (refer to Figure 6.16).

There are two ways you can create a master document. The first method is to create a new master document from a blank document when you begin a long document. This method is used if you have previously saved documents that you want to combine into one master document.

To work with a master document and subdocuments in a new document, complete the following steps:

1. Construct the master document with headings for the subdocuments:
   - Type headings on separate lines for each of the subdocuments.
   - Format each heading as a Heading 2 style because you want to reserve the Heading 1 style for Title.
2. Click the View tab. Click Outline in the Views group to display the Outlining tab on the ribbon.
3. Click Show Document in the Master Document group to display additional master document commands.
4. Place the insertion point below the first subdocument heading.
5. Click Insert in the Master Document group. Navigate and select the first subdocument.
6. Repeat Steps 4 and 5 to insert more subdocuments into the master document.
7. Click Collapse Subdocuments in the Master Document group to collapse the subdocuments in the master document and to display the name and path of each saved subdocument.
8. Save the master document and click Close Outline view in the Close group on the Outlining tab.

The second method to create a master document is to convert an existing document into a master document and add the appropriate headings and styles to the master document. This method creates a subdocument from each of the identified sections.

To work with a master document and subdocuments in an existing document, complete the following steps:

1. Format each heading as a Heading 2 style because you want to reserve the Heading 1 style for Title.
2. Click the View tab. Click Outline in the Views group to display the Outlining tab on the ribbon.
3. Click Show Document in the Master Document group to display additional master document commands.
4. Click Create in the Master Document group to display the individual subdocuments that were created for the selected headings.
5. Place the insertion point below the first subdocument heading.
6. Click Insert in the Master Document group. Navigate and select the first subdocument.
7. Repeat Steps 5 and 6 to insert more subdocuments into the master document.
8. Click Collapse Subdocuments in the Master Document group to collapse the subdocuments in the master document and to display the name and path of each saved subdocument.
9. Save changes to the master document and close Outline view.

Modify the Master Document and Subdocuments

Expanding the master document enables you to view and edit the contents of the subdocuments. You can make changes to the master document at any time. However, you can make changes to the subdocuments only when the subdocument is unlocked. You can lock the subdocuments to prevent changes to their content and also to prevent the subdocuments from being deleted from the master document. You have to place locks to each subdocument individually. Look carefully at the collapsed subdocuments in Figure 6.15. A padlock displays on the left of the collapsed subdocuments.

To lock or unlock a subdocument, complete the following steps:

1. Click Show Document on the Outlining tab and click Expand Subdocuments in the Master Document group.
2. Click anywhere in the subdocument that you want to lock or unlock.
3. Click Lock Document in the Master Document group. A padlock icon displays below the subdocument icon.
4. Click Lock Document in the Master Document group to toggle and unlock the subdocument.

You can make changes to a subdocument by expanding (and unlocking) the subdocument within a master document (refer to Figure 6.16). Another alternative is to open the subdocument as an independent document within Word. You can edit a master document either in Master Document view or Normal view. It is easier to use the Master Document view to review or revise the structure of a long document or to open specific subdocuments in the master document because you can see an outline of the current document and can easily open any subdocument. The Normal view enables you to work on the master document as a single long document. When the master document is opened in Normal view, the subdocuments are contained within section breaks, and you can see the properties and types of breaks with which you are working.

> **TIP: PRINTING A MASTER DOCUMENT**
> If you click Print when a master document is displayed and the subdocuments are collapsed, the message *Do you want to open the subdocuments before continuing with this command?* displays. Click Yes to open the subdocuments so that they will print as one long document. Click No to print the master document that lists the subdocument file names as they display on the screen.

In situations where there is no purpose to maintain the link between the master document and its subdocuments, you can unlink the subdocuments to convert them into regular text in the master document and also to remove the links between the master and subdocuments. Once the documents are unlinked, changes made in one document will not be reflected in the other. In Outline view with the subdocuments expanded, place the insertion point anywhere inside the subdocument that you want to unlink and click Unlink in the Master Document group on the Outlining tab. It is important to note that the unlink action cannot be undone.

Use the Master Document and Subdocuments with Extreme Care

If you use the Master Document feature, there are some necessary precautions to keep in mind to avoid major problems:

- Back up the original files before creating the master document.
- The newly created master document must be stored in the same directory as all the subdocuments.
- If you move or rename a subdocument separately after you create the master document, you will break the link in the master document. You can only restore the link by deleting and re-creating the link in the master document with the new file name.
- If you want to move the master document and subdocuments to a new location, you must first open the master document, and then save all the subdocuments to the new location.
- When you make changes to the links in the master document, you must delete all old subdocument files to avoid version confusion.
- Do not attempt to re-create the master document. If you do, you should delete all the files previously created and used in your last attempt to create the master document.

Using Navigational Tools

Not every document has a table of contents. And especially for long documents, it can be quite cumbersome to scroll through a document to find an exact location. You already know how to use the Find and Go To features in Word to locate and navigate to specific content in a document. There are other navigational tools in Word to assist in locating content quickly and easily.

STEP 4 Use the Navigation Pane

When you use the Find command, the Navigation Pane opens and shows the results of your search. The **Navigation Pane** is a tool that is used to navigate through a document by viewing headings, viewing pages, and browsing search results. You can open and close the Navigation Pane by selecting or unselecting the Navigation Pane check box on the View tab. You can also close the Navigation Pane by clicking the X at the top right corner of the pane. When displayed, the Navigation Pane contains three tabs: Headings, Pages, and Results.

There are two ways that you can use the Navigation Pane to navigate in a document:

- If a document is formatted with headings and you want to display the headings in a document, be sure the document is expanded to display the text of the whole document. The Navigation Pane displays headings only for documents that use the styles feature to format headings. The best way to format headings is to apply the built-in title or heading styles from the Styles group on the Home tab. When you are working with long documents, this view enables you to navigate quickly to a particular topic, as shown in Figure 6.17.

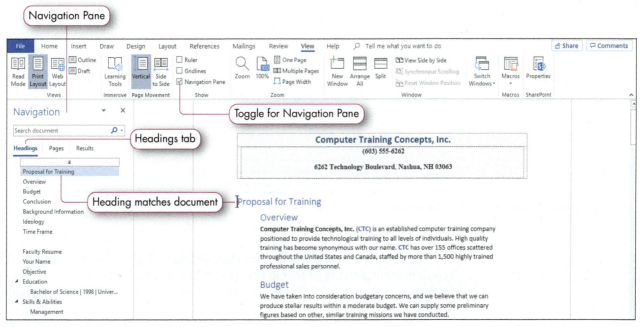

FIGURE 6.17 Browse a Document by Headings

- Alternatively, if your document does not have headings, or if it is easier to navigate with visuals of the document, click Pages in the Navigation Pane to display thumbnails of each page in your document. As with the headings, you can click a thumbnail to move the insertion point to the top of that page. Even though you cannot read the text on a thumbnail, you can see the layout of a page well enough to determine if it is the location you want to navigate to (see Figure 6.18). If you display revision marks and comments, the marks and comment balloons also display in the thumbnails. In addition to searching for text, you can use the search box to locate much more content, including graphics, tables, and comments.

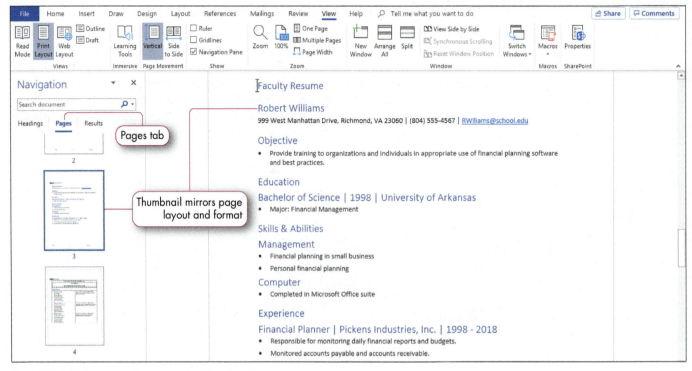

FIGURE 6.18 Browse a Document by Thumbnails

The third tab in the Navigation Pane displays the results of a search. When you type a word or a string of text in the Navigation search box, each occurrence displays, as shown in Figure 6.19. You can click the occurrence, and the text is highlighted in the document.

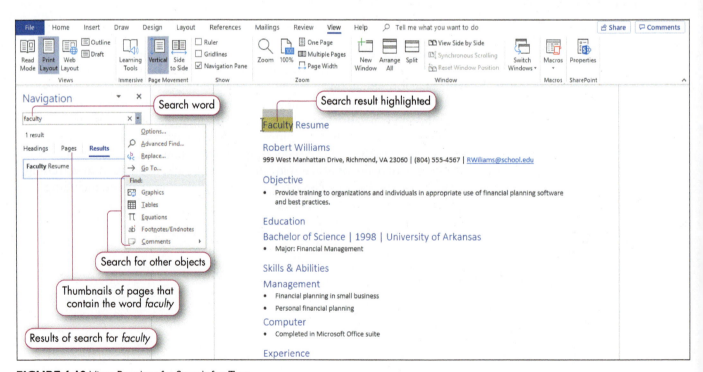

FIGURE 6.19 View Results of a Search for Text

386   **CHAPTER 6** • Time-Saving Tools

> **MAC TIP: NAVIGATION PANE** The Navigation Pane displays four options. Thumbnails Pane is similar to Pages, Document Map is similar to Headings, and Reviewing Pane is similar to Results. Find and Replace is similar to using the search box in the Navigation page.

Create Bookmarks

When you read a book, you use a bookmark to help you return quickly to the location where you left off. Word provides the ***bookmark*** feature as an electronic marker for a specific location in a document, enabling you to find that location quickly. You may also use bookmarks to create hyperlinks to specific places in a document.

Bookmarks are helpful to mark a location while you are working. You can scroll to other parts of a document, then quickly go back to the bookmarked location. It is common to bookmark headings, but bookmarks are also useful to mark parts of a document where a heading normally would not be applied. You can bookmark anything, including a paragraph, an image such as picture, an embedded chart, a table, an audio clip, or a video file. Bookmarks are inserted at the location of the insertion point. Creating a bookmark is necessary if you want to create a hyperlink to another location in a document.

> **To create a bookmark, complete the following steps:**
>
> 1. Put the insertion point in front of the word, phrase, or object (picture, table, or chart) that you want to add the bookmark. Note: If you want to bookmark a whole paragraph or a picture, select the whole paragraph or the object.
> 2. Click the Insert tab.
> 3. Click Bookmark in the Links group to display the Bookmark dialog box.
> 4. Type the word—or phrase (using an underscore between words)—that you want to use for the bookmark name and click Add. Repeat the preceding steps to add additional bookmarks.

You can sort the bookmarks according to the bookmark name (in alphabetical order) or the bookmark location in the document. You may also delete any unwanted bookmarks by selecting the unwanted bookmark and clicking Delete in the Bookmark dialog box (see Figure 6.20).

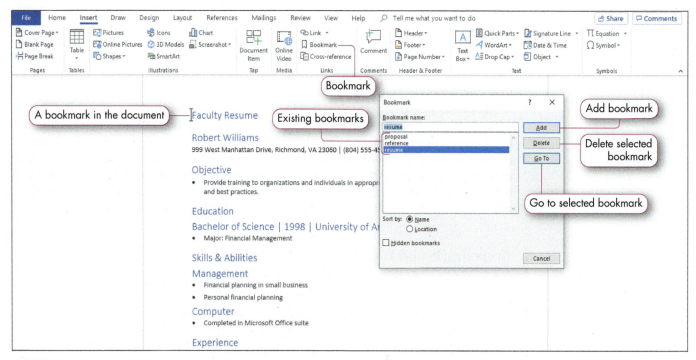

FIGURE 6.20 Bookmark a Location in the Document

> **TIP: USING NUMBERS IN BOOKMARK NAMES**
> You can use numbers within bookmark names, such as Quarter1. However, you cannot start a bookmark name with a number or use spaces in the bookmark name.

At any time after creating bookmarks, you can review the list of bookmarks and navigate to any of the bookmarked content. Use Bookmark in the Links group on the Insert tab to open the Bookmark dialog box. After selecting a bookmark in the Bookmark name list, click Go To to move the insertion point to the bookmarked location. Alternatively, you may navigate to a bookmark by pressing Ctrl+G to open the Go To tab of the Find and Replace dialog box. After selecting Bookmark in the *Go to what* section, click the *Enter bookmark name* arrow to select the bookmark that you want to view. You can then go to the bookmarked location by clicking Go To.

4. Contrast the process of comparing and combining as related to Word documents. **p. 379**
5. Explain why you would create a master document and several subdocuments. **p. 380**
6. Explain the purpose of creating a bookmark in a document. **p. 387**

Hands-On Exercises

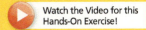

MyLab IT HOE2 Sim Training

Watch the Video for this Hands-On Exercise!

Skills covered: View Two Documents Side by Side • Combine Two Documents • Insert a File as an Object • Create a Master Document and Subdocuments • Use the Navigation Pane • Create Bookmarks

2 Multiple Documents

When setting up a prospective job proposal, Alexandra collects information about the company, the trainers who might work with the clients, and references from previous clients. After collecting this information, she forwards it to you to combine into one or more different documents. The final proposal is created from several files, and it is time-consuming to add page numbers to each one so that it looks like they all came from a single document. You use the master document feature to make this task easier.

STEP 1 VIEW TWO DOCUMENTS SIDE BY SIDE

Alexandra forwarded to you the documents that contain the information that should be included in the multipage proposal. Before you start the process of combining information, you decide to view the documents side by side so that you can identify any overlap in the content. Refer to Figure 6.21 as you complete Step 1.

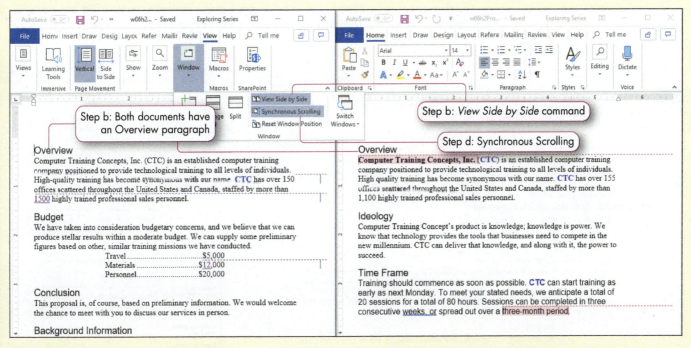

FIGURE 6.21 View Documents Side by Side

a. Start Word if you closed it at the end of Hands-On Exercise 1. Open the files *w06h2Proposal1* and *w06h2Proposal2* (in that order).

b. Click the **View tab** and click **View Side by Side** in the Window group.

> **MAC TROUBLESHOOTING:** View Side by Side is not available in Word for Mac.

Two windows display, containing the contents of each file. Both documents contain an Overview paragraph, otherwise they have different content, and the formatting is different too. Because w06h2Proposal2 is the last document that you open, it will become the active window. In the Window group of the active window, when you click Window, you see Synchronous Scrolling highlighted to indicate the setting is on. As you scroll in one document, the other will also scroll.

Hands-On Exercise 2   389

> **TROUBLESHOOTING:** If your view of one or both of the documents is insufficient, you can resize the window. Drag the border of the window until you reach an acceptable size to view the document information.

c. Click the active document and click the arrow at the bottom of the scroll bar several times to scroll to the bottom of the page.

Both documents scroll down at the same time, and you can view the footer of each document.

d. Click **Synchronous Scrolling** in the Window group in the active document to turn the toggle off.

Notice that Synchronous Scrolling is no longer highlighted. Now you can scroll through each document individually.

e. Close both documents without saving.

STEP 2 · COMBINE TWO DOCUMENTS AND INSERT A FILE AS AN OBJECT

Now that you know the two files you just viewed are not identical, you decide to use the Combine feature to pull all content into one document. You then make some minor formatting changes, insert the entire contents of another document, and save the file so that it is ready to accompany the other documents in the proposal. Refer to Figure 6.22 as you complete Step 2.

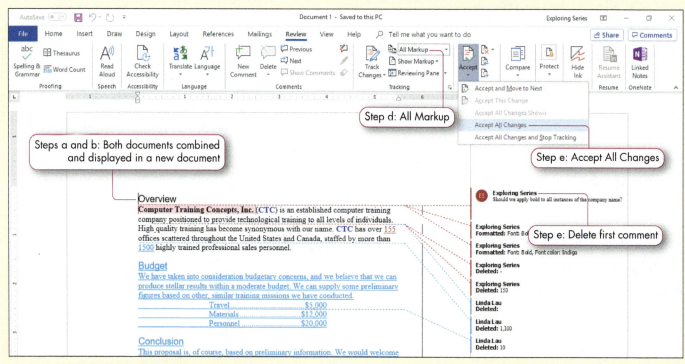

FIGURE 6.22 Combine Two Documents into One

a. Open a blank document. Combine the two documents you viewed in the last step by completing the following steps:

- Click the **Review tab**, click **Compare** in the Compare group, and then select **Combine** to display the Combine Documents dialog box.
- Click the **Browse folder icon** next to the Original document arrow, navigate to *w06h2Proposal1*, and then click **Open**.

- Click the **Browse folder icon** next to the Revised document arrow, navigate to *w06h2Proposal2*, and then click **Open**.
- Click **More** unless the Combine Document dialog box is already expanded and Less displays and ensure that **New document** below *Show changes in* is selected. Click **OK**.
- Click **Continue with Merge** in the Microsoft Word dialog box to accept the formatting changes from the w06h2Proposal1 file.

The combined document can only have one format. Because the two documents have different formats, you want to keep the formatting changes from the w06h2Proposal1 file. A new document (Combined Result1) displays with the Revisions pane open.

b. Click **Compare** in the Compare group on the Review tab if the two documents you just merged display in small windows on the right of the screen, point to **Show Source Documents**, and then select **Hide Source Documents** to close them. Click the **X** on the top right corner of the Revisions pane on the left to close it. Compare your screen to Figure 6.22.

The combined document now opens in a bigger window and displays all the changes and comments in the two documents. The two documents you just merged are now hidden on the screen.

> **TROUBLESHOOTING:** If the paragraphs in the document do not display in the same order as those in Figure 6.22, close the document and begin the process again. Make sure you select w06h2Proposal1 as the original document.

c. Ensure that **Simple Markup** in the Tracking group is selected.

The document in this view includes information from both files and is what you need to present to the customers. The document also contains markup balloons to indicate each difference in the two documents. Depending on your Track Changes settings, the balloons might display on either the left or right side of your document.

d. Click the **Display for Review arrow** in the Tracking group and select **All Markup**.

Notice the level of detail in the markup balloons increases when you switch between Simple Markup and All Markup. After some minor edits, the document will be ready for use.

e. Click the **Accept arrow** in the Changes group and select **Accept All Changes**. Place the insertion point in the first comment, click the **Delete arrow** in the Comments group, and then select **Delete All Comments in Document**.

All of the changes were accepted and the comments removed because everything looked good and now you are finalizing the document.

f. Press **Ctrl+End** and press **Enter** twice. Click the **Insert tab**, click **Object** in the Text group, and then click the **Create from File tab** in the Object dialog box. Navigate to *w06h2Faculty*, select the file, and click **Insert**. Click the **Link to file check box** to select it, and then click **OK**.

You insert the entire contents of the w06h2Faculty file at the bottom of the page because it contains information that you want to display with the rest of the proposal. For quick access, you also create a shortcut to the source of the file. You will revise the order of the paragraphs later.

g. Scroll up, right-click anywhere in the paragraph below the *Ideology* heading, and then click the **Format Painter**. Select the paragraph below the *Time Frame* heading to change the font from Arial to **Times New Roman**.

The Time Frame paragraph in the w06h2Proposal1 file was formatted as Arial. When you combined the two documents in Step a, you chose to keep the formatting changes in the w06h2Proposal1 file, but now you want to format this paragraph as Times New Roman.

h. Save the document as **w06h2FinalProposal_LastFirst** and close all files.

STEP 3: CREATE A MASTER DOCUMENT AND SUBDOCUMENTS

You now have the three main pieces of information (w06h2FinalProposal_LastFirst, w06h1ResumeRW_LastFirst, and w06h1References_LastFirst) that you will send to the potential client. You decide to create a master document so that you can insert each piece and make formatting modifications to the subdocuments. Refer to Figure 6.23 as you complete Step 3.

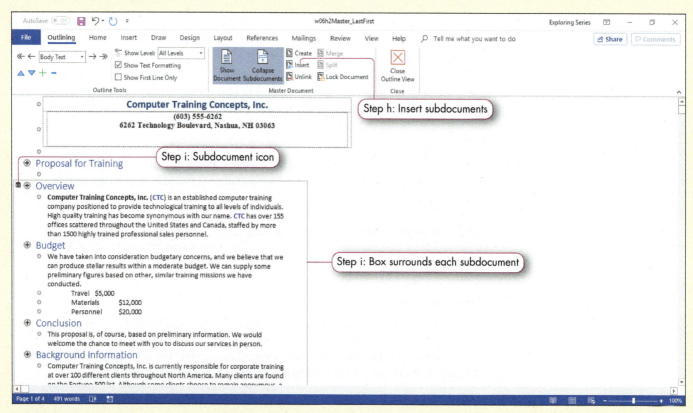

FIGURE 6.23 View Subdocuments in a Master Document

a. Open File Explorer. Create a folder named **w06h2Master_LastFirst**, and copy the following files to this folder:

w06h2FinalProposal_LastFirst

w06h1ResumeRW_LastFirst

w06h1References_LastFirst

Before you create a master document, you should create a folder and copy the files that you will insert into the master document to this folder because any changes made to the content in the master document will alter the original subdocuments.

b. Open a new blank document and save it as **w06h2Master_LastFirst** to the newly created w06h2Master_LastFirst folder.

c. Click the **Insert tab**, click **Quick Parts**, point at **AutoText**, and then select **CTC** to insert the building block that contains the company name and address.

d. Ensure the insertion point is below the CTC table and press **Enter** one time. Type the following headings, each on a separate line, for the subdocuments: **Proposal for Training**, **Faculty Resume**, and **References**.

e. Select the three headings you just typed and click **Heading 1** in the Styles group on the Home tab.

You want to create a separate section for each subdocument.

f. Click the **View tab** and click **Outline** in the Views group.

The Outlining tab displays, and the document text displays in Outline view.

392 CHAPTER 6 • Hands-On Exercise 2

g. Ensure that all three headings are selected. Click **Show Document** in the Master Document group to display more master document commands.

h. Place the insertion point at the end of the first subdocument heading, *Proposal for Training*, and press **Enter**. To insert the appropriate subdocument, complete the following steps:

- Click **Insert** in the Master Document group to display the Insert Subdocument dialog box.
- Select **w06h2FinalProposal_LastFirst** and click **Open**. If prompted to rename the style in the subdocument, click **Yes to All**.

The entire document displays under the Proposal for Training section of the master document.

i. Place the insertion point at the end of the second subdocument heading, *Faculty Resume* and press **Enter**. Repeat the steps above to insert the file **w06h1ResumeRW_LastFirst**. If prompted, click **OK** when the Microsoft Word information window displays indicating the subdocument has a different template than its master document. If prompted, click **Yes to All** when prompted to rename styles because there are several used in this document.

j. Place the insertion point at the end of the third subdocument heading, *References*, and press **Enter**. Repeat the steps above to insert the file **w06h1References_LastFirst**. If prompted, click **OK** when the Microsoft Word information window displays indicating the subdocument has a different template than its master document. If prompted, click **Yes to All** when prompted to rename styles because several are used in this document.

> **TROUBLESHOOTING:** Be sure to insert the w06h1References_LastFirst document, ending in *.docx*, and not the template, which ends in *.dotx*. To display file extensions, select the File name extensions check box on the View tab in File Explorer.

k. Click **Collapse Subdocuments** in the Master Document group to collapse the subdocuments in the document. Click **OK** if prompted to save changes to the master document.

Note that when you click Collapse Subdocuments, the name and path where each subdocument is saved displays.

l. Click **Expand Subdocuments** in the Master Document group to reopen and display the subdocuments. With the documents expanded, close Outline View. Click **Show/Hide** in the Paragraph group on the Home tab to turn on the non-printing characters.

Notice the section breaks after the Resume and Reference headings are (Next Page) section breaks, which need to be deleted.

m. Reopen the Outline view. Position the insertion point directly after the *Faculty Resume* heading, press **Delete twice** to remove the section break before the next page, and press **Enter** to put your name on the next paragraph. Replace *Your Name* at the top of the resume page with **Robert Williams**. Position the insertion point directly after the *References* heading, press **Enter**, and then press **Delete twice** to remove the section break before the company information.

> **MAC TROUBLESHOOTING:** Point to Faculty Resume in the left margin to display a pointing arrow and click, then press Delete. To delete the References heading, you can use Control+Click and click Cut.

n. Close the Outline view. Save the document.

STEP 4 USE THE NAVIGATION PANE AND CREATE BOOKMARKS

You remember that inserting bookmarks is a quick way to get to different pages in a document, so you add a bookmark to each heading so that you can easily navigate through the document. You display the Navigation Pane so that you can move quickly from one page to another to add the bookmarks. Refer to Figure 6.24 as you complete Step 4.

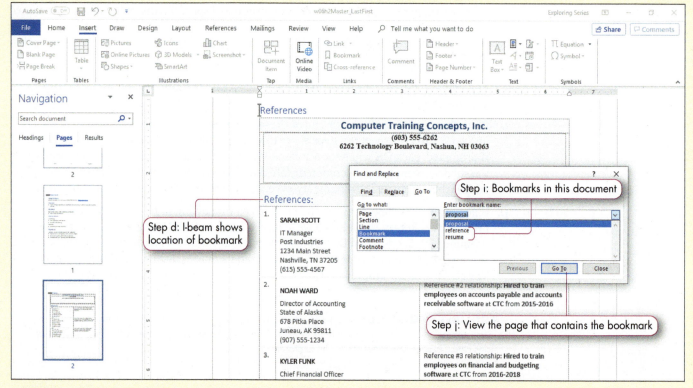

FIGURE 6.24 Create Bookmarks

a. Click the **View tab** and click **Navigation Pane** in the Show group to display the Navigation Pane on the left side of the window. Click **Headings** in the Navigation Pane to display all the headings in the master document.

The headings from the master document display in the pane. The heading of the paragraph where the insertion point displays is shaded.

> **MAC TROUBLESHOOTING:** Click Document Map on the Navigation Pane.

b. Click the **Proposal for Training heading** on the Navigation Pane.

c. Ensure that the insertion point is on the left of the *Proposal for Training* heading on the first page. Click the **Insert tab** and click **Bookmark** in the Links group. Type **proposal** in the Bookmark name box and click **Add**.

Word inserts a bookmark with the name you entered.

d. Click the **File tab**, scroll down, and click **Options**. Click **Advanced** in the Word Options dialog box, scroll down to display the Show document content section and click the **Show bookmarks check box** to select it. Click **OK** to save the settings and return to the document.

You changed a setting that enables the display of the bookmark indicators. A large gray I-beam indicates the location of the bookmark.

> **MAC TROUBLESHOOTING:** Click the Word menu and click Preferences. Under Authoring and Proofing Tools, click View. Under Show in Document, click the Bookmarks check box to check it and close the dialog box.

e. Click **Pages** on the Navigation Pane to display thumbnails of each page in the Navigation Pane. Click the thumbnail of page 3, the resume, to display the page and move the insertion point to the left of the Faculty Resume heading at the top of that page.

> **MAC TROUBLESHOOTING:** Click Thumbnails Pane in the Sidebar.

f. Click **Bookmark** in the Links group. Type **resume** in the Bookmark name box and click **Add**.

g. Type **reference** in the Search document box in the Navigation Pane. Click **Results** to view the results of the search. Click the second item listed, which is the label *References*, that displays at the top of page 4.

h. Click **Bookmark** in the Links group. Type **reference** in the Bookmark name box and click **Add**.

Notice the brackets that display around a block of text to show the location of the bookmark. When a block of text is selected when you insert a bookmark, brackets display around the text instead of a single I-beam, which displays at the location of the insertion point.

i. Press **Ctrl+G** to open the Find and Replace dialog box. Click **Bookmark** in the *Go to what* list.

Word displays the proposal bookmark in the Enter bookmark name box. If you click the Enter bookmark name arrow, the list displays all three bookmarks in alphabetical order: proposal, reference, resume.

j. Ensure that **proposal** is selected. Click **Go To**.

The insertion point moves to the proposal bookmark's location, and the Bookmark dialog box remains on the screen in case you want to go to another bookmark.

k. Click the resume and reference bookmarks and ensure that they work.

l. Click **Close** to remove the Find and Replace dialog box. Click **Close (X)** in the top-right corner of the Navigation Pane. Turn off the non-printing characters.

m. Save the document. Keep the document open if you plan to continue with the next Hands-On Exercise. If not, close the document, and exit Word.

Document Themes

To create a professional-looking document, you want to select features and styles that coordinate, but creating and managing document designs is time-consuming. Word contains several document themes that enable you to focus on the content of your document instead of spending time creating a design for it. You can also preview and apply style sets for the title, heading, and text body of a document. You can create your own theme by modifying several theme elements.

In this section, you will apply themes and style sets to a document. You will also create your own theme by customizing the theme elements.

Applying a Document Theme and Style Set

A **document theme** is a set of coordinating fonts, colors, and special effects, such as shadows or glows, that are combined into a package to provide a stylish appearance. Currently, several document themes are available in Word, but more themes are available for download at Office.com. Once you download a theme from Office.com, it is saved to your computer, ready to use another time.

STEP 1 Apply a Theme to a Document

It is important to select a theme that is appropriate for the purpose of the document. Depending on the theme you have selected, the coordinating font scheme, color scheme, and set of graphics effects in the theme can add either a bit of whimsy or help to enhance the appeal of your document and make it look more professional. Use Themes in the Document Formatting group on the Design tab to display a gallery of available document themes. You may apply a theme to your document by using one of the available themes or by clicking Browse for Themes to view and apply themes previously saved to your computer. On the other hand, you may select Reset to Theme from Template if you decide to revert to the default document theme. You may also use Page Color in the Page Background group to change the document background to a different color if you want to use a background color other than white.

> **TIP: ADDING A DOCUMENT THEME TO THE QAT**
> If you use the document theme frequently, you can add this feature to the Quick Access Toolbar (QAT) by right-clicking any of the theme's thumbnails and selecting Add Gallery to Quick Access Toolbar.

STEP 2 Apply a Style Set

A style set is a predefined combination of font style, color, and size for title, heading, and body text elements. A style set can be applied to any text in a document. Applying a new style set also changes the paragraph properties of the document. The Style Sets gallery is in the Document Formatting group on the Design tab. Other options in the Style Sets gallery include resetting to the default style set and saving a new style set.

> **TIP: PARAGRAPH SPACING AND SET AS DEFAULT**
> The Paragraph Spacing command in the Document Formatting group on the Design tab enables you to change the line and paragraph spacing of your entire document by selecting from a predefined set of values or customizing your own values. Below the Paragraph Spacing and Effects command is the Set as Default command, which saves your current settings and applies the saved settings to all your new documents. This feature is helpful to users who have a preferred font type or specified paragraph spacing.

Customizing Theme Colors and Theme Fonts, and Applying Theme Effects

When you create a blank new document, it is automatically formatted with the default Office document theme. If you want to change the document theme, you can try several themes before deciding on the best choice for your document. At any time, you can switch back to the original default document theme. If you want to make changes to any part of a theme design, you can modify and customize the theme elements individually. Word contains more than 20 color schemes and font combinations, in addition to 15 special effects, resulting in hundreds of available combinations.

STEP 3 Customize Theme Colors

Theme colors represent coordinated colors for the current text and background, accents, and hyperlinks and enable you to quickly change the look of the text and background of the document (see Figure 6.25). You can customize all these choices until you find something that you like by modifying any of the colors within a theme set or create an entirely new theme color set. The color combinations for the four text/background colors, six accent colors, and two hyperlink colors are numerous.

> **To create a custom theme color, complete the following steps:**
> 1. Click the Design tab.
> 2. Click Colors in the Document Formatting group.
> 3. Select any of the available predefined color schemes or select the Customize Colors option at the bottom of the gallery to modify the colors in the current theme.
> 4. Select colors for the text/background, accents, and hyperlinks in the Create New Theme Colors dialog box.
> 5. Type a new name for your custom theme color in the Name box.
> 6. Click Save to save the custom theme with a new name. The new color theme displays at the top of the theme color gallery.

> **MAC TIP:** Customizing theme colors is not available in Word for Mac.

Use the Reset button to undo any color changes or the Cancel button to exit the Create New Theme Colors dialog box without saving any changes.

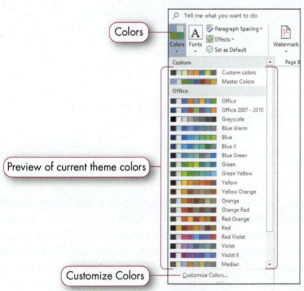

FIGURE 6.25 View and Customize Theme Colors

STEP 4 **Customize Theme Fonts**

Theme fonts contain a coordinating heading and body text font for each different theme. You can view the fonts used in the theme when you click Fonts in the Document Formatting group on the Design tab, as shown in Figure 6.26. Theme fonts display at the top of the font list when you click the Font arrow on the Home tab or on the Mini toolbar. As with theme colors, you can quickly change the text in your document by picking a new font set with a predefined font type. You can also create a new theme font set.

> **To create a custom theme font, complete the following steps:**
> 1. Click the Design tab.
> 2. Click Fonts in the Document Formatting group and select Customize Fonts.
> 3. Click the Heading font arrow to select a preferred font for all the headings.
> 4. Click the Body font arrow to select a font for the body text.
> 5. Type a new name for the custom theme font in the Name box.
> 6. Click Save to save the custom theme font with a new name. The new font theme displays at the top of the theme font gallery.

MAC TIP: Customizing theme fonts is not available in Word for Mac.

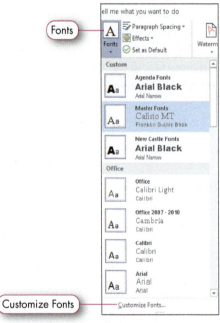

FIGURE 6.26 View and Customize Theme Fonts

Apply Theme Effects

Theme effects are another feature that you can incorporate into a document theme. ***Theme effects*** include lines, fill, and 3-D effects, such as shadows, glows, and borders. When you apply a theme effect, the selection affects objects such as shapes, SmartArt, and borders around graphics. Unlike theme colors and theme fonts, you cannot customize the set of theme effects, but you can choose and apply a theme effect from the built-in sets and then save it to your own document theme. When a shape or object is created, the theme effect is reflected in the Shape Styles gallery on the Format tab.

When you click Effects in the Document Formatting group on the Design tab, notice that the lines, fills, and special effects are represented in combinations of three shapes. The circle represents a line effect that includes the width or weight of the line, the rectangle represents effects such as bevels or shadows applied to an object, and the arrow displays the fill effects that might include gradients, as shown in Figure 6.27.

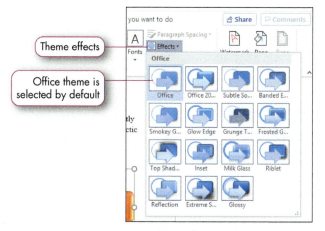

FIGURE 6.27 View and Apply Theme Effects

MAC TIP: Theme effects are not available in Word for Mac.

STEP 5 Save a Custom Theme

Once you have selected the theme colors, theme fonts, and maybe even the theme effects, you can save your changes as a custom theme. Themes are saved with a .thmx extension in the Templates folder in the subfolder Document Themes folder.

> **To save selected theme elements to a custom theme, complete the following steps:**
> 1. Click the Design tab.
> 2. Click Themes in the Document Formatting group.
> 3. Select Save Current Theme at the bottom of the gallery to save a theme.

TIP: DELETE CUSTOM THEME COLORS AND FONTS
You can easily delete a custom theme, a custom theme color set, or custom theme fonts. To remove these custom sets, click Themes (or Colors or Fonts) in the Document Formatting group on the Design tab, right-click the custom set that displays in the top of the gallery, and then select Delete. You will see a confirmation dialog box before the .thmx theme file is removed permanently. You cannot delete the themes, color themes, or font themes that are included in Word.

7. Describe the advantages of using document themes. ***p. 396***
8. Describe the purpose for creating your own custom themes. ***p. 396***
9. Explain why you want to customize theme colors or theme fonts. ***p. 397***

Hands-On Exercises

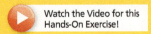

Skills covered: Apply a Theme to a Document • Apply a Style Set • Customize Theme Colors • Customize Theme Fonts • Save a Custom Theme

3 Document Themes

You are almost ready to print the proposal and send it to the potential client. But each subdocument that you inserted into the master document is formatted a bit differently, and you want the final document to have a consistent look. You apply a theme to the documents so they use the same style of fonts and colors to put the finishing touches on this proposal.

STEP 1 APPLY A THEME TO A DOCUMENT

Your proposal should have a professional look to it, so you apply one of the built-in themes in Word. By using the document theme, all colors in the resume template and the colors used for headings in the other documents will coordinate. You will format the document using the Organic theme. Refer to Figure 6.28 as you complete Step 1.

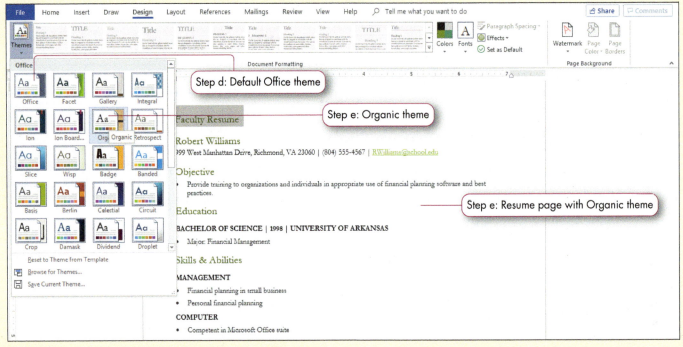

FIGURE 6.28 Select a New Theme

a. Open File Explorer. Make a copy of the w06h2Master_LastFirst folder and rename it w06h3Master_LastFirst, changing h2 to h3. Open w06h2Master_LastFirst in the w06h3Master_LastFirst folder and save it as **w06h3Master_LastFirst** in the same folder, changing h2 to h3.

b. Ensure that the **View tab** is selected and click **Outline** in the Views group to view the Outlining tab and commands. Click **Show Document** in the Master Document group on the Outlining tab and click **Expand Subdocuments** to view all of the content in the subdocuments. Click **Close Outline View** to return to Print Layout view.

The subdocuments are visible in the master document.

c. Press **Ctrl+G** and click **Bookmark** in the Go to what box. Click the **Enter bookmark name arrow** and select **resume**. Click **Go To** and the resume displays. Close the Find and Replace dialog box.

d. Click the **Design tab** and click **Themes** in the Document Formatting group.

The gallery of themes displays, and the Office theme is displayed as the first theme. This is the default theme and is applied to all Word documents when they are first created.

e. Point to the **Organic theme** to preview the effects. Click the **Organic theme**.

The Organic theme is applied to all pages in the master document.

f. Click the **View tab** and click **Multiple Pages** in the Zoom group. Click **Zoom**, change the percent to **38**, and then click **OK**.

You can see the subdocuments all at once, and you will notice how the resume features change to reflect the new theme.

g. Click **100%** in the Zoom group. Scroll through the document and preview the whole document.

The content for the Proposal for Training, Resume, and References sections are each on their own individual pages.

h. Save the document.

STEP 2 APPLY A STYLE SET

The Organic theme looks great on the master document, but you want to change the font style and paragraph properties of the document. You take steps to change the font style for the title, heading, and body text of the document. Refer to Figure 6.29 as you complete Step 2.

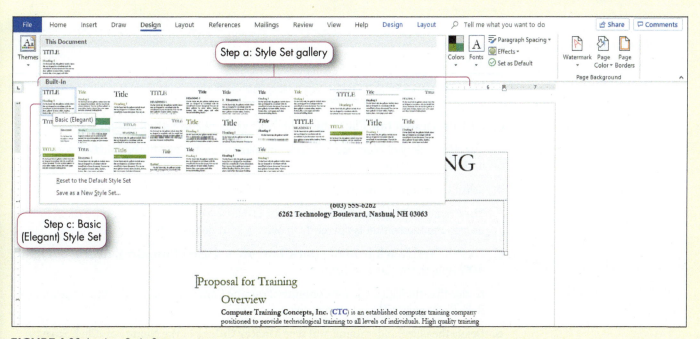

FIGURE 6.29 Apply a Style Set

a. Scroll to the resume page. Click the **Design tab**. Point to the **Style Set More arrow** in the Document Formatting group, read the description about style set, and then click the **Style Set More arrow**.

The Style Set gallery displays, with the current style set listed at the top and the built-in style sets created by Microsoft in the section below.

b. Point to several of the thumbnail images of the Style Set gallery to reveal the name of the individual style set and also to preview it.

c. Select the **Basic (Elegant) style set**.

The Basic (Elegant) style set is applied to the whole document.

d. Save the document.

STEP 3 CUSTOMIZE THEME COLORS

The Organic theme and Basic (Elegant) style set enhances the master document; however, you want to change a color to reflect colors used in other documents. You make a color change in the theme and you save the changes as a custom theme so that you can use it again in other documents. Refer to Figure 6.30 as you complete Step 3.

FIGURE 6.30 Customize Theme Colors

> **MAC TROUBLESHOOTING:** Customizing theme colors is not available in Word for Mac.

a. Click the **Design tab**. Click **Colors** in the Document Formatting group.

The color gallery displays, with the custom colors at the top and the built-in Office selections in the section below. You can select the colors for other built-in themes from this gallery.

b. Select **Customize Colors** at the bottom of the gallery.

The Create New Theme Colors dialog box displays. Now you can customize the colors used in the theme that is currently applied to your document.

c. Click the **Text/Background - Dark 2 arrow** and select **Blue-Gray, Accent 3, Lighter 40%** (fourth row, seventh column).

Notice that the Title style for Computer Training Concepts, Inc. on the first page and the References page reflects the new color.

d. Delete the placeholder name and type **Master Colors** in the Name box. Click **Save** to save this color scheme.

The Master Colors color theme is automatically applied to the document. When you click Theme Colors, the new color theme is listed under Custom at the top of the gallery.

e. Press **Ctrl+Home** to view the first page of the document. Select the title **Computer Training Concepts, Inc.**, click the **Home tab**, and then click the **Font Color arrow** in the Font group.

Notice the top of the box displays Theme Colors, so you know any color you select will coordinate with the document theme.

f. Select **Orange, Accent 5** from the first row. Deselect the report title.

g. Save the document.

STEP 4 CUSTOMIZE THEME FONTS

You notice the same font is used for headings and body text in the theme applied to this document. You make a change so a different yet coordinating font is used for the headings. Then the proposal is ready for the printer! Refer to Figure 6.31 as you complete Step 4.

FIGURE 6.31 Select Custom Fonts for a Theme

> **MAC TROUBLESHOOTING:** Customizing theme fonts is not available in Word for Mac.

a. Click the **Design tab**. Click **Fonts** in the Document Formatting group.

The custom fonts display at the top of the gallery, if any, followed by the Office and Office 2007–2010 theme fonts and then the other font groups.

b. Select **Customize Fonts** at the bottom of the gallery.

c. Click the **Heading font arrow** and select **Calisto MT**. Click the **Body font arrow** and select **Franklin Gothic Book**.

d. Delete the placeholder name and type **Master Fonts** in the Name box. Click **Save** to save this font scheme.

The title and the headings Proposal for Training, Resume, Resources, etc. change to reflect the new font. The body text font also changes to the new font.

e. Click **Fonts** in the Document Formatting group. Notice Master Fonts displays in alphabetical order in the custom fonts section at the top of the list, with blue shading to indicate it is in use. Press **Esc** to return to the document.

f. Save the document.

STEP 5: SAVE A CUSTOM THEME

Although the proposal is now ready, you made changes to both colors and fonts for this theme, so you want to take one more step and save the whole theme with a new name, so you can use it again without modifying the individual features. Refer to Figure 6.32 as you complete Step 5.

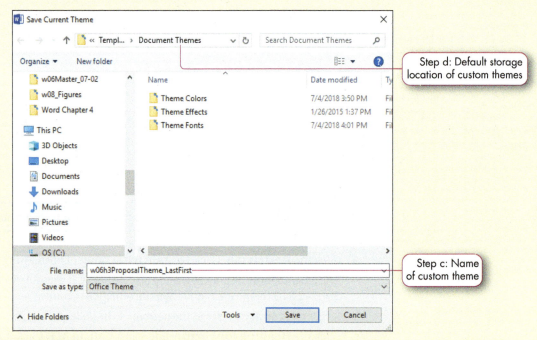

FIGURE 6.32 Save a Custom Theme

a. Click **Themes** in the Document Formatting group on the Design tab.

b. Select **Save Current Theme** at the bottom of the gallery.

The Save Current Theme dialog box displays. By default, the new themes are saved in the Document Themes folder for the current user. They are not stored in a folder with the themes that install with Word.

c. Type **w06h3MasterTheme_LastFirst** in the File name box and navigate to the w06h3Master_LastFirst folder.

d. Click **Save** to save the theme file with the .thmx extension.

e. Save and close the document. Zip all the files in the w06h3Master_LastFirst folder and name the zipped file as **w06h3Master_LastFirst**. Based on your instructor's directions, submit the following in the zipped file:

w06h1ResumeRW_LastFirst

w06h1References_LastFirst

w06h1ReferencesTemplate_LastFirst.dotx

w06h2FinalProposal_LastFirst

w06h3Master_LastFirst

w06h3MasterTheme_LastFirst.thmx

Chapter Objectives Review

After reading this chapter, you have accomplished the following objectives:

1. **Select a template.**
   - Select and download a template: You can use Word templates to create professional-looking documents such as letters, memos, reports, resumes, agendas, calendars, brochures, and checklists. Templates are available to download from the File tab or when you first open Word. They contain placeholders, a field or block of text, to determine the position of objects in a document.

2. **Create a Word template.**
   - Save a document as a template: If you create or use a particular document frequently, with only minor modifications each time, you should save the document as a template. You can insert placeholders for the information you change frequently.

3. **Use building blocks.**
   - Create and insert a custom building block: Building blocks are predefined objects to automate and streamline repetitive tasks that you perform frequently, such as inserting disclaimers, company addresses or logos, or your name and address. Each selection of text or graphics that you add to the Quick Parts gallery is stored in the Building Blocks Organizer and is assigned a unique name that makes it easy for you to find the content when you want to use it.

4. **View two documents side by side.**
   - The Side by Side feature enables you to view two versions of the same document on the same screen. It is useful when you want to compare the contents of two documents or if you want to cut or copy and paste text from one document to another. To view two documents side by side, they must both be open in Word. While in Side by Side view, you can resize and reset the two document windows.

5. **Merge documents.**
   - Compare two documents: When you have several copies of the same document submitted from different people, you can use the Compare and Combine features. The Compare feature evaluates the contents of two or more documents and displays markup balloons that show the differences between the documents. You can specify if the differences display in the original document, a revised document, or a new document.
   - Combine two documents: The Combine feature goes a step farther than the Compare feature and integrates all changes from multiple documents into one.
   - Insert a file as an object: You can quickly add the contents of a document to an open document by using the Object command on the Insert tab.
   - Create a master document and subdocuments: Another way to work with multiple documents, especially those that will be combined into one long document, is to create a master document that acts like a binder for managing smaller documents. The smaller document is called a subdocument and can be edited individually at any time.
   - Modify the master document and subdocuments: To modify the master and subdocuments, you can make changes to the master document at any time, but you can only make changes to the subdocuments when they are unlocked.
   - Use the master document and subdocuments with extreme care: Master documents and subdocuments can be very helpful, but they can also be problematic. Several precautions are to be observed when using this feature.

6. **Use navigational tools.**
   - Use the Navigation Pane: When you use the Browse the headings in your document feature, only the headings display. You can click a heading in the Navigation Pane to move the insertion point to that heading in the document. You also can use thumbnails to navigate quickly through a document. When you click a thumbnail, the insertion point moves to the top of that page. You can also navigate through a document using search keywords or phrases.
   - Create bookmarks: The Bookmark feature is an electronic marker for a specific location in a document. You can designate a bookmark in a location in a document and use the Go To command to return to that bookmark.

7. **Apply a document theme and style set.**
   - Apply a theme to a document: You can select a document theme from the Themes group on the Design tab. When you select a document theme, formatting occurs immediately.
   - Apply a style set: Style set enables you to change the font type and paragraph properties of the whole document.

8. **Customize theme colors and theme fonts, and apply theme effects.**
   - Customize theme colors: Theme colors represent the current text and background, accents, and hyperlinks. To create a custom color theme, you can modify the colors in the current theme and save the set with a new name.
   - Customize theme fonts: The theme fonts contain a coordinating heading and body text font for each theme. Theme fonts display at the top of the font list when you click the Font arrow on the Home tab or on the Mini toolbar.
   - Apply theme effects: The theme effects include lines and fill effects, such as shadows, glows, and borders. You cannot create your own set of theme effects, but you can choose from the built-in sets and apply it to the theme.
   - Save a custom theme: After you have chosen the theme colors, theme fonts, and maybe even the theme effects, you can save your changes as a custom theme.

Key Terms Matching

Match the key terms with their definitions. Write the key term letter by the appropriate numbered definition.

a. AutoText
b. Bookmark
c. Building block
d. Building Blocks Organizer
e. Combine
f. Compare
g. Document theme
h. Legal blacklining
i. Master document
j. Navigation Pane
k. Placeholder
l. Subdocument
m. Synchronous Scrolling
n. Template
o. Template thumbnail
p. Theme color
q. Theme effect
r. Theme font
s. View Side by Side

1. _____ A predefined block of text for standardized content that can be placed in any document. **p. 367**

2. _____ A feature that enables you to display two versions of the same document on the same screen. **p. 376**

3. _____ A feature that enables you to scroll through two documents at the same time using either of the two scroll bars. **p. 376**

4. _____ A feature that evaluates the contents of two versions of a document side by side for a line by line comparison and presents a merged version with markup and tracked changes showing the differences. **p. 377**

5. _____ A feature that integrates all changes from multiple authors or documents into one single document. **p. 379**

6. _____ A way to compare two documents and to display the changes between the two documents. **p. 377**

7. _____ A document that acts like a binder for managing smaller documents. **p. 380**

8. _____ A smaller document that is a part of a master document. **p. 380**

9. _____ A tool that is used to navigate through a document by viewing headings, viewing pages, and browsing search results. **p. 384**

10. _____ A small picture displays below the search box that matches the search term in the Search for online templates search box. **p. 366**

11. _____ A feature that provides an electronic marker for a specific location in a document. **p. 387**

12. _____ A partially completed document containing preformatted text or graphics. **p. 364**

13. _____ A field or block of text used to determine the position of objects in a document. **p. 364**

14. _____ A feature that displays a list of all the building blocks that are predefined in the templates stored in the current template location. **p. 368**

15. _____ A set of coordinating fonts, colors, and special effects, such as shadows or glows, that are combined into a package to provide a stylish appearance. **p. 396**

16. _____ A feature that represents coordinated colors for the current text and background, accents, and hyperlinks. **p. 397**

17. _____ A feature that contains a coordinating heading and body text font. **p. 398**

18. _____ A feature that includes lines or fill effects to incorporate into a document theme. **p. 398**

19. _____ A type of building block to store text or graphics that will be reused, such as a standard contract clause or a long distribution list. **p. 369**

Multiple Choice

1. You can obtain a document template in many ways, *except* which of the following?
   (a) Select it from the Insert tab.
   (b) Download it from Office.com.
   (c) Select it from the File tab.
   (d) Create a document yourself and save it as a template.

2. Which feature enables you to integrate all changes from multiple authors or documents into one single document?
   (a) Side by Side view
   (b) Compare
   (c) Combine
   (d) Subdocuments

3. Which of the document elements listed below can you find using the Go To command?
   (a) Placeholder
   (b) Bookmark
   (c) Content control
   (d) Picture

4. What file extension is given to a template?
   (a) .docx
   (b) .dotx
   (c) .xlsx
   (d) .html

5. When you use the Navigation Pane, you can navigate through the document by viewing headings or _____.
   (a) flags
   (b) extension
   (c) thumbnails
   (d) building blocks

6. What is the primary purpose of using a document theme?
   (a) To coordinate elements used in the document such as colors and fonts, and to give it a more professional appearance
   (b) To limit the number of colors allowed in the document
   (c) To merge information from a data source into a document
   (d) To easily create bookmarks

7. If you have created a customized cover page and you want to use the same cover page for all your reports, which productivity tool would best fit your need?
   (a) Document templates
   (b) Mail Merge
   (c) Document themes
   (d) Building blocks

8. Which of the following theme elements cannot be customized and saved?
   (a) Theme color
   (b) Theme font
   (c) Theme effect
   (d) Document theme

9. Which of the following features can be used to view small pictures of each page in your document?
   (a) View > Navigation Pane > Thumbnails
   (b) View > Navigation Pane > Headings
   (c) View > Navigation Pane > Search
   (d) View > Navigation Pane > Pages

10. What is the maximum number of documents that you can view side by side?
    (a) One
    (b) Two
    (c) Three
    (d) Four

Practice Exercises

1 My Home Town Cable Services

You work in the employee benefits department of the local cable provider, My Home Town Cable Services. You want to set up a form that all new and existing employees can use to document personal information and emergency contact numbers. Before you create a new form, you decide to look for an existing form in the Word templates gallery. You find just the right form and need to make only minor modifications, adding the company name and logo. You also insert the contents of another document to add insurance information, and the form is ready to be distributed to all employees. Refer to Figure 6.33 as you complete this exercise.

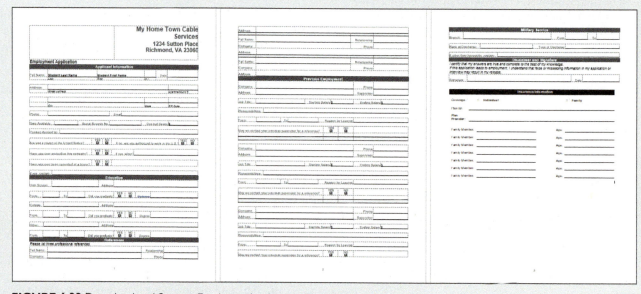

FIGURE 6.33 Download and Save an Employee Application Template

a. Start Word. Click **New**. Type **Employment Application** in the Search for online templates box and press **Enter**. Click the **Employment application (online)** to preview it and click **Create**. Close the Navigation Pane if it displays.

b. Click **Save**, click **Browse**, click the **Save as type arrow**, and then select **Word Template**. Type **w06p1EmployeeTemplate_LastFirst** in the File name box, navigate to the folder where you want to save this file, and click **Save**.

c. Select the border of the cell that displays *Your Logo Here*, and press **Delete**.

d. Select the text **Company Name**, and type the following:

   My Home Town Cable Services
   1234 Sutton Place
   Richmond, VA 23060

e. Insert a blank line after the zip code. Select the two paragraphs that contain the address, and click **Decrease Font Size** in the Font group once to decrease the font size.

f. Select the company name and address. Click the **Insert tab**. Click **Quick Parts** in the Text group and select **Save Selection to Quick Part gallery**.

g. Click the **Gallery arrow** in the Create New Building Block dialog box and select **Text Boxes**. Click the **Save In arrow**, select **Building Blocks**, and then click **OK**.

h. Press **Delete** to remove the company name and address. Click **Quick Parts** in the Text group, select the **Building Blocks Organizer**, and then click **Name** to sort the entries by name. Scroll down, click the **My Home Town Cable Services** entry, and then click **Insert**.

i. Select the whole document. Click the **Home tab**. Click the **Paragraph Dialog Box Launcher** in the Paragraph group. Set the Before and After Spacing to **0**. Click **OK**.

j. Press **Ctrl+End** to move to the end of the document. Press **Enter** twice. Click the **Insert tab**, click **Object** in the Text group, and then click the **Create from File tab**. Browse to the location where your data files are stored, select *w06p1Insurance*, click **Insert**, and then click **OK**.

k. Click the **View tab**, click **Navigation Pane** in the Show group to select it, click **Headings** on the Navigation Pane, and then click **Applicant Information** on the Navigation Pane. Click the **Insert tab** and click **Bookmark** in the Links group. Type **Applicant_Information** in the Bookmark name box and click **Add**. Create two more bookmarks for **Education** and **References**. Delete **Check3** and **Check4** under Bookmark name.

l. Click the **Home tab** and click **Replace** in the Editing group. Click the **Go To tab** in the Find and Replace dialog box. Click **Bookmark** in the *Go to what* list. Ensure that you have all three bookmarks. Click **Application Information**, click **Go To**, and then click **Close**. Click **Save**.

m. Click the **File tab**, click **Save As**, click **Browse**, and navigate to the folder where you want to save this file. Click the **Save as type arrow**, and select **Word document (*.docx)**. Type **w06p1Employee_LastFirst** (remove the word Template from the file name) in the File name box and click **Save**.

n. Position the insertion point on the line above *Last* under the *Applicant Information* section. Type your last name, press **Tab**, and then type your first name.

o. Save and close the file. Based on your instructor's directions, submit the following:
w06p1EmployeeTemplate_LastFirst.dotx
w06p1Employee_LastFirst

2 Cancer Information

You are a health care professional working at a local hospital, and you receive two documents from co-workers who searched for information about cancer on the Internet. The information is interesting and could be valuable to your patients, so you decide to create a well-formatted document that you can distribute to anyone who expresses an interest in basic information about cancer. You also apply a document theme so it will look more professional. Refer to Figure 6.34 as you complete this exercise.

FIGURE 6.34 Apply Theme to a Combined Document

a. Open both *w06p2Cancer1* and *w06p2Cancer2*. Click the **View tab** and click **View Side by Side** in the Windows group. Use synchronous scrolling to scroll down to view the contents of each. Click **Window** and select **View Side by Side** to turn off the feature. Close both documents.

b. Open a blank document. Click the **Review tab**, click the **Compare** in the Compare group, and then select **Combine**. Complete the following steps:
- Click **Browse** next to the Original document arrow, navigate to the *w06p2Cancer1* document, and then click **Open**.
- Click **Browse** next to the Revised document arrow, navigate to the *w06p2Cancer2* document, and then click **Open**.
- Click **More**, ensure that **New document** below *Show changes in* is selected, and click **OK**. Note: Disregard any entries for how to label unmarked changes because all changes will be accepted.

c. Save the document as **w06p2Cancer_LastFirst**. Position the insertion point at the beginning of the document. Click the **Review tab**. To accept and reject the tracked changes, complete the following steps:
- Review the first three track changes that describe the changes in Style Definition - Normal; Heading 1: Font color: Accent 1; and text Pattern: Clear (Accent 1). Click **Accept** three times to accept these three changes.
- Place the insertion point below the first paragraph starting with *Cancer is one of the scariest words*, and click **Reject and Move to Next** to remove the extra space below the first paragraph.
- Select the text highlighted by Move to Next and click **Accept** to keep the paragraphs with shading.
- Scroll down until you see a large amount of deleted text, starting with *What is cancer?* Right-click the selected text and select **Reject Deletion**.
- Click **Accept All Changes and Stop Tracking** in the Changes group on the Review tab to accept all remaining changes in the document and stop tracking.

d. Press **Ctrl+Home** to view the first page and scroll through the document to review the changes that you have made.

e. Click the **Design tab** and click **Themes** in the Document Formatting group. Select **Facet** to apply the theme. Modify theme features by completing the following steps:
- Click **Colors** in the Document Formatting group and select **Customize Colors** at the bottom of the gallery. Click the **Accent 1 arrow** and select **Dark Green, Accent 2, Lighter 40%** (fourth row, sixth column). Type **Cancer colors** in the Name box and click **Save**.
- Click **Fonts** in the Document Formatting group and select **Customize Fonts** at the bottom of the gallery. Click the **Heading font arrow** and select **Bookman Old Style**. Type **Cancer fonts** in the Name box and click **Save**.
- Click **Basic (Elegant) style set** in the Document Formatting group.
- Click **Themes** and select **Save Current Theme**. Navigate to the location in which you have saved your solution files, type **w06p2CancerTheme_LastFirst** in the File name box, and then click **Save**.

f. Save and close the file. Based on your instructor's directions, submit the following:
w06p2Cancer_LastFirst
w06p2CancerTheme_LastFirst.thmx

Mid-Level Exercises

1 Jeff's Food Truck in the Park

Your friend Jeffrey Woodman recently purchased a food truck. He prepared an information sheet to distribute to several office buildings downtown, and he asked you to review it and offer suggestions. Before you have a chance to review the information sheet, he sends another version with new changes. With two different documents, you use the Compare and Combine features to view them, consolidate the documents into one final copy, add your suggested changes, and return it to Jeffrey.

a. Use the Compare feature to open the two documents Jeffrey sends, *w06m1Truck* and *w06m1Truck Revision*, and display the results in a new document. View the differences, save the new document as **w06m1TruckCompare_LastFirst**, and then close the document.

b. Use the Combine feature to combine *w06m1Truck* (open this as the original document) and *w06m1TruckRevision*. Keep the formatting changes from the *w06m1Truck* document. Save the newly combined file as **w06m1TruckCombined_LastFirst**.

c. Accept and reject the following changes that display in the combined document:
   - Accept the tracked change *Formatted: Space Before: 24 pt*.
   - Reject the addition of text *on a daily basis* that displays above the SmartArt.
   - Reject the insertion of the SmartArt object that includes *Fresh Seafood, Homemade Soup, etc.*
   - Reject the tracked change that displays in the text *homey and* in the third paragraph.
   - Accept the tracked changes *Deleted: The* and *Deleted: the* in the last two paragraphs.
   - Accept the inclusion of the text *trendy-conscious people* in the last paragraph.
   - Accept the tracked change *Deleted: those in the know* in the last paragraph.
   - Accept all remaining changes in the document.

d. Apply the **Office theme** and **Frosted Glass effect** to the document.

e. Type **Jeffrey Woodman's** to replace *Jeff's* on the title line. Apply the **Black and White (Classic) style** from the style gallery in the Document Formatting group to the title line text and change the font color in the Font group to **Gold, Accent 4**.

f. Select the name *Jeffrey Woodman's* in the title line and save it as an AutoText entry in the Building Blocks in the Building Blocks Organizer.

g. Insert the building block in front of each occurrence of the Food Truck title throughout the document, replacing *Jeff's* and *Jeffrey's*, where necessary. Ensure that the inserted AutoText entry is bold.

h. Insert bookmarks for **lunch items** in the second paragraph and **owner** in the fourth paragraph. Review the list of bookmarks to ensure that both bookmarks are successfully created.

i. Save and close the file. Based on your instructor's directions, submit the following:
   w06m1TruckCombined_LastFirst
   w06m1TruckCompare_LastFirst

2 Custom Themes

Because you learned about the themes that Word provides, you decide that you need to use them more often and also to create your own custom theme. You download a letter that already incorporates a theme add a custom building block, and then make modifications to create your own custom theme that you can use in other documents. You also want to practice how to create a master document and subdocuments.

a. Open File Explorer. Create a folder named **w06m2MyMaster_LastFirst**, and copy the following data files to this folder:
   w06m2Employees
   w06m2Exceptions

b. Start Word. Search for and download the **Personal letterhead template**. Make certain the Save as type box displays **Word Template**, and save the file as a document template named **w06m2MyTemplate_LastFirst** to the w06m2MyMaster_LastFirst folder.

c. Replace the following text in the document template:

Replace This Text	With This Text
Your Name	Your First and Last Names
Street Address, City, ST ZIP Code	**101 Main Street, Liberty Town, VA 22222**
Telephone	**888-555-8888**
Email	**student@college.edu**

d. Insert a blank row after the email. Delete the comma and space after *Main Street* and press **Enter**. Create a building block that contains the address, telephone, and email address as an AutoText and save it in Building Blocks to your document. Name the building block **MyAddress**.

e. Display the Theme gallery and select the **Ion theme**. Apply the **Basic (Elegant) style set** to the document.

f. Display the Theme Colors gallery. Change the Text/Background - Dark 2 color to **Gold, Accent 3, Lighter 40%** (fourth row, seventh column). Save the theme color as **My Colors**.

g. Create a new theme font. Change the body font to **Arial**. Save the theme font as **My Fonts**.

h. Save the current document theme as **w06m2MyTheme_LastFirst** to your folder because you have personalized several pieces of the theme. Save the template.

i. Scroll to the bottom of the letter and insert a page break. Type **Employees** and **Exceptions** on separate paragraphs and format them with the **Heading 1 style**. Insert a blank line after each heading. Save the file as a Word document to your folder and name it **w06m2MyMaster_LastFirst**.

j. Insert the following two subdocuments into the master document using Outline view: *w06m2Employees* below the Employees heading and *w06m2Exeptions* below the Exceptions heading. If prompted to use the master document template, click **OK**. If prompted to rename the style in the subdocuments, click **Yes to All**.

k. Click **Collapse Subdocuments** in the Master Document group to collapse the subdocuments in the document. Click **OK** if prompted to save changes to the master document.

l. Click **Expand Subdocuments** in the Master Document group to reopen and display the subdocuments. With the documents expanded, close Outline view. Notice any excessive blank space or inappropriate section breaks in the document and make corrections.

m. Display the Outline view. Close the Outline view.

n. Type **09-01-2020** for Date on the first page. Scroll to the end of the document, press **Enter** once, and insert the MyAddress building block.

o. Save and close all files. Zip all the files in the w06m2MyMaster_LastFirst folder and name the zipped file as **w06m2MyMaster_LastFirst**. Based on your instructor's directions, submit the following in the zipped file:
w06m2Employees
w06m2Exceptions
w06m2MyMaster_LastFirst
w06m2MyTemplate_LastFirst.dotx
w06m2MyTheme_LastFirst.thmx

Running Case

New Castle County Technical Services

New Castle County Technical Services has been asked to participate in a technology fair at a local university. The fair is open to students and community members, many of whom are potential clients for New Castle's data and network solutions. You have been asked to take a rough draft of information related to data recovery solutions and use Word to create an attractive multi-page informational handout. Before you have a chance to review the information, your supervisor sent you another version of the same draft. With two different documents, you use the Compare and Combine features to view them, consolidate the documents into one final copy, and add your suggested changes. You apply a document theme, a theme effect, and a style set, and you also customize the fonts and colors to make the document more professional-looking.

a. Use the Compare feature to open the two documents, *w06r1NewCastle1* and *w06r1NewCastle2*, and display the results in a new document. View the differences, save the new document as **w06r1NewCastleCompare_LastFirst**, and then close the document.

b. Use the Combine feature to combine *w06r1NewCastle1* (open this as the original document) and *w06r1NewCastle2*. Keep the formatting changes from the *w06r1NewCastle1* document. Save the newly combined file as **w06r1NewCastleCombined_LastFirst**.

c. Accept all changes and stop tracking.

d. Select the **New Castle County Technical Services WordArt** at the top of the document and add it as a Quick Parts entry in the Building Blocks template. Name the building block as **NCCTS**.

e. Scroll down to the bottom of the second page and insert the New Castle building block right above the page break.

f. Insert bookmarks for **Our_Goal** in the last paragraph on the first page, and **What_is_Backup** and **What_is_Disaster_Recovery** on the left column of the last page. (Note: Do not select the text.) Review the list of bookmarks to ensure that these three bookmarks were successfully created.

g. Apply the **Organic theme** and **Reflection effect** to the document.

h. Apply the **Basic (Elegant) style set** to the document.

i. Modify the theme colors by changing the Text/Background - Light 1 color to **Black, Background 1** (first row, first column) and changing the Accent 1 color to **Orange, Accent 5, Darker 25%** (fifth row, ninth column). Save the color theme as **New Castle Colors**.

j. Create new Theme Fonts replacing the heading font with **Arial Black** and the body font with **Arial Narrow**. Save the font theme as **New Castle Fonts**.

k. Save the current document theme as **w06r1NewCastleTheme_LastFirst** because you have personalized several pieces of the theme.

l. Save and close all files. Based on your instructor's directions, submit the following:
   w06r1NewCastleCombined_LastFirst
   w06r1NewCastleCompare_LastFirst
   w06r1NewCastleTheme_LastFirst.thmx

Disaster Recovery

Planned Developments Guide

You work in the city's planning and zoning department as an analyst. You begin to prepare the *Guide to Planned Developments* document for posting on the city's intranet. The administrative clerk who typed the document attempted to use bookmarks for navigation purposes, but he did not test the bookmarks after inserting them. Open *w06d1Bookmarks*, review the document and repair the bookmarks, and save your revised document as **w06d1Bookmarks_LastFirst**. Close the document. Based on your instructor's directions, submit w06d1Bookmarks_LastFirst.

Capstone Exercise

MyLab IT Grader

Information Technologist Professionals

You have recently been elected secretary of the local professional chapter of Information Technologist Professionals (ITPs). You decide to send professional-looking documents to the other officers so they can prepare for meetings, as well as collect and distribute information. Your next meeting occurs in one week, so you begin the process of assembling your information.

Download a Word Template and Insert a File as an Object

You want to prepare a meeting agenda that is comprehensive, yet looks attractive and is easy to read. Instead of creating one from scratch, you download a meeting agenda document template from Office.com. Once you personalize the template with the organization name and logo, you save it as a custom template so you can use it for each monthly meeting.

1. Open a new blank document. Conduct a search for online templates using the key term **meeting agenda**. Download the **Formal meeting agenda template** and save it as a Word template named **w06c1AgendaTemplate_LastFirst**.

2. Replace the words *Company/Department Name* in the first paragraph with **Information Technologist Professionals**. On the left of this text, insert the graphic *w06c1Logo.png*. Position the image so that it is aligned with the upper-left corner of the template and change the text wrapping to tight. Resize the logo so that the height is **1"**. Insert the word **Chapter** in front of the words *Meeting Agenda* in the second paragraph.

3. Replace the following text in the document template:

Replace This Text	With This Text
Date	Every first Tuesday of the month
Time	7:00 p.m.
Invitees:	Location:
Names of Invitees	Student Union Building, Room III
IV. a) Description of open issue 1	Membership Update
IV. b) Description of open issue 2	Community Services
IV. c) Description of open issue 3	Fundraising Projects
V. a) Description of open issue 1	Upcoming Social Events

4. Create a building block consisting of the logo, and the meeting date and time. Name it **Meeting_Info** and save it as AutoText and put it in the Building Blocks template.

5. Remove the bullets and the two unused *Description of open issue 2 and 3* placeholders under *V. New Business*. Save and close the template.

Combine Documents to Create an Agenda with Minutes

After you create the agenda template, you send it to the president and vice president and ask them to revise it and add their topics for the meeting. When they each return their version to you, you combine them into one final agenda for the upcoming meeting. You also attach the minutes from the last meeting to the end of the agenda.

6. Use the **Combine feature** to view the returned agendas named *w06c1EileenAgendaTemplate* (as the original document) and *w06c1JohnAgendaTemplate* (as the revised document). Save the combined file as a Word document named **w06c1CombinedAgenda_LastFirst**.

7. Reject the following deletions: *Chairperson's Report*, *Rosemary Nursing Home*, and *Christmas Party*.

8. Accept the following additions: *Thanksgiving Turkeys*, and *Canned Goods Collection*. Change the date from Tuesday to **Wednesday**, and the time from 7:00 p.m. to **6:30 p.m.**

9. Insert a blank page after the agenda and remove the numbered list format. Change the top and bottom margins to **0.8"** so that the agenda is on one page.

10. Use the Create from File object feature to add the minutes of the meeting, stored in *w06c1Minutes*, to the end of the agenda. Type your name as Note taker/Secretary for the First Wednesday of September Minutes. Scroll to the end of the *Minutes* page, insert a blank paragraph, and insert the **Meeting_Info building block**.

Apply a Document Theme to the Meeting Agenda and Minutes

After you combine the agendas and insert the minutes, you decide to customize the document to reflect the national organization's colors. You begin by selecting a theme, but decide to modify it so your colors match and fonts are easier to read. You save your custom settings so that you can use them again on other documents.

11. Change the document theme to **Retrospect**.

12. Modify the colors used in this theme by changing the Text/Background - Light 1 color to **Black, Background 1** (first row, first column) and the Accent 1 color to **Orange, Accent 2, Lighter 60%** (third row, sixth column). Save the font colors as **Agenda Colors**.

13. Create new theme fonts by replacing the heading font with **Arial Black** and the body font with **Arial Narrow**. Save the theme font as **Agenda Fonts**.
14. Save the current theme, which includes the revisions you just made, as **w06c1AgendaTheme_LastFirst**.
15. Click the dark blue-colored logo graphic on the page where the agenda displays. Change the fill color to **Light Orange, Accent color 1 Light** (third row, second column in Recolor), and apply the **Photocopy Artistic Effects** (fifth row, second column). Save and close the file.

Use the Navigation Pane and Add Bookmarks to a Document

After the minutes for each meeting are approved, you are responsible for adding them to a document that holds the minutes for a whole year. The document becomes so lengthy that it is easier to navigate when bookmarks are applied to each month. You will add the minutes from the last meeting and add missing bookmarks.

16. Open *w06c1YearlyMinutes* and save it as **w06c1YearlyMinutes_LastFirst**. Add a page break at the beginning of the document, and then use the Create from File object to add the minutes of the September meeting, from the file *w06c1Minutes*.
17. Insert a bookmark named **August** at the left edge of the date *First Wednesday of August*, which displays on the next page. Continue to insert bookmarks for July and June. Type your name as the Note taker/Secretary in the August, July, and June minutes. Apply the **w06c1AgendaTheme_LastFirst** theme to this document.
18. Save and close all files. Based on your instructor's directions, submit the following:

    w06c1AgendaTemplate_LastFirst.dotx
    w06c1AgendaTheme_LastFirst.thmx
    w06c1CombinedAgenda_LastFirst
    w06c1YearlyMinutes_LastFirst

Word
Document Automation

LEARNING OUTCOME You will demonstrate how to use forms, macros, and document security features in a Word document.

OBJECTIVES & SKILLS: After you read this chapter, you will be able to:

Forms

OBJECTIVE 1: CREATE AN ELECTRONIC FORM 419
  Insert Content Controls, Perform Calculations with Content Control Data
OBJECTIVE 2: ENABLE FORM PROTECTION 424
  Protect Individual Controls on a Form, Protect an Entire Form, Complete an Electronic Form
HANDS-ON EXERCISE 1 426

Macros

OBJECTIVE 3: CREATE A MACRO 432
  Record a Macro, Run a Macro, Modify a Macro
OBJECTIVE 4: UNDERSTAND MACRO SECURITY 437
  Work with Security Settings
HANDS-ON EXERCISE 2 441

Document Protection and Authentication

OBJECTIVE 5: APPLY DOCUMENT RESTRICTIONS 445
  Mark a Document as Final, Set Formatting Restrictions, Set Editing Restrictions and Exceptions
OBJECTIVE 6: WORK WITH PASSWORDS 449
  Set a Password, Modify or Delete a Password
OBJECTIVE 7: USE A DIGITAL SIGNATURE TO AUTHENTICATE A DOCUMENT 451
  Attach a Digital Signature to a Document, Add a Signature Line
HANDS-ON EXERCISE 3 453

CASE STUDY | Oak Grove Products

Cassie Artman has purchased Oak Grove Products, Inc., a landscaping company that is opening a new line of products that includes tulip, hyacinth, and crocus bulbs. Cassie wants to take the company to the next level by automating some of the resources the company uses. One of the first projects she assigns to you, her technology coordinator, is to create a sales invoice that salespeople can fill out quickly while taking phone or online orders. The invoice will include check boxes, drop-down menus, and fields that calculate prices automatically. She also wants to incorporate an informational document about the products sold. When the form is complete, it should be protected so that variable data can be entered but the basic form structure cannot be changed.

CHAPTER 7

Using Forms, Macros, and Security Features

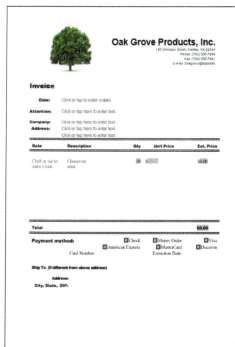

FIGURE 7.1 Oak Grove Document

top left: BeBoy/Fotolia; middle left: Monika Gniot/Shutterstock; middle right: Monia/Fotolia; bottom left: Leena Robinson/Shutterstock; bottom right: vic36/Fotolia

CASE STUDY | Oak Grove Products

Starting Files	Files to be Submitted
w07h1Invoice w07h3Tulip	w07h2Invoice_LastFirst.dotm w07h3Tulip_LastFirst

MyLab IT Grader An alternate version of this project is available as a MyLab IT Grader Assessment

Document Automation • Word 2019

Forms

A *form* is a document designed to collect data. You are likely to work with forms on a daily basis, in both print and electronic format. For example, you might open an account with an online retailer by visiting a website and providing information, or perhaps you complete a printed patient information form when you see a dentist for the first time. People often complete job applications in online format; you might even have applied for entry to a university by completing a form on the university website.

Microsoft Word includes design features that enable you to create well-structured forms that can be completed electronically or on paper. If designed to be completed on paper, a form would include formatting, labels, and blank spaces for writing or typing data. An online form, developed for data entry in electronic format, contains the same features as printed forms. In addition, an electronic form contains areas in which a user can type or otherwise indicate selections. Such a form can be designed to accept only certain types of input in restricted areas of the form. Figure 7.2 displays a completed form that is an invoice for goods or services.

FIGURE 7.2 Completed Form

In this section, you will create an electronic form that includes features that enhance the data entry process. You will learn to insert and customize content controls, perform calculations in a form, and restrict editing of the document to areas of variable data.

Creating an Electronic Form

When creating a form, regardless of whether it is intended for electronic or printed data entry, you define the standard layout, structure, and formatting of the document. If the form is designed for electronic data entry, you often establish settings to enable a user to enter data in specific places while preventing data entry or editing in others. Figure 7.3 shows a blank form that includes areas designed for data entry. Those areas are shown as blocks, referred to as *fields* or *content controls*.

FIGURE 7.3 Form Design

The Developer tab includes options that enable you to create a form. Although the Developer tab does not display by default on the ribbon, you can customize the ribbon to include it. Right-click an empty space on the ribbon and select Customize the Ribbon. Click the Developer check box on the right side of the dialog box to include the tab on the ribbon. Alternately, you can select Options from the File tab, click Customize Ribbon in the Word Options dialog box, and ensure that the Developer tab is selected from the options on the right side of the dialog box.

> **MAC TIP: DISPLAYING THE DEVELOPER TAB**
> Select Preferences from the Word menu and click Ribbon & Toolbar (under Authoring and Proofing Tools). Click the check box to select Developer in the Customize the Ribbon section.

Understand Content Controls

If your intent is to develop a form for use online, you will insert *content controls*. A content control provides a location for user interaction, just as a paper form would include blanks to be filled in. Content controls display prompts such as drop-down lists, date pickers, text boxes, and check boxes, as described in Table 7.1 and shown in Figure 7.4. Not all of these controls are available when working with a Mac.

TABLE 7.1 Content Controls

Control Type	Description
Rich Text	Enter a large amount of text—possibly even multiple paragraphs—that can be formatted. Entries can also include images and tables.
Plain Text	Enter text or numbers that can be read by any text or file editor. Limited formatting is possible.
Picture	Insert a picture in a field.
Building Block Gallery	Insert a building block item, which is a piece of content often designed to be used multiple times (such as a header or disclaimer).
Check Box	Select or deselect an item by clicking the check box that displays beside the item.
Combo Box	Combine a text box with a list box, requiring a user to click an arrow to display a list of items—but also enabling a user to type an entry in the text box instead of selecting from the list.
Drop-Down List	Select from a predefined list of choices that displays in a drop-down arrangement.
Date Picker	Select a date from a calendar.
Repeating Section	Designed to repeat content, often including other content controls, within a single control.

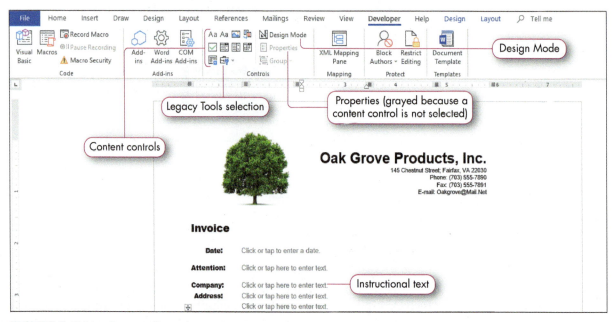

FIGURE 7.4 Using Content Controls

A **Rich Text content control** is often used to insert formatted text, images, and tables. The content control is useful when entering a large amount of text, as well. Conversely, a **Plain Text content control** enables data entry of a small amount of text that is readable by any text or file editor. Other items, such as images and tables, cannot be included.

A **Check Box content control**, as the name implies, consists of a box that is checked or unchecked to represent a preference or condition. For example, you might check *Yes* or *No* to indicate that you are, or are not, above the age of 18. You can customize check box form fields to be selected by default or to remain unchecked. You can also specify the size of a check box.

A **Combo Box content control** combines a text box with a list box, so that a user may choose from items displayed in a drop-down box or can type an entry instead of selecting from the list.

A ***Drop-Down List content control*** provides several options to choose from. A drop-down list is typically designed to display when you click an arrow. From that point, you select one option from the drop-down list. The selected option displays on the form.

The ***Date Picker content control*** displays a calendar from which a user can select a date. When entering data into a form that includes a date picker content control, you can select a Today option, facilitating quick selection of the current date. When designing a form, you can select from several date formats in the Properties dialog box, such as 3/2/2021 or 2-Mar-21.

In addition to the content controls described previously, you can also select from a small collection of Legacy Tools in the Controls group on the Developer tab (refer to Figure 7.4). Although ***Legacy Tools*** were originally developed in versions of Word prior to 2007, the Legacy form field selections can still be effectively used in form development today. In fact, forms are often developed using a combination of content controls and Legacy Tools because each type has unique characteristics that contribute to form design. For example, the Text Form Field content control, which is located in the Legacy Tools collection, is often included in forms that require numeric calculations as that field type is well suited for the purpose. In short, the choice of field type is dependent on the purpose of the form under development, but you can certainly choose from both content controls and Legacy fields if you understand the purposes and limitations of each.

> **TIP: USING ACTIVEX CONTROLS**
> ActiveX controls are available in the Legacy Tools collection, designed specifically for online forms although they can be used in other documents. ActiveX controls are useful when you need more flexible design requirements than those provided by other content controls. They are also beneficial when some type of response to user interaction is required. For example, you might include an ActiveX control in an online form so that different actions can be taken depending on which choice a user selects from a drop-down list. Or perhaps you choose to query a database to refill a combo box with items when a user clicks a button. Even so, Microsoft Edge does not support the inclusion of ActiveX controls, suggesting that the need for ActiveX controls has been significantly reduced by modern web standards that are more interoperable across browsers. You can still access an ActiveX add-on if you use the Internet Explorer browser.

STEP 1 Insert Content Controls

As you develop a form, you work in Design Mode, accessible as an option on the Developer tab (refer to Figure 7.4). ***Design Mode*** enables you to select control fields, positioning them in a document so you can make any necessary modifications to their layout or options. Design Mode is a toggle command; click it once to activate the feature and click it again to deactivate it. Having activated Design Mode, place the insertion point where you want to insert a content control and select an option from the Controls group. The Properties command enables you to customize a content control within a form. If you find it necessary to remove a content control, right-click the control and click Remove Content Control.

As a form designer, you should insert fields in the order in which they should be completed by a user. A user may complete an electronic form by clicking from field to field or by pressing tab. Tab order is determined by how form fields were created, so a user who is completing form data by tabbing from one field to another automatically progresses through fields in the order in which they were placed. Once a form is designed, the tab order is not evident and is time-consuming to modify. With that in mind, it is critical that you consider the way you intend users to work through a form before you create it.

> **TIP: COLOR A CONTENT CONTROL**
> You can change the color of a content control to add emphasis to the control or to adhere to your organization's color theme. To modify the color of a content control, select the control to be colored and ensure Design Mode is selected in the Control group on the Developer tab. Click Properties. Click the Color icon in the Content Control Properties dialog box and select a color.

> **TIP: MAKING A FORM ACCESSIBLE TO ALL**
> As with any document, it is important that a form is accessible to users, even those with vision impairment or other disabilities. You can add help text to Legacy fields in a form; text that is added will display on the status bar (if that option is selected as help text is created) or read by an assistive screen reader, if one is in use, as a user begins to complete the form. To add help text to a Legacy field, select the field and ensure that Design Mode is active. Click Properties and click Add Help Text.

When you insert a content control, the field displays instructional text, as shown in Figure 7.4. For example, having inserted a Rich Text content control, the field displays *Click or tap here to enter text*, which provides direction to a person completing the form. Suppose the content control is placed beside a *Company Name* label, which implies that the content control should contain a company name. You can change the field's instructional text, perhaps displaying *Enter company name* in the field, clearly defining the field's intended contents. To change instructional text in a field, select an inserted field and ensure that Design Mode is active. Edit the placeholder text and format it.

STEP 2 Perform Calculations with Content Control Data

A form can include fields that automatically calculate or update numeric values. The update can be set to occur when an area is clicked or upon exiting a form. For example, you might design a form to automatically calculate sales tax or total price when a user enters the cost of an item. If you intend to use formulas in a form, consider using a Word table for form design rather than text that is arranged otherwise. It simplifies the alignment of values. In addition, the use of Text Form Fields (available in the Legacy Tools collection on the Developer tab) is recommended when a form is collecting numeric data or completing a calculation. A Text Form Field enables you to define contents as numeric or as a calculation, in addition to various text formats. As you define properties for a Text Form Field, you will select from a Type list that includes Regular text, Number, Calculation, and others.

When defining the properties of a Text Form Field that has been inserted in a form and that is to represent numeric data, select the field and then click Properties in the Controls group on the Developer tab (refer to Figure 7.4). At that point, select Number as the data type and consider the assignment of a default value, as shown in Figure 7.5. For example, the inclusion of a Quantity field for an item that is most often purchased in units of 1 might be described with a default value of 1. Although the quantity can be changed by a user who is completing the form, the default value would often negate the need to do so, as it is most likely the choice that would be made anyway.

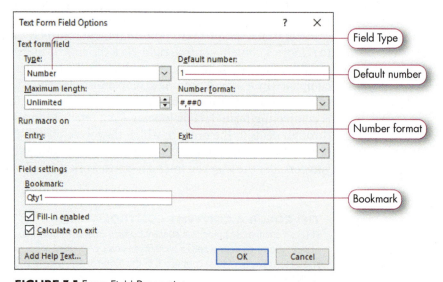

FIGURE 7.5 Form Field Properties

If the value in the Quantity field is to be included in a calculation in the form, you would also assign a bookmark name to the field. The bookmark name should uniquely describe the field so that it can be referred to in a calculation or other operation. Suppose the form has several rows, with each row including a Quantity field that is summarized in a calculation on the same row. Because each Quantity field occupies a different row, each one should be uniquely named—perhaps Qty1 for the first row's field, Qty2 for the second row, and so forth.

When defining the properties of a Text Form Field that is to be used as a calculation, perhaps to summarize a column of numbers or to multiply others, you would select Calculation as the data type. A field that has been defined as a calculation must include a formula or function as an expression, similar to the way formulas and functions can be included in a Word table. However, instead of using cell references in a calculation, as would be done in a Word table, a content control uses bookmarks. For example, having included a content control with the bookmark of *Qty1*, and another with the bookmark of *Price1*, you can insert a content control as a calculation with the expression, =*Qty1*Price1*, resulting in the amount owed. To total a column of values, a content control that is defined as a calculation might include a function of =*sum(above)*.

To include a calculation in a form, complete the following steps:

1. Insert Text Form Fields (available in the Legacy Forms group of the Legacy Tools collection in the Controls group) where applicable in a form to collect numeric data. Such data includes values like Quantity on Hand or Price—values that are not calculated, but simply entered.
2. Select a field that is to contain numeric data and click Properties in the Controls group. Click the Type arrow in the dialog box and select Number. Include an optional default value and assign a bookmark name if the value is to be used in a calculation. A bookmark name cannot contain spaces. Select *Calculate on exit*.
3. Insert a Text Form Field to serve as a calculation. For example, you might insert a Sales field to multiply Quantity1 by Price1, which are previously created and bookmarked fields.
4. Click Properties in the Controls group (with the calculating field selected). Click the Type arrow and select Calculation.
5. Type a formula in the Expression box, beginning with an equal sign (for example, =Quantity1*Price1).
6. Click the Number format arrow and select a result format. Optionally, enter a bookmark name for the calculation.

TIP: USING WORD LEARNING TOOLS
Documents that are intended for distribution, including forms, should be available to all readers, even those with limited reading skills. As you develop a form, you should consider using Word's Learning Tools to make the form more accessible. Including the option to have a form read aloud or using a modified page color that is more visible to those who are visually challenged, could greatly enhance a form's accessibility in many cases. Learning Tools are available on the View tab in the Immersive group. Tools include an option to have a document read aloud, broken into syllables, with increased text spacing, or with modified column width and page color. The language used is the default language of the operating system. Not all tools are available in all languages; for example, text spacing is not supported by languages with complex or connected scripts, such as Arabic.

Enabling Form Protection

The typical process in developing a form involves designing form content, including labels and controls for variable data, and then saving the document. Because you design a form to be a starting point for data entry, you may want to protect all or part of the form, enabling changes to occur only where user input is required. For example, a user would only be allowed to type data in locations that vary, such as when entering a name or selecting an option. Even as users enter data in certain controls, you might also want to protect those controls so they cannot be inadvertently deleted. You can protect a form's content with a password, providing access only when the password is entered. Be careful when using a password, though, because if you forget it, you will not be able to update the fields.

Protect Individual Controls on a Form

When designing a form for others to use, it is important to protect some areas from change while enabling data entry in others. For example, you would want to enable users to type a last name in the Last Name box, but not to modify the label *Last Name* that precedes the box.

A form is usually comprised of several fields designed to accept user input. Those fields, or controls, can be locked in several ways. Typically, you want to enable data entry in a field while ensuring that the field itself cannot be deleted. In other words, you want a user to be able to change the content of the field but not to remove the field. In rare cases, you might want to ensure that a user cannot change the contents of a field. For example, a field containing sales tax is not something that will be modified often, so you could protect the field contents from change. Options to lock fields in those ways are only available for newer content controls, but are not included in properties of Legacy fields. As a developer, you can lock a selected field when you click Properties in the Controls group on the Developer tab and select an option from the Locking section of the dialog box. You can prohibit the removal of a content control, and you can ensure that the contents of a field cannot be edited.

STEP 3 Protect an Entire Form

To protect an entire form so that only variable data can be entered by a user, click Restrict Editing in the Protect group on the Developer tab. Select *Allow only this type of editing in the document* from the Restrict Editing pane, shown in Figure 7.6, and click the arrow below. Select an editing type and click the command to begin enforcing protection. Enter and confirm a password or click OK to bypass password protection. Unless absolutely necessary, you should consider not assigning a password, because if you forget it the form will be unavailable for future editing. To remove protection from a form, click Restrict Editing to display the Restrict Editing task pane if it is not already shown, and choose to stop protection, entering a password if required.

FIGURE 7.6 Restrict Editing in a Form

STEP 4 Complete an Electronic Form

After an electronic form is created and protected, you can begin to use it. The form can be opened in Word, and then the user can navigate the form and input the requested data. To do so, press Tab or click to move from one field to another. Some controls, such as Drop-Down Lists or Combo Boxes, may require that you click an arrow to display a list from which you make a selection.

1. Describe the different considerations required in developing a form that will be printed out versus a form that will be accessed digitally. *p. 418*

2. Explain the purpose of using a bookmark when creating a field that is to be used in a calculation. *p. 423*

3. Describe areas of a form that are typically protected and provide rationale for such protection. *p. 424*

Hands-On Exercises

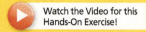

MyLab IT HOE1 Sim Training

Watch the Video for this Hands-On Exercise!

Skills covered: Insert Content Controls • Perform Calculations with Content Control Data • Protect an Entire Form • Complete an Electronic Form

1 Forms

Cassie asks you to update and automate the invoice form so that it is easier to use. You begin by inserting content controls and using automated calculations to summarize numeric data. You then save the document so that employees can open and enter data; however, you first protect the content and structure of the form so that only certain areas can be modified.

STEP 1 INSERT CONTENT CONTROLS

Cassie has given you a document to use as a starting point in developing an invoice form. You insert form controls for customer name, address, sales date, and order information in the document. Refer to Figure 7.7 as you complete Step 1.

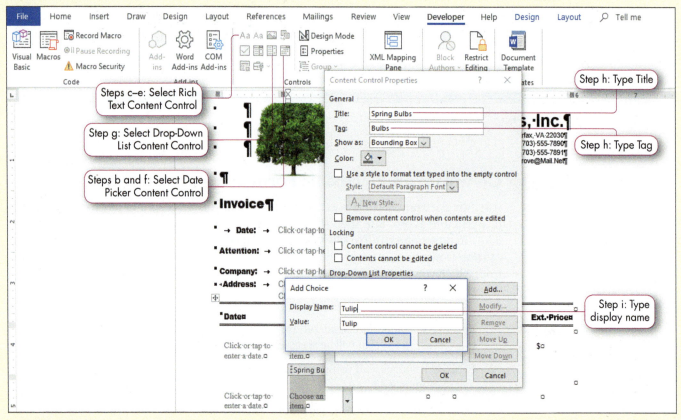

FIGURE 7.7 Insert Content Controls

a. Open *w07h1Invoice* and save it as **w07h1Invoice_LastFirst**. Ensure that nonprinting characters are displayed. Right-click a blank area of the ribbon and click **Customize the Ribbon**. Click the **Developer option** on the right side of the dialog box to select it (or confirm that it is already selected) and click **OK**.

> **TROUBLESHOOTING:** If you make any major mistakes in this exercise, you can close the file, open *w07h1Invoice*, and then start this exercise over.

> **MAC TROUBLESHOOTING:** To display the Developer tab, click the Word menu and select Preferences. Click Ribbon & Toolbar. Click to select the Developer check box in the Customize the Ribbon section of the Ribbon & Toolbar dialog box. Click Save.

b. Click before the paragraph mark after *Date*. Click the **Developer tab**. Click **Date Picker Content Control** in the Controls group.

> **MAC TROUBLESHOOTING:** The Date Picker Content Control is not available. To enter a date field, click Text Box in the Legacy Controls group. Click Options and select Date from the Type box. Click OK.

The control for choosing a date displays with a light border and the text *Click or tap to enter a date*.

c. Click before the paragraph mark after *Attention*. Click **Rich Text Content Control** in the Controls group. (On a Mac: Click Text Box.)

The control for entering text displays with a light border and the text *Click or tap here to enter text*.

d. Repeat the process described in Step c to insert *Rich Text* content controls after *Company* and *Address*.

e. Click before the paragraph mark below *Address*. Click **Rich Text Content Control** in the Controls group.

You insert a second text control for the final Address line, which enables a user to type the City, State, and Zip.

f. Click the first blank cell on the second row of the table, below *Date*. Click **Date Picker Content Control** from the Controls group. (On a Mac: Create a Text Box and format as a Date as in Step b above.) Click in the next blank cell on the third row of the table, below *Date*. Insert a **Date Picker Content Control**.

g. Click the next cell on the right, beside the first Date Picker content control in the table. Click **Drop-Down List Content Control** in the Controls group. Click **Properties** in the Controls group to display the Content Control Properties dialog box.

> **MAC TROUBLESHOOTING:** Click Combo Box and click Options. Read Step h and skip to Step i.

Users will select from a predefined list of products when selecting this control.

h. Type **Spring Bulbs** in the Title box. Type **Bulbs** in the Tag box.

Although the inclusion of a Title and Tag is optional, the *Spring Bulbs* text that you include as a Title will appear in a tab attached to the control in the Word document. It serves to identify the type of data that is available to a user who clicks the arrow beside the content control. Including text as a Tag—*Bulbs*, in this case—provides access to the control if its data ever needs to be collected within a computer program (or otherwise located and identified).

i. Click **Add** in the Drop-Down List Properties section to display the Add Choice dialog box. Type **Tulip** in the Display Name box and click **OK**.

> **MAC TROUBLESHOOTING:** Type Tulip in the drop-down item box and click the plus sign.

j. Repeat the process in Step i to add two more types of bulbs: **Hyacinth** and **Crocus**.

k. Click the cell on the next row, under *Description*, and insert a **Drop-Down List Content Control** and modify the properties as described in Steps h though j.

l. Click **OK**. Save the document.

STEP 2 PERFORM CALCULATIONS WITH CONTENT CONTROL DATA

The next section of the invoice reflects the quantity, unit price, and amount paid for products. Because these content controls are numeric, you define them as such when you insert the content controls and modify their properties. In doing so, you make them available for use in a calculation. You include a content control, defined as a calculation, to determine amount paid, and you include a total to sum the total amount paid. Refer to Figure 7.8 as you complete Step 2.

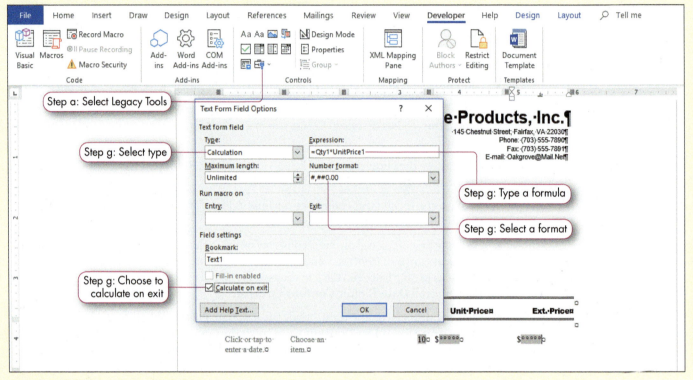

FIGURE 7.8 Work with a Calculation

a. Click the cell below *Qty*. Click **Legacy Tools** in the Controls group and click **Text Form Field** in the Legacy Forms section.

> **MAC TROUBLESHOOTING:** Click Text Box on the Developer Tab in the Legacy Controls group.

A Text Form Field, which is included in the Legacy Forms section of the Legacy Tools collection, is used when a form is to include numeric data, especially if it is to be used in a calculation. You can specify that the field is to only contain numbers and you can also define it as a calculation.

b. Click **Properties** in the Controls group. (On a Mac: Click Options.) Click the **Type arrow** and select **Number**. Type **10** in the Default number box.

Because the value in the field is expected to most often be *10*, setting it as a default value should minimize typing required of a user entering form data.

c. Click in the **Bookmark box**, remove any existing text, and then type **Qty1**. Ensure that there is no space between *Qty* and *1*. Click to select the **Calculate on exit check box** and confirm that **Fill-in enabled** is checked. Click **OK**.

Assigning a bookmark name to the field ensures that it can be used in a subsequent calculation. You select *Calculate on exit* to ensure that calculations are updated after values are entered.

> **TROUBLESHOOTING:** If you close the Properties dialog box before completing all steps, click Properties in the Controls group (with the control selected) and continue to make selections. Click OK when you have completed all entries.

d. Click in the cell on the next row, under *Qty*, and insert a **Legacy Tools Text Form Field**, modifying its properties as described in Steps b and c. The bookmark for the new entry is *Qty2*.

e. Click after the dollar sign in the cell below *Unit Price*. Click **Legacy Tools** in the Controls group and select **Text Form Field** in the Legacy Forms section. Click **Properties**. Click the **Type arrow** and select **Number**. Click the **Number format arrow** and select **#.##0.00**. Remove any existing text and type **UnitPrice1** in the Bookmark box. Click to select the **Calculate on exit check box** and confirm that **Fill-in enabled** is checked. Click **OK**.

The selected number format ensures that the result is shown with a comma if needed and two places to the right of the decimal place.

f. Repeat the process described in Step e, inserting a **Legacy Tools Text Form Field** on the next row under *Unit Price*, but assigning a bookmark of **UnitPrice2**.

g. Click after the dollar sign in the cell below *Ext. Price* and click **Legacy Tools** in the Controls group. Click **Text Form Field**. Click **Properties** and change the type to **Calculation**. Type **Qty1*UnitPrice1** after the equal sign in the Expression box. Select the number format **#,##0.00** in the Number Format list. Click to select the **Calculate on exit check box**. Click **OK**.

The equal sign in the Expression box indicates that a formula is to follow. The formula multiplies the value in the Qty1 field by the value of the UnitPrice1 field. Because you assigned bookmark names to the fields, you can use the bookmark names in the formula. The number format selected will display the result with a comma (if needed) and two places to the right of the decimal point.

h. Repeat the process described in Step g, inserting a **Legacy Tools Text Form Field** on the next row under *Ext. Price*, but assigning a calculation of **Qty2*UnitPrice2**.

i. Click after the dollar sign in the far-right cell on the *Total* row, at the bottom of the *Ext. Price* column. Click **Legacy Tools** in the Controls group and click **Text Form Field**. Right-click the new shaded field and select **Properties**. Change the type to **Calculation**. Type **sum(above)** after the equal sign in the Expression box. Select the number format **#,##0.00**. Click **OK**.

You use the =sum(above) function to total all values in the Ext. Price column. The result will display as a dollar value with two decimal places.

j. Save the document.

Hands-On Exercise 1

STEP 3 PROTECT AN ENTIRE FORM

Your changes to the invoice form are almost complete. You add a check box for the type of payment so that a user can easily indicate a method of payment. You protect the form to enable only those edits that are necessary. That way, the only changes that can be made are to those areas that are meant to collect variable data. Refer to Figure 7.9 as you complete Step 3.

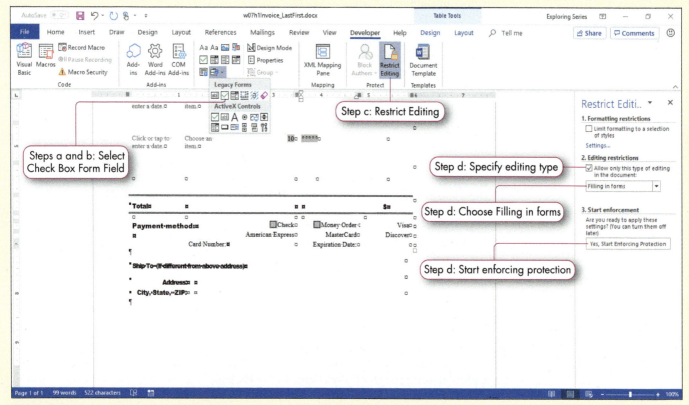

FIGURE 7.9 Protect a Form

a. Click before *Check* in the Payment method section near the bottom of the form. Click **Legacy Tools** and click **Check Box Form Field** in the Legacy Forms section.

This action inserts a Check Box content control at the left of the *Check* payment method section. A user can select the check box if paying by check.

b. Click before *Money Order*, click **Legacy Tools**, and then click **Check Box Form Field** in the Legacy Forms group.

You will include additional check boxes beside other payment methods in Hands-On Exercise 2.

c. Click **Restrict Editing** in the Protect group.

The Restrict Editing pane displays.

> **MAC TROUBLESHOOTING:** Click Protect Form in the Legacy Controls group. Skip to Step f.

d. Click the check box beside **Allow only this type of editing in the document**, which displays in the Editing restrictions section. Click the arrow in the box below this option and click **Filling in forms**. Click **Yes, Start Enforcing Protection**.

> **TROUBLESHOOTING:** If selections in the Restrict Editing pane are grayed out, click Design Mode in the Controls group to toggle the selection.

e. Click **OK** to close the Password dialog box without setting a password. Close the Restrict Editing pane.

The only areas in the document that are available for editing are the content controls. Therefore, a user can fill in the form but cannot change other text.

f. Save the document.

STEP 4 COMPLETE AN ELECTRONIC FORM

To test the electronic form, you enter fictional data into the form to ensure that calculations work correctly. Refer to Figure 7.10 as you complete Step 4.

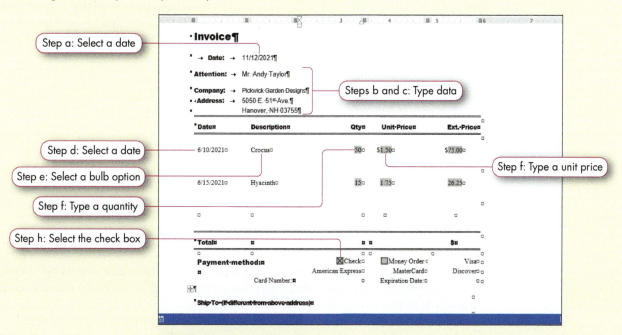

FIGURE 7.10 Complete a Form

a. Click the **Date Picker content control** (beside Date near the top of the document), click the arrow, and select **Today**.

b. Click the words **Click or tap here to enter text**, beside *Attention*, and type **Mr. Andy Taylor**. Press ↓ to move to the next field in the column.

c. Type **Pickwick Garden Designs** and press ↓. Type **5050 E. 51st Ave.** and press ↓. Type **Hanover, NH 03755** and press ↓.

d. Ensure that the **Date Picker content control** (in the table) is selected, click the arrow, and then select **June 10** of the current year.

e. Click the content control on the same row of the table under *Description*, click the arrow, and then select **Crocus**.

f. Double-click **10** in the Qty field on the same row, type **50**, and then press **Tab**. Type **1.50** and press **Tab**.

When you tab beyond the Unit Price field, the Ext. Price and Total fields automatically calculate.

g. Add the following record in the next row of the table:

Date	Description	Qty	Unit Price
June 15 (current year)	**Hyacinth**	**15**	**1.75**

h. Click the check box beside *Check*.

The customer is paying by check.

i. Save and close the document. Keep Word open if you plan to continue with the next Hands-On Exercise.

Macros

As you work with Word, you might find yourself repeating tasks, such as applying the same border within various sections of the same document. Even routine editing and formatting can become a repetitive task. Word's macro feature enables you to automate such tasks. A ***macro*** is a set of instructions, or a program, that you group together as a single command to execute a series of keystrokes. Using a macro in Word is like recording your favorite television show for later—even repeated—playback. Automating frequently executed tasks can save a great deal of time. However, because a macro is code that could be misused by those intent on causing mischief, it is also important to understand the security risks associated with macros and the protection that is available from Microsoft.

In this section, you will learn to create and modify a macro, and to test it for accuracy. You will explore the inherent security risks associated with the use of macros and identify methods of counteracting those risks.

Creating a Macro

If the set of steps you follow are routine and easily replicated, you can create a macro by recording the steps and providing a name for the macro so you can access it again. That way, you can repeat the task by running the macro. Before creating a macro, identify the task you want to record and rehearse the steps you will follow to accomplish the task. Doing so helps you create (record) the macro successfully the first time.

STEP 1 Record a Macro

When you record a macro, Word saves a series of keystrokes and command selections, converting them into coded statements that can be referred to by a group name. Recording a macro is similar to recording video or audio. You turn the recorder on by selecting Record Macro, which is a command located either in the Macros group on the View tab or in the Code group on the Developer tab, as shown in Figure 7.11. You can also record a macro by clicking the red button on the Word status bar (shown if the Macro Recording setting is selected on the Word status bar or if you have previously recorded a macro in Word). To customize Word so that you can record a macro by selecting from the status bar, right-click the status bar and click Macro Recording. While you are recording the macro, the command changes to Stop Recording, which you click when you have completed all the steps for the macro.

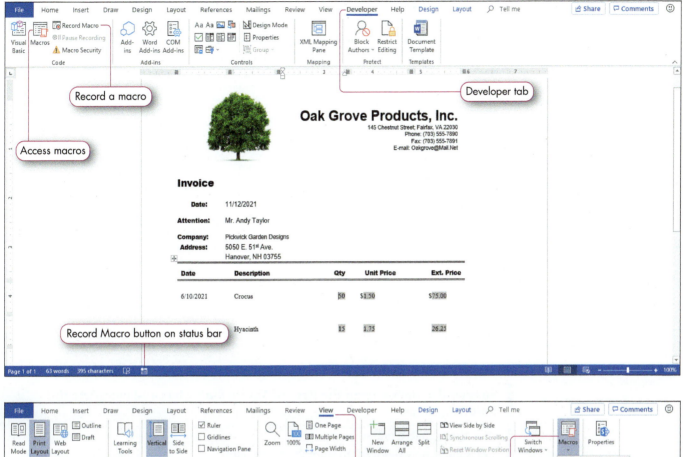

FIGURE 7.11 Using the Developer and View Tabs

When you begin to record a macro, the Record Macro dialog box opens, as shown in Figure 7.12. In the Record Macro dialog box, name the macro. A macro name must begin with a letter and must not contain any spaces or unusual characters. You can use letters, numbers, and underscores in a macro name. Make the name as descriptive as possible so its purpose will be obvious when you want to run it again. You can assign the macro to a button that can be placed on the Quick Access Toolbar, or you can assign a macro to a keyboard combination. Both options are available in the Record Macro dialog box. If you choose not to assign the macro to a button or a keyboard combination, the macro is still recorded and can be executed by clicking Macros, selecting the desired macro, and then clicking Run. You are not limited to selecting only one method for storing a macro. You can assign both a button and a keyboard combination to the same macro, although you must assign the macro to only one method first and use Word Options to add another method, as described in the next Tip box.

You also use the Record Macro dialog box to indicate where the macro will be stored—either in the current document only or within the Normal template that is available to all Word documents. By default, Word will assign the macro to the Normal template. If, instead, you want the macro to only be housed within the current document, you must make that selection.

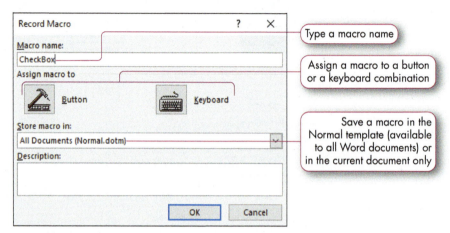

FIGURE 7.12 Creating a Macro

> **To record a macro, open the Record Macro dialog box and complete the following steps:**
>
> 1. Type a macro name.
> 2. Choose how you want to store the macro, either in the Normal template or the current document only.
> 3. Type a description (optionally).
> 4. Choose to assign the macro as follows:
>   - To assign a macro to a Quick Access Toolbar button, click Button. Click Normal.NewMacros <your macro name>, as shown in Figure 7.13. Click Add and click Modify. Select a button from the gallery of selections. Click OK twice. (On a Mac, it is not possible to assign a macro to a button prior to recording the macro.)
>   - To assign a macro to a keyboard combination, click Keyboard. Ensure that the insertion point is in the *Press new shortcut key:* box, as shown in Figure 7.14. Press the combination of keys that you want to use. Indicate whether to save changes in the Normal template or the current document only. Click Assign and click Close.
>   - To refrain from assigning a macro to either a button or keyboard combination, resulting in its only availability in the list of macros, move directly to Step 5.
> 5. Model the task you are recording by clicking commands or pressing keys for each step.
> 6. Click Stop Recording. You can also click Pause Recording to interrupt the recording temporarily and click Resume Recorder when you are ready to continue.

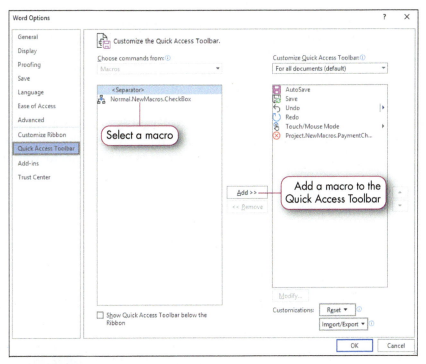

FIGURE 7.13 Assigning a Macro to a Button

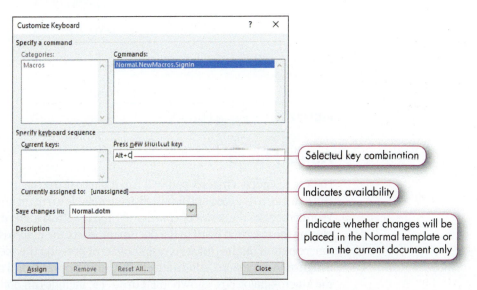

FIGURE 7.14 Assigning a Macro to a Key Combination

> **TIP: ASSIGNING A MACRO AFTER RECORDING**
> Until you are comfortable with the process of recording macros, you might find it easier to record a macro first and assign it to a button or keyboard combination only after you have perfected it, if you choose to do so at all. To assign an existing macro to a button, select Options from the File tab, and then click the Quick Access Toolbar. In the *Choose commands from* list, click Macros. Select the macro you want to assign to a button and proceed with the steps of assigning it. To assign an existing macro to a keyboard combination, select Options from the File tab and click Customize Ribbon. Click Customize. Scroll through the Categories list and select Macros. Select the macro you want to assign to a keyboard combination and proceed with the steps of assigning it.

As you model an activity for a macro, the pointer assumes the appearance of a tape used in a tape recorder. Word records everything—every keystroke and click of the mouse (including any errors and corrections to errors). For this reason, you do not want to perform any unnecessary actions while recording a macro. Practice the process, perhaps even recording keystrokes on paper, before recording it as a macro so you are less likely to make mistakes.

> **TIP: TYPING TEXT IN A MACRO**
> When recording a macro, you can type text to be included. If you plan to apply character attributes to the text, such as font color or boldface, turn on the attribute before typing, and then turn it off after typing. Macros do not record text selections made with a mouse, so any text you select in a macro should be selected using the keyboard.

If you make mistakes as you are recording, you can stop the process and re-record the macro or modify the macro code in VBA, which is addressed in the Modify a Macro section of this chapter. If you choose to re-record a macro, you can delete a faulty macro. To do so, open the Macro dialog box by clicking Macros on the Developer tab, select a macro to remove, and then click Delete (see Figure 7.15). At that point, you can begin the recording process again. You can also run or edit a macro from the Macros dialog box.

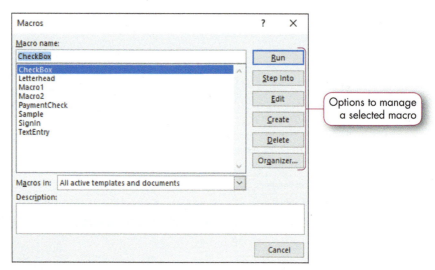

FIGURE 7.15 Managing Macros

Run a Macro

Having recorded a macro, you will run it to see if the macro performs the intended process. When a macro is tested and finalized, it is available to run at any time. When you run a macro, Word processes the series of commands and keystrokes saved in the macro. Run a macro by placing the insertion point in the document where the macro is to begin, and then clicking the macro button on the Quick Access Toolbar or pressing the specific key combination that you assigned to the macro. Alternatively, if a button or keyboard combination was not assigned, the Macros dialog box, shown in Figure 7.15, includes an option to run a selected macro.

> **TIP: SAVE BEFORE RUNNING A MACRO**
> Before running a macro, be sure to save the document. If the macro is incorrect, it could modify the document in unintended ways. In that case, you should close the document without saving it. Then you can reopen it in its original state.

STEP 2 Modify a Macro

As you test a macro and find that it does not work as intended, you might find it more efficient to modify the macro rather than re-recording it in its entirety, especially if only a slight change is necessary. Or perhaps the document affected by the macro has changed in such a way that the macro should be modified to ensure that it runs correctly. You might even find it necessary to create a new macro that is a modification of an existing macro. In any of these situations, you can access the code that the macro instructions are based on and edit them to generate the intended result.

Macro instructions are written in **Visual Basic for Applications (VBA)**, a subset of the Visual Basic programming language that is built into Microsoft Office. Fortunately, you do not have to be a programmer to use VBA, but it does help to be familiar with VBA code when editing a macro. As you record a macro, you code your actions in a VBA application. The code, shown as a series of programming statements, can be accessed in the Visual Basic Editor (see Figure 7.16). If you are even slightly familiar with Visual Basic, you can make minor adjustments to the code to modify a macro. To modify a macro, open the Macros dialog box, select a macro to edit, and then click Edit (refer to Figure 7.15). Make the necessary modifications to the macro, click Save Normal on the VBA toolbar, and then close all open VBA windows. After editing a macro in this manner, you should run the macro again to ensure that it works as intended.

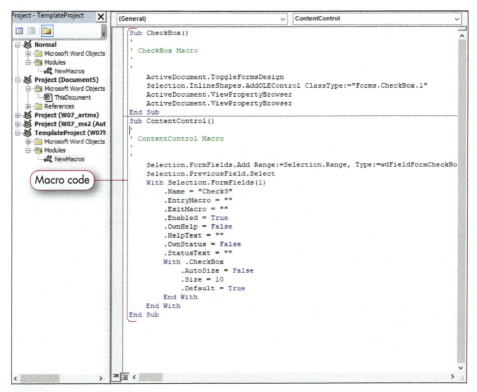

FIGURE 7.16 Macro VBA Code

Understanding Macro Security

Like a macro, a malicious program, such as a virus, is a series of coded steps. Because macros can contain malicious coding that, when run, can infect your system, macro security is of great importance in the Office environment. Especially when you download Word material from online sources or as an email attachment, you are at risk for transferring a malicious macro to your computer. Fortunately, you can use Word settings to protect your computer from malicious macros.

Work with Security Settings

When you download a Word document from an email attachment or an online source, a malicious virus could be hiding in a macro, quickly disabling your system. For that reason, Microsoft has added strong usability and security features to address any document containing macros, regardless of whether a macro is actually malicious. The level of threat posed by a macro cannot be determined ahead of time, so macro security is applied to all documents containing macros.

When you open a document that contains macros, you will see a yellow message bar below the ribbon with a security warning and an Enable Content button (see Figure 7.17). If you are sure the document is from a reliable source, click Enable Content. Doing so makes the file a trusted document, and when you open it again you will not see the same warning.

FIGURE 7.17 Document with Macros Disabled

Although in most cases Word's high security setting is desirable, at times you may want to modify it. For example, if you plan to transfer a file containing a macro between computers, or if the source of a macro is one that you trust, you can override the strict security setting so you can avoid having to enable content each time the document is opened. Microsoft's Trust Center, which contains security settings that you should not modify without good cause, is accessible in Word when you click File, Options, Trust Center, and Trust Center Settings. It is also available when you click Macro Security in the Code group on the Developer tab. Security options are shown in Figure 7.18. Keep in mind that security settings might not be available to you in a company or school, as the system administrator might have locked them. Table 7.2 describes Trust Center settings.

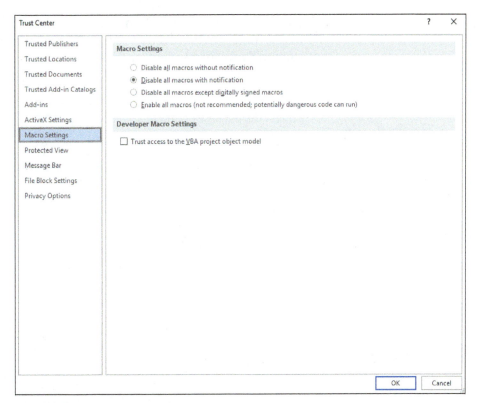

FIGURE 7.18 Using the Trust Center

TABLE 7.2 Trust Center Settings	
Macro Setting	**Description**
Disable all macros without notification	All macros and security alerts are disabled.
Disable all macros with notification	This is the default setting. All macros are disabled, but you are alerted when a document contains a macro. You can enable macros on a case-by-case basis.
Disable all macros except digitally signed macros	This setting works similarly to *Disable all macros with notification*; however, it enables macros to run if they are digitally signed by a trusted publisher. If you have not included the publisher in your trusted list, you will be alerted. The alert enables you to allow a macro or to include a publisher in your trusted list. All unsigned macros are disabled, and you will not see an alert.
Enable all macros (not recommended; potentially dangerous code can run)	This setting enables all macros to run regardless of their authenticity or signature. This option is not recommended because it exposes your computer to potential attacks by viruses.
Trust access to the VBA project object model	This setting is for use by developers only.

> **MAC TIP: MACRO SECURITY**
> To access Security & Privacy settings, click the Word menu, and then click Preferences. You can choose one of the following levels of Macro security:
> - Disable all macros without notification
> - Disable all macros with notification
> - Enable all macros (not recommended; potentially dangerous code can run)

When you save a document that you have created that includes macros, you should save it as a *Word Macro-Enabled Document* file type, which adds the *.docm* extension to the filename. By saving the file as a .docm file, the availability of macros included in the document is ensured.

Quick Concepts

4. Explain the purpose of developing macros. ***p. 432***
5. Explain why it is a good idea to save a document before running a macro. ***p. 436***
6. Explain why enhanced security is necessary for documents that contain macros. ***p. 437***

Hands-On Exercises

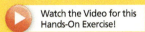

MyLab IT HOE2 Sim Training

Watch the Video for this Hands-On Exercise!

Skills covered: Record a Macro • Run a Macro • Modify a Macro

2 Macros

Your position at Oak Grove Products requires that you create forms frequently. As you work with the invoice form, you decide to automate the task of creating a check box for each payment method with a macro. After creating and testing the macro, you use the Visual Basic Editor to make a slight modification. Finally, you test the macro one last time before calling it final.

STEP 1 RECORD AND RUN A MACRO

You create a macro to insert a check box and change the property settings for that form control. Automating the process saves time, because there are several check boxes to insert, and ensures consistency. You begin the process of recording a macro to insert check boxes by assigning the macro to the current document. Refer to Figure 7.19 as you complete Step 1.

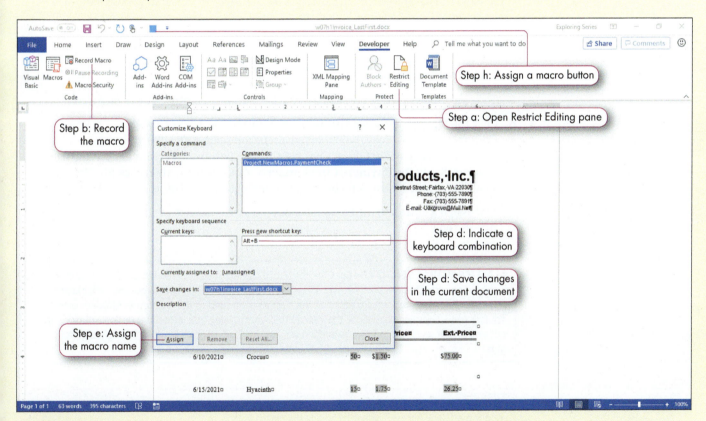

FIGURE 7.19 Record a Macro

    a. Open *w07h1Invoice_LastFirst*. Click the **Developer tab** and click **Restrict Editing** to display the Restrict Editing pane. Click **Stop Protection**, located at the bottom of the Restrict Editing pane, and close the Restrict Editing pane. (On a Mac: Click Protect Form on the Developer tab.)

    You must remove form protection so that you can edit the invoice.

    b. Place the insertion point at the left of the *Visa* payment method. Click **Record Macro** in the Code group.

    The Record Macro dialog box displays so that you can name the macro before you record it.

c. Type **PaymentCheck** in the Macro name box. Click the **Store macro in arrow** and select **w07h1Invoice_LastFirst (document)**.

d. Click **Keyboard**. Press **Alt+b** (On a Mac: Press option+control+b). Choose to save changes in **w07h1Invoice_LastFirst**.

e. Click **Assign** and click **Close**.

Word assigns the keyboard shortcut Alt+b to the PaymentCheck macro. The pointer resembles an arrow with an attached recorder. Any mouse or keyboard action will be recorded until the recording is stopped.

f. Click **Legacy Tools** in the Controls group and click to select **Check Box Form Field** in the Legacy Forms section. Click **Properties** in the Controls group. Select **Checked** in the default value section of the dialog box. Click **OK**.

You insert a Check Box control beside the Visa payment method and ensure that it is checked by default. Although it is not likely that you would often create a check box that is already checked, as you have done in this macro, you are doing so now so that you can explore editing a macro in subsequent steps of this exercise.

> **TROUBLESHOOTING:** If you click something unintentionally or find yourself off track, click Stop Recording in the Code group. Close the document without saving, open *w07h1Invoice_LastFirst*, and begin this step again.

g. Click **Stop Recording** in the Code group.

You can also click the square icon on the left side of the status bar to stop recording.

h. Click the **File tab** and click **Options**. Click the **Quick Access Toolbar**. Click the Customize Quick Access Toolbar arrow at the top right of the dialog box and select For w07h1Invoice_LastFirst.docx. Click the **Choose commands from arrow** and click **Macros**. Select the **PaymentCheck macro**, click **Add**, and then click **Modify**. Click a solid blue square button (or a button of your choice), click **OK**, and click **OK** again.

You assign a button to the PaymentCheck macro so that it is available on the Quick Access Toolbar.

> **MAC TROUBLESHOOTING:** Click the Word menu and select Preferences. Click Ribbon & Toolbar and click Quick Access Toolbar. Click the Choose command from arrow and click Macros. Select the PaymentCheck macro and click the right arrow to add to the Customize Quick Access Toolbar pane. Click Save and close the Word Preferences dialog box. Note that optional buttons are not available on the Mac. When you add a macro to the Quick Access Toolbar, it assigns a generic button.

> **TROUBLESHOOTING:** If you are working in a school computer lab, you may not be able to modify the Quick Access Toolbar by adding the macro button.

i. Click the **File tab** and click **Save As**. Change the file type to **Word Macro-Enabled Document** and save the document with the file name **w07h2Invoice_LastFirst**.

Because this document contains a macro, you change the file type accordingly.

j. Place the insertion point at the left of the American Express payment method. Click **Macros** in the Code group. Ensure that the macro related to PaymentCheck is selected. Click **Run**.

Having recorded a macro to insert a check box on the Oak Grove Products invoice, you run the macro to test it. Word runs the macro and inserts a Check Box control that is checked beside American Express.

> **TROUBLESHOOTING:** If the macro does not work as intended, click Macros, click Payment-Check, click Delete, and then click OK. Begin Step 1 again.

k. Place the insertion point at the left of the MasterCard payment method. Press **Alt+b** or click the **macro button** on the Quick Access Toolbar.

Word runs the macro again and inserts a Check Box control that is checked next to the MasterCard payment method.

l. Run the macro to place a checked check box beside Discover.

m. Save the document.

STEP 2 MODIFY A MACRO

The Oak Grove Products invoice is near completion. The macro works well, but because you want all payment methods to be available (unchecked) on the template, you need to ensure that check boxes are not checked by default. Rather than delete each check box control and begin again, you modify the macro using the Visual Basic Editor. Then you run the macro again to replace the incorrectly checked boxes. Refer to Figure 7.20 as you complete Step 2.

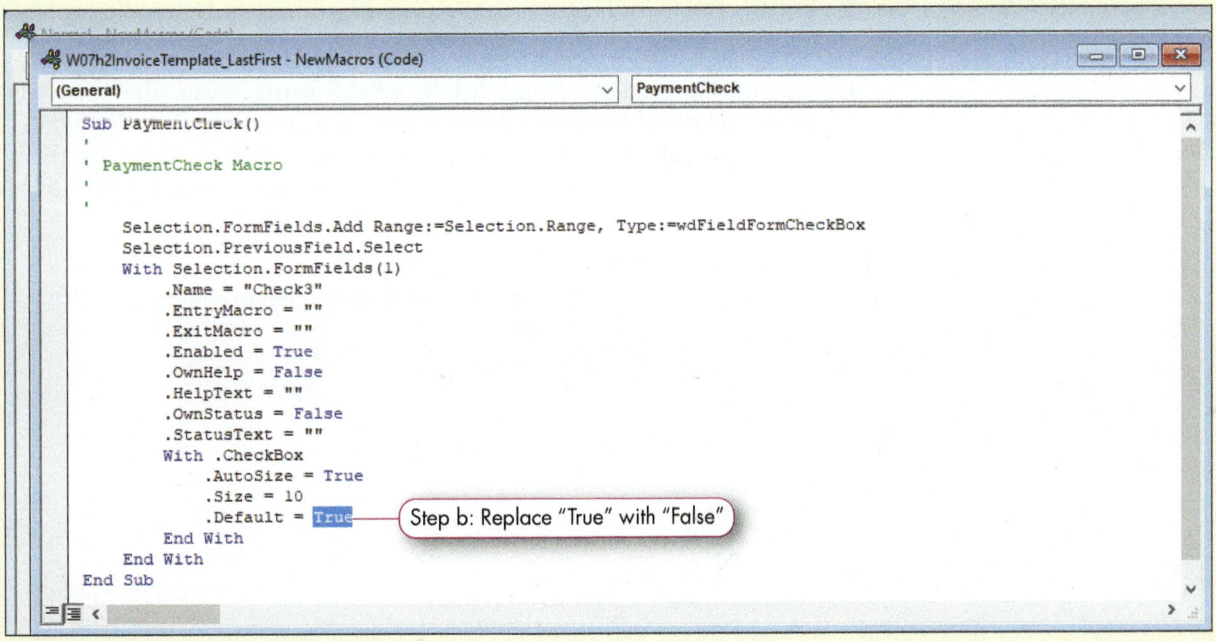

FIGURE 7.20 Modify a Macro

a. Click **Macros** in the Code group. Ensure that **PaymentCheck** is selected and click **Edit**.

The Visual Basic Editor program opens so that you can edit the programming statements.

b. Delete the word **True** at the end of the statement .Default = True and replace it with the word **False**.

You modify the Default statement near the end of the code, which shows a True value; this causes the box to display as checked. By changing the value to False, the box displays without a check.

> **TROUBLESHOOTING:** Do not delete any other part of the Default statement or any other programming statements. If you do, the macro may not run correctly. If you accidentally delete programming statements, refer to Figure 7.20 to retype them, and edit the Default statement again.

c. Close all open Visual Basic windows so that the change is saved and you return to the Word document.

You are ready to run the macro again to test the revised macro. Then you will run it repeatedly to replace the checked boxes with boxes that are not checked.

d. Drag to select the checked box beside Visa (or click at the left of the check box and press Shift+→) to select the checked box.

e. Click the **View tab**, click the **Macros arrow** in the Macros group, and then select **View Macros**.

The Macros dialog box displays so that you can run a macro.

f. Ensure that **PaymentCheck** is selected in the Macro name box and click **Run**.

The checked box is replaced by a box that does not display as checked.

g. Select the checked box that displays beside American Express and press **Alt+b** (or click the macro button on the Quick Access Toolbar).

h. Run the PaymentCheck macro to ensure that unchecked boxes display beside all other payment options.

i. Click the **Developer tab** and click **Restrict Editing**. Ensure that the editing restrictions allow filling in of forms only. Start protection without applying a password. Because you may be working in a school computer lab, you should remove the macro button from the Quick Access Toolbar. Right-click the macro button and click **Remove from Quick Access Toolbar**.

j. Save and close the document. You will submit this file to your instructor at the end of the last Hands-On Exercise. Keep Word open if you plan to continue with the next Hands-On Exercise.

Document Protection and Authentication

As you work with documents containing confidential information, you may want to protect those documents from unauthorized access. In other situations, you might need to store reference documents, such as policies and procedures, on an organization's network for others to read but not change. On occasion, you may need to assure document recipients that certain documents have come from you and have not been tampered with during transit. To assist in such situations, Word provides tools that enable you to protect documents on many levels.

In this section, you will learn to protect documents against unauthorized access, as well as changes to formatting or content. You will also learn to mark a document as final, set passwords, and add digital signatures.

Applying Document Restrictions

Word enables you to focus on the preparation and formatting of documents of all sorts. Some documents, such as contracts or other binding agreements, will undoubtedly contain text that should not be changed once the document is considered final. Other documents may contain formatting that should not be altered. Word includes features that enable you to finalize a document so that it cannot be changed. In addition, you can limit access to formatting features so that others cannot alter styles. You can use these restrictive features independently or in combination. Occasionally, you will want to enable editing by a select few while protecting a document from changes by others. Using Word, you can protect a document in a variety of ways.

STEP 1 ### Mark a Document as Final

When you want to share a document with others, but do not want them to make any changes, you create a read-only file. A read-only file lets recipients read but not change a document unless they remove the read-only status. Word provides a Mark as Final feature that enables you to designate a document as a read-only file. A document that has been marked as final is identified by a Final property on the status bar, as shown in Figure 7.21. The designation effectively identifies the document as a final copy, not a draft. The Mark as Final feature is found on the File tab in the Info section. On a Mac, use Always Open Read-Only on the Review tab to mark a document as final. When marked as final, editing and proofing marks do not display; all commands in the ribbon are grayed out; and the document cannot be modified unless the read-only status is removed. Click Edit Anyway, shown in Figure 7.21, to remove read-only status and edit a document.

Marking a document as final is not a security feature, as anyone who receives an electronic copy of the file can choose to edit the file by removing the read-only status from the file. Marking a document as final simply advises that the file should only be modified under allowable conditions.

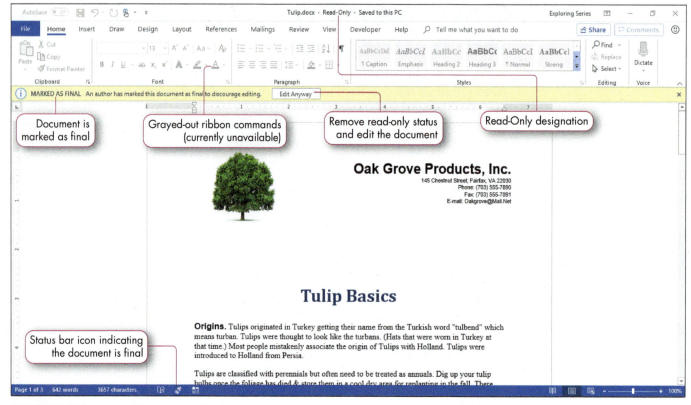

FIGURE 7.21 Marking a Document as Final

Because the Mark as Final setting can be bypassed by anyone, you should consider using the Restrict Editing command for document security, including preventing changes to a document. The Restrict Editing pane, shown in Figure 7.22, includes an option to apply a read-only setting to an open document. To open the Restrict Editing pane, do one of the following:

- Click Restrict Editing in the Protect group on either the Developer tab or the Review tab.
- Click Info from the File tab, click Protect Document, and click Restrict Editing.

FIGURE 7.22 Restrict Editing in a Document

446   **CHAPTER 7** • Document Automation

STEP 2 Set Formatting Restrictions

An organization may prefer to use certain styles and formatting, ensuring consistency among company documents. Some styles may even be unique to the organization. As such, it is likely that document formatting in some company documents should not be changed, intentionally or otherwise. As a document designer, you can limit the availability of styles, allowing others access to only a select few (if any) styles. For example, if you restrict the Heading 3 style, then no one can apply that style in the current document. To ensure that styles cannot be modified, you set *formatting restrictions* on documents. When you apply formatting restrictions, you identify styles that are available, restricting access to all others, as shown in Figure 7.23.

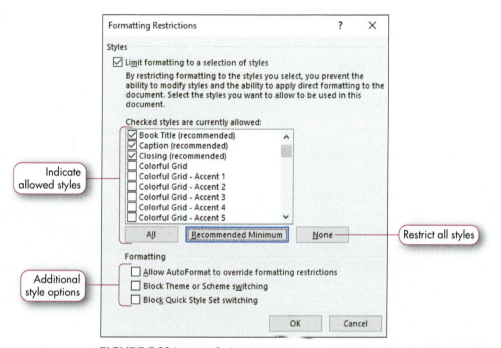

FIGURE 7.23 Limiting Styles

To apply formatting restrictions, complete the following steps:

1. Open the Restrict Editing pane and click the *Limit formatting to a selection of styles* check box to select it.
2. Click Settings and deselect any styles in the dialog box that should be restricted.
3. Apply other restrictions, as shown in Figure 7.23. Click OK to close the dialog box.
4. Click *Yes, Start Enforcing Protection* and enter a password (or click OK to bypass the password setting). If a password is entered, you must confirm it by typing it again.

MAC TIP: Restrict Editing to apply formatting restrictions is not an option in Word for Mac.

STEP 3 **Set Editing Restrictions and Exceptions**

Word enables you to set several levels of editing restrictions, limiting the types of changes that can be made to a document. For example, if you want to track changes a user makes to a document, even if the user neglects to activate Track Changes, you can ensure that the Track Changes feature is always active. Doing so keeps you apprised of changes made to collaborative documents. You can limit users to inserting comments without changing document content, or restrict data entry to areas of variable data in a form. To apply editing restrictions, display the Restrict Editing pane and click the *Allow only this type of editing in the document* check box to select it. Select a restriction as described in Table 7.3 and click Yes, Start Enforcing Protection.

TABLE 7.3	Editing Restrictions
Restriction Type	**Description**
Tracked changes	Enables the Track Changes feature automatically and marks the document with any changes made.
Comments	Enables users to add comments to the document but prohibits other changes.
Filling in forms	Enables users to fill in variable data on a form but prohibits other changes.
No changes (Read only)	Prohibits all changes to a document.

Even though a document is identified as a read-only file, you can extend editing privileges to a select group of individuals. A ***user exception*** is one or more persons who can edit all or specific parts of a restricted document. For example, you might want all team members to edit only a certain section of a collaborative document. You can create an exception by enabling users to edit that section only. It is possible to create various user exceptions throughout a document by enabling some individuals to edit certain text, while enforcing editing restrictions for others. Word color-codes text for which you create different user exceptions.

To apply user exceptions to document restrictions, complete the following steps:

1. Open the Restrict Editing pane. Click the *Editing restrictions* check box and indicate the editing to allow.
2. Select text that should be made available for editing to a select group of people. Complete one of the following:
   - Click the Everyone check box.
   - Click More users to open the Add Users dialog box. Type user names, domains, or email addresses for the individuals you want to add, separated by semicolons. Click OK.
3. Click Yes, Start Enforcing Protection and enter a password (or click OK to bypass the password setting).

MAC TIP: It is not possible to apply user exceptions to document restrictions in Word for Mac.

> **TIP: USING INFORMATION RIGHTS MANAGEMENT SERVICE**
> You can use Microsoft's Information Rights Management (IRM) service to restrict permission to document content to only those people who have been authorized through the service. IRM enables you to set permissions so that only intended recipients can edit the document content to which they are granted access. By using IRM, you can specify different users and the types of permissions granted to them, effectively enforcing corporate policy related to dissemination of confidential or proprietary content. To use the service, Microsoft Windows Rights Management Services (RMS) Client software must be installed.

You typically apply restrictions when a document is considered complete. Even so, you may occasionally need to make changes to a document that has been restricted. In that case, you must remove editing restrictions, applying them again after changes are complete. To remove editing restrictions, click Stop Protection in the Restrict Editing pane, entering a password if required.

Working with Passwords

For documents that are highly confidential or that contain sensitive information, you can set a password to limit access. A password is also helpful when you store a document on a network drive but want to restrict access to only those who are approved to view the document. In any situation where a document must be protected and made available to only a few, you should consider assigning a password, but be advised that once a password is set, you must remember it, as there is no way to retrieve the password and the file will become permanently unavailable. A password can include letters, numbers, and symbols; a strong password uses a combination of all three. A document password is case-sensitive, so it can, and should, include both uppercase and lowercase letters.

STEP 4 Set a Password to Protect or Modify a Document

You can set a password in several ways in Word, and you can indicate the type of protection a password applies. A password can protect an entire document so that no one can open the document without the proper password, or you can require a password to open the file for editing while enabling anyone to open a read-only copy of the document.

You can restrict access to an entire document in a couple of ways, either through a simple password or through encryption. Although the end result appears to be the same, the underlying principle is very different. Assigning a password to prevent users from modifying a document is like locking important papers in a safe, granting access only to those who know the combination. Encrypting contents of a document, however, is akin to shredding the important papers before locking them in a safe. A password still grants access, but the shredded bits must be put back together behind the scenes before the document is displayed for editing. In either case, through encryption or the use of a simple password, a user is still required to enter a password before access is granted. The strongest protection is through encryption, but a secure password is sufficient for most documents.

> **To create a password that encrypts and protects an entire document, complete the following steps:**
>
> 1. Click the File tab and ensure that Info is selected.
> 2. Click Protect Document.
> 3. Click Encrypt with a Password, type a password, and then click OK.
> 4. Retype the password to confirm and click OK.

To create a password that protects an entire document, although without encryption, complete the following steps:

1. Click the File tab and click Save As.
2. Click Browse and navigate to the save location, opening the Save As dialog box.
3. Click Tools (at the left of the Save button as shown in Figure 7.24) and click General Options.
4. Type a password in the *Password to open* box. Click OK, confirm the password, and click OK again.
5. Click Save.

On a Mac, to create a password to open a document, complete the following steps:

1. Click the Review tab and click Protect Document in the Protect group.
2. Click in the *Set a password to open this document* box and type a password.
3. Click OK, confirm the password and click OK.

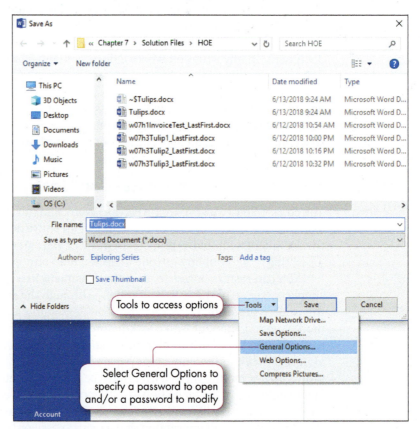

FIGURE 7.24 Saving with a Password

You may want to enable some users to open and edit a document, while others should be restricted to read-only access. Unlike marking a document as final, protecting a document with a password that specifies whether a user can modify or only read a document is a more effective way to ensure appropriate access.

To enable anyone to open a read-only copy of a document, but to require a password to modify contents, complete the following steps:

1. Click the File tab and click Save As.
2. Click Browse and navigate to the save location, opening the Save As dialog box.
3. Click Tools (at the left of the Save button) and click General Options.
4. Click in the *Password to modify* box and type a password. Click OK, confirm the password, and then click OK again.
5. Click Save.

On a Mac, to create a password to modify document contents, complete the following steps:

1. Click the Review tab and click Protect Document in the Protect group.
2. Click in the *Set a password to modify this document* box and type a password.
3. Click OK, confirm the password, and then click OK.

When saving a document, you can include both a password to open and another password to modify, which provides another level of protection. If the second password is not known, a user can click Read Only (see Figure 7.25) to view the file, and can then edit the document, but cannot save the document with changes in the same location from which it was opened. The document can be edited and saved in a different location but can only be opened again if the initial password to open the document is known.

FIGURE 7.25 Working with a Password

STEP 5 Modify or Delete a Password

If you know a document's password, you can change or delete it at any time. Especially for documents containing sensitive information, it is a good idea to change passwords periodically. Of course, the use of passwords carries the risk of forgetting them, so be sure to record any passwords in a secure place.

On occasion, you may want to remove password protection from a document. An unnecessary password can become cumbersome to remember and annoying to continually type when opening a document. Or perhaps you want to change the password. To remove or modify a password, follow the same steps you took to set it, but delete or change it in the password box.

Using a Digital Signature to Authenticate a Document

When a legal or otherwise official document is distributed electronically, the recipient often requires some guarantee that you initiated the document—in effect, an electronic "signature" to verify its authenticity. In addition, signing a document helps to ensure that the contents of an electronically transmitted document are confidential and that the document is not maliciously altered as it is transferred.

Word uses Microsoft Authenticode technology to attach a ***digital certificate***—a security feature that verifies the identity of the sender and maintains the integrity of an electronic document through encryption and security safeguards. A digital certificate is comprised of several identifiers, including personal information related to the sender, a public key (used to decode the digital certificate), and a digital signature. A ***digital signature*** is an electronic stamp that guarantees the authenticity of a file, providing a verifiable identifier that is linked to the organization's digital certificate. By adding a digital signature to a document, you confirm through electronic encryption that the information comes from you, is valid, and has not been changed after you signed it.

Attach a Digital Signature to a Document

You can obtain a digital certificate from a certificate authority (CA) that partners with Microsoft, such as Verisign, or you can create your own. However, creating your own digital certificate does not provide the same level of identity verification as that of a CA. The Microsoft tool SELFCERT.EXE enables you to create your own digital certificate. If this tool is not installed on your computer, you can search for and download it from the Internet. Some companies have in-house security administrators who issue company digital signatures using tools such as Microsoft Certificate Server.

When you attach a digital signature to a document, you are validating its contents, and the document remains signed until it is modified. Therefore, signing a document and attaching the signature should be the last action you take before you distribute it. Adding a digital signature causes the document to be marked as final, so it also becomes a read-only document. To attach a digital signature (if you have obtained a digital certificate), save the document, click the File tab, click Info and then click Protect Document. Select Add a Digital Signature and click OK.

Add a Signature Line in a Document

Word enables you to insert a signature line into a document. A ***signature line*** enables individuals and companies to distribute and collect signatures, then process forms or documents electronically without the need to print and fax or mail. The digital signatures, especially if verified by a CA, provide an authentic record of each signer and enable the document to be verified in the future.

When the document opens and the signature line displays, users can type a signature or select a digital image of a signature—or, if using a mobile device, write a signature. After the user inserts his or her signature, a digital signature tag attaches to the document to authenticate the identity of the signer, and the document becomes read-only to prevent modifications. After clicking the Add a Signature Line arrow in the Text group on the Insert tab, select Microsoft Office Signature Line. Complete the information in the Signature Setup dialog box and click OK.

7. Explain how you can restrict editing to a group of users and how they can be identified as belonging to the group. ***p. 448***

8. Compare encrypting with a password and applying a password without encryption. ***p. 449***

9. Provide rationale for using a digital signature, describing its use in verifying a sender's identity. ***p. 452***

Hands-On Exercises

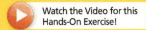

MyLab IT HOE3 Sim Training

Watch the Video for this Hands-On Exercise!

Skills covered: Mark a Document as Final • Set Formatting Restrictions • Set Editing Restrictions and Exceptions • Set a Password • Add a Signature Line

3 Document Protection and Authentication

The management of Oak Grove Products, Inc. has decided to include printed information related to tulip bulbs in each packet of tulip bulbs sold. You have received a tulip document with suggested changes that you have now incorporated. You mark the document as final while also setting formatting restrictions, applying editing exceptions, and setting a password. Finally you include a digital signature.

STEP 1 MARK A DOCUMENT AS FINAL

The document has been reviewed by several people and you are satisfied that this is the final version, so you mark it as final. Refer to Figure 7.26 as you complete Step 1.

FIGURE 7.26

a. Open *w07h3Tulip* and save it as **w07h3Tulip_LastFirst**. Close the Restrict Editing pane if it is shown.

b. Click the **File tab**, click **Info**, and then click **Protect Document**.

c. Click **Mark as Final**. Click **OK**. Click **OK** again. Click **Back**.

The yellow bar at the top of the document advises that the document has been marked as final.

d. Close the document.

MAC TROUBLESHOOTING: On a Mac, click Always Open Read-Only on the Review tab.

Hands-On Exercise 3   453

STEP 2: SET FORMATTING RESTRICTIONS

You are now ready to send the tulip information to the marketing manager so she can review the document and provide suggestions. However, you want to restrict editing to changes in styles. Refer to Figure 7.27 as you complete Step 2.

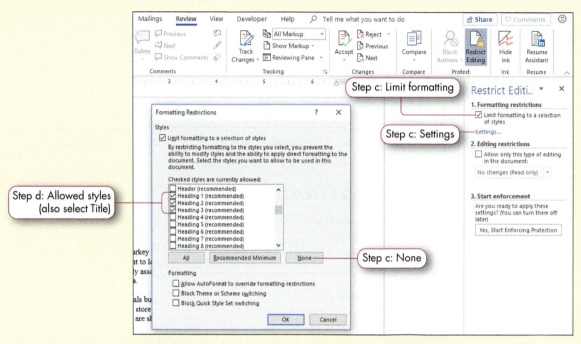

FIGURE 7.27 Limit Formatting

a. Open **w07h3Tulip_LastFirst** and click **Edit Anyway** in the yellow bar at the top of the document.

b. Click the **Review tab** and click **Restrict Editing** in the Protect group to display the Restrict Editing pane.

> **MAC TROUBLESHOOTING:** Restrict Editing is not available.

c. Click the check box beside **Limit formatting to a selection of styles** in the Restrict Editing pane. Click **Settings** to display the Formatting Restrictions dialog box. Click **None**. Do not click OK.

You remove the allowance that all styles can be changed, effectively restricting a user from changing any styles.

d. Scroll through the list of styles and select **Heading 1**, **Heading 2**, **Heading 3**, and **Title**. Click **OK**. Click **No** in the Microsoft Word dialog box that asks if you want to remove styles that are not allowed.

After removing all styles from the list that can be edited, you return access to only selected styles.

e. Click **Yes, Start Enforcing Protection** in the Restrict Editing pane. Click **OK** to refrain from setting a password.

f. Click the **Home tab**.

Most commands on the Home tab are grayed out, indicating that the document is restricted against formatting changes. The only styles shown in the Styles group are those that are currently available.

g. Place the insertion point in the title *Tulip Basics* and click **Title** in the Styles group.

Word enables you to apply a different style if that style was allowed when you edited restrictions; however, you cannot change character or paragraph formatting.

h. Save the document.

STEP 3: SET EDITING RESTRICTIONS AND EXCEPTIONS

You want the company botanist to review the tulip information for accuracy. The botanist has only basic Word skills, and you want to make sure he does not edit the content of the document. You use features to restrict the document to the insertion of comments only. Refer to Figure 7.28 as you complete Step 3.

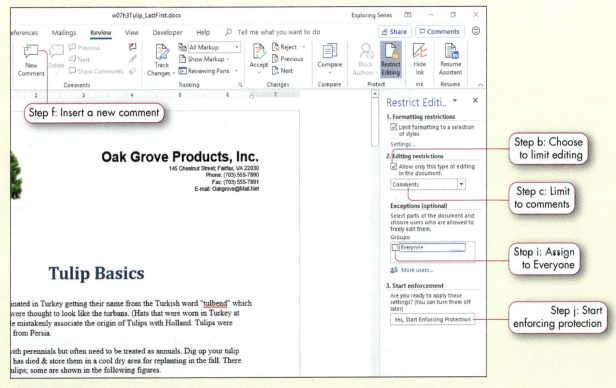

FIGURE 7.28 Limit to Comments

a. Click **Stop Protection**, which displays at the bottom of the Restrict Editing pane.

The formatting restriction is removed so that the entire document can be edited.

b. Click the check box beside **Allow only this type of editing in the document** in the Editing restrictions section of the Restrict Editing pane.

> **MAC TROUBLESHOOTING:** Click the Review tab and click Protect Document in the Protect group. Click to select the *Protect document for* check box. Click Comments. Click OK. Skip to Step e.

The Editing restrictions arrow is available so that you can specify the type of editing to restrict. Additionally, an Exceptions (optional) section displays on the pane so that you can apply user exceptions to the editing restrictions.

c. Click the **Editing restrictions arrow**, which displays *No changes (Read only)*, and click **Comments**.

d. Click **Yes, Start Enforcing Protection**. Click **OK** to bypass the step of adding a password.

The only change allowed is that of placing comments. Formatting restrictions are also in place once again.

e. Select the word **Origins** at the beginning of the first body paragraph and press **Delete**.

You cannot delete the text. The status bar displays the message *You can't make this change because the selection is locked*. The Restrict Editing pane now displays buttons to show document regions you can edit. However, because you restricted editing to comments only, no regions are available for editing.

f. Click the **Review tab**. Click **New Comment** and type **Use the word Beginnings.** (Include the period.)

The editing restrictions allow you to insert a comment.

g. Click **Stop Protection** in the Restrict Editing pane. Confirm that check boxes for Formatting restrictions and Editing restrictions in the Restrict Editing pane are checked.

> **MAC TROUBLESHOOTING:** Formatting restrictions and Editing restrictions are not available.

h. Scroll to the top of page 2 and select the three body paragraphs on the page (beginning with *Planting* and ending before the picture).

i. Click the check box beside **Everyone** in the *Exceptions (optional)* section of the Restrict Editing pane. Deselect the text.

Although you indicated earlier that the only change allowed is the addition of comments, you select a set of paragraphs and apply a user exception so that those paragraphs can be edited. The paragraphs you selected display with a light gray background, indicating that a user exception is applied to them.

> **TROUBLESHOOTING:** If you are unable to click the check box for *Everyone* in the *Exception* section of the Restrict Editing pane, make sure you have first selected text in the document.

j. Click **Yes, Start Enforcing Protection**. Click **OK** to bypass the selection of a password.

k. Select the picture of the green tulip bulbs, and press **Delete**.

You cannot delete the graphic because it is not included in the user exception and is protected against editing.

l. Click anywhere in the second paragraph of the available text (beginning with *Tulips prefer soil with reasonable drainage*). Click the **Home tab** and select **Heading 1** from the Styles group. Close the Restrict Editing pane.

Word enables this editing because you are a part of *Everyone* included in the user exception for the heading. You can use that particular style because it is allowed in the formatting restrictions.

STEP 4 SET A PASSWORD

The document is complete and ready for distribution. To protect against unauthorized access you set a password, ensuring that only those who should be allowed to modify the document are granted access. Refer to Figure 7.29 as you complete Step 4.

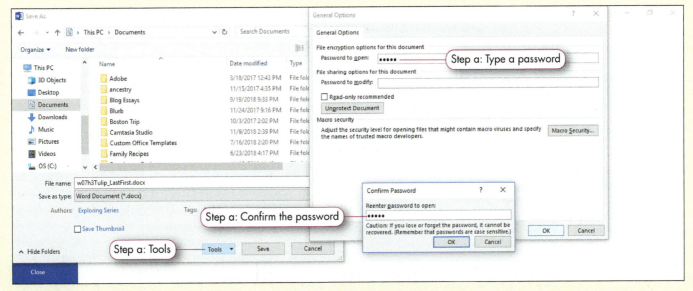

FIGURE 7.29 Set a Password

a. Click the **File tab** and click **Save As**. Click **Browse** and navigate to the location where you save your student files. Click **Tools** (near the bottom of the Save As dialog box). Click **General Options**. With the insertion point in the *Password to open* box, type **w07h3**. Click **OK**. Confirm the password and click **OK**. Save and close the document. If asked whether you want to replace the document, respond affirmatively.

> **MAC TROUBLESHOOTING:** Click the Review tab and click Protect Document in the Protect group. Click *Set a password to modify this document*. Type w07h3 in the password box. Click OK. Confirm the password and click OK. Close the document.

b. Open **w07h3Tulip_LastFirst**, type **w07h3** in the password box, and then click **OK**.

   Having supplied the password, you are able to open the document.

c. Repeat Step a, but instead of typing in the *Password to open* box, delete all characters (shown as solid round dots). Click **OK**. Save and close the document.

   You have removed the password.

d. Open **w07h3Tulip_LastFirst**. Click the **File tab** and click **Info**. Click **Protect Document**. Click **Encrypt with Password**. Type **w07h3** in the Encrypt Document box and click **OK**. Confirm the password. Save and close the document.

> **MAC TROUBLESHOOTING:** Encrypt with Password is not available.

Hands-On Exercise 3   457

e. Open **w07h3Tulip_LastFirst**. Type **w07h3** in the Password box and click **OK**.

The document opens after you supply the password.

f. Click the **File tab** and click Info. Click **Protect Document**. Click **Encrypt with Password**. Delete all characters (shown as solid round dots). Click **OK**. Save and close the document.

g. Open **w07h3Tulip_LastFirst**. You should not have to supply a password.

STEP 5 ADD A SIGNATURE LINE

You include a signature line at the end of the document so that those who edit or contribute to the document can sign to provide acknowledgment. Refer to Figure 7.30 as you complete Step 5.

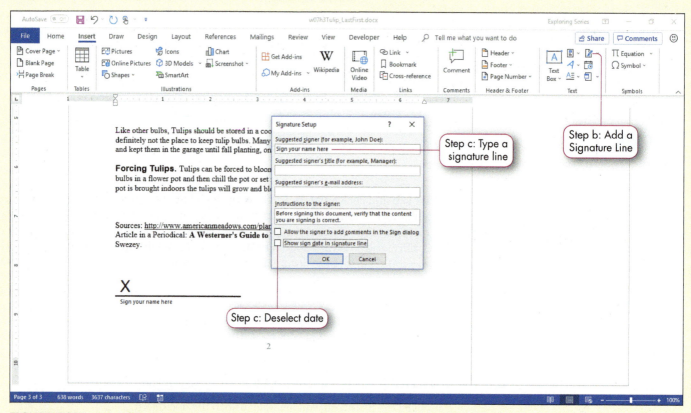

FIGURE 7.30 Include a Signature Line

a. Ensure that the Restrict Editing pane is open, click Stop Protection in the Restrict Editing pane, and close the Restrict Editing pane. Place the insertion point at the end of the document and press **Enter**.

> **MAC TROUBLESHOOTING:** Digital signatures are not available. Skip to Step d.

b. Click the **Insert tab** and click **Add a Signature Line** in the Text group.

c. Ensure that the insertion point is in the Suggested signer box. Type **Sign your name here**. (Do not type the period.) Deselect the **Show sign date in signature line check box**. Click **OK**.

d. Save and close the document. Based on your instructor's directions, submit the following:

w07h2Invoice_LastFirst.docm

w07h3Tulip_LastFirst

Chapter Objectives Review

After reading this chapter, you have accomplished the following objectives:

1. **Create an electronic form.**
   - Understand content controls: Content controls provide placeholders in a document for variable data that a user will supply. Various types of content controls are available.
   - Insert content controls: Content controls are inserted in a Word document to create a form or a collection of areas for variable data.
   - Perform calculations with content control data: Forms are often designed to include form fields that automatically calculate results based on the content of other fields.

2. **Enable form protection.**
   - Protect individual controls on a form: You can apply properties to a selected form field, protecting it against deletion or modification.
   - Protect an entire form: A form is often designed so that fields are available for data entry, but all other content is protected.
   - Complete an electronic form: A form is designed for data entry. Areas of variable data should be easily accessible for a user who is completing the form.

3. **Create a macro.**
   - Record a macro: A macro is a series of actions that can be recorded and assigned a name. Later, the steps can be repeated by running the macro.
   - Run a macro: Word enables you to refer to a macro by name or to activate it by a keyboard combination or button (depending on how it was created), so that the included tasks are repeated.
   - Modify a macro: After a macro is created, you can modify it by adjusting its underlying code.

4. **Understand macro security.**
   - Work with security settings: As a coded set of steps, a macro has the potential of being used as a vehicle for viruses and malicious software. Microsoft's Trust Center provides security settings that lessen the risk of damage from the use of macros in a document.

5. **Apply document restrictions.**
   - Mark a document as final: The Mark as Final command enables you to create a read-only file, with the status property set to Final. This is a helpful command for communicating to other people that the document is not a draft but a completed and final version.
   - Set formatting restrictions: You can set formatting restrictions to allow or disallow various document formatting features related to styles.
   - Set editing restrictions and exceptions: Editing restrictions specify conditions for users to modify a document, such as disallowing all restrictions except for comments, or the completion of form fields. Exceptions for individuals or groups can be made, so editing can occur in selected areas of a document.

6. **Work with passwords.**
   - Set a password to protect or modify a document: You can control access to a document by setting a password. A password can be used to protect the entire document from unauthorized access or to control access for modification.
   - Modify or delete a password: After a password is created, you can change it or delete it.

7. **Use a digital signature to authenticate a document.**
   - Attach a digital signature to a document: A digital signature, which is associated with a digital certificate, confirms the authenticity of a document.
   - Add a signature line in a document: A signature line enables individuals and companies to distribute and collect signatures, then process forms or documents electronically.

Key Terms Matching

Match the key terms with their definitions. Write the key term letter by the appropriate numbered definition.

- **a.** Check Box content control
- **b.** Content control
- **c.** Date Picker content control
- **d.** Design Mode
- **e.** Digital certificate
- **f.** Digital signature
- **g.** Drop-Down List content control
- **h.** Form
- **i.** Formatting restrictions
- **j.** Legacy Tools
- **k.** Macro
- **l.** Plain Text content control
- **m.** Rich Text content control
- **n.** Signature line
- **o.** User exception
- **p.** Visual Basic for Applications (VBA)

1. _____ Enables you to view and select control fields to allow for modifications to the control field layout or options. **p. 421**
2. _____ Provides a location for entry of various types of variable data. **p. 420**
3. _____ Consists of a box that can be checked or unchecked. **p. 420**
4. _____ Enables the user to choose from one of several existing entries, shown in a list format. **p. 421**
5. _____ Displays a calendar that a user can click rather than typing in a date. **p. 421**
6. _____ A document designed to collect data. **p. 418**
7. _____ Provides a set of controls that is accessible by both the current and earlier Word versions. **p. 421**
8. _____ Records a set of instructions that executes a specific task. **p. 432**
9. _____ The identification of styles that should be made available while restricting access to all others. **p. 447**
10. _____ Represents a macro in programming code. **p. 437**
11. _____ Comprises an individual or group that is allowed to edit all or specific parts of a restricted document. **p. 448**
12. _____ Enables the entry of text or numbers but allows only limited formatting. **p. 420**
13. _____ Verifies the identity of the sender and maintains the integrity of an electronic document through encryption and security safeguards. **p. 452**
14. _____ Electronic stamp that guarantees the authenticity of a file, providing a verifiable identifier that is linked to the organization's digital certificate. **p. 452**
15. _____ Enables individuals and companies to distribute and collect signatures, then process forms or documents electronically. **p. 452**
16. _____ Control that is often used to insert formatted text, images, and tables. **p. 420**

Multiple Choice

1. You can create a password to provide access to restricted areas of a form. In doing so, you must consider that:
   (a) a password cannot be deleted after it is set.
   (b) if you forget the password, the form will be permanently unavailable.
   (c) you must identify a password that is approved by the IRM.
   (d) a password cannot be changed after it has been established.

2. Why might you occasionally choose to modify Word's security settings related to opening a document that includes macros?
   (a) So that a document can be copied to an external disk drive or to online storage
   (b) So that a signature line can be included in the document
   (c) So that if you trust the source of a macro you do not need to enable the document each time you open it
   (d) So that the form can be used repeatedly for data entry

3. Why might a total field on a form not show a total, even though data has been entered in fields that are to be summed?
   (a) The total field includes an incorrect bookmark.
   (b) The total field is defined as a Text Form Field.
   (c) The total field is associated with a macro.
   (d) Fields associated with the total are not set to calculate on exit.

4. The Mark as Final feature:
   (a) enables you to designate a document as a read-only file.
   (b) makes it possible to include a digital signature.
   (c) requires that you protect the document with a password.
   (d) requires the use of Windows Rights Management Services (RMS) Client software.

5. As related to form design, a content control is used to:
   (a) restrict editing of the entire form to a particular set of users.
   (b) enable a document to be saved as a template.
   (c) provide a placeholder for variable data that a user will supply.
   (d) identify one or more people who can edit all or specific parts of a restricted document.

6. How does a digital signature help validate a document's authenticity?
   (a) It confirms through electronic encryption that the information is valid and has not been changed after signing.
   (b) It places the author's name in the document properties, confirming the document's owner.
   (c) It password protects and encrypts a document so that only the original signer can open the document later.
   (d) It restricts editing to areas in which variable data must be entered, ensuring much of the document remains unchanged.

7. Why would you consider changing a field's instructional text?
   (a) To more clearly define a field's intended contents
   (b) So that you can modify the field type
   (c) To ensure that a field can be included in a calculation
   (d) To ensure that the field is accessible to all

8. Which of the following is the least appropriate advice to give to someone who wants to learn how to create and run macros?
   (a) Decide what you want the macro to accomplish.
   (b) List the sequence of tasks you want to perform prior to recording the macro.
   (c) Change your macro security settings to enable all macros all the time.
   (d) Practice completing the steps before actually recording the macro.

9. Which two ribbon tabs include commands that enable you to record and modify macros?
   (a) Developer and Review
   (b) Home and Developer
   (c) View and Design
   (d) Developer and View

10. To modify Word's security settings related to macros, you can make selections in the:
    (a) Restrict Editing pane.
    (b) Trust Center.
    (c) Code group on the Developer tab.
    (d) Encryption Center.

Practice Exercises

1 Dinner to Go

You and a college friend have opened a new business, Dinner to Go: a service for busy people who want home-cooked meals. Your company contracts to provide biweekly, monthly, or special occasion meals with fresh ingredients prepared and served in private homes. Your personal chef service is marketed as a timesaver for busy professionals who value family time and want to avoid drive-thru meals. With various levels of service, you are prepared to assume the tasks of menu planning and grocery shopping, as well as meal preparation. You have prepared a document that describes the company and its services to potential clients; however, you plan to update it with current services, plans, and prices. You will create a macro to repeatedly apply heading formats. A signature line will be provided so that clients can confirm an appointment for one of your services. When the document is complete, you will mark it as final, and you will protect areas of the form to prevent editing. Refer to Figure 7.31 as you complete this exercise.

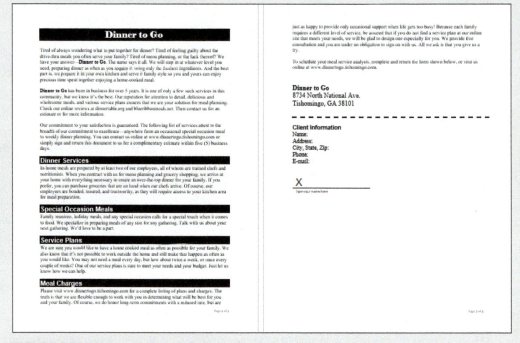

FIGURE 7.31 Dinner to Go Document

a. Open *w07p1Dinner*. Click the **File tab** and click **Save As**. Click **Browse** and navigate to the location where you save your files. Click the **Save as type arrow** and select **Word Macro-Enabled Document**. Change the file name to **w07p1Dinner_LastFirst** and click **Save**.

b. Ensure that the Developer tab displays on the ribbon. If it does not, click the **File tab**, click **Options**, click **Customize Ribbon**, and then check **Developer** in the right pane. Click **OK**. Ensure that nonprinting characters are shown.

c. Record a macro by completing the following steps:
   - Click before the heading *Dinner Services* on the first page.
   - Click the **Developer tab** and click **Record Macro** in the Code group.
   - Type **Heading** in the Macro name box.
   - Click the **Store macro in arrow**.
   - Click **w07p1Dinner_LastFirst.docm (document)**.
   - Click **Keyboard** to display the Customize Keyboard dialog box.
   - Press **Alt+h** to assign that keystroke combination to the macro.
   - Click the **Save changes in arrow**, click **w07p1Dinner_LastFirst.docm**, and then click **Assign**.
   - Click **Close** to return to the document, where the macro recording symbol displays with the pointer. You are now recording the macro.

- Click the **Home tab**, click the **Borders arrow**, and then click **Borders and Shading**.
- Click the **Shading tab**, click the **Style arrow**, click **Solid (100%)**, and then click **OK**.
- Click **Stop Recording** on the status bar (or click the **Developer** tab and click **Stop Recording**).

d. Click before the heading *Special Occasion Meals* on the first page. Press **Alt+h** to run the macro and apply the reverse effect to the heading. Similarly, run the macro on the headings *Service Plans* and *Meal Charges*.

e. Press **Ctrl+End** to move the insertion point to the end of the document. Click the **Insert tab** and click **Add a Signature Line** in the Text group.

> **MAC TROUBLESHOOTING:** On a Mac it is not possible to add a signature line.

f. Type **Type your name here** in the Suggested signer box in the Signature Setup dialog box and click **OK** to insert the signature line in the document.

g. Click the **File tab**, click **Info**, click **Protect Document**, and then click **Mark as Final**. Click **OK** when advised that the document has been marked as final. Click **OK**. Click **Back** to return to the document. On a Mac, use Always Open Read-Only.

h. Select the address for Dinner to Go on the second page, beginning with *Dinner to Go* and ending with *Tishomingo, GA 38101*. Press **Delete**. Because the document is marked as final, it is also protected from any changes. Text cannot be deleted or edited. Based on your instructor's directions, submit w07p1Dinner_LastFirst.docm.

2 Dinner to Go Service Plan

The marketing consultant you recently contracted with for your business, Dinner to Go, (as described in the previous exercise) has modified a summary document to include more detail for potential clients. The form will be made available both in print and online so that an interested party can indicate his or her meal planning needs. That way, you will have a bit of background before you call on the customer. You make the necessary modifications by replacing some bulleted items with check boxes and adding form controls to capture client contact data. You protect the form so that data can only be entered in form fields, and you finish by adding a signature line. Refer to Figure 7.32 as you complete this exercise.

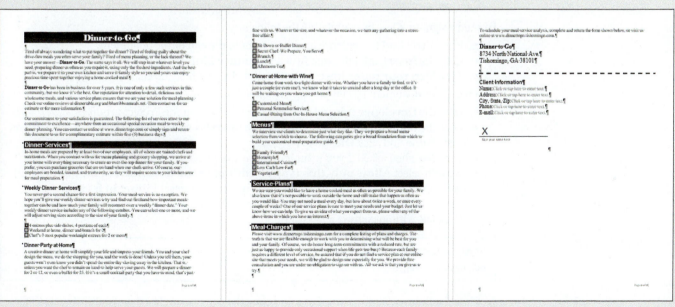

FIGURE 7.32 Dinner to Go Form

a. Open *w07p2Service*. Click **Edit Anyway** in the yellow bar at the top of the document. Click the **File tab** and click **Save As**. Click **Browse** and navigate to the location where you save your files. Click the **Save as type arrow** and select **Word Macro-Enabled Document**. Change the file name to **w07p2Service_LastFirst** and click **Save**.

b. Ensure that the Developer tab displays on the ribbon. If it does not, click the **File tab**, click **Options**, click **Customize Ribbon**, and then check **Developer** in the right pane. Click **OK**.

c. Click before the number *4* that begins the first bulleted item in the *Weekly Dinner Services* section on the first page. Record a macro by completing the following steps:
   - Click the **Developer tab** and click **Record Macro** in the Code group.
   - Type **CheckBox** in the Macro name box.
   - Click the **Store macro in arrow**.
   - Click **w07p2Service_LastFirst.docm** (**document**).
   - Click **Keyboard**.
   - Press **Alt+c**.
   - Click the **Save changes in arrow**, click **w07p2Service_LastFirst.docm**, click **Assign**, and then click **Close**.
   - Click the **Home tab**, click the **Bullets arrow**, and then select **None**.
   - Click the **Developer tab**, click **Legacy Tools** in the Controls group, and then click **Check Box Form Field**.
   - Press **Tab** and click **Stop Recording** in the Code group.

d. Click before the word *Weekend* on the next line. Press **Alt+c** to run the macro and replace the bullet with a check box. You will adjust the alignment of the check box in the next step.

e. Edit the macro by completing the following steps:
   - Click **Macros** in the Code group.
   - Click **CheckBox** and click **Edit**.
   - Select **Selection.TypeText Text:=vbTab**, and press **Delete**.
   - Close the Microsoft Visual Basic for Applications window.

f. Select the check box and tab that precedes *4 entrees plus side dishes*. Press **Delete**. Press **Alt+c** to replay the macro, which removes the tab between the check box and the service description. Select the check box and tab that precedes *Weekend at home, dinner and brunch for 2*. Run the macro. Click before *Chef's 3 most popular entrees* and run the macro.

g. Click after *Name:* in the Client Information section on the last page and press Space. Click **Rich Text Content Control** in the Controls group (use Text Box Content Control on a Mac). Add a space and a Rich Text Content Control for each of the remaining client information items. You will only need one content control for the City, State, Zip line.

h. Add a signature line by completing the following steps:
   - Press **Ctrl+End** to move the insertion point to the end of the document.
   - Click the **Insert tab** and click **Add a Signature Line** in the Text group.
   - Type **Sign your name here** in the Suggested signer box and click **OK**.

i. Protect the document by completing the following steps:
   - Click the **Developer tab** and click **Restrict Editing** in the Protect group.
   - Click the **Limit formatting to a selection of styles check box** to select it. Click **Settings**. Click **None** and click **OK**.
   - Click **No** when asked if you want to remove styles that are not allowed.
   - Click to select **Allow only this type of editing in the document** in the Restrict Editing pane. Click the **No changes (Read only) arrow** and select **Filling in forms**.
   - Click **Yes, Start Enforcing Protection** from the Start enforcement section.
   - Click **OK** without setting a password.

> **MAC TROUBLESHOOTING:** On a Mac, it is not possible to add a signature or to restrict editing in this way.

j. Close the Restrict Editing pane. Save and close the document. Based on your instructor's directions, submit w07p2Service_LastFirst.docm.

Mid-Level Exercises

1 Real Estate Appraisal

You are a real estate appraiser who estimates the value of residential homes. At the end of each week, you must submit a report to your supervisor of the properties you appraised during the past seven days. You decide to create a form that you can fill out quickly, even while you are on location with your laptop or tablet. You have a document containing a table for the information, which you decide to automate using form fields; you will then use features to protect the form and create a signature line prior to submitting it to your supervisor.

a. Open *w07m1Appraisal* and save the file as **w07m1Appraisal_LastFirst**. Ensure that nonprinting characters are displayed and that the Developer tab is displayed on the ribbon.

b. Insert a Rich Text Content Control (Mac users insert a Text Box) at the right of *Completed by* (after the two spaces).

c. Insert a Date Picker Content Control (Mac users insert a Text Box and format as a Date) at the right of *Week ending* (after the two spaces) and in each cell in the Date column in the table (excluding the Total Value of Appraisals row).

d. Insert a Rich Text Content Control (Mac users insert a Text Box) in each cell in the Address column (excluding the Total Value of Appraisals row).

e. Add a Drop-Down List Content Control (Mac users add a Combo Box and click Options) in each cell for *City*. Because you only assess homes in four cities, populate the City drop-down list box with **Ava**, **Salem**, **Ozark**, and **Nixa**. Add a Drop-Down List Content Control (Mac users add a Combo Box and click Options) in each *Zip* cell using **65800**, **65801**, **65802**, and **65803**. Insert the state abbreviation **MO** in each cell in the state column.

f. Insert a Text Form Field (a Legacy Tool) in each cell of the Appraised Value column, excluding the Total Value of Appraisals row (Mac users insert a Text Box). Select **Number** as the type and select a Number format of **#,##0.00**. Ensure that each field calculates on exit.

g. Insert a Text Form Field (a Legacy Tool) in the second column of the last row (the *Appraised Value* column) to provide a total of the Appraised Value column (Mac users insert a Text Box). The type is **Calculation**. The formula should be **=sum(above)**. Select a Number format of **#,##0.00**. Ensure that the sum calculates on exit.

h. Display the Restrict Editing pane and protect the document, allowing users to fill in form controls only. Start enforcing protection but do not apply a password.

> **MAC TROUBLESHOOTING:** Click the Review tab and click Protect Document in the Protect group. Click to select *Protect document for* and click Forms.

i. Complete the form with the following information:
   - Type your name in the **Completed by control**.
   - Select **Today** in the control for *Week ending*.
   - Type the following information into the first two table rows.

Address	City	State	Zip	Appraised Value	Date
1387 E. Main Street	Ava	MO	65803	129,900	Today
8977 N. Fremont Ave.	Ozark	MO	65801	225,000	Yesterday's Date

> **MAC TROUBLESHOOTING:** You cannot insert a signature line.

j. Click in a blank Appraised Value cell to ensure that the total calculates. Stop protection and close the Restrict Editing pane. Insert a signature line at the end of the document. Make no changes and accept all default settings.

k. Save and close the file. Based on your instructor's directions, submit w07m1Appraisal_LastFirst.

2 Game Assignments

The O'Neal Society is a student campus group that is affiliated with the Admissions Office. Students who are selected for the Society are considered leaders who exemplify the best characteristics of scholarship and dedication. They serve as campus guides and are always present at home football games to serve as hosts and to collect money to help support the two live lion mascots. O'Neal Society students are assigned to various student captains, who manage scheduling and attendance at ball games. To assist in that task, you are developing a monthly schedule of captain assignments and the number of Lion banks that should be available for each game. The schedule is maintained as a Word form so that others can complete it as needed. In addition, parts of the schedule will be automated with macros so that formatting tasks can be easily repeated. By protecting the document from unnecessary editing, you ensure that it is available in good form when needed.

a. Open *w07m2Assignments*. Save the file as a Word Macro-Enabled Document with the name **w07m2Assignments_LastFirst**. Ensure that nonprinting characters are displayed and that the Developer tab is displayed on the ribbon.

b. Insert a Rich Text Content Control (Mac users insert a Text Box) in each cell in the first column of the Fall 2021 table, from row 2 through 6 (under the Captain heading). Insert a Date Picker Content Control (Mac users insert a Text Box and format as a Date) in rows 2 through 6 of the second column (under the *Date* heading).

c. Insert a Combo Box Content Control (Mac users add a Combo Box and click Options) in rows 2 through 6 of the third column (under the *Flag Colors* heading). Values to add are **Purple**, **Gold**, **Crimson**, and **White**.

d. Insert a Text Form Field (from Legacy Tools) in rows 2 through 6 of the last column (Mac users insert a Text Box). The type is **Number**. There is no need to specify a number format. Be sure the field calculates on exit.

e. Add a row at the end of the table. Type **TOTAL** in the third cell on the new row. It is acceptable if the word is underlined. In the next cell on the same row, insert a Text Form Field from Legacy Tools (Mac users insert a Text Box). The type is **Calculation**. The expression is **=sum(above)**. There is no need to specify a number format. Be sure the field calculates on exit.

f. Restrict editing to filling in forms. Start protection but do not apply a password.

> **MAC TROUBLESHOOTING:** You cannot restrict editing.

g. Click in the first cell of the second row of the Fall 2021 table and type **Angela Hawkins**. The text may be underlined. Type the following data in the form:
   - The date is **9/17/2021**.
   - Flag color is **Gold**.
   - Lion banks needed is **14**.

h. Complete the next two rows as shown below. Note that because the color Blue is not included in the list that is displayed, you must type it.

| Mia Vest | 9/24/2021 | Purple | 12 |
| Clark Johnston | 10/1/2021 | Blue | 15 |

i. Click the last cell on row 4 (immediately above the total) to force the total to recalculate. Stop protection. If text is underlined, select the entire table and remove the underline formatting.

> **MAC TROUBLESHOOTING:** You cannot limit formatting.

j. Click the Editing restrictions box in the Restrict Editing pane to deselect it. Click the **Limit formatting to a selection of styles check box** to select it and display the settings. Ensure that no styles are selected and select only **Heading 1**, **Heading 2**, and **Heading 3** as allowable styles. Do not remove styles from any text that is already in place. Enforce protection without assigning a password.

k. Click before the first semester heading *Fall 2021*. Create a macro to apply the Heading 1 style to the semester heading. Name the macro **SemesterHeading** and store it in the current document. Also save all changes to the current document. Assign the keyboard combination of **Alt+h** to the macro.

l. Record the macro steps as follows:
- Click the **Home tab**.
- Click **Heading 1** in the Styles group.
- Click **Stop Recording** on the taskbar or click the **Developer tab** and click **Stop** Recording.

m. Click before *Winter 2021-2022* and run the macro. Edit the macro so that Heading 2 is selected instead of Heading 1. Run the macro for all four semester headings.

> **MAC TROUBLESHOOTING:** Use Always Open Read Only.

n. Close the Restrict Editing pane. Click the **File tab**, click **Info**, and mark the document as final. Based on your instructor's directions, submit w07m2Assignments_LastFirst.docm.

Running Case

New Castle County Technical Services

New Castle County Technical Services is continuing its outreach by collaborating with a local community college on a job fair at which area employers staff tables to promote their business and encourage applicants. The newsletter used at the recent technology fair is the perfect vehicle to generate interest in the upcoming job fair, so you plan to add a form that can be completed electronically to that document. That way, area businesses who already have an interest in your company can consider working with you to help make sure the job fair is a success—and they will have the added benefit of attracting qualified candidates for job opportunities. The form should be attractive and easy to complete. You have also become aware of a few formatting changes you would like to make to the newsletter, so you will automate those changes in a couple of macros. Finally, you will protect the document so that only certain changes can be made.

a. Open *w07r1NewCastle*. Save the document as a Word Macro-Enabled Document with the name **w07r1NewCastle_LastFirst**. Ensure that nonprinting characters are displayed and that the Developer tab is included on the ribbon.

b. Scroll to the last page of the document. Insert a Rich Text Content Control (Mac users insert a Text Box) after *Contact Name, Company, Phone, and Email*.

c. Click in the first cell on row 2, under the *Table Size Requested* heading and insert a Drop-Down List Content Control (Mac users insert a Combo Box and click Options). Open Properties and add a Title of **Table**, with a Tag of **Size**. Add the following options: **8x3**, **5x3**, and **Standard Round**. Ensure that the content control cannot be deleted.

d. Click in the second cell on row 2, under the *Cost/Table* heading. Insert a Text Form Field from the Legacy Tools collection (Mac users insert a Text Box). Ensure that the type is **Number** and the default value is **125**. Change the bookmark to **Cost1** and ensure that it calculates on exit. You do not need to specify a number format.

e. Click in the third cell on row 2, under the *NCCTS Discount* heading. Insert a Text Form Field from the Legacy Tools collection (Mac users insert a Text Box). Ensure that the type is **Number** and the default value is **15**. Change the bookmark to **Discount1** and ensure that it calculates on exit. You do not need to specify a number format.

f. Click in the fourth cell on row 2, under the *Total* heading. Insert a Text Form Field from the Legacy Tools collection (Mac users insert a Text Box). The type should be **Calculation** and the formula should subtract the NCCTS discount from the table cost. The field should calculate on exit. The number format should be **#,##0.00**.

g. Click in the fifth cell on row 2, under the Need Setup Assistance? heading. Insert a Drop-Down List Content Control (Mac users insert a Combo Box and click Options), with a title of **Setup** and a tag of **Setup**. Add two values, **Yes** and **No**.

h. Apply a table design of **Grid Table 6 Colorful** (row 6, column 1 under Grid Tables). Select row 1 and apply **Align Center alignment**.

i. Display the Restrict Editing pane and allow only filling in of forms. Start protection but do not assign a password.

> **MAC TROUBLESHOOTING:** You cannot restrict editing.

j. Click the field arrow in the first cell of the second row and select a table size of **8x3**. Click the *Need Setup Assistance control* in the last cell on the second row and select **No**.

k. Click the control beside *Contact Name* and type your first and last names. Click the control beside *Company* and type **Dryden Services**. Add a phone number of **601-555-3330**. Add an email address of **ddsinc@outlook.com**. Stop protection and close the Restrict Editing pane.

l. Move to page 1 of the document and click at the left of the word *Locally* in the first bulleted item. Record a macro, assigning the name **BulletFormat**. Store changes in **w07r1NewCastle_LastFirst.docm (document)** and assign a keyboard combination of **Alt+b**. Changes should be saved in **w07r1NewCastle_LastFirst.docm**.

m. The macro should follow the steps given below:
- Click the **Home tab**.
- Click the **Bullets arrow**.
- Click the **black checkmark** (or choose a clear round bullet if the checkmark is not shown).
- Click the **Bullets arrow** and click **Define New Bullet**.
- Click **Font**. Click the **Font color arrow**. Click **Red** (column 2 in Standard Colors).
- Click **OK**. Click **OK**.

n. Edit the VBA code for the BulletFormat macro so that the color is Blue instead of Red. You will find the coded instruction near the end of the VBA code in the line that reads *Color = wdColorRed*. Change the word *Red* in that instruction to **Blue**.

o. Run the macro to ensure that all bullets on page 1 are modified to blue.

p. Scroll to page 4 and click before the first bulleted item, beginning with *When was the last time your IT staff*. Run the BulletFormat macro.

q. Save the document. Based on your instructor's directions, submit w07r1NewCastle_LastFirst.docm.

Disaster Recovery

Purchase Order

A colleague wants to use a form as a purchase order for his small company. He created the form, but it does not work as he expected. The calculating fields do not function properly, the customer information does not display as a form field, and he is no longer able to type anything into his form. His frustration has forced him to ask you for advice. Your task is to troubleshoot the form and make corrections or additions that will turn it into a functional and professional-looking electronic form. Open *w07d1Problem* and save it as **w07d1Problem_LastFirst**. Correct problem areas on the form and apply formatting that improves the appearance. Consider and implement any editing restrictions that would ensure appropriate use, but do not apply a password. Based on your instructor's directions, submit w07d1Problem_LastFirst.

Capstone Exercise

MyITLab Grader

Stay at Home Pet Sitting

You and a friend are starting a pet sitting business in which you manage a crew of pet sitters. Much like a cleaning service, you accept clients who need pet sitting services in their homes either on an occasional or daily basis. Many of your clients need a pet sitter when they are away on business or vacation. As you are contacted by potential clients, you make it a point to visit their home to determine whether, or how, your service can assist them. You generally take your tablet and record a bit of information as you conduct the visit. You are designing a form on which you can collect and summarize information for later assignment of a pet sitter. The concisely designed form will be protected from inadvertent editing.

Design a Form

You want to only collect client information that is necessary to determine services and sitter assignment. The form should fit easily on a tablet screen and require minimal effort to complete. You begin with a basic document and develop a design that includes a table for ease of navigation between fields.

1. Open *w07c1Pet* and save the document as a Word Macro-Enabled Document with the name **w07c1Pet_LastFirst**. Ensure that nonprinting characters are displayed and that the Developer tab displays on the ribbon.

2. Click before *Online* and insert a Check Box Content Control. Add a Check Box Content Control before *Ad*, *Personal referral*, and *Other*. Click after the colon and the space following *Date* and insert a Date Picker Content Control. Insert a Rich Text Content Control after *Client Name*, *City*, *Phone*, and *Referral*.

3. Insert a Drop-Down List Content Control in the first cell on the third row (under *Pet Type*). The dropdown list should include **Cat**, **Dog**, and **Other**. You do not need to include a Title or Tag. Insert a Drop-Down List Control in the first cell on the fourth row, including the same values as the cell above.

4. Insert a Text Form Field, from the Legacy Tools collection, in the next cell (under *Number*). The type is **Number** and the bookmark is **Qty1**. You do not need to select a number format. Select **Calculate on exit**. Insert a Legacy Tools Text Form Field in the *Number* cell on the fourth row. The type is **Number** and the bookmark is **Qty2**. You do not need to select a number format. Select **Calculate on exit**.

5. Insert a Drop-Down List Content Control in every cell in the *Service Type* column (below the heading). Values to include are **Daily** or **Extended**.

6. Insert a Text Form Field from the Legacy Tools collection in the first cell under Daily Cost (est.). The type is **Calculation** and the formula is **Qty1 * 50**. You do not need to select a number format. Select **Calculate on exit**.

7. Insert a Text Form Field from the Legacy Tools collection in the second cell under *Daily Cost*. Repeat the same properties from the first cell but multiply Qty2 by 50.

8. Apply a table design of **Grid Table 4 - Accent 3** (row 4, column 4 under Grid Tables). Save the document.

> **MAC TROUBLESHOOTING:** You cannot restrict editing.

9. Display the Restrict Editing pane and restrict editing to filling in forms. Enforce protection without setting a password.

Complete a Form

To complete the form, you insert some fictitious data to see if it works as intended.

10. Click beside *Date* and select **April 29** of the current year. The Client Name is **Rita Baker**, whose City is **Jarvis**. Her phone is **331-555-0021**. She heard about Stay at Home Pet Sitting from a **Personal referral**. List **Jacob White** as the Referral.

11. Ensure the first pet listed is a **Dog**. Click in the next cell, *Number*, type **2**, and press **Tab**. The Service Type is **Daily**. The value in the last column should update. If necessary, click in another cell to force the update.

12. Ensure the second pet listed is a **Cat**. Click in the next cell, *Number*, type **1**, and press **Tab**. The Service Type is **Daily**. The value in the last column should update. If necessary, click in another cell to force the update.

13. Click **Stop Protection** in the Restrict Editing pane and save the document. Close the Restrict Editing pane.

Add and Edit a Macro

You will give a copy of the form to a potential client, but you want to make it clear that the form is only an estimate, as other considerations might modify the price later. You typically place a footer indicating that status, and since you do that so often, you will develop a macro to simplify the task.

14. Begin the process of recording a macro titled **EstimateFooter**. The macro should be stored in the current document. You will not assign the macro to either a button or a keyboard combination.

15. Design the macro by completing the following steps.
    - Click the **Insert tab**. Click **Footer** in the Header & Footer group.
    - Click **Edit Footer**.
    - Type **Estimate Only** in the footer area.
    - Click **Close Header and Footer** in the Header & Footer group.
16. Stop recording. Edit the macro to remove the word **Only** from the footer. Double-click in the footer and remove the footer. Close the footer.
17. Run the macro again to ensure that it correctly places the one-word footer.
18. Save the document.

Add a Signature Line

As you discuss your services with a client and prepare the estimate, you will ask the client to sign the form to agree that they have seen the estimate. You add a signature line for that purpose.

19. Place the insertion point at the end of the document and press **Enter**. Insert a signature line, accepting all defaults.

> **MAC TROUBLESHOOTING:** You cannot insert a signature line.

Protect a Document and Limit Editing

So that the document remains available, but editing is discouraged, you restrict editing so that it is in read-only mode when it is opened.

20. Turn off the display of nonprinting characters. Show the Restrict Editing pane and limit editing so that the document is in *Read only* format. Start enforcing protection without assigning a password.

> **MAC TROUBLESHOOTING:** You cannot restrict editing.

21. Save and close the document. Based on your instructor's directions, submit w07c1Pet_LastFirst.docm.

Word and the Internet

LEARNING OUTCOME: You will develop, enhance, and publish documents for the Web such as webpages and blogs.

OBJECTIVES & SKILLS: After you read this chapter, you will be able to:

Webpage Creation

OBJECTIVE 1: CUSTOMIZE THE RIBBON — 474
  Create a Custom Tab, Add Commands to a Group

OBJECTIVE 2: BUILD AND PUBLISH A WEBPAGE — 478
  Save a Document as a Webpage, Apply a Theme and Background Color to a Webpage, Insert Bookmarks in a Webpage and Add a Link to a Bookmark, Insert Hyperlinks to Other Webpages, Preview a Webpage

HANDS-ON EXERCISE 1 — 487

Webpage Enhancement

OBJECTIVE 3: ENHANCE A WEBPAGE — 496
  Download and Save a Template as a Document, Change a Template Picture, Use 3D Models, Insert Online Videos

OBJECTIVE 4: CREATE A BLOG POST — 499
  Download a Blog Post Template, Create a Blog Post

HANDS-ON EXERCISE 2 — 502

CASE STUDY | A Math Tutoring Club

You are working on your bachelor's degree to become a middle school teacher. You know that there is a need for math tutors, so you want to create a website to provide online resources to students who want to improve their math skills. Your plan is for a simple, static website to provide information about your new endeavor, information on how to request tutoring services, sample worksheets for students to practice, and other resources for students to consult. By keeping it simple, you can maintain and update it yourself using tools such as Microsoft Word.

Your knowledge of the Microsoft Office suite enables you to set up the webpages to be multifunctional and to format and organize information about your services in a way that displays well on a website. You will use these tools to create all the webpages as well as a blog to post more targeted notes and links about updates on your website.

CHAPTER 8

Creating and Enhancing Webpages and Blogs

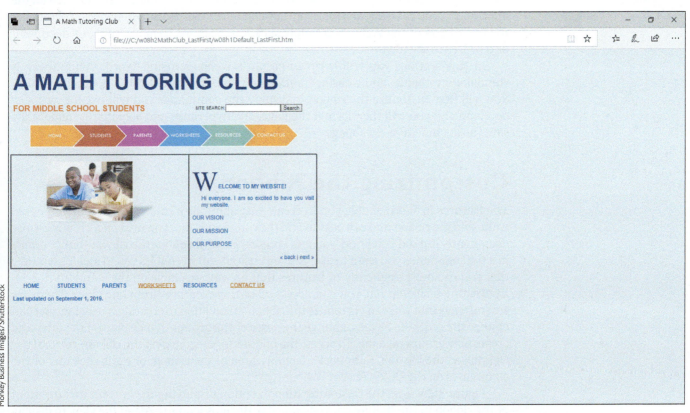

FIGURE 8.1 A Math Tutoring Club Webpage

CASE STUDY | A Math Tutoring Club

Starting Files	Files to be Submitted
Blank document Event flyer template w08h1ContactUs w08h1Default w08h1Worksheets w08h2Math	In the w08h2MathClub_LastFirst zipped file: w08h1ContactUs_LastFirst_files subfolder w08h1Worksheets_LastFirst_files subfolder w08h2Default_LastFirst_files subfolder w08h2Flyer_LastFirst_files subfolder w08h1ContactUs_LastFirst.htm w08h1Worksheets_LastFirst.htm w08h2Blog_LastFirst.docx w08h2Default_LastFirst.htm w08h2Flyer_LastFirst.htm

MyLab IT Grader An alternate version of this project is available as a MyLab IT Grader Assessment

Webpage Creation

For most students, the Internet is as much a part of the education process as books and teachers. As you probably know, the Internet is a network of networks that connects computers everywhere in the world. It is easy to connect your computer to the Internet, and that connection enables you to view an abundance of information about every imaginable topic.

The **World Wide Web (WWW)**, or simply the Web, is a very large subset of the Internet, consisting of special types of documents known as **webpages**. Any document that displays on the World Wide Web is a webpage. Webpages can be self-contained and provide all the information you need about a topic, or they can offer links to other webpages. Therein lies the fascination of the Web—you simply click link after link to move from one document or resource to the next.

In this section, you will learn to create a webpage using Word. While there is standalone webpage and website creation software, using Word is a good alternative. You will first customize the ribbon to display the commands you will use for webpage development; you will then format the page, add hyperlinks and bookmarks, and finally save the document as a webpage.

Customizing the Ribbon

The features in Word enable you to create just about any kind of document you could want, and the ribbon makes it easy to find the commands that you use when creating those documents. But did you know you can create a **custom tab** for the ribbon that contains just the commands you want to use? Ribbon customization enables you to include features that you use most frequently or features that are not available on the standard ribbon. By creating a custom tab, you can access all of these features from one place. There are several ways that you can customize the ribbon. In addition to creating a new tab, you can change the order of the tabs, change the order of the groups that display on the tabs, and create new groups on a tab. To access the options for customizing the ribbon, you can use Options on the File tab, right-click an empty area of the ribbon, or right-click any of the commands on the Quick Access Toolbar (QAT).

Figure 8.2 shows the Customize Ribbon option displaying the current arrangement of the ribbon in the right pane. You can click the plus icon to expand the view to display the groups within a tab or click the minus icon to collapse the view to hide the groups. To change the order of the existing tabs or groups, use the move up and move down arrows or drag and drop a selected tab and group to a new position.

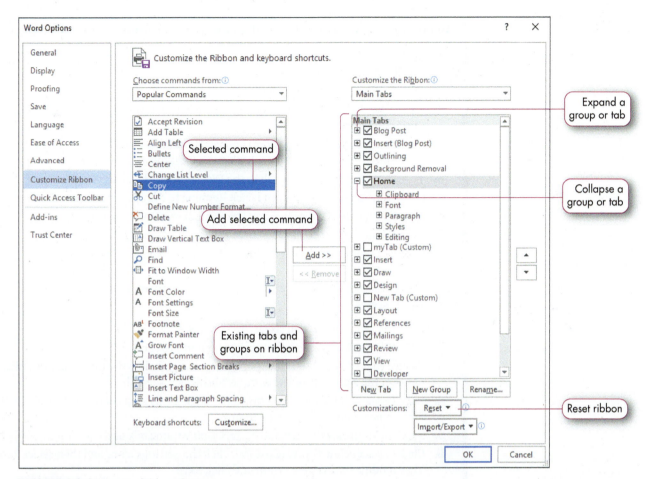

FIGURE 8.2 Customize Ribbon Options

> **TIP: RESTORE THE RIBBON**
> To restore the ribbon to its original arrangement, click Reset at the bottom of the Customize Ribbon view and select *Reset all customizations*. Reset also enables you to reset individual tabs.

STEP 1 Create a Custom Tab

To have easy access to the commands you use most, you can add a new tab to the ribbon, then add the frequently used commands to this newly created tab. When you create a new tab, you also automatically create a new group. You can select and add any frequently used commands to this group on the new tab. You can also add additional groups to the newly created tab. For instance, if you often use Word to create webpages, you may want to create a custom tab that contains Web-related commands, such as Bookmark, Horizontal Line, Link, Page Color, Themes, and Web Page Preview, and name the new tab as *Web*. It is always a good idea to rename new tabs and new groups using short and appropriate names. When you rename a group, you can also select a colorful symbol to represent the group's contents. You can reorder the tabs on the ribbon by selecting the tab and clicking the Move Up and Move Down arrows on the right side of Customize the Ribbon in the Word Options dialog box. Figure 8.3 displays a new tab containing a new group.

Webpage Creation • **Word 2019**

To create a new custom tab and a new group, complete the following steps:

1. Click the File tab.
2. Scroll down and click Options.
3. Click Customize Ribbon in the left pane.
4. Click New Tab below the Customize the Ribbon pane on the right side of the Word Options dialog box.
5. Click to select New Tab (Custom) and click Rename, which displays below the Customize the Ribbon pane, to display the Rename dialog box.
6. Type the name for the new tab in the Display name box and click OK.
7. Click New Group (Custom) and click Rename to display the Rename dialog box.
8. Select a symbol of your choice in the Symbol section (optional).
9. Type the name for the new group in the Display name box and click OK.
10. Click OK again to close the Word Options dialog box.

On a Mac, to create a new custom tab and custom group, complete the following steps:

1. Click the Word menu and select Preferences.
2. Click Ribbon & Toolbar in the Authoring and Proofing Tools.
3. Ensure that ribbon is selected. Click the plus sign below the Customize the Ribbon pane on the right side of the window and select New tab.
4. Click to select New Tab (Custom), click the Settings icon below the Customize the Ribbon pane, and then select Rename.
5. Type the name for the new tab in the Display name box and click Save.
6. Click to select New Group (Custom), click the Settings icon, and then select Rename. Type a name for the new group and click Save.
7. Click Save to close the Ribbon & Toolbar dialog box.

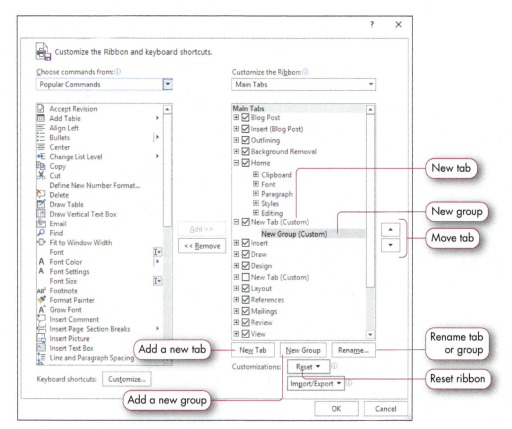

FIGURE 8.3 New Tab and Group Options

Add Commands to a Group

If you find that you predominantly work with the commands from one tab and use one or two other commands from another tab, you can add these commands to the tab that you use most often. Popular commands that you can add display in the default view under the *Choose commands from* selections in the Word Options dialog box. You can also click the *Choose commands from* arrow to choose from additional commands and macros. In addition, there is a category named Commands Not in the Ribbon. This is where you can find commands that are not on the default tabs, such as Web Page Preview, to add to the tab or group. Another option is the All Commands category, which lists all the commands available in Word. Figure 8.4 displays a customized tab with commands you will most likely use while creating webpages.

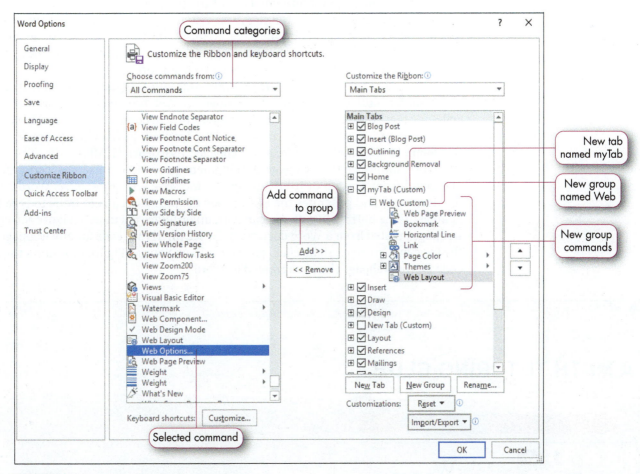

FIGURE 8.4 Customize Tab and Group

> **To add new commands to a tab, complete the following steps:**
>
> 1. Click to select the group in the Customize the Ribbon pane on the right.
> 2. Click the *Choose commands from* arrow to select the group of commands you want to choose from.
> 3. Scroll down the list of commands, find the command you want to add to the tab, and then click Add.
> 4. Repeat Step 3 to add more commands.
> 5. Confirm that the new tab is checked and click OK to close the Word Options dialog box.

> **TIP: EXPORT AND IMPORT A CUSTOM TAB**
> If you customize a tab or the Quick Access Toolbar (QAT), that customization is only applied to the Word application installed on that computer. You can export the customized tab or the QAT to a file that can be imported to a different computer. Click Import/Export at the bottom of the Word Options dialog box to save your customizations. Copy the file you save onto a different computer and click Import/Export again on the new computer to import your custom tab or QAT.

Building and Publishing a Webpage

Sooner or later, you might want to create a webpage or a website of your own. You can use any Web authoring software package to do so, but another option is to use Word. Word provides the tools necessary to create a basic webpage. You can use tables and SmartArt graphics to organize and lay out the page elements, add online images and your own pictures to enhance the page with visual elements, use bulleted and numbered lists to organize information on the page, create WordArt for text, and so on. Word has many useful tools for creating and updating your webpage, but if your webpage design is complex, you will want to use a full-featured Web authoring tool.

Webpage development uses ***HyperText Markup Language (HTML)***, which is a universal formatting instructional language for Web browsers. It consists of a set of codes (or tags) that are assigned to the content of a document. The codes describe how the document is to display when viewed in a browser. In the early years of Internet development, the only way to create a webpage was to learn HTML.

Word simplifies the webpage development process because you can create the document from scratch or from a template and save it as a webpage. Word converts the document and generates the HTML code for you. You can continue to type text or change the formatting just as you can with an ordinary document. Figure 8.5 shows a webpage created from a Word document. To see the HTML code for any webpage, open the page in a browser, right-click, and select View Source. Figure 8.6 shows the HTML code for the webpage that was created in Word.

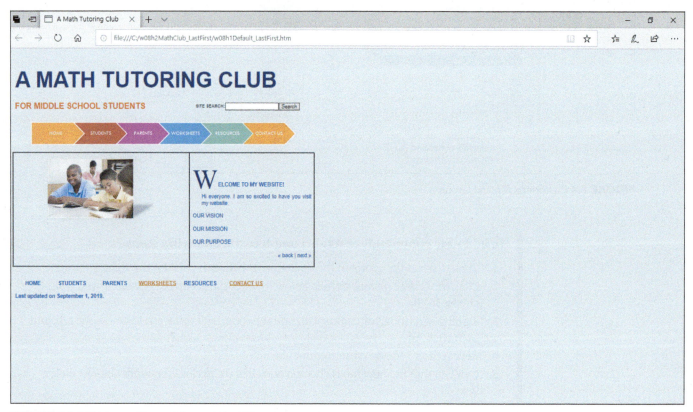

FIGURE 8.5 A Webpage Created from a Word Document

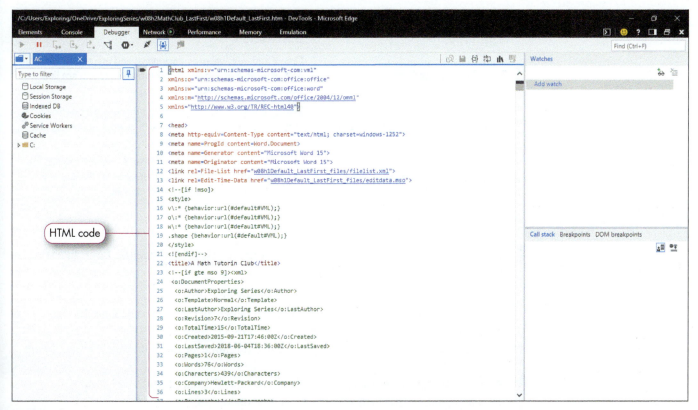

FIGURE 8.6 HTML Code for a Webpage

STEP 2 Save a Document as a Webpage

Any document you create in Word can be displayed in Web Layout view. This view enables you to continue using regular Word formatting features while displaying the document as it will be seen in a browser. Once you are finished creating and formatting the document in Web Layout view, you can save it as a webpage. When the document is saved as a webpage, there are three different Web formats from which to choose. Table 8.1 lists and describes the three Web file types. When you save your file as a Web Page in .htm or .html format, the source code is stored in one file and all the other webpage assets (images, Java applets, etc.) are stored in a separate folder. If you want the source code and all the assets to be saved in one file, then you will save your file as a single file webpage. The file extension for this type of file is .mht or .mhtml. Single file webpages have larger file sizes because all the images are embedded and saved in the file. If a large file size becomes an impediment to uploading to a Web server, you could save your file as a Web Page, Filtered. In a filtered webpage, Word keeps only the content and style instructions. All Word tags are removed, and only the HTML tags remain in the file. Therefore, the filtered file is small, without a lot of extra code. Images are saved in an accompanying folder, which must be saved in the same directory as the webpage on the server. The downsides are that some Office features may not be available when you reopen the filtered page and that you cannot edit a filtered webpage in Word.

It is good Web design practice to create a folder on your storage medium and save all your Word documents as individual webpages to this folder. One of these webpages is the homepage, which serves as an introductory page of a website and often contains a table of contents for it. The typical filename for the homepage is *default*. When you open a webpage, its name displays on the browser. Therefore, it is also a good idea to change the title of each page to reflect the content of the document.

TABLE 8.1 Options for Saving Webpages

File Type	Description
Web Page (*.htm; *.html)	Create and edit webpage documents and use regular Word editing tools. Keep saving in this format until you are finished preparing the document.
Single File Web Page (*.mht; *.mhtml)	Save all components of a webpage that are otherwise represented by external links (such as images, Java applets, audio files) in a single document.
Web Page, Filtered (*.htm; *.html)	Save the final webpage in this format to reduce the file size and Word editing options. Then upload this file and any corresponding folder(s) to a Web server.

To save the homepage for a website to a folder that has already been created, complete the following steps:

1. Open the document that will be the designated homepage.
2. Click the File tab, click Save As, and then navigate to the drive and folder that has already been created to store the webpage files.
3. Type Default in the File name box. The default name for the homepage is either *default* or *index*.
4. Click the *Save as type* arrow and select Web Page (*.htm; *.html).
5. Click Change Title to display the Enter Text dialog box.
6. Type the title of the webpage in the Page title text box.
7. Click OK and click Save.

MAC TIP: To change the title of a webpage, click the File menu and select Properties. Click the Summary tab and type the title in the Title box. Click OK.

TIP: AVOID SPACES IN FOLDER AND FILE NAMES
Many Web servers do not handle spaces well in folder and file names; they might replace each space with the %20 combination of characters. Therefore, it is a good habit to avoid using spaces when naming folders and files by substituting the spaces with underscores. Other options include using the PascalCase (each word starts with an uppercase letter) or the camelCase (the first word starts with a lowercase letter) notation or hyphens to replace the spaces.

STEP 3 Apply a Theme and Background Color to a Webpage

Webpages are more interesting when you add design elements such as background images, bullets, numbering, lines, and other graphical features. They also display better when colors and fonts are coordinated among the design elements. You can use Word themes while developing a webpage, which enables you to coordinate colors and fonts, as shown in Figure 8.7. To make sure themes are as effective as possible, you should format your document using Word heading styles, such as Heading 1, Heading 2, and so on. The process of applying formatting to a webpage is the same as for any Word document.

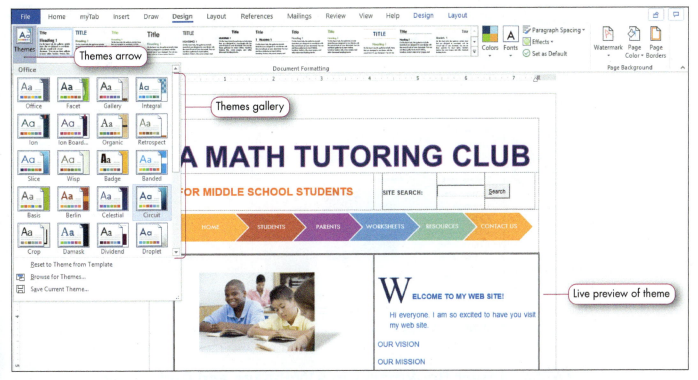

FIGURE 8.7 Apply a Theme to a Webpage

Themes assign colors to the elements on the webpage, such as text, numbers, and borders, and the colors enable you to emphasize key information. Themes do not automatically add a background to the webpage but they control the colors that can be used in the background. A **background** is a color, design, image, or watermark that displays behind text in a document or on a webpage. A colored background adds visual enhancement to the webpage. You can quickly add a background color to a webpage by using Page Color in the Page Background group on the Design tab. Point to any of the theme colors to see a Live Preview of the selected color or click the selected color to apply the new color to the webpage. If a theme has been selected, the Page Color palette automatically displays colors that coordinate with the theme.

On some occasions, you may want to match the background colors or design with those of other company documents. The More Colors command launches the Colors dialog box, which displays the Standard Colors along with the Theme colors. There is also an option for you to choose and mix a custom color. The Fill Effects command enables you to apply a gradient, texture, pattern, or picture background. Figure 8.8 shows the Gradient tab of the Fill Effects dialog box, where you can select from different color options as well as customize a gradient shading style to display on the background of your webpage. You want to carefully select a background color, pattern, or image so that it is not distracting and does not affect the readability of the contents on the page.

> **TIP: WEBPAGE BACKGROUND**
> The size of a webpage is not the same as a Word document. A Word document in portrait orientation has a standard dimension of 8 1/2" x 11", but a webpage is wider than that because it will fill up the whole monitor screen. Therefore, any color, pattern, or image you use as a background repeats itself so that it covers the entire webpage in a process called tiling.

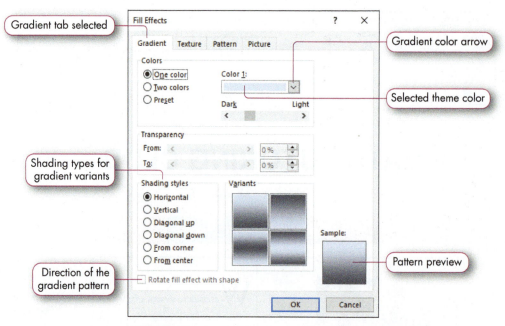

FIGURE 8.8 Apply a Color Gradient Background to a Webpage

STEP 4 Insert Bookmarks in a Webpage and Add a Link to a Bookmark

Some webpages are very lengthy and require the user to scroll to view all the contents on the page. You can help the viewer move to the top, bottom, or other part of that page by using a link to a specific location on a page or to a different page. A bookmark is used to mark the linked location. Recall from an earlier chapter that a **bookmark** is an electronic marker for a specific location in a document, enabling the user to go to that location quickly. As you learned earlier, bookmarks are helpful in long documents because they enable you to move easily from one place to another within that document without having to manually scroll. In websites, they are often used on FAQ (Frequently Asked Questions) webpages, which help the user to navigate quickly between a question and the corresponding answer. Another example of the use of bookmarks is shown in Figure 8.9. Each math category has a corresponding bookmark so that when you click any of the categories, the page view changes to that category and its subject topics further down the page. Additionally, the placement of a bookmark at the top of the page enables the user to click a link at the end of each category to return to the list of categories at the top of the page.

Creating a bookmark and linking to it is a two-step process. First you create the bookmark in the document, then you insert a link in some other part of the document that brings you back to that bookmark. (A bookmark for the top of the page generates automatically.) After you create the bookmarks, you can use the Go To command (Ctrl+G) in the Editing group on the Home tab to quickly jump to a bookmarked location in your document. After creating the bookmarks, you will create links that can be used with these bookmarks. In the next section, you will learn to create hyperlinks that can be used as references to other locations on the Web.

To create a bookmark in a webpage, complete the following steps:

1. Place the insertion point where you want to insert a bookmark.
2. Click the Insert tab.
3. Click Bookmark in the Links group.
4. Type the name of the bookmark in the Bookmark name box.
5. Click Add.

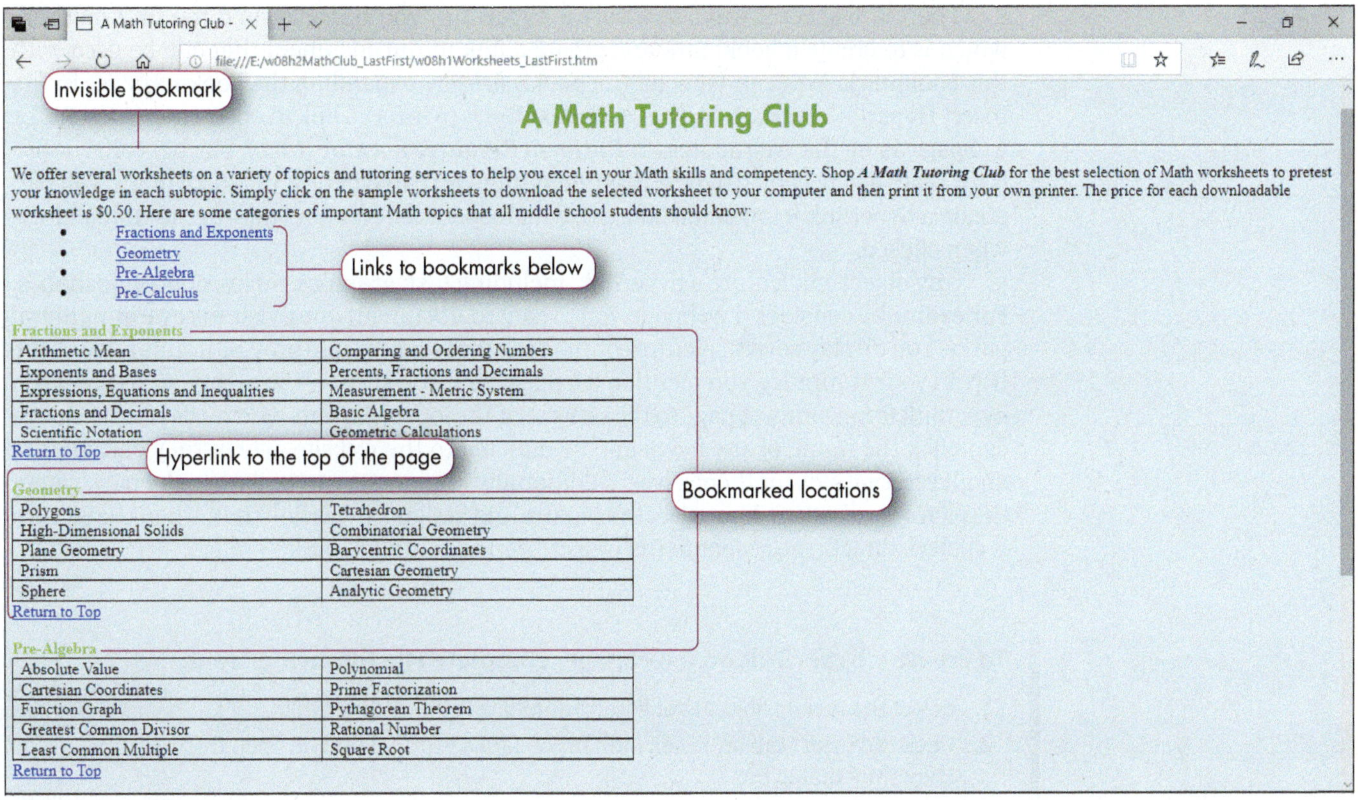

FIGURE 8.9 Use Bookmarks

> **TIP: BOOKMARK NAMES**
> You can use a combination of capital and lowercase letters, numbers, and the underscore character in bookmark names. Spaces and special characters, including hyphens, are not allowed. Also, you cannot begin the name of a bookmark with a number. You should create a descriptive name so you can identify the bookmark easily when you create a hyperlink to it. For example, a bookmark to Question 1 in a FAQ listing might be FAQ1.

After creating a bookmark, you will create a link to bring you back to a bookmark or another location within the same document. In the next section, you will learn to create hyperlinks that can be used as references to other locations on the Web.

To link to a bookmark in a webpage, complete the following steps:

1. Select the text or object that you want to link to a bookmark.
2. Click the Insert tab and click Link in the Links group. This will open the Insert Hyperlink dialog box.
3. Click Place in This Document in the Link to panel.
4. Click the bookmark in Select a page in this document.
5. Click OK.

STEP 5 Insert Hyperlinks to Other Webpages

One benefit of a webpage is that it contains references, called hyperlinks, to other webpages. **Hyperlinks** are electronic markers that, when clicked, do one of several actions: move the insertion point to a different location within the same document using a bookmark, open another document, or display a different webpage in a Web browser.

There are several ways to insert a hyperlink. You have learned the first method, which is to create a bookmark and create a link in the document that can be used with this bookmark. You can view all the bookmarks by expanding the bookmark list in the Insert Hyperlink dialog box. The second option is to insert a link to open an existing file or webpage using the Web address or **Uniform Resource Locator (URL)**. The next alternative is to create a hyperlink to a new document that you can edit now or later. Finally, you can create a hyperlink to an email address, which opens a new email message to that address when clicked.

Any object can feature a hyperlink, including text, graphics, tables, charts, or shapes. For example, consider a webpage you create to document your visit to several national parks. You display several pictures of the beautiful scenery and provide a summary of the trip. In your summary, you mention a lodge where you spent a few nights, so you create a hyperlink from your webpage to the website of the lodge. Anyone who reads your webpage can click the name of the lodge and be directed to the website, where they can inquire about reservations for themselves. Additionally, you create a hyperlink to the park where the picture was taken. You select the picture and assign a hyperlink that, when the picture is clicked, directs the reader to the website for that national park.

> **To create a hyperlink on a webpage, complete the following steps:**
> 1. Select the text or object that you want to display as a hyperlink.
> 2. Click the Insert tab and click Link in the Links group. This will open the Insert Hyperlink dialog box.
> 3. Select the type of hyperlink in the Insert Hyperlink dialog box (see Figure 8.10):
>   - Existing File or Web Page: Links to another webpage by inserting the address (or URL)
>   - Place in This Document: Links to another place within the same document using bookmarks
>   - Create New Document: Links to a new document that you can edit now or later
>   - E-mail Address: Links to an email address, which opens a new email message when clicked
> 4. Click OK.

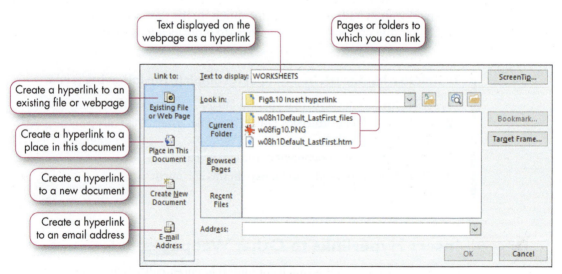

FIGURE 8.10 Insert Hyperlink Dialog Box

When you point to a hyperlink in a Word document, a ScreenTip displays that directs you to press Ctrl+Click to follow the link. If you right-click a hyperlink in a Word document, several options for working with the hyperlink are displayed, including Edit Hyperlink (which opens the Edit Hyperlink dialog box), Open Hyperlink (which opens the link in your default browser), Copy Hyperlink, and Remove Hyperlink (which removes the link but does not remove the text or graphic). You can also use the Link arrow in the Links group to view and insert documents from a list of recently visited URLs and files shared to the cloud.

> **TIP: HYPERLINK COLORS**
> When you add a hyperlink to text in a webpage, the text displays in a color that coordinates with the current theme. After you click the hyperlink, the color of the text changes to the theme or default color for a followed link.

STEP 6 Preview a Webpage

After finalizing pages for a website, you save the document(s) as described earlier. Web Layout view gives you a very accurate representation of how the page will look when published. You can also preview the page in a browser before you upload and publish it, so you can confirm it contains the correct content and is formatted to your specifications.

The Web Page Preview command is not on a ribbon tab or the QAT by default. If you work with webpages often, consider adding this command to a tab on the ribbon or the QAT for easier access during web page development. To view a webpage in Microsoft Edge or any other browser, open File Explorer, navigate to the folder that contains the webpages, and open the folder. Double-click the file name to open the file using the default browser. Another alternative is to select Open with from the shortcut menu to choose your preferred browser to view the webpage (see Figure 8.11).

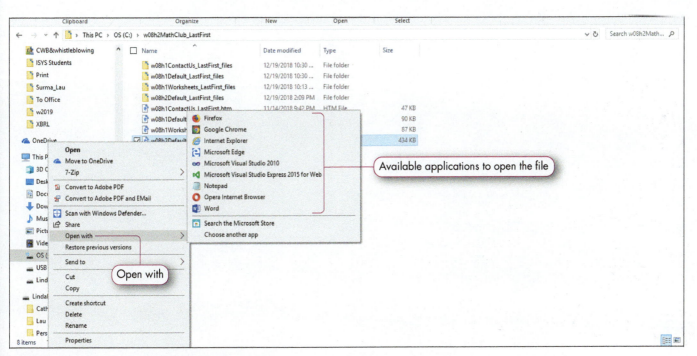

FIGURE 8.11 Open a Webpage from File Explorer

Publish a Webpage

To view pages on the Internet, you must save or publish the pages to a **Web server**, which is a computer system that hosts webpages so that they are available for viewing by anyone who has an Internet connection. You will need additional information from your instructor about how to obtain an account on a Web server at your school, if available, as well as how to upload the pages from your computer to the server. The most common method of uploading webpages to the server is by using **File Transfer Protocol (FTP)**, a process that uploads files from a computer to a server or downloads files from a server to a computer.

1. Describe the advantages of using Word to create a webpage. **p. 478**
2. Describe the benefits of using a Word theme in a webpage. **p. 480**
3. Explain the reason for inserting bookmarks and hyperlinks in a webpage. **p. 482**

Hands-On Exercises

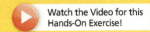

MyLab IT HOE1 Sim Training

Watch the Video for this Hands-On Exercise!

Skills covered: Create a Custom Tab • Add Commands to a Group • Save a Document as a Webpage • Apply a Theme and Background Color to a Webpage • Insert Bookmarks in a Webpage and Add a Link to a Bookmark • Insert Hyperlinks to Other Webpages • Preview a Webpage

1 Webpage Creation

You are designing a website for your math tutoring club. You want a simple design that provides basic information about your service. You have a few documents started but need to refine each one to use a common theme, add color, and add general Web components such as bookmarks and hyperlinks. When complete, you will preview the results to make sure the website is ready to go live on the Web.

STEP 1 CREATE A CUSTOM TAB AND ADD COMMANDS TO A GROUP

Before you begin designing a webpage, you want to organize the tools that will enable you to work quickly and efficiently. You decide to create a custom tab and add commands to it to display the commands you will use most frequently while designing the website. Refer to Figure 8.12 as you complete Step 1.

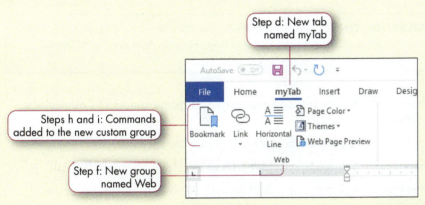

FIGURE 8.12 Custom Tab Containing Web Development Commands

a. Start Word and open a new blank document.

You can create a custom tab or group in any open document. Even if you do not save this document, the new settings will be available every time Word is used on this computer.

b. Click the **File tab**, click **Options**, and then click **Customize Ribbon**.

The available Word commands display in the pane on the left side. On the right side, you customize the tabs and groups with the available commands.

> **MAC TROUBLESHOOTING:** Click the Word menu and select Preferences. Click Ribbon & Toolbar in the Authoring and Proofing Tools. Ensure that ribbon is selected. Click the plus sign below the Customize the Ribbon pane on the right side of the window and select New tab.

> **TROUBLESHOOTING:** If you work in a lab environment where you are unable to customize the applications on your computer, read through the remainder of Step 1.

c. Click **New Tab**, which displays below the Customize the Ribbon pane on the bottom right side of the Word Options dialog box.

A new tab is created in the Main Tabs list and positioned between the Home tab and the Insert tab. The tab is named *New Tab (Custom)* and contains a new group named *New Group (Custom)*.

d. Click **New Tab (Custom)**, and click **Rename**, which displays below that pane. Type **myTab** in the Display name box and click **OK**.

The new tab displays as *myTab (Custom)*.

> **MAC TROUBLESHOOTING:** Click to select New Tab (Custom), click the Settings icon below the Customize the Ribbon pane, and select Rename. Type myTab in the Display name box and click Save.

e. Click **New Group (Custom)** and click **Rename**.

The Rename dialog box opens. You can select a symbol from the Symbol gallery to represent the tab.

f. Type **Web** in the Display name box and click **OK**.

The group displays as *Web (Custom)*.

> **MAC TROUBLESHOOTING:** Type myTab in the Display name box and click Save. Click to select New Group (Custom), click the Settings icon, and select Rename. Type Web in the Display name box and click Save.

g. Click the **Choose commands from arrow in the left pane** and select **Commands Not in the Ribbon**.

All the commands that are not on the ribbon display in the left panel.

h. Scroll down the list of commands, select **Web Page Preview**, and then click **Add**.

The Web Page Preview command now displays in the Web (Custom) group on the myTab (Custom) tab.

i. Click **Choose commands from arrow** and select **All Commands**. Select each of the following commands and click **Add** to display them in the Web (Custom) group on the myTab (Custom) tab:

- **Bookmark** . . . (followed by ellipsis)
- **Horizontal Line** (Note: Make sure that you select the Horizontal Line, NOT the *Horizontal Line* . . . (followed by ellipsis) command.)
- **Link**
- **Page Color** (Note: Make sure that you select the Page Color Picker, NOT the Page Color in the Learning Tools tab command.)
- **Themes**
- **Web Layout**

j. Ensure that the myTab tab is selected so that it will display on the ribbon and click **OK** in the right pane to close the Word Options dialog box.

k. Click the **myTab tab** and ensure that the Web group contains seven commands. Click the **File tab**, click **Options**, and then click **Customize Ribbon**.

The Word Options dialog box opens.

l. Click the **plus sign** to display all commands in the Web (Custom) group under the myTab (Custom) tab.

> **MAC TROUBLESHOOTING:** Click the Word menu and select Preferences. Click Ribbon & Toolbar. Click the myTab (Custom) arrow and click the Web(Custom) arrow to display all commands in the Web (Custom) group under the MyTab (Custom) tab.

m. Click to select **Link** and drag and drop it above Horizontal Line. Drag **Web Page Preview** and drop it above Web Layout. Right-click **Web Layout** and select **Remove**. Click **OK** to close the Word Options dialog box.

> **MAC TROUBLESHOOTING:** Click Web Layout and use the minus sign to remove it from a group.

Notice that Web Layout has been removed from the myTab tab because you changed your mind and decided it was not needed. The order in which the commands display on the tab has also changed.

n. Close the blank document without saving.

STEP 2: SAVE A DOCUMENT AS A WEBPAGE

You have a few documents prepared as a foundation for the website, but before you create the homepage, you first create a folder for storing all the webpage files. You open each document and save it as a webpage, which places it in the proper format for viewing in a browser. You add a title for each page, knowing it will display in the title bar of the browser. Refer to Figure 8.13 as you complete Step 2.

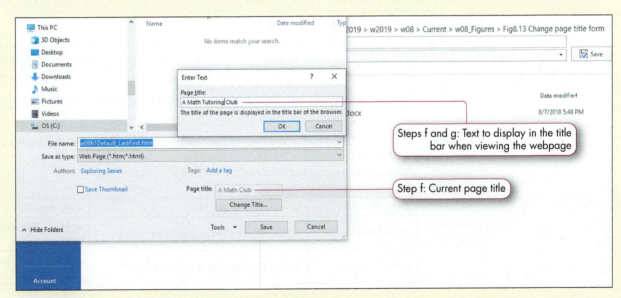

FIGURE 8.13 Change the Page Title in the Enter Text Dialog Box

a. Open *w08h1Default*.

This document is designed to be the homepage for the *A Math Tutoring Club* website.

b. Click the **File tab**, click **Save As**, and then click **Browse**. In the Save As dialog box, navigate to the drive and folder in which you want to create a folder.

Before you start creating Web documents, you need to create a folder to store all Web documents for a specific website.

c. Click **New folder** on the Save As dialog box toolbar, and type the folder name **w08h2MathClub_LastFirst**, and then press **Enter**. Click **Open** or double-click the new folder to open it.

Be aware that the folder name has a *2* after the letter *h*. This is because you will use the same folder name for both Hands-On Exercises 1 and 2. Usually, you will have many files when you create webpages, so it is a good idea to put all the files and subfolders in the same folder.

d. Click the **Save as type arrow** and select **Web Page (*.htm; *.html)**. Do not click Save or press Enter.

When you save as a webpage, the Save As dialog box displays the Page title text area and the Change Title button.

> **TROUBLESHOOTING:** If the (*.htm; *.html) extension does not display, you can change the setting in File Explorer to reveal the file extension. Open File Explorer, and in the Show/hide group on the View tab, click to select File name extensions.

e. Name the file as **w08h1Default_LastFirst.htm**.
f. Click **Change Title** to display the Enter Text dialog box.

In this dialog box, you can edit the webpage title—the text that appears on the browser's title bar when the webpage displays.

> **MAC TROUBLESHOOTING:** Click the File menu, click Properties, and then click the Summary tab. Enter Tutoring in the Page title box.

g. Place the insertion point before the word *Club* in the Page title box, type **Tutoring**, and then press **Spacebar** to add a space between words as appropriate. Click **OK** and click **Save**.

The page displays in Web Layout view and you have changed the title to *A Math Tutoring Club* by adding the word Tutoring.

h. Open the Word documents listed in the following table. Save each document as a webpage in the **w08h2MathClub_LastFirst** folder. Assign new file names and webpage titles using the information in the following table.

Open This File	Save as Web Page (.htm)	Web Page Title
w08h1Worksheets	w08h1Worksheets_LastFirst.htm	A Math Tutoring Club - Worksheets
w08h1ContactUs	w08h1ContactUs_LastFirst.htm	A Math Tutoring Club - Contact Us

The w08h2MathClub_LastFirst folder now contains three webpages that you will use to complete your website. This folder also contains three subfolders with the same webpages' names ending in *_files*. You should not change the webpages' names; otherwise, the connection to these subfolders will be lost.

STEP 3 APPLY A THEME AND BACKGROUND COLOR TO A WEBPAGE

Now that your webpages are saved with the proper file type, you select a common theme to use on each one. You also select a background color that gives a distinct look to your simple pages. Refer to Figure 8.14 as you complete Step 3.

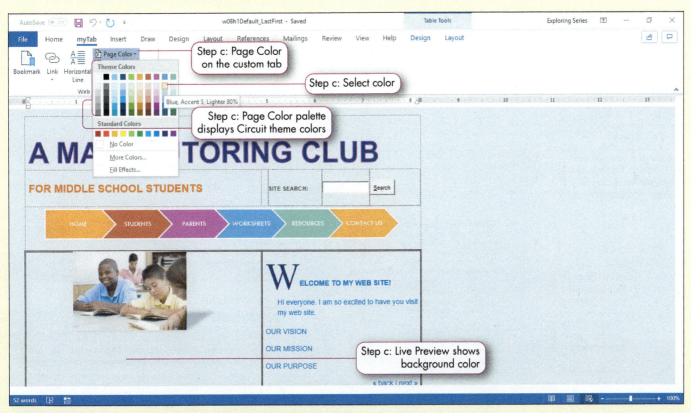

FIGURE 8.14 Select a Background Color and Theme for a Webpage

a. Click the **View tab**, click **Switch Windows** in the Window group, and then select **w08h1Default_LastFirst.htm** from the list of open files.

b. Click the **myTab tab**, click **Themes** in the Web group, and then select **Circuit**.

   The *A Math Tutoring Club* title and text below it display in colors represented in the Circuit theme.

c. Click **Page Color** in the Web group. Select **Blue, Accent 5, Lighter 80%** (second row, ninth column).

   You applied a light blue background color that covers the entire page.

d. Save the document.

e. Press **Alt+Tab** repeatedly until the **w08h1ContactUs_LastFirst.htm** document displays. Repeat Steps b and c to apply the same theme and background color to the page. Save the document.

   When you press Alt+Tab, you move from one open window to another. You may also use Task View on the taskbar.

f. Press **Alt+Tab** repeatedly until the **w08h1Worksheets_LastFirst.htm** document displays. Repeat Steps b and c to apply the theme and background color to the page. Save the document.

Hands-On Exercise 1   491

STEP 4: INSERT BOOKMARKS IN A WEBPAGE AND ADD A LINK TO A BOOKMARK

The content in the Worksheets webpage cannot be displayed on one screen and you must scroll down to view the remaining content. You know that good Web design assists the viewer in navigating up and down the page without having to scroll. With that in mind, you will incorporate bookmarks to help the reader move from section to section on the page. You will then create hyperlinks using the bookmarks to navigate within the webpage. Refer to Figure 8.15 as you complete Step 4.

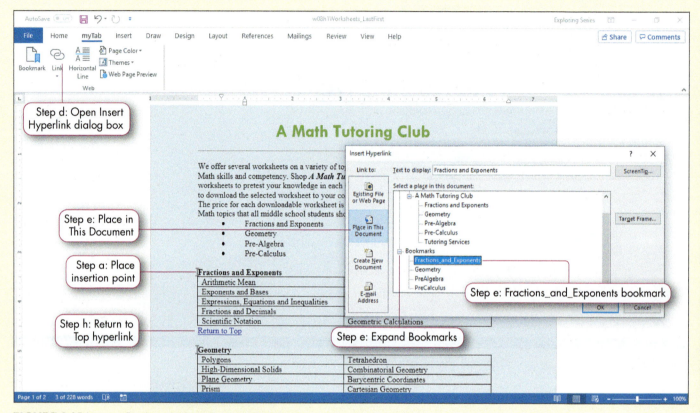

FIGURE 8.15 Insert a Bookmark Hyperlink on a Webpage

a. Place the insertion point on the left side of the first table heading, *Fractions and Exponents*, on the Worksheets page.

This table describes the variety of worksheets that are available on the A Math Tutoring Club website. Make sure that you do not select *Fractions and Exponents* in the bulleted list above the table.

b. Click **Bookmark** in the Web group, type **Fractions_and_Exponents** in the Bookmark name box, and then click **Add**.

> **TROUBLESHOOTING:** If you did not type the underscores, the Add button will not display and you cannot add this bookmark to the webpage. Remember that spaces and special characters such as hyphens are not allowed in bookmark names. If you forgot to type the underscore for *Fractions and Exponents*, you will need to re-create the bookmark using underscores between words.

c. Repeat Step b to create bookmarks at the beginning of the table headings that display down the page for *Geometry*, *Pre-Algebra*, and *Pre-Calculus*. Remember to use Pascal Case (note: PreCalculus and PreAlgebra) to replace the hyphen sign in *Pre-Calculus* and *Pre-Algebra*. Do not create a bookmark for *Tutoring Services*.

d. Press **Ctrl+Home** to view the top of the page. Select **Fractions and Exponents** in the bulleted list and click **Link** from the Web group on the myTab tab.

The Insert Hyperlink dialog box displays. You will select the bookmark to create a link from the words *Fractions and Exponents* to the location in the document where the subtopics for Fractions and Exponents display.

e. Click **Place in This Document** in the Link to panel of the Insert Hyperlink dialog box. Ensure that Bookmarks is expanded. Click **Fractions_and_Exponents** and click **OK**.

Fractions and Exponents displays as a hyperlink, and the text color changes to blue.

f. Point to the **Fractions and Exponents** hyperlink and view the ScreenTip that displays the name of the bookmark and *Ctrl+Click to follow link*. Press **Ctrl** and click the hyperlink to move the insertion point to the listing of *Fractions and Exponents*.

The heading Fractions and Exponents displays near the top of the screen, and the insertion point moves as well. This simplifies navigation on the page. Additionally, the color of the hyperlink changes as a visual indication that it has been clicked.

g. Repeat Steps d and e to create hyperlinks for each bulleted list item to the corresponding bookmark for that item.

h. Select the text **Return to Top** that displays below the *Fractions and Exponents* table. Click **Link** in the Web group, scroll to the top of the *Select a place in this document* list, click **Top of the Document**, and then click **OK**.

This bookmark to the top of the page generates automatically when you save a document as a webpage. When you click this link, the page scrolls to the very top and displays the page heading. This enables you to return to the top of the page after you view content anywhere in the page.

i. Repeat Step h to create a hyperlink from each occurrence of *Return to Top* that displays below each table.

j. Save the webpage.

STEP 5: INSERT HYPERLINKS TO OTHER WEBPAGES

Your last modification is the addition of hyperlinks to bookmarked locations. You want the viewer to click from one page to another in this site with ease, so you add hyperlinks on each page that link to the others. Refer to Figure 8.16 as you complete Step 5.

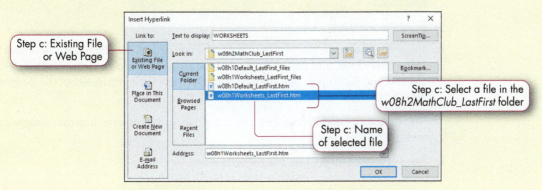

FIGURE 8.16 Insert a Hyperlink to the Worksheets Webpage

a. Point to the **Word icon** on the taskbar and select **w08h1Default_LastFirst.htm**.

b. Select **WORKSHEETS** at the bottom of the page and click **Link** in the Web group on the myTab tab.

c. Click **Existing File or Web Page** in the Link to panel of the Insert Hyperlink dialog box and select **w08h1Worksheets_LastFirst.htm**. Click **OK**.

> **MAC TROUBLESHOOTING:** Click Select and click *w08h1Worksheets_LastFirst.htm*. Click Open.

By creating this link, the Worksheets page displays when you click Worksheets on the homepage.

> **TROUBLESHOOTING:** If you select the w08h1Worksheets_LastFirst folder instead of the Worksheet webpage, the hyperlink will not work. Right-click the hyperlink, click Edit Hyperlink, and then select the Worksheet webpage in the Edit Hyperlink dialog box.

d. Repeat Steps b and c to create a hyperlink from *CONTACT US* on the Default page to the **w08h1ContactUs_LastFirst.htm** webpage. Save the webpage.

You will create a link for Resources using the webpage to be created in a future exercise.

e. Point to the Word icon on the taskbar and select **w08h1ContactUs_LastFirst.htm** to display the ContactUs webpage. Complete the following steps to create a link to the Default page:

- Press **Ctrl+End** and press **Enter**.
- Type **Return to Homepage**
- Select the text **Return to Homepage** and click **Link** in the Web group on the myTab tab.
- Select **w08h1Default_LastFirst.htm** and click **OK**.

f. Press **Enter** two times to move the insertion point below the hyperlink. Click **Horizontal Line** in the Web group.

A straight line displays below the Return to Homepage link. Now you have a second line in the document that matches the graphic that displays below the *A Math Tutoring Club* heading.

g. Save the webpage.

h. Press **Alt+Tab** repeatedly until the *w08h1Worksheets_LastFirst.htm* document displays. Press **Ctrl+End,** and press **Enter** one time. Type **Return to Homepage**, select the text you just typed, and then click **Link** in the Web group. Select the document **w08h1Default_LastFirst.htm** and click **OK**.

The ContactUs and Worksheets pages each include a link back to the homepage of the website.

i. Save and close all documents and exit Word.

STEP 6 PREVIEW A WEBPAGE

With your changes and edits complete, you decide to take a look at the final webpages. All files are saved in the *w08h2MathClub_LastFirst* folder, so you can open and preview them from within a browser. Refer to Figure 8.17 as you complete Step 6.

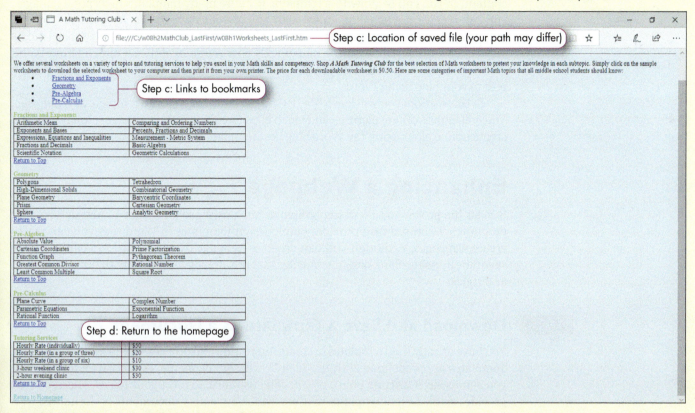

FIGURE 8.17 Preview a Webpage in Microsoft Edge

a. Open File Explorer, navigate to the **w08h2MathClub_LastFirst** folder, and open the folder. Select and double-click **w08h1ContactUs_LastFirst.htm**.

The browser window opens and the page displays. Look closely at the components of the URL in the Address bar, reading from right to left. The w08h1ContactUs_LastFirst.htm document is stored locally in the w08h2MathClub_LastFirst folder. That means you are viewing the site locally, as opposed to seeing it on a Web server.

b. Click the **Return to Homepage link** to make sure it works properly.

The homepage, w08h1Default_LastFirst.htm, displays.

c. Click the **WORKSHEETS page hyperlink** at the bottom on the homepage. Once the Worksheets page displays, click the hyperlinks to navigate to the various bookmarks.

You are now in the Worksheets page. When you click each of the hyperlinks in this page, the hyperlinks will bring you to the place where you inserted the bookmarks.

> **TROUBLESHOOTING:** If your link does not open your webpage in a browser, right-click the hyperlink and select Edit Hyperlink, which displays the Edit Hyperlink dialog box and enables you to revise the link. Remove Hyperlink also displays when you right-click a hyperlink, and this enables you to remove the hyperlink completely.

d. Click **Return to Homepage** to verify the link to the default page works.

You are now back to the homepage, w08h1Default_LastFirst.htm.

e. Click the **CONTACT US hyperlink** at the bottom of the homepage. Click **Return to Homepage** to verify the link to the default page works.

f. Exit the browser.

All opened webpages in the browser close automatically.

Hands-On Exercise 1   495

Webpage Enhancement

You can create a webpage from a blank Word document, using and arranging your own content, or you can begin with a template. Because many templates incorporate images, you can replace the template image with any of your own choice. In addition, you can further enhance your webpage by adding videos and 3D models. Postings to social media services become easier when you can quickly post your blog or tweet directly from Word. Although there is special software that you can use to create blogs, you can also create a post to your blog using Word.

In this section, you will learn how to save a blank design Word template as a webpage. You will embed online pictures and video clips to enhance the webpage. Finally, you will create online blogs using the Word blog post template.

Enhancing a Webpage

Besides the professional-looking templates such as those for resumes, newsletters, and brochures, Microsoft also provides blank design templates in Word that you can use to create webpages. Although you can create a webpage from scratch, you can certainly save time by using blank design templates that are already formatted with design elements and styles.

STEP 1 Download and Save a Template as a Document

You have already used templates to create interesting and professional-looking documents. Templates are predefined with useful styles, design elements, and creative themes that you can use as a starting point, or you can customize to meet your needs. Microsoft also provides blank design templates to users, which are empty documents preformatted with frequently used styles. You can search for blank design templates by typing *Blank* in the *Search for online templates* box on the New dialog box in Backstage view. After you select and download a design template, you can type your content into the blank template and not have to worry about formatting the document. The predefined heading styles save to the Style gallery on the Home tab and you can easily apply them to the content of the document.

You can download any of the professionally created or blank design templates and save them as regular Word documents or webpages. Therefore, instead of creating your webpage from scratch, you have the option of downloading a template that is nearly completed or a blank template that has been formatted to some specific standards. Both options make webpage creation more time efficient.

> **TIP: PIN A DESIGN TEMPLATE**
> If you find a design template that you want to use often, you can pin it to Backstage view by clicking *Pin to list* so that it is always at the top portion of your template selection list.

STEP 2 Change a Template Picture

Templates often include placeholder pictures that may not meet your specific needs. Therefore, you might want to swap out the picture on the template with an image that is more directly suited to your purpose. There are also occasions where you want to exchange an existing picture for another image without having to redo the sizing and formatting. You can replace a picture using the Change Picture command in the Adjust group on the Picture Tools Format tab (see Figure 8.18). In addition to using pictures stored on your device, you can insert any picture that you have saved to your Facebook or OneDrive account, or from some of the popular online sites such as Office.com and Bing.

FIGURE 8.18 Change a Template Picture

> **TIP: THE PICKIT IMAGES APP**
> Besides Bing Search in Word, the Pickit Images App is a convenient add-in app for finding and inserting permission-approved images from the Internet that you are legally allowed to use for any purpose. If you believe you will use this resource quite often, it may be a good idea to add it to your ribbon by clicking Get Add-ins on the File tab and then selecting Pickit in the Office Add-ins dialog box. However, PickIt requires a fee after a brief free trial period.

STEP 3 Use 3D Models

3D Models is a feature in Word that enables you to include different perspectives of the same object by manipulating it in three dimensions. After you insert the 3D model from your own computer or an external source such as Microsoft's Remix 3D (https://www.remix3d.com) into your document, use the controls to manipulate the object to display a different view or perspective on the object. For instance, you can click and drag the 3D control to rotate the object 360 degrees or tilt it up or down in any direction to display a specific feature of the object (see Figure 8.19). Similarly, you can also use the rotation handle to rotate the object clockwise or counterclockwise and the image handles to resize the object. With the object selected, the object anchor enables you to anchor the selected object to the related document text.

On the 3D Model Tools Format tab, the 3D Models command in the Adjust group opens the Insert 3D Model dialog box so that you can select and replace the selected 3D image. If you change your mind, select Reset 3D Model in the Adjust group to revert back to the original setting. The 3D Model Views gallery is a collection of preset views that you can apply to the image. Launching the 3D Model Views dialog box will open the Format 3D Model task pane, enabling you to make adjustments to the look of the 3D object.

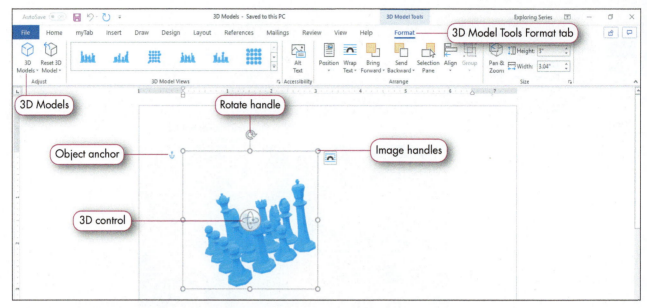

FIGURE 8.19 3D Models

STEP 4 Insert Online Videos

Using video on a webpage is a way to communicate a message or process. In addition to creating your own videos, you can select from a range of interesting and useful online videos to help you make a point. Word makes it easy to insert and embed an online video, rather than having to link the video to an external website. Once you have searched for and embedded a video from a Web source such as YouTube into your document, you can view the video directly within the context of the document itself. When users do not have to leave an open document to go to another window, they stay focused on the content.

Click Online Video in the Media group on the Insert tab. The Insert Video dialog box displays, and you have instant access to online video from YouTube. You can also access a video clip directly using an embed code, which works like a URL when you paste it into a browser to insert a video. Many online video sources, such as YouTube, will generate the embedded HTML code for a video for you to use. If you already have the embed code for a video clip, you can paste the embed code of the video into the *From a Video Embed Code* text box. Figure 8.20 shows a video clip embedded in a Word document.

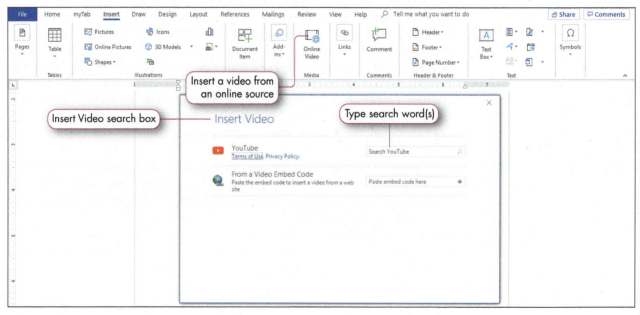

FIGURE 8.20 Embed a Video Clip

CHAPTER 8 • Word and the Internet

To search for and insert a video clip in a webpage, complete the following steps:

1. Click the Insert tab.
2. Click Online Video in the Media group.
3. Do one of the following in the Insert Video dialog box:
   - Type the key search word(s) in the Search YouTube box and press Enter.
   - Paste the embed code in the *From a Video Embed Code* box and press Enter.
4. Click Insert to insert the video into the document.

TIP: WATCHING AN ONLINE VIDEO IN A WORD DOCUMENT
Although an online video clip is embedded into the document, it is not stored on your hard drive. Therefore, you still need to have Internet access to watch the video. Certain browsers work better with online videos than others, so you might need to change your default browser to improve the video display.

Creating a Blog Post

Anyone can post information on the Internet about themselves, their thoughts, their interests, or simply whatever they want to make public. The chronological publication of personal thoughts and Web links is called a **blog**. The term *blog* derives from the phrase *Web log*, which refers to publishing personal information on the Web. Blogs can provide a vehicle to display the works of current or future journalists and authors, or they can simply reflect the emotions and ideas of an individual at a particular point in time.

Before you can publish your blog posts, you must have a blog account with one of the several blog service providers. To learn about and find service providers, perform an Internet search, or ask your friends which service they use. Once you have an established a blog account with a blog service provider, you can register and publish blogs directly from Word. You can register several blog accounts in Word. After they are registered, you can use the Manage Accounts command in Word to change them, delete them, and set one account as your default blog location. Word supports several blogging sites, including but not limited to SharePoint Blog, Telligent Community, TypePad, and WordPress.

STEP 5 — Download a Blog Post Template

One convenient feature of Word is the Blog post template. It is very beneficial to users who are accustomed to working in Word and who also publish blogs on a frequent basis. The Blog post template is predesigned with a certain style and format that makes it easy for you to write effective blogs quickly. Besides enabling you to personalize your content, it also provides a consistent and familiar format for your readers.

To download the Blog post template, complete the following steps:

1. Click the File tab and click New.
2. Type blog in the *Search online templates* search box and press Enter.
3. Click the Blog post template.
4. Click Create to download the blog template.
5. Click Register Later in the Register a Blog Account dialog box. You will be prompted for this information again the first time you post.

When you open the Blog post template, you will note that the ribbon only displays tabs that are necessary to complete the blog post. The Blog Post tab contains commands that you use to format text and that enable you to publish your blog directly to the host server for your blog, as shown in Figure 8.21. It is a good idea to proofread your blog using the Spelling and Grammar command in the Proofing group before posting it to the Internet.

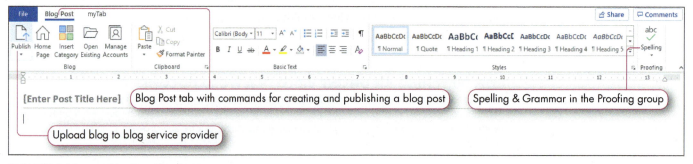

FIGURE 8.21 New Blog Post Window

Create and Set Up a Blog Account

After completing your first blog post by using the Word Blog post template, the blog registration wizard prompts you for the service provider and your blog account information. If you use a service not listed, you can click Manage Accounts, click New, select Other in the Blog list, click Next, and then type the blog post URL, your user name, and your password (see Figure 8.22). Click OK to complete the registration process and click Close to exit the registration process.

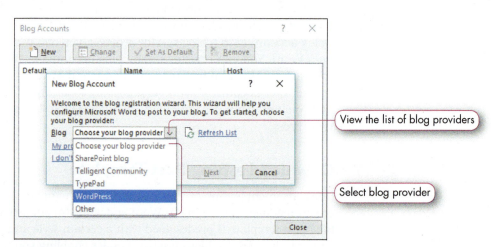

FIGURE 8.22 New Blog Account Dialog Box

> **TIP: REGISTER YOUR BLOG ACCOUNT**
> To sign up for a blog account, you will select Manage Accounts in the Blog group on the Blog Post tab to create a new account. You can select your preferred blog service provider from the list in the New Account dialog box. You will type your user name and password in the New Blogger Account dialog box to activate the new account.

Create a Blog Post

Using the blog post template, you can create a blog on any topic or subject of interest. Some blogs include pictures. Even though they display with the blog post, pictures are stored in a separate folder from the blog text. Your blog service provider might supply storage space for images, or you might have a completely different service provider for images. In the New Account dialog box, you can click Picture Options and specify the picture provider location where you store the images that display with the blog.

> **TIP: IMAGE PROVIDER CONSIDERATIONS**
> If you sign up for an account with an image provider, pay special attention to the terms and conditions for using the service. Some free services might impose a limit on the maximum size of files, total amount of storage, or the types of files you can store.

Publish a Blog Post

After you have set up a blog account and added content to your blog post, you are ready to publish to your blog. But always remember that it is a good idea to use the Spell Check tool before publishing your blog.

> **To publish a blog post, complete the following steps:**
> 1. Click Publish in the Blog group on the Blog Post tab.
> 2. Type your user name and password in the appropriate boxes in the Connect to dialog box. Click the Remember Password box (optional). Click OK.
> 3. Click OK to save and post the blog.
> 4. Click Yes in the Word dialog box that alerts you to the possibility that the information you send to your blog service provider could be seen by other people. Click *Don't show this message again* if you want to avoid clicking Yes at this dialog box each time you post a blog entry.
> 5. Click Home Page on the Blog Post tab to display the blog in a separate browser window.

You may also create and publish a blog by clicking the File tab, and then click Share, click Post to Blog, and click Post to Blog again. A new blog post template displays, and the Register your account dialog box prompts you to log on to your blog service provider.

4. Describe the reasons for using a blank design Word template. ***p. 496***
5. Explain the reason for changing the picture in a Word template. ***p. 496***
6. Explain the advantages of embedding a video into a Word document. ***p. 498***
7. Describe the purpose of writing a blog. ***p. 499***

Hands-On Exercises

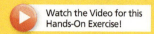

MyLab IT HOE2 Sim Training

Watch the Video for this Hands-On Exercise!

Skills covered: Download and Save a Template as a Document • Change a Template Picture • Use 3D Models • Insert Online Videos • Download a Blog Post Template • Create a Blog Post

2 Webpage Enhancement

The webpages for *A Math Tutoring Club* are businesslike and you want to present your math tutoring services to a larger group of participants. You want to enhance the webpages with a flyer template but change the picture to reflect your math content, insert a 3D model, and embed an instructional video in one of your webpages. It is also important to link your flyer page back to the homepage and to put the flyer link on the homepage. Finally, you want to start a blog to post topics of interest and to conduct ongoing discussions with your students.

STEP 1 DOWNLOAD AND SAVE A TEMPLATE AS A DOCUMENT

Instead of creating a webpage from scratch, you will search and download a flyer template to take advantage of the design templates available. Refer to Figure 8.23 as you complete Step 1.

FIGURE 8.23 Download the Event Flyer Template

a. Click the **File tab** and click **New**. Click in the **Search online templates box**, type **event flyer**, and then press **Enter**.

You have already created several pages for your A Math Tutoring Club website. You searched for a template to use to insert and display your content instead of creating the webpage from scratch.

b. Locate and click **Event flyer** and click **Create** to download the template.

TROUBLESHOOTING: Several templates come under the category of Event flyer. It is important that you select the flyer template named exactly as Event flyer.

> **MAC TROUBLESHOOTING:** Open the Event flyer template from the student data files.

c. Click **Save**, click **Browse**, and then navigate to the **w08h2MathClub_LastFirst** folder.

This is the same folder where you saved the other webpages completed in Hands-On Exercise 1. You need to save all your documents together in the same folder to keep all the pages for the website organized in one place. It also is easier if you later upload the files to a server or email all the webpages to someone else in a zipped file.

d. Double-click the **w08h2MathClub_LastFirst folder** to open it.

e. Type **w08h2Flyer_LastFirst** in the File name box. Make sure that it is saved as a Word document (.docx) file.

You save this file as a Word document file first, and you will save it as a webpage later.

f. Click **Save**.

STEP 2: CHANGE A TEMPLATE PICTURE

The event flyer template includes a photo. You will search for another photo online that is more appropriate for your webpage to replace the current photo. This process is easier because you are using a design layout template that was predefined. Refer to Figure 8.24 as you complete Step 2.

FIGURE 8.24 Change an Online Picture

a. Change a picture by completing the following steps:
   - Click the photo located on the template.
   - Click the **Format tab** and click **Change Picture** in the Adjust group. Select **From Online Sources** and type **homework problem** in the Bing Search box. Press **Enter**.
   - Review the list of images and click the image of the little boy, as seen in Figure 8.24, to insert it into the document. If you do not find the same image that displays in Figure 8.24, you may substitute a similar image.
   - Click **Insert** to insert the image into your document.
   - Select and delete the additional text box that may display below the image.

b. Click the **Picture Tools Format tab**. Click and type **4"** in the **Shape Height box** in the Size group.

c. Click the **Insert tab**, click **Text Box** in the Text group, and then insert a **Simple Text Box**. Position the text box to the right of the image. Ensure that the text box is aligned so the top is approximately even with the top of the image.

You inserted the text box to write your own content.

d. Click in the text box. Ensure that the sample text is selected and type **This boy must be thinking, "I should get a tutor from A Math Tutoring Club to help me with my math homework!"** Select the text that you just typed, and format it as **Times New Roman** and **26 pt**. Change Line spacing to **Single**. Select and **bold**. Click and type **4"** in the text *A Math Tutoring Club*.

e. Select the text box. Click the **Drawing Tools Format tab** and type **4"** in the **Height box** in the Size group. Click and type **2.5"** in the **Width box**. Click **Layout Options** and select **Square**.

You size the text box and aligned it with the image.

f. Save the document.

STEP 3 USE 3D MODELS

After you replace the photo, you want to further enhance the webpage by using a 3D model. Refer to Figure 8.25 as you complete Step 3.

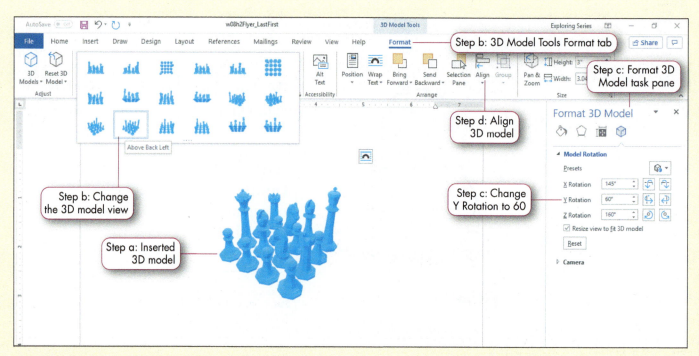

FIGURE 8.25 Insert a 3D Model

> **MAC TROUBLESHOOTING:** 3D Models are not available in Word for Mac.

a. Insert a 3D model by completing the following steps:

- Insert a blank page at the end of the document. Position the insertion point on the blank page.
- Click the **Insert tab**. Click the **3D Models arrow** in the Illustrations group and select **From a File**. Scroll to the *Chess Set.3mf* file and select it to insert it into the document.

You searched and inserted a 3D model from your computer onto your document. You can also search other online sites such as www.Remix3D.com for more freely shared 3D models from the creative community.

b. Ensure that the 3D model is selected and the Format tab is displayed. Click **More** in the 3D Model Views group and then click **Above Back Left** (third row, second column).

You want to apply a different view to the image to give it an additional touch.

c. Click the **3D Model Views dialog box launcher** to open the Format 3D Model task pane. Change the Y Rotation in Model Rotation to **60**.

You want to rotate the image by an additional 30 degrees.

d. Close the task pane. Click **Align** in the Arrange group and select **Align Center**.

e. Save the document.

STEP 4 INSERT ONLINE VIDEOS

You know that many students learn their math by watching someone teach them and they can also watch the same video again if needed. You will search online for a video clip on learning algebra and insert the instructional video into the event flyer document. You will then save the document as a webpage so that viewers can watch the video clip from the webpage itself. You will create a link to the homepage, as well as a hyperlink on the homepage to the flyer page. Refer to Figure 8.26 as you complete Step 4.

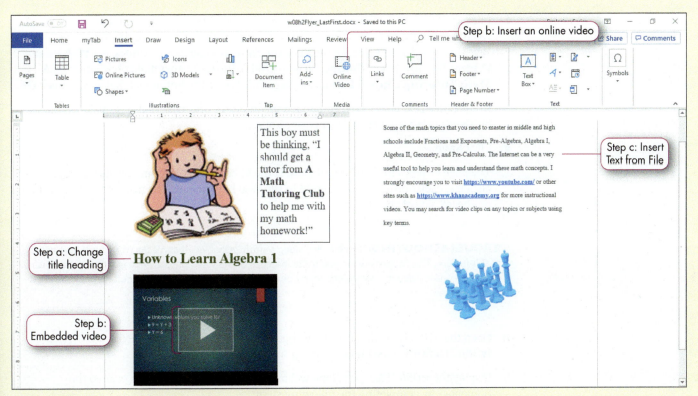

FIGURE 8.26 Insert an Online Video Clip

a. Scroll up to the first page. Click the **Title heading** below the picture and type **How to Learn Algebra 1**. Format the title heading as **Times New Roman** and **36 pt**. Change Line spacing to **1.5** and After spacing to **0**. Select and delete the first two placeholders and their paragraph marks below the title heading. Select and delete the third placeholder below the title heading but keep the paragraph mark.

b. Position the insertion point in the paragraph below the title heading. Click the **Insert tab** and click **Online Video** in the Media group. Type **How to Learn Algebra 1** in the Search YouTube box and press **Enter**. Select any appropriate video and click **Insert**.

You inserted the video from Search YouTube box into your document, but you could also have inserted a video clip that you created on your own.

c. Position the insertion point in the paragraph below the video. Click the **Insert tab**, click **Object** in the Text group, and then click **Text from File**. Navigate to your student files and select the *w08h2Math* file. Click **OK**.

Instead of using copy and paste, you insert all the content of the w08h2Math file onto the flyer without opening the file. Notice that the font size of the inserted text changes from 12 to 16 and the line spacing from 1.08 to 1.8.

d. Delete the page break below the inserted file so that the 3D model stays at the bottom of page 2.

The document will look more professional if you display the 3D model at the bottom of page 2.

e. Click the **myTab tab**, click **Themes** in the Web group, and then select **Circuit**. Click **Page Color** in the Web group and click **Blue, Accent 5, Lighter 80%** (second row, ninth column). Save the document.

You apply a theme and page color to the flyer, and then save it with its added elements as a Word document before saving it as a webpage.

f. Click the **File tab**, click **Save As**, and then click **Browse**. Navigate to the w08h2MathClub_LastFirst folder in the Save As dialog box to save the file. You will save the file with the same name. Click the **Save as type arrow** and select **Web Page (*.htm; *.html)**. Click **Change Title** to display the Enter Text dialog box and type **A Math Tutoring Club - Flyer** in the Page Title box in the Enter Text dialog box. Click **OK**.

In the Enter Text dialog box, you added the webpage title, which also displays on the browser's title bar when the webpage displays.

g. Click **Save**.

The page displays in Web Layout view. If the Microsoft Word Compatibility Checker displays, click Continue. Notice that in the Web Layout view, the inserted text box is now on the left side of the little boy's picture.

> **TROUBLESHOOTING:** If the online video button is disabled, that means you do not have access to this feature. This happens when you try to insert an online video onto a webpage. If you intend to embed an online video in a Word document or template, you must insert the video before you save it as a webpage.

h. Open the *w08h1Default_LastFirst* webpage in Word and save the file as **w08h2Default_LastFirst** by changing h1 to h2.

i. Display the *w08h2Flyer_LastFirst* webpage and create a link on this page to the homepage by completing the following steps:

- Position the insertion point at the end of the paragraph above the 3D model on page 2, press **Enter**, and then type **Return to Homepage**. (Omit the period.) Select the typed text and change the font to **Times New Roman**.
- Select the **Return to Homepage text** you just typed, click the **Insert tab**, and then click **Link** in the Links group to display the Insert Hyperlink dialog box.
- Click **Existing File or Web Page** in the Link to panel of the Insert Hyperlink dialog box. Scroll to and click the **w08h2Default_LastFirst.htm** file. Click **OK**.

By creating this link, you ensure that the homepage displays when you click Return to Homepage on the Flyer webpage.

j. Create a link from the homepage to the Flyer page by completing the following steps:

- Click the **Word icon** on the taskbar and select **w08h2Default_LastFirst.htm**.
- Select **RESOURCES** at the bottom of the page, right-click to display the shortcut menu, and then select **Link** to display the Insert Hyperlink dialog box.
- Click **Existing File or Web Page** in the Link to panel of the Insert Hyperlink dialog box and click **w08h2Flyer_LastFirst.htm**. Click **OK**.
- You will see two w08h2Flyer_LastFirst files in this folder. One is a Word document, and the other is a webpage. Make sure that you select the webpage file.
- Save and close both documents.

Now the homepage has a link to the page that contains the 3D model and the embedded video clip.

STEP 5: DOWNLOAD A BLOG POST TEMPLATE AND CREATE A BLOG POST

It is time for you to start sharing information that your students will enjoy viewing. You are going to introduce your newly created website to your students, and to encourage them to review the math worksheets. You create a blog by downloading and using a blog post template. Refer to Figure 8.27 as you complete Step 5.

FIGURE 8.27 First Blog Entry for *A Math Tutoring Club*

> **MAC TROUBLESHOOTING:** Blog Post Template and the ability to create a blog post are not available in Word for Mac.

a. Click the File tab. Click New. Type **blog** in the *Search online templates* box and press **Enter**. Click the **Blog post template**. Click **Create** to download the blog template. A Register a Blog Account dialog box displays; click **Register Later**.

b. Click the placeholder **Enter Post Title Here** and type **My Math Tutoring Club Website**. (Omit the period.) Click anywhere in the document to deselect the post title you just typed.

c. Type the following text at the insertion point (below the title):

Welcome to my Math Tutoring Club!

I have created a website so that both parents and students can have access to various resources that might be helpful to you. Visit my website at http://www.AMathTutoringClub.net. Feel free to contact me if you have any questions about my website.

After you type the website address, notice that it automatically turned into a hyperlink. (Note: This link does not actually open a live website.)

d. Click **Spelling** in the Proofing group on the Blog Post tab. When the spell check is complete, click **OK**.

e. Click the **File tab**, click **Save As**, click **Browse** to navigate to the folder *w08h2MathClub_LastFirst*, and then type **w08h2Blog_LastFirst** in the File name box. Click **Save** to save the post until you are ready to publish.

f. Open **File Explorer** and navigate to the *w08h2MathClub_LastFirst* folder. Double-click **w08h2Flyer_LastFirst.htm** to open it in a browser to preview the webpage. Click the **Return to Homepage hyperlink page** to navigate back to the homepage. Close Microsoft Edge.

g. Open Word. Click the **File tab**, click **Options**, and then click **Customize Ribbon**. Click **Reset** and select **Reset all Customizations** to reset the ribbon back to the default ribbon setting and click **OK**. Close all files and exit Word.

h. Save and close all documents. Exit Word.

i. Go to **File Explorer** and navigate to the **w08h2MathClub_LastFirst** folder. Select the folder, right-click to display the shortcut menu, click **Send to**, and then select **Compressed (zipped) folder**.

All the files and webpages for the *A Math Tutoring Club* website are now contained in a zipped file.

j. Based on your instructor's directions, submit the following in the w08h2MathClub_LastFirst zipped file:

w08h1ContactUs_LastFirst_files subfolder

w08h1Worksheets_LastFirst_files subfolder

w08h2Default_LastFirst_files subfolder

w08h2Flyer_LastFirst_files subfolder

w08h1ContactUs_LastFirst.htm

w08h1Worksheets_LastFirst.htm

w08h2Blog_LastFirst.docx

w08h2Default_LastFirst.htm

w08h2Flyer_LastFirst.htm

Chapter Objectives Review

After reading this chapter, you have accomplished the following objectives:

1. **Customize the ribbon.**
   - Create a custom tab: You can create a custom tab for the ribbon that contains only the features that you use frequently or that are not available on the default ribbon. You can also create new groups within the custom tab.
   - Add commands to a group: In addition to changing the order of the tabs or groups that display within the tabs, you can add commands that are not on the default tabs to a group on your personalized tab, and export and import custom tabs.

2. **Build and publish a webpage.**
   - Save a document as a webpage: Word provides all the tools necessary to create a basic webpage, convert the document, and generate the HTML (HyperText Markup Language) code for you. You can easily save a document as a webpage to be published to the Internet to be accessed by anyone online.
   - Apply a theme and background color to a webpage: Use the Word themes to coordinate colors and fonts for webpages. A colored background adds visual enhancement to the webpage.
   - Insert bookmarks in a webpage and add a link to a bookmark: A bookmark is an electronic marker for a specific location in a document, enabling the user to go to that location quickly. Bookmarks are helpful in long webpages because they enable users to move easily from one location to another within that webpage, without having to manually scroll through the document.
   - Insert hyperlinks to other webpages: Hyperlinks are electronic markers that, when clicked, move the insertion point to a different location within the same document, open another document, or display a different webpage in a browser.
   - Preview a webpage: As you prepare a webpage, Web Layout view displays an accurate representation of how the page will look when published. You can preview the page in a browser before you upload and publish it so that you can confirm that it contains the correct content and is formatted to your specifications.
   - Publish a webpage: To view the pages on the Internet, you must save or publish them to a Web server, which is a computer system that hosts pages so that they are available for viewing by anyone who has an Internet connection.

3. **Enhance a webpage.**
   - Download and save a template as a document: Design templates are documents preformatted with frequently used styles and design elements. It is more time efficient to use a predefined template and save it as a webpage.
   - Change a template picture: Templates are often preloaded with pictures that may not be suitable to your needs. You can quickly change any picture by using the Change Picture command.
   - Use 3D Models: 3D Models is a feature in Office 365 that enables you to bring animation to your object.
   - Insert online videos: In Word you can insert or embed an online video into a document or webpage so that your audience can view the video clips without having to leave the document page.

4. **Create a blog post.**
   - Download a blog post template: A blog post template downloaded from Microsoft can be beneficial to you if you are accustomed to working in Word and publish blogs frequently.
   - Create and set up a blog account: You must establish a blog account with one of several blog service providers before you can register and publish blogs directly from Word.
   - Create a blog post: You can use the blog post template to create a blog. You can write about any topic and even include pictures. Pictures are stored in a file separate from the blog text.
   - Publish a blog post: When you are ready, you can publish your blog post from Word by clicking Publish on the Blog Post tab.

Key Terms Matching

Match the key terms with their definitions. Write the key term letter by the appropriate numbered definition.

- **a.** Background
- **b.** Blog
- **c.** Bookmark
- **d.** Custom tab
- **e.** File Transfer Protocol (FTP)
- **f.** Hyperlink
- **g.** HyperText Markup Language (HTML)
- **h.** Uniform Resource Locator (URL)
- **i.** Webpage
- **j.** Web server
- **k.** World Wide Web (WWW)

1. _____ A tab on the ribbon created by the user that contains the commands he/she wants to use. **p. 474**

2. _____ A computer system that hosts pages for viewing by anyone with an Internet connection. **p. 486**

3. _____ The chronological publication of personal thoughts and Web links. **p. 499**

4. _____ A process that uploads files from a computer to a server or download files from a server to a computer. **p. 486**

5. _____ A color, design, image, or watermark that displays behind text in a document or on a webpage. **p. 481**

6. _____ An electronic marker that points to a different location within the same document using a bookmark, opens another document, or displays a different webpage in a Web browser. **p. 483**

7. _____ A very large subset of the Internet that stores webpage documents. **p. 474**

8. _____ A universal formatting instructional language for Web browsers. **p. 478**

9. _____ Any document that displays on the World Wide Web. **p. 474**

10. _____ An electronic marker for a specific location in a document, enabling the user to go to that location quickly. **p. 482**

11. _____ A Web resource used to specify addresses on the World Wide Web. **p. 484**

Multiple Choice

1. While you are creating and editing documents that will be part of a website, you should save them in which format?
   - (a) XML
   - (b) HTML
   - (c) Compatibility Mode
   - (d) Text

2. Which of the following is *not* a legitimate object to use in a hyperlink?
   - (a) A blog post
   - (b) An email address
   - (c) A webpage
   - (d) A bookmark

3. What is the advantage of applying a theme to a webpage?
   - (a) It adds a background color to the webpage automatically.
   - (b) It cannot be removed after you apply it.
   - (c) It enables you to coordinate colors and fonts.
   - (d) It is automatically applied to each additional webpage you create.

4. If you view a webpage and hyperlinks display in two different colors, what is the most likely explanation?
   - (a) One of the hyperlinks has a different theme applied to it.
   - (b) One of the hyperlinks is invalid.
   - (c) One of the hyperlinks was previously visited.
   - (d) One of the hyperlinks is a bookmark.

5. Which of the following is *not* a format used to save documents as webpages?
   - (a) Web Template
   - (b) Single File Web Page
   - (c) Web Page
   - (d) Web Page, Filtered

6. What information is relayed to the browser by HTML tags?
   - (a) How to categorize the data on the webpage
   - (b) How to save the information on the webpage
   - (c) How to transfer the data to a Web server
   - (d) How to format the information on the webpage

7. Which of the following statements about online video is *false*?
   - (a) Once an online video is embedded into a webpage, it can be viewed without Internet access.
   - (b) To insert an online video, click Online Video in the Media group.
   - (c) You can insert videos from YouTube directly onto a Word document.
   - (d) You can manually insert the video HTML code into the Insert Video dialog box.

8. Which of the following statements about custom tab is *true*?
   - (a) Once a custom tab is added to the ribbon, it cannot be removed.
   - (b) The maximum number of commands that you can add to a custom tab is five.
   - (c) You can select a colorful symbol to represent a group's contents.
   - (d) When you create a new tab, you must also create a new group.

9. What type of website enables you to view the frequent, chronological publication of personal thoughts?
   - (a) A search engine
   - (b) An FTP
   - (c) A Web server
   - (d) A blog

10. What feature should you change in order to display information about your website at the top of the Microsoft Edge window?
    - (a) The XML element
    - (b) The file name
    - (c) The page title
    - (d) The document theme

Practice Exercises

1 Williamson Realtors

Samuel Williamson owns a large real estate company in Colorado. The company offers a comprehensive list of services beyond the standard commercial and residential real estate sales and listings, including management of retirement community properties and commercial properties. Sam wants to take advantage of the Internet to advertise his services and attract more clients. Sam is quite tech-savvy, so he wants to create and establish a simple website by himself and then contract a Web designer to enhance the site if it starts to generate business. Sam takes the following steps to turn a few basic Word documents into webpages. Refer to Figure 8.28 as you complete this exercise.

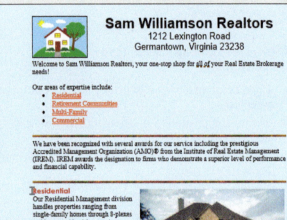

FIGURE 8.28 Sam Williamson Realtors Website

a. Open *w08p1Default*.

b. Customize the ribbon by completing the following steps:
- Click the **File tab**, click **Options**, and then click **Customize Ribbon**.
- Click **View** in the Main Tabs list on the right. Click **New Group** and click **Rename**. Type **Web** in the Display name box in the right pane and click **OK**.
- Click the **Choose commands from arrow** in the left pane and select **Commands Not in the Ribbon**.
- Scroll down and click **Web Page Preview**. Click **Add** to add the command to the Web group in the View tab.
- Click **OK** to close the Word Options dialog box.

c. Click the **File tab**, click **Save As**, and then click **Browse**. In the Save As dialog box, navigate to the drive and folder in which you want to create a folder to organize your webpages. Click **New folder** on the Save As dialog box toolbar, type **w08p1Realtor_LastFirst**, and then press **Enter**. Click **Open**.

d. Type **w08p1Default_LastFirst** in the File name box. Click the **Save as type arrow** and select **Web Page (*.htm; *.html)**. Click **Change Title** to display the Enter Text dialog box. Type **Sam Williamson Real Estate – Homepage** in the Page title box and click **OK**. Click **Save**.

e. Open *w08p1Services* and save it as a webpage named **w08p1Services_LastFirst** in the w08p1Realtor_LastFirst folder. Click **Change Title**, type **Sam Williamson Real Estate - Services**, click **OK**, and then click **Save**.

f. Apply themes and color to the Default webpage by completing the following steps:
- Click the **View tab**, click **Switch Windows** in the Window group, and then select **w08p1Default_LastFirst**. Click the **Design tab**, click **Themes** in the Document Formatting group, and then select **Vapor Trail**.
- Click **Page Color** in the Page Background group. Select **Fill Effects** to display the Fill Effects dialog box, and ensure that the **Gradient tab** is selected.
- Click **Two colors** in the Colors section. Click the **Color 1 arrow** and select **Blue, Accent 6, Lighter 80%** (second row, tenth column). Click the **Color 2 arrow** and select **Blue, Accent 6, Lighter 40%** (fourth row, tenth column).
- Ensure that **Horizontal** in the Shading styles section is selected. Click the **square in the top-right corner** in the Variants section. Click **OK** to apply the background.
- Save the changes to w08p1Default_LastFirst.htm.

g. Repeat Step f to apply the theme and background color to the Services page. Save the Services page.

h. Display the w08p1Default_LastFirst file. Select **Real Estate Services** and click **Link** in the Links group on the Insert tab. Click **Existing File or Web Page** in the Link to panel of the Insert Hyperlink dialog box. Click the **w08p1Realtor_LastFirst folder**, click the **w08p1Services_LastFirst.htm file**, and then click **OK**.

i. Display the Services page. Place the insertion point on the left side of the second instance of the word *Residential* (in red text), which displays as a heading for a paragraph. Click the **Insert tab**, click **Bookmark**, type **residential** in the Bookmark name box, and then click **Add**.

j. Repeat Step i to insert bookmarks at the beginning of the red headings *Retirement Communities*, *Multi-Family*, and *Commercial* that display down the page. The bookmarks should be named **retirement**, **multi_family**, and **commercial**, respectively.

k. Select **Residential** in the bulleted list near the top of the page and click **Link** from the Links group. Click **Place in This Document** in the Link to panel of the Insert Hyperlink dialog box. Click **residential** under Bookmarks and click **OK**.

l. Repeat Step k to create hyperlinks from each bulleted list item to the corresponding bookmarks *retirement*, *multi_family*, and *commercial* for the bulleted text *Retirement Communities*, *Multi-Family*, and *Commercial*.

m. Select the text **Return to Top** that displays below the *Residential* paragraph. Click **Link** in the Links group; scroll to the top of the *Select a place in this document* list, click **Top of the Document**, and then click **OK**.

n. Repeat Step m to create a hyperlink from each of the 3 occurrences of Return to Top that displays throughout the Services page.

o. Press **Ctrl+End** to move the insertion point to the end of the document, press **Enter**, type **HOME**. Select **HOME**. Click **Link**. Click **Existing File or Web Page**. Click **w08p1Default_LastFirst**. Click **OK**.

p. Save and close the webpages.

q. Use File Explorer to locate the **w08p1Default_LastFirst webpage** in your w08p1Realtor_LastFirst folder. Double-click the webpage to preview it in a browser window. Click the **Real Estate Services hyperlink** to view the Services page. Click the various hyperlinks on the Services page to navigate the webpage. Close the browser.

r. Switch to File Explorer and navigate to the w08p1Realtor_LastFirst folder. Select the folder, right-click to display the shortcut menu, click **Send to**, and then select **Compressed (zipped) folder**.

s. Select the zipped file name and rename the zipped file **w08p1Realtor_LastFirst**. Based on your instructor's directions, submit the following in the zipped file:

w08p1Default_LastFirst_files subfolder

w08p1Services_LastFirst_files subfolder

w08p1Default_LastFirst.htm

w08p1Services_LastFirst.htm

2 China Blog Post

You are participating in a study abroad program at Illinois State University this fall and will spend the semester in China. You are excited about the opportunities to learn about a different country and its people, language, and culture, and you can travel and see as much of the country as possible. Your parents are nervous about your time away and want you to write home as much as possible. Your friends are also eager to hear about your experiences. You have decided that the most convenient and efficient way to communicate with everyone is to post blog entries frequently. You can use Word on your laptop to quickly write your blog entries, which you can then publish to your WordPress account later. Refer to Figure 8.29 as you complete this exercise.

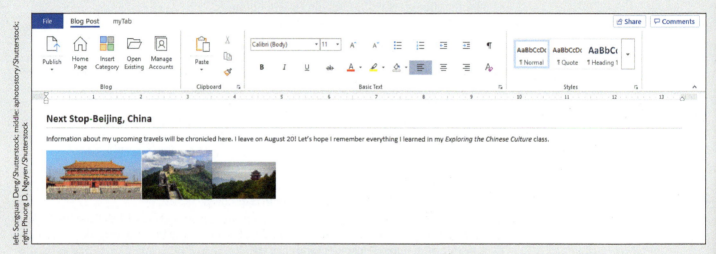

FIGURE 8.29 Blog Post for China Trip

a. Start Word. Click **New**. Type **blog** in the Search online templates box and press **Enter**. Click the **Blog post template**. Click **Create** to download the blog template. If the Register a Blog Account dialog box displays, click **Register Later**. If you have already created a blog account, the Register a Blog Account dialog box does not display.

b. Click the **Enter Post Title Here placeholder** and type the text **Next Stop–Beijing, China**. (Omit the period.)

c. Click anywhere below the title and then type the following text at the insertion point: **Information about my upcoming travels will be chronicled here. I leave on August 20! Let's hope I remember everything I learned in my Exploring the Chinese Culture class.** (Include the period.)

d. Press **Enter**. Click the **Insert tab**, and click **Pictures** in the illustration group. Locate and select the **w08p2ForbiddenCity** image in your data folder, and click **Insert**. Repeat and insert the **w08p2GreatWall** and **w08p2SummerPalace** images next to each other in the same row. Size the height of the three images to **1"**.

e. Select the text **Exploring the Chinese Culture** in the last sentence that you typed and click **Italic** from the mini toolbar.

f. Click **Spelling** in the Proofing group on the Blog Post tab.

g. Click the **File tab**, click **Save As**, and navigate to the folder where you want to organize your blog posts. Type **w08p2ChinaBlog_LastFirst** in the File name box. Click **Save** to save the post until you are ready to publish.

h. Close the document. Based on your instructor's directions, submit w08p2ChinaBlog_LastFirst.

Mid-Level Exercises

1 FlyRight Airways Website

 CREATIVE CASE

The marketing manager at a fledgling airline company is hosting a competition that awards a prize to the employee who designs the best homepage for the company's website. The manager gives each person a document with a description of the company, which should display in the final version. Take the following steps to develop the page you will submit.

a. Open *w08m1Airline*, and save the document as a **Single File Web Page (*.mht; *.mhtml)** with the file name **w08m1Airline_LastFirst**. Change the page title to **Take Off with FlyRight Airways**. (Omit the period.)

b. Customize the ribbon to place the buttons you use most on one custom tab with groups. You can modify the myTab tab you created in Hands-On Exercise 1 or reset the ribbon to its original state and create a new tab with groups.

c. Apply the **Office theme** to the page. Apply the **Black & White (Capitalized) style** to the company name displayed at the top of the document and increase the font size to **20**. Use a different style if you do not find Black & White (capitalized) on the list of styles.

d. Apply a background color to the page. Use a Gradient Fill Effect that uses two colors. Select **Blue-Gray, Text 2, Lighter 80%** (second row, fourth column) for Color 1 and **Blue-Gray, Text 2, Lighter 40%** (fourth row, fourth column) for Color 2. Use a **Diagonal down shading style** and select **variant effect** in the top-left corner.

e. Select the text **Contact us** displayed near the top of the document. Insert a hyperlink that links to the email address **help@flyrightairways.org** and that contains the subject **Request for Information**.

f. Perform a Web search to find website addresses for the two companies mentioned—Boeing and FlightAware—in the third paragraph. Create hyperlinks to those companies after you find their website addresses. The FlightAware site enables you to track a flight from takeoff to landing.

g. Create bookmarks named **b737** and **b767** at the beginning of the paragraphs at the bottom of the page that describe the two types of aircraft. Create hyperlinks to these bookmarks from the text *Boeing 737* and *Boeing 767* displayed in the first paragraph.

h. Insert the **boeing.com hyperlink** to Boeing.com in the fourth paragraph. Save and close the document.

i. Start File Explorer, navigate to the folder containing your webpage, and double-click the file you just created to display the webpage in a browser. Look carefully at the Address bar and note the local address, as opposed to a Web address. Test all links.

j. Close the browser. Based on your instructor's directions, submit w08m1Airline_LastFirst.mht.

2 Introduce Myself Blog

 CREATIVE CASE

FROM SCRATCH

You are enrolled in a social media marketing class at the local university. Companies in the area often use popular social media tools such as blogs, Facebook, Foursquare, Google+, Instagram, LinkedIn, Pinterest, Tumblr, Twitter, Yelp, and YouTube to advertise products. Therefore, the first assignment in this marketing course is to "sell" yourself to your instructor and your classmates. Your instructor suggests that you use a blog to advertise yourself. You may write about your hobbies, interests, strengths, classes you are taking, and your career goals. Also, to put a face to a name, you need to insert a reasonably sized (e.g., a height of 2") photo of yourself on a blog post. Because this is a marketing class, feel free to use any kind of Word features to enhance your blog post. However, remember that you are treading a very fine line in this assignment—you want to present enough information to "sell" yourself, but you need to be careful not to reveal information that may be considered private. After all the blogs are posted, students will evaluate the blog posts and will vote on them using "likes" or "dislikes."

a. Download the **Blog post template** and save it as **w08m2MyselfBlog_LastFirst**.

b. Write several paragraphs in your blog about things that you want others to know about you.

c. Use graphics or a table to tabulate data or information to present your case.

d. Insert a picture of yourself at the bottom of the blog page. Resize the picture to roughly **2"** in height.
e. Type your first and last name as the post title.
f. Save your blog entry.
g. Close the document. Based on your instructor's directions, submit w08m2MyselfBlog_LastFirst.

Running Case

New Castle County Technical Services

New Castle County Technical Services has been asked to participate in a technology fair at a local university. The fair is open to students and community members, many of whom are potential clients for New Castle's data and network solutions. Your manager wants to take advantage of the Internet to advertise this fair and attract more participants, and he wants you to create and publish a simple website.

a. Create a folder named **w08r1NewCastle_LastFirst**.
b. Customize the ribbon to place the buttons you use most on one custom tab with groups. You can modify the myTab tab you created in Hands-On Exercise 1 or reset the ribbon to its original state and create a new tab with groups.
c. Open *w08r1Default* and save it as a webpage named **w08r1Default_LastFirst** in the w08r1NewCastle_LastFirst folder. Change the page title to **New Castle – Homepage**. (Omit the period.)
d. Open *w08r1Preserve* and save it as a webpage named **w08r1Preserve_LastFirst** to the w08r1NewCastle_LastFirst folder. Change the page title to **New Castle – Preserving Data**. (Omit the period.)
e. Open *w08r1FinalNote* and save it as **w08r1FinalNote_LastFirst** to the w08r1NewCastle_LastFirst folder. You will save this document as a webpage after you insert a 3D model later.
f. Apply the following formatting to the default page:
   - **Ion document theme**.
   - A background color that uses a Gradient Fill Effect that uses two colors. Select **Light Gray, Background 2** (first row, third column) for Color 1 and **Light Gray, Background 2, Darker 10%** (second row, third column) for Color 2. Use a **Diagonal down shading style** and select **variant effect** in the top-left corner.
g. Repeat Step f to apply the same theme and background color formats to the Preserve page and the FinalNote document.
h. Display the w08r1FinalNote_LastFirst file, go to the bottom of the document, and then insert the *Space Shuttle.3mf* 3D model from your computer. Change the X Rotation to **90**, and both the Y and Z Rotations to **60**. Apply **Dotted: 5% Pattern fill** (first row, first column) to the image. Close the task pane and apply Align Center to the 3D image on the document. Save the document.
i. Save the w08r1FinalNote_LastFirst file as a webpage in the w08r1NewCastle_LastFirst folder and change the page title to **New Castle – Final Note**. (Omit the period.)
j. Display the w08r1Default_LastFirst file. Select the text *Contact us* displayed at the bottom of the document. Insert a hyperlink that links to the email address **support@NewCastle.com** and that contains the subject **Request for Information**.

k. Create a hyperlink from *Preserving Data* to the w08r1Preserve_LastFirst webpage and another from *Final Note* to the w08r1FinalNote_LastFirst webpage.
l. Display the w08r1FinalNote_LastFirst webpage. Create a hyperlink from *Preserving Data* at the bottom of the document to the w08r1Preserve_LastFirst webpage and another from *HOME* to the default page.
m. Display the w08r1Preserve_LastFirst file. Create a hyperlink from *Final Note* at the bottom of the document to the w08r1FinalNote_LastFirst webpage and another from *HOME* to the default page.
n. Add the following three bookmarks to the related headings in the document: **We_Are_Here_to_Help**, **What_is_Backup**, and **What_is_Disaster_Recovery**.
o. Create six hyperlinks from each of the six bullets in the first paragraph to their corresponding bookmarks.
p. Save and close all documents.
q. Open File Explorer, navigate to the w08r1NewCastle_LastFirst folder, and double-click the default file to display the homepage in a browser. Look carefully at the Address bar and note the local address, as opposed to a Web address. Test all links. Close the browser.
r. Save and close all files. Zip all the files in the w08r1NewCastle_LastFirst folder and name the zipped file as **w08r1NewCastle_LastFirst**. Based on your instructor's directions, submit the following in the zipped file:

   w08r1Default_LastFirst_files subfolder

   w08r1Preserve_LastFirst_files subfolder

   w08r1FinalNote_LastFirst_files subfolder

   w08r1Default_LastFirst.htm

   w08r1Preserve_LastFirst.htm

   w08r1FinalNote_LastFirst.htm

   w08r1FinalNote_LastFirst.docx

Disaster Recovery

Modify a Video Clip

You are a member of the Web design team for the Christmas Candle website. One of the junior Web designers had embedded a video clip from YouTube that has since been removed from the website. Create a folder named **w08d1ChristmasCandle_LastFirst**. Open the *w08d1Default.mht* file, save it **w08d1Default_LastFirst.docx** to the newly created folder. Search the Internet using a search engine such as Bing or Google for a video clip that emphasizes safety when lighting candles at home. Locate the nonworking video on your document and replace it with the new video clip. Save the Word document as a mht webpage and test the new video. Save and close all files. Based on your instructor's directions, submit w08d1Default_LastFirst.mht.

Capstone Exercise

MyLab IT Grader

Sam's Gym Website

Sam's Gym is a family-owned fitness center and you are the newly hired membership director. You have collected information and put together a membership package providing essential information about the gym and its services. Because of your extensive experience with Word, you want to create a website to add visibility and publicity to the gym.

Create a Folder

You begin by creating a folder to contain all files for the website.

1. Create a folder named **w08c1Fitness_LastFirst**.

Design a Set of Webpages

You will convert existing documents to webpages for Sam's Gym, but before you save them as webpages, you redesign the documents to incorporate visual enhancements such as color and graphics. You will also create bookmarks and hyperlinks on the webpages.

2. Open *w08c1Default* and save it as a webpage named **w08c1Default_LastFirst** in the w08c1Fitness_LastFirst folder. Change the page title to **Sam's Gym – Homepage**. (Omit the period.)
3. Customize the ribbon to place the buttons you use most on one custom tab with groups. You can modify the myTab tab you created in Hands-On Exercise 1 or reset the ribbon to its original state and create a new tab with groups.
4. Apply the **Frame theme**. Apply a background color using the **Newsprint Texture Fill Effects** (fourth row, first column). Increase the font size of the heading *Sam's Gym* to **36** and apply the text effect **Fill: Black, Text color 1, Outline: White, Background color 1; Hard Shadow: White, Background color 1** (third row, first column).
5. Select the first picture and use the picture formatting tools to resize the picture height to **2.5"** and apply the **Beveled Oval, Black picture style**.
6. Open *w08c1Activities* and save it as a webpage named **w08c1Activities_LastFirst** in the w08c1Fitness_LastFirst folder. Change the page title to **Sam's Gym – Activities**. Apply the same formatting used in Step 4 for the homepage.
7. Open *w08c1Hours* and apply the same formatting used in Step 4 for the homepage to this document. You will save this document as a webpage after you insert an online video later.

Add Navigation Elements to Webpages

Your pages are looking good. Now you want to add the ability to navigate within a long page and to navigate easily among the pages.

8. Display the Default page. Press **Ctrl+End** to move the insertion point to the end of the document, press **Enter**, and then type View Our Activities and Hours Information on two separate lines, with a blank line in between. Create a **hyperlink to the Activities webpage** from *View Our Activities*.
9. Display the Activities page. Create two bookmarks, **Beginners** and **Intermediate**, in front of the following two paragraphs: *The following classes are suitable for beginners or senior citizens* and *The following classes are suitable for intermediate participants*.
10. Create a hyperlink from each of the following two bullets in the first paragraph to the corresponding bookmarks: *Classes for Beginners or Senior Citizens* and *Classes for Intermediate Participants*.
11. On the Activities page, go to the end of the document, and then type **Back to Top** and **HOME** on two separate lines. Insert a **Top of the Document hyperlink** to navigate back to the top of the document and create a **hyperlink from HOME** to the Default page. Save the page.
12. Display the Hours page. Go to the bottom of the document, type **HOME**, and then create a hyperlink from the Hours page to the Default page. Save the page.

Replace a Photo and Remove Background on Photos

You want to replace the photo on the Activities page with the same photo on the default page.

13. Display the Activities page. Select the first picture and replace it with the **w08c1SamGym image** in your data folder. Resize the picture height to **2.5"** and apply **Top and Bottom Text Wrapping**.

Add an Online Video to the Services Page

You want to include a video on yoga on the Hours page.

14. Display the Hours page and place the insertion point above the *HOME* hyperlink. Conduct a search on YouTube using the key words **yoga**. Select any of the videos, insert the video into the Hours page and save the document. Center the video and change the height to **3"**.
15. Save the document as a webpage in the w08c1Fitness_LastFirst folder and change the page title to **Sam's Gym – Hours**.
16. Display the Default page. Create a hyperlink from *Hours Information* on the default page to the Hours page.

Document Progress in a Blog Post

The owner of Sam's Gym wants you to create a blog and share the new website with employees and clients. You start the blog and then find the server is down for maintenance, so you save your work so that you can post it at a later time.

17. Open a new blog post document. Type the text **Sam's Gym Website** as the title of the blog post. Type the following sentence for the post: **Welcome to our Fitness Center Website! I used Word to design the website, and I used features such as background color, themes, hyperlinks, and bookmarks to make the process easy for me. I hope you like our website, and please contact me if you have any questions about our website or would like to check out our facilities.**

18. Save the blog post in the w08c1Fitness_LastFirst folder as **w08c1FitnessBlog_LastFirst**. Save and close all files. Preview all your webpages and test all links.

19. Zip all the files in the w08c1Fitness_LastFirst folder and name the zipped file as **w08hc1Fitness_LastFirst**. Based on your instructor's directions, submit the following in the zipped file:

    w08c1Default_LastFirst_files subfolder
    w08c1Activities_LastFirst_files subfolder
    w08c1Hours_LastFirst_files subfolder
    w08c1Default_LastFirst.htm
    w08c1Activities_LastFirst.htm
    w08c1FitnessBlog_LastFirst.docx
    w08c1Hours_LastFirst.docx
    w08c1Hours_LastFirst.htm

Word Application Capstone Exercise (Chs. 1–4)

MyLab IT Grader

You are enrolled in an independent study graduate class in which you are reading and analyzing a book, *Cognitive Creativity*. As the final project for the class, you prepare a paper providing an overview of the book and its application to decision-making strategy. You will use MLA style as a basis for the paper, but you are allowed to deviate from the style with respect to the inclusion of a cover page and various other elements. A table included in the paper summarizes data and includes a formula to provide numerical analysis.

Edit and Format the Document

The rough draft includes text that you will begin with, but you must format the text and you will reword a bit as well. Because headings are formatted in preset styles, you will modify those styles to suit your purposes. By adjusting paragraph and line spacing, you will produce an attractive document that is well designed.

1. Open *wApp_Cap1_Thinking* and save it as **wApp_Cap1_Thinking_LastFirst**.
2. Display nonprinting characters. Note that the document includes a blank first page, as evidenced by the page break designation on the first page. Change the document theme to **Retrospect** and select Colors of **Blue Warm**. Select all text in the document and change the font to **Times New Roman**. View the Ruler.
3. Remove the word *why* from the second sentence in the first body paragraph on page 2. Change the word *believes* in the *Prospect Theory* section on page 3 to **proposes**.
4. Remove the space following the word *Cognitive* in the last sentence of the first body paragraph on page 2 and insert a **Nonbreaking Space symbol** between *Cognitive* and *Creativity*.
5. Insert **black check mark bullets** on the three single-line paragraphs following the first body paragraph, beginning with *the irrationality of humans* and ending with *the nature of well-being*. Decrease indent to position bullets at the left margin and ensure that each bulleted text begins with a capital letter.
6. Change margins to **1"** top, bottom, left, and right. Change to **Outline View**. Change the Show Level setting to **Level 2**. Drag *Stages of Prospect Theory* directly below the heading *Prospect Theory* so that it becomes the first sublevel in the *Prospect Theory* section. Close Outline View.
7. **Bold** the bulleted items on page 2. Select all text in the document and adjust paragraph spacing Before and After to **0 pt**. **Double-space** the document. Add a First line indent of **0.5"** to the first body paragraph on page 2 (beginning with *The study of behavioral economics*).
8. Center the title and subtitle (*Cognitive Creativity* and *An Analysis*). Change the line spacing of the *Cognitive Creativity* title to **1.0**.
9. Modify document properties to include **Parker Adams** as the author, removing any existing author.
10. Modify Heading 1 style to include a font of **Times New Roman**, **14 pt**, **Black, Text 1**. Modify Heading 2 style to include a font of **Times New Roman** with a font color of **Black, Text 1**. Changes in style should apply to the current document only.

Insert and Format a Table

To support the report summary, you will develop a table to describe various decision-making strategies. You will ensure that the table is well organized and attractive, inserting rows where appropriate and merging and splitting others. A table style adds to the design, while borders improve the table's readability. You will also include a formula to summarize a column numerically.

11. Select the lines of tabbed text near the top of page 3 (beginning with *System 1* and ending with *0.39*). Whether you select the final paragraph mark on the last line is irrelevant. Convert the selection to a table, accepting all default settings.
12. Insert a row above the first row of the new table, merge all cells, and then type **Systems of Decision Making**. Apply **Align Center** alignment to text in the first row.

13. Insert a row below the first row. Split cells in the new row, adjusting the number of columns shown in the dialog box to **4** and ensuring that *Merge cells before split* is selected. Select the table and choose **Distribute Columns** on the Table Tools Layout tab to align all columns.
14. Type the following text in row 2:

    | System Theory | Characterized by | Percentage Employed | Probability Factor |

15. Insert a row at the end of the table and merge the first three cells in the row. Type **Average Probability** in the merged cell on the last row and apply **Align Center** alignment to the text. In the last cell on the last row, include a formula to average numbers in the column above. You do not need to select a number format.
16. Apply a table style of **List Table 3 – Accent 1**. Deselect **First Column** in the Table Style Options group to remove bold formatting from the first column. **Bold** text on the second row. Select the table and change the font size to **10 pt**. Apply **Align Center** alignment to all text in rows 2, 3, and 4. Apply **Align Center** alignment to the numeric value in the last cell on the last row.
17. Add a caption below the table of **Table 1: Decision-Making Strategies**.
18. Change the probability factor for *System 1* (in row 3) to **0.62**. Update the field in the last cell on the last row to reflect the change in probability.
19. Select **rows 2**, **3**, and **4**, click the **Table Tools Design tab**, and then choose a Pen Color of **Black, Text 1**. Ensure that the line style is a single line and the line weight is **½ pt**. Apply the border selection to **All Borders**.

Edit and Format a Report

The report is near completion but must be formatted to adhere to guidelines supplied by your instructor and loosely based on the MLA writing style. You will include a header to identify yourself as the author and you will provide a footnote with additional information on a report topic. Including a table of contents assists readers with moving quickly to topics, while a cover page provides an introduction to the report. You will include a picture as a design element on the cover page and insert a watermark to identify the report as a draft copy. You will include citations to properly acknowledge sources and include those sources in a Works Cited page.

20. Click after the period that ends the last sentence in the first body paragraph under *System Biases* (ending in *economical solutions to problems*). Insert a footnote with the text, **For more information on theory-induced blindness, visit http://cognitivecreativity.com/theory.** (Include the period.) Right-click the footnote and modify the style to include **Times New Roman, 12 pt font**.
21. Shade the first two lines on page 2, *Cognitive Creativity* and *An Analysis* in **Blue, Accent 2, Lighter 60%**. Add a **½ pt Box border** to the shaded text, ensuring that the color is **Black, Text 1**.
22. Insert a **DRAFT 1 watermark**, colored **Red** (second column in Standard Colors).
23. Click before the *Cognitive Creativity* heading at the top of page 2 (in the shaded area) and insert a page break. Click before the new page break indicator on the newly inserted page 2 and insert a Table of Contents, selecting **Automatic Table 1**. (On a Mac, select Classic.)
24. Click before the word *Contents* at the top of the table of contents and insert a **Continuous section break**. Click before the page break indicator on the first page and insert text from the file *wApp_Cap1_Cover*. Choose from options in the Page Setup dialog box to center the cover page vertically. Ensure that the settings apply to the current section only. (On a Mac, click before the word Table at the top of the table of contents.)

25. Click before the fourth blank paragraph below the words *An Analysis* on the Cover page. Insert the picture file *wApp_Cap1_QuestionMark.png*. Change the picture height to **1.5"** and choose **Top and Bottom text wrapping**. Apply an artistic effect of **Paint Strokes** to the picture (row 2, column 2).
26. Add an unformatted right-aligned header. Type **Parker Adams** and include a space following the name. Insert a page number in the current position, selecting the **Plain Number** option. Ensure that the header does not show on the first page. It is possible that the watermark is removed as well. Close the header.
27. Click before *Submitted by Parker Adams* at the end of the document. Insert a right tab at **5.5"**. Press **Tab** to align the text at the right tab stop.
28. Change the writing style to **MLA**. Click before the period ending the first sentence in the paragraph under the *Decision Systems* heading on page 3 (ending in *and decisions are made*). Insert a citation, using the existing source of *Daniel Conner*. Edit the citation to show page **157** and to suppress **Author**, **Year**, and **Title**.
29. Click before the period ending the first sentence the first paragraph under the *System Biases* heading (ending in *theory-induced bias*). Insert a citation to a new source as follows:

    Type: **Article in a Periodical**
    Author: **Leo James**
    Title: **Decision-Making Strategies**
    Periodical Title: **Journal of Behavioral Economics**
    Year: **2020**
    Month: **April**
    Day: **21**
    Pages: **45–52**

30. Insert a page break at the end of the document. Insert a bibliography, selecting the **Insert Bibliography** option so that a title is not included. Click before the first source on the Bibliography page and press **Enter**. Click the new blank paragraph at the top of the page and type **Works Cited**. (Do not type the period.) Center the *Works Cited* line. Select all text on the Works Cited page and change the font to **Times New Roman 12 pt**. (On a Mac, select Works Cited bibliography and center the title.)
31. Select the heading *Decision Systems* on page 3. Insert the comment **This is often referred to as Decision Support Strategies**. (Include the period.)
32. Check spelling and grammar, correcting at least two spelling errors and one grammatical error, but not accepting clarity and conciseness suggestions. The word *spills* is correctly used so you should ignore the error, if presented.
33. Save and close the document. Based on your instructor's directions, submit wApp_Cap1_Thinking_LastFirst.

Word Comprehensive Capstone Exercise (Chs. 5–8)

MyLab IT Grader

You are the newly hired volunteer director of a local hospital and one of your responsibilities is to put together a hospital volunteer orientation package that provides essential information to new volunteers. Your supervisor had previously conducted some research and written a short draft. You collected information from various other sources and wrote your own draft about the hospital's volunteer program and its services. Now you are ready to combine the two drafts and format the combined document to enhance readability. You will apply several Word features and insert appropriate images to make the document look more professional. You will then insert several form controls into the Total Your Volunteer Hours table and create a macro to align the document. Finally, you will restrict editing so that volunteers can only type the date, shift, location, and work hours into the Total Your Volunteer Hours table.

Combine Two Documents into a New Document

You will combine the content from two documents to create the volunteer orientation document.

1. Start Word and open a blank document. Combine the contents of the *wApp_Cap2_Volunteer1* (original document) and the *wApp_Cap2_Volunteer2* (revised document) documents into a new document. Save the combined document as **wApp_Cap2_Volunteer_LastFirst**.
2. Reject all the changes and stop tracking.
3. Format the entire document as follows:
   - Change the font type to **Times New Roman** and font size to **11**.
   - Set Spacing Before to **6 pt** and Line spacing to **Single**.
   - Change the margins to **Normal**.

Insert a Cover Page, and Apply a Document and a Font Theme

You want to include a cover page, which will display the title of the document and the date that you are preparing the document. You will then apply a document theme and a font theme to the document so that all the features in the Word document are color-coordinated.

4. Insert a cover page by performing the following steps:
   - Insert the **Slice (Light)** Cover Page.
   - Type **HOSPITAL VOLUNTEER PROGRAM** in the Document Title placeholder.
   - Delete the **Document subtitle content control** and the **textbox containing the School and Course title content controls**.
   - Apply the **Slice theme** to the document.
   - Apply a page background color that uses the **Parchment texture fill effect**. (On a Mac, apply a page background color of Orange, Accent 2, Lighter 80%.)

Insert a WordArt Object and a Text Box

You will improve the appearance of the document with a masthead created using WordArt, and format a selected paragraph using a text box and shading.

5. Insert a WordArt object on page 3 by performing the following steps:
   - Delete the text *Our Mission* on page 3 and insert the **Gradient Fill: Orange, Accent color 5, Reflection WordArt** (second row, second column).
   - Type **Our Mission** as the text for the WordArt.
   - Change the font size to **40**.
   - Ensure that the width of the WordArt is **3"**.

- Apply the **Square Text Wrapping style** and the **Top Center alignment** to the object.
- Position the insertion point in front of the paragraph beginning with *To provide excellent and compassionate healthcare services* and press **Enter**.

6. Format the *Our Mission* statement under the Our Mission WordArt using a text box and shading by performing the following steps:
   - Cut the whole paragraph below the Our Mission WordArt, insert a **Simple Text Box** (on a Mac, draw a text box), and then paste the content into the text box.
   - Format the height of the text box as **1.1"** and the width as **5"**.
   - Apply the **Top and Bottom Text Wrapping style** to the text box and delete three blank paragraphs below the text box.
   - Apply the **Subtle Effect – Dark Blue, Accent 1 Shape Style** (fourth row, second column).
   - Apply the **Tight Reflection: Touching Shape Effects**.

Format a Section into Two Columns

You want to format the text in the Our Core Values section on page 3 into two columns.

7. Select the seven bullets in Our Core Values section, and format them into two equal columns with a line between. Delete the extra bullet if it is created.

Insert a Picture and a 3D Model, and Change a Picture

Carefully selected images will improve the visibility of the document, so you want to insert a picture and replace another image in the document.

8. Insert the picture *wApp_Cap2_Snow.jpg* to the left of the paragraph below the *Attendance and Inclement Weather* heading on page 5.
   - Change the width of the picture to **2"**.
   - Change text wrapping to **Tight** and apply the **Center Shadow Rectangle Picture Style** and the **Film Grain Artistic Effect**. (On a Mac, use the Quick Style.)
   - Position the picture below the *Attendance and Inclement Weather* heading.
9. Replace the picture on page 2 with the file *wApp_Cap2_Hospital.jpg*. Ensure that the picture stays at the top left of the page. Position the insertion point in front of the paragraph beginning with *We are pleased to have you* and press **Enter** four times.
10. Insert the *wApp_Cap2_Doctor's bag.glb* 3D model image below the *Resources* section on page 6. Open the Format 3D Model task pane and change the X Rotation to **30** and both Y and Z Rotations to **60**. Adjust the width of the model image to **3"**. Apply the **Dotted grid Pattern fill** (seventh row, second column) to the image. Close the task pane and apply the **Square Text Wrapping style** and the **Bottom Center alignment** to the 3D image.

Create and Insert a Subdocument

The Reporting Volunteer Hours section is in another file and you want to insert it as a subdocument into the document that you are currently working on.

11. Create a subdocument by performing the following steps:
    - Go to the end of the document and insert a page break.
    - Type the heading **Reporting Volunteer Hours** on the last page and press **Enter**. Ensure that the typed heading is formatted as Heading 1.
    - Switch to Outline view to create and insert the subdocument. Ensure that the Reporting Volunteer Hours heading is selected, click **Show Document**, and click **Insert** to insert the subdocument *wApp_Cap2_Hours* into the current document.

- Click **Yes to All** if prompted to rename the styles. When prompted, click **OK** to use the master document template.
- Unlink the subdocument. Close Outline view.
- Select all the content on the last page (except the *Reporting Volunteer Hours* heading) and apply the **Normal font style**.

Insert Form Fields

You want to insert several form fields into the Total Your Volunteer Hours table on the last page. For instance, you want to use a Date Picker content control for the date, a Drop-Down List content control to list item choices available to volunteers, a Text Form field to display the hours worked, and another Text Form field to calculate the total hours worked for the month.

12. Insert a Date Picker content control by performing the following steps:
    - Display the Developer tab on the ribbon and turn on Design Mode.
    - Insert a **Date Picker Content Control** in the table cell immediately below *Date*. (On a Mac, click Text Box Form Field. Click Options and select Date from the Type box. Click OK.)
13. Insert a Drop-Down List Content Control by performing the following steps:
    - Insert a **Drop-Down List Content Control** in the table cell immediately below *Shift*. (On a Mac, use the Combo Box Form Field.)
    - Set the properties for the drop-down list to display **Shift** as the title. Type the word **Type** in the Tag box. (On a Mac, Title and Tag options are not available.)
    - Add the following items to the list in the order given:
      8:00–10:00 am
      10:00–12:00 pm
      12:00–2:00 pm
      2:00–4:00 pm
      4:00–6:00 pm
14. Insert a Drop-Down List Content Control by performing the following steps:
    - Insert a **Drop-Down List Content Control** in the table cell immediately below *Location*. (On a Mac, use the Combo Box Form Field.)
    - Set the properties for the drop-down list to display **Location** as the title. Type the word **Type** in the Tag box. (On a Mac, Title and Tag options are not available.)
    - Add the following items to the list in the order given:
      Emergency Room
      Flower Shop
      Gift Shop
      Information Desk
      Pharmacy
      Others
15. Insert a Legacy Tools Text Form Field by performing the following steps:
    - Insert the **Legacy Tools Text Form Field** in the table cell immediately below *Hours*. (On a Mac, use the Text Box Form Field.)
    - Set the properties of the text form field to be a **Number**, the default number to **0**, and the number format to **0.00**.
    - Replace the contents of the Bookmark box with **Hour1** and select the option to **Calculate on exit**.

16. Insert a Legacy Tools Text Form Field by performing the following steps:
    - Insert the **Legacy Tools Text Form Field** in the table cell to the right of *Total Hours*. (On a Mac, use the Text Box Form Field.)
    - Set the properties of the text form field to be a **Calculation**, the expression to **=sum(above)** and the number format to **0.00**.
    - Replace the contents of the Bookmark box with **TotalHours** and select the option to **Calculate on exit**.
17. Copy and paste the four controls in the second row of the table to the next five rows. Turn off Design Mode. Select and right-align the seven cells below *Hours* in the fourth column.

Create a Macro

You will create a macro to align the adjustment of the document and edit the macro using the Visual Basic Editor (VBE). You will also save the document as a macro-enabled document.

18. Move to the beginning of the document, and create a new macro by performing the following steps:
    - Select **Record Macro**.
    - Name the macro **Alignment**.
    - Store the macro in **wApp_Cap2_Volunteer_LastFirst (document)**.
    - Type the description of the macro as **Change document alignment** (no period).
    - Select the entire document and change the paragraph alignment of the entire document to **Center**.
    - Stop recording the macro.
    - Save the document as a macro-enabled document using the filename **wApp_Cap2_Volunteer_LastFirst.docm**.
19. Edit the macro by performing the following steps:
    - Open the **Alignment** macro in the VBE.
    - Edit the text *Selection.ParagraphFormat.Alignment = wdAlignParagraphCenter* to read **Selection.ParagraphFormat.Alignment = wdAlignParagraphLeft**.
    - Save the macro.
20. Copy the entire Alignment macro from the *Sub* statement to the *End Sub* statement and paste the code onto a blank page below the *Total Your Volunteer Hours* table. Close the VBE window and run the **Alignment** macro. Save the document.

Restrict Editing

You do not want the volunteers to make any editorial changes to the document, but at the same time, you want them to be able to record their volunteer hours.

21. Restrict editing by performing the following steps:
    - Click the **Review tab**. Restrict editing in the document to **Limit formatting to a selection of styles**.
    - Allow filling in forms as the only type of editing in the document.
    - Start enforcing protection, leaving the password boxes blank.
22. Save and close the document. Based on your instructor's directions, submit wApp_Cap2_Volunteer_LastFirst.docm.

Microsoft Office 2019 Specialist Word

Online Appendix materials can be found in the Student Resources located at **www.pearsonhighered.com/exploring**.

MOS Obj #	MOS Objective	Exploring Chapter	Exploring Section Heading
1.	**Manage Documents**		
1.1	**Navigate within documents**		
1.1.1	Search for text	Online Appendix	Online Appendix
1.1.2	Link to locations within documents	**Chapter 6**: Time-Saving Tools **Chapter 8**: Word and the Internet	Create Bookmarks Insert Bookmarks in a Webpage and Add a Link to a Bookmark; Insert Hyperlinks to Other Webpages
1.1.3	Move to specific locations and objects in documents	**Chapter 6**: Time-Saving Tools	Use the Navigation Pane
1.1.4	Show and hide formatting symbols and hidden text	**Chapter 1**: Introduction to Word	Create a Document
1.2	**Format documents**		
1.2.1	Set up document pages	**Chapter 1**: Introduction to Word	Adjust Margins Change Page Orientation
1.2.2	Apply style sets	**Chapter 2**: Document Presentation	Use a Style Set
1.2.3	Insert and modify headers and footers	**Chapter 1**: Introduction to Word	Insert Headers and Footers
1.2.4	Configure page background elements	**Chapter 1**: Introduction to Word	Insert a Watermark
1.3	**Save and share documents**		
1.3.1	Save documents in alternative file formats	**Chapter 1**: Introduction to Word	Ensure Document Compatibility
1.3.2	Modify basic document properties	**Chapter 1**: Introduction to Word	Modifying Document Properties
1.3.3	Modify print settings	**Chapter 1**: Introduction to Word	Select Print Options
1.3.4	Share documents electronically	**Chapter 4**: Research and Collaboration	Sharing Documents Use Word Online
1.4	**Inspect documents for issues**		
1.4.1	Locate and remove hidden properties and personal information	**Chapter 1**: Introduction to Word	Run the Document Inspector
1.4.2	Locate and correct accessibility issues	**Chapter 1**: Introduction to Word	Ensure Document Accessibility
1.4.3	Locate and correct compatibility issues	**Chapter 1**: Introduction to Word	Ensure Document Compatibility
2.	**Insert and Format Text, Paragraphs, and Sections**		
2.1	**Insert text and paragraphs**		
2.1.1	Find and replace text	Online Appendix	Online Appendix
2.1.2	Insert symbols and special characters	**Chapter 1**: Introduction to Word	Insert a Symbol

MOS Obj #	MOS Objective	Exploring Chapter	Exploring Section Heading
2.2	**Format text and paragraphs**		
2.2.1	Apply text effects	**Chapter 2**: Document Presentation	Change Text Appearance
2.2.2	Apply formatting by using Format Painter	**Chapter 2**: Document Presentation	Create a New Style from Text
2.2.3	Set line and paragraph spacing and indentation	**Chapter 2**: Document Presentation	Select Line and Paragraph Spacing Select Indents
2.2.4	Apply built-in styles to text	**Chapter 2**: Document Presentation	Select and Modify Styles
2.2.5	Clear formatting	**Chapter 2**: Document Presentation	Change Text Appearance
2.3	**Create and configure document sections**		
2.3.1	Format text in multiple columns	**Chapter 5**: Document Publications	Apply and Modify Column Layout
2.3.2	Insert page, section, and column breaks	**Chapter 5**: Document Publications	Insert a Section Break; Insert a Column Break
2.3.3	Change page setup options for a section	**Chapter 1**: Introduction to Word	Using Features that Improve Readability
3.	**Manage Tables and Lists**		
3.1	**Create tables**		
3.1.1	Convert text to tables	**Chapter 3**: Document Productivity	Convert Text to a Table and Convert a Table to Text
3.1.2	Convert tables to text	**Chapter 3**: Document Productivity	Convert Text to a Table and Convert a Table to Text
3.1.3	Create tables by specifying rows and columns	**Chapter 3**: Document Productivity	Create or Draw a Table
3.2	**Modify tables**		
3.2.1	Sort table data	**Chapter 3**: Document Productivity	Sort Data in a Table
3.2.2	Configure cell margins and spacing	**Chapter 3**: Document Productivity	Format Table Text
3.2.3	Merge and split cells	**Chapter 3**: Document Productivity	Merge and Split Cells
3.2.4	Resize tables, rows, and columns	**Chapter 3**: Document Productivity	Change Row Height and Column Width
3.2.5	Split tables	Online Appendix	Online Appendix
3.2.6	Configure a repeating row header	**Chapter 3**: Document Productivity	Include a Recurring Table Header
3.3	**Create and modify lists**		
3.3.1	Format paragraphs as numbered and bulleted lists	**Chapter 2**: Document Presentation	Create Bulleted and Numbered Lists
3.3.2	Change bullet characters and number formats	**Chapter 2**: Document Presentation	Create Bulleted and Numbered Lists
3.3.3	Define custom bullet characters and number formats	**Chapter 2**: Document Presentation	Create Bulleted and Numbered Lists
3.3.4	Increase and decrease list levels	**Chapter 2**: Document Presentation	Create Bulleted and Numbered Lists
3.3.5	Restart and continue list numbering	**Chapter 2**: Document Presentation	Create Bulleted and Numbered Lists
3.3.6	Set starting number values	**Chapter 2**: Document Presentation	Create Bulleted and Numbered Lists

MOS Obj #	MOS Objective	Exploring Chapter	Exploring Section Heading
4. Create and Manage References			
4.1 Create and manage reference elements			
4.1.1	Insert footnotes and endnotes	**Chapter 4**: Research and Collaboration	Create Footnotes and Endnotes
4.1.2	Modify footnote and endnote properties	**Chapter 4**: Research and Collaboration	Create Footnotes and Endnotes
4.1.3	Create and modify bibliography citations sources	**Chapter 4**: Research and Collaboration	Create a Source and Include a Citation
4.1.4	Insert citations for bibliographies	**Chapter 4**: Research and Collaboration	Create a Source and Include a Citation
4.2 Create and manage reference tables			
4.2.1	Insert tables of contents	**Chapter 4**: Research and Collaboration	Create a Table of Contents
4.2.2	Customize tables of contents	**Chapter 4**: Research and Collaboration	Create a Table of Contents
4.2.3	Insert bibliographies	**Chapter 4**: Research and Collaboration	Create a Bibliography
5. Insert and Format Graphic Elements			
5.1 Insert illustrations and text boxes			
5.1.1	Insert shapes	**Chapter 5**: Document Publications	Insert Drawing Shapes
5.1.2	Insert pictures	**Chapter 5**: Document Publications	Include Images
5.1.3	Insert 3D models	**Chapter 5**: Document Publications	Include 3D Models
5.1.4	Insert SmartArt graphics	**Chapter 5**: Document Publications	Insert SmartArt
5.1.5	Insert screenshots and screen clippings	**Chapter 5**: Document Publications	Applying Design Features
5.1.6	Insert text boxes	**Chapter 5**: Document Publications	Insert a Text Box
5.2 Format illustrations and text boxes			
5.2.1	Apply artistic effects	**Chapter 2**: Document Presentation	Modify a Picture
5.2.2	Apply picture effects and picture styles	**Chapter 2**: Document Presentation	Modify a Picture
5.2.3	Remove picture backgrounds	**Chapter 2**: Document Presentation	Modify a Picture
5.2.4	Format graphic elements	**Chapter 5**: Document Publications	Manipulating Graphic Objects
5.2.5	Format SmartArt graphics	**Chapter 5**: Document Publications	Insert SmartArt
5.2.6	Format 3D models	**Chapter 5**: Document Publications	Include 3D Models
5.3 Add text to graphic elements			
5.3.1	Add and modify text in text boxes	**Chapter 5**: Document Publications	Insert a Text Box
5.3.2	Add and modify text in shapes	**Chapter 5**: Document Publications	Insert a Text Box
5.3.3	Add and modify SmartArt graphic content	**Chapter 5**: Document Publications	Insert SmartArt

MOS Obj #		MOS Objective	Exploring Chapter	Exploring Section Heading
5.4	Modify graphic elements			
	5.4.1	Position objects	**Chapter 5**: Document Publications	Insert Drawing Shapes
	5.4.2	Wrap text around objects	**Chapter 5**: Document Publications	Insert a Text Box
	5.4.3	Add alternative text to objects for accessibility	Online Appendix	Online Appendix
6.	**Manage Document Collaboration**			
6.1	Add and manage comments			
	6.1.1	Add comments	**Chapter 4**: Research and Collaboration	Add a Comment
	6.1.2	Review and reply to comments	**Chapter 4**: Research and Collaboration	View Comments Reply to Comments
	6.1.3	Resolve comments	**Chapter 4**: Research and Collaboration	View Comments Reply to Comments
	6.1.4	Delete comments	**Chapter 4**: Research and Collaboration	Add a Comment
6.2	Manage change tracking			
	6.2.1	Track changes	**Chapter 4**: Research and Collaboration	Use Track Changes
	6.2.2	Review tracked changes	**Chapter 4**: Research and Collaboration	Use Track Changes
	6.2.3	Accept and reject tracked changes	**Chapter 4**: Research and Collaboration	Accept and Reject Changes
	6.2.4	Lock and unlock change tracking	**Chapter 4**: Research and Collaboration	Tracking Changes

Microsoft Office 2019 Expert Word

MOS Obj #	MOS Objective	Exploring Chapter	Exploring Section Heading
1.	**Manage Document Options and Settings**		
1.1	**Manage documents and templates**		
1.1.1	Modify existing document templates	**Chapter 6**: Time Saving Tools	Selecting Templates
1.1.2	Manage document versions	**Chapter 1**: Introduction to Word	Understand Document Retrieval
1.1.3	Compare and combine multiple documents	**Chapter 6**: Time Saving Tools	Merging Documents
1.1.4	Link to external document content	**Chapter 8**: Word and the Internet	Building and Publishing a Webpage
1.1.5	Enable macros in a document	**Chapter 7**: Document Automation	Understanding Macro Security
1.1.6	Customize the Quick Access toolbar	Office 2019 Common Features	Using Common Interface Components
1.1.7	Display hidden ribbon tabs	**Chapter 7**: Document Automation	Creating an Electronic Form
1.1.8	Change the Normal template default font	Online Appendix	Online Appendix
1.2	**Prepare documents for collaboration**		
1.2.1	Restrict editing	**Chapter 7**: Document Automation	Applying Document Restrictions
1.2.2	Protect documents by using passwords	**Chapter 7**: Document Automation	Applying Document Restrictions
1.3	**Use and configure language options**		
1.3.1	Configure editing and display languages	Online Appendix	Online Appendix
1.3.2	Use language-specific features	Online Appendix	Online Appendix
2.	**Use Andvanced Editing and Formatting Features**		
2.1	**Find, replace, and paste document content**		
2.1.1	Find and replace text by using wildcards and special characters	Online Appendix	Online Appendix
2.1.2	Find and replace formatting and styles	Online Appendix	Online Appendix
2.1.3	Apply Paste Options	Online Appendix	Online Appendix
2.2	**Configure paragraph layout options**		
2.2.1	Configure hyphenation and line numbers	Online Appendix	Online Appendix
2.2.2	Set paragraph pagination options	Online Appendix	Online Appendix

MOS Obj #	MOS Objective	Exploring Chapter	Exploring Section Heading
2.3	**Create and manage styles**		
2.3.1	Create paragraph and character styles	**Chapter 2**: Document Presentation	Applying Styles
2.3.2	Modify existing styles	**Chapter 2**: Document Presentation	Applying Styles
2.3.3	Copy styles to other documents or templates	**Chapter 2**: Document Presentation	Applying Styles
3.	**Create Custom Document Elements**		
3.1	**Create and modify building blocks**		
3.1.1	Create QuickParts	**Chapter 6**: Time Saving Tools	Using Building Blocks
3.1.2	Manage building blocks	**Chapter 6**: Time Saving Tools	Using Building Blocks
3.2	**Create custom design elments**		
3.2.1	Create custom color sets	**Chapter 6**: Time Saving Tools	Customizing Theme Colors and Theme Fonts, and Applying Theme Effects
3.2.2	Create custom fonts sets	**Chapter 6**: Time Saving Tools	Customizing Theme Colors and Theme Fonts, and Applying Theme Effects
3.2.3	Create custom themes	**Chapter 6**: Time Saving Tools	Customizing Theme Colors and Theme Fonts, and Applying Theme Effects
3.2.4	Create custom style sets	**Chapter 6**: Time Saving Tools	Applying a Document Theme and Style Set
3.3	**Create and manage indexes**		
3.3.1	Mark index entries	**Chapter 4**: Research and Collaboration	Exploring Special Features
3.3.2	Create indexes	**Chapter 4**: Research and Collaboration	Exploring Special Features
3.3.3	Update indexes	**Chapter 4**: Research and Collaboration	Exploring Special Features
3.4	**Create and manage tables of figures**		
3.4.1	Insert figure and table captions	**Chapter 3**: Document Productivity	Enhancing Table Data
3.4.2	Configure caption properties	**Chapter 3**: Document Productivity	Enhancing Table Data
3.4.3	Insert and modify a table of figures	Online Appendix	Online Appendix
4.	**Use Advanced Word Features**		
4.1	**Manage forms, fields, and controls**		
4.1.1	Add custom fields	**Chapter 7**: Document Automation	Creating an Electronic Form
4.1.2	Modify field properties	**Chapter 7**: Document Automation	Creating an Electronic Form
4.1.3	Insert standard content controls	**Chapter 7**: Document Automation	Creating an Electronic Form
4.1.4	Configure standard content controls	**Chapter 7**: Document Automation	Creating an Electronic Form

MOS Obj #	MOS Objective	Exploring Chapter	Exploring Section Heading
4.2	**Create and modify macros**		
4.2.1	Record simple macros	**Chapter 7**: Document Automation	Creating a Macro
4.2.2	Name simple macros	**Chapter 7**: Document Automation	Creating a Macro
4.2.3	Edit simple macros	**Chapter 7**: Document Automation	Creating a Macro
4.2.4	Copy macros to other documents or templates	**Chapter 7**: Document Automation	Understanding Macro Security
4.3	**Perform mail merges**		
4.3.1	Manage recipient lists	**Chapter 3**: Document Productivity	Creating a Mail Merge Document
4.3.2	Insert merged fields	**Chapter 3**: Document Productivity	Completing a Mail Merge
4.3.3	Preview merge results	**Chapter 3**: Document Productivity	Completing a Mail Merge
4.3.4	Create merged documents, labels, and envelopes	**Chapter 3**: Document Productivity	Completing a Mail Merge

Glossary

Accessibility Checker A feature that locates elements in a document that might cause difficulty for people with disabilities to read.

Add-in A custom program or additional command that extends the functionality of a Microsoft Office program.

Alignment The positioning of the text relative to the margins.

Alignment guide A horizontal or vertical green bar that displays as you move an object, assisting with aligning the object with text or with another object.

All Markup A markup view that shows the document with all the revisions, markups, and comments using the formats predefined in Track Changes options.

APA (American Psychological Association) A writing style established by the American Psychological Association with rules and conventions for documenting sources and organizing a research paper (used primarily in business and the social sciences).

Argument A positional reference contained within parentheses in a function such as a cell reference or value, required to complete a function and produce output.

AutoCorrect A feature that automatically corrects standard spelling and word usage errors as they are typed.

AutoRecover A feature that enables Word to recover a previous version of a document.

AutoSave A feature that saves files every few seconds if those files are housed on OneDrive, OneDrive for Business, or SharePoint Online.

AutoText A type of building block to store text or graphics that will be reused, such as a standard contract clause or a long distribution list.

Background A color, design, image, or watermark that displays behind text in a document or on a webpage.

Backstage view A component of Office that provides a concise collection of commands related to an open file.

Bibliography A list of sources consulted by an author during research for a paper.

Blog A chronological publication of personal thoughts and Web links.

Bookmark A feature that provides an electronic marker for a specific location in a document, enabling the user to go to that location quickly.

Border Lines that display at the top, bottom, left, or right of a paragraph, a page, a table, or an image.

Border Painter A feature that enables you to choose border formatting and click on any table border to apply the formatting.

Building block A predefined block of text for standardized content that can be placed in any document.

Building Blocks Organizer A feature that displays a list of all the predefined building blocks in the templates stored in the current template location.

Bulleted list A list of points that is not sequential; each point is typically identified by a graphic element that itemizes and separates bulleted items.

Caption A descriptive title for a table.

Cell The intersection of a column and row in a Word table, PowerPoint table, or an Excel worksheet.

Center alignment A setting that positions text horizontally in the center of a line, with an equal distance from both the left and right margins.

Check Box content control A form element that consists of a box that can be checked or unchecked.

Chicago Manual of Style A writing style established by the University of Chicago with rules and conventions for preparing an academic paper for publication.

Citation A brief, parenthetical reference placed at the end of a sentence or paragraph that directs a reader to a source of information you used.

Cloud storage A technology used to store files and to work with programs that are stored in a central location on the Internet.

Column A format that separates document text into side-by-side vertical blocks, often used in newsletters.

Combine A feature that integrates all changes from multiple authors or documents into one single document.

Combo Box content control A content control that combines a text box with a list box, so that a user may choose from items displayed in a drop-down box or can type an entry instead of selecting from the list.

Command A button or area within a group that you click to perform tasks.

Comment A note, annotation, or additional information to the author or another reader about the content of a document.

Comment balloon A feature that displays as a boxed note in the margin and, when selected, highlights the text to which the comment is applied.

Compare A feature that evaluates the contents of two versions of a document side-by-side for a line-by-line comparison and displays a merged version with markup and tracked changes showing the differences between them.

Content control A form element that displays prompts such as drop-down lists, date pickers, text boxes, and check boxes so that users can quickly fill out electronic forms.

Contextual tab A tab that contains a group of commands related to the selected object.

Copy A command used to duplicate a selection from the original location and place it in the Office Clipboard.

Cover page The first page of a report, including the report title, author, and other identifying information.

Crop The process of trimming edges that you do not want to display.

Current List A list that includes all citation sources you use in the current document.

Custom tab A tab on the ribbon created by the user that contains the commands he or she wants to use.

Cut A command used to remove a selection from the original location and place it in the Office Clipboard.

Data source A list of information that is merged with a main document during a mail merge procedure.

Date Picker content control A form element that displays a calendar that can be used to select a date.

Design Mode The setting that enables users to view, insert, and modify content controls.

Desktop publishing A process that uses software, such as Word, to design commercial-quality printed material.

Dialog box A box that provides access to more precise, but less frequently used, commands.

Dialog Box Launcher A button that, when clicked, opens a corresponding dialog box.

Digital certificate A security feature that verifies the identity of the sender and maintains the integrity of an electronic document through encryption and security safeguards.

Digital signature An electronic stamp that guarantees the authenticity of a file, providing a verifiable identifier that is linked to the organization's digital certificate.

Document Inspector A feature that checks for and removes certain hidden and personal information from a document.

Document properties Data elements that are saved with a document but do not appear in the document as it is shown onscreen or is printed.

Document theme A unified set of design elements, including font style, color, and special effects, that is applied to an entire document.

Draft view A view that shows a great deal of document space, but no margins, headers, footers, or other special features.

Drop cap A very large capital letter at the beginning of a paragraph.

Drop-Down List content control A form element that enables choices from one of several existing entries.

Embed A process that brings an object or data from another application or file into a document, enabling the object to be edited without changing the source.

Endnote A citation that appears at the end of a document.

Enhanced ScreenTip A small message box that displays when you place the pointer over a command button. The purpose of the command, short descriptive text, or a keyboard shortcut, if applicable, will display in the box.

File Transfer Protocol (FTP) A process that uploads files from a computer to a server or downloads files from a server to a computer.

First line indent A setting that marks the location to indent only the first line in a paragraph.

Font A combination of typeface and type style.

Footer Information that displays at the bottom of a document page.

Footnote A citation that displays at the bottom of a page.

Form A document designed to collect data.

Form letter A document used in a mail merge process including standard text that is personalized with recipient information.

Format Painter A feature that enables you to quickly and easily copy all formatting from one area to another in Word, PowerPoint, and Excel.

Formatting The process of modifying text by changing font and paragraph characteristics.

Formatting restriction A setting that limits the types of styles users can apply in a document.

Formula A combination of cell references, operators, values, and/or functions used to perform a calculation.

Function A predefined computation that simplifies creating a complex calculation and produces a result based on inputs known as arguments.

Gallery An Office feature that displays additional formatting and design choices.

Group (Common Features) A subset of a tab that organizes similar tasks together.

Group (Word) The process of combining selected objects so they appear as a single object.

Hanging indent A setting that aligns the first line of a paragraph at the left margin, indenting remaining lines in the paragraph.

Header An area with one or more lines of information at the top of each page.

Header row The first row in a data source that contains labels describing the data in rows beneath.

Hyperlink An electronic marker that points to a different location within the same document using a bookmark, opens another document, or displays a different webpage in a browser.

HyperText Markup Language (HTML) A universal formatting instructional language that describes how a document appears when viewed in a browser.

Immersive Reader A document view that is an add-in learning tool designed to help readers pronounce words correctly, read quickly and accurately, and understand what is read.

Indent A setting associated with how part of a paragraph is distanced from the margin.

Index An alphabetical listing of topics covered in a document, along with the page numbers on which the topic is discussed.

Insert control An indicator that displays between rows or columns in a table, enabling you to insert one or more rows or columns.

Insertion point A blinking bar that indicates where text that you next type will appear.

Justified alignment A setting that spreads text evenly between the left and right margins, so that text begins at the left margin and ends uniformly at the right margin.

Keyboard shortcut A combination of two or more keys pressed together to initiate a software command.

Landscape orientation A document layout in which a page is wider than it is tall.

Layer The process of placing one object on top of another.

Leaders The series of dots or hyphens that leads the reader's eye across the page to connect two columns of information.

Left alignment A setting that begins text evenly at the left margin, with a ragged right edge.

Left indent A setting that positions all text in a paragraph at an equal distance from the left margin.

Legacy Tools A set of controls that is accessible by both current and earlier Word versions.

Legal blacklining A way to compare two documents and to display the changes between the two documents.

Line spacing The vertical space between lines in a paragraph.

Link A process that brings an object or data from another application or file into a document, retaining a connection to the source data.

Live Layout A feature that enables you to watch text flow around an object as you move it, so you can position the object exactly as you want it.

Live Preview An Office feature that provides a preview of the results of a selection when you point to an option in a list or gallery. Using Live Preview, you can experiment with settings before making a final choice.

Macro A set of instructions that executes a specific task or series of keystrokes; often used to automate repetitive tasks using only a button click or keyboard combination.

Mail Merge A process that combines content from a main document and a data source.

Main document A document that contains the information that stays the same for all recipients in a mail merge.

Margin The area of blank space that displays to the left, right, top, and bottom of a document or worksheet.

Markup A feature to help customize how tracked changes are displayed in a document.

Master document A document that acts like a binder for managing smaller documents.

Master List A database of all citation sources created in Word on a particular computer.

Masthead The identifying information at the top of a newsletter or other periodical.

Merge field An item that serves as a placeholder for the variable data that will be inserted into the main document during a mail merge procedure.

Microsoft Access A relational database management system in which you can record and link data, query databases, and create forms and reports.

Microsoft Excel An application that makes it easy to organize records, financial transactions, and business information in the form of worksheets.

Microsoft Office A productivity software suite including a set of software applications, each one specializing in a particular type of output.

Microsoft PowerPoint An application that enables you to create dynamic presentations to inform groups and persuade audiences.

Microsoft Word A word processing software application used to produce all sorts of documents, including memos, newsletters, forms, tables, and brochures.

Mini Toolbar A toolbar that provides access to the most common formatting selections, such as adding bold or italic, or changing font type or color. Unlike the Quick Access Toolbar, the Mini Toolbar is not customizable.

MLA (Modern Language Association) A writing style established by the Modern Language Association, with rules and conventions for preparing research papers (used primarily in the area of humanities).

Navigation Pane A feature that enables you to navigate through a document by viewing headings, viewing pages, and browsing search results.

No Markup A markup view that provides a completely clean view of a document, temporarily hiding all comments and revisions, and displays the document as it would if all changes were applied and does not show any of the markups or comments.

Numbered list A list that sequences items by displaying a successive number beside each item.

Object An item, such as a picture or text box, that can be individually selected and manipulated in a document.

Object Linking and Embedding (OLE) A feature in Microsoft Office that enables you to insert an object into a presentation either as an embedded or linked object.

Office Clipboard An area of memory reserved to temporarily hold selections that have been cut or copied and enables you to paste the selections.

OneDrive Microsoft's cloud storage system. Saving files to OneDrive enables them to sync across all Windows devices and to be accessible from any Internet-connected device.

Order of operations A set of rules that controls the sequence in which arithmetic operations are performed. Also called the *order of precedence*.

Original Markup A markup view that displays the document in its original form, as it was before any changes were applied.

Outline view A structural view of a document that can be collapsed or expanded as necessary.

Paragraph spacing The amount of space before or after a paragraph.

Paste A command used to place a cut or copied selection into another location.

PDF (Portable Document Format) A file type that was created for exchanging documents independent of software applications and operating system environments.

PDF Reflow A Word feature that converts a PDF document into an editable Word document.

Picture A graphic file that is retrieved from storage media or the Internet and placed in an Office project.

Placeholder A field or block of text used to determine the position of objects in a document.

Plagiarizing The act of using and documenting the works of another as one's own.

Plain Text content control A form element that enables all types of data entry but prohibits formatting.

Portrait orientation A document layout in which a page is taller than it is wide.

Print Layout view A view that closely resembles the way a document will look when printed.

Pull quote A phrase or sentence taken from an article to emphasize a key point.

Quick Access Toolbar A toolbar located at the top-left corner of any Office application window; provides fast access to commonly executed tasks such as saving a file and undoing recent actions.

Range A group of adjacent or contiguous cells in a worksheet. A range can be adjacent cells in a column (such as C5:C10) or row (such as A6:H6), or a rectangular group of cells (such as G5:H10).

Read Mode A view in which text reflows automatically between columns to make it easier to read.

Real-time co-authoring A Word feature that shows several authors simultaneously editing the document in Word or Word Online.

Real Time Typing A Word feature that shows where co-authors are working, and what their contributions are as they type.

Record A group of related fields representing one entity, such as data for one person, place, event, or concept.

Revision mark A mark that indicates where text is added, deleted, or formatted while the Track Changes feature is active.

Ribbon The command center of Office applications. It is the long bar located just beneath the title bar, containing tabs, groups, and commands.

Rich Text content control Control that is often used to insert formatted text, images, and tables.

Right alignment A setting that begins text evenly at the right margin, with a ragged left edge.

Right indent A setting that positions all text in a paragraph at an equal distance from the right margin.

Sans serif font A font that does not contain a thin line or extension at the top and bottom of the primary strokes on characters.

Section A part of a document that contains its own page format settings, such as those for margins, columns, and orientation.

Section break An indicator that divides a document into parts, enabling different formatting for each section.

Serif font A font that contains a thin line or extension at the top and bottom of the primary strokes on characters.

Shading A background color that appears behind text in a paragraph, page, or table element.

Shape A geometric or non-geometric object, such as a rectangle or an arrow, used to create an illustration or highlight information.

Shortcut menu A menu that provides choices related to the selection or area at which you right-click.

Sidebar Supplementary text that appears along the side of a document.

Signature line Enables individuals and companies to distribute and collect signatures, and then process forms or documents electronically without the need to print and fax or mail.

Simple Markup A Word feature that simplifies the display of comments and revision marks, resulting in a clean, uncluttered look.

Sizing handle A series of dots on the outside border of a selected object; enables the user to adjust the height and width of the object.

SmartArt A visual representation of information that can be created to effectively communicate a list, process, or relationship.

Smart Lookup A feature that provides information about tasks or commands in Office and can also be used to search for general information on a topic, such as *President George Washington*.

Source A publication, person, or media item that is consulted in the preparation of a paper and given credit.

Status bar A bar located at the bottom of the program window that contains information relative to the open file. It also includes tools for changing the view of the file and for changing the zoom size of onscreen file contents.

Style A named collection of formatting characteristics that can be applied to text or paragraphs.

Style manual A guide to a writing style outlining required rules and conventions related to the preparation of papers.

Style set Predefined combinations of font, style, color, and font size that can be applied to selected text.

Subdocument A smaller document that is a part of a master document.

Symbol A character or graphic not normally included on a keyboard.

Synchronous scrolling A feature that enables you to scroll through two documents at the same time using either of the two scroll bars.

Tab Located on the ribbon, each tab is designed to appear much like a tab on a file folder, with the active tab highlighted.

Tab selector The small box at the leftmost edge of the horizontal ruler.

Tab stop A marker on the horizontal ruler specifying the location where the insertion point stops after Tab is pressed to align text in a document.

Table A grid of columns and rows that organizes data.

Table alignment The horizontal position of a table between the left and right margins.

Table of contents A page that lists headings in the order in which they appear in a document and the page numbers on which the entries begin.

Table style A named collection of color, font, and border designs that can be applied to a table.

Tag A data or metadata element that is added as a document property. Tags help in indexing and searching.

Tell me box A box located to the right of the last tab that enables you to search for help and information about a command or task you want to perform and displays a shortcut directly to that command.

Template A predesigned file that contains preformatted text and/or graphics such as a theme and layout, and may include content that can be modified.

Template thumbnail A small picture displayed below the search box that matches the search term in the *Search for online templates* search box.

Text box A rectangular object that contains text and that can display in any location within a document; if text changes, the box dimensions automatically adjust to accommodate.

Text pane A pane that displays beside a SmartArt diagram, enabling you to enter text.

Theme A collection of design choices that includes colors, fonts, and special effects used to give a consistent look to a document, workbook, presentation, or database form or report.

Theme color A feature that represents coordinated colors for the current text and background, accents, and hyperlinks.

Theme effect A feature that includes lines or fill effects to incorporate into a document theme.

Theme font A feature that contains a coordinating heading and body text font.

Thesaurus A tool used to quickly find a synonym (a word with the same meaning as another) for a selected word.

Three-part indent marker An icon located at the left side of the ruler that enables you to set a left indent, a hanging indent, or a first line indent.

Title bar The long bar at the top of each window that displays the name of the folder, file, or program displayed in the open window and the application in which you are working.

Toggle command A button that acts somewhat like light switches that you can turn on and off. You select the command to turn it on, then select it again to turn it off.

Track Changes A Word feature that monitors all additions, deletions, and formatting changes you make in a document.

Ungroup A process that divides a combined single object into individual objects that comprise it.

Uniform Resource Locator (URL) A Web resource used to specify addresses on the World Wide Web.

User exception An individual or group that can edit all or specific parts of a restricted document.

View The various ways a file can display on the screen.

View Side by Side A feature that enables you to display two versions of the same document on the same screen.

Visual Basic for Applications (VBA) A programming language that is built into Office and used to code and edit macros.

Watermark Text or graphics that display behind text.

Web Layout view A view that displays the way a document will look when posted on the Internet.

Webpage Any document that displays on the World Wide Web.

Web server A computer system that hosts pages for viewing by anyone with an Internet connection.

WordArt A feature that modifies text to include special effects, such as color, shadow, gradient, and 3-D appearance.

Word Online An online component of Office Online consisting of a Web-based version of Word with sufficient capabilities to enable you to edit and format a document online.

Word processing software A computer application, such as Microsoft Word, used primarily with text to create, edit, and format documents.

Word wrap The feature that automatically moves words to the next line if they do not fit on the current line.

Works Cited A list of sources cited by an author in his or her work.

World Wide Web (WWW) A very large subset of the Internet that stores webpage documents.

Writing style Provides a set of rules that results in standardized documents that present citations in the same manner and that include the same general page characteristics.

Zoom slider A feature that displays at the far right side of the status bar. It is used to increase or decrease the magnification of the file.

Index

A

Accept Changes feature, 272
Accessibility Checker, 105–107, 114–115
ActiveX controls, 421
add-ins in Microsoft Office, 17–18
alignment
 center alignment, 135
 justified alignment, 135
 left alignment, 135
 paragraphs, 135, 145–146
 right alignment, 135
 table alignment, 202
alignment guides, 169
All Commands function, 12
All Markup, 273, 274
APA (American Psychological Association) style, 253
argument, defined, 212
authentication of document, 445–459
AutoCorrect, 34, 80–81
automate document creation
 authentication in, 445–459
 building blocks, 367–370, 374–375
 introduction to, 364
 multiple documents, 376–395
 templates, 364–367
AutoRecover, 109
AutoSave, 7, 109
AutoText, 369

B

background color for webpages, 480–482
Backstage Navigation Pane, 25–26, 50
Backstage view, 6, 51–52
backup copy of document, 110
bibliography for research papers, 256–257, 259, 266–267
blank document, 6
blog posts on webpages, 499–501, 507–508
bookmarks, 387–388, 394–395, 482–483, 492–493
Border Painter, 214
Border Sampler, 216
borders
 manipulating, 333
 in newsletters, 317, 318, 324–325
 paragraph formatting, 141–142, 146–148
 in tables, 214–216, 222–224
building blocks, 367–370, 374–375
Building Blocks Organizer, 368–370
built-in formatting styles, 106
bulleted lists, 142–143, 148

C

calculations with content control data, 422–423, 428–429
captions, 217–218
Cell Margins, 203
cells
 defined, 196
 merge cells, 199, 206–207
 split cells in tables, 199, 206–207
center alignment, 135
charts in newsletters, 317
Check Box content control, 420
Check Compatibility, 107
Check Document, 32–34
Chicago writing style, 253
Choose commands from feature, 477
citations for research papers, 254–255, 264–266
cloud storage, 6
co-authoring documents, 292
color
 applying to webpages, 480–482, 491
 for content control, 421
 for hyperlinks, 485
 Text Highlight Color, 133
 in themes, 397, 402
columns
 break in, 316, 321–322
 changing, 199–200
 formatting, 152
 inserting, 198–199
 layout of, 314–315, 320–321
 sorting, 213
combining documents, 379, 390–391
Combo Box content control, 420
commands to a group, 477–478, 487–489
comment balloon, 277
comments
 adding in a document, 275–276, 281–282
 reply to a comment, 277–278, 281–282
 User Name in, 276
 viewing a comment, 277, 281–282
common interface components, 9–15
comparing documents, 377–378
Compatibility Mode, 108
Compress Pictures, 36
Computer Training Concepts, Inc. case study, 362–363
content controls, 420–423, 426–429
contextual tabs, 10
copy/paste object, 343, 345–346
copy text, 30, 40–41
counting words, 79
cover page in research papers, 262–263, 270
crop, defined, 170
Crop tool, 36
cropping handles, 170
Current List, 255
custom tab, 12, 474–476, 487–489
custom theme, 399, 404
cut text, 30, 40–41

D

data
 calculations with content control data, 422–423, 428–429
 enhancing table data, 214–218
 managing data, 210–214
 sorting data, 213, 221–222
data source in Microsoft Excel, 228
data source in Microsoft Word, 227–229, 233
Date Picker content control, 421
Design Mode, 421
desktop publishing
 column break, 316, 321–322
 column layout, 314–315, 320–321
 defined, 312
 design features, 316–319
 document layout, 313–314
 drop caps, 318, 323–324
 mastheads, 317, 322–323
 newsletter design, 313–316
 section break, 315–316, 321–322
Developer tab, 419, 421
Dialog Box Launcher, 10
dialog box, 10–11, 48
digital signature, 451–452
document. *see also* reviewing a document
 Accessibility Checker, 105–106, 114–115
 adding text and navigating, 76, 83–84
 applying styles, 152–157
 creating in Microsoft Word, 73–75, 82
 ensure compatibility, 107–108
 font attributes, 130–134
 formatting a document, 149–152
 inserting pictures, 34–35, 43, 165–166, 174–175
 manage page flow, 94
 objects, 164–173
 paragraph formatting, 134–143
 preparing for distribution, 105–112
 retrieval of, 108–110, 115
 save as webpage, 479–480, 489–490
 saving as templates, 367, 373–374
 select view, 91–92
 sharing in OneDrive, 286–289
 themes, 396–403
 viewing in Microsoft Word, 91–95

Index **539**

document automation
　applying restrictions, 445–449
　content controls, 420–423, 426–429
　digital signature, 451–452
　editing restrictions/exceptions, 448–449, 455–456
　formatting restrictions on, 447, 454–455
　forms, 418–431
　macros, 432–444
　marking as final, 445–446, 453
　protection and authentication, 445–459
Document Inspector, 110, 116
document productivity
　completion of mail merge, 230–231
　create mail merge document, 226–229
　enhancing table data, 214–218
　formatting tables, 200–203
　inserting tables, 196–200
　managing table data, 210–214
document properties in Microsoft Office, 50–51, 56
document properties in Microsoft Word
　introduction to, 103–104
　printing, 104–105, 111–112, 113–114
　view and edit, 50–51
document sharing
　co-authoring documents, 292
　inviting others to share, 287–288
　Microsoft OneDrive, 286–289
　send as attachment, 289–290
　using a link, 288–289
　Word Online, 287, 290–293
document tracking
　OneDrive, 284–286
　PDF document, 271, 278–279, 282–283
　reviewing a document, 273–279
　tracking changes, 271–273, 280–281
document views, 45, 46
Draft view, 91
Drawing Tools Format tab, 329
drop caps, 318, 323–324
Drop-Down List content control, 421

editing restrictions/exceptions, 448–449, 455–456
effects for themes, 398–399
electronic forms, 419–423, 425, 431
embedding objects, 342–346
endnotes for research papers, 258–260
Enhanced ScreenTips, 17

F

FAQ (Frequently Asked Questions) webpages, 482
field, defined, 227
File Explorer in Microsoft OneDrive, 6, 284–286, 294–295

File Transfer Protocol (FTP), 486
files/folders in Microsoft Office
　creating new file, 6
　open saved file, 7–8, 20–21
　previewing and printing, 51–52, 57
　saving file, 7, 19–20
　working with, 6–9
files/folders in Microsoft Word, 108, 289, 380
fills, in text boxes, 333
first line indents, 137
Font Dialog Box Launcher, 10, 132
Font group, 9
fonts
　commonly accessed commands, 132–134
　defined, 130
　font options, 130–132
　theme fonts, 398, 403
footers in Microsoft Office, 49–50, 55
footers in Microsoft Word, 86–88, 96–97
footnotes for research papers, 258–260, 267–268
form letter, 226
Format Painter, 17, 155
formatting
　columns, 152
　Microsoft Office, 28–29, 39–40
　restrictions on documents, 447, 454–455
　sections, 150–151
　theme selection, 149–150, 158–159
forms
　automation of, 418–431
　content controls, 420–423, 426–429
　electronic forms, 419–423, 425, 431
　enabling protection, 424–425, 430–431
　individual controls on, 424
　introduction to, 418
formulas, 210–212, 219–220
functions, 210, 212–213, 219–220

gallery, defined, 11
Get Add-ins, 17
grammar check in Microsoft Office, 32–34, 42
grammar check in Microsoft Word, 77–79, 84–85
graphic objects
　inserting, 326–333
　introduction to, 326
　manipulating, 333–335, 339–340
　SmartArt, 316, 326–327, 336–337
　text box, 328–329, 330
　3D models, 332–333
　WordArt, 172–173, 179, 316, 328, 337–338
Greenways case study, 310–311
group, defined, 9
grouping shapes/objects, 334–335, 341

hanging indents, 137
header row in mail merge, 227
headers in Microsoft Office, 49–50, 55
headers in Microsoft Word, 86–88, 96–97
Help tab, 16
Home tab, 9
hyperlinks, 106, 483–485, 493–494
HyperText Markup Language (HTML), 478–480

icons, 165
images in newsletters, 316, 319, 324–325
Immersive Reader, 291
indents, in paragraph formatting, 137–138, 145–146
index in research papers, 262, 268–269
individual controls on forms, 424
insert control, 198–199
insert object, 343–344, 346
insert pictures, 34–35
insertion point, 76

J

justified alignment, 135

K

keyboard shortcuts, 14–15

L

landscape orientation, 47, 88, 89
layering objects, 335
layout of documents, 313–314
Layout Options, 171, 319
leaders, 140
Learning Tools, 423
left alignment, 135
left indents, 137
Legacy Tools, 421
legal blacklining, 377
line spacing, 137
linking objects, 342–347
lists in newsletters, 317
literature analysis case study, 250
Live Layout, 169
Live Preview, 11, 131

Mac-based Office applications, 4
macros
　automation of, 432–444
　creation of, 432–437
　modifying, 436–437, 443–444
　recording of, 432–436, 441–443
　running of, 436, 441–443
　security protection, 437–440

540　Index

mail merge
  Access Database as data source, 228
  completion of, 231, 235
  create document, 226–229
  create/select recipient list, 227, 232–233
  defined, 226
  editing data source, 229, 233
  insert merge fields, 230–231, 234
  Microsoft Excel as data source, 228
  Word table/Outlook list as data source, 228
margins, 47, 88, 97
Mark as Final feature, 445–446, 453
Markup feature, 271, 273–275
master document, 380–384, 392–393
Master List in document, 255
mastheads, 317, 322–323
merge cells, 199, 206–207
merge fields, 230–231
merging documents, 377–384
Microsoft Access, 4
Microsoft account, 5–6, 286
Microsoft Excel
  add-ins, 17
  changing document views, 45
  inserting into document, 197
  introduction to, 4
  order of operations, 211
  spelling/grammar check, 32
  worksheet as data source, 228
Microsoft Office
  add-ins, 17–18
  changing document views, 45–46
  common interface components, 9–15
  customizing ribbon, 12–13
  dialog box, 10–11, 21–22
  document properties, 50–51
  Enhanced ScreenTips, 17
  headers and footers, 49–50, 55
  Help tab, 16
  introduction to, 4–5
  keyboard shortcuts, 14–15
  Microsoft account, 5–6
  Mini Toolbar, 29
  modifying text, 27–29
  Office Clipboard, 31
  page layout, 46–48
  Quick Access Toolbar, 13–14, 22
  relocating text, 30–31
  reviewing a document, 32–34
  ribbon, 9–10
  shortcut menu, 14, 23
  spelling/grammar check, 32–34, 42
  starting an application, 5–6
  Tell me box, 15–16, 24
  templates, 25–26, 37–38
  themes, 26, 38
  updates to, 107
  Visual Basic for Applications, 437
  working with files, 6–9
  working with pictures, 34–36, 43–44

Microsoft OneDrive
  access to, 4, 6–7
  document sharing, 286–289
  document tracking, 284–286
  File Explorer and, 6, 284–286, 294–295
  mobile devices, 284
  photos saved in, 319
  saving file to, 7
  Word Online, 287, 290–293, 295–296
Microsoft PowerPoint, 4, 17, 32, 45
Microsoft Word
  beginning and editing, 73–79
  borders, 141–142, 146–148
  creating a document, 73–75, 82
  customizing, 79–81
  document properties, 103–104
  headers/footers, 86–88, 96–97
  introduction to, 4, 72–73
  preparing document for distribution, 105–112
  readability features, 86–90
  spelling and grammar check, 77–79, 84–85
  templates, 75–76
  viewing documents, 91–95
  Word options, 79–81
  zoom setting, 92–93, 101–102
Mini Toolbar, 29, 79
MLA (Modern Language Association) style, 252–253
multiple documents
  combining documents, 379, 390–391
  comparing documents, 377–378
  creating bookmarks, 387–388, 394–395
  insert file as object, 380
  introduction to, 376
  master document, 380–384, 392–393
  merging documents, 377–384
  Navigation Pane, 384–387, 394–395
  subdocument, 380–384, 392–393
  View Side by Side, 376–377, 389–390
My Add-ins, 17

N

Navigation Pane, 384–387, 394–395
newsletter design, 313–316
No Markup, 273, 274–275
Normal template, 364
number formats in Microsoft Excel, 211
numbered lists, 142–143, 148

O

Oak Grove Products, Inc. case study, 416–417
Object Linking and Embedding (OLE), 342–347
objects
  defined, 164
  embedding, 342–347
  grouping/ungrouping, 334–335, 341
  insert file as, 380
  linking, 342–347
  move, align, resize, 167–170, 175–176
  pictures, 165–166
  resizing, 334
  screenshots, 166–167
  text box, 170–172, 178
  WordArt, 172–173, 179
Office Clipboard, 31
online videos, 498–499, 505–507
open saved file, 7–8
order of operations, 211
orientation in page layouts, 47, 88–89
Original Markup, 273, 275
Outline Tools group, 381
Outline view, 91, 156–157, 162–163
Outlining tab, 381

P

Page Movement group, 314
pages/page layout in Microsoft Office
  dialog box, 48
  manage page flow, 94–95
  margins, 47
  orientation changes, 47, 54–55, 98–99
  overview of, 46–48
pages/page layout in Microsoft Word. see also webpages
  cover page in research papers, 262–263, 270
  cover page/title page, 262–263, 270
  manage page flow, 94–96
paragraph formatting
  borders and shading, 141–142, 146–148
  bulleted and numbered lists, 142–143, 148
  commands, 134
  indents, 137–138, 145–146
  selecting alignment, 135–136, 145–146
  spacing, 136–137, 145–146
  tab stops, 139–140
parenthetical citations for research papers, 258–259
password protection, 449–451, 457–458
Paste arrow, 10
paste object, 343, 345–346
paste text, 30–31, 40–41
PDF (Portable Document Format), 108, 271, 278–279, 282–283
Phillips Studio L Photography case study, 128–129
Pickit Images App, 17, 319, 497
pictures in Microsoft Office, 34–35, 43, 44
pictures in Microsoft Word
  inserting into document, 165–166, 174–175
  modifying, 170, 176–177
  move, align, resize, 167–170, 175–176
placeholder, 364–365, 496–497

Index **541**

plagiarizing, defined, 252
Plain Text content control, 420
Portable Document Format (PDF). *see* PDF
portrait orientation, 47, 88–89
PowerPoint Themes gallery, 11
previewing files, 51–52, 57
Print Layout view, 91, 314
print/printing
    document properties and, 104–105, 111–112, 113–114
    previewing files and, 51–52, 57
    Quick Access Toolbar, 13–14
Protect group, 424
protection
    digital signature, 451–452
    documentation automation, 445–458
    forms, 424–425, 430–431
    password protection, 449–451, 457–458
pull quote, 330, 338–339

Q

Quick Access Toolbar (QAT)
    customizing ribbon, 12, 474, 485
    defined, 9
    file saving, 7
    shared files, 289
    use and customizing, 13–14, 22

R

ranges, defined, 212
Read Mode, 91
readability features, 86–90
real-time co-authoring, 292
Real Time Typing, 292
Recent Documents list, 8–9
recipient list in mail merge, 227
Record Macro dialog box, 432–436, 441–443
records, defined, 227
recurring table headers, 214
Reject Changes feature, 272
relocating text, 30–31
research papers
    basics of, 252
    cover page/title page, 262–263, 270
    footnotes and endnotes, 258–260, 267–268
    index, 262, 268–269
    special features, 260–263
    table of contents, 260–261, 268–269
    writing style, 252–257, 264–266
Resume Assistant, 365
resume templates, 365
retrieval of documents, 108–110, 115
reusing text, 75
reviewing a document
    adding a comment, 275–276, 281–282
    Markup feature, 273–275
    PDF document, 271, 278–279, 282–283
    reply to a comment, 277–278, 281–282
    viewing a comment, 277, 281–282
revision marks, 272
ribbon
    changing document views, 45
    customizing ribbon, 12–13
    defined, 9
    modifying files, 20–21
    tabs on, 9–10
ribbon customization, 12–13, 474–478
Rich Text content control, 420
Rich Text Format (RTF), 108
right alignment, 135
right indents, 137
rows, 198–200, 213

S

sans serif font, 130
Screen Clipping, 166
screenshots, 166, 317
sections/section break, 150–151, 315–316
security protection for macros, 437–440
select text in Microsoft Office, 27–28
serif font, 130
shading
    in newsletters, 317, 318, 324–325
    paragraph formatting, 141–142, 146–148
    in tables, 214–216, 222–224
shapes, 316, 331–332, 334–335
shortcut menu, 14, 23
Show Training, 16
Side by Side view, 314, 376–377, 389–390
sidebar, 330
Simple Markup, 273
sizing handles, 169
Smart Lookup, 16
SmartArt, 316, 326–327, 336–337
Source Manager, 256
sources for research papers, 252, 254–256, 264–266
spacing of paragraphs, 136–137, 145–146
spell check
    Microsoft Office, 32–34, 42
    Microsoft Word, 77–79, 84–85
split cells in tables, 199, 206–207
Spotted Begonia Art Gallery case study, 2–3
status bar, 46, 314
style manual, 252
style sets, 155, 161–162, 396, 401
styles
    creation of, 155–156
    defined, 152
    in newsletters, 317
    outline view, 156–157, 162–163
    selecting and modifying, 153–155, 160–161
    style set, 155, 161–162, 396, 401
    table styles, 200–201, 208–209
subdocuments, 380–384, 392–393
Swan Creek National Wildlife Refuge case study, 70–71
symbols, insertion of, 90, 100
Synchronous scrolling, 376

T

tab selector, 139
tab stops, 139–140
table alignment, 202
table of contents, 260–261, 268–269
table styles, 200–201
Table Tools Layout tab, 203
tables
    adjusting/position/alignment, 202
    applying/modifying styles, 200–201, 208–209
    borders and shading, 214–216, 222–224
    calculating/using formulas, 210–212, 219–220
    calculating/using functions, 210, 212–213, 219–220
    convert text to, 216–217, 225
    convert to text, 216–217
    creating/drawing, 197–198, 204–206
    as data source for mail merge, 228
    defined, 196
    enhancing table data, 214–218
    formatting, 200–203
    include caption, 217–218
    inserting, 196–200
    managing data, 210–214
    merge/split cells, 199, 206–207
    in newsletters, 316
    recurring table headers, 214
    row height/column width changes, 199–200
    rows/columns, 198–199
    sorting data, 213, 221–222
tabs on ribbon, 9–10
Tell me box, 15–16, 24
templates in Microsoft Office, 25–26, 37–38
templates in Microsoft Word
    for blog posts, 499–500, 507–508
    change placeholder picture, 496–497, 503–504
    creating in Word, 366–367
    defined, 364
    downloading, 365–366, 371–372, 496, 502–503
    overview of, 75–76
    save as document, 496, 502–503
    saving document as, 367, 373–374
    selection of, 364–366, 371–372
    thumbnails, 366
text box, 170–172, 178, 328–329, 330, 333

Text Form Field, 422–423
Text Highlight Color, 133
text in Microsoft Office, 27–29, 39–40
text in Microsoft Word
  adding and navigating, 76, 83–84
  changing appearance of, 132–134, 144–145
  convert table to, 216–217
  convert to table, 216–217, 225
  reusing text, 75, 82
  in tables, 203
  typing into macros, 436
text pane, 327
themes in Microsoft Office, 25, 26–27, 38
themes in Microsoft Word
  applying to webpages, 480–482, 491
  custom theme, 399, 404
  customizing colors, 397, 402
  effects for, 398–399
  fonts for, 398, 403
  formatting, 149–150, 158–159
  style sets, 396, 401
thesaurus tool, 78
3D models, 332–333, 497–498, 504–505
three-part indent marker, 138
time-saving tools, 364–375
title bar, defined, 9
title page in research papers, 262–263
toggle commands, 29
Track Changes feature, 271–272, 280–281
Traylor University economic impact study, 194–195
typography, 313, 317

ungrouping objects, 335
Uniform Resource Locator (URL), 484
user exception, 448
user name in comments, 276

videos on webpages, 498–499, 505–507
Visual Basic for Applications (VBA), 437

watermark, 89, 99
Web Layout view, 91
Web log, 499
Web server, 486
webpages
  blog posts, 499–501
  bookmarks and, 482–483, 492–493
  building/publishing, 478–486
  case study, 472–473
  commands to a group, 477–478, 487–489
  custom tab, 12, 474–475, 487–489
  customizing ribbon, 12, 474–478
  defined, 474
  download/save template as document, 496, 502–503
  enhancement of, 496–508
  hyperlinks and, 483–485, 493–494
  online videos, 498–499, 505–507
  placeholder picture in templates, 496–497, 503–504
  previewing, 485, 495
  publishing, 486
  save document as, 479–480, 489–490
  theme/background color, 480–482, 491
  3D models, 497–498, 504–505
Windows-based Office applications, 4
Word Online, 287, 290–293, 295–296
Word options, 79–80
word wrap feature, 73
WordArt, 172–173, 179, 316, 328, 337–338
works cited for research papers, 256–257
World Wide Web (WWW), 474, 484
wrap text, 73
writing style for research papers
  bibliography, 256–257, 259, 266–267
  creating sources and citations, 254–255
  formatting of, 254
  parenthetical citations, 258–259
  selection of, 252–253
  sharing sources and citations, 255–256, 264–266

zoom setting, 92–93, 101–102
zoom slider, 46